Cisco CCNP SWITCH Simplified

Your Complete Guide to Passing the 642-813 SWITCH Exam

Paul Browning (LLB Hons) CCNP, MCSE
Farai Tafa dual CCIE

ISBN: 978-0-9557815-6-8

Published by:
Reality Press Ltd.
Midsummer Court
314 Midsummer Blvd.
Milton Keynes
MK9 2UB
help@reality-press.com

LEGAL NOTICE
The advice in this book is designed to assist you in reaching the required standard for the CCNP SWITCH exam. The labs are designed to illustrate various learning points and are not suggested configurations to apply to a production network. Please check all your configurations with a qualified Cisco professional.

These labs are designed to be used on your own private home labs or rental racks and NOT on production networks. Many of the commands including debug commands can cause serious performance issues on live networks.

Introduction

Firstly, we want to say congratulations for investing in yourself and your future. Actions speak far louder than words and you have already taken a very important step towards your future as a Cisco Certified Network Professional.

The new CCNP track has been developed based on continuing feedback from Cisco customers who inform Cisco about what skills and abilities they want to see in their engineers. Over the past few years, Cisco exams have become increasingly harder and, of course, your certification expires every three years, so many engineers who have not kept themselves up-to-date have struggled to maintain their certification.

The objective for us, as with all of our Cisco Simplified manuals, is to help you do two things. First and foremost, our goal is to equip you with the skills, knowledge, and ability to carry out the day-to-day role of a Cisco network engineer. We don't want you to be a walking manual, but we do want you to know how to do the stuff that we consider the "bread and butter" jobs a CCNP engineer would need to carry out.

Secondly, of course, we want you to pass your Cisco exams. The mistake many Cisco students make is to do whatever it takes to pass the exam. Even if that approach did work, people taking this tack often sell themselves short. The reason is that most job interviews nowadays consist of both a hands-on and a theoretical test. If a student doesn't have a grasp of how the technology works, he or she has no hope of success in the real world.

These are the current exams you need to pass in order to become a CCNP:

642-902 ROUTE—Implementing Cisco IP Routing
642-813 SWITCH—Implementing Cisco IP Switched Networks
642-832 TSHOOT—Troubleshooting and Maintaining Cisco IP Networks

Each exam features theoretical questions as well as multiple hands-on labs where you could be asked to configure or troubleshoot any of the technologies in the syllabus. In addition, you have only 120 minutes to complete all of the tasks and answer all of the questions.

Each chapter is broken down into an overview and then the main theory discussion before moving on to a review section covering the main learning points. Be patient with yourself because there is a lot to learn. If you put about two hours aside every day to study, you should be ready to attempt the exam in approximately 60 days from the day you start. If you take days off or holidays, then of course it will take much longer.

Almost every topic is applied to how you would use the knowledge in real life, which is an area you will find missing from almost every other Cisco textbook. We design, install, and troubleshoot Cisco networks on a daily basis and have been doing so for many years. We don't fill your head full of useless jargon and fluff just to boast about how much we know. Although we do spend a little time teaching, for the most part, we are Cisco consultants out in the field.

If you are a member of www.howtonetwork.net, then please use the tools, such as the flash cards, practice exams, and videos, found on the site to help you through the exam. You will find them to be vital study tools. Please use the CCNP SWITCH discussion forum if you have any questions you need help with. Farai and I monitor the forum on a daily basis.

Lastly, make sure you register your book at the link below in order to receive free updates on it for life.

http://www.howtonetwork.net/public/2240.cfm

Best of luck with your studies. See you at the top.

Paul Browning

Farai Tafa

About the Authors

Paul Browning

Paul Browning is the author of *CCNA Simplified,* which is one of the industry's leading CCNA study guides. Paul previously worked for Cisco TAC but left in 2002 to start his own Cisco training company in the UK. Paul has taught over 2,000 Cisco engineers with both his classroom-based courses and his online Cisco training site, www.howtonetwork.net. Paul lives in the UK with his wife and daughter.

Farai Tafa

Farai Tafa is a Dual CCIE in both Routing and Switching and Service Provider. Farai currently works for one of the world's largest telecoms companies as a network engineer. He has also written workbooks for the CCNA, CCNP, and Cisco Security exams. Farai lives in Washington, D.C. with his wife and daughter.

Table of Contents

PART 1

Theory

CHAPTER 1

Campus LAN Switching Basics

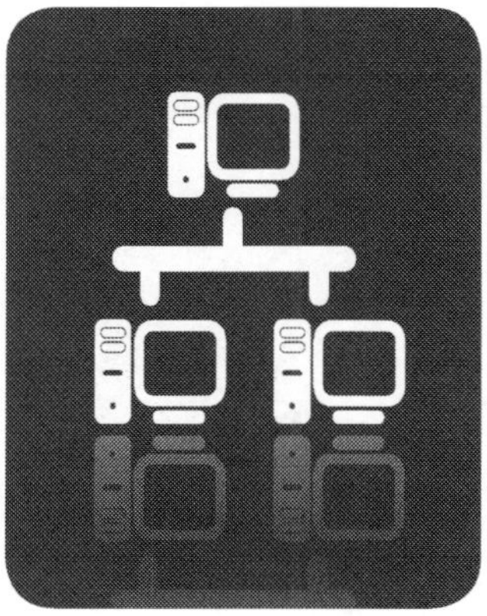

Welcome to the SWITCH course of the Cisco Certified Network Professional certification program. The focus of this guide is to pick up LAN switching concepts where the Cisco Certified Network Associate certification program left off, as well as to introduce and explain, in detail, additional LAN switching and other relevant concepts that are mandatory requirements of the current SWITCH certification exam. The foundation topics that will be covered in this chapter are as follows:

- Internetwork Switching Methods
- Local Area Network Switching Fundamentals
- Switch Table Architectures
- Segmenting the LAN Using Bridges and Switches
- The Hierarchical LAN Design Model
- The Enterprise Composite Model
- Switched LAN Design Considerations
- Campus Switched LAN Topologies

Internetwork Switching Methods

In telecommunications terminology, a switch is a device that forwards incoming data from any of multiple input ports to a specific output port that will take the data toward its destination.

Although the most common form of switching is Layer 2 switching, it is important to know that switching can also be performed as Layers 1, 3, and 4 or the OSI Model. The different methods of internetwork switching described in this section are as follows:

- Physical Layer (Layer 1) Switching
- Data Link Layer (Layer 2) Switching
- Network Layer (Layer 3) Switching
- Transport Layer (Layer 4) Switching
- Multilayer Switching (MLS)

Layer 1 Switching

Physical Layer Switching operates at Layer 1 of the OSI Model and allow users to connect any port to any other port within the system. Layer 1 switches use cross-connects to create connections from any port to any other port on the device. In addition to this, Layer 1 switches also have the ability to convert one media type to another (e.g. Ethernet to Fiber) using cross-connects. This provides Physical Layer switches the ability to adapt to changes in the network that could occur over time.

Layer 2 Switching

Although the most commonly known type of Data Link Switching is LAN switching, keep in mind that WAN protocols, such as Frame Relay, also switch packets at the Data Link Layer. Given that the SWITCH exam is focused only on LAN switching, this guide will be restricted to only that form of Layer 2 switching.

A LAN switch is, in many ways, similar to a bridge. Both devices allow you to segment the LAN and create multiple collision domains. However, LAN switches do have several advantages over bridges, which include the following:

- More ports than a bridge would ever be capable of supporting
- Microsegmentation by allowing individual hosts to be connected to individual ports
- Operating at hardware speed using ASICs, versus the software used by bridges
- Supporting Layer 3 and Layer 4 packet switching by including Multilayer features
- Using VLANs to create smaller logical broadcast domains

By default, the implementation of both switches and bridges creates a single broadcast domain, which is simply a logical division of a network in which all hosts can reach each other by broadcasting at the Data Link Layer. Broadcast domains either can reside within the same LAN segment or can be bridged to other LAN segments.

While both switches and bridges create a single broadcast domain, switches support Virtual Local Area Networks (VLANs), which can be used to create multiple logical broadcast domains. A detailed understanding of VLANs is required for the SWITCH exam; therefore, they will be described in detail later in this guide. The three primary functions of LAN switches are as follows:

1. MAC Address Learning
2. MAC Address Forwarding and Filtering
3. Loop Avoidance and Detection

LAN switches learn Media Access Control (MAC) addresses by examining the source address of each frame received on the interface and using that address to build their forwarding tables. Switches note the incoming port of frames sourced from a MAC address when the device connected to that port sends a frame to another MAC address. This concept is illustrated in Figure 1-1 below:

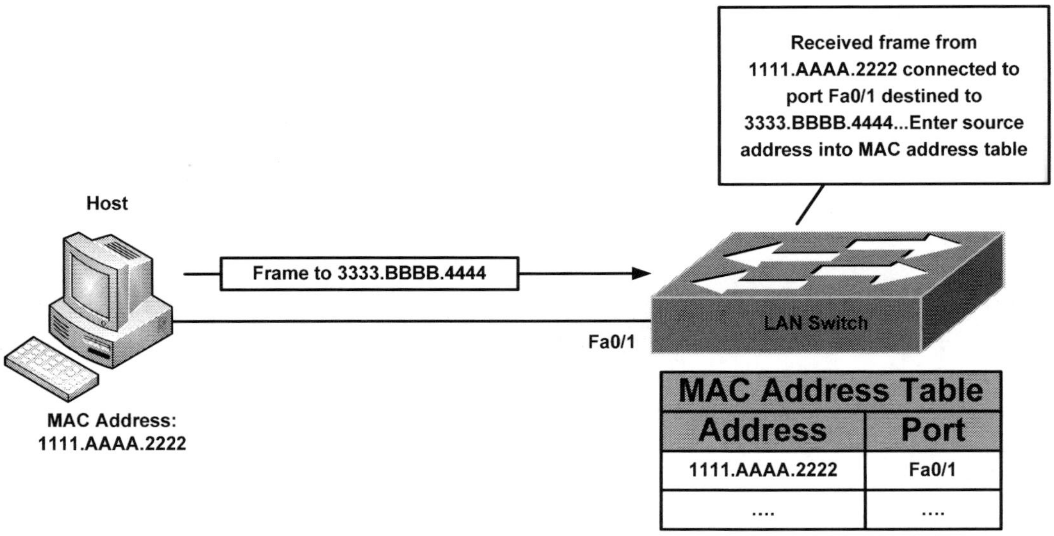

Fig. 1-1. Switches Learn MAC Address of Connected Devices

Because they initially have no idea where the destination device is, switches broadcast the received frame out of every port, except for the port on which the frame was received. This is illustrated in Figure 1-2 below:

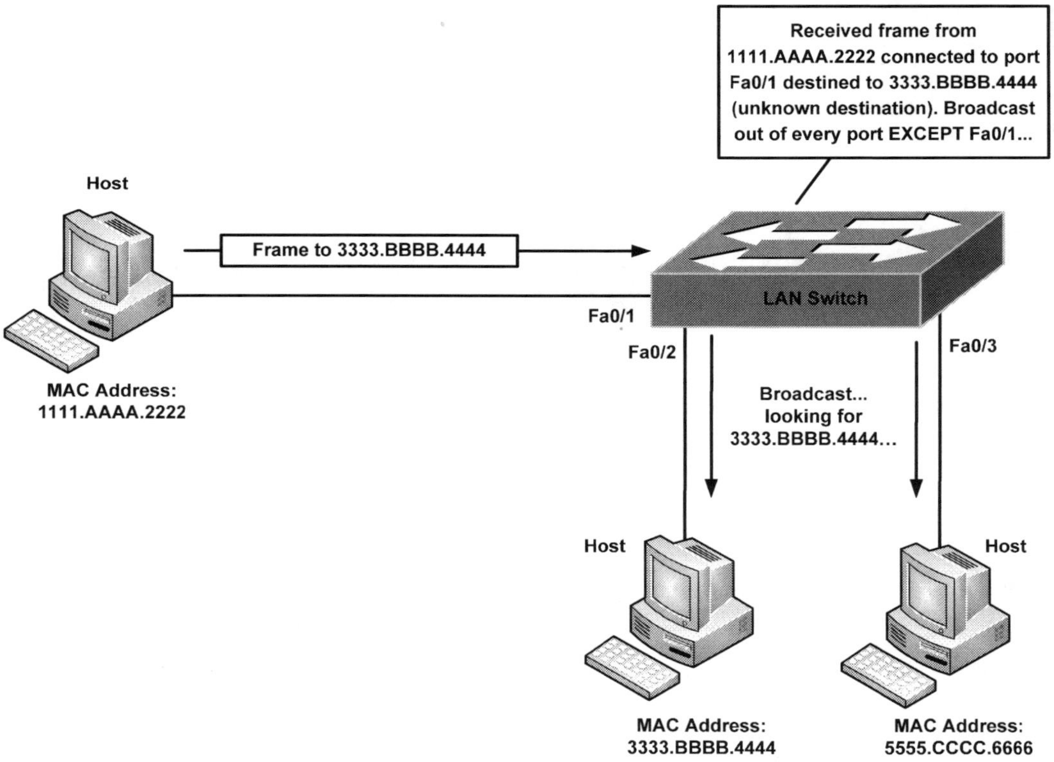

Fig. 1-2. Switches Send Broadcasts until They Build a MAC Address Table

After the switch has flooded the broadcast packet, it will wait for a device to respond. When the intended destination device responds to the broadcast packet, the switch will note the port the response was received on and place that address into the forwarding table, which is also called the MAC address table. This concept is illustrated in Figure 1-3 below:

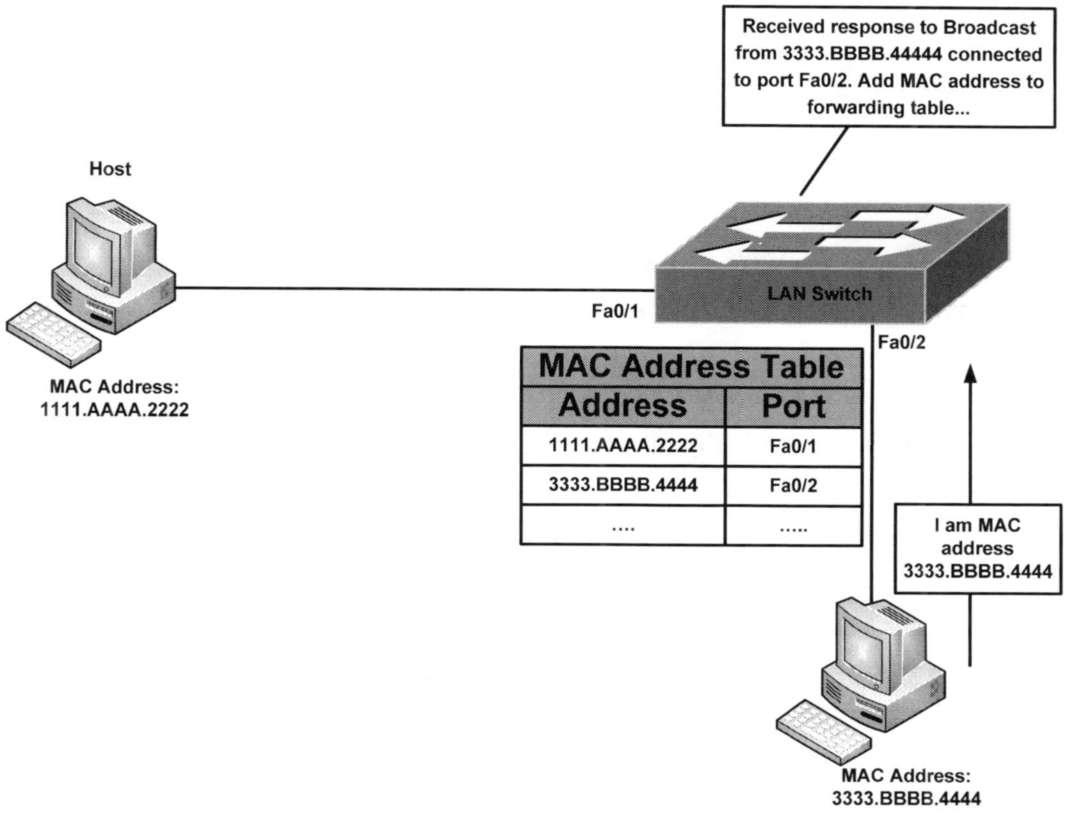

Fig. 1-3. Switches Build Their MAC Address Tables

This same process is repeated until the switch has learned the MAC addresses of all devices connected to all of its ports.

> **NOTE:** Switches will never learn a Broadcast address because this can never belong to any single host. If a switch receives a frame with a source address of FFFF-FFFF-FFFF from a port, it will not place that address in the forwarding table. Only Unicast and Multicast addresses are learned and placed in the forwarding table.

Once the switch has learned all the addresses of the devices connected to it, it builds a MAC address table, which lists the MAC addresses of connected devices and the ports they are connected to. The switch MAC address table uses either Content Addressable Memory or Ternary Content Addressable Memory. Content Addressable Memory and Ternary Content Addressable Memory will be described in detail later in this chapter.

When a switch receives a frame and the destination port is in the MAC address table, which means it is a known destination, the frame is transmitted out of the destination interface. However, if a switch receives a frame and the destination port is the same as the source port, that frame is filtered out and is not forwarded out of any interfaces. This is the address forwarding and filtering functionality provided by LAN switches.

The third primary function of LAN switches is Layer 2 loop avoidance. A Layer 2 loop occurs when there are multiple redundant paths in the Layer 2 network and the paths are all in a forwarding state at the same time. If this happens, the links will continuously forward frames, resulting in the creation of a network loop. To prevent such incidents from occurring, LAN switches use the Spanning Tree Protocol (STP). Intimate knowledge of STP is a mandatory SWITCH exam requirement; therefore, STP and all relevant STP-related technologies and protocols will be described in detail later in this guide.

Layer 3 Switching

Network Layer Switching is similar to the routing of packets at Layer 3 by routers, with the exception that it is performed using dedicated hardware Application Specific Integrated Circuits (ASICs), which are dedicated pieces of hardware designed for a specific purpose.

At a very basic level, Layer 3 switches are simply routers that allow for the faster forwarding of packets by using hardware instead of software. In traditional network routers, before a packet is forwarded, the router must perform a route lookup, decrement the packet TTL, recalculate the checksum, and then the frame can be forwarded using the appropriate Layer 2 information. The processor or CPU, using software, typically performs all of these functions.

In Layer 3 switches, these same functions can be performed using dedicated hardware, which offloads the processor-intensive packet routing functionality from traditional network routers. Although Layer 3 Cisco switches, such as the Catalyst 6500 series, still use standard routing protocols (e.g. OSPF and EIGRP) to determine the best path to the destination, they use dedicated hardware to forward packets whenever a complete switched path exists between two hosts. This allows packets to be forwarded at Layer 2 speeds, although Layer 3 protocols are still used to determine the best path to the destination. Layer 3 switching provides the following advantages over Layer 3 routing:

- Hardware-based packet forwarding
- High-performance packet switching
- High-speed scalability
- Low latency
- Lower per-port cost
- Flow accounting

- Security
- Quality of Service (QoS)

Cisco Express Forwarding (CEF) is an example of a Layer 3 switching technology supported in Cisco IOS devices, which will be described in detail later in this guide.

Layer 4 Switching

Layer 4 Switching provides additional routing above Layer 3 by using the port numbers found in the Transport Layer header to make routing decisions. Packets are forwarded, in hardware, based on Network Layer addressing and Transport Layer application information, protocol types, and segment headers.

The largest benefit of Layer 4 Switching is that the network administrator can configure a Layer 4 switch to prioritize data traffic by application, which means a QoS can be defined for each user. However, this also means that Layer 4 switches require a lot of memory in order to keep track of application information and conversations.

Layer 4 switches can use information up to Layer 7 to perform packet switching. These switches are typically referred to as Layer 4-7 switches, content switches, content services switches, web switches, or application switches. Examples of Layer 4 or Layer 4-7 switches include the standalone Cisco Content Services Switch and the Content Switching Modules that can be installed into the Catalyst 6500 series switches or 7600 series routers.

Going into detail on Layer 4 or Layer 4-7 switching is beyond the scope of the SWITCH exam requirements. These switching methods will not be described in further detail in this guide.

Multilayer Switching

Multilayer Switching (MLS) combines Layer 2, Layer 3, and Layer 4 switching technologies to forward packets at wire speed using hardware. Cisco supports MLS for both Unicast and Multicast traffic flows.

In Unicast transmission, a flow is a unidirectional sequence of packets between a particular source and destination that share the same protocol and Transport Layer information. These flows are based only on Layer 3 address information.

In Multicast transmission, a flow is a unidirectional sequence of packets between a Multicast source and the members of a destination Multicast group. Multicast flows are based on the IP address of the source device and the destination IP Multicast group address.

In MLS, a Layer 3 switching table, referred to as an MLS cache, is maintained for the Layer 3-switched flows. The MLS cache maintains flow information for all active flows and includes entries for traffic statistics that are updated in tandem with the switching of packets. After the MLS cache is created, any packets identified as belonging to an existing flow can be Layer 3-switched based on the cached information.

In Cisco Catalyst switches, MLS requires the following components:

- Multilayer Switching-Switching Engine (MLS-SE)
- Multilayer Switching-Route Processor (MLS-RP)
- Multilayer Switching Protocol (MLSP)

The MLS-SE is responsible for the packet switching and rewrite functions in ASICs. The MLS-SE is also capable of identifying Layer 3 flows.

The MLS-RP informs the MLS-SE of MLS configuration and runs routing protocols, which are used for route calculation.

The MLSP is a Multicast protocol that is used by the MLS-RP to communicate information, such as routing changes, to the MLS-SE, which then uses that information to reprogram the hardware dynamically with the current Layer 3 routing information. This is what allows for faster packet processing.

Multilayer switching will be described in detail later in this chapter.

Local Area Network Switching Fundamentals

LAN switching is a form of packet switching used in Local Area Networks. LAN switching is performed using hardware at the Data Link Layer. Because LAN switching is hardware-based, it uses MAC addresses, which are used by LAN switches to forward frames.

LAN switches provide much higher port density at a lower cost than traditional bridges, which allows LAN switches to accommodate network designs featuring fewer users per segment (microsegmentation), thereby increasing the average available bandwidth per user. Switches can use three main forwarding techniques, as follows:

- Store-and-Forward Switching
- Cut-Through Switching
- Fragment-Free Switching

Store-and-Forward Switching

This LAN switch forwarding method copies the entire frame into the switch buffer and performs a Cyclic Redundancy Check (CRC) for errors within the frame. Because of the CRC, this method of forwarding is the slowest and most processor-intensive.

However, the plus side to this method is that it is also the most efficient because it avoids forwarding frames with errors. For example, if a received frame is less than 64 bytes in length (which is considered a runt) or more than 1518 bytes in length (which is considered a giant), then the switch will discard the frame.

Cut-Through Switching

In cut-through switching, the frame header is inspected and the Destination Address (DA) of the frame is copied into the internal memory of the switch before the frame is forwarded.

Because only the frame header is inspected before the switch begins to forward the frame, once it reads the destination MAC address, this forwarding method is very fast and reduces latency, which is the amount of time it takes a packet to travel from source to destination.

This is the fastest switching method and is sometimes referred to as Fast Forward or Real Time switching. However, with speed comes some consequence in that the switch also forwards frames with errors. It is up to the destination switch to discard received frames with errors.

Fragment-Free Switching

Fragment-free switching waits for the collision window, which is the first 64 bytes of a frame, to be accepted before forwarding the frame to its destination. The fragment-free switching method holds the packet in memory until the data portion reaches the switch.

This switching method was primarily developed to address and solve the problem encountered with late collisions, which occur when another system attempts to transmit a frame after a host has transmitted at least the first 60 bytes of its frame.

Any network device will create some latency, and switches are no exception. The cut-through and fragment-free switching methods were primarily used in older switches to reduce latency when forwarding frames. However, as faster processors and ASICs were developed and introduced into newer switches, latency became a non-factor. Instead, greater emphasis was placed on efficiency and data integrity, and as a result, all new Cisco Catalyst switches utilize store-and-forward switching.

Symmetric and Asymmetric LAN Switching

LAN switching can be characterized based on the proportion of bandwidth that is allocated to each port. LAN switching can therefore be classified into one of two categories, as follows:

1. Symmetric LAN Switching
2. Asymmetric LAN Switching

Symmetric switching provides evenly distributed bandwidth to each port on the switch. A symmetric LAN switch provides switched connections between ports with the same bandwidth, such as all FastEthernet ports, for example. Symmetric switching is therefore optimized for a reasonably distributed traffic load, such as one found in a peer-to-peer desktop environment. This concept is illustrated in Figure 1-4 below:

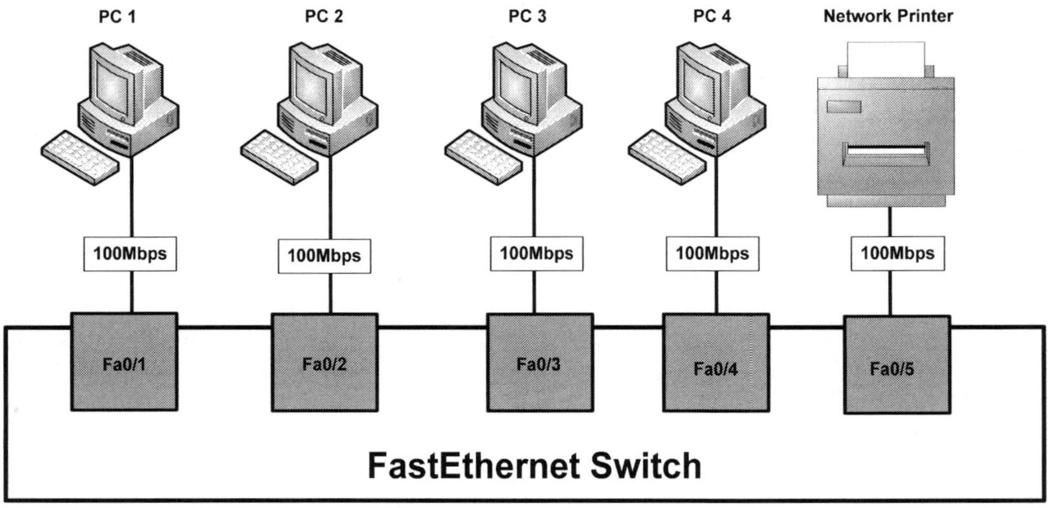

Fig. 1-4. Switching in a Peer-to-Peer Environment

The diagram above illustrates a typical peer-to-peer LAN using symmetric switching. The symmetric LAN switch provides switched connections between the 100Mbps ports.

Asymmetric switching provides unequal bandwidth between ports on a switch. An asymmetric LAN switch provides switched connections between ports of unlike bandwidths, such as a combination of Ethernet, FastEthernet, and even GigabitEthernet ports, for example. This type of switching is also called 10/100/1000 switching in that some hosts may be using 10Mbps connections, others 100Mbps connections, and others 1000Mbps connections. This is the most common type of switching.

Asymmetric switching is optimized for client-server environments in which multiple clients simultaneously communicate with a server, which requires that more bandwidth be dedicated to the server port to prevent a bottleneck at that port. The asymmetric switching concept is illustrated in Figure 1-5 below:

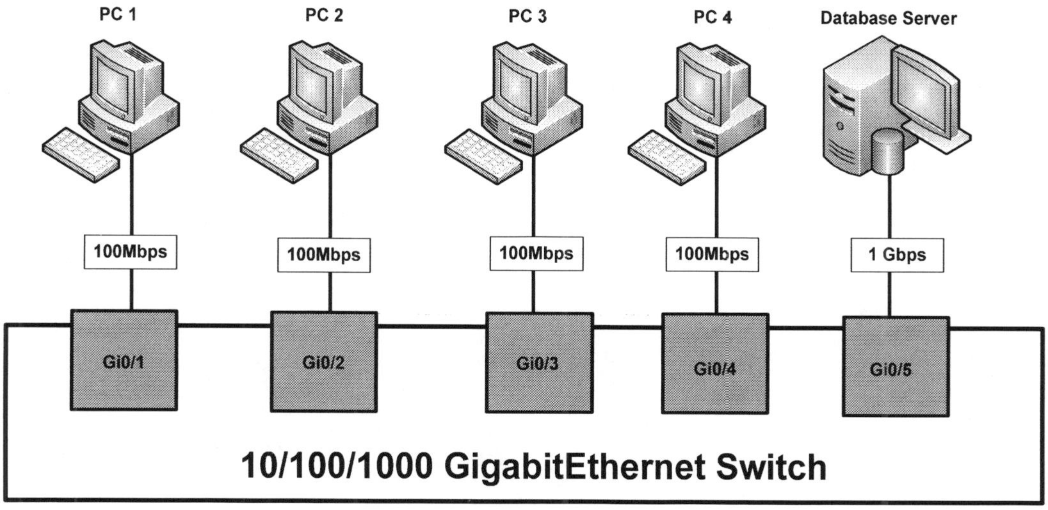

Fig. 1-5. Asymmetric Switching

In the diagram illustrated above, asymmetric switching is being used in a client-server environment. The client machines are all connected using FastEthernet links, while the server is connected using a GigabitEthernet link. The asymmetric LAN switch provides switched connections between the different bandwidth ports.

Switch Table Architectures

In the Catalyst switch architecture, when routing, switching, or ACL tables are built, the collected information is stored in high-speed table memory, which allows lookups to be performed using efficient search algorithms. The two types of tables are Content Addressable Memory (CAM) and Ternary Content Addressable Memory (TCAM).

CAM uses a key to perform a table lookup. For example, the destination MAC address could be used as the key for a Layer 2 table lookup, which is based on an exact match made on Binary operation (i.e. a 0 or a 1 value). The key is fed into a hashing algorithm, which produces a pointer that points to a specific memory location in the CAM table. That location in the CAM table shows the result, so searching the entire table is unnecessary. This operation allows for very high speed lookups in very large tables.

CAM and TCAM perform the same functionality; however, TCAM offers an enhancement over CAM. Because the CAM table lookup is based on an exact match, it does have a limitation in that some of the information that should be looked up is essential while some of it can be ignored. An example of this might be a situation where the first 16 bits of an IP address must be matched, but the last 16 bits can be ignored. In this case, CAM cannot ignore the last 16 bits since it is based on an exact match; however, TCAM has the ability to do so.

TCAM is so named because the word Ternary literally means 'composed of three items.' Unlike CAM, which is based on two values (0 and 1), TCAM is based on three values (0, 1, and x). The x represents the wildcard value. The TCAM memory structure is divided into a series of patterns and masks. The masks are shared among a specific number of patterns and are used to mark some content fields as wildcard fields. This allows TCAM to ignore these wildcard fields while comparing other fields. This concept is illustrated in Figure 1-6 below:

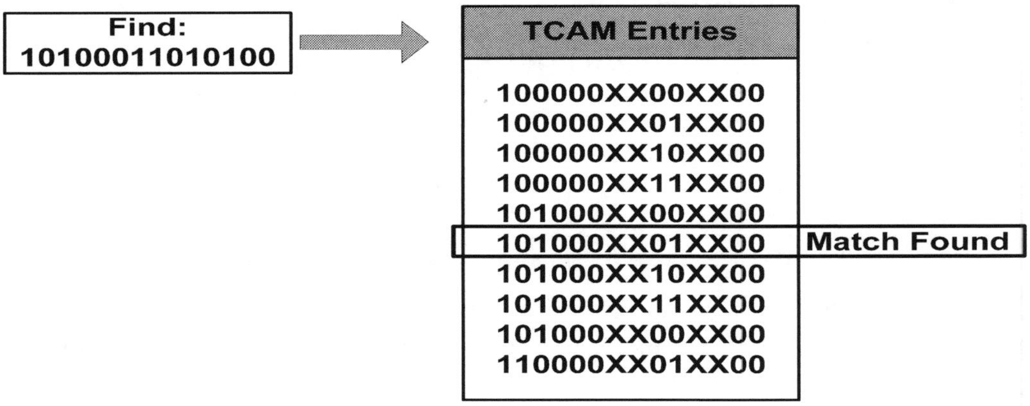

Fig. 1-6. TCAM Ignores Wildcard Fields

In the diagram above, the packet lookup is based on the address 10100011010100. Even though TCAM has the ability to ignore certain fields, the longest match lookup is still performed for CEF and ACLs. Additionally, because all entries are checked in parallel, this results in the same performance regardless of the number of entries.

NOTE: You are not required to demonstrate detailed knowledge of CAM or TCAM architecture as part of the SWITCH exam requirements.

Segmenting the LAN Using Bridges and Switches

When designing the networks of yesteryear, network engineers had only a limited number of hardware options when purchasing technology for their campus networks. In most cases, hubs were used to connect all network hosts, such as user workstations and network printers, to a single, shared LAN, while routers were used to segment the network as well as to provide connectivity between the LANs.

However, the increasing power of desktop machines and the increased need for more bandwidth has quickly highlighted the fact that shared media or a shared network model of LAN design has both distance limitations and limitations on the number of devices that can be connected to a single LAN. Thus, these networks are incapable of supporting these technological advances adequately.

To address these issues, LAN switches were developed in 1990. These were Layer 2 devices, referred to as bridges, and they were primarily dedicated to solving desktop bandwidth issues. One of the advantages offered by bridges was the ability to segment the LAN. Segmentation is the process by which the LAN is broken down into smaller, more manageable pieces. These segments are then interconnected by internetworking devices that enable communication between LANs while blocking other types of traffic. Segmenting LANs divides users into two or more separate LAN segments, reducing the number of users contending for bandwidth.

The rule of thumb when designing bridged networks was the 80/20 rule. This rule stipulated that while 80% of network traffic remained on the local network segment, up to 20% of network traffic needed to be bridged across segments or routed across the network backbone. Figure 1-7 below illustrates LAN design based on the 80/20 rule:

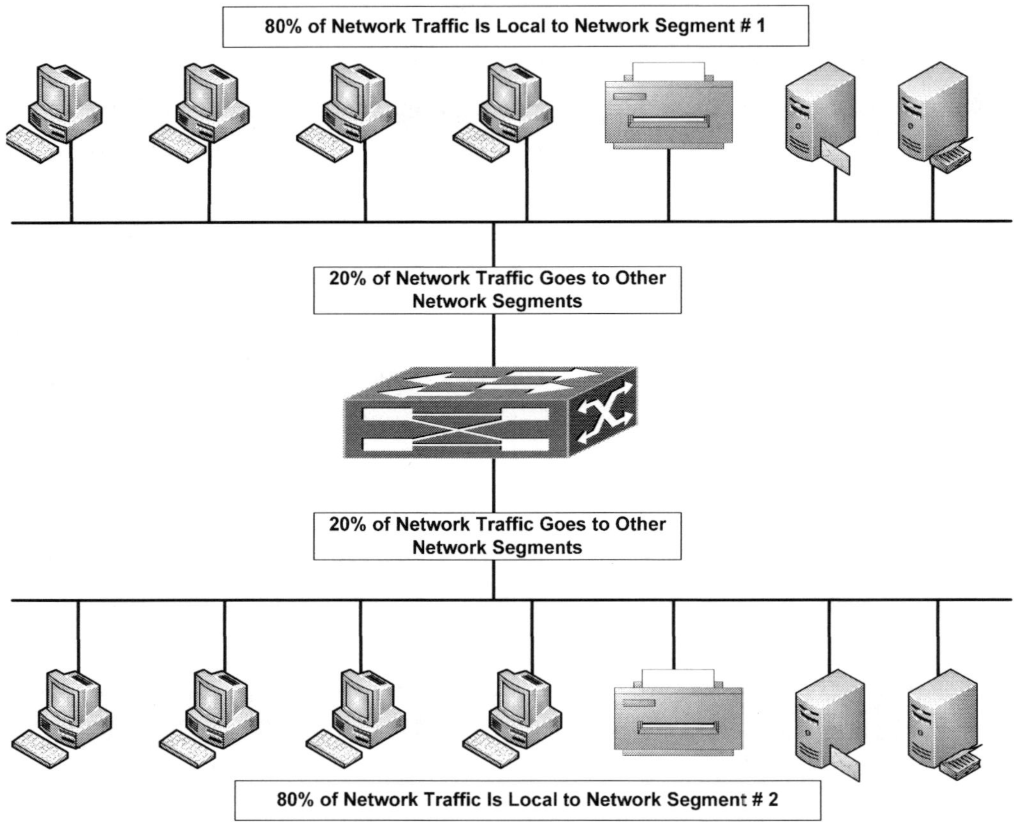

Fig. 1-7. 80/20 Design Rule

In the diagram above, local servers and other network devices, such as printers, are present on each LAN segment. These serve the clients, such as workstations, on those respective LAN segments. Because of localized servers and applications, 80 % of network traffic is restricted to the local segment. This means that only up to 20 % of network traffic will ever need to be bridged, switched, or routed between network segments.

As technology continued to evolve, along with the increasing power of desktop processors, the requirements of client-server and multimedia applications, and the need for greater bandwidth, it was clear that bridges alone were incapable of addressing such needs. This prompted network engineers to replace bridges with LAN switches.

Switches segment LANs in a manner similar to bridges. However, unlike bridges, switches are hardware-based, making them much faster. Switches also go one step further with LAN segmentation by allowing microsegmentation, which further segments the LAN by allowing individual hosts to be connected to individual switch ports. In other words, each individual host device is connected to its own switch port. Each switch port, therefore, provides a dedicated Ethernet segment.

LAN switches allow dedicated communication between devices using full-duplex operations, multiple simultaneous conversations, and media-rate adaption. In addition to this, it is also important to remember that Multilayer switches are capable of handling protocol issues involved in high-bandwidth applications that have historically been solved by network routers. In modern day networks, LAN switches, not hubs or bridges, are used in the wiring closet primarily because user applications demand greater bandwidth.

The demand for greater bandwidth has stemmed from the exponential growth of the Internet, as well as faster, more processor-intensive applications, which have fueled the implementation of server farms. A server farm, also called a server cluster, is a group of servers that is kept in a centralized location, such as a data center. These servers are networked together, making it possible for them to meet server needs that are difficult or impossible to handle with just one server. With a server farm, workload is distributed among multiple server components, providing expedited computing processes.

These two factors, the Internet and server farms, have resulted in modern networks being designed based on the 20/80 rule instead. Based on the 20/80 rule, up to 20 % of the network traffic is local to the network segment, while 80 % of the network traffic is destined to other network segments or traverses the network backbone. This type of LAN design places a greater burden on the network backbone than that imposed by the 80/20 rule.

In addition to this, network engineers should also understand that Layer 3 forwarding (routing) is slower than Layer 2 forwarding (switching), and so greater consideration must be given to the LAN design to avoid bottlenecks within the backbone. To assist in design, Cisco has created a hierarchical model for internetwork design to allow for designing internetworks in layers. This is described in detail in the following section.

The Hierarchical LAN Design Model

The hierarchical model follows the same basic concept of the OSI Reference Model, which is layering. Because each layer is responsible for a particular function, or sets of functions, a layered approach simplifies the tasks required for hosts to communicate, as well as other basic networking tasks such as troubleshooting connectivity issues between the hosts. The LAN hierarchical model is no different.

By using a hierarchical network design, network changes are easier to make and implement. Additionally, such a design allows network engineers to create design elements that can be replicated as the network grows. As each element in the network design requires change, the cost and complexity of making the upgrade is constrained to a small subset of the overall network, whereas in a large, flat or meshed network, such changes tend to impact a large number of systems. The LAN hierarchical model is comprised of the following three layers:

1. The Core Layer
2. The Distribution Layer
3. The Access Layer

The core, or backbone, layer provides optimal transport between sites. It is a high-speed switching backbone and should be designed to switch packets as fast as possible. This layer of the network should not perform any packet manipulation, such as access lists and filtering, that would slow down the switching of packets.

The distribution layer provides policy-based connectivity. That is, the distribution layer is the place at which packet manipulation can take place. The distribution layer provides boundary definition and is the demarcation point between the access and core layers. This layer also helps to define and differentiate the core layer. In a campus network environment, the distribution layer can include several functions, as follows:

- Address or area aggregation
- Departmental or workgroup access
- VLAN routing
- Broadcast or Multicast domain definition
- Media transitions
- Security

In a non-campus environment, the distribution layer can be a redistribution point between routing domains or the demarcation between static and dynamic routing protocols. The distribution layer can also be the point at which remote sites access the corporate network.

The access layer provides workgroup or user access to the LAN. In other words, the access layer is the point at which local users physically connect to the network. The access layer may also use access lists or filters, such as MAC address filters, to optimize the needs of a particular set of users or to provide security. In a campus network environment, access layer functions can include the following:

- Shared bandwidth (i.e. via hub connectivity)
- Switched bandwidth (i.e. using LAN switches)
- MAC layer and MAC address filtering
- Microsegmentation

In the non-campus environment, the access layer can give remote sites access to the corporate network via WAN technologies, such as Frame Relay. Figure 1-8 below illustrates the interaction of these three layers in a typical enterprise LAN:

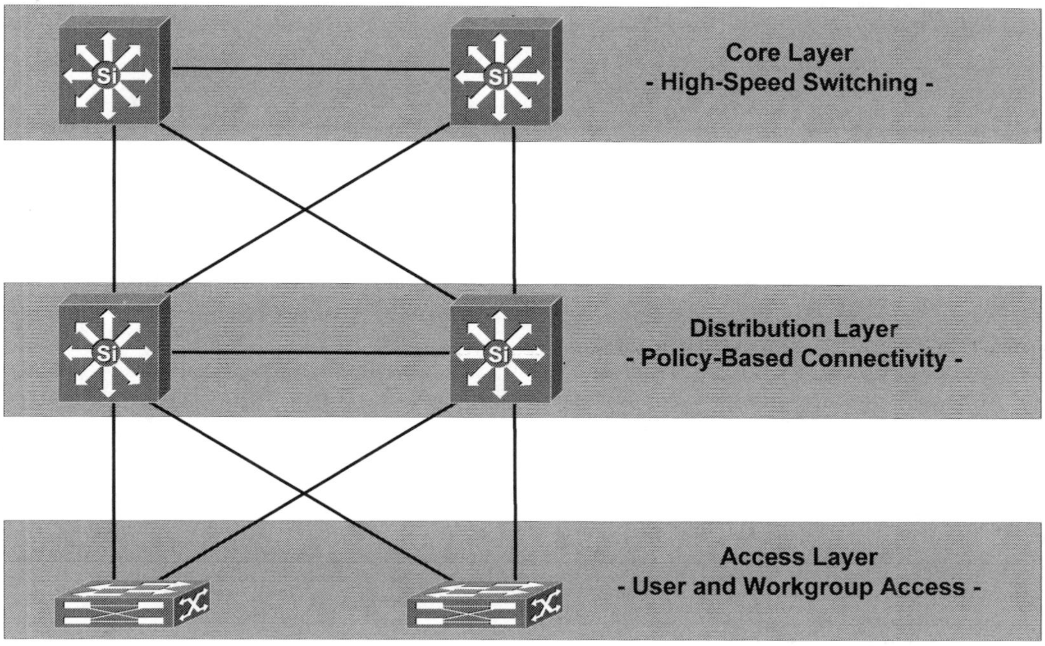

Fig. 1-8. Three-Layer Model in an Enterprise LAN

It is commonly believed that the three layers must exist as clear and distinct physical entities; in fact, this is not always practical or applicable. For example, in medium-sized networks, it is common to find the core and distribution layer functions incorporated into the same physical devices, resulting in a collapsed core. This concept is illustrated in Figure 1-9 below:

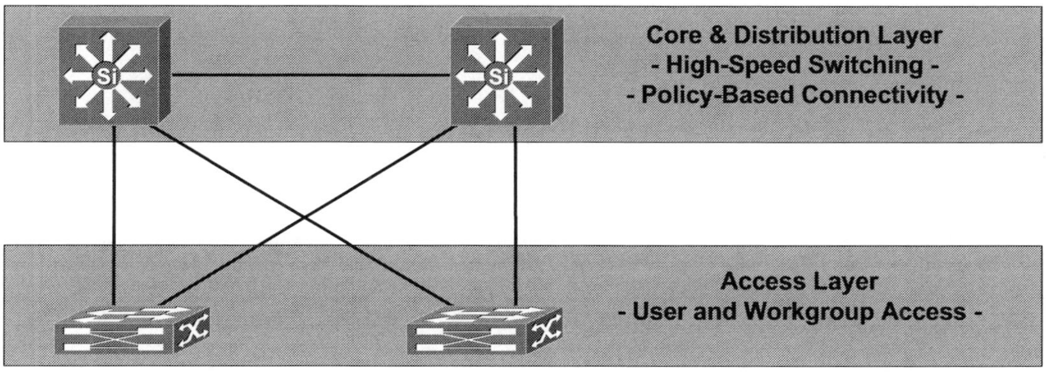

Fig. 1-9. Two Layers Can Be Used for Smaller LANs

Based on the diagram illustrated above, it is important to understand and remember that the layers in the hierarchical model are implemented based on the needs of the network being designed. A medium-sized network, as illustrated above, may have only a collapsed core and access layer, while an even smaller network may have only a single switch performing the functions of the access layer, distribution layer, and core layer at the same time.

In a manner similar to the OSI Model, the layers in the hierarchical model are defined to assist with successful network design and represent the functionality that should exist in a switched network. Additionally, this model also simplifies the identification of failures or problems by structuring the network into smaller, easy-to-understand elements.

The Enterprise Composite Model

The Cisco Enterprise Composite Model (ECM) or Enterprise Composite Network Model (ECNM) provides a detailed design for the campus for a converged, intelligent infrastructure to access IT resources across enterprise locations. This model expands on the traditional hierarchical concepts of core, distribution, and access layers and is based on the principles described in Cisco's description of converged networks. It is therefore important to keep in mind that this is not an industry standard but, rather, a Cisco recommendation.

The model provides a framework for the recommended design and implementation of an enterprise campus network. The enterprise network comprises two functional areas, which are the enterprise campus and the enterprise edge. These two areas are further divided into modules or blocks that define the various functions of each area in detail. The enterprise campus is comprised of the following modules:

- The Building or Switch Module
- The Core Module
- The Management Module
- The Server Module
- The Enterprise Edge Distribution Module

The building or switch module is defined as the portion of the network that contains end-user workstations, phones, and their associated Layer 2 access points. Its primary goal is to provide services to end users. This module is comprised of access layer switches as well as their related distribution layer switches.

The core module is the portion of the network that routes and switches traffic as fast as possible from one network to another. This is simply the core layer in the hierarchical network model.

The management module allows for the secure management of all devices and hosts within the enterprise. Within this module, logging and reporting information flows from the devices to the management hosts, while content, configurations, and new software flows to the devices from the management hosts.

The server, or server farm, module provides application services to end users and devices. Traffic flows on the server module are inspected by on-board intrusion detection within the Layer 3 switches. This module is tied into the switch block.

The enterprise edge distribution module aggregates connectivity from the various elements at the network edge, which may include external-facing routers or firewalls. At the enterprise edge distribution module, network traffic is filtered and routed from the edge modules to the core modules. Figure 1-10 below illustrates the modules within an enterprise campus:

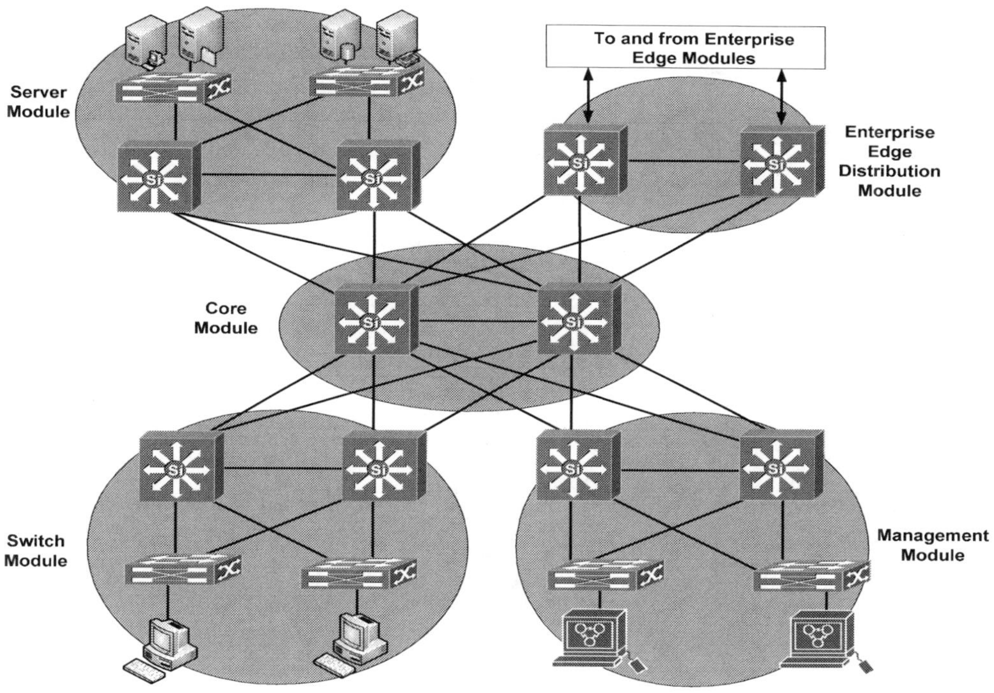

Fig. 1-10. The Enterprise Edge Distribution Module

The enterprise edge distribution module is comprised of the following modules:

- The Corporate Internet Module
- The VPN and Remote Access Module
- The WAN Module
- The E-Commerce Module

The corporate Internet module provides internal users with connectivity to Internet services. It also provides Internet users access to information on the corporate public servers, such as public-facing E-Mail servers, for example. To protect these servers, security devices such as Intrusion Detection Systems (IDS) or Intrusion Prevention Systems (IPS), as well as firewalls, are typically integrated into the design of this module.

Inbound traffic flows from this module to the VPN and remote access module, where VPN termination takes place. It is important to remember that this module is not designed to serve E-Commerce-type applications. Figure 1-11 below illustrates an example of how the corporate Internet module might be implemented:

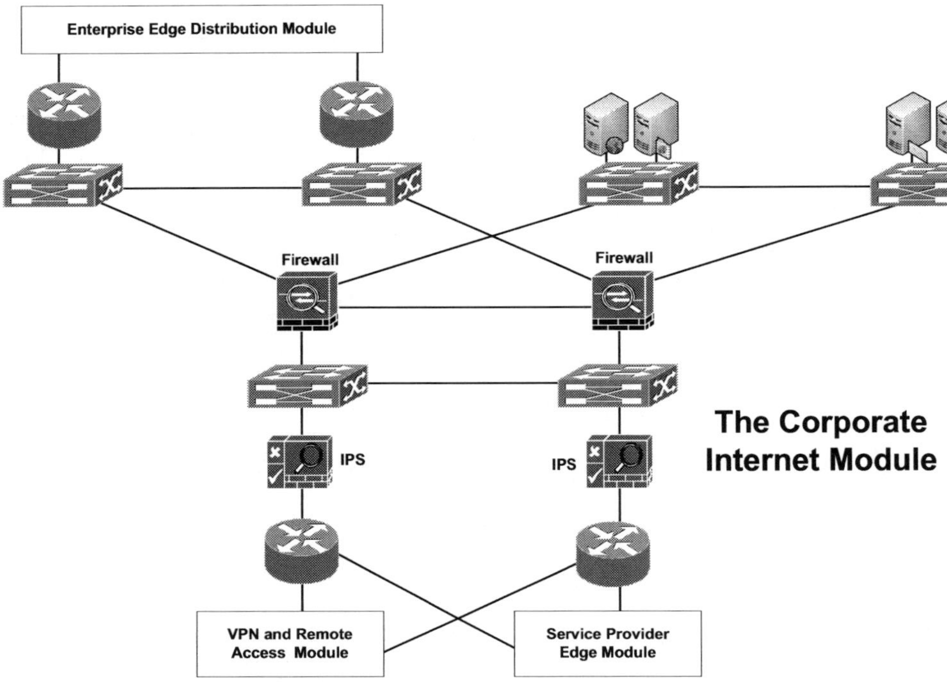

Fig. 1-11. The Corporate Internet Module

NOTE: In referencing this diagram, keep in mind that security requirements differ depending on the objectives and type of business. No standard template is applicable to all business types or organizations.

The VPN and remote access block is responsible for terminating VPN traffic from remote users, providing a hub for terminating VPN traffic from remote sites, and terminating traffic from dial-in users. All traffic forwarded to the enterprise edge distribution module is from remote corporate users that are authenticated in some fashion before being allowed through the firewall. Figure 1-12 below is an example of how the VPN and remote access block might be designed:

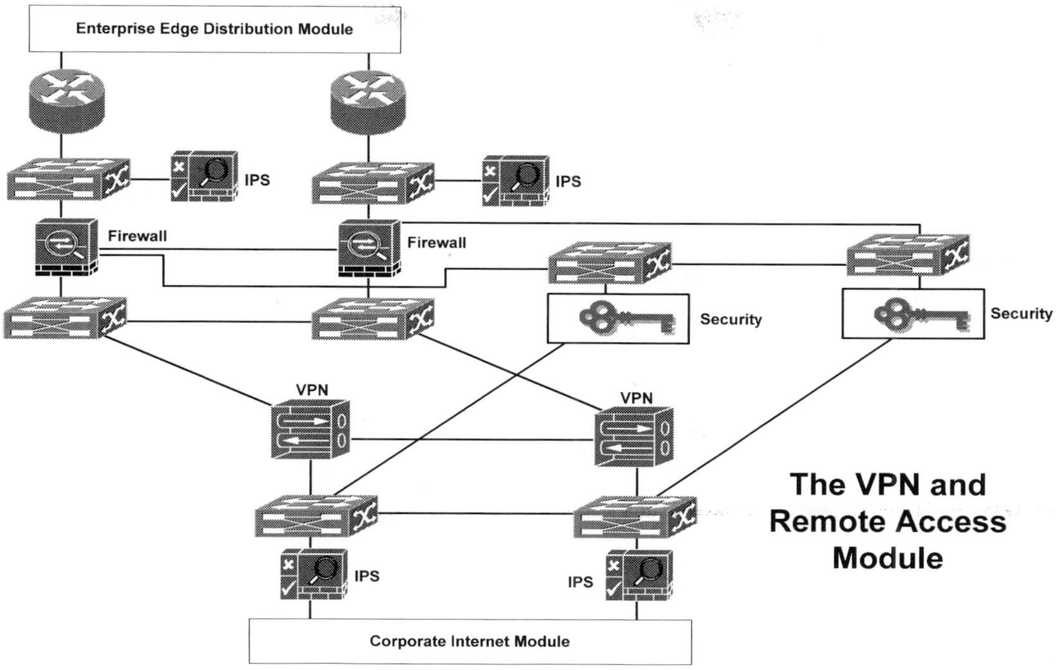

Fig. 1-12. The VPN and Remote Access Module

The WAN module is the simplest. It provides and allows for WAN termination via ATM and Frame Relay, for example. The WAN module is used for network connectivity between the central (hub) site and remote (spoke) sites. Figure 1-13 below illustrates the WAN module:

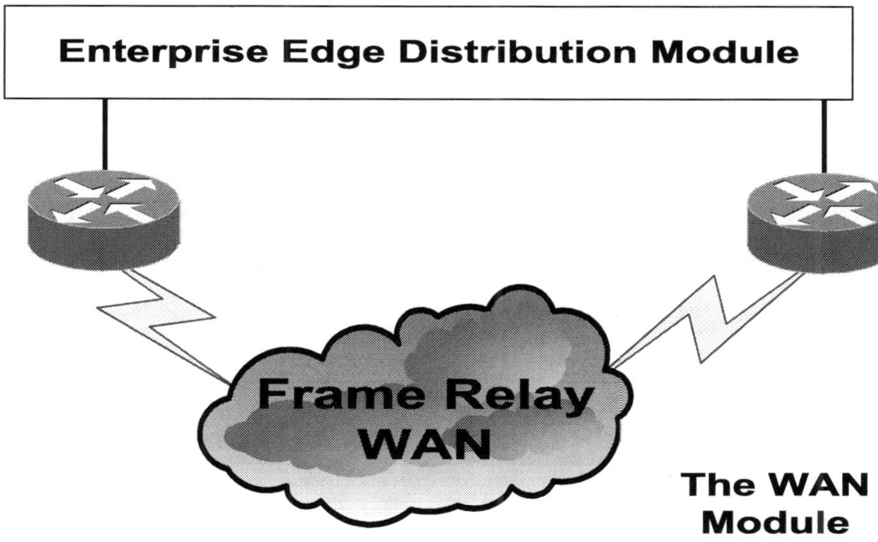

Fig. 1-13. The WAN Module

The E-Commerce module, used for E-Commerce, interfaces with the enterprise edge distribution module and the service provider edge module. Figure 1-14 below illustrates how the E-Commerce module might be implemented:

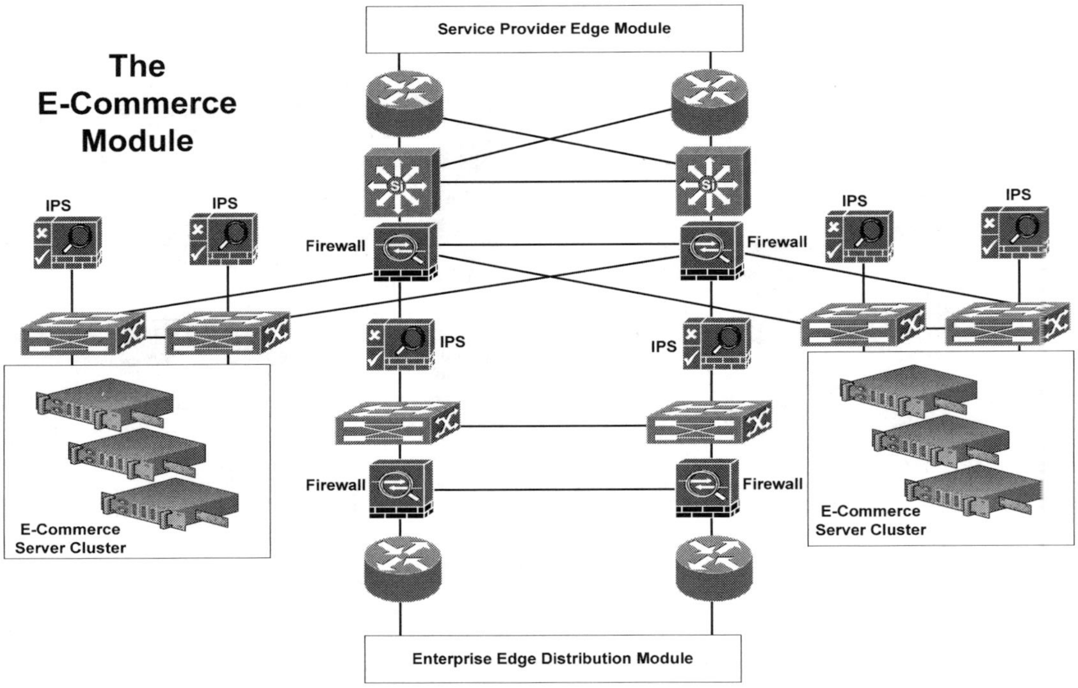

Fig. 1-14. The E-Commerce Module

As has been demonstrated in this section, LAN design and implementation is simply more than interconnecting switches and connecting network hosts to these switches. Instead, considerable thought and planning should go into the design of the enterprise LAN.

The Enterprise Composite Model (ECM) divides functional areas of the LAN into modules. This allows for easier implementation of other network functions, such as security, on a module-by-module basis, rather than attempting to do so all at once on the entire network.

The ECM provides several advantages. The first is that it addresses performance by dividing functional areas into modules and connecting them together over a high-speed backbone. This allows for efficient summarization of networks and more efficient use of high-speed uplink ports. Secondly, with its modular approach, the ECM allows for network scalability by allowing administrators to add on more function modules easily, as required. And finally, the ECM allows for high availability within the network, as different modules can be connected in a redundant fashion to the core and distribution layers with relative ease.

Switched LAN Design Considerations

An internetwork consists of different types of media, such as Ethernet, Token Ring, and FDDI, connected together by routers, enabling these different standards to communicate in a manner that is transparent to the end user. The term 'internetworking' refers to the industry, products, and procedures that meet the challenge of creating and administering internetworks.

A switched internetworking solution is comprised of both routers and switches. The routers and switches used within the internetwork are responsible for the following:

- The switching of data frames
- The maintenance of switching operations

The switching of data frames is typically performed in a store-and-forward operation in which a frame arrives on an input media and is transmitted to an output media. The two most common methods of switching data frames are Layer 2 switching and Layer 3 switching.

As described in the previous section, the primary difference between Layer 2 switching and Layer 3 switching is the information used to determine the output interface. In Layer 2 switching, the destination Layer 2 address (MAC address) is used to determine the egress interface of the frame, while in Layer 3 switching, the Layer 3 address (Network address) is used to determine the egress interface of the frame.

Switches maintain switching operations by building and maintenance of switching tables, as well as preventing loops within the switched network. Routers support switching operations by building and maintaining routing tables and service tables, such as ARP tables, for example. Within the switched internetwork, switches offer the following benefits:

- High bandwidth
- Quality of Service (QoS)
- Low cost
- Easy configuration

Routers (or Multilayer switches) also provide several benefits, which include the following:

- Broadcast prevention
- Hierarchical network addressing
- Internetworking
- Fast convergence

- Policy routing
- Quality of Service routing
- Security
- Redundancy and load balancing
- Traffic flow management
- Multimedia group membership

When designing a switched LAN, it is important to be familiar with the following:

- The differences between LAN switches and routers
- The advantages of using LAN switches
- The advantages of using routers
- The benefits of VLANs
- How to implement VLANs
- General network design principles
- Switched LAN network design principles

The Differences between LAN Switches and Routers

In modern-day networks, Multilayer switches, such as the Cisco Catalyst 6500 series switches, merge router and switch functionality. Because of this blurred line, it becomes even more important for network engineers to have a solid understanding of the differences between LAN switches and network routers when it comes to addressing the following design concerns:

- Network loops
- Network convergence
- Broadcast traffic
- Inter-subnet communication
- Network security
- Media dependence

LAN switches use the Spanning Tree Protocol (STP) to prevent Layer 2 loops. This is performed by the Spanning Tree Algorithm (STA), which places redundant links in a blocked state. Although this does prevent network loops, it also means that only a subset of the network topology is used for forwarding data. Routers, on the other hand, do not block redundant network paths; instead, they rely on routing protocols in order to use the optimum path and to prevent loops.

A switched network is said to be converged when all ports are in a forwarding or blocking state, while a routed network is said to be converged when all routers have the same view of the network.

Depending on the size of the switched network, convergence might take a very long time. Routers have the advantage of using advanced routing protocols, such as OSPF, that maintain a topology of the entire network, allowing for rapid convergence.

By default, LAN switches will forward Broadcast Multicast and unknown Unicast frames. In large networks with many of these types of packets, the LAN can quickly become saturated, resulting in poor performance, packet loss, and an unpleasant user experience. Because routers do not forward Broadcasts by default, they can be used to break up Broadcast domains.

Although multiple physical switches can exist on the same LAN, they provide connectivity to hosts on the assumption that they are all on the same logical network. In other words, Layer 2 addressing assumes a flat address space with universally unique addresses. Routers can use a hierarchical addressing structure, which allows them to associate a logical addressing structure to a physical infrastructure so that each network segment has an IP subnet. This provides a routed network a more flexible traffic flow because routers can use the hierarchy to determine optimal paths depending on dynamic factors, such as bandwidth, delay, etc.

Both LAN switches and routers can provide network security, but it is based on different information. Switches can be configured to filter based on many variables pertaining to Data Link Layer frames. Routers can use Network and Transport Layer information. Multilayer switches have the capability to provide both types of filtering.

When designing switched internetworks, it is imperative to ensure that network hosts use the MTU representing the lowest common denominator of all the switched LANs that make up the internetwork. When using switches, however, this results in poor performance and limits throughput, even on fast links. Unlike LAN switches, however, most Layer 3 protocols can fragment packets that are too large for a particular media type, so routed networks can accommodate different MTUs, which allow them to maximize throughput in internetworks.

Table 1-1 below lists the minimum and maximum frame size for common types of media that may be found within internetworks:

Table 1-1. Frame Size for Common Media Types

Media Type	Minimum Valid Frame Size	Maximum Valid Frame Size
Ethernet	46 bytes	1500 bytes
Token Ring	32 bytes	16 KB theoretical, 4 KB normal
Fast Ethernet	46 bytes	1500 bytes
FDDI	32 bytes	4468 bytes
Serial HDLC	14 bytes	No limit, 4.5 KB normal

The Advantages of Using LAN Switches

LAN switches provide several advantages over bridges. These advantages include increased bandwidth to users via microsegmentation and supporting VLANs, which increase the number of Broadcast domains while reducing their overall size. In addition to these advantages, Cisco Catalyst switches also support Automatic Packet Recognition and Translation (APaRT).

Cisco's APaRT technology recognizes and converts a variety of Ethernet protocol formats into industry-standard CDDI and FDDI formats. Not all switches can provide these functions.

The Advantages of Using Routers

Even within switched LANs, the importance of routers cannot be ignored. Routers, or Multilayer switches, provide the following critical functions in switched LANs:

- Broadcast and Multicast control
- Media transition
- Network segment services

By default, routers do not forward Broadcast or Multicast packets. Instead, routers control Broadcast and Multicast packets via the following three methods:

1. By caching the addresses of remote hosts and responding on behalf of remote hosts
2. By caching advertised network services and responding on behalf of those services
3. By providing special protocols, such as IGMP and PIM

Both routers and Multilayer switches can be used to connect networks of different media types, such as Fiber, Ethernet, and Token Ring, for example. Therefore, if a requirement for a switched campus network design is to provide high-speed connectivity between unlike media, these devices play a significant part in the design.

Routers are also responsible for providing Broadcast services, such as Proxy ARP, to a local network segment. When designing the switched LAN, it is important to consider the number of routers that can provide reliable services to a given network segment or segments.

The Benefits of VLANs

VLANs solve some of the scalability problems of large, flat networks by breaking down a single bridged domain into several smaller bridged domains. However, it is important to understand that routing is instrumental in the building of scalable VLANs because it is the only way to impose hierarchy on the switched VLAN internetwork. The advantages provided by implementing VLANs include the following:

- They increase network security by logical segmentation
- They increase network flexibility and scalability
- They can be used to enhance or improve network performance
- They reduce the size of broadcast domains
- They allow for differentiation between traffic types, such as voice and data
- They aid in the ease of network administration and management

NOTE: These advantages will be described in detail in the following chapter.

How to Implement VLANs

In addition to understanding the advantages or benefits of using VLANs, it is also important to understand the different ways in which VLANs can be implemented within the switched LAN. VLANs can be defined based on port, protocol, or user-defined values. It is therefore important to understand the network requirements in order to determine which method best suits the network and user requirements. These three concepts will be described in detail in the following chapter.

General Network Design Principles

While different vendors have different thoughts and inputs on network design principles, Cisco recommends that the following general design principles be taken into consideration when designing a switched LAN:

- Examine the single points of failure carefully
- Characterize application and protocol traffic
- Analyze bandwidth availability
- Build networks using a hierarchical or modular model

It is important to examine all single points of failure to ensure that a single failure does not isolate any portion of the network. Single points of failure can be avoided by implementing alternative or backup paths, or by implementing load balancing.

Characterizing application and protocol traffic assists in efficient resource allocation within the switched network. Various QoS mechanisms can be used to ensure that critical and sensitive traffic, such as voice and video traffic, is allocated the desired preference and bandwidth resources within the switched LAN environment.

When talking about switches, the bandwidth of the switch refers to the capacity of the switch fabric (or backplane) and not to the cumulative bandwidth of the ports, as often mistakenly assumed. It is important to ensure that there is enough bandwidth across the different layers of the hierarchical model to accommodate user and network traffic.

NOTE: The switch fabric will be described later in this guide.

Building the switched network using a hierarchical model allows autonomous segments to be internetworked together, simplifies troubleshooting, and improves performance. It is highly recommended that some form of hierarchical model be used in switched LAN design.

Campus Switched LAN Topologies

There are three types of topologies that can be used in campus switched LAN design, as follows:

1. Scaled Switching
2. Large Switching with Minimal Routing
3. Distributed Routing and Switching

Scaled Switching

In a scaled switching LAN design, the entire LAN is comprised of only switches at all layers. No routers are used or integrated into the LAN. This design requires no knowledge of the addressing structure (since it is essentially a flat network), is low cost (from a monetary or financial point of view), and is very easy to manage.

However, the downside is that the entire campus LAN is still a single Broadcast domain. Even if VLANs were used, users in one VLAN would not be able to communicate with users in another VLAN without the use of routers.

Large Switching with Minimal Routing

The large switching with minimal routing design deploys switching at the access, distribution, and core layers. At the distribution layer, routers are used to allow for inter-VLAN communication. In this topology, routing is used only in the distribution layer, and the access layer depends on bandwidth through the distribution layer in order to gain access to high-speed switching functionality in the core layer.

This design scales well when VLANs are designed so that the majority of resources are available in the VLAN. In other words, this design is suited for networks adhering to the legacy 80/20 rule. In modern-day client-server networks, this design would not be very scalable and therefore would not be recommended.

Distributed Routing and Switching

The distributed routing and switching design follows the LAN hierarchical network model both physically and logically, which allows this design to scale very well.

This design is optimized for networks that adhere to the 20/80 rule, which is the majority of modern-day client-server networks. This is the most common campus LAN design model in modern-day networks.

Chapter Summary

The following section is a summary of the major points you should be aware of in this chapter.

Internetwork Switching Methods

- Switching can be performed at Layers 1 through 4 of the OSI Model
- The different types of switching are:
  1. Physical Layer (Layer 1) Switching
  2. Data Link (Layer 2) Switching
  3. Network Layer (Layer 3) Switching
  4. Transport Layer (Layer 4) Switching
  5. Multilayer Switching (MLS)

- Physical Layer switches operate at Layer 1 of the OSI Model
- Physical Layer switches can convert one media type to another
- LAN switches operate at the Data Link layer
- LAN bridges and switches allow you to segment the LAN
- LAN switches have several advantages over bridges:
  1. More ports than a bridge would ever be capable of supporting
  2. Microsegmentation by allowing individual hosts to be connected to individual ports
  3. Operating at hardware speed using ASICs, versus the software used by bridges
  4. Supporting Layer 3 and Layer 4 packet switching by including Multi-Layer features
  5. Using VLANs to create smaller logical broadcast domains

- The three primary functions of LAN switches are:
  1. MAC Address Learning
  2. MAC Address Forwarding and Filtering
  3. Layer 2 Loop Avoidance and Detection

- Network Layer Switching is similar to the routing of packets at Layer 3
- Layer 3 switching is performed using hardware ASICs
- Layer 3 switching provides the following advantages over Layer 3 routing:
  1. Hardware-based packet forwarding
  2. High-performance packet switching
  3. High-speed scalability
  4. Low latency
  5. Lower per-port cost
  6. Flow accounting
  7. Security
  8. Quality of service (QoS)

- Layer 4 switching provides additional routing above Layer 3
- Layer 4 switching is also sometimes referred to as Layer 4-7 switching
- Layer 4 switches require a lot of memory
- Multilayer Switching, or MLS, combines Layer 2, Layer 3, and Layer 4 switching
- Cisco supports MLS for both Unicast and Multicast
- In MLS switching, an MLS cache, is maintained for the Layer 3-switched flows
- In Cisco Catalyst switches, MLS requires the following components:
  1. Multilayer Switching Engine (MLS-SE)
  2. Multilayer Switching Route Processor (MLS-RP)
  3. Multilayer Switching Protocol (MLSP)

Local Area Network Switching Fundamentals

- LAN switching is a form of packet switching used in Local Area Networks
- LAN switches provide much higher port density at a lower cost than traditional bridges
- There are three main forwarding techniques that can be used by switches:
  1. Store-and-Forward Switching
  2. Cut-Through Switching
  3. Fragment-Free Switching

- LAN switching can be characterized as either symmetric or asymmetric
- Symmetric switching provides evenly distributed bandwidth to each port on the switch
- Symmetric switching is typically used in a peer-to-peer desktop environment
- Asymmetric switching provides unequal bandwidth between ports on a switch
- Asymmetric switching is the most common type of switching
- Asymmetric switching is optimized for client-server environments

Switch Table Architectures

- The two table architectures supported by Catalyst switches are:
  1. Content Addressable Memory (CAM)
  2. Ternary Content Addressable Memory (TCAM)

- CAM uses a key to perform a table lookup
- The key is fed into a hashing algorithm
- The CAM table lookup is based on an exact match
- Ternary CAM (TCAM) offers an enhancement over CAM
- TCAM is based on three values, which are 0, 1, or X
- The TCAM memory structure is divided into a series of patterns and masks
- TCAM has the ability to ignore certain fields
- TCAM uses the longest match rule to match against packets

Segmenting the LAN using Bridges and Switches

- The rule of thumb when designing bridged networks was the 80/20 rule
- The Internet and server farms have resulted in modern networks using the 20/80 rule
- The 20/80 rule places a greater burden on the network backbone

The Hierarchical LAN Design Model

- In using a hierarchical network design, network changes are easier to make and implement
- The LAN hierarchical model is comprised of the following three layers:
    1. The Core Layer
    2. The Distribution Layer
    3. The Access Layer

- The core, or backbone, layer provides optimal transport between sites
- The distribution layer provides policy-based connectivity
- The access layer provides workgroup or user access to the LAN

The Enterprise Composite Model

- The ECM provides a framework for the design of an enterprise network
- The enterprise network comprises the enterprise campus and the enterprise edge
- The enterprise campus is comprised of the following modules or blocks:
    1. The Building or Switch Block or Module
    2. The Core Block or Module
    3. The Management Block or Module
    4. The Server or Server Farm Block or Module
    5. The Enterprise Edge Distribution Block or Module

- The enterprise edge is comprised of the following modules or blocks:
    1. The Corporate Internet Module or Block
    2. The VPN and Remote Access Module or Block
    3. The WAN Module or Block
    4. The E-Commerce Module or Block

Switched LAN Design Considerations

- An internetwork consists of different types of media
- The routers and switches used within the internetwork are responsible for:
    1. The switching of data frames
    2. The maintenance of switching operations

- The switching of data frames is typically performed in a store-and-forward operation
- The most common methods of switching frames are Layer 2 and Layer 3 switching
- Within the switched internetwork, switches offer the following benefits:
  1. High bandwidth
  2. Quality of Service (QoS)
  3. Low cost
  4. Easy configuration

- Routers (or Multilayer switches) also provide several benefits, which include:
  1. Broadcast Prevention
  2. Hierarchical Network Addressing
  3. Internetworking
  4. Fast Convergence
  5. Policy Routing
  6. Quality of Service Routing
  7. Security
  8. Redundancy and Load Balancing
  9. Traffic Flow Management
  10. Multimedia Group Membership

- When designing a switched LAN, it is important to be familiar with the following:
  1. The differences between LAN Switches and Routers
  2. The Advantages of Using LAN Switches
  3. The Advantages of Using Routers
  4. The Benefits of VLANs
  5. How to Implement VLANs
  6. General Network Design Principles
  7. Switched LAN Network Design Principles

Campus Switched LAN Topologies

- There are three types of topologies that can be used in campus switched LAN design:
  1. Scaled Switching
  2. Large Switching with Minimal Routing
  3. Distributed Routing and Switching

CHAPTER 2

VLANs and the VLAN Trunking Protocol

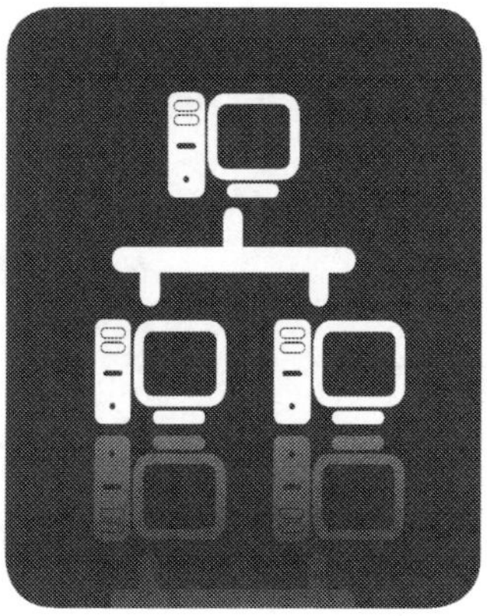

In this chapter, we are going to be learning about Virtual Local Area Networks (VLANs) and the VLAN Trunking Protocol (VTP). A VLAN is a logical grouping of hosts that appear to be on the same LAN regardless of their physical location. The VLAN Trunking Protocol is a Cisco proprietary Layer 2 messaging protocol that manages the addition, deletion, and renaming of VLANs on a network-wide scale. The following is the core SWITCH exam objective covered in this chapter:

- Implement a VLAN-based solution, given a network design and a set of requirements

This chapter will be divided into the following sections:

- Understanding Virtual LANs (VLANs)
- Configuring and Verifying VLANs
- Configuring and Verifying Trunk Links
- VLAN Trunking Protocol (VTP)
- Configuring and Verifying VTP Operation
- Troubleshooting and Debugging VTP

SWITCH Exam Objective	Chapter Section(s) Covered
Determine network resources needed for implementing a VLAN-based solution on a network	• Understanding Virtual LANs (VLANs)
Create a VLAN-based implementation plan	• Configuring and Verifying Trunk Links • Configuring and Verifying VTP Operation
Create a VLAN-based verification plan	• Configuring and Verifying VLANs • Configuring and Verifying Trunk Links • Configuring and Verifying VTP Operation
Configure Access Ports for the VLAN-based solution	• Configuring and Verifying VLANs
Verify the VLAN-based solution was implemented properly using show and debug commands	• Configuring and Verifying VLANs • Configuring and Verifying Trunk Links • Configuring and Verifying VTP Operation • Troubleshooting and Debugging VTP
Document results of VLAN implementation and verification	• Configuring and Verifying VLANs • Configuring and Verifying Trunk Links • Configuring and Verifying VTP Operation • Troubleshooting and Debugging VTP

Understanding Virtual LANs (VLANs)

In this section, the following topics pertaining to VLANs will be described:

- Switch Port Types and VLAN Membership
- VLAN Numbers and Ranges
- Extended and Internal VLANs
- VLAN Trunks
- VLANs and Network Addressing
- Implementing VLANs

The integration of bridges and switches into the LAN allows administrators to segment the LAN and create multiple collision domains. Unlike bridges, switches provide the additional advantage of allowing individual hosts to be connected to their own dedicated ports. This concept is referred to as microsegmentation.

Despite this added advantage, by default, the implementation of switches still results in a single Broadcast domain. This means that any Broadcast frames that are generated by hosts connected to the LAN switch are propagated to all other hosts connected to the same switch as illustrated in Figure 2-1 below:

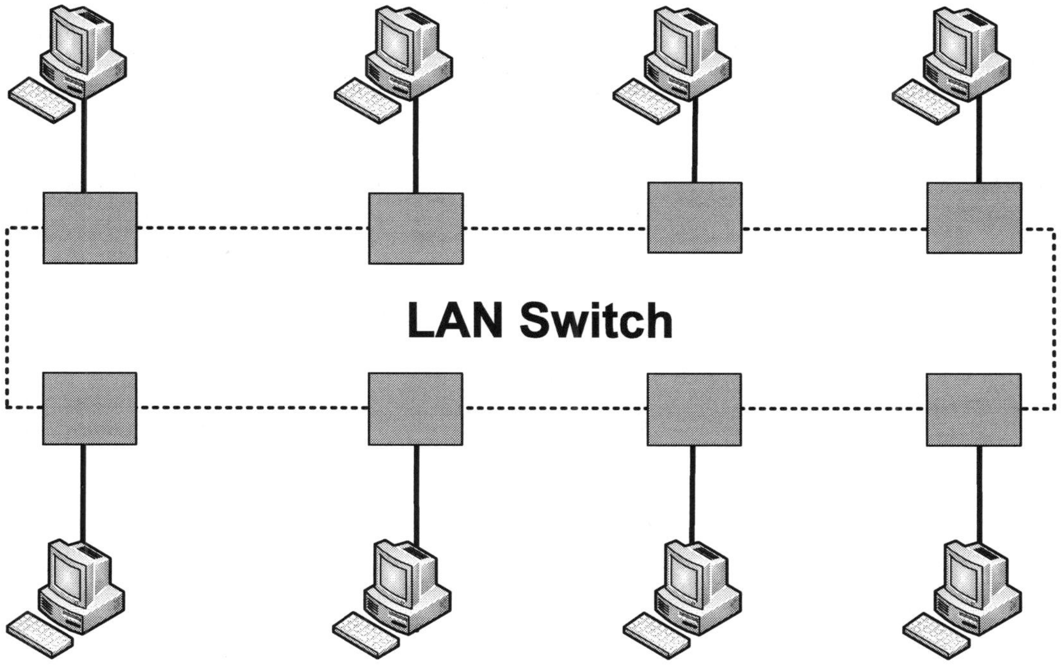

Fig. 2-1. Broadcast Frames Are Sent to All Devices

Referencing Figure 2-1, a Broadcast frame sent by any host connected to the LAN switch will be forwarded out of all ports, except the port on which the frame is received. This is the default method of operation for all LAN switches.

On small LANs with a few hosts, this method of operation is typically not an issue. However, on larger LANs with hundreds, or even thousands, of hosts, the sheer number of Broadcast packets can result in packet loss, latency, and performance issues.

To address all of these issues, LAN switches can employ Virtual Local Area Networks (VLANs), which increase the number of Broadcast domains but reduce their overall size. A VLAN is a logical grouping of hosts that appear to be on the same LAN, regardless of their physical location. Each VLAN is its own separate Broadcast domain. Therefore, if a switched network has 10 VLANs, then there will be 10 separate Broadcast domains. By default, any Broadcast packets that are generated by hosts within the VLAN will not cross into any other VLAN. This concept is illustrated in Figure 2-2 below:

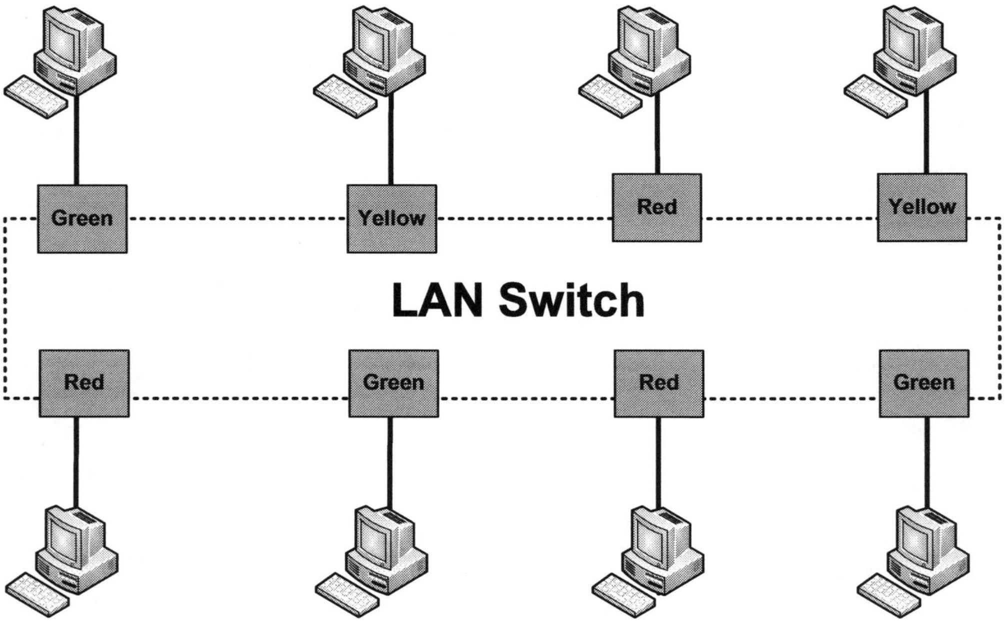

Fig. 2-2. Broadcast Packets Never Leave the VLAN

Figure 2-2 illustrates hosts connected to a switch configured with three VLANs: the green VLAN, the red VLAN, and the yellow VLAN. While the implementation of VLANs on the LAN switch has increased the number of Broadcast domains, it has also resulted in an overall reduction of the VLANs as each contains fewer hosts.

For example, if the switch receives a Broadcast frame from a host connected to the green VLAN, that Broadcast frame will be flooded only to other ports associated with that VLAN, except for the port on which it was received, and will not cross over into any other VLAN. This concept is also applicable to all Broadcast frames that are sent in the red and yellow VLANs.

Switch Port Types and VLAN Membership

The two primary VLAN switch port types are as follows:

1. Access Ports
2. Trunk Ports

Access ports are switch ports that are assigned to a single VLAN. These ports can only belong to a single VLAN. Switch access ports are typically used to connect network hosts, such as printers, computers, IP phones, and wireless access points to the LAN switch. However, in some cases, access ports can also be used to interconnect LAN switches, although going into the details pertaining to this configuration is beyond the scope of the SWITCH certification requirements. The following two methods are used to assign individual switch access ports to a particular VLAN:

- Static VLAN Assignment
- Dynamic VLAN Assignment

Static VLAN assignment consists of the network administrator manually configuring a switch port to be part of a VLAN. This is the most common method of assigning ports on a switch to a particular VLAN. Static VLAN assignment is also referred to as port-based VLAN membership because each device connected to a particular switch port is automatically a member of the VLAN that the port has been assigned to.

Static VLAN membership must be manually implemented by the network administrator. This method of VLAN membership is typically handled via hardware in the switch, which negates the need for complex table lookups because all port mappings are done at the hardware level, resulting in increased switch performance. Static VLAN membership configuration and verification will be illustrated in detail later in this chapter.

Dynamic VLAN assignment consists of using a VLAN Management Policy Server (VMPS) to assign a desired VLAN to users connected to a switch. This dynamic assignment is based on the MAC address of the user machine or network device.

Dynamic VLAN assignment allows for centralized management in that network administrators simply enter the MAC addresses into a database on the VMPS. Therefore, when a user connects to the switch, the switch simply checks with the VMPS and the user is automatically assigned to the desired

VLAN based on the MAC address of the connected end system. Flexibility is also afforded by this solution in that when a host moves from a port on one switch in the network to a port on another switch in the network, the switch dynamically assigns the new port to the proper VLAN for that host.

Despite the advantages of using dynamic VLAN assignment, it is also important to understand that this method requires considerable administrative overhead. For example, in a company with several thousand users and devices, populating and keeping the VMPS database correct and up-to-date becomes a labor- and resource-intensive task.

Unlike access ports, which can only belong to a single VLAN at any given time, trunk ports are ports on switches that are used to carry traffic from multiple VLANs. Trunk ports are typically used to connect switches to other switches or routers. Additionally, in some situations, trunk ports can be used to connect network hosts and devices, such as IP phones to LAN switches, especially in legacy networks. VLAN trunks and trunking configuration will be described in detail later in this chapter.

VLAN Numbers and Ranges

When VLANs are configured, they must be assigned a valid number within a specified range. Cisco Catalyst switches use VLANs in the range of 0 – 4095; however, only VLANs 1 – 4094 are user-configurable VLANs. Table 2-1 below illustrates VLAN numbers and ranges, along with their descriptions as supported in Cisco Catalyst switches:

Table 2-1. VLAN Numbers and Ranges

VLAN Number or Range	Type	Description
0	Reserved	This VLAN is reserved and is not configurable; it is for IEEE 802.1p priority tagging for voice traffic. 802.1p will be described in detail later in this guide.
1	Normal	This is the default Cisco native VLAN. It can be used but cannot be deleted.
2 – 1001	Normal	By default, these VLANs can be created, used, and deleted on all Cisco Catalyst switches.
1002 – 1005	Normal	These are the default Token Ring and FDDI VLANs. They cannot be deleted. Both Token Ring and FDDI are beyond the scope of the SWITCH certification requirements and will not be described further in this guide.
1006 – 4094	Extended	This extended range is used for Ethernet VLANs only. These VLANs can be created, used, and deleted.
4095	Reserved	This VLAN is reserved for system use and cannot be configured.

NOTE: Although VLANs 0 and 4095 are reserved system VLANs, these VLANs cannot be seen in the output of any show commands that pertain to VLANs.

Extended and Internal VLANs

By default, switches are required to create a unique Bridge ID (BID) for each configured VLAN. The BID is comprised of the Bridge Priority and a unique MAC address. The format of the BID is illustrated in Figure 2-3 below:

Fig. 2-3. Bridge ID Format

Because of this requirement, switches need up to 4096 different MAC addresses in order to create a unique BID for every VLAN that can be created.

When the extended system ID or MAC address reduction feature is enabled, the switch instead uses the extended system ID, (which is the VLAN ID), the switch priority, and a single MAC address to build a unique BID for all potential 4094 VLANs. All VLANs are thus able to have a unique BID because the VLAN ID used for each individual VLAN will be unique. Therefore, even though the same MAC address is used for all BIDs, the requirement that the BID be unique for all VLANs is still maintained.

While both Spanning Tree Protocol (STP) and BID will be described in detail later in this guide, Figure 2-4 below illustrates how the normal STP BID is built using the 2-byte Bridge Priority and a system MAC address (see Figure 2-3 above). When the extended system ID feature is enabled, the BID is built as follows:

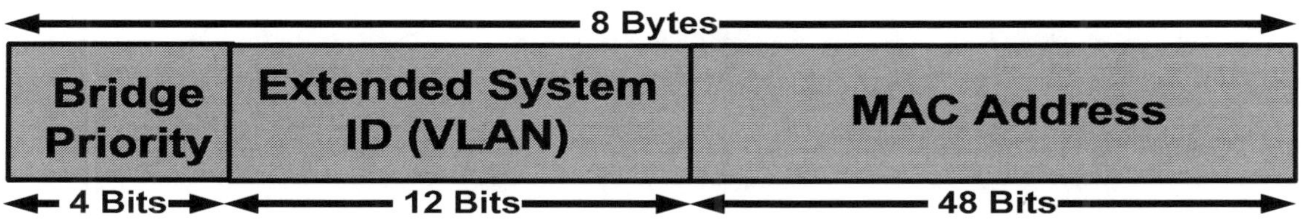

Fig. 2-4. Bridge ID with Extended System ID

In Figure 2-4, the BID becomes a 4-bit value when the extended system ID is enabled. Additionally, a 12-bit extended system ID field, which is the extended VLAN number, is now part of the BID. The MAC address used for all VLANs can now be the same, negating the need for so many MAC addresses, hence the term 'MAC address reduction.'

The extended system ID or MAC address reduction feature is enabled by default in Cisco IOS switches via the `spanning-tree extend system-id` global configuration command.

Cisco's flagship Catalyst switches, the Catalyst 6500 series switches, use certain VLAN numbers internally to represent Layer 3 ports. These VLANs are referred to as internal VLANs and are selected from the extended VLAN range (i.e. the range 1006 – 4094).

Once selected and in use by the switch, the extended VLAN can no longer be used for any other purpose. Figure 2-5 below illustrates how the different types of VLANs can be used, and are allocated internally, on Cisco Catalyst 6500 switches:

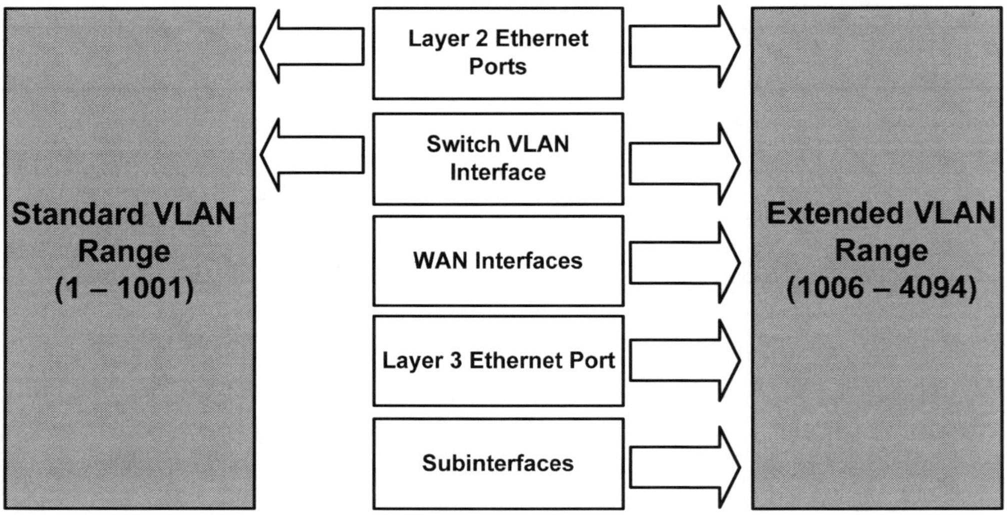

Fig. 2-5. VLAN Use and Allocation

Referencing Figure 2-5, keep in mind the following when implementing or designing an internetwork using Catalyst 6500 series switches:

- Layer 2 Ethernet ports can be assigned into any VLAN—standard or extended
- VLAN interface numbers can use any VLAN number—standard or extended
- WAN interfaces consume one extended VLAN number
- Layer 3 Ethernet ports consume one extended VLAN number
- Subinterfaces consume one extended VLAN number

As previously stated, once an extended VLAN is used by a Layer 3 port, it cannot be used for any other purpose. This presents a problem in that the administrator might want to use certain VLANs for his or her design. To address this, Cisco Catalyst switches allow network administrators to configure the switch such that extended VLANs required for internal use can be allocated in an ascending or descending order as illustrated in Figure 2-6 below:

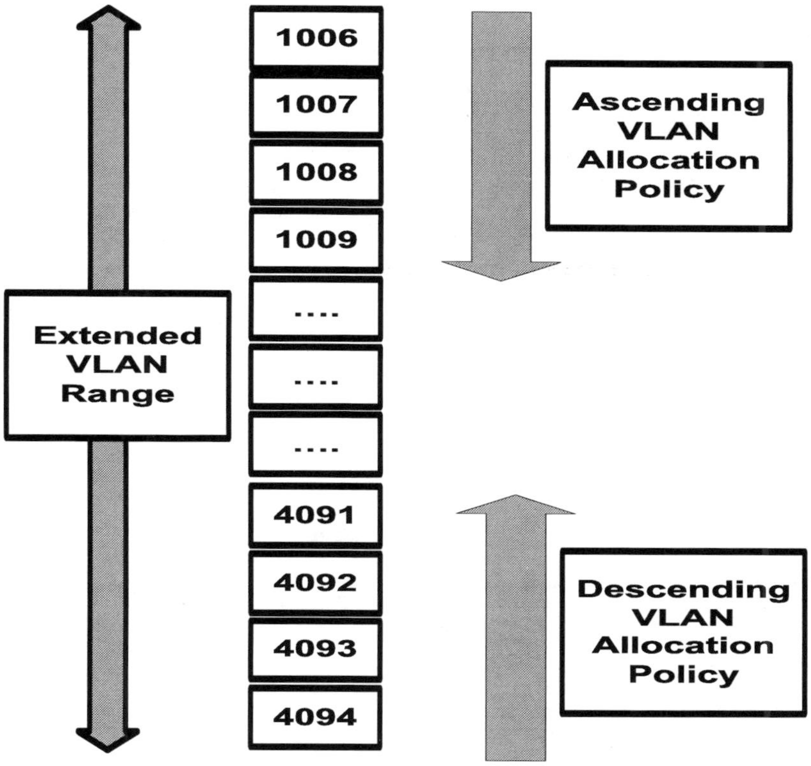

Fig. 2-6. Extended VLANs in Ascending or Descending Order

In Figure 2-6, Catalyst 6500 series switches can be configured for an ascending VLAN allocation policy, in which the switch will allocate internal VLANs from 1006 and up. Alternatively, the VLAN allocation policy can be configured for descending, causing the switch to allocate internal VLANs from 4094 and down.

By default, internal VLANs are allocated in ascending order. However, as previously stated, this can be changed. If the allocation order is changed, the switch must be rebooted before the change can take effect. To display information about the internal VLAN allocation, use the `show vlan internal usage` command as illustrated in the following output:

```
Cat6k#show vlan internal usage

VLAN Usage
```

```
---- --------------------
1006 online diag vlan0
1007 online diag vlan1
1008 online diag vlan2
1009 online diag vlan3
...
...
1016 GigabitEthernet5/1
1018 GigabitEthernet1/1
```

NOTE: Although internal VLAN configuration has been described in this section, keep in mind that the configuration of the internal VLAN allocation order is beyond the scope of the SWITCH exam requirements and will not be illustrated in this guide. Extended VLANs, however, are within the scope of the SWITCH exam requirements and will be illustrated later in this chapter.

VLAN Trunks

VLAN trunks are used to carry data from multiple VLANs. In order to differentiate one VLAN frame from another, all frames sent across a trunk link are specially tagged so that the destination switch knows which VLAN the frame belongs to. The following two primary methods can be used to ensure that VLANs that traverse a switch trunk link can be uniquely identified:

- Inter-Switch Link
- IEEE 802.1Q

Inter-Switch Link (ISL) is a Cisco proprietary protocol that is used to preserve the source VLAN identification information for frames that traverse trunk links. Although ISL is a Cisco proprietary protocol, it is not supported on all Cisco platforms. For example, Catalyst 2940 and 2950 series switches support only 802.1Q trunking and do not support ISL trunking.

ISL operates in a point-to-point environment and can support up to 1000 VLANs. When using ISL, the original frame is encapsulated and an additional header is added before the frame is carried over a trunk link. At the receiving end, the header is removed and the frame is forwarded to the assigned VLAN. This encapsulated frame may be anywhere between 1 and 24,575 bytes in order to accommodate Ethernet, Token Ring, and FDDI; however, if only Ethernet packets are encapsulated, the range of ISL frame size is between 94 and 1548 bytes.

The ISL protocol uses Per VLAN Spanning Tree (PVST), which allows for optimization of root switch placement for each VLAN and supports the load balancing of VLANs over multiple trunk links. PVST is a core SWITCH exam concept that will be described in detail later in this chapter.

The ISL frame consists of the following three primary fields:

- The ISL header, which is used to encapsulate the original frame
- The encapsulation frame, which is the original frame
- The Frame Check Sequence (FCS), used for error checking at the end

When further expanded, the ISL header includes many more fields as illustrated in Figure 2-7 below, showing the encapsulation of a SNAP (AAAA03) frame using ISL:

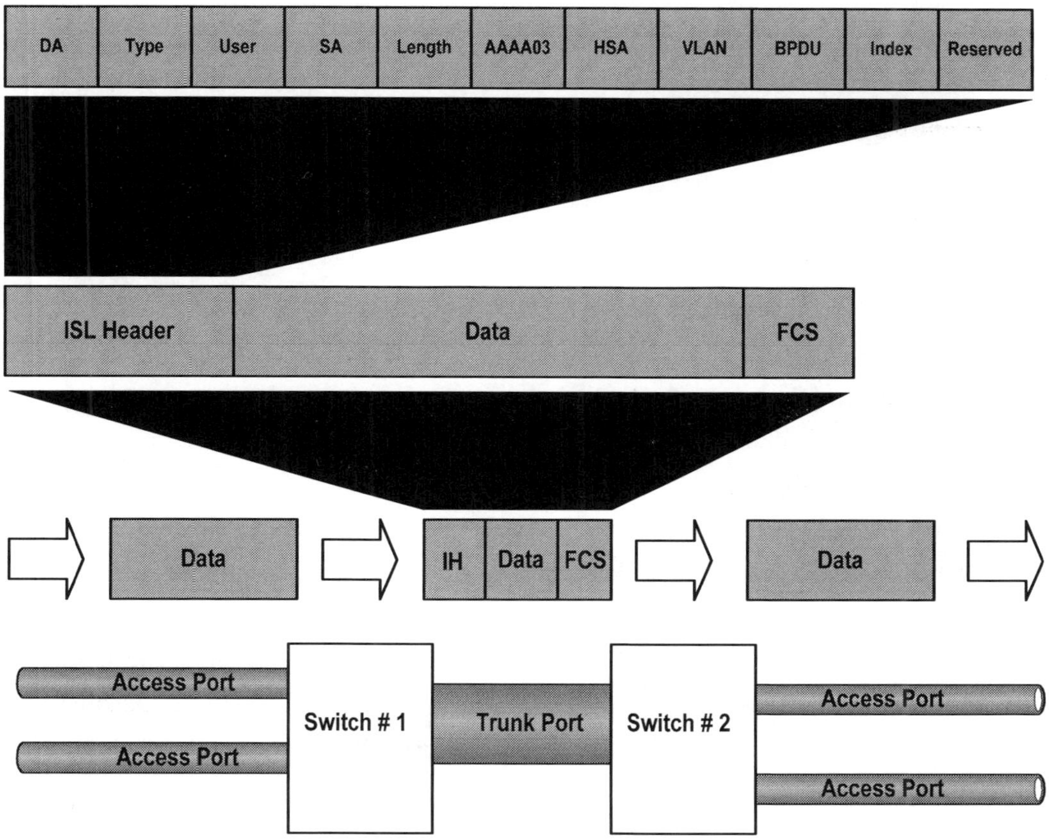

Fig. 2-7. SNAP Frame Using ISL

- The Destination Address (DA) field of the ISL packet is a 40-bit destination address. The DA is a Multicast address and is set to either 0x01-00-0C-00-00 or 0x03-00-0C-00-00. The first 40 bits of the DA field signal to the receiver that the packet is in ISL format.

- The Type field consists of a 4-bit code that indicates the type of frame that is encapsulated. This field can also be used in the future to indicate alternative encapsulations. A Type Code of 0000 indicates an Ethernet Frame, a Type Code of 0001 indicates a Token Ring frame, and a Type Code of 0010 indicates an FDDI frame.

- The User field consists of a 4-bit code that is used to extend the meaning of the TYPE field. The default USER field value is 0000. For Ethernet frames, the USER field bits "0" and "1" indicate the priority of the packet as it passes through the switch. Whenever traffic can be handled in a manner that allows it to be forwarded more quickly, the packets with this bit-set should take advantage of the quick path.

- The Source Address (SA) field is the source address of the ISL packet. The field should be set to the 802.3 MAC address of the switch port that transmits the frame. It is a 48-bit value. The receiving device may ignore the SA field of the frame.

- The Length field stores the size of the original packet as a 16-bit value. This field represents the length of the packet in bytes, with the exclusion of the DA, TYPE, USER, SA, LENGTH, and FCS fields. The total length of the excluded fields is 18 bytes, so the LENGTH field represents the total length minus 18 bytes.

- The AAAA03 SNAP field is a 24-bit constant value of 0xAAAA03.

- The High Bits of Source Address (HSA) field is a 24-bit value that represents the manufacturer ID portion of the SA field. This field contains the value 0x00-00-0C.

- The VLAN field contains the VLAN ID of the packet. This is a 15-bit value that is used to distinguish frames. The VLAN ID is commonly referred to as the color of the frame.

- The bit in the BPDU field is set for all BPDU packets that are encapsulated by the ISL frame. The BPDUs are used by the Spanning Tree Algorithm (STA) to determine information about the topology of the network. This bit is also set for CDP and VLAN Trunk Protocol (VTP) frames that are encapsulated.

- The Index field indicates the port index of the source of the packet as it exits the switch. This field is used for diagnostic purposes only and may be set to any value by other devices. It is a 16-bit value and is ignored in received packets.

- The Reserved field is a 16-bit value that is used when Token Ring or FDDI packets are encapsulated with an ISL frame. For Ethernet packets, this field should be set to all zeros.

The ISL header is 26 bytes in length, while the FCS is 4 bytes in length, which means that the ISL frame encapsulation is a total of 30 bytes in length. The FCS is generated over the DA, SA, LENGTH or TYPE, and DATA fields. When an ISL header is attached, a new FCS is calculated over the entire

ISL packet and added to the end of the frame. Additionally, a second FCS is calculated after the packet has been encapsulated in ISL.

However, the addition of the new FCS by ISL does not alter the original FCS that is contained within the encapsulated frame; instead, the encapsulated frame includes its own cyclical redundancy check (CRC) value that remains completely unmodified during encapsulation. Therefore, if the original data does not contain a valid CRC, the invalid CRC is not detected until the ISL header is stripped off and the end device checks the original data FCS. This typically is not a problem for switching hardware but can be difficult for devices such as routers and network servers.

Because ISL both prepends and appends a 'tag' to the front and the back of the frame, it is often referred to as a double-tagging or two-level tagging mechanism. Before moving on to the next method of VLAN identification, the following is a summary of ISL capabilities:

- ISL can support up to 1000 VLANs
- ISL is a Cisco-proprietary protocol
- ISL encapsulates the frame; it does not modify the original frame in any way
- ISL operates in a point-to-point environment

802.1Q is an IEEE standard for VLAN tagging. Unlike ISL, 802.1Q, or dot1q as it is commonly referred to as, inserts a single 4-byte tag into the original frame between the SA field and the TYPE or LENGTH fields, depending on the Ethernet frame type. For this reason, 802.1Q is also referred to as a one-level, internal-tagging or single-tagging mechanism.

Given that the length of the 802.1Q tag is 4 bytes, the resulting Ethernet frame can be as large as 1522 bytes, while the minimum size of the Ethernet frame with 802.1Q tagging is 68 bytes. In addition, it is important to remember that because the frame has been modified, the trunking device must recalculate the FCS before it sends the frame over the trunk link. Figure 2-8 below illustrates how the 802.1Q tag is inserted into a frame:

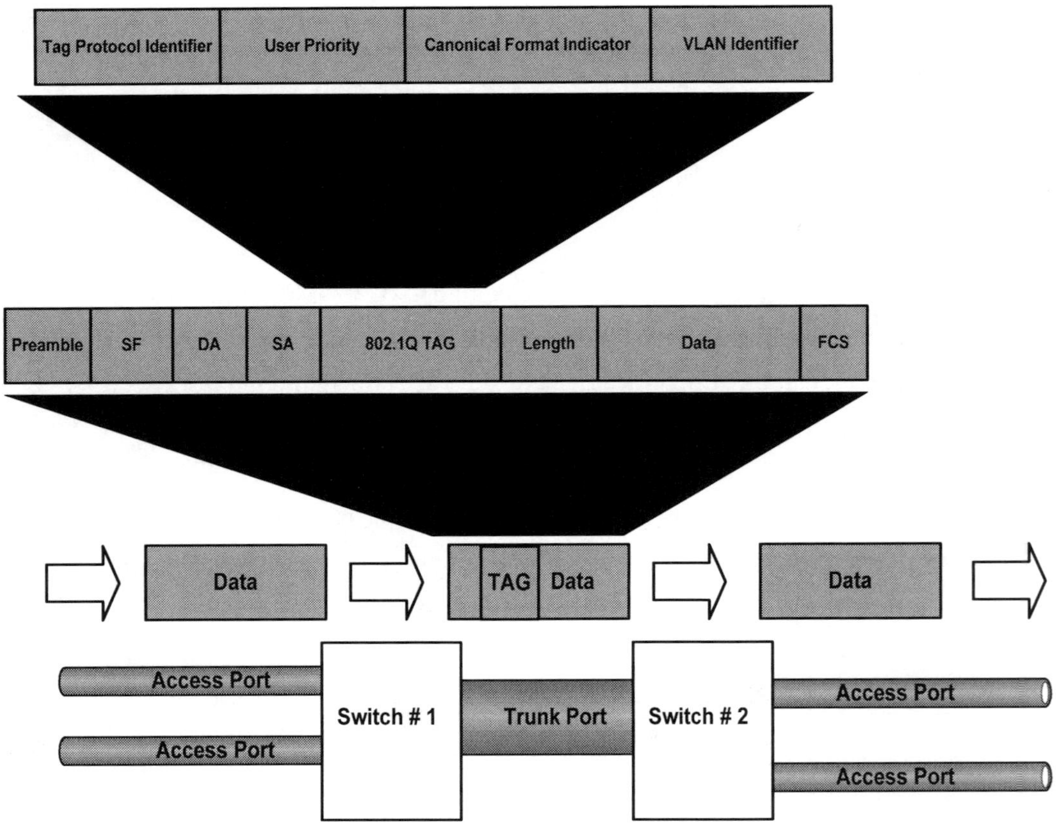

Fig. 2-8. 802.1Q Tag Inserted into a Frame

- The Tag Protocol Identifier (TPID) is a 16-bit field. It is set to a value of 0x8100 in order to identify the frame as an IEEE 802.1Q-tagged frame.

- The User Priority, or simply Priority, field is a 3-bit field that refers to the IEEE 802.1p priority. This field indicates the frame priority level that can be used for the prioritization of traffic. The field can represent 8 levels (0 through 7). 802.1p will be described in detail later in this guide.

- The Canonical Format Indicator (CFI) field is a 1-bit field. If the value of this field is 1, the MAC address is in non-canonical format. Alternatively, if the value is 0, then the MAC address is in canonical format. Ethernet uses a canonical format while Token Ring uses a non-canonical format.

- The VLAN Identifier (VID) field is a 12-bit field that uniquely identifies the VLAN to which the frame belongs. The field can have a value between 0 and 4095; keep in mind that VLAN 0 and VLAN 4095 are reserved VLANs.

802.1Q differs from ISL in several ways. The first significant difference is that 802.1Q supports up to 4096 VLANs. Another significant difference is that of the native VLAN concept used in 802.1Q. By default, all frames from all VLANs are tagged when using 802.1Q. The only exception to this rule is frames that belong to the native VLAN, which are not tagged. By default, in Cisco LAN switches, the native VLAN is VLAN 1. Therefore, by default, frames from VLAN 1 are not tagged.

However, keep in mind that it is possible to specify which VLAN will not have frames tagged by specifying that VLAN as the native VLAN on a particular trunk link. For example, to prevent tagging of frames in VLAN 400 when using 802.1Q, you would configure that VLAN as the native VLAN on a particular trunk. IEEE 802.1Q native VLAN configuration will be illustrated in detail later in this chapter. The following summarizes some 802.1Q features:

- It can support up to 4096 VLANs
- It uses an internal tagging mechanism, modifying the original frame
- It is an open standard protocol developed by the IEEE
- It does not tag frames on the native VLAN; however, all other frames are tagged

ADDITIONAL REAL-WORLD TECHNOLOGIES

Yet another VLAN tagging mechanism can be used. This mechanism is called 802.1Q-in-802.1Q, or QinQ, and it adds another layer of IEEE 802.1Q tag (referred to as the metro tag or PE-VLAN) to the 802.1Q tagged packets that enter the network.

The purpose is to expand the VLAN space by tagging the tagged packets, resulting in double-tagged frames, which allows the Service Provider to provide certain services, such as Internet access on specific VLANs for specific customers, yet still allows other types of services for their other customers on other VLANs. QinQ configuration is beyond the scope of the SWITCH certification requirements and will not be illustrated in this guide.

By default, Cisco's ISL and 802.1Q are not interoperable; however, there may be cases in which networks are comprised of both ISL and 802.1Q VLANs. This may be the case, for example, when migrating from ISL to IEEE 802.1Q. In such networks, Cisco Catalyst 6500 series switches can be configured to map 802.1Q VLANs to ISL VLANs. These mappings are then stored in a mapping table. This concept is illustrated in Figure 2-9 below:

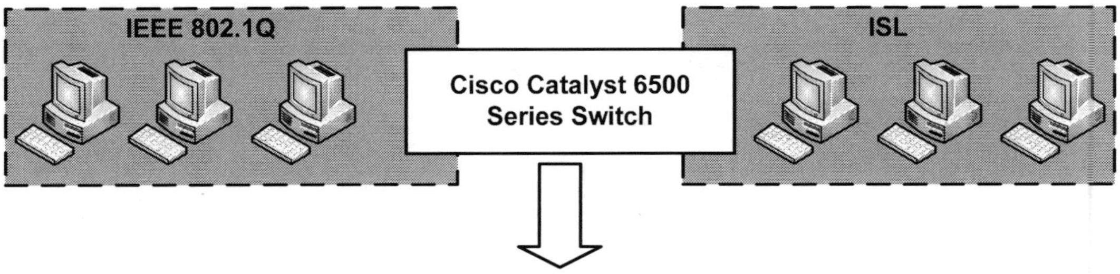

Mapping Table	
802.1Q	ISL
200	100
201	101
202	102
203	103
etc...	etc...
etc...	etc...

Fig. 2-9. 802.1Q Mappings

The `show vlan mapping` command can be used to display the VLAN mapping table information as illustrated in the following output:

```
Cat6k#show vlan mapping

802.1q vlan      ISL vlan        Effective

------------------------------------------

3000             300             true
```

NOTE: The configuration of VLAN mapping is beyond the scope of the SWITCH certification requirements; however, ensure that you are familiar with the basic concept.

VLANs and Network Addressing

While VLANs pertain to Layer 2, it is important to understand that from a design perspective, Layer 3 must also be considered when designing the LAN. The following two methods can be used when designing a Network Layer addressing schema for VLAN-based networks:

- Assigning a single subnet to each individual VLAN
- Assigning multiple subnets per VLAN

The most common practice when designing LANs is to assign a single, unique network to each individual VLAN. The size of the network depends on the number of network hosts that will reside in the VLAN. This solution allows for all hosts within the same VLAN to communicate, at both Layer 2 and Layer 3; however, in order for hosts within one VLAN (and network) to communicate with hosts in another VLAN (and network), a Layer 3 device, such as a router or a Multilayer switch, must be used in the LAN as illustrated in Figure 2-10 below:

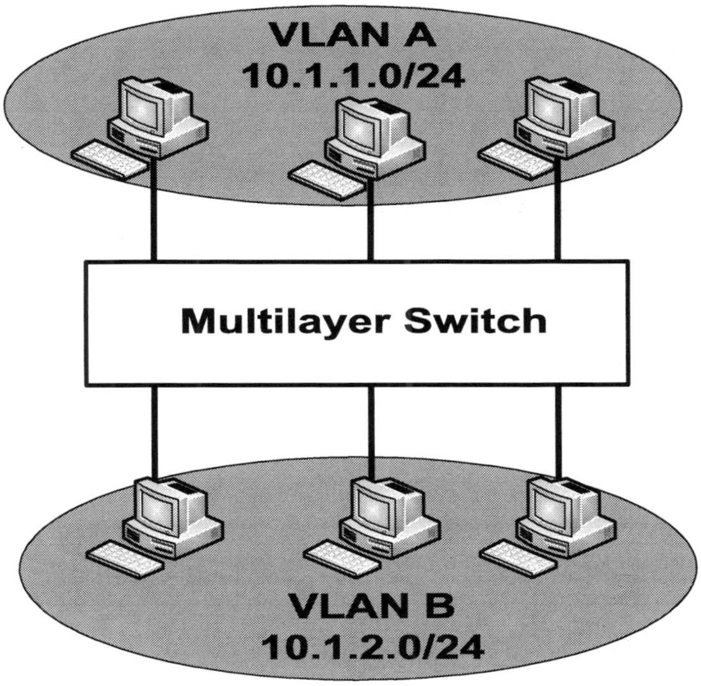

Fig. 2-10. Layer 3 Device Required for Inter-VLAN Communication

In some networks, however, it is possible for multiple IP subnets to be allocated to the same VLAN. In such networks, hosts using the same network address space within the VLAN can communicate with each other; however, a Layer 3 device is still required to allow communication between the subnets, even though the hosts reside in the same VLAN. This concept is illustrated in Figure 2-11 below:

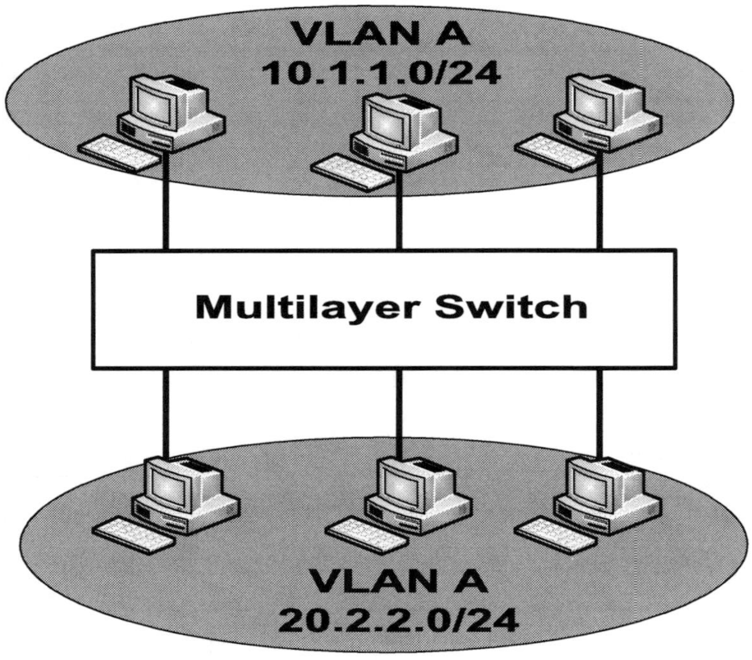

Fig. 2-11. Layer 3 Device Required for Communication between Subnets

Although both techniques do have their advantages and disadvantages, Cisco recommends that a one-to-one mapping between VLANs and subnets be maintained when designing and implementing the switched LAN. Instead of using multiple subnets per VLAN, the preferred solution would be to use a subnet mask that accommodates the actual number of hosts that will reside in the VLAN or VLANs.

Implementing VLANs

Following are two ways of implementing VLANs that should be taken into consideration when designing the switched LAN:

- End-to-End VLANs
- Local VLANs

End-to-end VLANs are VLANs that span the entire switch fabric of a network. These VLANs are also commonly referred to as campus-wide VLANs, as they sometimes span the entire campus LAN so that network hosts and their servers remain in the same VLAN (logically), even though the devices may physically reside in different buildings, for example. End-to-end VLAN implementation is based on the 80/20 rule and therefore requires that each VLAN exist at the access layer in every switch block.

The primary reason for end-to-end VLAN implementation is to support maximum flexibility and the mobility of end devices. These VLANs have the following characteristics:

- They allow the grouping of users into a single VLAN independent of physical location
- They are difficult to implement and troubleshoot
- Each VLAN provides common security and resource requirements for members
- They becomes extremely complex to maintain as the campus network grows

Unlike end-to-end VLANs, local VLANs are based on geographic locations by demarcation at a hierarchical boundary. These VLANs are designed for modern-day networks that adhere to the 80/20 rule, where end users typically require greater access to resources outside of their local VLAN. With local VLANs, up to 80% of the traffic is destined to the Internet or other remote network locations while no more than 20% of the traffic remains local.

Despite the name, local VLANs are not restricted to a single switch and can range in size from a single switch in a wiring closet to an entire building. This VLAN implementation method provides maximum availability by using multiple paths to destinations, maximum scalability by keeping the VLAN within a switch block, and maximum manageability.

Configuring and Verifying VLANs

In this section, we are going to be learning about the configuration of VLANs and some of their characteristics in Cisco IOS Catalyst switches. When configuring Ethernet VLANs, keep in mind that Ethernet VLAN 1 uses only default values. This means that you cannot change the default values assigned to VLAN 1 as illustrated in the output below:

```
VTP-Switch-1(config)#vlan 1
VTP-Switch-1(config-vlan)#mtu 1518
Default VLAN 1 may not have its MTU changed.
VTP-Switch-1(config-vlan)#name TEST
Default VLAN 1 may not have its name changed.
VTP-Switch-1(config-vlan)#
```

NOTE: In order to configure VLANs, the switch must be in either VTP server mode, which is the default, or the VTP must be disabled. In order to configure extended range VLANs, the VTP must be disabled. VTP will be described in detail in the following section. This section is restricted to the configuration of VLANs only. Additionally, all VLAN configuration examples will be illustrated on a switch acting as a VTP server.

Creating and Naming VLANs

VLANs are configured by issuing the `vlan [number]` global configuration command. Although the VLAN number can be either a standard or an extended range VLAN number, keep in mind that extended VLANs can only be configured on a switch that has the VTP disabled. This will be illustrated in detail later in this guide.

When configuring a VLAN, it is always good practice to assign the VLAN a meaningful name via the `name` VLAN configuration command. The assigned VLAN name must be in the form of an ASCII string from 1 to 32 characters and must be unique within the administrative domain. The following output illustrates how to configure several standard range VLANs on a Cisco Catalyst switch running IOS software:

```
VTP-Server(config)#vlan 10
VTP-Server(config-vlan)#name Test-VLAN-10
VTP-Server(config-vlan)#exit
VTP-Server(config)#vlan 20
VTP-Server(config-vlan)#name Test-VLAN-20
VTP-Server(config-vlan)#exit
VTP-Server(config)#vlan 30
VTP-Server(config-vlan)#name Test-VLAN-30
VTP-Server(config-vlan)#exit
VTP-Server(config)#vlan 40
VTP-Server(config-vlan)#name Test-VLAN-40
VTP-Server(config-vlan)#exit
VTP-Server(config)#vlan 50
VTP-Server(config-vlan)#name Test-VLAN-50
VTP-Server(config-vlan)#exit
```

Once the VLANs have been configured, the `show vlan brief` command can be used to view a summary of these configured VLANs, along with default VLANs, on the switch as illustrated in the following output:

```
VTP-Server#show vlan brief

VLAN Name                             Status    Ports
---- -------------------------------- --------- -------------------------------
1    default                          active    Fa0/2, Fa0/3, Fa0/4, Fa0/5
                                                Fa0/6, Fa0/7, Fa0/8, Fa0/9
                                                Fa0/10, Fa0/11, Fa0/12, Fa0/13
                                                Fa0/14, Fa0/15, Fa0/16, Fa0/17
                                                Fa0/18, Fa0/19, Fa0/20, Fa0/21
                                                Fa0/22, Fa0/23, Fa0/24, Gi0/1
                                                Gi0/2
10   Test-VLAN-10                     active
20   Test-VLAN-20                     active
30   Test-VLAN-30                     active
```

```
40   Test-VLAN-40                     active
50   Test-VLAN-50                     active
1002 fddi-default                     active
1003 trcrf-default                    active
1004 fddinet-default                  active
1005 trbrf-default                    active
```

To view detailed information on a VLAN, such as the MTU, ports assigned to the VLAN, state of the VLAN, name, and the type of VLAN, the show vlan id [number] command is used as illustrated in the following output:

```
VTP-Server#show vlan id 10

VLAN Name                             Status    Ports
---- -------------------------------- --------- -------------------------------
10   Test-VLAN-10                     active    Fa0/1

VLAN Type  SAID       MTU   Parent RingNo BridgeNo Stp  BrdgMode Trans1 Trans2
---- ----- ---------- ----- ------ ------ -------- ---- -------- ------ ------
10   enet  100010     1500  -      -      -        -    -        0      0

Remote SPAN VLAN
----------------
Disabled

Primary Secondary Type              Ports
------- --------- ----------------- ------------------------------------------
```

This same information can also be provided by issuing the `show vlan name [name]` command as illustrated in the following output:

```
VTP-Server#show vlan name Test-VLAN-10

VLAN Name                             Status    Ports
---- -------------------------------- --------- -------------------------------
10   Test-VLAN-10                     active    Fa0/1

VLAN Type  SAID       MTU   Parent RingNo BridgeNo Stp  BrdgMode Trans1 Trans2
---- ----- ---------- ----- ------ ------ -------- ---- -------- ------ ------
10   enet  100010     1500  -      -      -        -    -        0      0

Remote SPAN VLAN
----------------
Disabled

Primary Secondary Type              Ports
------- --------- ----------------- ------------------------------------------
```

Assigning Ethernet Ports to Configured VLANs

Once the VLAN has been created, the next configuration step is to assign one or more access ports to the VLAN. By default, only trunk ports are assigned to VLANs since they carry traffic for multiple VLANs; however, access ports must be statically assigned to VLANs by the administrator or dynamically assigned using dynamic VLAN assignment (VMPS). Trunk ports will be described in detail later in this chapter, but VMPS configuration is beyond the scope of the SWITCH exam requirements and will not be illustrated in this guide.

VLANs pertain to the Data Link Layer, and therefore only Layer 2 ports can be assigned to VLANs. This is typically not an issue in Layer 2-only switches, such as the Catalyst 2950 switches; however, on Layer 3-capable and Multilayer switches, such as Catalyst 3750 and Catalyst 6500 series switches, ports on the switch must be designated as Layer 2 before they can be assigned to a particular VLAN. This is performed by issuing the `switchport` interface configuration command.

By default, ports on Cisco Catalyst switches default to a dynamic desirable mode, which means that the switch will attempt to convert the link into a trunk link if possible. In production networks, this is not a desirable trait; therefore, it is always recommended that all ports that will be used on the switch always be statically configured as either access ports or trunk ports. This default setting can be viewed in the output of the `show interfaces [name] switchport` command as illustrated in the following output:

```
VTP-Server#show interfaces gigabitethernet 0/1 switchport
Name: Gi0/1
Switchport: Enabled
Administrative Mode: dynamic desirable
Operational Mode: down
Administrative Trunking Encapsulation: dot1q
Negotiation of Trunking: On
Access Mode VLAN: 1 (default)
Trunking Native Mode VLAN: 1 (default)
Voice VLAN: none
Administrative private-vlan host-association: none
Administrative private-vlan mapping: none
Operational private-vlan: none
Trunking VLANs Enabled: ALL
Pruning VLANs Enabled: 2-1001
Capture Mode Disabled
Capture VLANs Allowed: ALL

Protected: false

Voice VLAN: none (Inactive)
Appliance trust: none
```

NOTE: This is the default for all ports, regardless of whether they are connected.

Statically configuring a switch port as an access port requires that the `switchport mode access` interface configuration command be issued under the desired port (interface).

Next, the port can then be assigned to the desired VLAN by issuing the `switchport access vlan [number]` interface configuration command. The following output illustrates how to configure and assign a Layer 2 access port (interface) to a VLAN on a Layer 2-only switch:

```
VTP-Server(config)#interface fastethernet0/2
VTP-Server(config-if)#switchport mode access
VTP-Server(config-if)#switchport access vlan 20
VTP-Server(config-if)#exit
```

The following output illustrates how to configure and assign a Layer 2 access port (interface) to a VLAN on a Layer 2-capable or Multilayer switch:

```
VTP-Server(config)#interface fastethernet0/2
VTP-Server(config-if)#switchport
VTP-Server(config-if)#switchport mode access
VTP-Server(config-if)#switchport access vlan 20
VTP-Server(config-if)#exit
```

Once configured, the `show interfaces [name] switchport` command can be used to validate the configuration on the switch as illustrated in the following output:

```
VTP-Server#show interfaces fastethernet 0/2 switchport
Name: Fa0/2
Switchport: Enabled
Administrative Mode: static access
Operational Mode: static access
Administrative Trunking Encapsulation: dot1q
Operational Trunking Encapsulation: native
Negotiation of Trunking: Off
Access Mode VLAN: 20 (Test-VLAN-20)
Trunking Native Mode VLAN: 1 (default)
Voice VLAN: none
Administrative private-vlan host-association: none
Administrative private-vlan mapping: none
Operational private-vlan: none
Trunking VLANs Enabled: ALL
Pruning VLANs Enabled: 2-1001
Capture Mode Disabled
Capture VLANs Allowed: ALL

Protected: false
```

```
Voice VLAN: none (Inactive)
Appliance trust: none
```

Suspending Configured VLANs

When a VLAN is configured, it can be in one of two states: active or suspended. By default, all VLANs are in an active state when configured. However, Cisco IOS software allows administrators to change this default behavior after the VLAN is configured by suspending it.

In an active state, a VLAN passes all packets that are sent within it. However, if a VLAN is suspended, it will cease to pass any packets. This state will be replicated throughout the VTP domain and no packets will be passed within that VLAN on a network-wide basis.

Suspending the VLAN retains the configuration, such as all access ports assigned to the VLAN, but prevents the VLAN from passing traffic until it is manually transitioned to an active state. This makes VLAN suspension a powerful tool for administrators who understand its capabilities; however, it can also make it a very dangerous tool for those who do not. VLANs can be suspended in VLAN configuration mode by issuing the `state suspend` command.

NOTE: Extended range VLANs cannot be suspended; this applies only to standard VLAN ranges.

Although VTP will be described in the following section, the following network, illustrated in Figure 2-12, is comprised of two switches (VTP server and VTP client) and will be used to demonstrate the effect of suspending a VLAN on switches within the same VTP domain:

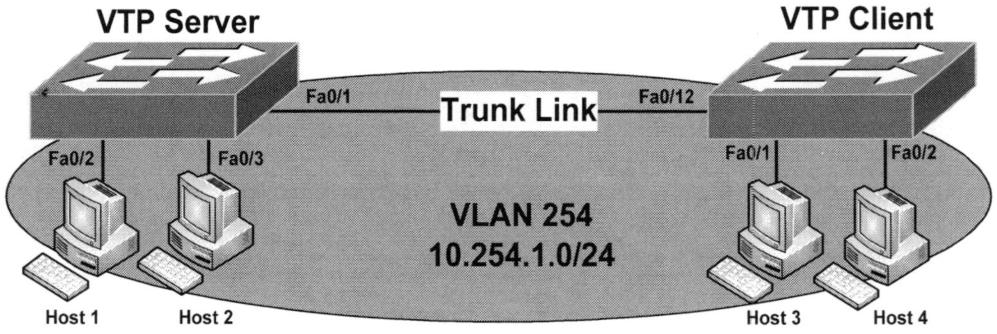

Fig. 2-12. Suspending a VLAN on Switches in the Same VTP Domain

In the switched LAN diagram illustrated in Figure 2-12, a trunk is configured between the VTP server and VTP client switches. VLAN 254 is configured on the VTP server switch and is propagated to the VTP client switch via the trunk link. Hosts 1 and 2 are connected to ports FastEthernet0/2 and FastEthernet0/3, respectively, on the VTP server switch, while Hosts 3 and 4 are connected to ports FastEthernet0/1 and FastEthernet0/2.

The VLAN information on the VTP server switch is is illustrated in the following output:

```
VTP-Server#show vlan brief

VLAN Name                             Status    Ports
---- -------------------------------- --------- -------------------------------
1    default                          active    Gi0/1, Gi0/2
10   Test-VLAN-10                     active    Fa0/4, Fa0/5, Fa0/6
20   Test-VLAN-20                     active    Fa0/7, Fa0/8, Fa0/9
30   Test-VLAN-30                     active    Fa0/10, Fa0/11, Fa0/12, Fa0/13
                                                Fa0/14, Fa0/15
40   Test-VLAN-40                     active    Fa0/16, Fa0/17, Fa0/18, Fa0/19
50   Test-VLAN-50                     active    Fa0/20, Fa0/21, Fa0/22, Fa0/23
                                                Fa0/24
254  VLAN_Suspension_Example          active    Fa0/2, Fa0/3
1002 fddi-default                     active
1003 trcrf-default                    active
1004 fddinet-default                  active
1005 trbrf-default                    active
```

On the VTP client switch, the same VLAN information is present as illustrated in the following output:

```
VTP-Client#show vlan brief
VLAN Name                             Status    Ports
---- -------------------------------- --------- -----------------------------
1    default                          active    Fa0/4, Fa0/10, Fa0/11, Gi0/1,
                                                Gi0/2
10   Test-VLAN-10                     active    Fa0/6
20   Test-VLAN-20                     active    Fa0/7
30   Test-VLAN-30                     active    Fa0/8
40   Test-VLAN-40                     active    Fa0/3, Fa0/9
50   Test-VLAN-50                     active    Fa0/5
254  VLAN_Suspension_Example          active    Fa0/1, Fa0/2
1002 fddi-default                     active
1003 trcrf-default                    active
1004 fddinet-default                  active
1005 trbrf-default                    active
```

As can be seen in the output above, the VLAN is active on both the VTP server and the VTP client. This means that Hosts 1, 2, 3, and 4 can all communicate with each other, as the VLAN allows packets by default.

If a VLAN is suspended on the VTP server, this suspended state information will be propagated throughout the entire VTP domain and the VLAN will also be suspended on the VTP client switch.

The following configuration illustrates the suspension of VLAN 254 on the VTP server:

```
VTP-Server(config)#vlan 254
VTP-Server(config-vlan)#state suspend
VTP-Server(config-vlan)#exit
```

The suspended state can be validated by issuing the `show vlan brief`, `show vlan id [number]` or `show vlan name [name]` commands on the VTP server switch. The following output shows the suspended state in the output of the `show vlan id [number]` command:

```
VTP-Server#show vlan id 254

VLAN Name                             Status    Ports
---- -------------------------------- --------- -----------------------------
254  VLAN_Suspension_Example          suspended Fa0/1, Fa0/2, Fa0/3

VLAN Type  SAID       MTU   Parent RingNo BridgeNo Stp  BrdgMode Trans1 Trans2
---- ----- ---------- ----- ------ ------ -------- ---- -------- ------ ------
254  enet  100254     1500  -      -      -        -    -        0      0

Remote SPAN VLAN
----------------
Disabled

Primary Secondary Type              Ports
------- --------- ----------------- ------------------------------------------
```

The same state for this single VLAN is also propagated to the VTP client in the following output:

```
VTP-Client#show vlan brief
VLAN Name                             Status    Ports
---- -------------------------------- --------- -----------------------------
1    default                          active    Fa0/4, Fa0/10, Fa0/11, Gi0/1,
                                                Gi0/2
10   Test-VLAN-10                     active    Fa0/6
20   Test-VLAN-20                     active    Fa0/7
30   Test-VLAN-30                     active    Fa0/8
40   Test-VLAN-40                     active    Fa0/3, Fa0/9
50   Test-VLAN-50                     active    Fa0/5
254  VLAN_Suspension_Example          suspended Fa0/1, Fa0/2
1002 fddi-default                     active
1003 trcrf-default                    active
1004 fddinet-default                  active
1005 trbrf-default                    active
```

The result of this configuration is that all hosts in VLAN 254 will not be able to communicate since suspended VLANs do not pass packets. However, all other hosts in all other VLANs that are still in the active state are still able to communicate.

The primary advantage of suspending a VLAN is that it blocks traffic while negating the need to delete the VLAN manually, to shut down ports assigned to the VLAN, or to filter the propagation of the VLAN throughout the switched LAN. When administrators want to allow hosts in the VLAN to resume communication, the state can simply be changed to active.

Shutting Down Configured VLANs

In the previous section, we learned about suspending VLANs. While VLAN suspension does have its advantages, the fact that this state change is propagated throughout the entire VTP domain may be viewed as a disadvantage, especially in cases where the objective is simply to prevent packets from passing in a particular VLAN on the local switch, versus the entire network.

To prevent packets from being forwarded in a VLAN on the local switch without affecting the forwarding of packets for all other hosts in that VLAN throughout the entire switched LAN, administrators can simply shut down the VLAN. This can be performed in global configuration mode via the `shutdown vlan [number]` command, or in VLAN configuration mode via the `shutdown` command. Either command performs the same action.

The following output illustrates how to shut down VLAN switching in global configuration mode:

```
VTP-Server(config)#shutdown vlan ?
  <2-1001>   VLAN ID of the VLAN to shutdown
```

The following output illustrates how to shut down VLAN switching in VLAN configuration mode:

```
VTP-Server(config)#vlan 254
VTP-Server(config-vlan)#shutdown ?
  <cr>
```

The VLAN shutdown feature is illustrated in Figure 2-13 below:

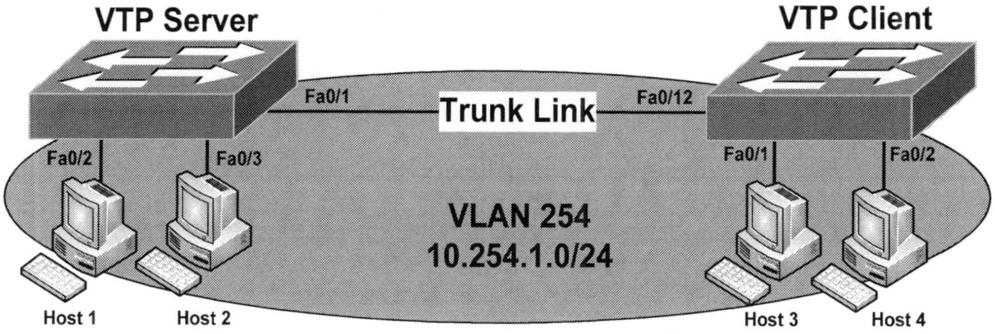

Fig. 2-13. VLAN Shutdown Feature

Figure 2-13 is the same topology as that used in Figure 2-12. This time, instead of suspending VLAN 254, it will be shut down on the VTP server, preventing only locally connected hosts from communicating but not affecting the hosts residing in the same VLAN on the VTP client switch. This is performed as follows:

```
VTP-Server(config)#shutdown vlan 254
```

NOTE: The same action can be performed in VLAN configuration mode as follows:

```
VTP-Server(config)#vlan 254
VTP-Server(config-vlan)#shutdown
```

The VLAN state can then be validated on the VTP server as follows:

```
VTP-Server#show vlan brief

VLAN Name                             Status    Ports
---- -------------------------------- --------- -------------------------------
1    default                          active    Gi0/1, Gi0/2
10   Test-VLAN-10                     active    Fa0/4, Fa0/5, Fa0/6
20   Test-VLAN-20                     active    Fa0/7, Fa0/8, Fa0/9
30   Test-VLAN-30                     active    Fa0/10, Fa0/11, Fa0/12, Fa0/13
                                                Fa0/14, Fa0/15
40   Test-VLAN-40                     active    Fa0/16, Fa0/17, Fa0/18, Fa0/19
50   Test-VLAN-50                     active    Fa0/20, Fa0/21, Fa0/22, Fa0/23
                                                Fa0/24
254  VLAN_Suspension_Example          act/lshut Fa0/2, Fa0/3
1002 fddi-default                     active
1003 trcrf-default                    active
1004 fddinet-default                  active
1005 trbrf-default                    active
```

The `act/lshut` status indicates that the VLAN is still active but is locally shut down. This state, therefore, does not affect any other switch in the network, as can be seen on the VTP client in the following output:

```
VTP-Client#show vlan brief
VLAN Name                             Status    Ports
---- -------------------------------- --------- -------------------------------
1    default                          active    Fa0/4, Fa0/10, Fa0/11, Gi0/1,
                                                Gi0/2
10   Test-VLAN-10                     active    Fa0/6
20   Test-VLAN-20                     active    Fa0/7
30   Test-VLAN-30                     active    Fa0/8
```

```
40   Test-VLAN-40                       active    Fa0/3, Fa0/9
50   Test-VLAN-50                       active    Fa0/5
254  VLAN_Suspension_Example            active    Fa0/1, Fa0/2
1002 fddi-default                       active
1003 trcrf-default                      active
1004 fddinet-default                    active
1005 trbrf-default                      active
```

The result of the VLAN shutdown configuration is that only hosts that are locally connected to ports assigned to VLAN 254 on the VTP server will be unable to pass packets; however, all other hosts assigned to the same VLAN on any other switches in VLAN 254 will still be able to pass packets and communicate with each other.

ADDITIONAL REAL-WORLD TECHNOLOGIES

Cisco Catalyst 6500 series switches support an additional feature called VLAN locking that allows administrators to provide an extra level of verification when moving ports from one VLAN to another. This feature, which is enabled via the `vlan port provisioning` global configuration command, requires that the VLAN name, NOT number, be entered when a port is moved from one VLAN to another via the `switchport access vlan [VLAN NAME]` interface configuration command. VLAN locking configuration is beyond the scope of the SWITCH certification requirements and will not be illustrated in this guide.

Configuring and Verifying Trunk Links

A trunk is a switch port that can carry multiple traffic types, each tagged with a unique VLAN ID. As data is switched across the trunk port or trunk link, it is tagged (or colored) by the egress switch trunk port, which allows the receiving switch to identify that it belongs to a particular VLAN. On the receiving switch ingress port, the tag is removed and the data is forwarded to the intended destination.

The first configuration task when implementing VLAN trunking in Cisco IOS Catalyst switches is to configure the desired interface as a Layer 2 switch port. This is performed by issuing the `switchport` interface configuration command.

NOTE: This command is required only on Layer 3-capable or Multilayer switches. It is not applicable to Layer 2-only switches, such as the Catalyst 2950 series.

The second configuration task is to specify the encapsulation protocol that the trunk link should use. This is performed by issuing the `switchport trunk encapsulation [option]` command.

The options available with this command are as follows:

```
Cat6-Distribution(config)#interface fastethernet 1/1
Cat6-Distribution(config-if)#switchport trunk encapsulation ?
  dot1q      Interface uses only 802.1q trunking encapsulation when trunking
  isl        Interface uses only ISL trunking encapsulation when trunking
  negotiate  Device will negotiate trunking encapsulation with peer on
             interface
```

The `dot1q` keyword forces the switch port to use IEEE 802.1Q encapsulation. The `isl` keyword forces the switch port to use Cisco ISL encapsulation. The `negotiate` keyword is used to specify that if the Dynamic Inter-Switch Link Protocol (DISL) and Dynamic Trunking Protocol (DTP) negotiation fail to successfully agree on the encapsulation format, then ISL is the selected format. DISL simplifies the creation of an ISL trunk from two interconnected Fast Ethernet devices. DISL minimizes VLAN trunk configuration procedures because only one end of a link needs to be configured as a trunk.

DTP is a Cisco proprietary point-to-protocol that negotiates a common trunking mode between two switches. DTP will be described in detail later in this chapter. The following output illustrates how to configure a switch port to use IEEE 802.1Q encapsulation when establishing a trunk:

```
Cat6-Distribution(config)#interface fastethernet 1/1
Cat6-Distribution(config-if)#switchport
Cat6-Distribution(config-if)#switchport trunk encapsulation dot1q
```

This configuration can be validated via the `show interfaces [name] switchport` command as illustrated in the following output:

```
Cat6-Distribution#show interfaces fastethernet 1/1 switchport
Name: Fa0/2
Switchport: Enabled
Administrative Mode: dynamic desirable
Operational Mode: trunk
Administrative Trunking Encapsulation: dot1q
Operational Trunking Encapsulation: dot1q
Negotiation of Trunking: On
Access Mode VLAN: 1 (default)
Trunking Native Mode VLAN: 1 (default)
...
[Output Truncated]
```

The third trunk port configuration step is to implement configuration in order to ensure that the port is designated as a trunk port. This can be done in one of two ways:

- Manual (Static) Trunk Configuration
- Dynamic Trunking Protocol (DTP)

Manual (Static) Trunk Configuration

The manual configuration of a trunk is performed by issuing the `switchport mode trunk` interface configuration command on the desired switch port. This command forces the port into a permanent (static) trunking mode. The following configuration output shows how to configure a port statically as a trunk port:

```
VTP-Server(config)#interface fastethernet 0/1
VTP-Server(config-if)#switchport
VTP-Server(config-if)#switchport trunk encapsulation dot1q
VTP-Server(config-if)#switchport mode trunk
VTP-Server(config-if)#exit
VTP-Server(config)#
```

This configuration can be validated via the `show interfaces [name] switchport` command as illustrated in the following output:

```
VTP-Server#show interfaces fastethernet 0/1 switchport
Name: Fa0/1
Switchport: Enabled
Administrative Mode: trunk
Operational Mode: trunk
Administrative Trunking Encapsulation: dot1q
Operational Trunking Encapsulation: dot1q
Negotiation of Trunking: On
Access Mode VLAN: 1 (default)
Trunking Native Mode VLAN: 1 (default)
...
[Truncated Output]
```

Although manual (static) configuration of a trunk link forces the switch to establish a trunk, Dynamic ISL and Dynamic Trunking Protocol (DTP) packets will still be sent out of the interface. This is performed so that a statically configured trunk link can establish a trunk with a neighboring switch that is using DTP, as will be described in the following section. This can be validated in the output of the `show interfaces [name] switchport` command as illustrated in the following output:

```
VTP-Server#show interfaces fastethernet 0/1 switchport
Name: Fa0/1
Switchport: Enabled
Administrative Mode: trunk
Operational Mode: trunk
Administrative Trunking Encapsulation: dot1q
Operational Trunking Encapsulation: dot1q
Negotiation of Trunking: On
Access Mode VLAN: 1 (default)
Trunking Native Mode VLAN: 1 (default)
...
[Truncated Output]
```

In the output above, the text in bold indicates that despite the static configuration of the trunk link, the port is still sending out DTP and DISL packets.

In some cases, this is considered undesirable. Therefore, it is considered good practice to disable the sending of DISL and DTP packets on a port statically configured as a trunk link by issuing the `switchport nonegotiate` interface configuration command as illustrated in the following output:

```
VTP-Server(config)#interface fastethernet 0/1
VTP-Server(config-if)#switchport
VTP-Server(config-if)#switchport trunk encapsulation dot1q
VTP-Server(config-if)#switchport mode trunk
VTP-Server(config-if)#switchport nonegotiate
VTP-Server(config-if)#exit
VTP-Server(config)#
```

Again, the `show interfaces [name] switchport` command can be used to validate the configuration, as follows:

```
VTP-Server#show interfaces fastethernet 0/1 switchport
Name: Fa0/1
Switchport: Enabled
Administrative Mode: trunk
Operational Mode: trunk
Administrative Trunking Encapsulation: dot1q
Operational Trunking Encapsulation: dot1q
Negotiation of Trunking: Off
Access Mode VLAN: 1 (default)
Trunking Native Mode VLAN: 1 (default)
...
[Truncated Output]
```

Dynamic Trunking Protocol (DTP)

DTP is a Cisco proprietary point-to-protocol that negotiates a common trunking mode between two switches. This dynamic negotiation can also include the trunking encapsulation. The two DTP modes that a switch port can use, depending on the platform, are as follows:

- Dynamic Desirable
- Dynamic Auto

When using DTP, if the switch port defaults to a dynamic desirable state, the port will actively attempt to become a trunk if the neighboring switch is set to dynamic desirable or dynamic auto mode. If the switch ports default to a dynamic auto state, the port will revert to being a trunk only if the neighboring switch is set to dynamic desirable mode.

Figure 2-14 below illustrates the DTP mode combinations that will result in a trunk either establishing or not establishing between two Cisco Catalyst switches:

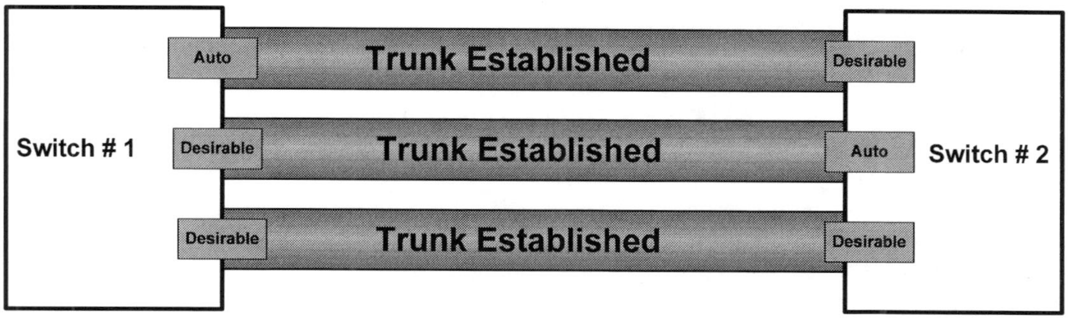

Fig. 2-14. DTP Mode Combinations

Figure 2-15 below illustrates the valid combinations that will result in the successful establishment of a trunk link between two neighboring switches—one using DTP and the other statically configured as a trunk port:

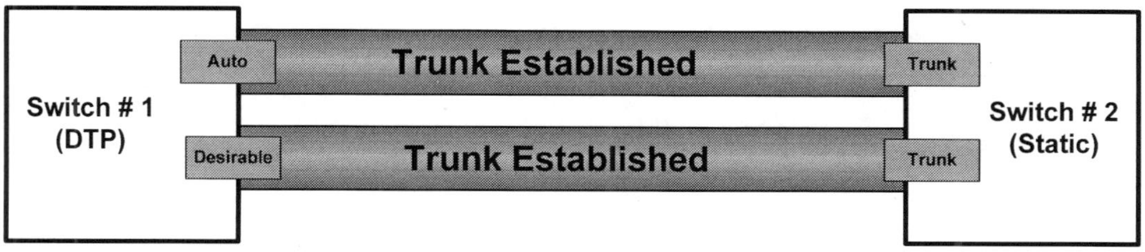

Fig. 2-15. DTP Mode Combinations 2

In addition to these various combinations that can be used to establish a trunk link between two neighboring switches, it is important to know that if the switches are both set to dynamic auto, they will not be able to establish a trunk between them.

This is because unlike dynamic desirable mode, dynamic auto mode is a passive mode that waits for the other side to initiate trunk establishment. Therefore, if two passive ports are connected, neither will ever initiate trunk establishment and the trunk will never be formed. Similarly, if a statically configured switch port is also configured with the `switchport nonegotiate` command, it will never form a trunk with a neighboring switch using DTP because this prevents the sending of DISL and DTP packets out of that port.

When using DTP in a switched LAN, the `show dtp [interface <name>]` command can be used to display DTP information globally for the switch or for the specified interface. The following output shows the information printed by the show dtp command:

```
VTP-Server#show dtp
Global DTP information
        Sending DTP Hello packets every 30 seconds
        Dynamic Trunk timeout is 300 seconds
        4 interfaces using DTP
```

Based on the output above, the switch is sending DTP packets every 30 seconds. The timeout value for DTP is set to 300 seconds (5 minutes), and 4 interfaces are currently using DTP. The `show dtp interface [name]` command prints DTP information about the specified interface, which includes the type of interface (trunk or access), the current port DTP configuration, the trunk encapsulation, and DTP packet statistics as illustrated in the following output:

```
VTP-Server#show dtp interface fastethernet0/1
DTP information for FastEthernet0/1:
  TOS/TAS/TNS:                              TRUNK/ON/TRUNK
  TOT/TAT/TNT:                              802.1Q/802.1Q/802.1Q
  Neighbor address 1:                       000000000000
  Neighbor address 2:                       000000000000
  Hello timer expiration (sec/state):       7/RUNNING
  Access timer expiration (sec/state):      never/STOPPED
  Negotiation timer expiration (sec/state): never/STOPPED
  Multidrop timer expiration (sec/state):   never/STOPPED
  FSM state:                                S6:TRUNK
  # times multi & trunk                     0
  Enabled:                                  yes
  In STP:                                   no

  Statistics
  ----------
  0 packets received (0 good)
  0 packets dropped
      0 nonegotiate, 0 bad version, 0 domain mismatches, 0 bad TLVs, 0 other
  764 packets output (764 good)
      764 native, 0 software encap isl, 0 isl hardware native
  0 output errors
  0 trunk timeouts
  2 link ups, last link up on Mon Mar 01 1993, 00:00:22
  1 link downs, last link down on Mon Mar 01 1993, 00:00:20
```

IEEE 802.1Q Native VLAN

Earlier in this chapter, we learned that 802.1Q, or VLAN tagging, inserts a tag into all frames and all frames, except those in the native VLAN, are tagged. The IEEE defined the native VLAN to provide for connectivity to old 802.3 ports that did not understand VLAN tags.

By default, an 802.1Q trunk uses VLAN 1 as the native VLAN. The default native VLAN on an 802.1Q trunk link can be verified by issuing the `show interfaces [name] switchport` or the `show interfaces trunk` command as illustrated in the following output:

```
VTP-Server#show interfaces fastethernet 0/1 switchport
Name: Fa0/1
Switchport: Enabled
Administrative Mode: trunk
Operational Mode: trunk
Administrative Trunking Encapsulation: dot1q
Operational Trunking Encapsulation: dot1q
Negotiation of Trunking: On
Access Mode VLAN: 1 (default)
Trunking Native Mode VLAN: 1 (default)
Voice VLAN: none
...
[Truncated Output]
```

The native VLAN is used by the switch to carry specific protocol traffic like Cisco Discovery Protocol (CDP), VLAN Trunking Protocol (VTP), Port Aggregation Protocol (PAGP), and Dynamic Trunking Protocol (DTP) information. CDP and PAGP will be described in detail later in this guide. Although the default native VLAN is always VLAN 1, the native VLAN can be manually changed to any valid VLAN number that is not in the reserved range of VLANs.

However, it is important to remember that the native VLAN must be the same on both sides of the trunk link. If there is a native VLAN mismatch, Spanning Tree Protocol (STP) places the port in a port VLAN ID (PVID) inconsistent state and will not forward the link. Additionally, CDP v2 passes native VLAN information between switches and will print error messages on the switch console if there is a native VLAN mismatch. The default native VLAN can be changed by issuing the `switchport trunk native vlan [number]` interface configuration command on the desired 802.1Q trunk link as illustrated in the following output:

```
VTP-Server(config)#interface fastethernet 0/1
VTP-Server(config-if)#switchport trunk native vlan ?
  <1-4094>  VLAN ID of the native VLAN when this port is in trunking mode
```

Filtering VLANs on Trunk Links

By default, all trunk ports on Cisco Catalyst switches allow traffic from all VLANs as illustrated in the output of the `show interfaces trunk` command:

```
VTP-Server#show interfaces trunk

Port        Mode         Encapsulation  Status        Native vlan
Fa0/1       on           802.1q         trunking      1
Fa0/2       desirable    802.1q         trunking      1
Fa0/3       desirable    802.1q         trunking      1

Port        Vlans allowed on trunk
Fa0/1       1-4094
```

```
Fa0/2       1-4094
Fa0/3       1-4094

Port        Vlans allowed and active in management domain
Fa0/1       1,10,20,30,40,50
Fa0/2       1,10,20,30,40,50
Fa0/3       1,10,20,30,40,50

Port        Vlans in spanning tree forwarding state and not pruned
Fa0/1       1,10,20,30,40,50
Fa0/2       1
Fa0/3       none
```

In the output above, three trunk links have been established on the switch. By default, all three trunk links allow traffic from the entire range of VLANs without any explicit configuration. While this default behavior is generally acceptable, in some environments, such as those that require high levels of network security, for example, it may not be acceptable.

Cisco IOS software allows administrators to configure manually the VLANs that are allowed on specific trunk links via the `switchport trunk allowed vlan` interface configuration command. The options available with this command are as follows:

```
VTP-Server(config)#interface fastethernet0/1
VTP-Server(config-if)#switchport trunk allowed vlan ?
  WORD     VLAN IDs of the allowed VLANs when this port is in trunking mode
  add      add VLANs to the current list
  all      all VLANs
  except   all VLANs except the following
  none     no VLANs
  remove   remove VLANs from the current list
```

The first available option allows for specifying the VLANs that will be allowed to traverse the trunk link. The `add` keyword allows for adding additional VLANs to those that are already allowed to traverse the trunk link. The `all` keyword specifies that all VLANs are allowed across the trunk link. This is the default behavior. The `except` keyword is used to allow all VLANs except for the VLANs specified following this keyword. The `none` keyword prevents any VLANs from traversing the trunk link. The `remove` keyword removes previously allowed VLANs from the trunk link.

The following configuration output illustrates how to allow VLANs 1, 10, 20, 30, 40, and 50 to traverse a configured trunk link:

```
VTP-Server(config)#interface fastethernet 0/1
VTP-Server(config-if)#switchport
VTP-Server(config-if)#switchport trunk encapsulation dot1q
VTP-Server(config-if)#switchport mode trunk
VTP-Server(config-if)#switchport trunk allowed vlan 1,10,20,30,40,50
VTP-Server(config-if)#exit
```

The following configuration output illustrates how to permit all VLANs except for VLANs 100 through 200 on a configured trunk link:

```
VTP-Server(config)#interface fastethernet 0/2
VTP-Server(config-if)#switchport
VTP-Server(config-if)#switchport trunk encapsulation dot1q
VTP-Server(config-if)#switchport mode trunk
VTP-Server(config-if)#switchport trunk allowed vlan except 100-200
VTP-Server(config-if)#exit
```

The following configuration output illustrates how to remove VLANs 1, 3, 5, and 7–9 from the VLANs permitted to traverse a trunk link:

```
VTP-Server(config)#interface fastethernet 0/3
VTP-Server(config-if)#switchport
VTP-Server(config-if)#switchport trunk encapsulation dot1q
VTP-Server(config-if)#switchport mode trunk
VTP-Server(config-if)#switchport trunk allowed vlan remove 1,3,5,7-9
```

These configurations can be validated by issuing the `show interfaces trunk` command as illustrated in the following output:

```
VTP-Server#show interfaces trunk

Port        Mode          Encapsulation  Status        Native vlan
Fa0/1       on            802.1q         trunking      1
Fa0/2       desirable     802.1q         trunking      1
Fa0/3       desirable     802.1q         trunking      1

Port        Vlans allowed on trunk
Fa0/1       1,10,20,30,40,50
Fa0/2       1-99,201-4094
Fa0/3       2,4,6,10-4094

Port        Vlans allowed and active in management domain
Fa0/1       1,10,20,30,40,50
Fa0/2       1,10,20,30,40,50
Fa0/3       10,20,30,40,50

Port        Vlans in spanning tree forwarding state and not pruned
Fa0/1       1,10,20,30,40,50
Fa0/2       1
Fa0/3       none
```

VLAN Trunking Protocol (VTP)

VTP is a Cisco proprietary Layer 2 messaging protocol that manages the addition, deletion, and renaming of VLANs on switches in the same VTP domain. VTP allows VLAN information to propagate through the switched network, which reduces administration overhead in a switched network, while enabling switches to exchange and maintain consistent VLAN information. Figure 2-16 below shows a packet capture of a VTP frame:

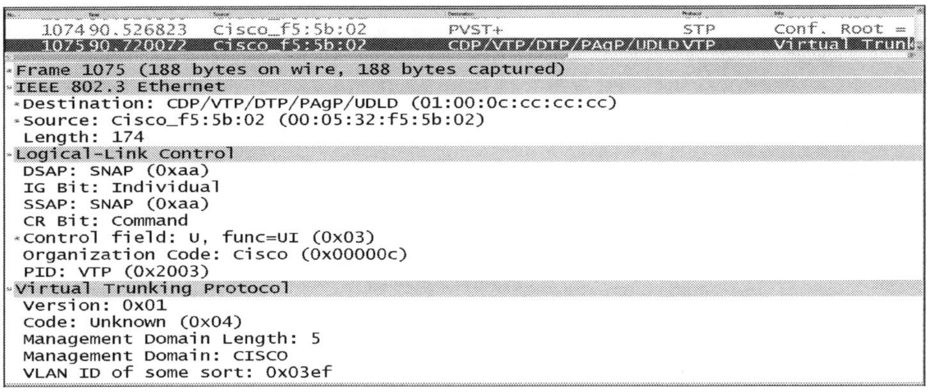

Fig. 2-16. VTP Frame

VTP Domain

The VTP domain consists of a group of adjacent connected switches that are part of the same VTP management domain. A switch can belong to only one VTP domain at any one time and will reject or drop any VTP packets received from switches in any other VTP domains. Figure 2-17 below illustrates how the VLAN Trunking Protocol is used to propagate VLAN information between switches within the same VTP domain:

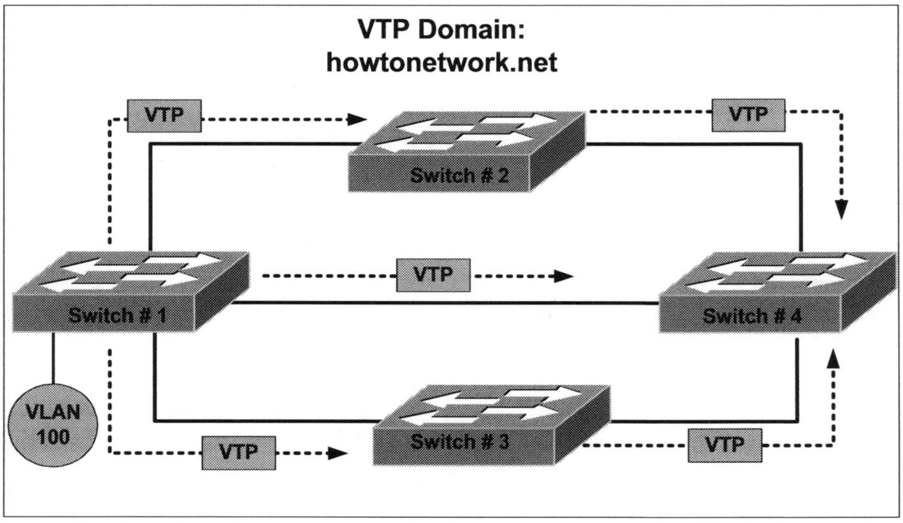

Fig. 2-17. VTP Propagating VLAN Information

Referencing Figure 2-17, 4 switches—switch 1, switch 2, switch 3, and switch 4—all reside within the VTP domain howtonetwork.net. VLAN 100 is configured on switch 1. Using VTP, this information is dynamically propagated throughout the VTP domain so that in the end, switches 2, 3, and 4 receive this information and add VLAN 100 to their VLAN databases. In order to pass VTP advertisements, the links configured between the switches must all be trunk links.

Two methods via which a switch can be configured within the VTP domain are dynamic domain assignment and, the most common method, manual configuration. Dynamic VTP domain configuration occurs on switches that have no default VTP domain configured. When the switch is added to the switched network and establishes a trunk link with another switch in defined VTP domain, it becomes part of the VTP domain that is identified in the update that they receive from their adjacent connected switch. This concept is illustrated in Figure 2-18 below:

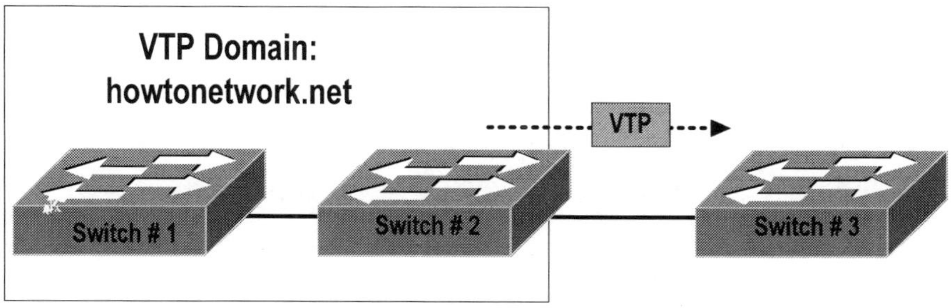

Fig. 2-18. Dynamic VTP

In Figure 2-18, switch 1 and switch 2 belong to the VTP domain howtonetwork.net. Switch 3 is added to the network and a trunk connection is configured between it and switch 2. Because switch 2 has no default VTP domain information configured, when it receives its first VTP update from an adjacent switch, it will become part of the VTP domain identified in the update. In this case, the switch will automatically join the howtonetwork.net VTP domain.

Using this same automatic method, if the switch is connected to two switches in two different VTP domains, it will join the VTP domain listed in the first VTP update that it receives. This concept is illustrated in Figure 2-19 below:

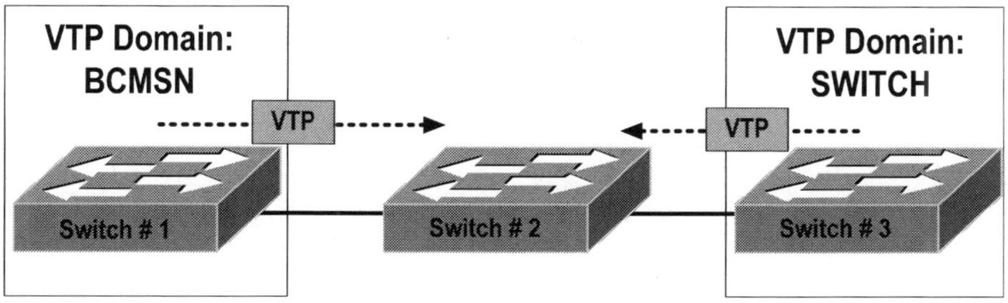

Fig. 2-19. Switch Joins VTP Domain Sending First VTP Update

Referencing Figure 2-19, switch 2 is connected to switch 1 and switch 3 via trunk links. This switch has no default VTP domain information. If this switch receives VTP updates from switch 1 and switch 3, it will join the VTP domain based on the first VTP update that it receives. If, for example, switch 3 sends the first VTP update, switch 2 will join VTP domain SWITCH and reject updates from switch 1 because it is in another VTP domain. This is illustrated in Figure 2-20 below:

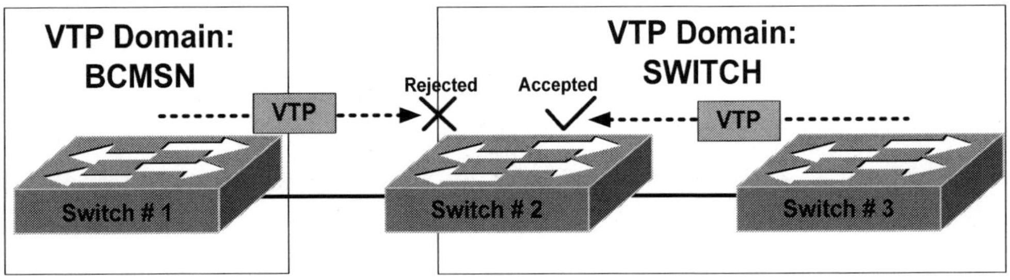

Fig. 2-20. VTP Updates Rejected

Manual VTP domain configuration is the most commonly used method of assigning a switch to a VTP domain. In Cisco IOS software, this is performed by manually configuring the VTP domain name on each individual switch that will be in that domain via the `vtp domain [name]` global configuration command as illustrated in the following output:

```
VTP-Server(config)#vtp domain ?
  WORD  The ascii name for the VTP administrative domain.
```

The VTP domain can be any ASCII string from 1 to 32 characters. In addition to this, it is also important to remember that the domain name is case sensitive. Once configured, the VTP domain, as well as other VTP parameters (which will be described later in this chapter), can be viewed by issuing the `show vtp status` command as illustrated below:

```
VTP-Server#show vtp status
...
VTP Domain Name                 : howtonetwork.net
VTP Pruning Mode                : Enabled
VTP V2 Mode                     : Enabled
VTP Traps Generation            : Disabled
MD5 digest                      : 0x3B 0x6E 0xE4 0x6A 0x41 0xE1 0xA5 0x73
Configuration last modified by 10.1.1.1 at 3-1-93 02:28:44
Local updater ID is 10.1.1.1 on interface Vl10 (lowest numbered VLAN
interface found)
```

VTP Modes

In order to participate in the VTP domain, switches must be configured for a specific VTP mode, each with its own characteristics. A switch can be configured by one of the following three VTP modes:

- VTP Server
- VTP Client
- VTP Transparent

VTP server mode is the default VTP mode for all Cisco Catalyst switches. VTP server switches control VLAN creation, modification, and deletion for their respective VTP domain. Switches operating in VTP server mode store the VLAN database in NVRAM and advertise VTP information to all other switches within the VTP domain. Although each VTP domain must have at least a single VTP server switch, there is no restriction on the number of VTP server switches that can exist within the VTP domain. However, it is considered good practice to have no more than two switches configured as VTP servers – one primary and the other secondary.

VTP clients advertise and receive VTP information; however, they do not allow VLAN creation, modification, or deletion. This means that VTP clients cannot modify or store the VTP database in NVRAM. Additionally, it is important to remember that VTP client switches can receive VLAN information only from VTP server switches within the same VTP domain.

VTP transparent mode is not really a true VTP mode in that it is actually the disabling of VTP on the switch. While a switch that is configured for VTP transparent allows for the creation, modification, and deletion of VLANs in the same manner as on a VTP server switch, it is different in that it ignores VTP updates, and all VLANs that are created on the switch are locally significant and are not propagated to other switches in the VTP domain.

NOTE: VTP can only support up to 1000 VLANs. In order to support the expanded range of VLANs, VTP must be disabled on the switch. This operation is referred to as VTP transparent mode. However, even though VTP is disabled, switches still relay VTP messages.

Table 2-2 below summarizes the capabilities of switches in these three VTP modes:

Table 2-2. Switch Capabilities

Capability	VTP Server	VTP Client	VTP Transparent
Sending VTP Messages	Yes	Yes	No
Listening to VTP Messages	Yes	Yes	No
Creating VLANs	Yes	No	Yes (locally)
Deleting VLANs	Yes	No	Yes (locally)
Modifying VLANs	Yes	No	Yes (locally)
Storing VLANs	Yes	No	Yes (locally)

Figure 2-21 below illustrates the roles played by several switches operating in different modes within the VTP domain howtonetwork.net:

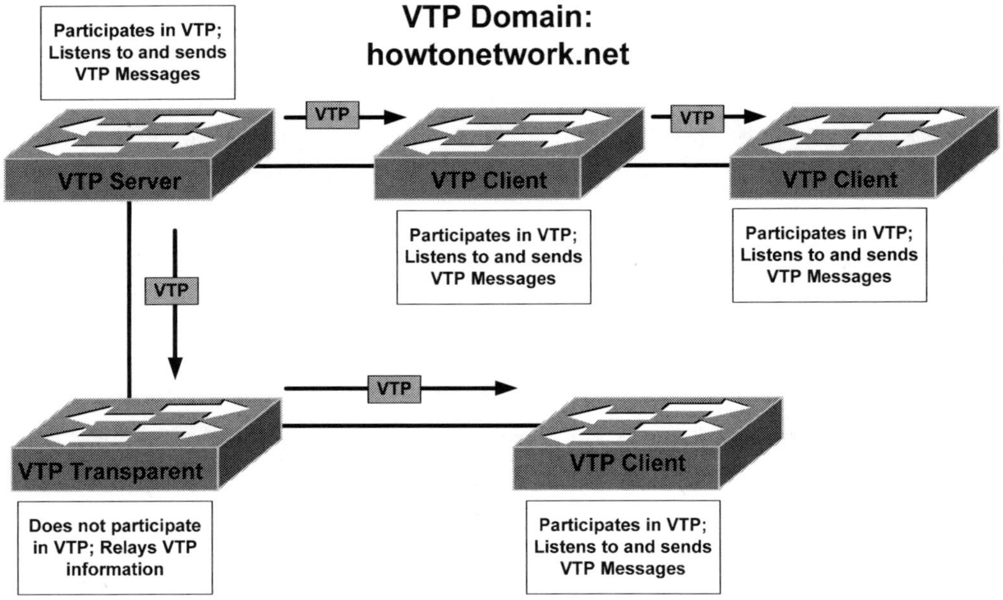

Fig. 2-21. Switch Roles in Different Modes

VTP Advertisements

VTP advertisements are sent out periodically by each switch in the VTP domain via its trunk(s) link to the reserved Multicast address 01-00-0C-CC-CC-CC. These packets are sent with an LLC code of SNAP AA and a type of 0x2003. This information is illustrated in Figure 2-22 below, a screenshot that displays a VTP frame showing advertisement:

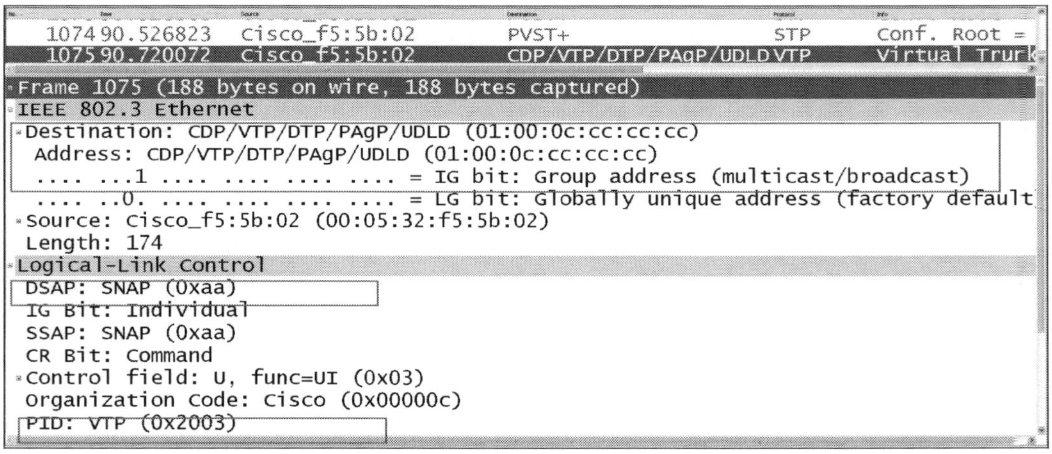

Fig. 2-22. VTP Frame Showing Advertisement

Switches use the configuration revision number to keep track of the most recent information in the VTP domain. Every switch in the VTP domain stores the configuration revision number that it last heard from a VTP advertisement and this number is incremented every time new information is received.

The configuration revision number will always begin at zero. Within the VTP domain, the switch with the highest configuration revision number is considered the switch with the most up-to-date information. When any switch in the VTP domain receives an advertisement message with a higher configuration revision number than its own, it will overwrite any stored VLAN information and synchronize its own stored VLAN information with the information received in the advertisement message.

This means that if a new, non-configured switch is introduced into the VTP domain and it has a configuration revision number that is greater than the other switches in the domain, they will all overwrite their local VLAN information and replace it with the information received in the advertisement message. This is referred to as a VTP synchronization problem and it can wreak havoc in the VTP domain if administrators do not reset the configuration revision number of any new switches to 0 prior to integrating them into the network. This is done by performing one of two actions on the new switch, as follows:

- Changing the switch to VTP transparent mode and then changing it back to VTP server mode via the `vtp mode [mode]` global configuration command; or

- Changing the VTP domain name to a temporary name and then changing it back to the desired VTP domain name via the `vtp domain [name]` global configuration command

NOTE: Although VTP clients do not store VLAN information in NVRAM, they still retain the VTP configuration number. Therefore, simply rebooting a VTP client will not reset the configuration revision number. In other words, even on a VTP client, the configuration revision number must be manually reset using one of the two methods listed in the previous section.

The VLAN Trunking Protocol uses three types of messages to communicate VLAN information throughout the VTP domain. These three message types, which are collectively referred to simply as VTP advertisements, are as follows:

1. VTP Advertisement Requests
2. VTP Summary Advertisements
3. VTP Subset Advertisements

VTP advertisement requests are requests for configuration information. These messages are sent by VTP clients to VTP servers to request VLAN and VTP information they may be missing. A VTP advertisement request is sent out when the switch resets, the VTP domain name changes, or in the event that the switch has received a VTP summary advertisement frame with a higher configuration revision than its own.

Unlike VTP clients, VTP servers store the VTP database in NVRAM, in the vlan.dat file. This file is located in Flash memory as illustrated in the following output:

```
Cat2950-VTP-Server#show flash

Directory of flash:/

    2  -rwx    2888547   Mar 01 1993 00:03:33  c2950-i6q4l2-mz.121-13.EA1.bin
    3  -rwx        273   Jan 01 1970 00:01:35  env_vars
    4  -rwx        924   Mar 01 1993 02:28:44  vlan.dat
    5  -rwx       2477   Mar 03 1993 02:45:24  config.text
    6  -rwx          5   Mar 03 1993 02:45:24  private-config.text
    7  drwx        832   Mar 01 1993 00:04:29  html
   21  -rwx        109   Mar 01 1993 00:04:31  info
   22  -rwx        109   Mar 01 1993 00:04:31  info.ver

7741440 bytes total (2867200 bytes free)
```

This means that the VLAN and VTP information is retained across VTP server switches reboots, which is not the case for VTP client switches. After receiving the VTP advertisement request message(s) from the VTP client, VTP servers respond via summary and subset advertisements. Figure 2-23 below shows the format of a VTP advertisement request:

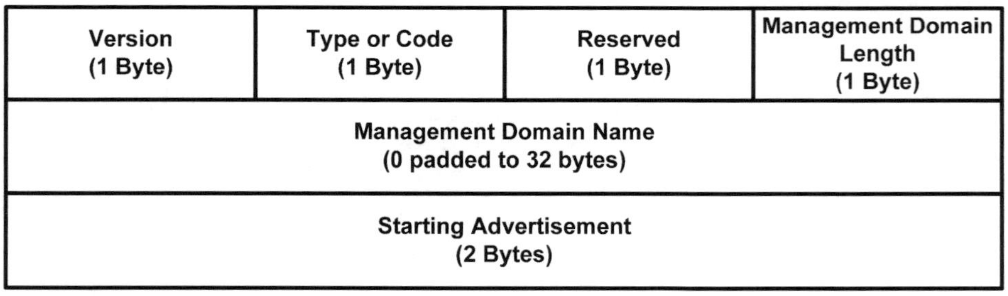

Fig. 2-23. VTP Advertisement Request

- Within the VTP advertisement request, the version field is used to indicate the VTP version number, which can be either version 1 or version 2.
- The type or code field contains the value 0x03, which indicates that this is an advertisement request frame.

These same fields are illustrated in Figure 2-24 below, a screenshot that shows the format of an advertisement request:

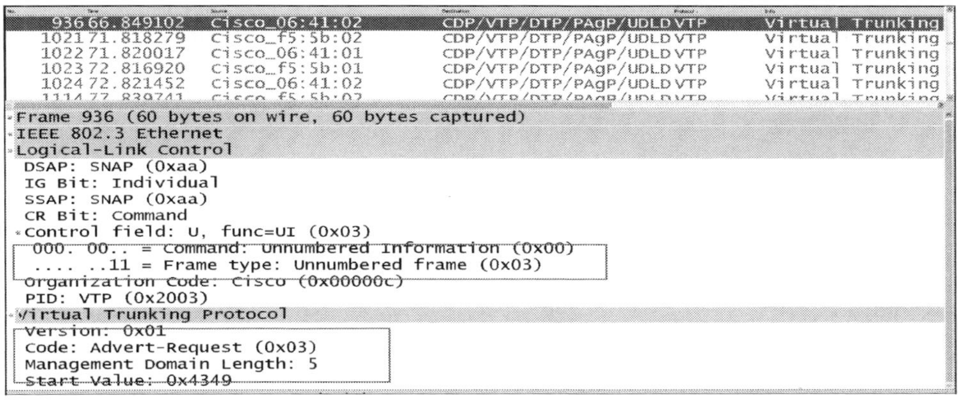

Fig. 2-24. Format of Advertisement Request

- The management domain length field is used to specify the length of the VTP management domain, while the management domain name field specifies the actual name of the VTP management domain.
- The starting advertisement field, or start byte, as it is sometimes referred to, contains the starting VLAN ID of the first VLAN for which information is requested.

VTP summary advertisements are sent out by VTP servers every 5 minutes, by default. VTP summary advertisement messages are used to tell an adjacent switch of the current VTP domain name, the configuration revision number, and the status of the VLAN configuration, as well as other VTP information, which includes the time stamp, the MD5 hash, and the number of subset advertisements to follow. Figure 2-25 below illustrates the format of this message type:

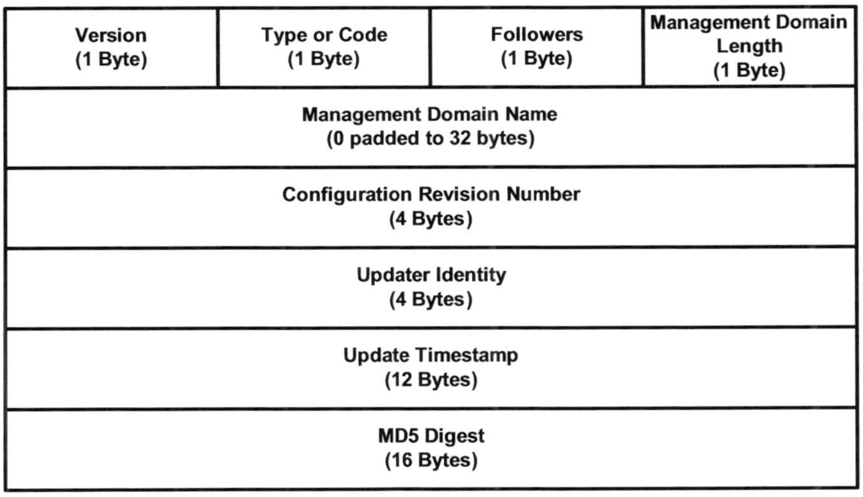

Fig. 2-25. VTP Summary Advertisement

- The version field indicates the version number, which is version 1 or version 2.
- The type or code field indicates that this is a summary advertisement. The value contained in this field is 0x01.
- The followers field indicates that this packet is followed by a VTP Subset Advertisement packet.
- The management domain length field is used to specify the length of the VTP management domain, while the management domain name field specifies the actual name of the VTP management domain.
- The configuration revision number field contains the revision number of this configuration update.
- The updater identity field contains the IP address of the switch that is the last to have incremented the configuration revision.
- The update timestamp field contains the timestamp of the last update, which is essentially the date and time of the last increment of the configuration revision.
- The MD5 digest field carries the VTP password, if MD5 is configured and is used for VTP authentication.

VTP subset advertisements are sent out by VTP servers when VLAN configuration changes, such as when a VLAN is added, suspended, changed, deleted, or other VLAN-specific parameters, such as the VLAN MTU, have changed. One or several VTP subset advertisements will be sent following the VTP summary advertisement.

A VTP subset advertisement contains a list of VLAN information. If there are several VLANs, more than one subset advertisement may be required in order to advertise all the VLANs. Figure 2-26 below illustrates the frame format of the VTP subset advertisement:

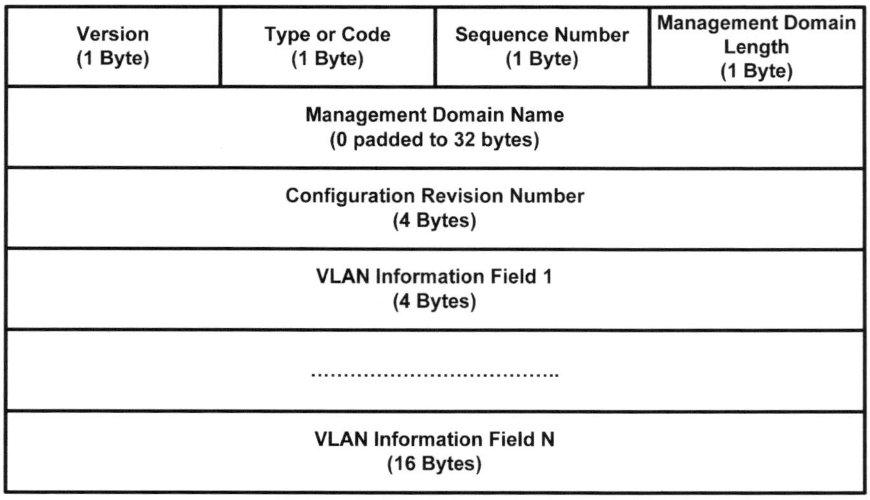

Fig. 2-26. VTP Subset Advertisement

NOTE: For brevity, only the fields unique to this frame will be described in the section below.

- The type or code field indicates that this is a subset advertisement. The value contained in this field is 0x02.
- The sequence number field contains the sequence of the packet in the stream of packets that follow a summary advertisement. The sequence starts with 1.

Each VLAN information field contains information for a different VLAN. It is ordered so that lowered-valued ISL VLAN IDs occur first. Figure 2-27 below illustrates the information that is contained in the VLAN information field of each subset advertisement:

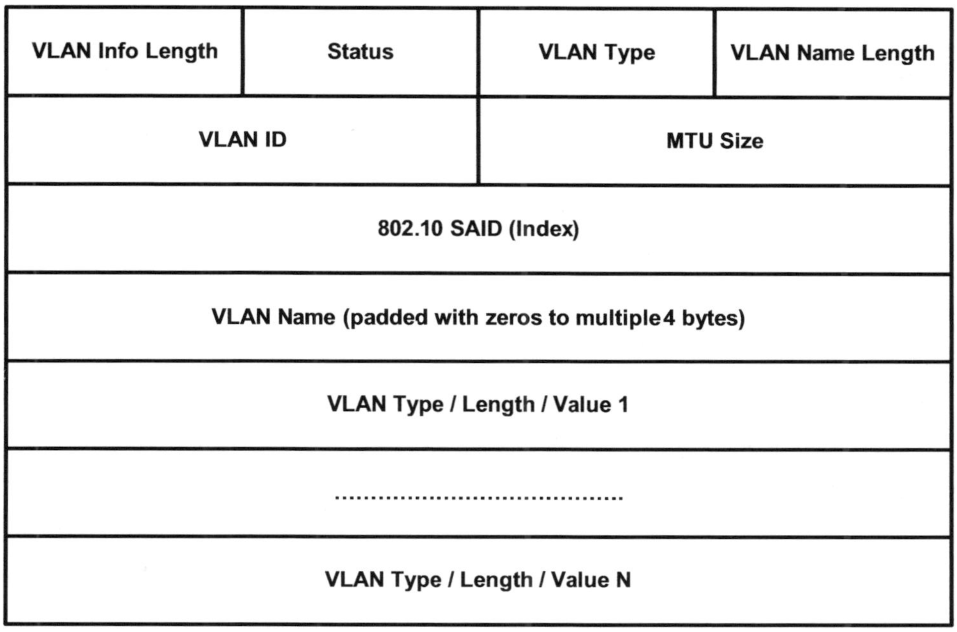

Fig. 2-27. VLAN Information Field

As can be seen in the figure above, these fields are self-explanatory. Although going into further detail on VTP packets is beyond the scope of the SWITCH exam requirements, ensure that you are familiar with the different messages and what they are used for. To assist with this, Figure 2-28 below summarizes the usage of the different packet types described in this section:

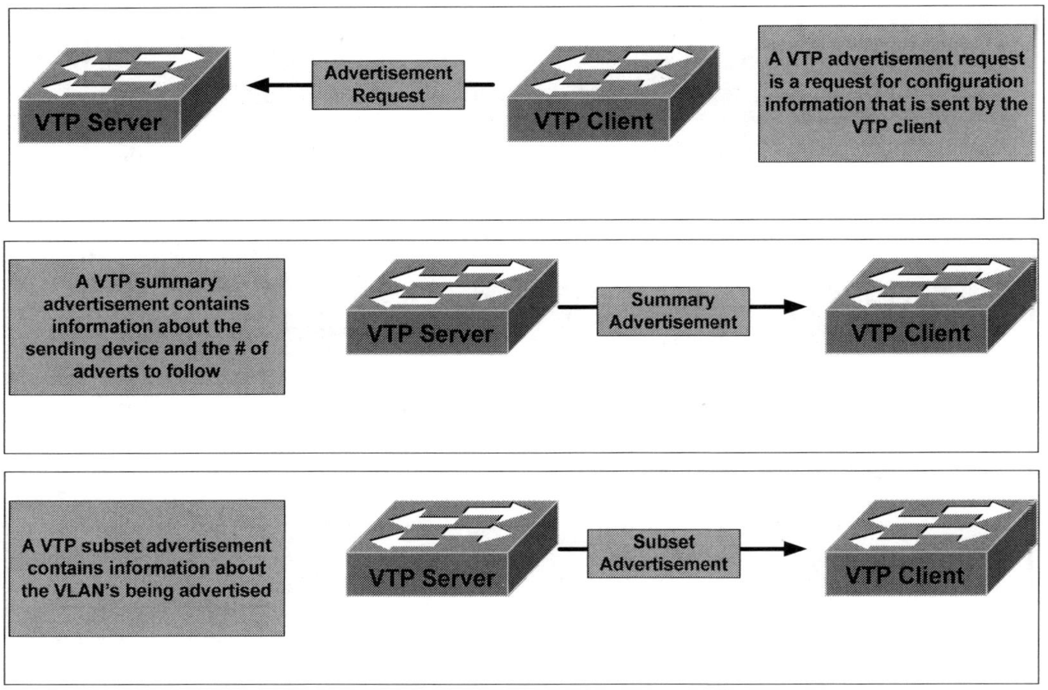

Fig. 2-28. VTP Packet Type Usage

VTP Passwords

VTP passwords are embedded in messages and are used to authenticate incoming VTP messages. It is important to know that although a password is configured locally on the switch, the actual password itself is not actually sent out. Instead, an MD5 hash code is generated and sent out in VTP advertisements. This hash code is then used by the local switch to validate incoming VTP messages.

VTP passwords can only be configured on VTP servers and clients. Because servers send out VTP advertisements and clients receive them, it is always recommended that if you are planning to secure the VTP domain using a password, you configure the password on the server first, and then on the client switches.

The VTP password can be an ASCII string from 1 to 32 characters. When configuring the VTP password, it is important to remember that it is case sensitive.

VTP Versions

There are three versions of VTP, which are versions 1, 2, and 3. As of the time of this writing, the default version used by Cisco Catalyst switches is VTP version 1. This can be validated in the output of the `show vtp status` command as illustrated below:

```
Catalyst2950-VTP-Server#show vtp status
VTP Version                     : 2
Configuration Revision          : 16
Maximum VLANs supported locally : 250
Number of existing VLANs        : 11
VTP Operating Mode              : Server
VTP Domain Name                 : howtonetwork.net
VTP Pruning Mode                : Enabled
VTP V2 Mode                     : Disabled
VTP Traps Generation            : Disabled
MD5 digest                      : 0x35 0xB6 0x39 0xCD 0x53 0x40 0x79 0x4F
Configuration last modified by 10.1.1.1 at 3-1-93 22:25:33
Local updater ID is 10.1.1.1 on interface Vl10 (lowest numbered VLAN
interface found)
```

The first line in bold text is confusing, as it shows that the VTP version is VTP version 2. However, this line simply indicates that this switch is version 2-capable. To determine whether VTP version 2 is enabled, the '`VTP V2 Mode`' line should be referred to. In the output printed above, this shows '`Disabled`', meaning that even though the switch is version 2-capable, as is stated in the first line, it is still running the default version (1) and version 2 is disabled.

VTP version 2 is similar in basic operation to version 1 but provides additional capabilities and features over version 1. The first additional feature supported in VTP version 2 is Token Ring support. VTP version 2 supports Token Ring switching and Token Ring Bridge Relay Function (TrBRF) and Token Ring Concentrator Relay Function (TrCRF). Token Ring is beyond the scope of the SWITCH exam requirements and will not be described any further in this guide.

The second VTP version 2 feature is version-dependent transparent mode. When using VTP version 1, switches in transparent mode forward only VTP packets that match their domain name and VTP version. This is because version 1 supports multiple domains.

VTP version 2 supports only a single VTP domain, which means that all switches assume that they are in the same VTP domain. If the domain name is not the same, DTP will not be able to successfully establish a trunk link and VTP packets will not be relayed by . If VTP debugging is enabled on the switch, the following error messages will be printed on the console:

```
Catalyst2950-VTP-Server#debug sw-vlan vtp packets
Catalyst2950-VTP-Server#debug sw-vlan vtp events

%DTP-5-DOMAINMISMATCH: Unable to perform trunk negotiation on port Fa0/8
because of VTP domain mismatch.
VTP LOG RUNTIME: Dropping packet received on trunk Fa0/8 - not in domain VTP-
V2-DOMAIN
VTP LOG RUNTIME: Dropping packet received on trunk Fa0/8 - not in domain VTP-
V2-DOMAIN
```

However, although the domain name must be the same, with VTP version 2, Catalyst switches in Transparent mode ignore the VTP version and forward VTP messages regardless. This concept is illustrated in Figure 2-29 below:

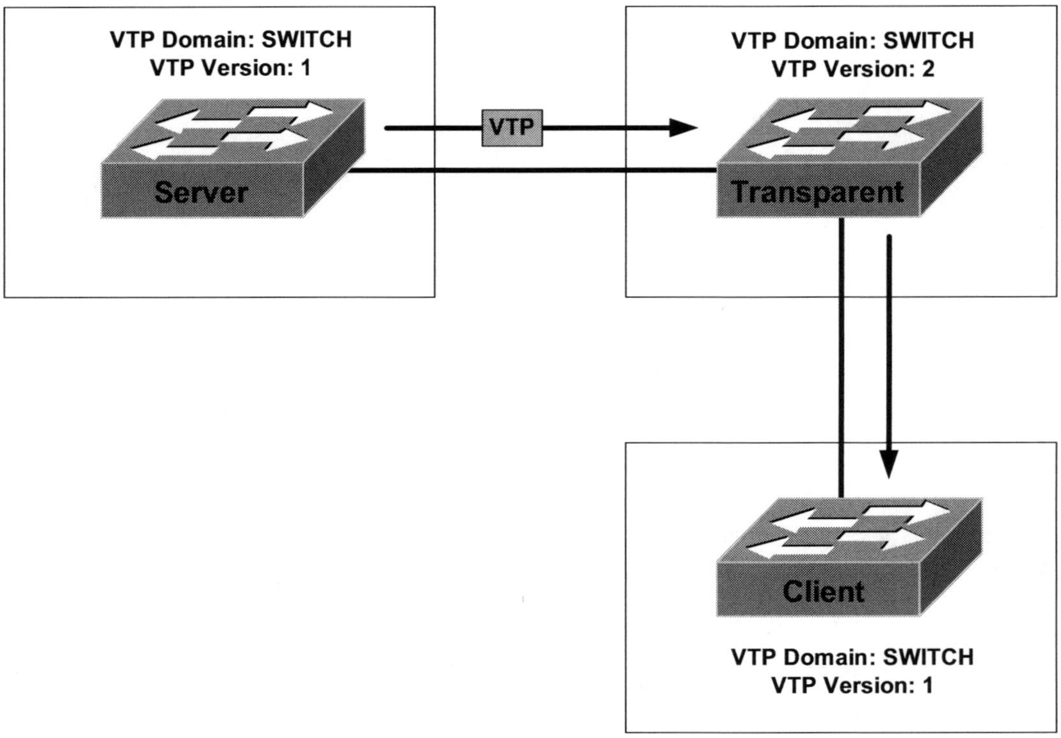

Fig. 2-29. VTP Version Ignored in Transparent Mode

In summation, version-dependent mode means that while the VTP domain name must match, the VTP version does not have to be the same for a version 2 transparent switch to relay received VTP packets.

The third VTP feature is that unlike VTP version 1, VTP version 2 also provides consistency checks. This means that when a VLAN change is entered via CLI or SNMP, VTP version 2 will check that VLAN names and values entered are consistent with its current VLAN knowledge. This feature prevents errors from being propagated to other switches within the VTP domain. Keep in mind, however, that consistency checks are not performed on incoming VTP messages or when the switch reads VLAN information from its local NVRAM.

The final feature available in VTP version 2 that is not available in version 1 is unrecognized Type/Length/Value (TLV) support. In version 2, a VTP server will propagate TLVs, even those it does not understand. It also saves them in NVRAM when the switch is in VTP server mode. This could be useful if not all devices are at the same version or release level.

IMPORTANT NOTE: Although VTP version 3 is technically beyond the scope of the SWITCH certification exam because of its limited support in Cisco switches, it is still important to have a basic understanding of some of the differences between this and versions 1 and 2. The section that follows provides an overview of VTP version 3.

VTP version 3 is the third version of the VLAN trunk protocol. This version of VTP enhances its initial functions well beyond the handling of VLANs. VTP version 3 adds a number of enhancements to VTP version 1 and VTP version 2, which include the following:

- Support for a structured and secure VLAN environment (Private VLAN, or PVLAN)
- Support for up to 4000 VLANs
- Feature enhancement beyond support for a single database or VTP instance
- Protection from unintended database overrides during insertion of new switches
- Option of clear text or hidden password protection
- Configuration option on a per-port basis instead of only a global scheme
- Optimized resource handling and more efficient transfer of information

VTP version 3 differs from VTP versions 1 and 2 in that it distributes a list of opaque databases over an administrative domain in situations where VTP version 1 and VTP version 2 interacted with the VLAN process directly. By offering a reliable and efficient transport mechanism for a database, usability can be expanded from just serving the VLAN environment.

VTP version 3 uses the same concept of domains as those used in VTP versions 1 and 2, where only devices belonging to the same VTP domain are able to exchange and process VTP information. However, unlike versions 1 and 2, which allow a new switch with the default domain name to configure itself with the domain name in the first received VTP message, VTP version 3 requires that the domain name be explicitly configured on each switch. This means that the VTP domain name must be configured before VTP version 3 can be enabled.

In addition to the traditional VTP roles of sever, client, and transparent, VTP version 3 supports an additional switch role called 'off.' This mode is similar to transparent mode; however, unlike a transparent mode switch that relays any received VTP messages, a switch in off mode simply terminates the received messages and does not relay or forward them. With VTP version 3, off mode can be configured globally or on a per-port basis. Turning VTP to off allows a VTP domain to connect to devices in a different administrative domain.

VTP Pruning

VTP pruning is the process of removing VLANs from the VLAN database of the local switch when no local ports are part of that VLAN. The primary goal of VTP pruning is to increase the efficiency of trunk links by eliminating unnecessary Broadcast, Multicast, and unknown traffic from being propagated across the network. VTP pruning is a feature that is used in order to eliminate or prune this unnecessary traffic. Figure 2-30 below illustrates the forwarding of traffic in a network that does not have VTP pruning enabled:

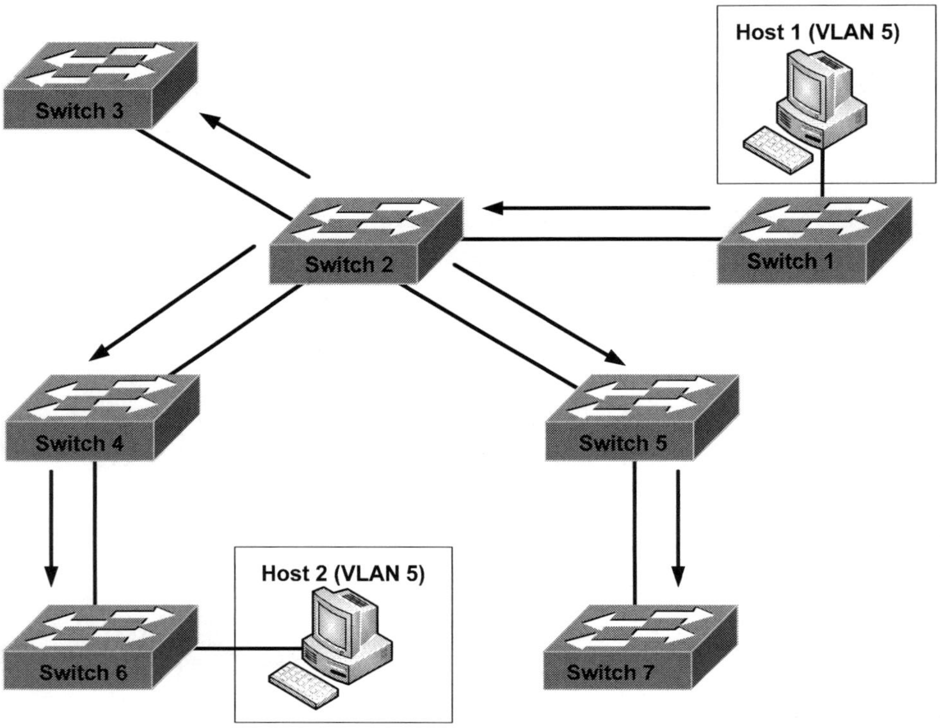

Fig. 2-30. Traffic Forwarding With No VTP Pruning

In Figure 2-30, Host 1 and Host 2 reside in VLAN 5, which is propagated throughout the VTP domain. Without pruning enabled in the VTP domain, all switches forward traffic for this VLAN on their trunk links, even though they have no hosts connected to this VLAN locally.

When VTP pruning is enabled on the VTP server, pruning is enabled for the entire management domain. Each switch will advertise which VLANs it has active to neighboring switches. The neighboring switches will then prune VLANs that are not active across that trunk, thus saving bandwidth. If a VLAN is then added to one of the switches, the switch will then re-advertise its active VLANs so that pruning can be updated by its neighbors. Figure 2-31 below illustrates the propagation of a Broadcast frame sent by Host 1 in VLAN 5 when VTP pruning has been enabled in the management domain:

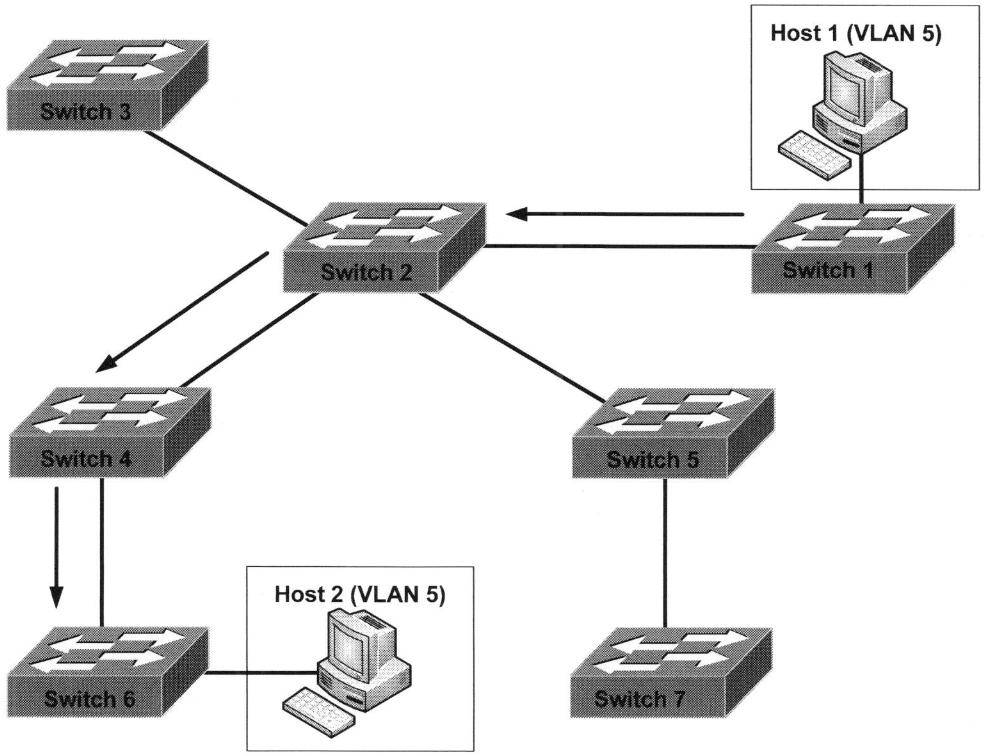

Fig. 2-31. Forwarding with VTP Pruning

This time, the Broadcast is not forwarded to all switches that do not have attached devices in VLAN 5. When implementing VTP pruning, it is important to remember that VLAN 1 and VLANs 1002 to 1005 are always pruning-ineligible. In other words, traffic from these VLANs cannot be pruned. Traffic from any other VLAN, however, can be pruned.

Configuring and Verifying VTP Operation

VTP configuration is very straightforward and is performed by issuing the `vtp [keyword]` global configuration command. The keywords available with this command are illustrated in the following switch output:

```
VTP-Server(config)#vtp ?
  domain     Set the name of the VTP administrative domain.
  file       Configure IFS filesystem file where VTP configuration is stored.
  interface  Configure interface as the preferred source for the VTP IP
             updater address.
  mode       Configure VTP device mode
  password   Set the password for the VTP administrative domain
  pruning    Set the administrative domain to permit pruning
  version    Set the administrative domain to VTP version
```

The options printed above will be described in the following section.

Configuring the VTP Domain Name

The VTP domain is configured via the `vtp domain [name]` global configuration command. The domain name is a case sensitive ASCII string from 1 to 32 characters. The following output illustrates how to configure a switch with the VTP domain name howtonetwork.net:

```
VTP-Server(config)#vtp domain howtonetwork.net
Changing VTP domain name from cisco to howtonetwork.net
VTP-Server(config)#exit
```

The configuration VTP domain name can be viewed in the output of the `show vtp status` command as illustrated below:

```
VTP-Server#show vtp status
...
VTP Domain Name                 : howtonetwork.net
VTP Pruning Mode                : Enabled
VTP V2 Mode                     : Disabled
VTP Traps Generation            : Disabled
MD5 digest                      : 0x8E 0x85 0x23 0xAA 0x6E 0x7F 0xBF 0x16
Configuration last modified by 10.1.1.1 at 3-2-93 05:53:25
...
```

Renaming the VTP Database

By default, VTP and VLAN information is stored in the vlan.dat file in Flash memory. This file can be seen in the output of the `show flash` command as illustrated below:

```
VTP-Server#show flash

Directory of flash:/

    2  -rwx    2888547   Mar 01 1993 00:03:33  c2950-i6q4l2-mz.121-13.EA1.bin
    3  -rwx        273   Jan 01 1970 00:01:35  env_vars
    4  -rwx        916   Mar 02 1993 05:44:29  vlan.dat
    5  -rwx       2477   Mar 03 1993 02:45:24  config.text
    6  -rwx          5   Mar 03 1993 02:45:24  private-config.text
    7  drwx        832   Mar 01 1993 00:04:29  html
   21  -rwx        109   Mar 01 1993 00:04:31  info
   22  -rwx        109   Mar 01 1993 00:04:31  info.ver

7741440 bytes total (2867200 bytes free)
```

The vtp filename [name] global configuration command can be used to change this default name to any other desired name. Although the file name can be changed, it is important to remember that this command cannot be used to load a new database. In other words, the same information is retained, only in a file with a different name. The following output illustrates how to rename the VLAN configuration file:

```
VTP-Server(config)#vtp file myvlaninfo
Setting device to store VLAN database at filename myvlaninfo.
VTP-Server(config)#exit
```

Again, the `show flash` command can be used to verify the file in Flash memory as follows:

```
VTP-Server#show flash

Directory of flash:/

     2  -rwx    2888547   Mar 01 1993 00:03:33  c2950-i6q412-mz.121-13.EA1.bin
     3  -rwx        273   Jan 01 1970 00:01:35  env_vars
     4  -rwx        916   Mar 02 1993 05:44:29  vlan.dat
     5  -rwx       2477   Mar 03 1993 02:45:24  config.text
     6  -rwx          5   Mar 03 1993 02:45:24  private-config.text
     7  drwx        832   Mar 01 1993 00:04:29  html
    21  -rwx        109   Mar 01 1993 00:04:31  info
    22  -rwx        109   Mar 01 1993 00:04:31  info.ver
    23  -rwx        916   Mar 02 1993 05:50:02  myvlaninfo
```

NOTE: In the output above, notice that the vlan.dat file is also still present. The renamed file contains all the VLAN information from the vlan.dat file but all new changes, etc., are stored in the new file and not the vlan.dat file. For example, if several new VLANs were created on the switch, only the size of the newly named file would increment as illustrated below:

```
VTP-Server(config-vlan)#vlan 60
VTP-Server(config-vlan)#name Test-VLAN-60
VTP-Server(config-vlan)#vlan 70
VTP-Server(config-vlan)#name Test-VLAN-70
VTP-Server(config-vlan)#vlan 80
VTP-Server(config-vlan)#name Test-VLAN-80
VTP-Server(config-vlan)#vlan 90
VTP-Server(config-vlan)#name Test-VLAN-90
VTP-Server(config-vlan)#end
VTP-Server#
VTP-Server#show flash:

Directory of flash:/

     2  -rwx    2888547   Mar 01 1993 00:03:33  c2950-i6q412-mz.121-13.EA1.bin
     3  -rwx        273   Jan 01 1970 00:01:35  env_vars
     4  -rwx        916   Mar 02 1993 05:44:29  vlan.dat   <<<<< File size same
                          as before
     5  -rwx       2477   Mar 03 1993 02:45:24  config.text
```

```
 6   -rwx          5   Mar 03 1993 02:45:24  private-config.text
 7   drwx        832   Mar 01 1993 00:04:29  html
21   -rwx        109   Mar 01 1993 00:04:31  info
22   -rwx        109   Mar 01 1993 00:04:31  info.ver
23   -rwx       1156   Mar 02 1993 05:53:25  myvlaninfo <<<<< File size has
                       increased

7741440 bytes total (2865664 bytes free)
```

Changing the VTP IP Updater Address

The `vtp interface [name] [only]` global configuration command is used to specify the name of the interface providing the VTP ID updated for this device. The `[only]` keyword provides an additional capability to force the switch to use only the IP address of the specified interface as the VTP IP updater. The following output illustrates how to force the switch to use only the IP address of interface VLAN 10 as the VTP IP updater:

```
VTP-Server#conf t
Enter configuration commands, one per line.  End with CNTL/Z.
VTP-Server(config)#vtp interface vlan10 only
VTP-Server(config)#exit
```

This option allows administrators to specify a desired interface, such as the IP address of the management VLAN, on switches with multiple interfaces. This configuration can be validated in the following output illustrating the `show vtp status` command:

```
VTP-Server#show vtp status
...
[Truncated Output]
Configuration last modified by 10.1.1.1 at 3-2-93 05:53:25
Local updater ID is 10.1.1.1 on interface Vl10 (preferred interface)
Preferred interface name is vlan10 (mandatory)
```

Configuring the VTP Mode

By default, all Cisco Catalyst switches default to a VTP mode of server. This default behavior can be adjusted via the `vtp mode [mode] global` configuration command. The following configuration output illustrates how to disable VTP on the switch (i.e. transparent mode):

```
VTP-Server(config)#vtp mode transparent
Setting device to VTP TRANSPARENT mode.
VTP-Server(config)#exit
```

The configured VTP mode can be viewed in the following output illustrating the `show vtp status` command:

```
VTP-Server#show vtp status
...
VTP Operating Mode              : Transparent
VTP Domain Name                 : howtonetwork.net
VTP Pruning Mode                : Enabled
VTP V2 Mode                     : Disabled
VTP Traps Generation            : Disabled
MD5 digest                      : 0x8E 0x85 0x23 0xAA 0x6E 0x7F 0xBF 0x16
Configuration last modified by 10.1.1.1 at 3-2-93 05:53:25
```

Configuring the VTP Password

The `vtp password [password]` global configuration command is used to set the administrative domain password for the generation of the 16-byte secret value used in MD5 digest calculation to be sent in VTP advertisements and to validate received VTP advertisements. The VTP password can be an ASCII string from 1 to 32 characters. The password is case sensitive. The following output illustrates how to configure the VTP password on a switch:

```
VTP-Server(config)#vtp password ccnp-here-i-come
Setting device VLAN database password to ccnp-here-i-come
VTP-Server(config)#exit
```

The `show vtp password` command is used to view the current VTP password in plaintext as follows:

```
VTP-Server#show vtp password
VTP Password: ccnp-here-i-come
```

Configuring VTP Pruning

VTP pruning is enabled globally on the VTP server via the `vtp pruning` global configuration command. By default, VLAN 1 and VLANs 1002 to 1005 are always pruning-ineligible; however, any other VLANs can be pruned. The following configuration output demonstrates how to enable VTP pruning on a VTP server:

```
VTP-Server#conf t
Enter configuration commands, one per line.  End with CNTL/Z.
VTP-Server(config)#vtp pruning
Pruning switched on
VTP-Server(config)#exit
```

This configuration can be validated using the `show vtp status` command as follows:

```
VTP-Server#show vtp status
...
VTP Operating Mode              : Server
```

```
VTP Domain Name                 : howtonetwork.net
VTP Pruning Mode                : Enabled
...
```

This same state can also be verified on all VTP clients in the management domain as illustrated in the following output:

```
VTP-Client#show vtp status
...
VTP Operating Mode              : Client
VTP Domain Name                 : howtonetwork.net
VTP Pruning Mode                : Enabled
...
```

In some cases, administrators may want to change the default pruning of all prune-eligible VLANs. Cisco IOS software provides this flexibility via the use of the `switchport trunk pruning vlan` interface configuration command. The options available with this command are as follows:

```
VTP-Server(config)#interface fastethernet 0/1
VTP-Server(config-if)#switchport trunk pruning vlan ?
  WORD     VLAN IDs of the allowed VLANs when this port is in trunking mode
  add      add VLANs to the current list
  except   all VLANs except the following
  none     no VLANs
  remove   remove VLANs from the current list
```

The VLAN list allows administrators to manually specify the VLANs they want pruned when pruning has been enabled. The `add` keyword is used to add to the current list of VLANs being pruned. The `except` keyword excludes the specified VLANs from being pruned. The none keyword prevents all VLANs from being pruned on the trunk link. The `remove` keyword removes prune-eligible VLANs from the current pruned VLAN list.

The following output illustrates how to prevent all VLANs from being pruned on a trunk interface (port):

```
VTP-Server(config)#interface fastethernet0/1
VTP-Server(config-if)#switchport trunk pruning vlan none
VTP-Server(config-if)#exit
```

The following output illustrates how to allow only VLANs 10, 20, and 30 to be pruned:

```
VTP-Server(config)#interface fastethernet 0/2
VTP-Server(config-if)#switchport trunk pruning vlan 10,20,30
VTP-Server(config-if)#exit
```

Pruning configuration applied to trunk ports can be validated by issuing the `show interfaces [name] switchport` command as illustrated in the following output:

```
VTP-Server#show interfaces fastethernet 0/1 switchport
Name: Fa0/1
Switchport: Enabled
Administrative Mode: trunk
Operational Mode: trunk
Administrative Trunking Encapsulation: dot1q
Operational Trunking Encapsulation: dot1q
...
Trunking VLANs Enabled: 1,10,20,30,40,50
Pruning VLANs Enabled: NONE
...
VTP-Server#
VTP-Server#
VTP-Server#show interfaces fastethernet 0/2 switchport
Name: Fa0/2
Switchport: Enabled
Administrative Mode: dynamic desirable
Operational Mode: trunk
Administrative Trunking Encapsulation: dot1q
Operational Trunking Encapsulation: dot1q
...
Trunking VLANs Enabled: 1-99,201-4094
Pruning VLANs Enabled: 10,20,30
...
```

Additionally, the `show interfaces trunk` command can be used to view trunking information, including pruning configuration, for all configured trunks on the switch:

```
VTP-Server#show interfaces trunk

Port        Mode          Encapsulation  Status        Native vlan
Fa0/1       on            802.1q         trunking      1
Fa0/2       desirable     802.1q         trunking      1
Fa0/3       desirable     802.1q         trunking      1

Port        Vlans allowed on trunk
Fa0/1       1,10,20,30,40,50
Fa0/2       1-99,201-4094
Fa0/3       2,4,6,10-4094

Port        Vlans allowed and active in management domain
Fa0/1       1,10,20,30,40,50
Fa0/2       1,10,20,30,40,50,60,70,80,90,254
Fa0/3       10,20,30,40,50,60,70,80,90,254

Port        Vlans in spanning tree forwarding state and not pruned
Fa0/1       1,10,20,30,40,50
Fa0/2       1,40,50,60,70,80,90,254
Fa0/3       none
```

Configuring the VTP Version

The default VTP version used in Cisco Catalyst switches is VTP version 1. To change the default VTP version, the `vtp version [version]` global configuration command can be used as illustrated in the following output:

```
VTP-Server(config)#vtp version ?
  <1-2>  Set the administrative domain VTP version number
```

NOTE: Keep in mind that VTP version 3 is available only in a select few Cisco Catalyst switches, such as the Catalyst 6500 series switches.

Troubleshooting and Debugging VTP

The `show vtp status` command provides information on VTP defaults and configuration. This information includes the VTP version enabled on the switch, the VTP domain name (if one is configured), the IP address of the updater, the configuration revision number, the number of VLANs, and the VTP operating mode of the switch. The information printed by this command is illustrated in the following output:

```
Catalyst2950-VTP-Server#show vtp status
VTP Version                     : 2
Configuration Revision          : 23
Maximum VLANs supported locally : 250
Number of existing VLANs        : 15
VTP Operating Mode              : Server
VTP Domain Name                 : howtonetwork.net
VTP Pruning Mode                : Enabled
VTP V2 Mode                     : Enabled
VTP Traps Generation            : Disabled
MD5 digest                      : 0x82 0xCD 0xAE 0xE1 0x20 0x44 0x71 0xE0
Configuration last modified by 10.1.1.1 at 3-2-93 06:54:09
Local updater ID is 10.1.1.1 on interface Vl10 (lowest numbered VLAN
interface found)
```

In addition to the `show vtp status` command, the `show vtp counters` command is also a useful VTP troubleshooting tool. This command prints local VTP statistics, such as the number of messages sent and received, as well as errors and VTP pruning packet statistics as illustrated in the following output:

```
Catalyst2950-VTP-Server#show vtp counters
VTP statistics:
Summary advertisements received    : 526
Subset advertisements received     : 50
```

```
Request advertisements received    : 0
Summary advertisements transmitted : 543
Subset advertisements transmitted  : 58
Request advertisements transmitted : 4
Number of config revision errors   : 2
Number of config digest errors     : 1
Number of V1 summary errors        : 0

VTP pruning statistics:

Trunk            Join Transmitted Join Received    Summary advts received from
                                                   non-pruning-capable device
---------------- ---------------- ---------------- ---------------------------
Fa0/1               14447            14452             0
Fa0/2               15082            15071             0
Fa0/3               15073            15082             0
```

As is the case with all forms of troubleshooting, debugging should be considered when all other troubleshooting mechanisms have been exhausted. VTP debugging is enabled by issuing the `debug sw-vlan vtp` privileged EXEC command. The available options with this command are as follows:

```
Catalyst2950-VTP-Server#debug sw-vlan vtp ?
  events    vtp events
  packets   vtp packets
  pruning   vtp pruning events
  xmit      vtp packets transmitted
```

The following shows a sample output of the information printed on the console when VTP debugging is enabled on a VTP server switch:

```
Catalyst2950-VTP-Server#show debugging
Generic VLAN Manager:
  vtp packets debugging is on
  vtp events debugging is on
Catalyst2950-VTP-Server#
1d07h: VTP LOG RUNTIME: Transmit vtp summary, domain howtonetwork.net, rev
26, followers 1
   MD5 digest calculated = 2B 94 D7 D4 BD A0 ED AA 5F 2B 9E A9 82 F5 36 C7

1d07h: VTP LOG RUNTIME: Transmit vtp summary, domain howtonetwork.net, rev
26, followers 1
   MD5 digest calculated = 2B 94 D7 D4 BD A0 ED AA 5F 2B 9E A9 82 F5 36 C7

1d07h: VTP LOG RUNTIME: Transmit vtp summary, domain howtonetwork.net, rev
26, followers 1
   MD5 digest calculated = 2B 94 D7 D4 BD A0 ED AA 5F 2B 9E A9 82 F5 36 C7

1d07h: %SYS-5-CONFIG_I: Configured from console by console
1d07h: VTP LOG RUNTIME: Summary packet received, domain = howtonetwork.net,
rev = 26, followers = 1
```

```
1d07h:
1d07h: summary: 02 01 01 10 68 6F 77 74 6F 6E 65 74 77 6F 72 6B    ....
howtonetwork
1d07h: summary: 2E 6E 65 74 00 00 00 00 00 00 00 00 00 00 00 00
.net............
1d07h: summary: 00 00 00 00 00 00 00 1A 0A 01 01 01 39 33 30 33
............9303
1d07h: summary: 30 32 30 37 31 31 31 36 2B 94 D7 D4 BD A0 ED AA    02071116+.
WT= m*
1d07h: summary: 5F 2B 9E A9 82 F5 36 C7 00 00 00 01 06 01 00 01    _
+.).u6G........
1d07h:
1d07h: VTP LOG RUNTIME: Summary packet rev 26 equal to domain howtonetwork.
net rev 26

1d07h: VTP LOG RUNTIME: Subset packet received, domain = howtonetwork.net,
rev = 26, seq = 1, length = 484

1d07h: subset: 02 02 01 10 68 6F 77 74 6F 6E 65 74 77 6F 72 6B    ....
howtonetwork
1d07h: subset: 2E 6E 65 74 00 00 00 00 00 00 00 00 00 00 00 00
.net............
1d07h: subset: 00 00 00 00 00 00 00 1A 14 00 01 07 00 01 05 DC
...............\
1d07h: subset: 00 01 86 A1 64 65 66 61 75 6C 74 00 18 00 01 0C
...!default.....
1d07h: subset: 00 0A 05 DC 00 01 86 AA 54 65 73 74 2D 56 4C 41
...\...*Test-VLA
1d07h: subset: 4E 2D 31 30 18 00 01 0C 00 14 05 DC 00 01 86 B4    N-
10.......\...4
```

Chapter Summary

The following section is a summary of the major points you should be aware of in this chapter.

Understanding Virtual LANs (VLANs)

- There are two primary types of switch VLAN port types:
  1. Access Ports
  2. Trunk Ports

- Access ports are switch ports that are assigned to a single VLAN
- Access ports can only belong to a single VLAN
- The two methods that can be used to assign access port to VLANs are:
  1. Static VLAN Assignment
  2. Dynamic VLAN Assignment

- Trunk ports are ports on switches that are used to carry traffic from multiple VLANs
- Trunk ports are typically used to connect switches to other switches or routers
- Cisco Catalyst switches use VLANs in the range of 0 – 4095
- VLANs 1 - 4094 are user-configurable VLANs
- VLANs 0 and 4096 are reserved system VLANs
- Extended VLANs requires that the switch be enabled to use the extended system-id
- The extended system ID feature is based on the 802.1t standard
- Catalyst 6500 series switches use extended VLANs for internal VLAN assignments
- In Catalyst 6500 switches, the following use extended VLANs for internal use:
  1. WAN interfaces
  2. Layer 3 Ethernet ports
  3. Subinterfaces

- VLAN trunks are used to carry data from multiple VLANs
- The two most common trunk encapsulation methods are:
  1. Inter-Switch Link
  2. IEEE 802.1Q

- Inter-Switch Link (ISL) is a Cisco proprietary protocol
- The ISL header is 26 bytes in length, while the FCS is 4 bytes in length
- The following is a summary of ISL capabilities:
  1. ISL can support up to 1000 VLANs
  2. ISL is a Cisco-proprietary protocol
  3. ISL encapsulates the frame, it does not modify the original frame in any way
  4. ISL operates in a point-to-point environment

- 802.1Q is an IEEE standard for VLAN tagging
- 802.1Qinserts a single 4-byte tag into the original frame
- The following summarizes some 802.1Q features:
    1. It can support up to 4096 VLANs
    2. It uses an internal tagging mechanism, modifying the original frame
    3. It is an open standard protocol developed by the IEEE
    4. It does not tag frames on the native VLAN, however, all other frames are tagged

- Two methods that can be used to address VLANs are:
    1. Assigning a single subnet to each individual VLAN
    2. Assigning multiple subnets per VLAN

- The two methods of implementing VLANs are:
    1. End-to-end VLANs
    2. Local VLANs

Configuring and Verifying VLANs

- The following should be taken into consideration when configuring VLANs:
    1. In Cisco Catalyst switches, Ethernet VLAN 1 uses only default values
    2. Except for the VLAN name, Ethernet VLANs 1006 through 4094 use only default values
    3. You can configure the VLAN name for Ethernet VLANs 1006 through 4094

Configuring and Verifying Trunk Links

- DISL simplifies the creation of an ISL trunk from two interconnected Fast Ethernet devices
- DTP is a Cisco proprietary point-to-protocol that negotiates trunking between two switches
- Trunk ports can be configured using one of two methods:
    1. Manual (Static) Trunk Configuration
    2. Dynamic Trunking Protocol (DTP)

VLAN Trunking Protocol (VTP)

- VTP is a Cisco proprietary Layer 2 messaging protocol
- VTP manages addition, deletion, and renaming of VLANs on switches in the same domain
- The VTP domain consists of a group of adjacent connected switches
- The three VTP modes are:
    1. VTP Server
    2. VTP Client
    3. VTP Transparent

- VTP server mode is the default VTP mode for all Cisco Catalyst switches
- VTP clients receive VTP information from VTP servers
- VTP transparent mode disables VTP on the switch
- VTP advertisements are sent out periodically by each switch in the VTP domain
- VTP packets are sent to the Multicast address 01-00-0C-CC-CC-CC
- Switches use the configuration revision number to keep track of the most recent information
- There are three types of VTP messages:
  1. VTP Advertisement Requests
  2. VTP Summary Advertisements
  3. VTP Subset Advertisements

- Advertisement requests are requests for configuration information
- Summary advertisement messages are used to provide current VTP information
- VTP summary advertisements are sent out by VTP servers every 5 minutes
- VTP subset advertisements are sent out by VTP servers when VLAN configuration changes
- A VTP subset advertisement contains a list of VLAN information
- VTP passwords are embedded in messages
- VTP passwords are used to authenticate incoming VTP messages
- VTP passwords can only be configured on VTP servers and clients
- The VTP password can be an ASCII string from 1 to 32 characters
- There are three versions of VTP, which are versions 1, 2, and 3
- The default version used by Cisco Catalyst switches is VTP version 1
- VTP version 2 provides additional capabilities over version 1 which include:
  1. Token Ring support
  2. Version-dependent transparent mode
  3. Consistency checks
  4. Unrecognized Type/Length/Value (TLV) support

- VTP version 3 adds a number of enhancements to VTP which include:
  1. Support for a structured and secure VLAN environment (Private VLAN, or PVLAN)
  2. Support for up to 4000 VLANs
  3. Feature enhancement beyond support for a single database or VTP instance
  4. Protection from unintended database overrides during insertion of new switches
  5. Option of clear text or hidden password protection
  6. Configuration option on a per port base instead of only a global scheme
  7. Optimized resource handling and more efficient transfer of information

- VTP pruning is a feature that you use in order to eliminate or prune this unnecessary traffic

CHAPTER 3

IEEE 802.1D Spanning Tree Protocol

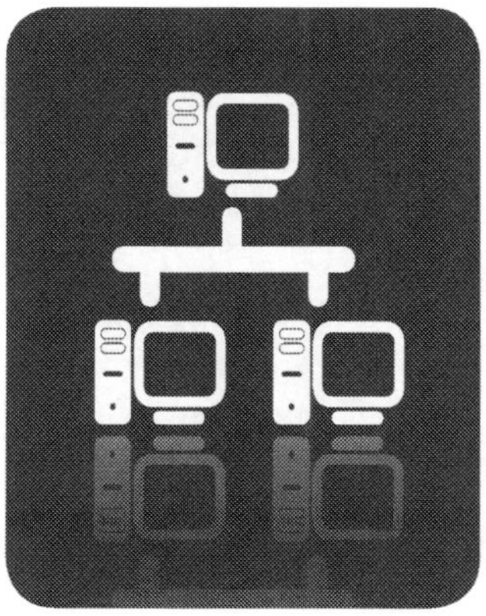

The Spanning Tree Protocol (STP) is used in switched networks to prevent loops that may be caused by having multiple redundant paths between source and destination stations. This chapter focuses on the theoretical aspects as well as the configuration of basic and advanced STP within the switched LAN. The following core SWITCH exam objective will be covered in this chapter:

- Implement VLAN-based solution, given a network design and a set of requirements

This chapter will be divided into the following sections:

- An Introduction to the Spanning Tree Protocol
- Spanning Tree Bridge Protocol Data Units
- Spanning Tree Port States
- Understanding the Spanning Tree Bridge ID
- IEEE 802.1t and the Extended System ID
- Spanning Tree Root Bridge Election
- Understanding Spanning Tree Cost and Priority
- Spanning Tree Root and Designated Ports
- Spanning Tree Timers
- Understanding the Spanning Tree Diameter
- Cisco Spanning Tree Enhancements
- Unidirectional Link Detection (UDLD)
- Configuring Spanning Tree Protocol
- Troubleshooting Spanning Tree Networks

SWITCH Exam Objective	Chapter Section(s) Covered
Configure loop prevention for the VLAN-based solution	• An Introduction to the Spanning Tree Protocol • Spanning Tree Bridge Protocol Data Units • Spanning Tree Port States • Understanding the Spanning Tree Bridge ID • IEEE 802.1t and the Extended System ID • Spanning Tree Root Bridge Election • Understanding Spanning Tree Cost and Priority • Spanning Tree Root and Designated Ports • Spanning Tree Timers • Understanding the Spanning Tree Diameter • Cisco Spanning Tree Enhancements • Unidirectional Link Detection (UDLD) • Configuring Spanning Tree Protocol • Troubleshooting Spanning Tree Networks

An Introduction to the Spanning Tree Protocol

Spanning Tree Protocol (STP) is defined in the IEEE 802.1D standard. The primary purpose of STP is to attempt to provide a loop-free topology in a redundant Layer 2 network environment. The word 'attempt' is used because implementing STP does not always guarantee a loop-free switched network. This is because STP operates by making the following assumptions about the network:

- All links are bidirectional and can both send and receive BPDUs
- The switch is able to regularly receive, process, and send BPDUs

NOTE: BPDU is the acronym for Bridge Protocol Data Unit. Spanning Tree BPDUs will be described in detail later in this chapter.

If any of these two assumptions are not true (e.g. there may be a unidirectional Fiber link), then STP may fail and a network loop may be created. To address this, Cisco IOS software supports several stability features, such as Unidirectional Link Detection (UDLD), that are recommended in STP networks. UDLD and other STP stability and enhancement features will be described in detail later in this chapter.

Spanning Tree Bridge Protocol Data Units

All switches that reside in the Spanning Tree domain communicate and exchange messages using Bridge Protocol Data Units (BPDUs). The exchange of BPDUs is used by STP to determine the network topology. The topology of an active switched network is determined by the following three variables:

1. The unique MAC address (switch identifier) that is associated with each switch
2. The Path Cost to the Root Bridge associated with each switch port
3. The port identifier (MAC address of the port) associated with each switch port

In the Spanning Tree domain, all switches send BPDUs to the STP Multicast destination address 01-80-C2-00-00-00. The source address of the BPDU will be set to the MAC address of the port that sends the BPDU. Figure 3-1 below shows a BPDU being sent to the STP Multicast address 01-80-C2-00-00-00:

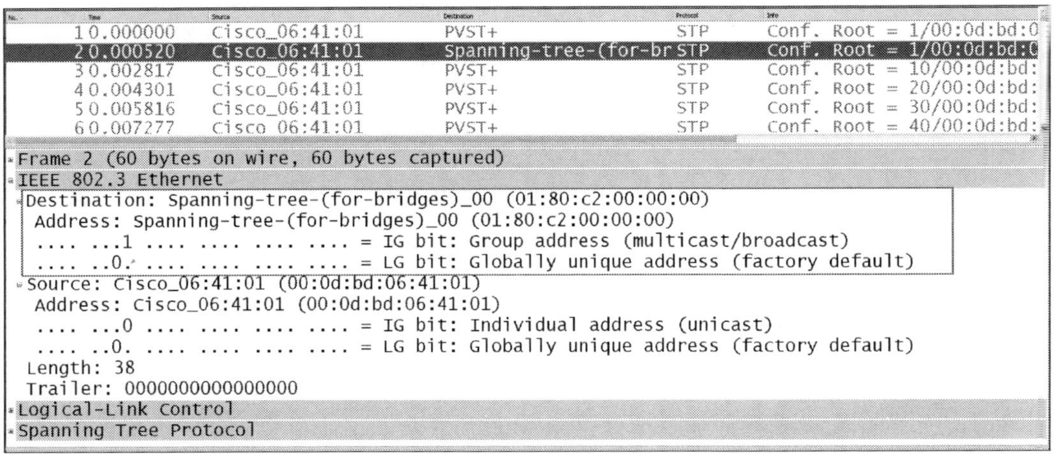

Fig. 3-1. IEEE 802.1D BPDU Destination Address

BPDUs are sent every 2 seconds, which allows for rapid network loop detection and topology information exchanges. There are two types of BPDUs, which are Configuration BPDUs and Topology Change Notification BPDUs. These are described in the following sections.

IEEE 802.1D Configuration BPDUs

Configuration BPDUs are sent by LAN switches and are used to communicate and compute the Spanning Tree topology. After the switch port initializes, the port is placed into the Blocking state and a BPDU is sent to each port in the switch. By default, all switches initially assume that they are the Root of the Spanning Tree until they exchange Configuration BPDUs with other switches. As long as a port continues to see its Configuration BPDU as the most attractive, it will continue sending Configuration BPDUs. Switches determine the best Configuration BPDU based on the following four factors (in the order listed):

1. Lowest Root Bridge ID
2. Lowest Root Path Cost to Root Bridge
3. Lowest Sender Bridge ID
4. Lowest Sender Port ID

The completion of the Configuration BPDU exchange results in the following actions:

- A Root Switch is elected for the entire Spanning Tree domain
- A Root Port is elected on every Non-Root Switch in the Spanning Tree domain
- A Designated Switch is elected for every LAN segment
- A Designated Port is elected on the Designated Switch for every segment
- Loops in the network are eliminated by blocking redundant paths

NOTE: These characteristics will be described in detail as we progress through this chapter.

Once the Spanning Tree network has converged, which happens when all switch ports are in a Forwarding or Blocking state, Configuration BPDUs are sent by the Root Bridge every Hello Time interval, which defaults to 2 seconds. This is referred to as the origination of Configuration BPDUs. The Configuration BPDUs are forwarded to downstream neighboring switches via the Designated Port on the Root Bridge.

When a Non-Root Bridge receives a Configuration BPDU on its Root Port, which is the port that provides the best path to the Root Bridge, it sends an updated version of the BPDU via its Designated Port(s). This is referred to as the propagation of BPDUs.

The Designated Port is a port on the Designated Switch that has the lowest Path Cost when forwarding packets from that LAN to the Root Bridge.

Once the Spanning Tree network has converged, a Configuration BPDU is always transmitted away from the Root Bridge to the rest of the switches within the STP domain. The simplest way to remember the flow of Configuration BPDUs after the Spanning Tree network has converged is to memorize the following four rules:

1. A Configuration BPDU originates on the Root Bridge and is sent via the Designated Port.
2. A Configuration BPDU is received by a Non-Root Bridge on a Root Port.
3. A Configuration BPDU is transmitted by a Non-Root Bridge on a Designated Port.
4. There is only one Designated Port (on a Designated Switch) on any single LAN segment.

Figure 3-2 below illustrates the flow of the Configuration BPDU in the STP domain, demonstrating the four simple rules listed above:

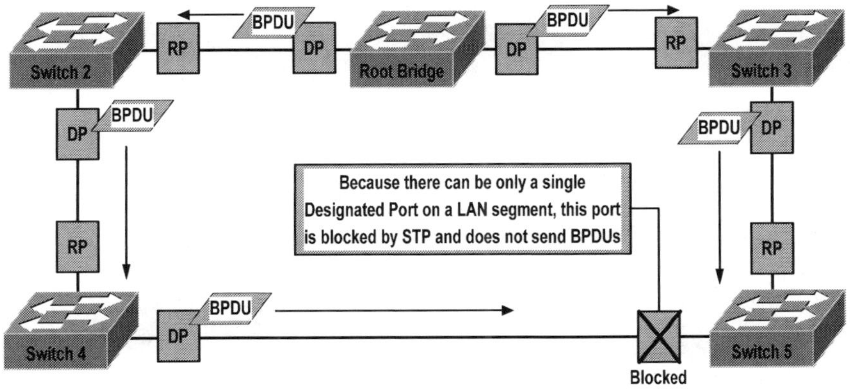

Fig. 3-2. BPDU Flow throughout the STP Domain

1. Referencing Figure 3-2, the Configuration BPDU is originated by the Root Bridge and sent out via the Designated Ports on the Root Bridge toward the Non-Root Bridge switches, Switch 2 and Switch 3.
2. Non-Root Bridge switches, Switch 2 and Switch 3, receive the Configuration BPDU on their Root Ports, which provide the best path to the Root Bridge.
3. Switch 2 and Switch 3 modify (update) the received Configuration BPDU and forward it out of their Designated Ports. Switch 2 is the Designated Switch on the LAN segment for itself and Switch 4, while Switch 3 is the Designated Switch on the LAN segment for itself and Switch 5. The Designated Port resides on the Designated Switch and is the port that has the lowest Path Cost when forwarding packets from that LAN segment to the Root Bridge.
4. On the LAN Segment between Switch 4 and Switch 5, Switch 4 is elected Designated Switch and the Designated Port resides on that switch. Because there can be only a single Designated Switch on a segment, the port on Switch 5 for that LAN segment is blocked. This port will not forward any BPDUs.

EXCEPTION BPDU PROCESSING

Although it has been stated that Configuration BPDUs originate only from the Root Bridge, you should also be aware that, based on a Spanning Tree exception, Configuration BPDUs may also be sent out by Non-Root Bridges. This occurs when a Non-Root Bridge receives an inferior BPDU from another switch. A common example would be an inferior BPDU that is received from a new switch that has just been added to the network.

In such cases, the Designated Switch for the segment will send out a Configuration BPDU that contains the identity of the current Root Bridge. This exception rule prevents false information from being injected into the Spanning Tree domain as well as from creating network loops. This concept is illustrated in the following network diagram:

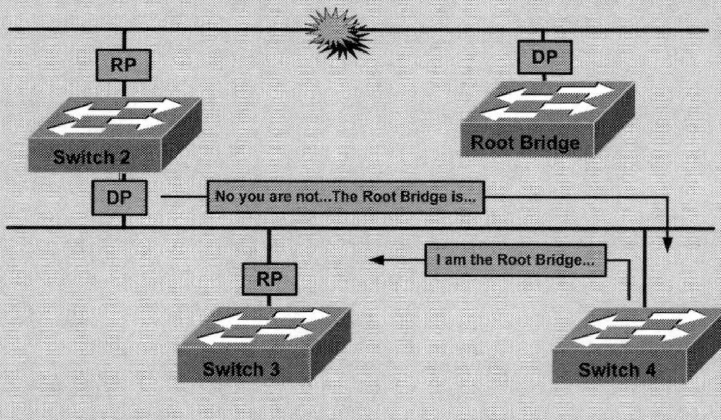

In the diagram above, Switch 4 is added to the network segment that Switch 2 and Switch 3 reside on via a hub, for example. Switch 2 is the Designated Switch for this segment. By default, at port initialization, Switch 4 will send out a BPDU stating that it is the Root Bridge. Even though Switch 2 has lost communication with the Root Bridge, which effectively stops the sending of Configuration BPDUs, as long as Switch 2 still has a copy of the information provided by the Root Bridge and is the Designated Port, it can send out a Configuration BPDU advising the new switch (Switch 4) that it is incorrect, refuting the inferior BPDU.

Table 3-1 below lists the fields contained in the Spanning Tree Configuration BPDU, and the size of these fields, and provides a description of the information contained in each field:

Table 3-1. IEEE 802.1D BPDU Fields

Field	Size	Description
Protocol Identifier (ID)	2 Bytes	This field identifies the STP Algorithm and Protocol. This field is always set to 0.
Protocol Version Identifier	1 Byte	This field identifies the STP Protocol Version. This field is always set to 0.
BPDU Type	1 Byte	This field identifies the type of BPDU. It is set to 0 for a Configuration BPDU.
Flags	1 Byte	This field is used for the Topology Change and Topology Change ACK flag. LSB = Topology Change (TC) flag and MSB = Topology Change Acknowledgment (TCA) flag.
Root Identifier	8 Bytes	This field is used to state the Bridge ID of the current Root Bridge.
Root Path Cost	4 Bytes	This field contains the cumulative cost, or Path Cost, to the Root Bridge.
Sender Bridge Identifier (ID)	8 Bytes	This field contains the Bridge ID of the current bridge (i.e. the Bridge ID of the sender).
Port Identifier (ID)	2 Bytes	This field contains the unique ID for the port that sent this BPDU.
Message Age	2 Bytes	This field contains the time since the Root Bridge-created the BPDU (i.e. the age of the Root BPDU).
Maximum Age (Max Age)	2 Bytes	This field contains the maximum time to save BPDU information. The default value is 20 seconds.
Hello Time	2 Bytes	This field specifies the time between sending BPDUs. The default value is 2 seconds.
Forward Delay	2 Bytes	This field specifies the time spent in the Listening and Learning states. The default value is 15 seconds.

The fields described in Table 3-1 are illustrated in Figure 3-3 below:

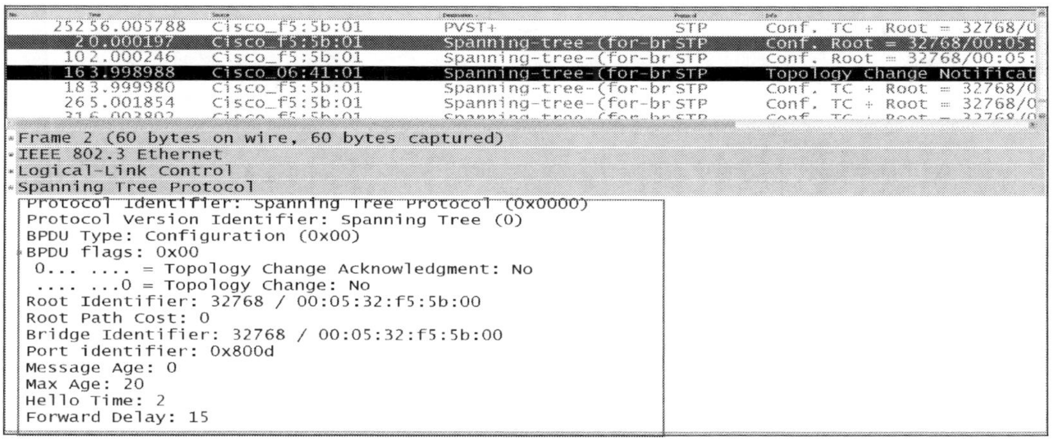

Fig. 3-3. IEEE 802.1D BPDU Fields

If the current Root Bridge fails, Configuration BPDUs stop being sent throughout the network. This state will persist until another switch assumes the role of Root Bridge for the Spanning Tree domain. If the physical link to the Root Bridge fails or communication with the Root Bridge is lost, but the Root Bridge itself is still operational, Configuration BPDUs will cease being sent through the network until an alternate path to the Root Bridge is placed into the forwarding state. However, if there is no alternate path to the Root Bridge, the switched network is partitioned (divided up) and Root Bridges are elected for the different network segments.

IEEE 802.1D Topology Change Notification BPDUs

In a stable and 'healthy' switched network, the majority of the BPDUs sent by switches should be Configuration BPDUs. However, another type of BPDU, the Topology Change Notification (TCN) BPDU may also be sent by switches. The TCN BPDU plays a key role in handling changes in the active topology. This BPDU is used to inform downstream switches of a change in the Spanning Tree network topology. A switch originates a TCN BPDU in the following two conditions:

- It transitions a port into the Forwarding state and it has at least one Designated Port
- It transitions a port from either the Forwarding or Learning states to the Blocking state

These situations indicate a change in the active switch topology and require a notification to be sent to the Root Bridge, assuming that the local switch is not the Root Bridge, which then propagates this information to the rest of the switches within the Spanning Tree domain.

Unlike Configuration BPDUs, which are always originated by the Root Bridge and are received on the Root Port of a Non-Root Bridge, TCN BPDUs are originated by any switch and are sent upstream toward the Root Bridge via the Root Port to alert the Root Bridge that the active topology has changed. Once the Root Bridge acknowledges the TCN, it propagates it to all the other switches in the Spanning Tree domain. The BPDU flow will be described further, beginning with Figure 3-4 illustrated below:

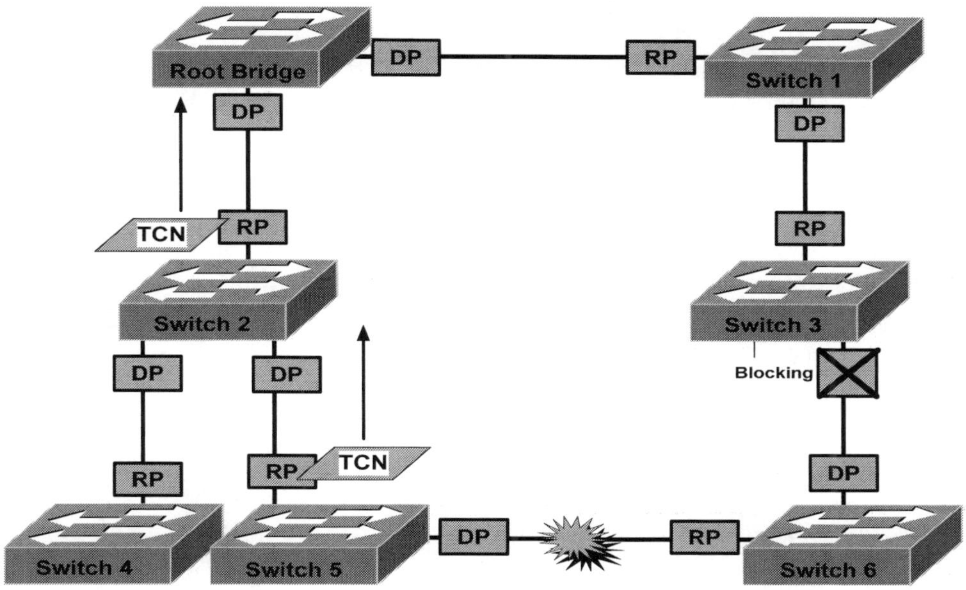

Fig. 3-4. IEEE 802.1D TCN BPDU Flow to the Root Bridge

Referencing Figure 3-4, Switch 5 detects a link failure for the connection between it and Switch 6 and sends out a TCN BPDU via its Root Port toward the Root Bridge. This TCN BPDU is received by Switch 2, which regenerates the TCN BPDU and forwards it to the Root Bridge.

When the Root Bridge receives the TCN BPDU, it confirms receipt by sending back an acknowledgement (ACK). The TCN ACK is received by Switch 2, which relays it to Switch 5. This process is illustrated in Figure 3-5 below:

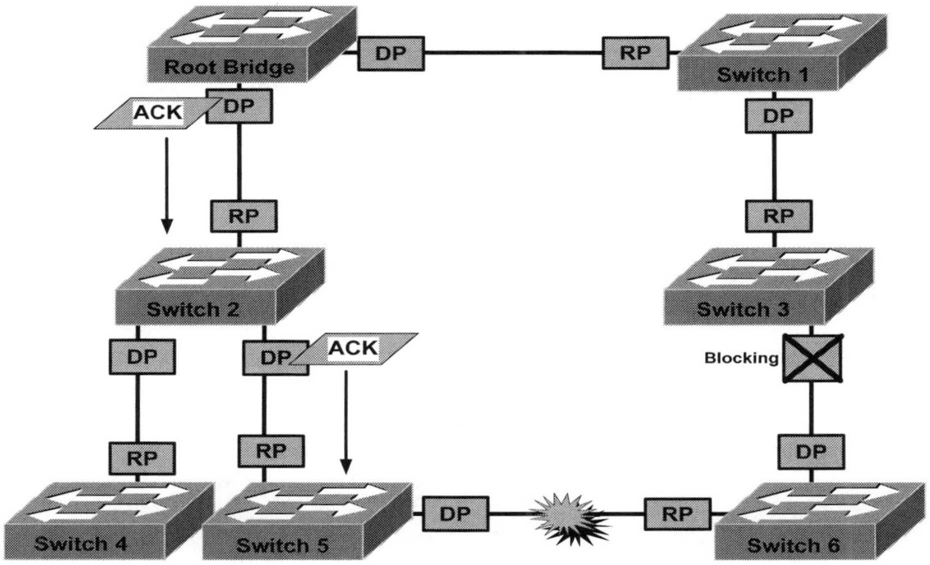

Fig. 3-5. IEEE 802.1D TCN Ack Propagation

The Root Bridge then sends out a Configuration BPDU that has the TCN Flag set. The Root Bridge continues to set the TCN flag in all Configuration BPDUs that it sends out for a total of Forward Delay + Max Age seconds (35 seconds). Forward Delay and Max Age will be described in detail later in this chapter.

The TCN flag instructs all switches to shorten their MAC address table aging process from the default value of 300 seconds to the current Forward Delay value, which is 15 seconds. The switch ports on the switches transition through the Listening and Learning states in order to regenerate a loop-free topology. This is illustrated in Figure 3-6 below:

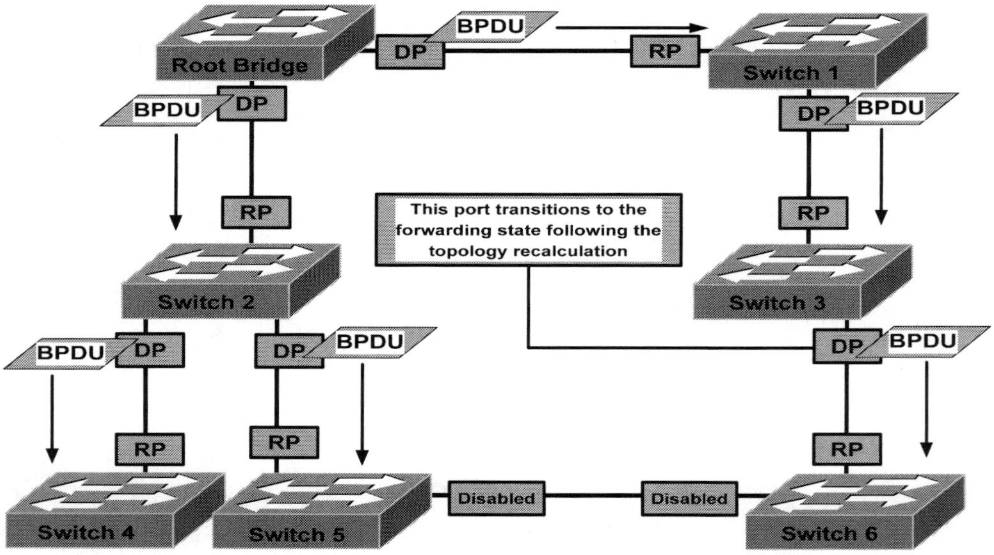

Fig. 3-6. IEEE 802.1D TCN BPDU Propagation from the Root Bridge

The Flag field in the Configuration BPDU is used for the Topology Change (TC) and Topology Change Acknowledgement (TCA) flags. If the Least Significant Bit (LSB) is enabled, this indicates a TC BPDU. However, if the Most Significant Bit (MSB) is enabled, then it indicates a TCA BPDU. It is possible for a single Configuration BPDU to be set with both of these fields in place. Figure 3-7 below illustrates the layout of the Configuration BPDU Flag field:

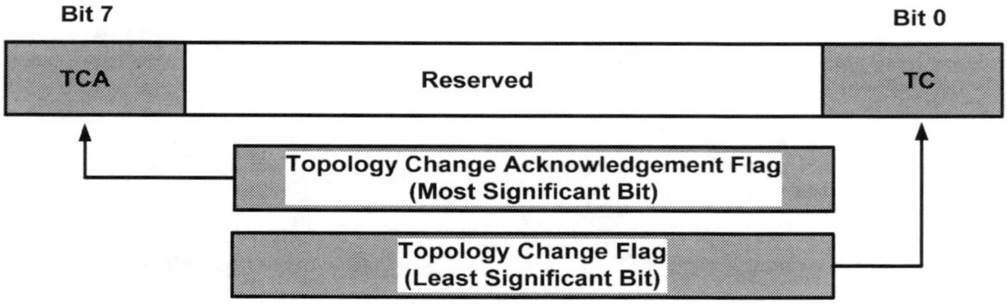

Fig. 3-7. IEEE 802.1D BPDU Flag Field Format

The format of the TCN BPDU is simpler than that of the Configuration BPDU and consists of only three fields. These fields are listed and described in Table 3-2 below:

Table 3-2. IEEE 802.1D BPDU Flag Field Description

Field	Size	Description
Protocol Identifier (ID)	2 Bytes	This field identifies the STP Algorithm and Protocol. This field is always set to 0.
Protocol Version Identifier	1 Byte	This field identifies the STP Protocol Version. This field is always set to 0.
BPDU Type	1 Byte	This field identifies the type of BPDU. It is set to 0x80 for a TCN BPDU.

The TYPE field in the TCN BPDU contains the Binary value 1000 0000, which translates to the value 80 in hexadecimal as can be seen in Figure 3-8 below:

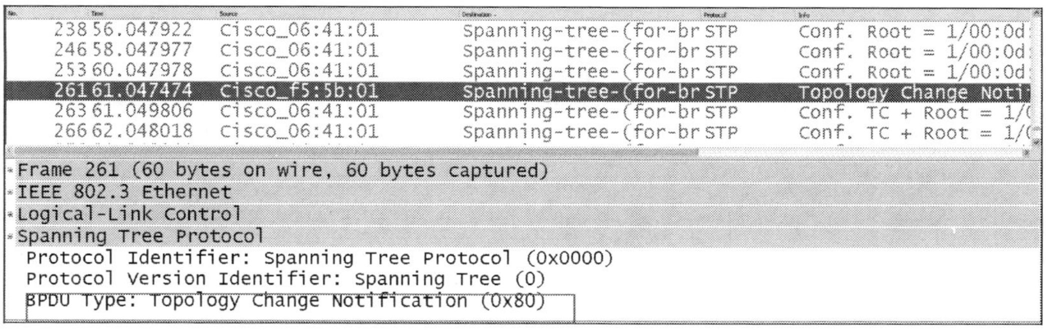

Fig. 3-8. IEEE 802.1D TCN BPDU Hexadecimal Value

Figure 3-9 below illustrates the LSB set in the Configuration BPDU, which indicates that this is a TCN BPDU:

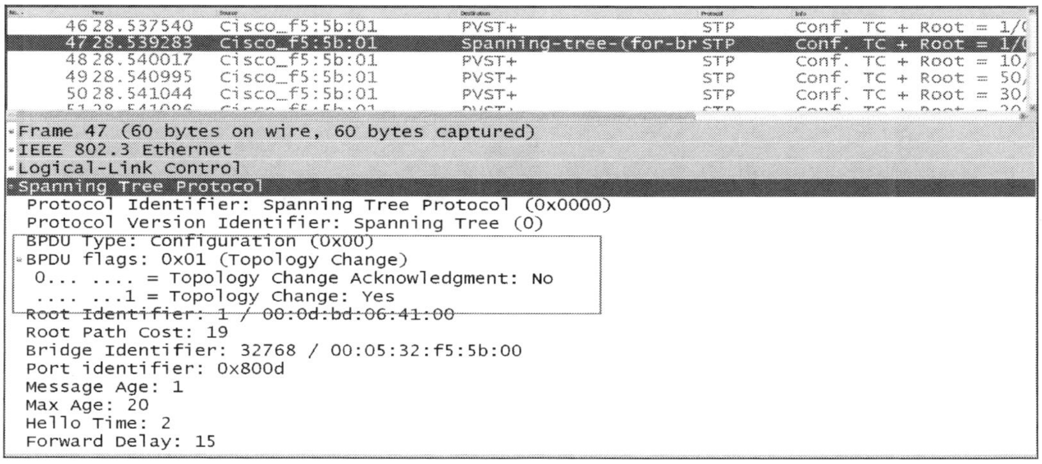

Fig. 3-9. IEEE 802.1D TCN BPDU LSB Field

Figure 3-10 below shows a Configuration BPDU with both the LSB and the MSB set, which indicates that it is used as both a TC BPDU and a TCA BPDU:

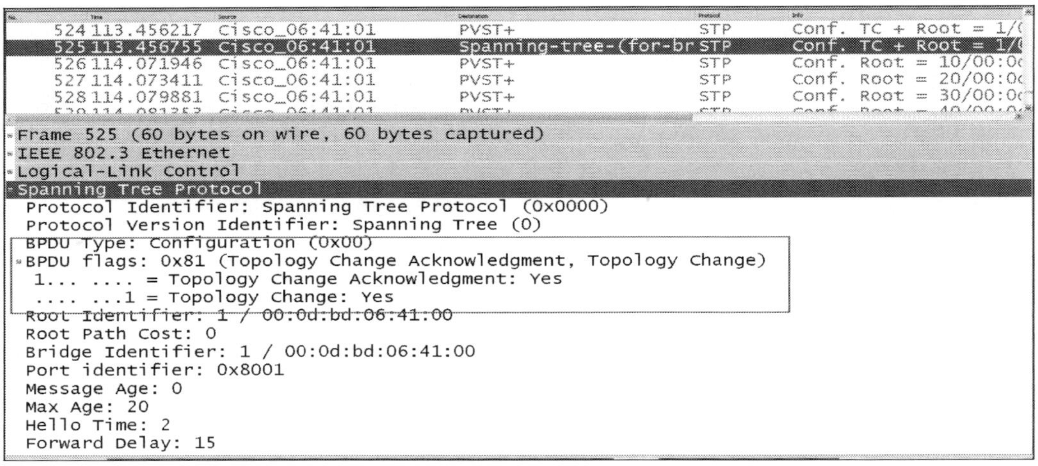

Fig. 3-10. IEEE 802.1D BPDU LSB and MSB Fields

NOTE: In the real world, most people often refer to Configuration BPDUs simply as BPDUs. Unless explicitly stated otherwise, any time the acronym 'BPDU' is used in this chapter, and throughout the remainder of this guide, assume that it is referring to a Configuration BPDU.

Spanning Tree Port States

The Spanning Tree Algorithm defines a number of states that a port under STP control will progress through before being in an active forwarding state. These port states are as follows:

- Blocking
- Listening
- Learning
- Forwarding
- Disabled

A port moves through these states in the following manner:

1. From initialization to Blocking
2. From Blocking to either Listening or Disabled
3. From Listening to either Learning or Disabled
4. From Learning to either Forwarding or Disabled
5. From Forwarding to Disabled

Spanning Tree Blocking State

A switch port that is in the Blocking state performs the following actions:

- Discards frames received on the port from the attached segment
- Discards frames switched from another port
- Does not incorporate station location into its address database
- Receives BPDUs and directs them to the system module
- Does not transmit BPDUs received from the system module
- Receives and responds to network management messages

Spanning Tree Listening State

The Listening state is the first transitional state that the port enters following the Blocking state. The port enters this state when STP determines that the port should participate in frame forwarding. A switch port that is in the Listening state performs the following actions:

- Discards frames received on the port from the attached segment
- Discards frames switched from another port
- Does not incorporate station location into its address database
- Receives BPDUs and directs them to the system module
- Receives, processes, and transmits BPDUs received from the system module
- Receives and responds to network management messages

Spanning Tree Learning State

The Learning state is the second transitional state the port enters. This state comes after the Listening state and before the port enters the Forwarding state. In this state, the port learns and installs MAC addresses into its forwarding table. A switch port that is in the Learning state performs the following actions:

- Discards frames received from the attached segment
- Discards frames switched from another port
- Incorporates (installs) station location into its address database
- Receives BPDUs and directs them to the system module
- Receives, processes, and transmits BPDUs received from the system module
- Receives and responds to network management messages

Spanning Tree Forwarding State

The Forwarding state is the final transitional state the port enters after the Learning state. A port in the Forwarding state forwards frames. A switch port that is in the Forwarding state performs the following actions:

- Forwards frames received from the attached segment
- Forwards frames switched from another port
- Incorporates (installs) station location information into its address database
- Receives BPDUs and directs them to the system module
- Processes BPDUs received from the system module
- Receives and responds to network management messages

Spanning Tree Disabled State

The Disabled state is not part of the normal STP progression for a port. Instead, a port that is administratively shut down by the network administrator, or by the system because of a fault condition, is considered to be in the Disabled state. A disabled port performs the following actions:

- Discards frames received from the attached segment
- Discards frames switched from another port
- Does not incorporate station location into its address database
- Receives BPDUs but does not direct them to the system module
- Does not receive BPDUs from the system module
- Receives and responds to network management messages

Understanding the Spanning Tree Bridge ID

Switches in a Spanning Tree domain have a Bridge ID (BID), which is used to uniquely identify the switch within the STP domain. The BID is also used to assist in the election of an STP Root Bridge, which will be described later in this chapter. The BID is an 8-byte field that is composed from a 6-byte MAC address and a 2-byte Bridge Priority. The BID is illustrated in Figure 3-11 below:

Fig. 3-11. Bridge ID Format

The Bridge Priority is the priority of the switch in relation to all other switches. The Bridge Priority values range from 0 to 65,535. The default value for Cisco Catalyst switches is 32,768. Figure 3-12 below illustrates how the Bridge Priority values are calculated:

Bridge Priority															
Bit 16	Bit 15	Bit 14	Bit 13	Bit 12	Bit 11	Bit 10	Bit 9	Bit 8	Bit 7	Bit 6	Bit 5	Bit 4	Bit 3	Bit 2	Bit 1
32768	16384	8192	4096	2048	1024	512	256	128	64	32	16	8	4	2	1

Fig. 3-12. Calculating the Bridge Priority Values

The MAC address is the hardware address derived from the switch backplane or supervisor engine. In the 802.1D standard, each VLAN requires a unique BID. Figure 3-13 below illustrates the BID format in a Spanning Tree BPDU:

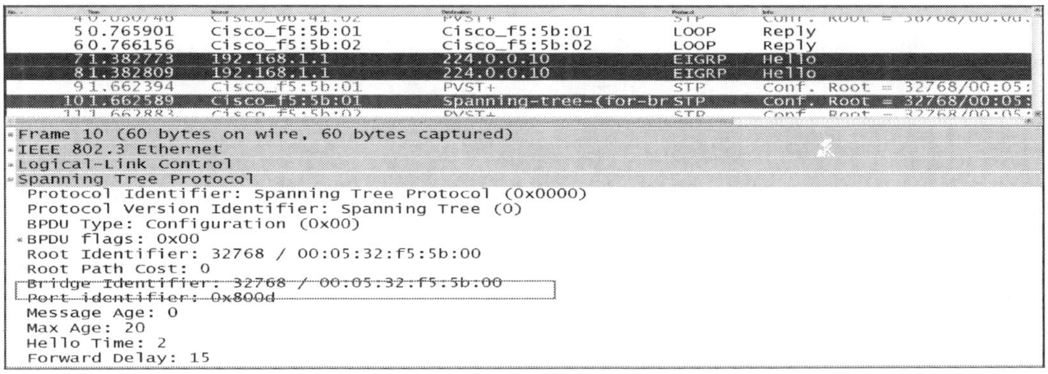

Fig. 3-13. Viewing the BID Format

Most Cisco Catalyst switches have a pool of 1,024 MAC addresses that can be used as bridge identifiers for VLANs. These MAC addresses are allocated sequentially, with the first MAC address in the range assigned to VLAN 1, the second to VLAN 2, the third to VLAN 3, and so forth. This provides the capability to support the standard range of VLANs, but more MAC addresses would be needed to support the extended range of VLANs. This issue was resolved in the 802.1t standard, which is described next.

IEEE 802.1t and the Extended System ID

The 802.1t standard introduced the extended system ID to conserve MAC addresses while still allowing for a unique BID for each VLAN. In order to support extended VLANs, the Bridge Priority is reduced to a 4-bit value and a 12-bit Extended System ID field is added. STP then uses the extended system ID, the switch priority, and a single MAC address to make a unique BID for each VLAN. This is illustrated in Figure 3-14 below:

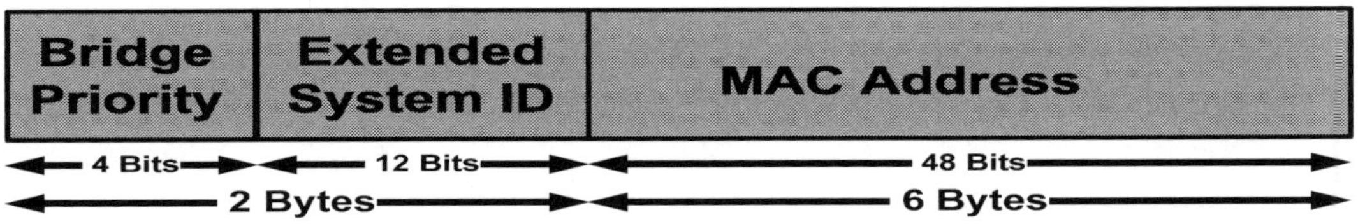

Fig. 3-14. 802.1t BID Composition

With extended system ID enabled, the Bridge Priority is set either to 4,096 as a minimum or to a multiple of 4,096, depending on which Bridge Priority bits are set. Figure 3-15 below illustrates how the Bridge Priority value is calculated with the extended system ID feature:

Bridge Priority				Extended System ID (Set to VLAN ID)											
Bit 16	Bit 15	Bit 14	Bit 13	Bit 12	Bit 11	Bit 10	Bit 9	Bit 8	Bit 7	Bit 6	Bit 5	Bit 4	Bit 3	Bit 2	Bit 1
32768	16384	8192	4096	2048	1024	512	256	128	64	32	16	8	4	2	1

Fig. 3-15. Calculating the 802.1t BID

On Cisco Catalyst switch platforms that have the extended system ID feature enabled (which is the majority of all currently supported Cisco switches), the format of the Bridge ID can be viewed in the `show spanning-tree vlan [number] [address]` command in the following output:

```
VTP-Access-Switch-1#show spanning-tree vlan 10

VLAN0010
  Spanning tree enabled protocol ieee
  Root ID     Priority     0
              Address      0005.32f5.5b01
              Cost         19
              Port         1 (FastEthernet0/1)
              Hello Time    2 sec  Max Age 20 sec  Forward Delay 15 sec

  Bridge ID   Priority     4106   (priority 4096 sys-id-ext 10)
              Address      000d.bd06.4100
              Hello Time    2 sec  Max Age 20 sec  Forward Delay 15 sec
              Aging Time 300
```

```
...
[Truncated Output]
VTP-Switch-1#
VTP-Switch-1#
VTP-Switch-1#show spanning-tree vlan 10 bridge

                                                   Hello  Max  Fwd
Vlan                         Bridge ID              Time  Age  Dly  Protocol
---------------- --------------------------------- ----- ---  ---  --------
VLAN0010               4106 (4096,10) 000d.bd06.4100    2    20   15  ieee
```

In the output above, we can see that because the extended system ID feature is enabled, the BID is comprised of the Bridge Priority (4096), the VLAN ID (10), and the MAC address (000d.bd06.4100). It is important to remember that this same format is used for standard range VLANs as long as the extended system ID feature is enabled on the switch. Because the extended system ID is used, do not assume that the BID incorporates only extended VLAN range numbers. This is a common but false assumption. Make sure you do not make the same error.

REAL WORLD IMPLEMENTATION

The MAC address reduction feature is used on Catalyst 6500 switches to enable extended-range VLAN identification. When MAC address reduction is enabled, it disables the pool of MAC addresses used for the VLAN Spanning Tree, leaving a single MAC address that identifies the switch. If you have a Catalyst 6500 switch in your network and you have MAC address reduction enabled on it, you should also enable MAC address reduction on all other switches to avoid problems in the Spanning Tree topology. By default, MAC address reduction is enabled in later versions of Cisco IOS software; however, if not enabled it can also be manually enabled by issuing the spanning-tree extend system-id or the set spantree macreduction enable CatOS configuration commands in Cisco IOS software.

Spanning Tree Root Bridge Election

By default, following initialization, all switches initially assume that they are the Root of the Spanning Tree until they exchange BPDUs with other switches. When switches exchange BPDUs, an election is held and the switch with the highest Bridge Priority is elected the STP Root Bridge. If two or more switches have the same priority, the switch with the lowest order MAC address is chosen. This concept is illustrated in Figure 3-16 below:

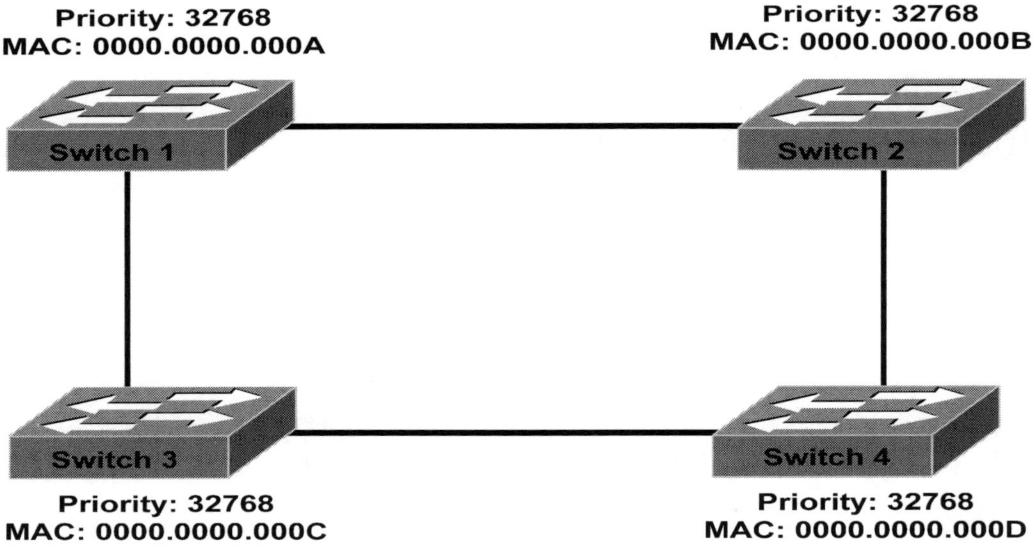

Fig. 3-16. Electing the STP Root Bridge

In Figure 3-16, four switches—Switch 1, Switch 2, Switch 3, and Switch 4—are all part of the same STP domain. By default, all switches have a Bridge Priority of 32,768. In order to determine which switch will become the Root Bridge, and thus break the tie, STP will select the switch based on the lowest order MAC address. Based on this criterion, and referencing the information printed in Figure 3-16, Switch 1 will be elected Root Bridge.

Once elected, the Root Bridge becomes the logical center of the Spanning Tree network. This is not to say that the Root Bridge is physically at the center of the network. Make sure that you do not make that false assumption.

NOTE: It is important to remember that during STP Root Bridge election, no traffic is forwarded over any switch in the same STP domain.

The Cisco IOS software allows administrators to influence the election of the Root Bridge. In addition to this, administrators can also configure a backup Root Bridge. The backup Root Bridge is a switch that administrators would prefer to become the Root Bridge in the event that the current Root Bridge failed or was removed from the network.

It is always good practice to configure a backup Root Bridge for the Spanning Tree domain. This allows the network to be deterministic in the event that the Root Bridge fails. The most common practice is to configure the highest priority (lowest numerical value) on the Root Bridge and then the second highest priority on the switch that should assume Root Bridge functionality in the event that the current Root Bridge fails. This is illustrated in Figure 3-17 below:

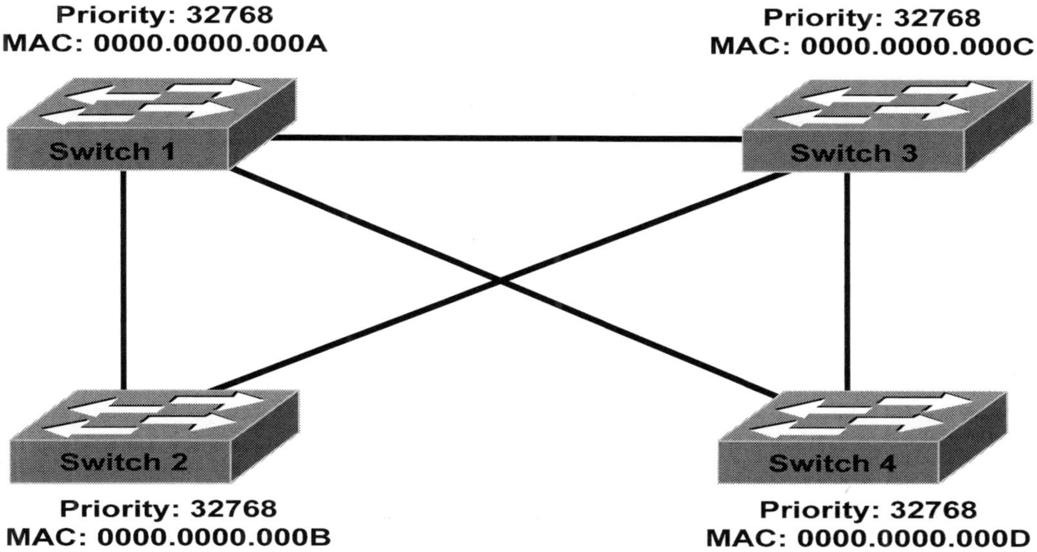

Fig. 3-17. Electing the STP Root Bridge (Contd.)

Based on the configuration in Figure 3-17, the most likely switch to be elected Root Bridge in this network is Switch 1. This is because, although all priority values are the same, this switch has the lowest order MAC address. In the event that Switch 1 failed, STP would elect Switch 2 as the Root Bridge, because it has the second-lowest MAC address. However, this would result in a sub-optimal network topology.

To address this, administrators can manually configure the priority on Switch 1 to the lowest possible value (0) and that of Switch 2 to the second-lowest possible value (4096). This will ensure that in the event that the Root Bridge (Switch 1) fails, Switch 2 will be elected as the Root Bridge. Because administrators are aware of the topology and know which switch would assume Root Bridge functionality, they create a deterministic network that is easier to troubleshoot. The Root ID is carried in BPDUs and includes the Bridge Priority and MAC address of the Root Bridge. This is illustrated in Figure 3-18 below:

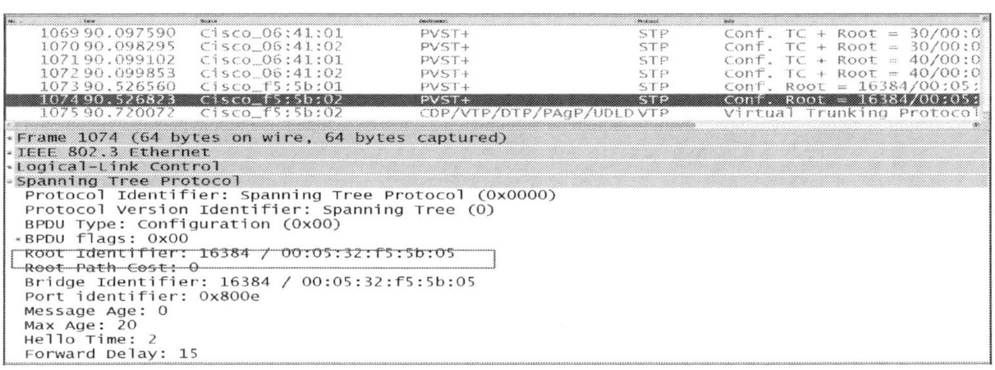

Fig. 3-18. Viewing the Root ID in a BPDU

When referencing the backup Root Bridge, it is important to understand that this switch will function in the same manner as any other Non-Root Bridge until it assumes the role of Root Bridge. Spanning Tree Root Bridge and backup Root Bridge configuration will be illustrated in detail later in this chapter.

Understanding Spanning Tree Cost and Priority

STP uses cost and priority values to determine the best path to the Root Bridge. These values are then used in the election of the Root Port, which will be described in the following section. It is important to understand the calculation of the cost and priority values in order to understand how Spanning Tree selects one port over another, for example.

One of the key functions of the Spanning Tree Algorithm (STA) is to attempt to provide the shortest path to each switch in the network from the Root Bridge. Once selected, this path is then used to forward data while redundant links are placed into a Blocking state. STA uses two values to determine which port will be placed into a Forwarding state (i.e. is the best path to the Root Bridge) and which port(s) will be placed into a Blocking state. These values are the port cost and the port priority. Both are described in the section that follows.

Spanning Tree Port Cost

The 802.1D specification assigns 16-bit (short) default port cost values to each port that is based on the port's bandwidth. Because administrators also have the capability to manually assign port cost values (between 1 and 65,535), the 16-bit values are used only for ports that have not been specifically configured for port cost. Table 3-3 below lists the default values for each type of port when using the short method to calculate the port cost:

Table 3-3. Default STP Port Cost Values

Bandwidth	Default Port Cost
4 Mbps	250
10 Mbps	100
16 Mbps	62
100 Mbps	19
1 Gbps	4
10 Gbps	2

The 802.1t standard assigns 32-bit (long) default port cost values to each port using a formula that is based on the bandwidth of the port. The formula for obtaining default 32-bit port costs is to divide the bandwidth of the port by 200,000,000.

As with the 802.1D (short) method, administrators can also manually configure the port cost using the long method; this time, however, the range that can be configured is from 1 to 200,000,000. Table 3-4 below lists the default values for each type of port when using the long method to calculate the port cost:

Table 3-4. Default STP 802.1t Port Cost Values

Bandwidth	Default Port Cost
4 Mbps	5000000
10 Mbps	2000000
16 Mbps	1250000
100 Mbps	200000
1 Gbps	20000
10 Gbps	2000

In Cisco IOS Catalyst switches, default port cost values can be verified by issuing the `show spanning-tree interface [name]` command as illustrated in the following output, which shows the default short port cost for a FastEthernet interface:

```
VTP-Server#show spanning-tree interface fastethernet 0/2

Vlan             Role Sts Cost      Prio.Nbr Type
---------------- ---- --- --------- -------- --------------------------------
VLAN0050         Desg FWD 19        128.2    P2p
```

The same can be viewed in a Spanning Tree BPDU shown in Figure 3-19 below:

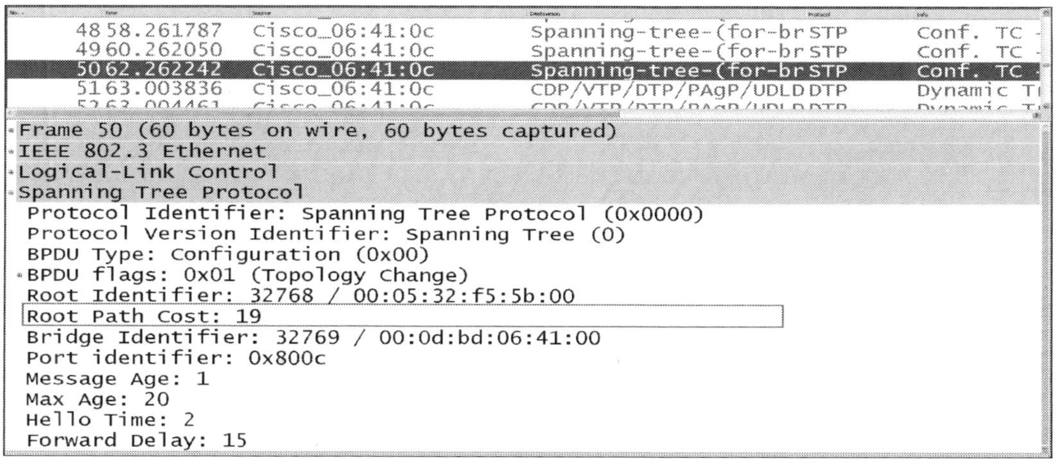

Fig. 3-19. Viewing the Root Path Cost in a BPDU

The following output shows the same for long port cost assignment:

```
VTP-Server#show spanning-tree interface fastethernet 0/2

Vlan             Role Sts Cost      Prio.Nbr Type
---------------- ---- --- --------- -------- --------------------------------
VLAN0050         Desg FWD 200000    128.2    P2p
```

The same can be viewed in a Spanning Tree BPDU illustrated in Figure 3-20 below:

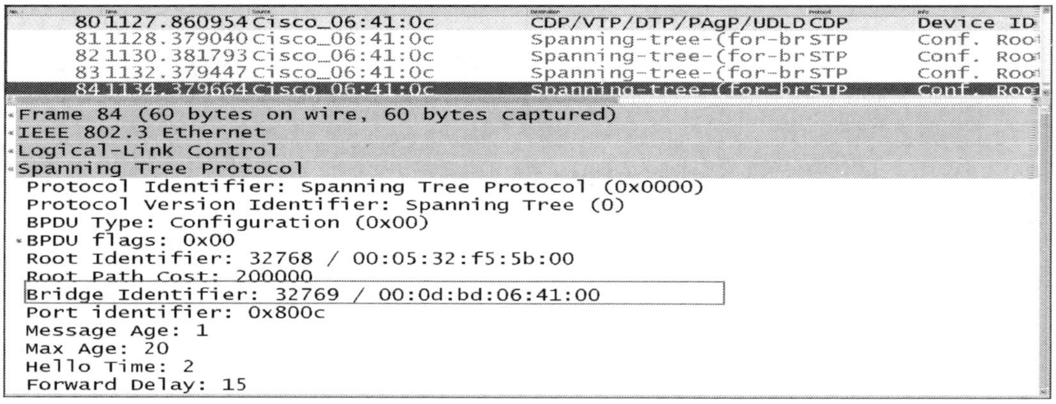

Fig. 3-20. Viewing the Root Path Cost in a BPDU When Using the Long Method

NOTE: By default, the short method will be used. This can be configured by manually issuing the `spanning-tree pathcost method [long|short]` global configuration command as illustrated in the following output:

```
VTP-Server(config)#spanning-tree pathcost method ?
  long   Use 32 bit based values for default port path costs
  short  Use 16 bit based values for default port path costs
```

In both the short and long methods of port cost assignment, it is important to remember that ports with lower (numerically) costs are more preferred and the lower the port cost, the higher the probability of that particular port being elected the Root Port. The Root Port will be described in detail later in this chapter.

The port cost value is globally significant and affects the entire Spanning Tree network. This value is configured on all Non-Root Switches in the Spanning Tree domain. This statement will be explained in greater detail later in this chapter and illustrated in the configuration outputs.

Spanning Tree Port Priority

In the event that multiple ports have the same port cost, STP considers the port priority when selecting which port to put into the Forwarding state. The valid port priority range is from 0 to 240 and the Cisco IOS default value is 128. This value can be manually adjusted by the administrator to influence which port is selected by the STA—the lower the numerical number, the more preferred the port. The default port priority is adjusted in increments of 16.

In traditional STP, the 8-bit port priority and the 8-bit port number are combined to create the 16 bit port identifier (port ID). However, as switches became capable of supporting more and more ports, it was evident that this value needed to be changed. With 802.1t, the port priority is further reduced to 4 bits, which allows 12 bits to be used for the port number, effectively increasing the number of ports that can be supported. The differences between the two standards described here are illustrated in Figure 3-21 below:

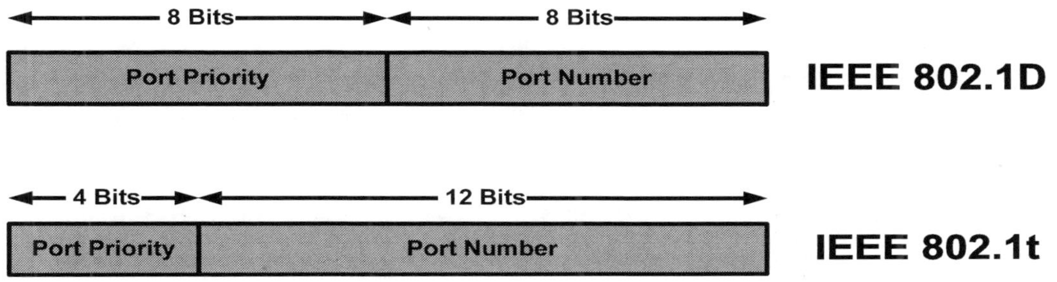

Fig. 3-21. Differences between 802.1D and 802.1t Port Priority

> **NOTE:** If all LAN ports have the same priority value, STP puts the LAN port with the lowest port number into the Forwarding state and blocks other ports.

In Cisco IOS Catalyst switches, default port priority values can be verified by issuing the `show spanning-tree interface [name] [detail]` command as illustrated in the following output, which shows the default port priority for an interface:

```
VTP-Server#show spanning-tree interface fastethernet 0/2 detail
 Port 2 (FastEthernet0/2) of VLAN0050 is forwarding
   Port path cost 200000, Port priority 128, Port Identifier 128.2.
   Designated root has priority 50, address 000d.bd06.4100
   Designated bridge has priority 50, address 000d.bd06.4100
...
[Truncated Output]
```

The port priority is locally significant between two switches. If a switch is connected via multiple links to another switch, it uses the following tiebreaker mechanisms to determine which link to place into the Forwarding state:

- Lowest Root Bridge ID
- Lowest Root Path Cost to Root Bridge
- Lowest Sender Bridge ID
- Lowest Sender Port ID

Figure 3-22 below will be used to explain this concept:

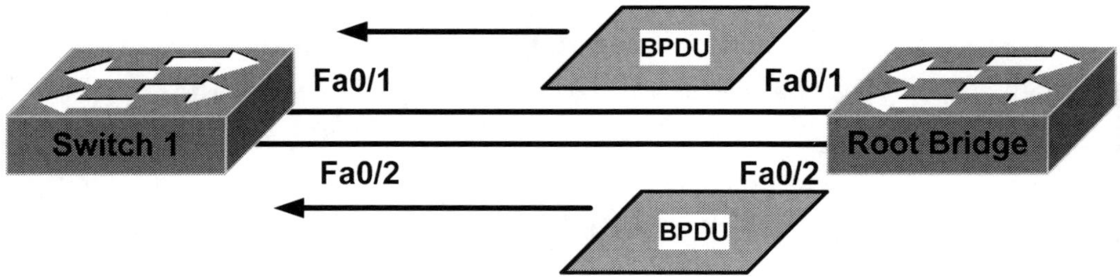

Fig. 3-22. Understanding How the Port Priority Is Used

In Figure 3-22, Switch 1 receives two BPDUs from the Root Bridge. To determine which port to place into the Forwarding state, it considers the received Root Bridge ID. Because the BPDU is originated from the same switch (Root Bridge), these values will be the same. Next, it considers the Root Path Cost. Because both links to the Root Bridge are the same, they have the same Path Cost, which results in another tie.

Next, it considers the Sender BID. However, this is also the same, and so there is yet another tie. Finally, Spanning Tree considers the lowest Sender Port ID, which is comprised of the port priority value and the port number. The Sender Port ID of FastEthernet0/1 would be 128.1 and the sender priority of FastEthernet0/2 would be 128.2. The lower sender ID is FastEthernet0/1 and so this port would be placed into the Forwarding state. The default port priority on all Cisco Catalyst switches is 128.

Spanning Tree Root and Designated Ports

Spanning Tree elects two types of ports that are used to forward BPDUs: the Root Port, which points toward the Root Bridge; and the Designated Port, which points away from the Root Bridge. It is important to understand the functionality of these two port types and how they are elected by STP.

Spanning Tree Root Port Election

STA defines three types of ports: the Root Port, the Designated Port, and the Non-Designated Port. These port types are elected by the STA and placed into the appropriate state (e.g. Forwarding or Blocking). During the Spanning Tree election process, in the event of a tie, the following values will be used (in the order listed) as tie-breakers:

- Lowest Root Bridge ID
- Lowest Root Path Cost to Root Bridge
- Lowest Sender Bridge ID
- Lowest Sender Port ID

NOTE: It is important to remember these tiebreaking criteria in order to understand how Spanning Tree elects and designates different port types in any given situation. Not only is this something that you will most likely be tested on, but also it is very important to have a solid understanding in order to design, implement, and support internetworks in the real world.

The Spanning Tree Root Port is the port that provides the best path, or lowest cost, when the device forwards packets to the Root Bridge. In other words, the Root Port is the port that receives the best BPDU for the switch, which indicates that it is the shortest path to the Root in terms of Path Cost. The Root Port is elected based on the Root Path Cost.

The Root Path Cost is calculated based on the cumulative cost (Path Cost) of all the links leading up to the Root Bridge. The Path Cost is the value that each port contributes to the Root Path Cost. Because this concept is often quite confusing, it is illustrated in Figure 3-23 below:

NOTE: All links illustrated in Figure 3-23 are GigabitEthernet links. It should be assumed that the traditional 802.1D (short) method is used for port cost calculation. Therefore, the default port cost of GigabitEthernet is 4 while that of FastEthernet is 19.

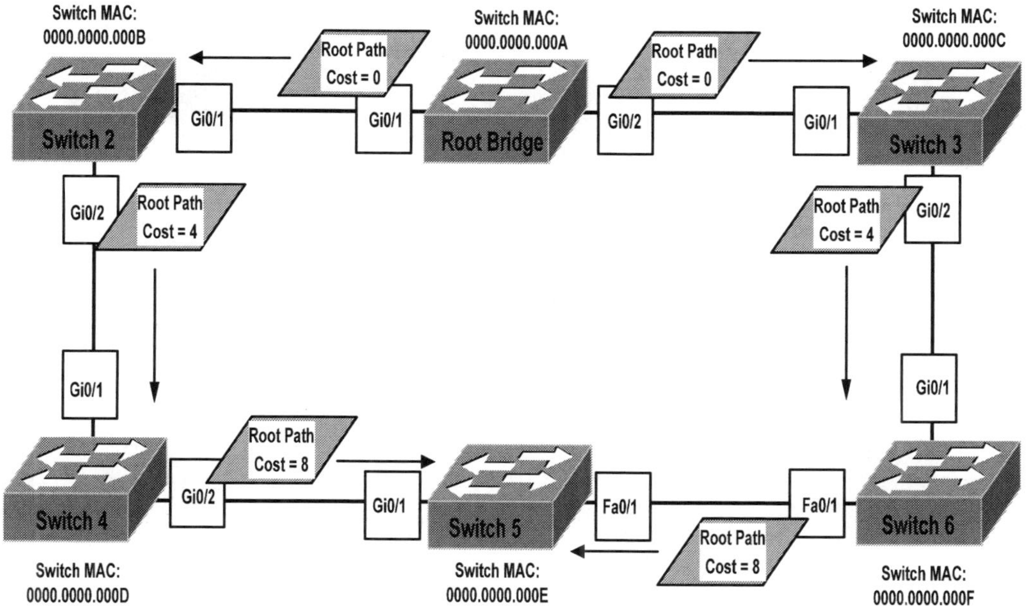

Fig. 3-23. Spanning Tree Root Port Election

NOTE: The following explanation illustrates the flow of BPDUs between the switches in the network. Along with other information, these BPDUs contain the Root Path Cost information, which is incremented by the ingress port on the receiving switch.

1. The Root Bridge sends out a BPDU with a Root Path Cost value of 0 because its ports reside directly on the Root Bridge. This BPDU is sent to Switch 2 and Switch 3.

2. When Switch 2 and Switch 3 receive the BPDU from the Root Bridge, they add their own Path Cost based on the ingress interface. Because Switch 2 and Switch 3 are both connected to the Root Bridge via GigabitEthernet connections, they add the Path Cost value received from the Root Bridge (0) to their GigabitEthernet Path Cost values (4). The Root Path Cost from Switch 2 and Switch 3 via GigabitEthernet0/1 to the Root Bridge is 0 + 4 = 4.

3. Switch 2 and Switch 3 send out new BPDUs to their respective neighbors, which are Switch 4 and Switch 6, respectively. These BPDUs contain the new cumulative value (4) as the Root Path Cost.

4. When Switch 4 and Switch 6 receive the BPDUs from Switch 2 and Switch 3, they increment the received Root Path Cost value based on the ingress interface. Since GigabitEthernet connections are being used, the value received from Switch 2 and Switch 3 is incremented by 4. The Root Path Cost to the Root Bridge on Switch 4 and Switch 6 via their respective GigabitEthernet0/1 interfaces is therefore 0 + 4 + 4 = 8.

5. Switch 5 receives two BPDUs: one from Switch 4 and the other from Switch 6. The BPDU received from Switch 4 has a Root Path Cost of 0 + 4 + 4 + 4 = 12. The BPDU received from Switch 6 has a Root Path Cost of 0 + 4 + 4 + 19 = 27. Because the Root Path Cost value contained in the BPDU received from Switch 4 is better than that received from Switch 6, Switch 5 elects GigabitEthernet0/1 as the Root Port.

NOTE: Switches 2, 3, 4, and 6 will all elect their GigabitEthernet0/1 ports as Root Ports.

FURTHER EXPLANATION

To further explain and help you to understand the election of the Root Port, let's assume that all ports in the diagram used in the example above are GigabitEthernet ports. This would mean that in Step 5 above, Switch 5 would receive two BPDUs with the same Root Bridge ID, both with a Root Path Cost value of 0 + 4 + 4 + 4 = 12. In order for the Root Port to be elected, STP will progress to the next option in the tiebreaker criteria. The criteria is listed below, with the first two options (which have already been used) crossed out:

- Lowest Sender Bridge ID
- Lowest Sender Port ID

Based on the third selection criteria, Switch 5 will prefer the BPDU received from Switch 4 because its BID (0000.0000.000D) is lower than that of Switch 6 (0000.0000.000F). Switch 5 elects port GigabitEthernet0/1 as the Root Port.

Spanning Tree Designated Port Election

Unlike the Root Port, the Designated Port is a port that points away from the STP Root. This port is the port via which the designated device is attached to the LAN. It is also the port that has the lowest Path Cost when forwarding packets from that LAN to the Root Bridge.

NOTE: Some people refer to the Designated Port as the Designated Switch. The terms are interchangeable and refer to the same thing; that is, this is the switch, or port, that is used to forward frames from a particular LAN segment to the Root Bridge.

The primary purpose of the Designated Port is to prevent loops. When more than one switch is connected to the same LAN segment, all switches will attempt to forward a frame received on that segment. This default behavior can result in multiple copies of the same frame being forwarded by multiple switches—resulting in a network loop. To avoid this default behavior, a Designated Port is elected on all LAN segments. By default, all ports on the Root Bridge are designated ports. This is because the Root Path Cost will always be 0. The STA election of the Designated Port is illustrated in Figure 3-24 below:

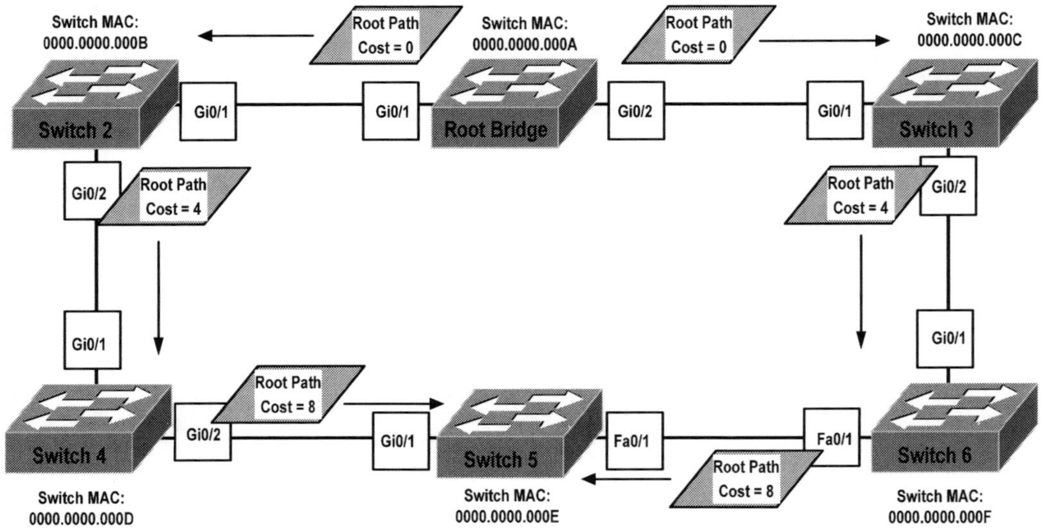

Fig. 3-24. Spanning Tree Designated Port Election

1. On the segment between the Root Bridge and Switch 2, the Root Bridge GigabitEthernet0/1 is elected as the Designated Port because it has the lower Root Path Cost, which is 0.

2. On the segment between the Root Bridge and Switch 3, the Root Bridge GigabitEthernet0/2 is elected as the Designated Port because it has the lower Root Path Cost, which is 0.

3. On the segment between Switch 2 and Switch 4, the GigabitEthernet0/2 port on Switch 2 is elected as the Designated Port because Switch 2 has the lowest Root Path Cost, which is 4.

4. On the segment between Switch 3 and Switch 6, the GigabitEthernet0/2 port on Switch 3 is elected as the Designated Port because Switch 3 has the lowest Root Path Cost, which is 4.

5. On the segment between Switch 4 and Switch 5, the GigabitEthernet0/2 port on Switch 4 is elected as the Designated Port because Switch 4 has the lowest Root Path Cost, which is 8.

6. On the segment between Switch 5 and Switch 6, the GigabitEthernet0/2 port on Switch 6 is elected as the Designated Port because Switch 6 has the lowest Root Path Cost, which is 8.

The Non-Designated Port is not really a Spanning Tree Port type. Instead, it is a term that simply means a port that is not the Designated Port on a LAN segment. This port will always be placed into a Blocking state by STP. Based on the calculation of Root and Designated Ports, the resultant Spanning Tree topology for the switched network that was used in the Root Port and Designated Port election examples is shown in Figure 3-25 below:

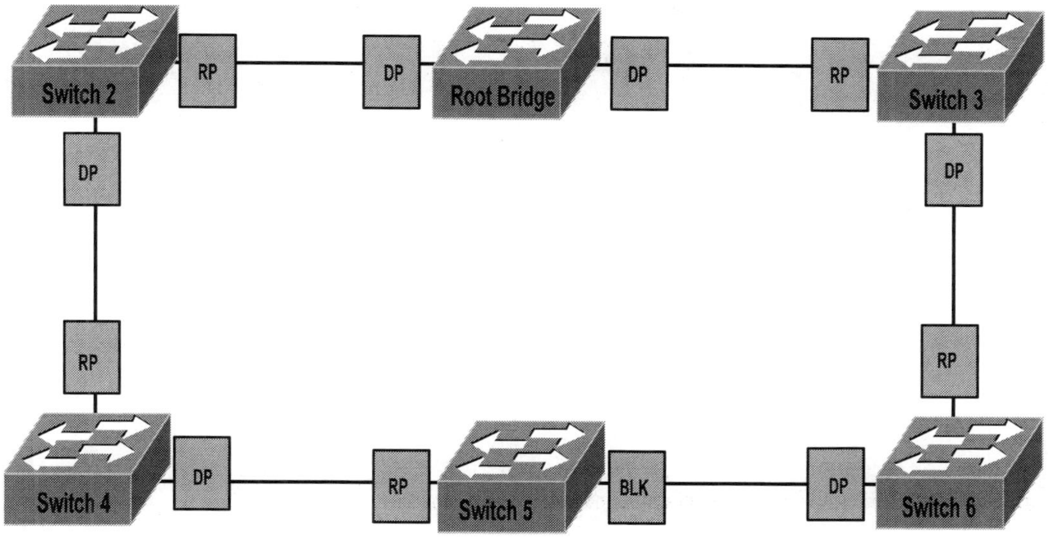

Fig. 3-25. Converged Spanning Tree Network

Spanning Tree Timers

Spanning Tree BPDUs include several timers that play an integral role in the operation of the protocol. The Spanning Tree timer values are contained in the last three fields of a BPDU. Within the Spanning Tree domain, the only timer values that are important are those that are sent by the Root Bridge. In other words, Non-Root Bridges are not concerned with locally configured timer values.

The default Spanning Tree timers go hand-in-hand with the IEEE 802.1D specification that recommends a maximum network diameter of 7. The Spanning Tree diameter is the maximum distance that any two single switches can be from each other. A maximum diameter of 7 means that two distinct switches cannot be more than seven hops away from each other. This concept will be described in detail later in this chapter.

Because all other switches in the Spanning Tree domain use the timer values advertised by the Root Bridge, the modification of any of these values should always be made at the Root Bridge. By setting these values in the STP Root, these values will be passed (via BPDUs) to other switches in the STP domain. The three configurable Spanning Tree timer values are as follows:

1. The Hello Time
2. The Forward Delay
3. The Max Age

In addition to these three configurable timers, BPDUs also include a Message Age timer. This timer is unique in that it is modified by every switch that receives and propagates a BPDU. This timer cannot be configured by the administrator. The Message Age timer is used in conjunction with the Max Age timer. This correlation will be described later in this chapter. Figure 3-26 below shows the STP timer fields in a BPDU:

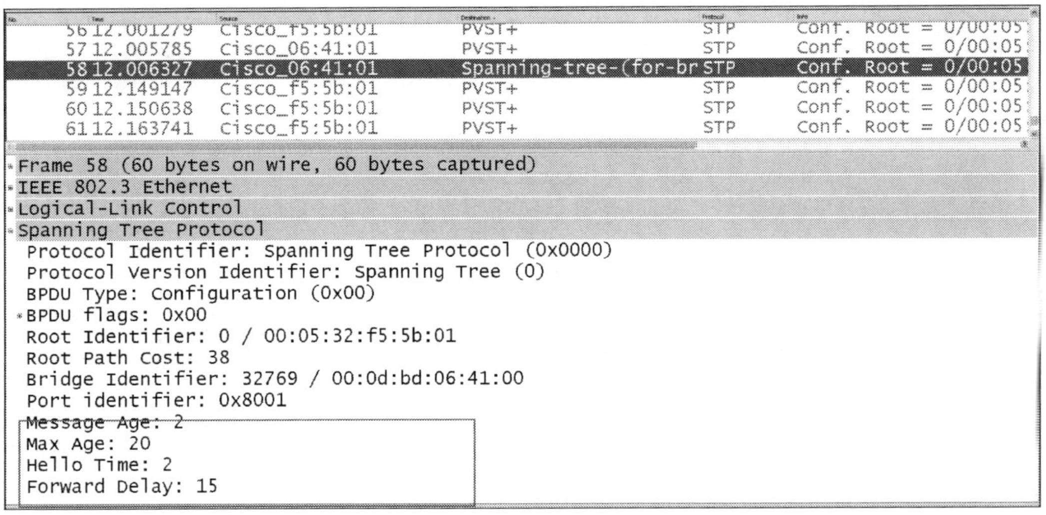

Fig. 3-26. Spanning Tree BPDU Timer Fields

The `show spanning-tree vlan [number]` command can also be used to verify the Hello Time, Forward Delay, and Max Age timers as illustrated in the following output:

```
VTP-Switch-1#show spanning-tree vlan 80

VLAN0080
  Spanning tree enabled protocol ieee
  Root ID     Priority    80
              Address     000d.bd06.4100
              This bridge is the root
              Hello Time   2 sec  Max Age 20 sec  Forward Delay 15 sec

  Bridge ID   Priority    80     (priority 0 sys-id-ext 80)
              Address     000d.bd06.4100
              Hello Time   2 sec  Max Age 20 sec  Forward Delay 15 sec
              Aging Time 300
...
 [Truncated Output]
```

NOTE: The Message Age is not included in the output of any `show` commands.

The Hello Time

The Hello Time is the time between each BPDU that is sent. This time is equal to 2 seconds (sec) by default, but it can be set to be between 1 and 10 seconds. While the Hello Time received in the BPDU from the Root Bridge is propagated unchanged throughout the Spanning Tree domain, all switches have their own local Hello Time for TCN BPDUs that the switches transmit.

The IEEE 802.1D standard specifies a default Hello Time value of 2 seconds based on a recommended Spanning Tree diameter of 7 switches.

By decreasing the Hello Time to the lowest possible value, which is 1 second, administrators can reduce the interval between BPDU updates on a port. However, this effectively doubles the number of BPDUs that are sent and received by each bridge, which can cause an additional load on the CPU of the switches. This additional load can cause instability in a network with a large number of VLANs and trunk links due to the added load to the switch CPUs.

The Forward Delay

The Forward Delay is the time that is spent in the Listening and Learning state. When the port transitions to the Listening state, it indicates a change in the current Spanning Tree topology and that the port will go from a Blocking state to a Forwarding state. The Forward Delay is used to cover the period between the Blocking and Forwarding states, which includes the Listening and Learning states.

This time is set to 15 seconds (sec) by default but can be manually set to be between 4 and 30 seconds. As is the case with the Hello Time, the default Forward Delay value is based on the IEEE Spanning Tree diameter of 7 switches. This is derived via the following formula:

Forward Delay = ((4 * hello) + (3 * Diameter)) / 2

Assuming all the default values, we can calculate the Forward Delay as follows:

Forward Delay = ((4 * hello) + (3 * Diameter)) / 2
Forward Delay = ((4 * 2) + (3 * 7)) / 2
Forward Delay = ((8) + (21)) / 2
Forward Delay = 29 / 2
Forward Delay = 29 / 2
Forward Delay = 14.5 seconds (rounded up to 15 seconds)

The Max Age and Message Age Timers

When switches execute STP, they save a copy of the best BPDU that is received. In addition to the two timers previously described, the BPDU also contains the Message and Max Age timers.

The Max Age time is set in the BPDU by the Root Bridge and defaults to 20 seconds. This timer can be manually set to any number between 6 and 40 seconds. The Max Age value remains the same for all BPDUs that are propagated by all switches in the Spanning Tree domain. Any changes to this value on the Root Bridge are propagated to the other switches in the Spanning Tree domain. The default Max Age is based on the IEEE Spanning Tree diameter of 7 switches. This is derived via the following formula:

Max Age = (4 * Hello) + (2 * Diameter) – 2

Assuming the default STP values, the Max Age is calculated as follows:

Max Age = (4 * Hello) + (2 * Diameter) – 2
Max Age = (4 * 2) + (2 * 7) – 2
Max Age = 8 + 14 – 2
Max Age = 20 seconds

The Message Age timer displays the age of the Root Bridge BPDU. Unlike the Max Age timer, the Message Age timer is incremented by 1 by each switch that propagates it to any other downstream switch within the STP domain.

The Root Bridge sends BPDUs with a Message Age value of 0. Non-Root Bridges that are directly connected to the Root Bridge will receive the BDPU with a Message Age of 0 on their Root Port. These switches then increment this value by 1 before propagating the BPDU to downstream neighbors. This process is repeated by every switch that receives and propagates the Bridge Protocol Data Unit. This concept is illustrated in Figure 3-27 below:

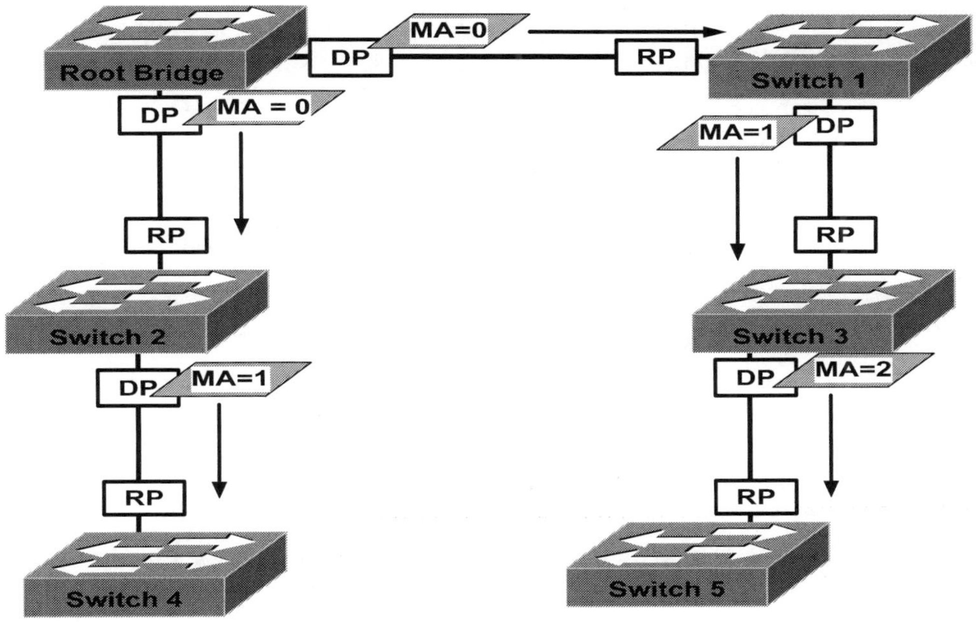

Fig. 3-27. Spanning Tree BPDU Message Age Propagation

Referencing Figure 3-27, the Message Age is propagated as follows:

1. The Root Bridge sends out a BPDU on its Designated Ports to Switch 1 and Switch 2. This BPDU contains the default STP timers and a Message Age value of 0.

2. Switch 1 and Switch 2 receive the BPDU from the Root Bridge on their respective Root Ports. The BPDU contains the STP timers set by the Root Bridge and a Message Age of 0. Both switches increment the Message Age value by 1 before propagating the BPDU downstream.

3. Switch 3 and Switch 4 receive the BPDU on their respective Root Ports from their upstream neighbors, which are Switch 1 and Switch 2. This BPDU contains the STP timers set by the Root Bridge and an incremented Message Age value of 1. Switch 3 increments the Message Age by 1 before propagating the BPDU downstream.

4. Switch 5 receives the BPDU from Switch 3 on its Root Port. The BPDU contains the STP timers set by the Root Bridge and the incremented Message Age value of 2.

The Message Age timer can be used to determine the following two variables:

1. How far away the switch is from the Root Bridge
2. The time before the received BPDU is aged out on the port

Because each switch that forwards the Configuration BPDU increments the Message Age field by 1, the value contained in this field that is received by a downstream switch can be used to determine how far away that switch is from the Root Bridge. For example, Switch 1 receives the BPDU with a Message Age of 0. This indicates that Switch 1 is zero hops away from (i.e. directly connected to) the Root Bridge. The Message Age value of 1 received on Switch 4 indicates that the switch is one hop away from the Root Bridge, and the Message Age value of 2 that is received on Switch 5 indicates the switch is two hops away from the Root Bridge.

When a switch receives a BPDU, the BPDU contains the Max Age timer, which is set by the Root Bridge and never changes, and the Message Age, which is incremented by all other upstream switches. To determine the time before information received on that port is aged out, the switch subtracts the Message Age from the Max Age. Table 3-5 below shows how the switches illustrated in Figure 3-27 would calculate their aging times based on the Message Age and Max Age values in the received BPDUs:

Table 3-5. Aging Times

Switch	Max (Maximum) Age	Message Age	Aging Time
Switch 1	20	0	(20 – 0) = 20 seconds
Switch 2	20	0	(20 – 0) = 20 seconds
Switch 3	20	1	(20 – 1) = 19 seconds
Switch 4	20	1	(20 – 1) = 19 seconds
Switch 5	20	2	(20 – 2) = 18 seconds

Understanding the Spanning Tree Diameter

The IEEE 802.1D specification recommends a maximum network diameter of 7 switches. The term 'diameter' refers to the maximum number of switches a frame would have to travel to get from one end of the network to the other. A network diameter of 7 switches means that no two distinct switches can be more than seven hops away from each other. To understand this concept, consider the switched network illustrated in Figure 3-28 below:

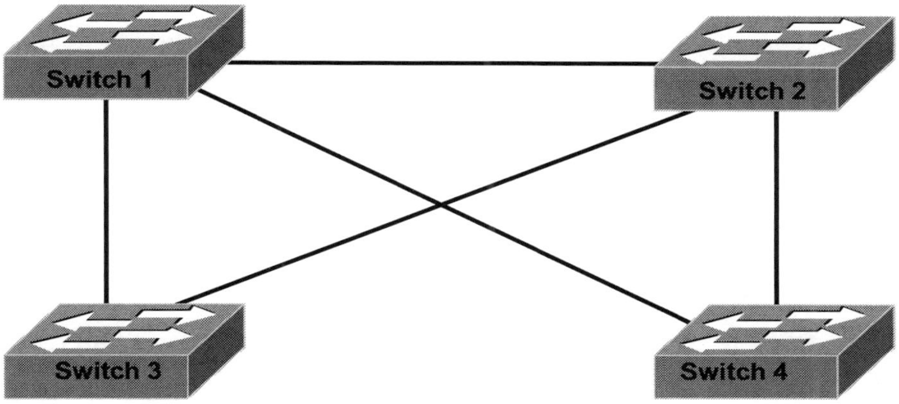

Fig. 3-28. Understanding the STP Diameter

In Figure 3-28, the diameter is 4. This means that if a frame travelled from one end of the network to the other, going through all switches, it would only transit a maximum of 4 switches. For example, the longest path that a frame would take to go from Switch 3 to Switch 4 could be either of the following:

- Switch 3 > Switch 1 > Switch 2 > Switch 4
- Switch 3 > Switch 2 > Switch 1 > Switch 4

The number seven is derived from a series of calculations based on various timers being tuned to their default values. The default Spanning Tree diameter is determined based on the Max Age and Forward Delay timers. These two values can be used to calculate the diameter using the following two formulas:

Diameter = (Max Age + 2 - (4 * Hello)) / 2
Diameter = ((2 * Forward Delay) - (4 * Hello)) / 3

Based on the default values for these timers, the STP network diameter is calculated as follows:

Diameter = (Max Age + 2 - (4 * Hello)) / 2 Diameter = (20 + 2 - (4 * 2)) / 2 Diameter = (22 - 8) / 2 Diameter = 14 / 2 Diameter = 7 seconds	Diameter = ((2 * Forward Delay) - (4 * Hello)) / 3 Diameter = ((2 * 15) - (4 * 2)) / 3 Diameter = (30 - 8) / 3 Diameter = 22 / 3 Diameter = 7.33 (rounded down to 7) seconds

This maximum network diameter restricts how far away from each other bridges in the network can be. However, the network diameter may be higher than 7 although this is not recommended, as it could result in Spanning Tree convergence issues. Cisco IOS software allows network administrators to change the Spanning Tree diameter when configuring the Root Bridge. When you specify the network diameter, the switch automatically sets an optimal Hello Time, Forward Delay time, and Max Age time for a network of that diameter, which can significantly reduce the convergence time.

STP TIMER WARNING

When working with STP in live networks, it is important that you do not arbitrarily adjust the default Spanning Tree parameters. These values are perfectly fine for almost every network. Changing these values, without a solid understanding of the implications, may cause unexpected results, even as far as a complete network meltdown. If you do not want to be remembered as the person who brought down the network, then it is recommended that you do not change these values without absolute justification or guidance from the Cisco Technical Assistance Center (TAC).

Cisco Spanning Tree Enhancements

As stated earlier in this chapter, the Spanning Tree protocol makes two assumptions about the environment in which it has been enabled, as follows:

- All links are bidirectional and can both send and receive Bridge Protocol Data Units
- All switches can regularly receive, process, and send Bridge Protocol Data Units

In real-world networks, these two assumptions are not always correct. In situations where that is the case, STP may not be able to prevent loops from being formed within the network. Because of this possibility, and to improve performance of the basic IEEE 802.1D STP Algorithm, Cisco has introduced a number of enhancements to the IEEE 802.1D standard. These enhancements are described in this section.

Port Fast

Port Fast is a feature that is typically enabled only for a port or interface that connects to a host. When the link comes up on this port, the switch skips the first stages of the STA and directly transitions to the Forwarding state. Contrary to popular belief, the Port Fast feature does not disable Spanning Tree on the selected port.

This is because even with the Port Fast feature, the port can still send and receive BPDUs. This is not a problem when the port is connected to a network device that does not send or respond to BPDUs, such as the NIC on a workstation, for example. However, this may result in a switching loop if the port is connected to a device that does send BPDUs, such as another switch. This is because the port skips the Listening and Learning states and proceeds immediately to the Forwarding state. Port Fast simply allows the port to begin forwarding frames much sooner than a port going through all normal STA steps.

BPDU Guard

The BPDU Guard feature is used to protect the Spanning Tree domain from external influence. BPDU Guard is disabled by default but is recommended for all ports on which the Port Fast feature has been enabled. When a port that is configured with the BPDU Guard feature receives a BPDU, it immediately transitions to the errdisable state.

This prevents false information from being injected into the Spanning Tree domain on ports that have Spanning Tree disabled. The operation of BPDU Guard, in conjunction with Port Fast, is illustrated in Figures 3-29, 3-30, and 3-31 below and following:

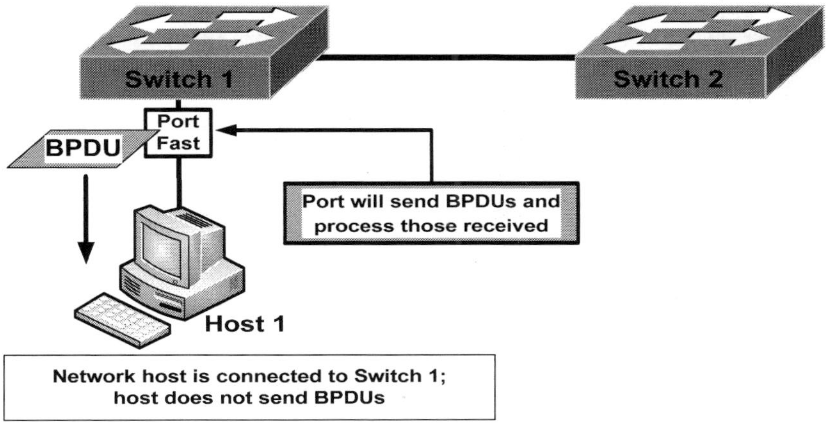

Fig. 3-29. Understanding BPDU Guard

In Figure 3-29, Port Fast is enabled on Switch 1 on its connection to Host 1. Following initialization, the port transitions to a Forwarding state, which eliminates 30 seconds of delay that would have been encountered if STA was not bypassed and the port went through the Listening and Learning states. Because the network host is a workstation, it sends no BPDUs and so disabling Spanning Tree on that port is not an issue.

Either by accident or due to some other malicious intent, Host 1 is disconnected from Switch 1. Using the same port, Switch 3 is connected to Switch 1. Switch 3 is also connected to Switch 2. Because Port Fast is enabled on the port connecting Switch 1 to Switch 3, this port moves from initialization to the Forwarding state, bypassing normal STP initialization. This port will also receive and process any BPDUs that are sent by Switch 3 as illustrated in Figure 3-30 below:

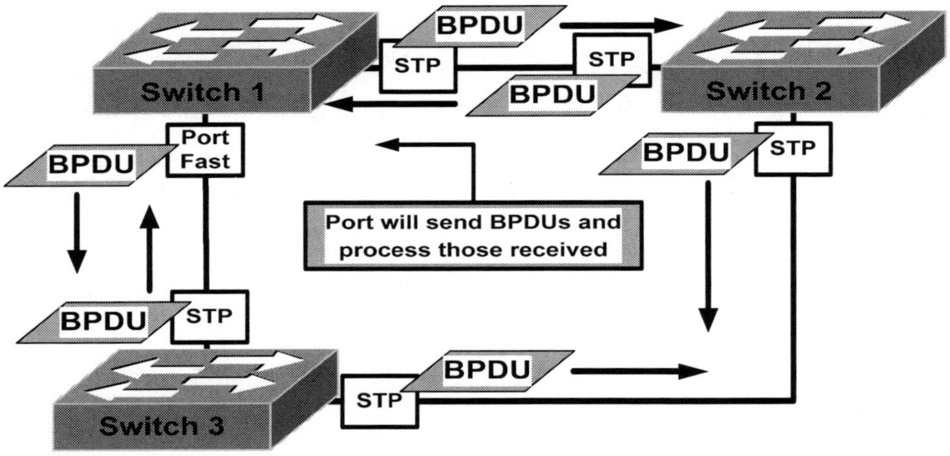

Fig. 3-30. Understanding BPDU Guard (Contd.)

Based on the port states illustrated above, and referencing the first lesson in this chapter, on bridging loops, we can quickly see how a loop would be created in this network. To prevent this from occurring, BPDU Guard should be enabled on all ports with Port Fast enabled. This is illustrated in Figure 3-31 below:

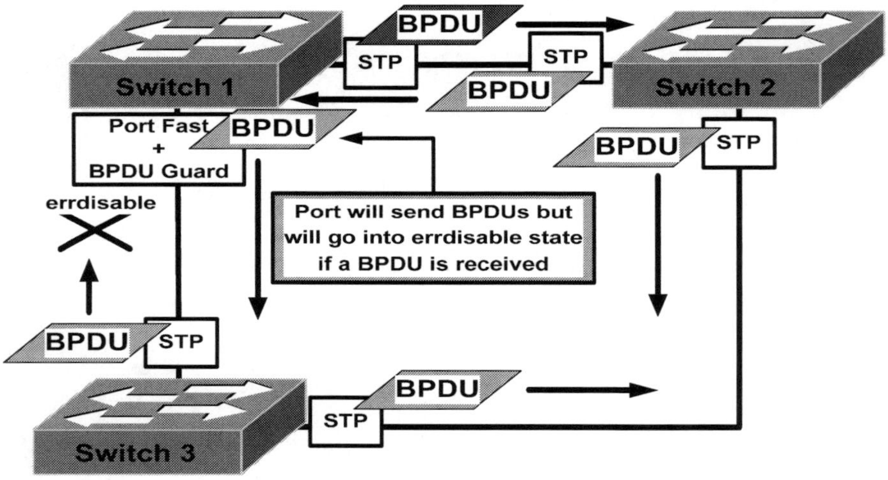

Fig. 3-31. Understanding BPDU Guard (Contd.)

With BPDU Guard enabled on the Port Fast port, when Switch 1 receives a BPDU from Switch 3, it immediately transitions the port into an errdisabled state. The result is that the STP calculation is not affected by this redundant link and the network will not have any loops.

BPDU Filter

The BPDU Guard and BPDU Filter features are often confused or even thought to be the same. They are, however, different, and it is important to understand the differences between them.

When Port Fast is enabled on a port, the port will send out BPDUs and will accept and process received BPDUs. The BPDU Guard feature prevents the port from receiving any BPDUs but does not prevent it from sending them. If any BPDUs are received, the port will be errdisabled.

The BPDU Filter feature effectively disables STP on the selected ports by preventing them from sending or receiving any BPDUs. This is illustrated in Figure 3-32 below:

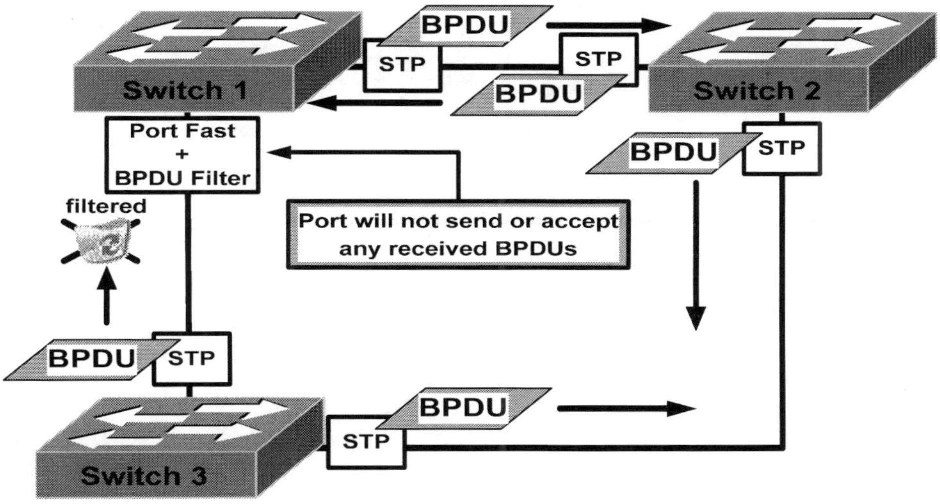

Fig. 3-32. Understanding BPDU Filter

Loop Guard

The Loop Guard feature is used to prevent the formation of loops within the Spanning Tree network. Loop Guard detects Root Ports and blocked ports, and ensures they continue to receive BPDUs. When switches receive BPDUs on blocked ports, the information is ignored because the best BPDU is still being received from the Root Bridge via the Root Port.

If the switch link is up and no BPDUs are received (due to a unidirectional link), the switch assumes that it is safe to bring this link up and the port transitions to the Forwarding state and begins relaying received BPUDs. If a switch is connected to the other end of the link, this effectively creates a Spanning Tree loop. This concept is illustrated in Figure 3-33 below:

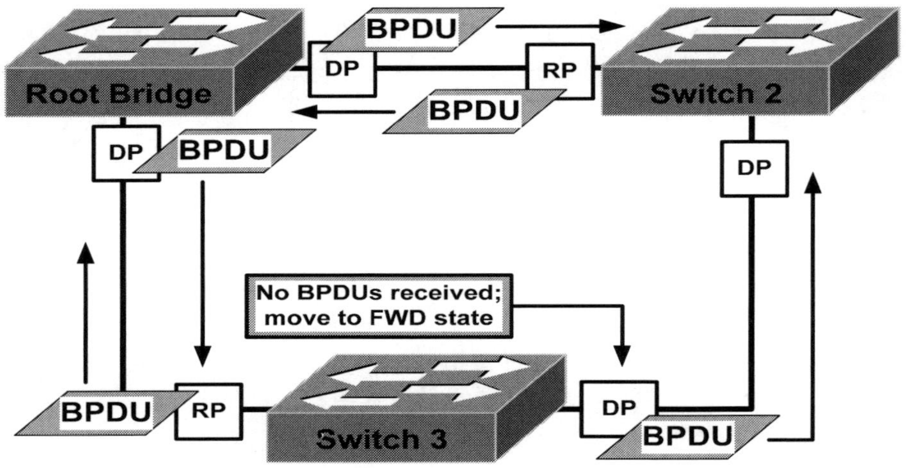

Fig. 3-33. Understanding Loop Guard

In Figure 3-33, the Spanning Tree network has converged and all ports are in a Blocking or Forwarding state. However, the Blocking port on Switch 3 stops receiving BPDUs from the Designated Port on Switch 2 due to a unidirectional link. Switch 3 assumes that the port can be transitioned into a Forwarding state and so begins this move. The switch then relays received BPDUs out of that port, resulting in a network loop.

When Loop Guard is enabled, the switch keeps track of all Non-Designated Ports. As long as the port continues to receive BPDUs it is fine; however, if the port stops receiving BPDUs, it is moved into a loop-inconsistent state. In other words, when Loop Guard is enabled, the STP port state machine is modified to prevent the port from transitioning from the Non-Designated Port role to the Designated Port role in absence of BPDUs. When implementing Loop Guard, you should be aware of the following implementation guidelines:

- Loop Guard cannot be enabled on a switch that also has Root Guard enabled
- Loop Guard does not affect Uplink Fast or Backbone Fast operation
- Loop Guard must be enabled on point-to-point links only
- Loop Guard operation is not affected by the Spanning Tree timers
- Loop Guard cannot actually detect a unidirectional link
- Loop Guard cannot be enabled on Port Fast or Dynamic VLAN ports

Root Guard

The Root Guard feature prevents a Designated Port from becoming a Root Port. If a port on which the Root Guard feature receives a superior BPDU, it moves the port into a root-inconsistent state, thus maintaining the current Root Bridge status quo. This concept is illustrated in Figure 3-34 below:

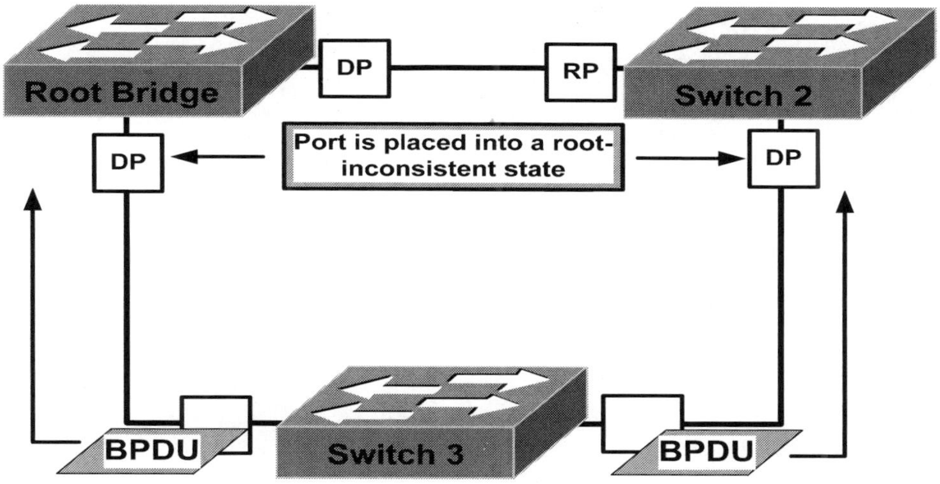

Fig. 3-34. Understanding Root Guard

In Figure 3-34, Switch 3 is added to the current STP network and sends out BPDUs that are superior to those of the current Root Bridge. Under ordinary circumstances, STP would recalculate the entire topology and Switch 3 would be elected Root Bridge. However, because the Root Guard feature is enabled on the Designated Ports on the current Root Bridge, as well as on Switch 2, both switches will place these ports into a root-inconsistent state when they receive the superior BPDUs from Switch 3. This preserves the Spanning Tree topology.

The Root Guard feature prevents a port from becoming a Root Port, thus ensuring that the port is always a Designated Port. Unlike other STP enhancements, which can also be enabled on a global basis, Root Guard must be manually enabled on all ports where the Root Bridge should not appear. Because of this, it is important to ensure a deterministic topology when designing and implementing STP in the LAN.

Uplink Fast

The Uplink Fast feature provides faster failover to a redundant link when the primary link fails. The primary purpose of this feature is to improve the convergence time of STP in the event of the failure of an uplink. This feature is of most use on Access switches with redundant uplinks to the Distribution layer, hence the name.

When Access layer switches are dual-homed to the Distribution layer, one of the links is placed into a Blocking state by STP to prevent loops. When the primary link to the Distribution layer fails, the port in the Blocking state must transition through the Listening and Learning states before it begins forwarding traffic. This results in a 30-second delay before the switch is able to forward frames destined to other network segments. Uplink Fast operation is illustrated in Figure 3-35 below:

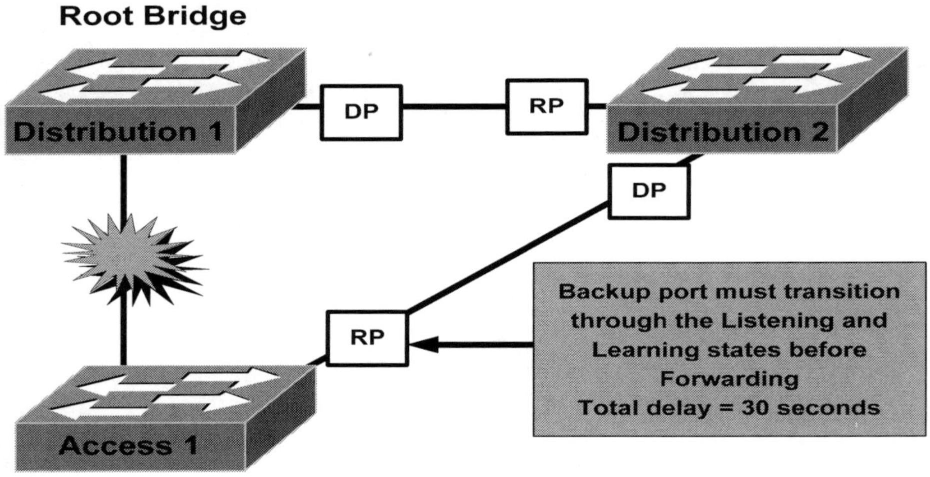

Fig. 3-35. Understanding Uplink Fast

In Figure 3-35, a failure on the link between Access 1 and Distribution 1, which is also the STP Root Bridge, would mean that STP would move the link between Access 1 and Distribution 1 into a Forwarding state (i.e. Blocking > Listening > Learning > Forwarding). The Listening and Learning states take 15 seconds each, so the port would begin to forward frames only after a total of 30 seconds had elapsed. When the Uplink Fast feature is enabled, the backup port to the Distribution layer is immediately placed into a Forwarding state, resulting in no network downtime. This concept is illustrated in Figure 3-36 below:

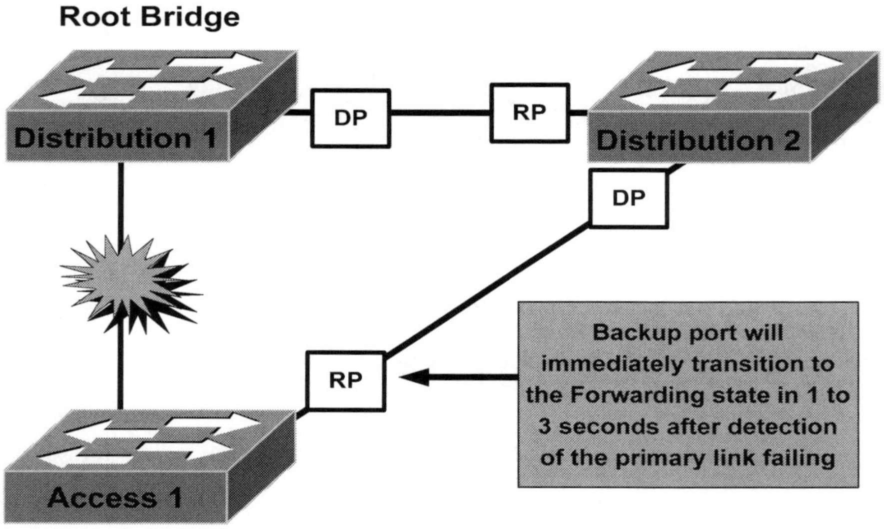

Fig. 3-36. Understanding Uplink Fast (Contd.)

Backbone Fast

The Backbone Fast feature provides fast failover when an indirect link failure occurs. Failover occurs when the switch receives an inferior BPDU from its designated bridge. An inferior BPDU indicates that the designated bridge has lost its connection to the Root Bridge. This is illustrated in Figure 3-37 below:

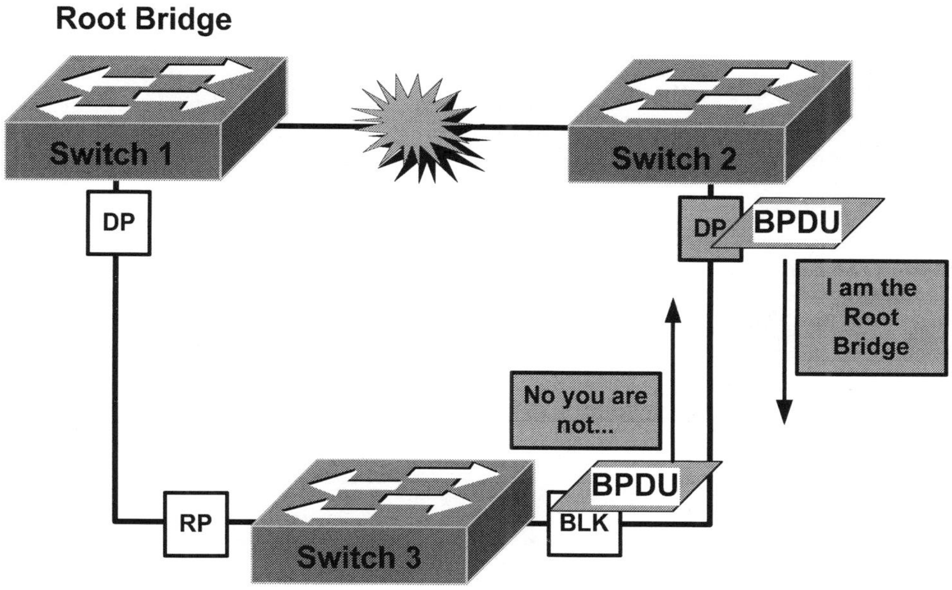

Fig. 3-37. Understanding Backbone Fast

In Figure 3-37, the link between Switch 1 and Switch 2 fails. Switch 2 detects this and sends out BPDUs indicating that it is the Root Bridge. The inferior BPDUs are received on Switch 3, which still has the BPDU information received from Switch 1 saved.

Switch 3 will ignore the inferior BPDUs until the Max Age value expires. During this time, Switch 2 continues to send BPDUs to Switch 3. When the Max Age expires, Switch 3 will age out the stored BPDU information from the Root Bridge and transition into a Listening state, and then will send out the received BPDU from the Root Bridge out to Switch 2.

Because this BPDU is better than its own, Switch 2 stops sending BPDUs and the port between Switch 2 and Switch 3 transitions through the Listening and Learning states and, finally, into the Forwarding state. This default method of operation by the STP process will mean that Switch 2 will be unable to forward frames for at least 50 seconds.

The Backbone Fast feature includes a mechanism that allows for an immediate check to see if the BPDU information stored on a port is still valid if an inferior BPDU is received. This is implemented with a new PDU and the Root Link Query, which is referred to as the RLQ PDU.

Upon receipt of an inferior BPDU, the switch will send out an RLQ PDU on all Non-Designated Ports, except for the port on which the inferior BPDU was received. If the switch is either the Root Bridge or has lost its connection to the Root Bridge, it will respond to the RLQ. Otherwise, the RLQ will be propagated upstream. If the switch receives an RLQ response on its Root Port, connectivity to the Root Bridge is still intact. If the response is received on a Non-Root Port, it means connectivity to the Root Bridge is lost, and the local switch Spanning Tree must be recalculated on the switch and the Max Age timer expired so that a new Root Port can be found. This concept is illustrated in Figure 3-38 below:

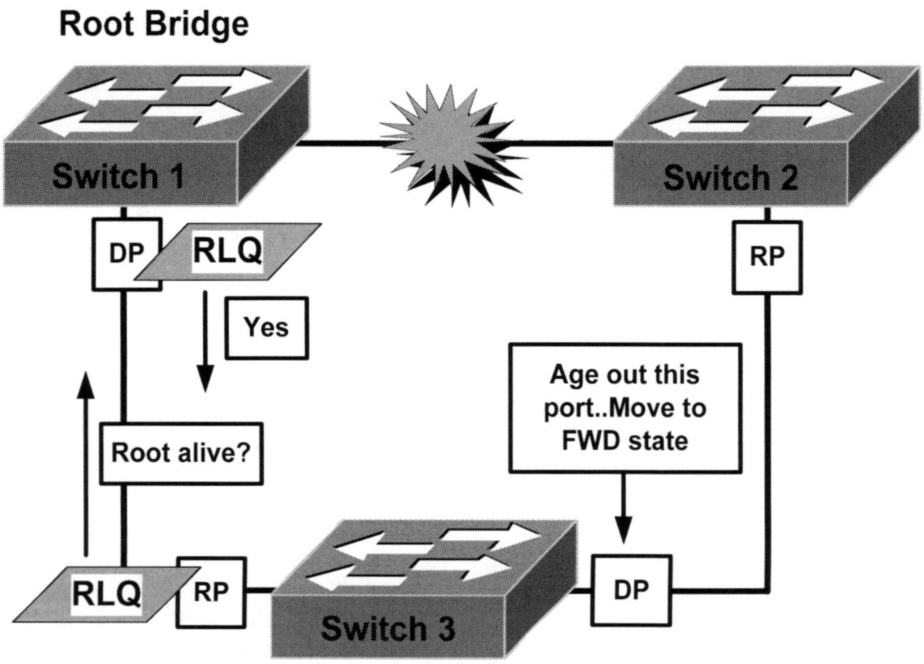

Fig. 3-38. Understanding Backbone Fast (Contd.)

Referencing Figure 3-38, upon receipt of the inferior BPDU, Switch 3 sends out an RLQ request on all Non-Designated Ports, except for the port on which the BPDU was received. The Root Bridge responds via an RLQ response sent out of its Designated Port. Because the response is received on the Root Port of Switch 3, it is considered a positive response. However, if the response was received on a Non-Root Port, the response would be considered negative and the switch would need to go through the whole Spanning Tree calculation again.

Based on the positive response received on Switch 3, it can age out the port connected to Switch 2 without waiting for the Max Age timer to expire. The port, however, must still go through the Listening and Learning states. By immediately aging out the Max Age timer, Backbone Fast reduces the convergence time from 50 seconds (20 seconds Max Age + 30 seconds Listening and Learning) to 30 seconds (the time for the Listening and Learning states).

There are two types of RLQs: RLQ requests and RLQ responses. RLQ requests are typically sent out on the Root Port to check for connectivity to the Root Bridge. All RLQ responses are sent out on Designated Ports. Because the RLQ request contains the BID of the Bridge that sent it, if another switch in the path to the Root Bridge can still reach the Root Bridge specified in the RLQ response, it will respond back to the sending switch. If this is not the case, the switch simply forwards the query toward the Root Bridge through its Root Port.

NOTE: The RLQ PDU has the same packet format as a normal BPDU, with the only difference being that the RLQ contains two Cisco SNAP addresses that are used for requests and replies.

Unidirectional Link Detection (UDLD)

Unidirectional Link Detection (UDLD) is a Layer 2 protocol designed to detect unidirectional link failures. UDLD performs tasks that Layer 1 mechanisms, such as auto negotiation, cannot perform. These tasks include detecting the identities of neighbors and shutting down misconnected ports. When UDLD and auto-negotiation are enabled, both Layer 1 and Layer 2 detections work together to prevent physical and logical unidirectional connections and the malfunctioning of other protocols.

UDLD exchanges protocol packets between the neighboring switches. These messages are sent out every 15 seconds. If the messages are echoed back within a specific timeframe but they lack specific acknowledgment (echo), the link is flagged as unidirectional and the port is shut down. If messages are not received within the timeout interval (45 seconds), the port is also disabled.

The 45 seconds it takes to detect a unidirectional link and errdisable the port is less than the 50 seconds it would take for STP to transition the port to a Forwarding state, which is based on 20 seconds for Max Age + 30 seconds for Listening and Learning. This prevents a loop that would otherwise be caused if STP transitioned the port into the Forwarding state because of a lack of received BPDUs.

In order for UDLD to work, both devices on the link must support UDLD and UDLD must be enabled on both sides of the link. Each switch port configured for UDLD sends out UDLD protocol packets that contain the port's own device and port ID, and the neighbor's device and port IDs seen by UDLD on that port.

By default, UDLD messages are sent to the destination MAC address 01-00-0C-CC-CC-CC. The neighboring ports should see their own device and port ID (echo) in the packets received from the other side, which indicates that the link is bidirectional. Table 3-6 below lists and describes the fields and information that is contained in a UDLD frame:

Table 3-6. Fields in the UDLD Frame

Field	Description
Device ID	This field contains the MAC address of the sending device.
Port ID	This field contains the module and port number of the sending device.
Echo	This field contains the module and port pair known by the sending device.
Message Interval	This field contains the transmit interval of the sending device.
Timeout Interval	This field contains the timeout interval of the sending device.
Device Name	This field contains the CDP Device ID string of the sending device.
Sequence Number	This field contains the number used to validate discovery packets.
Reserved	These fields are reserved for future use.

The destination MAC address and other fields are illustrated in Figure 3-39 below:

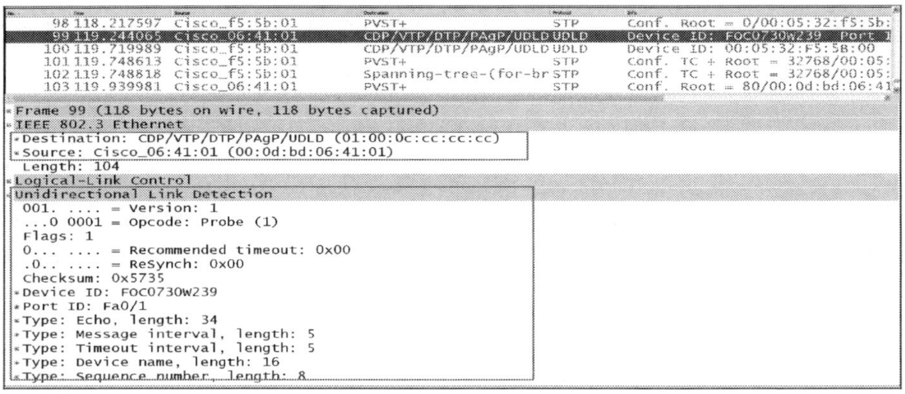

Fig. 3-39. The UDLD Frame

If the port does not see its own device and port ID in the incoming UDLD packets for a specific duration of time (timeout interval), the link is considered unidirectional and is disabled. The following section describes the detection and the disabling of a unidirectional link by UDLD. The examples in this section are based on Figure 3-40 below:

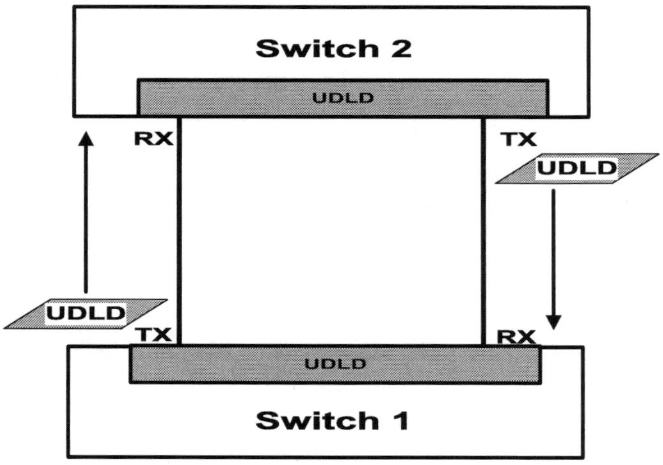

Fig. 3-40. Understanding UDLD Operation

Figure 3-40 shows two switches connected via a Fiber link. UDLD is enabled on both ends of the link. Switch 1 sends out UDLD packets that include its port and device ID, and the same parameters for its neighbor. These packets are received by Switch 2, which echoes the UDLD packet back to Switch 1. Because both switches see their own device and port ID in the incoming UDLD packets, the link is considered bidirectional and remains up.

If, for example, there is a failure between the TX end of Switch 2 and the RX end of Switch 1, the switches will not be able to send or receive UDLD messages using this link. In this case, Switch 2 receives the UDLD packets from Switch 1, but Switch 1 does not receive the UDLD packets from Switch 2. UDLD detects this and the link is flagged as unidirectional and the port is shut down. This is illustrated in Figure 3-41 below:

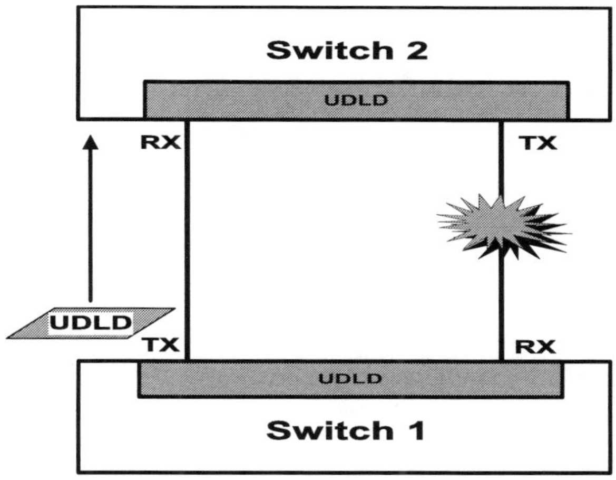

Fig. 3-41. Understanding UDLD Operation (Contd.)

This UDLD echo-algorithm allows for unidirectional link detection due to the following:

- When the link is up on both sides; however, packets are being received by only one side
- When receive and transmit Fibers are not connected to the same port on the remote side

Once the unidirectional link is detected by UDLD, the respective port is disabled and remains disabled until it is manually re-enabled, or until errdisable timeout expires (if configured). UDLD can operate in either normal or aggressive mode. These two modes of operation are described in the following section.

UDLD Normal Mode

In UDLD normal mode, when a unidirectional link condition is detected, the port is allowed to continue its operation. UDLD merely marks the port as having an undetermined state and generates a syslog message. In other words, in normal mode, no action is taken by UDLD and the port is allowed to continue behaving according to its Spanning Tree state.

UDLD Aggressive Mode

UDLD aggressive mode is configured on point-to-point links. This mode comes into play after a UDLD neighbor stops receiving UDLD updates from its adjacent peer. In aggressive mode, the local device will attempt to re-establish the UDLD connection eight times. If the switch is unable to re-establish the connection within this timeframe, it will proceed and errdisable the port.

`UDLD aggressive` mode adds additional detection when the port is stuck (i.e. one side of the port neither transmits nor receives; however, the link is `up` on both ends) or when the link is `up` on one side and `down` on the other side, which is typically seen on Fiber connections only, as Copper ports are normally not susceptible to this type of issue because they use Ethernet link pulses to monitor the link.

Configuring Traditional Spanning Tree Protocol

By default, in Cisco Catalyst switches, a single STP instance is enabled for each configured VLAN. This is referred to as Per VLAN Spanning Tree Plus (PVST+), which simply means a single Spanning Tree instance for every individual VLAN.

NOTE: PVST+ is a Cisco proprietary protocol that supports 802.1Q. It is an extension of PVST, which is also a Cisco proprietary protocol that supports ISL. PVST is described in detail in the CCNA guide. There is no explicit configuration command required to enable PVST+. A sample PVST+ frame is illustrated in Figure 3-42 below:

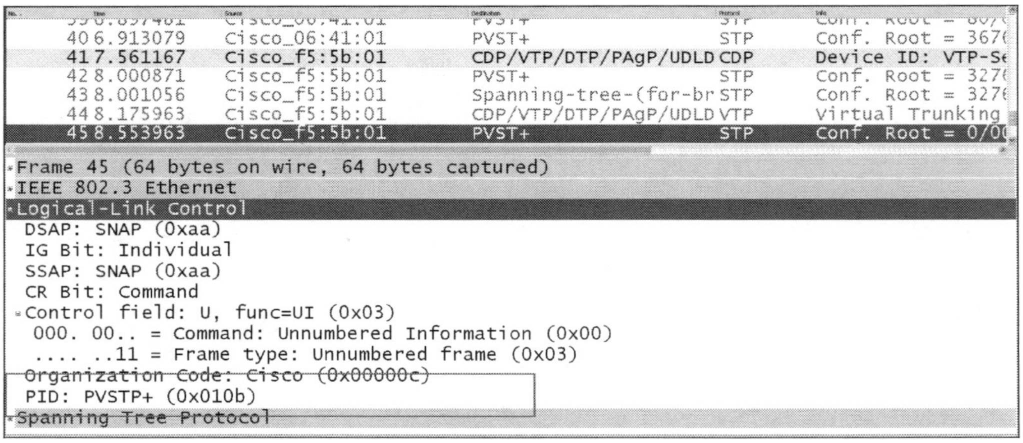

Fig. 3-42. PVST+ Frame Format

Configuring the Spanning Tree Root Bridge

Root Bridge election can be influenced by administrators in one of two ways:

1. By manually configuring the Bridge Priority
2. By using the macro available in Cisco IOS software

In Cisco IOS software, administrators can manually configure the Bridge Priority of the switch they want to become elected Root Bridge via the `spanning-tree vlan [number] priority [number]` global configuration command. The switch with the highest priority will be elected Root Bridge for that particular VLAN. The priority value must be configured in increments of 4,096, with 0 being the lowest possible value and 61,440 being the highest possible value. The following output illustrates how to configure a switch as the Root Bridge for standard VLAN 80:

```
VTP-Switch-1#config t
Enter configuration commands, one per line.  End with CNTL/Z.
VTP-Switch-1(config)#spanning-tree vlan 80 priority 0
VTP-Switch-1(config)#exit
```

The `show spanning-tree vlan [number] [detail]` command can be used to validate the Root Bridge configuration as illustrated in the following output:

```
VTP-Switch-1#show spanning-tree vlan 80 detail

 VLAN0080 is executing the ieee compatible Spanning Tree protocol
  Bridge Identifier has priority 0, sysid 80, address 000d.bd06.4100
  Configured hello time 2, max age 20, forward delay 15
  We are the root of the spanning tree
  Topology change flag not set, detected flag not set
  Number of topology changes 1 last change occurred 00:24:30 ago
          from FastEthernet0/1
  Times:  hold 1, topology change 35, notification 2
          hello 2, max age 20, forward delay 15
  Timers: hello 1, topology change 0, notification 0, aging 300
...
...
[Truncated Output]
```

There is a macro available in Cisco IOS software that allows the software to configure dynamically the priority of the Root Bridge or secondary (backup) Root Bridge. The Root Bridge is configured dynamically via the `spanning-tree vlan [number] root [primary|secondary]` global configuration command. When this command is executed using the [primary] keyword, Cisco IOS software checks the switch priority of the current Root Switch for the specified VLAN.

Because of the extended system ID support, the switch sets the switch priority for the specified VLAN to 24,576 if this value will cause this switch to become the Root Bridge for the specified VLAN. However, if the Root Switch for the specified VLAN has a priority lower than 24,576, the switch sets its own priority for the specified VLAN to 4,096 less than the lowest switch priority. This continues until the switch has a lower priority than the current Root Bridge and is itself elected Root Bridge.

To demonstrate how this Cisco IOS macro works, we will use the topology in Figure 3-43 below:

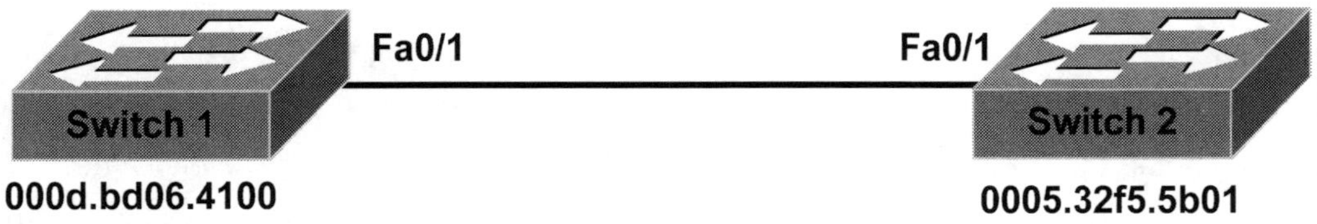

Fig. 3-43. Configuring the Root Bridge Using the Cisco IOS Macro

In Figure 3-43, Switch 1 and Switch 2 are connected via their respective FastEthernet0/1 ports. Both of the switches reside in the same VTP domain and a trunk has been successfully configured between the two. Both switches are configured as VTP servers. VLAN 10 is configured and because the Bridge Priority values are the same (32,768), Switch 2 is elected Root Bridge because it has a lower MAC address. This is reflected in the `show spanning-tree vlan [number]` command on Switch 1 as illustrated in the following output:

```
VTP-Switch-1#show spanning-tree vlan 10

VLAN0010
  Spanning tree enabled protocol ieee
  Root ID     Priority     32768
              Address      0005.32f5.5b01
              Cost         19
              Port         1 (FastEthernet0/1)
              Hello Time    2 sec   Max Age 20 sec   Forward Delay 15 sec

  Bridge ID   Priority     32778  (priority 32768 sys-id-ext 10)
              Address      000d.bd06.4100
              Hello Time    2 sec   Max Age 20 sec   Forward Delay 15 sec
              Aging Time 300

Interface          Role Sts Cost       Prio.Nbr Type
----------------   ---- --- ---------  -------- --------------------------------
Fa0/1              Root FWD 19         128.1    P2p
```

The `spanning-tree vlan 10 root primary` command is executed on Switch 1 to allow Cisco IOS software to dynamically configure Switch 1 to become the Root Bridge for this VLAN. This is illustrated in the following output:

```
VTP-Switch-1#conf t
Enter configuration commands, one per line.  End with CNTL/Z.
VTP-Switch-1(config)#spanning-tree vlan 10 root primary
VTP-Switch-1(config)#exit
```

Once executed, the `show spanning-tree vlan 10` command is used to validate that this switch that has now been elected Root Bridge, as shown in the following output:

```
VTP-Switch-1#show spanning-tree vlan 10

VLAN0010
  Spanning tree enabled protocol ieee
  Root ID     Priority     24586
              Address      000d.bd06.4100
              This bridge is the root
              Hello Time    2 sec  Max Age 20 sec  Forward Delay 15 sec

  Bridge ID   Priority     24586  (priority 24576 sys-id-ext 10)
              Address      000d.bd06.4100
              Hello Time    2 sec  Max Age 20 sec  Forward Delay 15 sec
              Aging Time 15

Interface         Role Sts Cost      Prio.Nbr Type
----------------- ---- --- --------- -------- --------------------------------
Fa0/1             Desg FWD 19        128.1    P2p
```

In the output above, we can see that the priority for the VLAN has been set to 24,576 and this switch is elected Root Bridge. Now, suppose Switch 2 was manually configured in the manner illustrated in the following output:

```
VTP-Switch-2#conf t
Enter configuration commands, one per line.  End with CNTL/Z.
VTP-Switch-2(config)#spanning-tree vlan 10 priority 8192
VTP-Switch-2(config)#exit
```

The result of this manual change is that Switch 2 becomes the Root Bridge for this VLAN. This is because the macro works only once. In other words, the Cisco IOS macro works only once, each time it is executed, and does not continually check to see if any other switches have had their priority values changed so that it can adjust the local switch priority accordingly in order to ensure that it remains the Root Bridge. Switch 1 retains the priority value set by the macro but is now no longer the Root Bridge for VLAN 10, as shown in the following output:

```
VTP-Switch-1#show spanning-tree vlan 10

VLAN0010
  Spanning tree enabled protocol ieee
```

```
  Root ID    Priority    8192
             Address     0005.32f5.5b01
             Cost        19
             Port        1 (FastEthernet0/1)
             Hello Time   2 sec  Max Age 20 sec  Forward Delay 15 sec

  Bridge ID  Priority    24586  (priority 24576 sys-id-ext 10)
             Address     000d.bd06.4100
             Hello Time   2 sec  Max Age 20 sec  Forward Delay 15 sec
             Aging Time 15

Interface        Role Sts Cost      Prio.Nbr Type
---------------- ---- --- --------- -------- --------------------------------
Fa0/1            Root FWD 19        128.1    P2p
```

To configure Switch 1 as the Root Bridge, the macro command must be entered again. This is illustrated in the following output:

```
VTP-Switch-1#conf t
Enter configuration commands, one per line.  End with CNTL/Z.
VTP-Switch-1(config)#spanning-tree vlan 10 root primary
VTP-Switch-1(config)#exit
```

The priority is lowered by 4,096 and Switch 1 becomes Root Bridge for VLAN 10 again. This is shown in the following output:

```
VTP-Switch-1#show spanning-tree vlan 10

VLAN0010
  Spanning tree enabled protocol ieee
  Root ID    Priority    4106
             Address     000d.bd06.4100
             This bridge is the root
             Hello Time   2 sec  Max Age 20 sec  Forward Delay 15 sec

  Bridge ID  Priority    4106   (priority 4096 sys-id-ext 10)
             Address     000d.bd06.4100
             Hello Time   2 sec  Max Age 20 sec  Forward Delay 15 sec
             Aging Time 15
...
[Truncated Output]
```

When the `spanning-tree vlan [number] root secondary` command is executed, the software changes the switch priority from the default value of 32,768 to 28,672. Assuming all defaults, this value would be the next best priority value in the Spanning Tree domain, after the value of 24,576 that is assigned to the Root Bridge by the `spanning-tree vlan [number] root primary` command. If the Root Bridge should fail, this switch becomes the next Root Bridge.

Configuring the Spanning Tree Port Cost

The Root Path Cost value is contained in the STP BPDU. This value is calculated using the Path Cost. Administrators can adjust the Spanning Tree port cost to allow for load balancing between different links within the Spanning Tree domain. In Figure 3-44 below, Switch 1 and Switch 2 reside within the same STP domain. The switches have two links between them, FastEthernet0/1 and FastEthernet0/2. VLAN 20 is configured on both switches (VTP servers) and Switch 2 is elected Root Bridge for the VLAN.

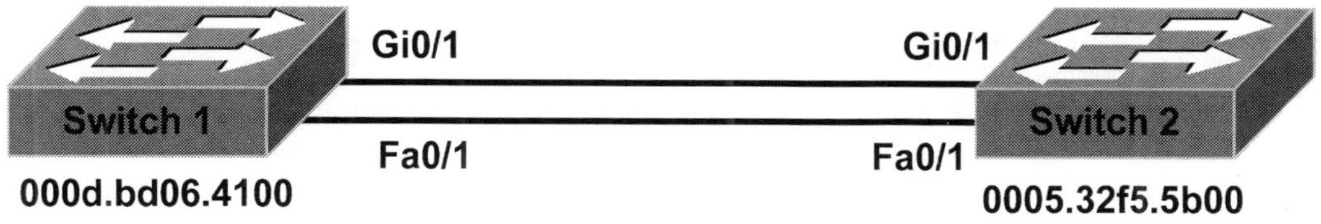

Fig. 3-44. Configuring the Spanning Tree Port Cost

By default, GigabitEthernet0/1 will be placed into a Forwarding state by Switch 1 because this port has a lower cost value (4) than that of the FastEthernet0/1 interface (19). The `spanning-tree vlan [number] cost [value]` interface configuration command can be used to manipulate the interface that is placed into the Forwarding state by STP for a specified VLAN. For example, the cost on port FastEthernet 0/1 can be lowered to a value less than 4, making it preferred over GigabitEthernet0/1 for all traffic in VLAN 20. This would be implemented using the configuration commands shown in the following output:

```
VTP-Switch-1(config)#interface fastethernet 0/1
VTP-Switch-1(config-if)#spanning-tree vlan 20 cost 1
VTP-Switch-1(config-if)#exit
```

The lower cost value assigned to FastEthernet0/1 means that it is moved into a Forwarding state for VLAN 20 while GigabitEthernet0/1 is moved into the Blocking state for VLAN 20. This configuration can be validated by using the `show spanning-tree vlan [number]` command as illustrated in the following output:

```
VTP-Switch-1#show spanning-tree vlan 20

VLAN0020
  Spanning tree enabled protocol ieee
  Root ID    Priority    32768
             Address     0005.32f5.5b02
             Cost        1
             Port        1 (FastEthernet0/1)
             Hello Time   2 sec  Max Age 20 sec  Forward Delay 15 sec

  Bridge ID  Priority    32788  (priority 32768 sys-id-ext 20)
```

```
                  Address     000d.bd06.4100
                  Hello Time   2 sec  Max Age 20 sec  Forward Delay 15 sec
                  Aging Time 300

Interface        Role Sts Cost      Prio.Nbr Type
---------------- ---- --- --------- -------- --------------------------------
Fa0/1            Root FWD 1         128.1    P2p
Gi0/1            Altn BLK 4         128.25   P2p
```

Although FastEthernet0/1 is elected Root Port for VLAN 20, GigabitEthernet0/1 is still elected as the Root Port for all other VLANs because the port cost for those VLANs has not been modified. This is shown in the following output:

```
VTP-Switch-1#show spanning-tree vlan 40

VLAN0040
  Spanning tree enabled protocol ieee
  Root ID    Priority    32768
             Address     0005.32f5.5b04
             Cost        4
             Port        25 (GigabitEthernet0/1)
             Hello Time   2 sec  Max Age 20 sec  Forward Delay 15 sec

  Bridge ID  Priority    32808  (priority 32768 sys-id-ext 40)
             Address     000d.bd06.4100
             Hello Time   2 sec  Max Age 20 sec  Forward Delay 15 sec
             Aging Time 300

Interface        Role Sts Cost      Prio.Nbr Type
---------------- ---- --- --------- -------- --------------------------------
Gi0/1            Root FWD 4         128.25    P2p
Fa0/1            Altn BLK 19        128.1    P2p
```

In addition to manipulating the cost value for individual VLANs, Cisco IOS software allows administrators to manipulate the interfaces via which all VLAN traffic is forwarded. This is performed by issuing the `spanning-tree cost [number]` interface configuration command on the desired interface. This is illustrated in the following output:

```
VTP-Switch-1(config)#interface fastethernet 0/1
VTP-Switch-1(config-if)#spanning-tree cost 1
VTP-Switch-1(config-if)#exit
```

Based on this configuration, FastEthernet0/1 would be elected Root Port for all VLANs and port GigabitEthernet0/1 would be placed into a Blocking state.

Changing the cost value is not typically recommended as this does have an effect on the entire Spanning Tree domain. By default, when a Switch receives a BPDU, it adds its local cost value to the received Root Path Cost value before propagating it downstream. If this cost value is incorrect, then the Spanning Tree network might not be able to select the most optimal path. Consider the network topology illustrated in Figure 3-45 below:

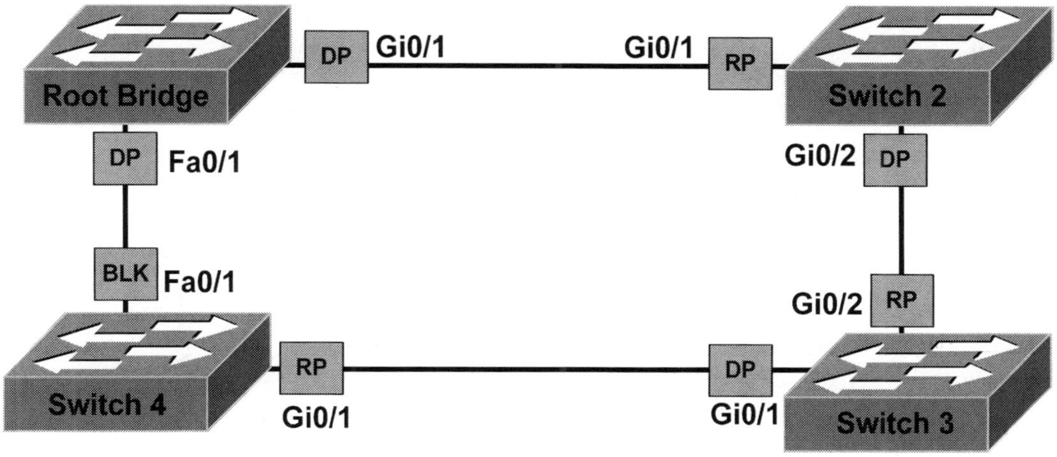

Fig. 3-45. Understanding the Effects of Changing the STP Port Cost

Figure 3-45 shows four switches in a network. Based on the inter-switch links, STP will proceed and elect the following Root Ports on the switches:

- Switch 4—Interface GigabitEthernet0/1 (Root Path Cost of 12)
- Switch 3—Interface GigabitEthernet0/2 (Root Path Cost of 8)
- Switch 2—Interface GigabitEthernet0/1 (Root Path Cost of 4)

NOTE: FastEthernet has a Spanning Tree cost of 19, so the Root Path Cost via FastEthernet0/1 on Switch 4 would be 0 + 19, which equals 19, whereas the Root Path Cost via GigabitEthernet0/1 is 0 + 4 + 4 + 4 = 12. This value is better than 19, so GigabitEthernet0/1 wins.

If the port cost on Switch 4 was changed to force it to use port FastEthernet0/1 as the Root Port interface instead, this would impact the entire Spanning Tree topology. For example, the cost for FastEthernet0/1 is changed to 1 for all VLANs as illustrated in the following output:

```
VTP-Switch-4(config)#interface fastethernet 0/1
VTP-Switch-4(config-if)#spanning-tree cost 1
VTP-Switch-4(config-if)#exit
```

This Path Cost value results in a Root Path Cost of 1 for FastEthernet0/1. This BPDU shows a Root Path Cost of 1 from Switch 4 as illustrated in Figure 3-46 below:

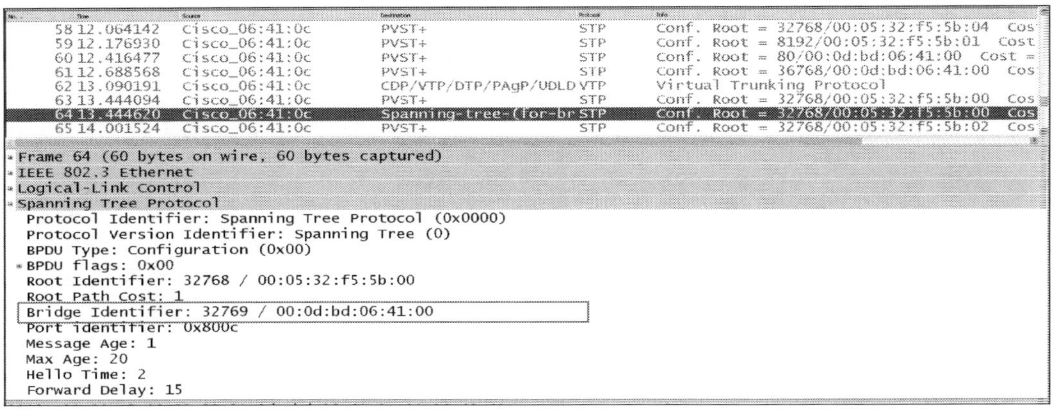

Fig. 3-46. Verifying the Spanning Tree Port Cost (Contd.)

Switch 4 propagates the BPDU to Switch 4 and STP then selects the following Root Ports for each Switch:

- Switch 4—Interface FastEthernet0/1 (New Root Path Cost of 1)
- Switch 3—Interface GigabitEthernet0/1 (Root Path Cost of 5)
- Switch 2—Interface GigabitEthernet0/1 (Root Path Cost of 4)

The Spanning Tree network topology is recalculated and changed as shown in Figure 4-47 below:

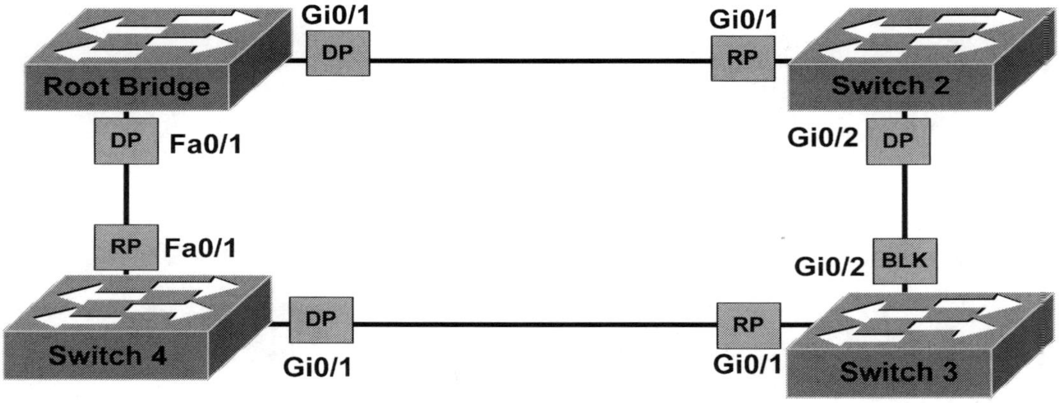

Fig. 3-47. Understanding the Effects of Changing the STP Port Cost (Contd.)

Naturally, this is a suboptimal path because a FastEthernet interface has less bandwidth than GigabitEthernet interface; however, because the cost values have been changed, the Spanning Tree calculation deems this the best (least cost) path to the Root Bridge. It is very important to understand the network topology before manipulating Spanning Tree cost values.

FURTHER TOPIC EXPLANATION

Earlier in this chapter, it was stated that the port cost should only be configured on the Root Bridge. This is because port cost is the Path Cost. It is used in the calculation of the Root Path Cost, which leads to the election of the Root Port.

The Root Bridge originates BPDUs and there is no Root Port on the Root Bridge. In other words, the Root Bridge will never receive a BPDU from another switch and needs to determine which path to use to get to the Root Bridge, because it is the Root already.

Configuring the Spanning Tree Port Priority

In the event that ports have the same cost value, the port priority is used as a tiebreaker to determine which port will be placed into the Forwarding state. This priority is locally significant for the connection between two switches and has no effect on the remainder of the Spanning Tree domain. Figure 3-48 below will be used to illustrate this concept.

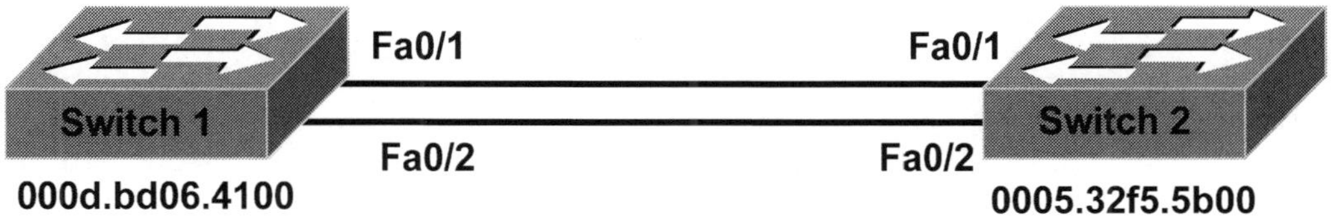

Fig. 3-48. Manipulating the Default Spanning Tree Port Priority

In Figure 3-48, Switch 1 and Switch 2 are connected using two FastEthernet links. Switch 2 is the Root Bridge for VLAN 20. By default, Switch 1 places port FastEthernet0/1 into the Forwarding state because it is the port that has the lower port ID. Remember, as stated earlier, the port ID is comprised of the port priority and the port number. This concept is illustrated in the following output:

```
VTP-Switch-1#show spanning-tree vlan 20

VLAN0020
  Spanning tree enabled protocol ieee
  Root ID    Priority    32768
             Address     0005.32f5.5b02
             Cost        19
             Port        1 (FastEthernet0/1)
             Hello Time   2 sec  Max Age 20 sec  Forward Delay 15 sec

  Bridge ID  Priority    32788  (priority 32768 sys-id-ext 20)
             Address     000d.bd06.4100
             Hello Time   2 sec  Max Age 20 sec  Forward Delay 15 sec
             Aging Time 300
```

```
Interface        Role Sts Cost      Prio.Nbr Type
---------------- ---- --- --------- -------- --------------------------------
Fa0/1            Root FWD 19        128.1    P2p
Fa0/2            Altn BLK 19        128.2    P2p
```

Switch 1 places FastEthernet0/1 into the Forwarding state because the port ID of FastEthernet0/1 (128.1) is lower than that of FastEthernet0/2 (128.2). The tiebreaker values used are as follows:

- Lowest Root Bridge ID—The BPDUs are originated from the same switch; this is equal
- Lowest Root Path Cost to Root Bridge—Both ports are FastEthernet; this is equal
- Lowest Sender Bridge ID—The BPDUs are originated from the same switch; this is equal
- Lowest Sender Port ID—The PID of Fa0/1 is 128.1; the PID of Fa0/2 is 128.2. Fa0/1 is better

The `spanning-tree vlan [number] port-priority [value]` interface configuration command can be used to manipulate the port that Spanning Tree places into the Forwarding state when multiple equal cost paths exist between two switches. However, this must be done on the switch sending the BPDUs, effectively influencing the inbound path of the remote switch. The higher the priority (which is the lower numerical value) the more preferred the BPDU.

As an example, the priority of FastEthernet0/2 can be changed to 96 on Switch 2 to influence Switch 1 to place FastEthernet0/2 into the Forwarding state for VLAN 20 as illustrated in the following output:

```
VTP-Switch-2#conf t
Enter configuration commands, one per line.  End with CNTL/Z.
VTP-Switch-2(config)#interface fastethernet 0/2
VTP-Switch-2(config-if)#spanning-tree vlan 20 port-priority 96
VTP-Switch-2(config-if)#exit
```

NOTE: The priority value is entered in increments of 16, as stated earlier in this chapter.

The result of this configuration changes the election process as follows:

- Lowest Root Bridge ID—The BPDUs are originated from the same switch; this is equal
- Lowest Root Path Cost to Root Bridge—Both ports are FastEthernet; this is equal
- Lowest Sender Bridge ID—The BPDUs are originated from the same switch; this is equal
- Lowest Sender Port ID—The PID of Fa0/1 is 128.1, the PID of Fa0/2 is 96.2. Fa0/2 is better

This result is reflected on Switch 1, which has now placed FastEthernet0/2 into a Forwarding state for VLAN 20. Port FastEthernet0/1 is placed into a Blocking state. This is illustrated in the following output:

```
VTP-Switch-1#show spanning-tree vlan 20

VLAN0020
  Spanning tree enabled protocol ieee
  Root ID     Priority     32768
              Address      0005.32f5.5b02
              Cost         19
              Port         2 (FastEthernet0/2)
              Hello Time    2 sec  Max Age 20 sec  Forward Delay 15 sec

  Bridge ID   Priority     32788  (priority 32768 sys-id-ext 20)
              Address      000d.bd06.4100
              Hello Time    2 sec  Max Age 20 sec  Forward Delay 15 sec
              Aging Time 300

Interface         Role Sts Cost       Prio.Nbr Type
----------------  ---- --- ---------  -------- --------------------------------
Fa0/1             Altn BLK 19         128.1    P2p
Fa0/2             Root FWD 19         128.2    P2p
```

NOTE: You will not see the priority value configured on the remote switch (Switch 2) on the local switch (Switch 1). This is used in the internal STP calculation and is not reflected in the `show spanning-tree vlan [number]` output.

Adjusting Spanning Tree Timers

The Spanning Tree timers (which should never be changed without due cause) can be adjusted in global configuration mode via the `spanning-tree vlan [number] [forward-time| hello-time| max-age]` global configuration command. These values should always be adjusted on the Root Bridge, which will then send them out in the Configuration BPDUs. These options are illustrated in the following output:

```
Root-Bridge(config)#spanning-tree vlan 10 ?
  forward-time  Set the forward delay for the spanning tree
  hello-time    Set the hello interval for the spanning tree
  max-age       Set the max age interval for the spanning tree
```

Adjusting the Spanning Tree timers requires careful thought and consideration because they are used in the calculation of the Spanning Tree diameter. The following output illustrates how to change the Spanning Tree Hello Time interval to 1 second for a specified VLAN:

```
Root-Bridge#conf t
Enter configuration commands, one per line.  End with CNTL/Z.
Root-Bridge(config)#spanning-tree vlan 10 hello-time 1
Root-Bridge(config)#exit
```

NOTE: These values should always be changed on the Root Bridge.

Once adjusted, the `show spanning-tree vlan [number]` command can be used to verify the timers set on the Root Bridge. The following output shows the Hello Time change implemented on the Root Bridge reflected on a Non-Root Bridge in the Spanning Tree domain:

```
VTP-Client-Switch-1#show spanning-tree vlan 10

VLAN0010
  Spanning tree enabled protocol ieee
  Root ID     Priority     8192
              Address      0005.32f5.5b01
              Cost         19
              Port         1 (FastEthernet0/1)
              Hello Time    1 sec   Max Age 20 sec   Forward Delay 15 sec

  Bridge ID   Priority     32778  (priority 32768 sys-id-ext 10)
              Address      000d.bd06.4100
              Hello Time    2 sec   Max Age 20 sec   Forward Delay 15 sec
              Aging Time 300

Interface          Role Sts Cost        Prio.Nbr Type
----------------- ---- --- --------- -------- --------------------------------
Fa0/1              Root FWD 19          128.1    P2p
Fa0/2              Altn BLK 19          128.2    P2p
Fa0/12             Desg FWD 19          128.12   P2p
```

NOTE: In the output above, the Hello Time from the Root Bridge is used; however, we can also see that the switch has its own locally set values. These values are not used in relayed BPDUs.

Changing the Spanning Tree Diameter

As is the case with Spanning Tree timers, changing the Spanning Tree Protocol diameter is not recommended without just cause or guidance from the Cisco TAC. However, in the event that the diameter does need to be changed, this can be performed via the `spanning-tree vlan [number] root [primary|secondary] diameter [value]` global configuration command on either the Root Bridge or backup Root Bridge for a specified VLAN. The following output shows how to change the default Spanning Tree diameter to 2 on the Root Bridge:

```
VTP-Switch-1#conf t
Enter configuration commands, one per line.  End with CNTL/Z.
VTP-Switch-1(config)#spanning-tree vlan 80 root primary diameter 2
VTP-Switch-1(config)#exit
```

By default, when the diameter is changed, Cisco IOS software automatically calculates the appropriate values for the Hello Time, Forward Delay, and Max Age timers. These dynamic changes are illustrated in the following output:

```
VTP-Switch-1#show spanning-tree vlan 80

VLAN0080
  Spanning tree enabled protocol ieee
  Root ID     Priority     80
              Address      000d.bd06.4100
              This bridge is the root
              Hello Time    2 sec   Max Age 10 sec   Forward Delay  7 sec

  Bridge ID   Priority     80       (priority 0 sys-id-ext 80)
              Address      000d.bd06.4100
              Hello Time    2 sec   Max Age 10 sec   Forward Delay  7 sec
              Aging Time 300
...
[Truncated Output]
```

These changes are propagated in all BPDUs sent out by the Root Bridge. Figure 3-49 below illustrates an STP BDPU that reflects the adjusted timer values:

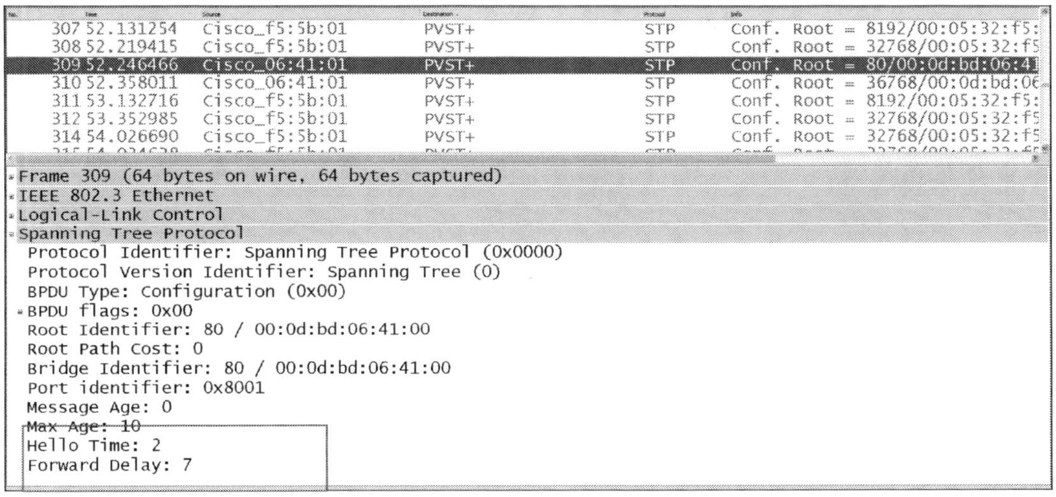

Fig. 3-49. STP BPDU Parameters after Changing the STP Diameter

NOTE: After you change the diameter, you can also use the `spanning-tree vlan [number] hello-time [seconds]` command to reduce the Hello Time if so desired.

Configuring Port Fast

The Port Fast feature can be enabled on a per-port basis or globally, for the entire switch. If you enable Port Fast globally, it is enabled for all ports on the switch. This operation may create loops in redundant Spanning Tree networks and the Cisco IOS software warns of this. To enable Port Fast globally, the `spanning-tree portfast default` command must be issued. This is illustrated in the following output:

```
VTP-Switch-1#conf t
Enter configuration commands, one per line.  End with CNTL/Z.
VTP-Switch-1(config)#spanning-tree portfast default
%Warning: this command enables portfast by default on all interfaces. You
 should now disable portfast explicitly on switched ports leading to hubs
 switches and bridges as they may create temporary bridging loops.

VTP-Switch-1(config)#exit
```

NOTE: Notice the warning message issued by the switch when this is performed.

To enable Port Fast on a per-interface basis, the `spanning-tree portfast` interface configuration command must be applied to the desired interface(s). This is illustrated in the following output:

```
VTP-Switch-1(config)#interface fastethernet 0/5
VTP-Switch-1(config-if)#spanning-tree portfast
%Warning: portfast should only be enabled on ports connected to a single
 host. Connecting hubs, concentrators, switches, bridges, etc... to this
 interface when portfast is enabled can cause temporary bridging loops.
 Use with CAUTION

%Portfast has been configured on FastEthernet0/5 but will only
 have effect when the interface is in a non-trunking mode.
Switch-1(config-if)#exit
```

NOTE: It is also important to remember that the Port Fast feature (although not recommended) can also be manually enabled on a trunk link by issuing the `spanning-tree portfast trunk` interface configuration command to the desired interface(s). This is illustrated in the following output:

```
Switch-1(config)#interface gigabitethernet 0/1
Switch-1(config-if)#switchport
Switch-1(config-if)#switchport mode trunk
Switch-1(config-if)#spanning-tree portfast trunk
%Warning: portfast should only be enabled on ports connected to a single
 host. Connecting hubs, concentrators, switches, bridges, etc... to this
 interface when portfast is enabled can cause temporary bridging loops.
 Use with CAUTION

Switch-1(config-if)#exit
```

Although Cisco IOS allows you to do so, keep in mind that enabling Port Fast on a trunk link is not recommended. The only way to validate Port Fast configuration is to look at the switch configuration. There are no Cisco IOS `show` commands to verify Port Fast configuration. The following output shows how to look at the configuration to verify Port Fast configuration:

```
VTP-Switch-1#show running-config interface gigabitethernet 0/1
Building configuration...

Current configuration : 118 bytes
!
interface GigabitEthernet0/1
 switchport mode trunk
 no ip address
 no keepalive
 spanning-tree portfast trunk
end
```

Configuring BPDU Guard

The BPDU Guard feature can also be enabled globally or on a per-port basis. To enable BPDU Guard in global configuration mode, the `spanning-tree portfast bpduguard default` command must be issued on the switch. This is illustrated in the following output:

```
VTP-Switch-1#conf t
Enter configuration commands, one per line.  End with CNTL/Z.
VTP-Switch-1(config)#spanning-tree portfast bpduguard default
VTP-Switch-1(config)#exit
```

Global configuration of the BPDU Guard feature can be validated by issuing the `show spanning-tree summary` command. This verification is shown in the following output:

```
VTP-Switch-1#show spanning-tree summary
Switch is in pvst mode
Root bridge for: VLAN0080, VLAN4000
EtherChannel misconfiguration guard is enabled
Extended system ID   is enabled
Portfast             is enabled by default
PortFast BPDU Guard  is enabled by default
Portfast BPDU Filter is disabled by default
Loopguard            is disabled by default
UplinkFast           is disabled
BackboneFast         is disabled
Pathcost method used is short
...
[Truncated Output]
```

BPDU Guard can also be enabled on a per-port basis via the `spanning-tree bpduguard enable` interface configuration command. This is illustrated in the following output:

```
VTP-Switch-1#conf t
Enter configuration commands, one per line.  End with CNTL/Z.
VTP-Switch-1(config)#int fast 0/2
VTP-Switch-1(config-if)#spanning-tree bpduguard enable
VTP-Switch-1(config-if)#exit
VTP-Switch-1(config)#
```

If the port receives a BPDU, an error message will be printed on the console. The following output shows a typical error message printed on the console when a BPDU is received on a port that has had the BPDU Guard feature enabled:

```
00:23:23: %SPANTREE-2-BLOCK_BPDUGUARD: Received BPDU on port FastEthernet0/2
          with BPDU Guard enabled. Disabling port.
00:23:23: %PM-4-ERR_DISABLE: bpduguard error detected on Fa0/2, putting Fa0/2
          in err-disable state
00:23:24: %LINEPROTO-5-UPDOWN: Line protocol on Interface FastEthernet0/2,
          changed state to down
00:23:25: %LINK-3-UPDOWN: Interface FastEthernet0/2, changed state to down
```

The port is then placed into an errdisable state as illustrated in the following output:

```
VTP-Switch-1#show interface fastethernet 0/2
FastEthernet0/2 is down, line protocol is down (err-disabled)
  Hardware is Fast Ethernet, address is 000d.bd06.4102 (bia 000d.bd06.41C2)
  MTU 1500 bytes, BW 100000 Kbit, DLY 1000 usec,
     reliability 255/255, txload 1/255, rxload 1/255
  Encapsulation ARPA, loopback not set
  Keepalive set (10 sec)
  Auto-duplex, Auto-speed
  input flow-control is off, output flow-control is off
  ARP type: ARPA, ARP Timeout 04:00:00
  Last input 00:03:20, output 00:03:21, output hang never
  Last clearing of 'show interface' counters never
  Input queue: 0/75/0/0 (size/max/drops/flushes); Total output drops: 0
  Queueing strategy: fifo
...
[Truncated Output]
```

To re-enable the port, one of two actions can be taken. The first is that the administrator can manually re-enable the interface by performing a `shut` and `no shut` on the interface. These configuration steps are illustrated in the following output:

```
VTP-Switch-1#conf t
Enter configuration commands, one per line.  End with CNTL/Z.
VTP-Switch-1(config)#int f0/2
VTP-Switch-1(config-if)#shut
VTP-Switch-1(config-if)#no shut
VTP-Switch-1(config-if)#exit
VTP-Switch-1(config)#exit
VTP-Switch-1#
VTP-Switch-1#show interface fastethernet 0/2
FastEthernet0/2 is up, line protocol is up (connected)
  Hardware is Fast Ethernet, address is 000d.bd06.4102 (bia 000d.bd06.4102)
  MTU 1500 bytes, BW 100000 Kbit, DLY 1000 usec,
     reliability 255/255, txload 1/255, rxload 1/255
  Encapsulation ARPA, loopback not set
```

```
    Keepalive set (10 sec)
    Full-duplex, 100Mb/s
    input flow-control is off, output flow-control is off
    ARP type: ARPA, ARP Timeout 04:00:00
    Last input 00:00:00, output 00:00:00, output hang never
    Last clearing of 'show interface' counters never
    Input queue: 0/75/0/0 (size/max/drops/flushes); Total output drops: 0
    Queueing strategy: fifo
...
[Truncated Output]
```

The second option is to enable automatic errdisable recovery in Cisco IOS software via the `errdisable recovery cause [reason]` global configuration command. The following output shows how to configure the switch to enable errdisabled ports automatically:

```
VTP-Switch-1(config)#errdisable recovery cause ?
  all                 Enable timer to recover from all causes
  bpduguard           Enable timer to recover from BPDU Guard error disable
                      state
  channel-misconfig   Enable timer to recover from channel misconfig disable
                      state
  dtp-flap            Enable timer to recover from dtp-flap error disable
                      state
  gbic-invalid        Enable timer to recover from invalid GBIC error disable
                      state
  link-flap           Enable timer to recover from link-flap error disable
                      state
  loopback            Enable timer to recover from loopback detected disable
                      state
  pagp-flap           Enable timer to recover from pagp-flap error disable
                      state
  psecure-violation   Enable timer to recover from psecure violation disable
                      state
  security-violation  Enable timer to recover from 802.1x violation disable
                      state
  udld                Enable timer to recover from udld error disable state
  vmps                Enable timer to recover from vmps shutdown error
                      disable state
```

The `errdisable recovery cause` command configures Cisco IOS software to re-enable ports that have been placed into the errdisable state automatically by any one of the options above. By default, Cisco IOS software will re-enable the ports after 300 seconds (5 minutes). The following output illustrates how to enable errdisable recovery for BPDU Guard:

```
VTP-Switch-1(config)#errdisable recovery cause bpduguard
```

The errdisable configuration is validated using the `show errdisable recovery` command as shown in the following output:

```
VTP-Switch-1#show errdisable recovery
ErrDisable Reason    Timer Status
-----------------    --------------
udld                 Disabled
bpduguard            Enabled
security-violatio    Disabled
channel-misconfig    Disabled
vmps                 Disabled
pagp-flap            Disabled
dtp-flap             Disabled
link-flap            Disabled
gbic-invalid         Disabled
psecure-violation    Disabled
loopback             Disabled

Timer interval: 300 seconds

Interfaces that will be enabled at the next timeout:

Interface     Errdisable reason    Time left(sec)
---------     -----------------    --------------
Fa0/2         bpduguard             277
```

From the output above, we can see that errdisable recovery is enabled for BPDU Guard. We can also see that the default timer (i.e. when Cisco IOS software will re-enable the affected port(s)) is 5 minutes. And finally, we can see that FastEthernet0/2, which has been placed into the errdisable state because it has BPDU Guard enabled and received a BPDU, will be re-enabled in 277 seconds by the Cisco IOS software.

NOTE: Keep in mind, however, that if the port is automatically re-enabled and the same condition still exists (i.e. it receives another BPDU) it will be errdisabled again.

To adjust the default errdisable timer, use the `errdisable recovery interval [seconds]` command as illustrated in the following output:

```
VTP-Switch-1#conf t
Enter configuration commands, one per line.  End with CNTL/Z.
VTP-Switch-1(config)#errdisable recovery interval 60
VTP-Switch-1(config)#exit
```

Again, the `show errdisable recovery` command can be used to validate this configuration as illustrated in the following output:

```
VTP-Switch-1#show errdisable recovery
ErrDisable Reason    Timer Status
-----------------    --------------
```

```
udld                    Disabled
bpduguard               Enabled
security-violatio       Disabled
channel-misconfig       Disabled
vmps                    Disabled
pagp-flap               Disabled
dtp-flap                Disabled
link-flap               Disabled
gbic-invalid            Disabled
psecure-violation       Disabled
loopback                Disabled

Timer interval: 60 seconds

Interfaces that will be enabled at the next timeout:

Interface     Errdisable reason      Time left(sec)
---------     -----------------      --------------
Fa0/2         bpduguard               4
```

Configuring BPDU Filter

Unlike the BPDU Guard feature, which allows a Port Fast interface to still send BPDUs but errdisables the port in the event that it receives BPDUs, the BPDU Filter feature prevents the port from both sending and receiving BPDUs.

By default, the BPDU Filter feature is disabled on all ports. However, this feature can be enabled by issuing the `spanning-tree portfast bpdufilter default` global configuration command, or on a per-port basis via the `spanning-tree bpdufilter enable` interface configuration command. The following output illustrates how to enable the BPDU Filter on a global basis:

```
VTP-Switch-1#conf t
Enter configuration commands, one per line.  End with CNTL/Z.
VTP- Server-1(config)#spanning-tree portfast bpdufilter default
VTP- Server-1(config)#exit
```

The following output illustrates how to configure the BPDU Filter on a per-port basis:

```
VTP-Switch-1#conf t
Enter configuration commands, one per line.  End with CNTL/Z.
VTP-Switch-1(config)#int f0/4
VTP-Switch-1(config-if)#spanning-tree bpdufilter enable
VTP-Switch-1(config-if)#exit
```

This configuration can be validated by looking at the switch configuration or via the `show spanning-tree summary` command as illustrated in the following output:

```
VTP-Switch-1#show spanning-tree summary
Switch is in pvst mode
Root bridge for: VLAN0001
EtherChannel misconfiguration guard is enabled
Extended system ID   is enabled
Portfast             is disabled by default
PortFast BPDU Guard  is disabled by default
Portfast BPDU Filter is enabled by default
Loopguard            is disabled by default
UplinkFast           is disabled
BackboneFast         is disabled
Pathcost method used is short
```

Configuring Loop Guard

By default, the Loop Guard feature is disabled. However, it can be enabled either globally or on a per-port basis. To enable Loop Guard globally, use the `spanning-tree loopguard default` global configuration command. To enable Loop Guard on a per-port basis, use the `spanning-tree guard loop` interface configuration command. The following output illustrates how to enable Loop Guard globally on the switch:

```
VTP-Switch-1#conf t
Enter configuration commands, one per line.  End with CNTL/Z.
VTP-Switch-1(config)#spanning-tree loopguard default
VTP-Switch-1(config)#exit
```

The following output illustrates how to enable Loop Guard on a per-port basis:

```
VTP-Switch-1#conf t
Enter configuration commands, one per line.  End with CNTL/Z.
VTP-Switch-1(config)#int f0/2
VTP-Switch-1(config-if)#spanning-tree guard loop
VTP-Switch-1(config-if)#exit
```

The `show spanning-tree summary` command can be used to verify Loop Guard configuration. This is illustrated in the following output:

```
VTP-Switch-1#show spanning-tree summary
Switch is in pvst mode
Root bridge for: VLAN0080, VLAN4000
EtherChannel misconfiguration guard is enabled
Extended system ID   is enabled
Portfast             is disabled by default
PortFast BPDU Guard  is disabled by default
Portfast BPDU Filter is disabled by default
Loopguard            is enabled by default
UplinkFast           is disabled
BackboneFast         is disabled
Pathcost method used is short
...
[Truncated Output]
```

Configuring Root Guard

The Root Guard feature is disabled by default. This feature is used to prevent a Designated Port from becoming a Root Port. If a switch advertises a superior BPDU, or one with a lower BID, on a port where Root Guard is enabled, the local switch will not allow the new switch to become the Root Bridge. Instead, the port will be placed into a root-inconsistent state and will remain in this state as long as it continues to receive those BPDUs.

The port, however, can continue to relay received BPDUs to downstream switches. The Root Guard feature can only be enabled on a per-port basis. This is performed by issuing the `spanning-tree guard root` interface configuration command. The following output illustrates how to enable Root Guard on a port:

```
VTP-Switch-1#conf t
Enter configuration commands, one per line.  End with CNTL/Z.
VTP-Switch-1(config-if)#spanning-tree guard root
VTP-Switch-1(config-if)#exit
```

There is no `show` command that can be used to verify which ports are configured with the Root Guard feature. However, this can be validated by looking at the switch configuration. This is illustrated in the following output:

```
VTP-Switch-1#show running-config interface fastethernet 0/2
Building configuration...

Current configuration : 97 bytes
!
interface FastEthernet0/2
 switchport mode trunk
 no ip address
 spanning-tree guard root
end
```

If there are any ports that are configured for Root Guard and placed into the root-inconsistent state, they can be viewed by issuing the `show spanning-tree inconsistentports` command, which is shown in the following output:

```
VTP-Switch-1#show spanning-tree inconsistentports

Name                 Interface              Inconsistency
-------------------- ---------------------- ------------------
VLAN0001             FastEthernet0/2        Root Inconsistent
VLAN0010             FastEthernet0/2        Root Inconsistent
VLAN0020             FastEthernet0/2        Root Inconsistent
VLAN0030             FastEthernet0/2        Root Inconsistent
VLAN0040             FastEthernet0/2        Root Inconsistent
Number of inconsistent ports (segments) in the system : 5
```

Although the port is placed into a root-inconsistent state, it is important to know that it is not err-disabled. This still allows the port to retain the ability to relay BPDUs downstream as shown in the following output:

```
VTP-Switch-1#show interfaces fastethernet 0/2
FastEthernet0/2 is up, line protocol is up (connected)
  Hardware is Fast Ethernet, address is 000d.bd06.4102 (bia 000d.bd06.41C2)
  MTU 1500 bytes, BW 100000 Kbit, DLY 1000 usec,
     reliability 255/255, txload 1/255, rxload 1/255
  Encapsulation ARPA, loopback not set
  Keepalive set (10 sec)
  Full-duplex, 100Mb/s
  input flow-control is off, output flow-control is off
  ARP type: ARPA, ARP Timeout 04:00:00
  Last input 00:00:00, output 00:00:01, output hang never
  Last clearing of 'show interface' counters never
  Input queue: 0/75/0/0 (size/max/drops/flushes); Total output drops: 0
  Queueing strategy: fifo
...
[Truncated Output]
```

Configuring Uplink Fast

Uplink Fast is enabled on Access layer switches and keeps track of possible paths to the Root Bridge. Once the Uplink Fast feature is enabled globally, it is enabled for the entire switch and all VLANs. By default, when Uplink Fast is enabled, Cisco IOS software performs the following actions on the local switch:

- The Bridge Priority of the switch is raised to 49,152
- The Port Cost of all VLANs is increased by 3,000

These two actions ensure that the switch will never be elected Root Bridge, and it makes the path through this switch as undesirable as possible for any downstream switches. For this reason, Uplink Fast should never be enabled on the Root Bridge because it will lose its Root status or lose switches that have other downstream switches connected to them. The following output illustrates how to enable Uplink Fast on an Access layer switch:

```
VTP-Switch-1#conf t
Enter configuration commands, one per line.  End with CNTL/Z.
VTP-Switch-1(config)#spanning-tree uplinkfast
VTP-Switch-1(config)#exit
```

The Bridge Priority and port cost adjustments by Uplink Fast are reflected in the `show spanning-tree` command as illustrated in the following output:

```
VTP-Access-Switch-1#show spanning-tree

VLAN0001
  Spanning tree enabled protocol ieee
  Root ID    Priority    32768
             Address     0005.32f5.5b00
             Cost        3019
             Port        1 (FastEthernet0/1)
             Hello Time   2 sec  Max Age 20 sec  Forward Delay 15 sec

  Bridge ID  Priority    49153  (priority 49152 sys-id-ext 1)
             Address     000d.bd06.4100
             Hello Time   2 sec  Max Age 20 sec  Forward Delay 15 sec
             Aging Time 300
  Uplinkfast enabled

Interface        Role Sts Cost      Prio.Nbr Type
---------------- ---- --- --------- -------- --------------------------------
Fa0/1            Root FWD 3019      128.1    P2p
Fa0/2            Altn BLK 3019      128.2    P2p

VLAN0010
  Spanning tree enabled protocol ieee
  Root ID    Priority    0
             Address     0005.32f5.5b01
             Cost        3019
             Port        1 (FastEthernet0/1)
             Hello Time   2 sec  Max Age 20 sec  Forward Delay 15 sec

  Bridge ID  Priority    49162  (priority 49152 sys-id-ext 10)
             Address     000d.bd06.4100
             Hello Time   2 sec  Max Age 20 sec  Forward Delay 15 sec
             Aging Time 300
  Uplinkfast enabled

Interface        Role Sts Cost      Prio.Nbr Type
---------------- ---- --- --------- -------- --------------------------------
Fa0/1            Root FWD 3019      128.1    P2p
Fa0/2            Altn BLK 3019      128.2    P2p

VLAN0020
  Spanning tree enabled protocol ieee
  Root ID    Priority    0
             Address     0005.32f5.5b02
             Cost        3019
             Port        1 (FastEthernet0/1)
             Hello Time   2 sec  Max Age 20 sec  Forward Delay 15 sec

  Bridge ID  Priority    49172  (priority 49152 sys-id-ext 20)
             Address     000d.bd06.4100
             Hello Time   2 sec  Max Age 20 sec  Forward Delay 15 sec
             Aging Time 300
  Uplinkfast enabled

Interface        Role Sts Cost      Prio.Nbr Type
---------------- ---- --- --------- -------- --------------------------------
Fa0/1            Root FWD 3019      128.1    P2p
Fa0/2            Altn BLK 3019      128.2    P2p
```

Uplink Fast configuration can be validated by issuing the `show spanning-tree uplinkfast` command. The information printed by this command is illustrated in the following output:

```
VTP-Access-Switch-1#show spanning-tree uplinkfast
UplinkFast is enabled

Station update rate set to 150 packets/sec.

UplinkFast statistics
-----------------------
Number of transitions via uplinkFast (all VLANs)            : 0
Number of proxy multicast addresses transmitted (all VLANs) : 0

Name                 Interface List
-------------------- ------------------------------------
VLAN0001             Fa0/1(fwd), Fa0/2
VLAN0010             Fa0/1(fwd), Fa0/2
VLAN0020             Fa0/1(fwd), Fa0/2
```

By transitioning the port to a Forwarding state almost immediately, the Uplink Fast feature presents the potential problem of incorrect entries in the CAM tables of the other switches because they have not had an opportunity to re-learn the new path for the MAC addresses of the devices connected to the Access switch.

To prevent this, the Access layer switch on which the Uplink Fast feature is enabled floods dummy frames with the different MAC addresses that it has in its CAM as a source. The frames are sent to the Multicast address 01-00.0C-CD-CD-CD and appear to originate from the hosts connected to the switch so all the upstream switches can learn of these addresses through the new port. This message is shown in Figure 3-50 below:

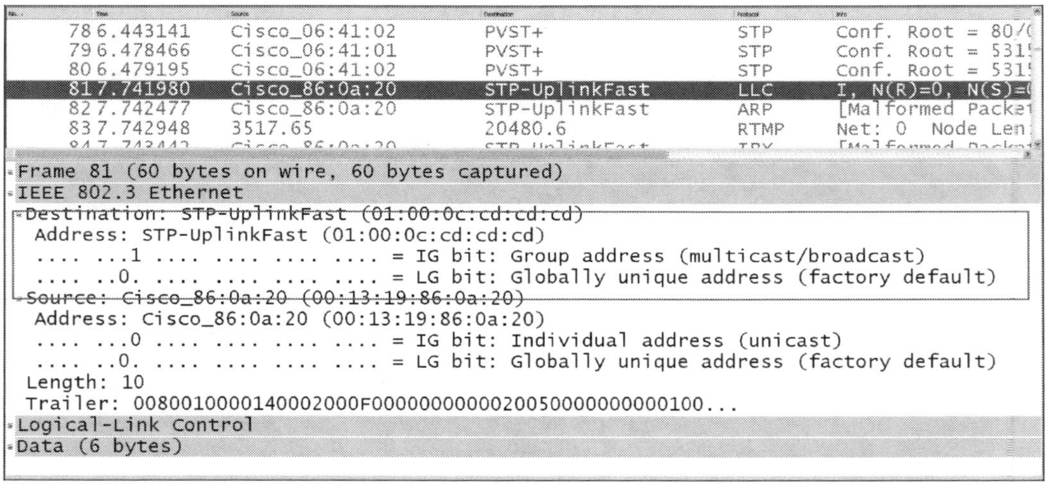

Fig. 3-50. Uplink Fast Destination Address

By default, the switch sends out these Multicast frames at a rate of 150 packets per second (pps). However, this value can be adjusted by using the `spanning-tree uplinkfast max-update-rate [rate]` global configuration command. The following output illustrates how to change the number of packets sent to 500 pps on the Access switch:

```
VTP-Access-Switch-1#conf t
Enter configuration commands, one per line.  End with CNTL/Z.
VTP-Switch-1(config)#spanning-tree uplinkfast max-update-rate 500
VTP-Switch-1(config)#exit
```

This configuration is reflected in the output of the `show spanning-tree uplinkfast` command. The output is shown in the following output:

```
VTP-Access-Switch-1#show spanning-tree uplinkfast
UplinkFast is enabled

Station update rate set to 500 packets/sec.

UplinkFast statistics
-----------------------
Number of transitions via uplinkFast (all VLANs)            : 15
Number of proxy multicast addresses transmitted (all VLANs) : 12

Name                 Interface List
-------------------- ------------------------------------
VLAN0001             Fa0/1(fwd), Fa0/2
VLAN0010             Fa0/1(fwd), Fa0/2
VLAN0020             Fa0/1(fwd), Fa0/2
```

Configuring Backbone Fast

The Spanning Tree Backbone Fast feature is used to speed up convergence in the event of an indirect link failure to the Root Bridge. By immediately aging out the Max Age timer, this feature speeds up convergence from 50 seconds to 30 seconds.

By default, the Backbone Fast feature is disabled on all switches. However, if enabled, then it should be enabled on all switches in the STP domain. This enables the use of the Root Link Query protocol on all switches, which allows them to process RLQ packets. The Backbone Fast feature is enabled globally on the switch via the `spanning-tree backbonefast` global configuration command. The following output illustrates how to enable Backbone Fast on a switch:

```
VTP-Switch-1#conf t
Enter configuration commands, one per line.  End with CNTL/Z.
VTP-Switch-1(config)#spanning-tree backbonefast
VTP-Switch-1(config)#exit
```

This configuration is validated using the `show spanning-tree summary` or the `show spanning-tree backbonefast` commands as shown in the following output:

```
VTP-Switch-1#show spanning-tree summary
Switch is in pvst mode
Root bridge for: VLAN0080, VLAN4000
EtherChannel misconfiguration guard is enabled
Extended system ID   is enabled
Portfast             is disabled by default
PortFast BPDU Guard  is disabled by default
Portfast BPDU Filter is disabled by default
Loopguard            is disabled by default
UplinkFast           is disabled
BackboneFast         is enabled
Pathcost method used is short

Name                   Blocking Listening Learning Forwarding STP Active
---------------------- -------- --------- -------- ---------- ----------
VLAN0001               1        0         0        2          3
VLAN0010               1        0         0        1          2
VLAN0020               1        0         0        1          2
VLAN0030               1        0         0        1          2
VLAN0040               1        0         0        1          2
VLAN0080               0        0         0        2          2
VLAN4000               0        0         0        2          2
---------------------- -------- --------- -------- ---------- ----------
7 vlans                5        0         0        10         15
VTP-Switch-1#
VTP-Switch-1#
VTP-Switch-1#show spanning-tree backbonefast
BackboneFast is enabled

BackboneFast statistics
-----------------------
Number of transitions via backboneFast (all VLANs)          : 0
Number of inferior BPDUs received (all VLANs)               : 0
Number of RLQ request PDUs received (all VLANs)             : 0
Number of RLQ response PDUs received (all VLANs)            : 0
Number of RLQ request PDUs sent (all VLANs)                 : 0
Number of RLQ response PDUs sent (all VLANs)                : 0
```

Configuring Unidirectional Link Detection

By default, UDLD is disabled on all switch ports. This feature can be enabled globally for all Fiber-connected ports or on a per-port basis. UDLD normal mode is enabled globally via the `udld enable` command, while UDLD aggressive mode is enabled via the `udld aggressive` global configuration command. The following output illustrates how to enable UDLD normal mode (which is the default UDLD mode of operation) on a switch:

```
VTP-Switch-1#conf t
Enter configuration commands, one per line.  End with CNTL/Z.
VTP-Switch-1(config)#udld enable
VTP-Switch-1(config)#exit
```

The following output illustrates how to configure UDLD aggressive mode on a switch:

```
VTP-Switch-1#conf t
Enter configuration commands, one per line.  End with CNTL/Z.
VTP-Switch-1(config)#udld aggressive
VTP-Switch-1(config)#exit
```

To enable UDLD on a per-port basis, issue the `udld port [aggressive]` interface configuration command. This command cannot be used for Fiber-connected ports, as they enable or disable UDLD operation based on the `udld enable` or `udld aggressive` global configuration commands. The following output illustrates how to enable UDLD normal mode on a point-to-point link between two FastEthernet switches:

```
VTP-Switch-1(config)#interface fast 0/1
VTP-Switch-1(config-if)#description 'Point-to-Point Link To VTP-Switch-2'
VTP-Switch-1(config-if)#udld port
VTP-Switch-1(config-if)#exit

VTP-Switch-2(config)#interface fast 0/1
VTP-Switch-2(config-if)#description 'Point-to-Point Link To VTP-Switch-2'
VTP-Switch-2(config-if)#udld port
VTP-Switch-2(config-if)#exit
```

The `show udld [interface]` command can be used to view UDLD configuration parameters. This is shown in the following output:

```
VTP-Switch-1#show udld fastethernet 0/1

Interface Fa0/1
---
Port enable administrative configuration setting: Enabled
Port enable operational state: Enabled
Current bidirectional state: Bidirectional
Current operational state: Advertisement - Single neighbor detected
Message interval: 15
Time out interval: 5

    Entry 1
    ---
    Expiration time: 121
    Device ID: 1
```

```
    Current neighbor state: Bidirectional
    Device name: 00:05:32:F5:5B:00
    Port ID: Fa0/1
    Neighbor echo 1 device: FOC0730W239
    Neighbor echo 1 port: Fa0/1

    Message interval: 5
    CDP Device name: VTP-Server-2
```

To adjust the default UDLD timers, the `udld message time [seconds]` command can be used. The following output illustrates how to change the time interval between UDLD probe messages on UDLD ports to 10 seconds:

```
VTP-Switch-1#conf t
Enter configuration commands, one per line.  End with CNTL/Z.
VTP-Switch-1(config)#udld message time 10
VTP-Switch-1(config)#exit
```

The `show udld [interface]` command can be used to view UDLD configuration parameters. The following output shows how to verify the UDLD message interval time:

```
VTP-Switch-1#show udld

Interface Fa0/1
---
Port enable administrative configuration setting: Enabled
Port enable operational state: Enabled
Current bidirectional state: Bidirectional
Current operational state: Advertisement - Single neighbor detected
Message interval: 10
Time out interval: 5

    Entry 1
    ---
    Expiration time: 169
    Device ID: 1
    Current neighbor state: Bidirectional
    Device name: 00:05:32:F5:5B:00
    Port ID: Fa0/1
    Neighbor echo 1 device: FOC0730W239
    Neighbor echo 1 port: Fa0/1

    Message interval: 5
    CDP Device name: VTP-Server-2
```

Troubleshooting Spanning Tree Networks

While we will not be going into detail on Spanning Tree troubleshooting in this guide, because that has been moved to the new TSHOOT certification exam, there are some commands with which you should be familiar in order to support and troubleshoot the STP network. These commands will be described and illustrated in this section. The following output shows the different options available with the `show spanning-tree` command:

```
VTP-Switch-1#show spanning-tree ?
  active              Report on active interfaces only
  backbonefast        Show spanning tree backbonefast status
  blockedports        Show blocked ports
  bridge              Status and configuration of this bridge
  detail              Detailed information
  inconsistentports   Show inconsistent ports
  interface           Spanning Tree interface status and configuration
  mst                 Multiple spanning trees
  pathcost            Show Spanning pathcost options
  root                Status and configuration of the root bridge
  summary             Summary of port states
  uplinkfast          Show spanning tree uplinkfast status
  vlan                VLAN Switch Spanning Trees
  |                   Output modifiers
  <cr>
```

The `show spanning-tree active [detail]` command prints out information on active STP interfaces (i.e. interfaces that are either in a Forwarding or Blocking state). This command basically prints out the same information as the `show spanning-tree vlan [number]` command. The information printed by this command is illustrated in the following output:

```
VTP-Switch-1#show spanning-tree active

VLAN0001
  Spanning tree enabled protocol ieee
  Root ID    Priority    32768
             Address     0005.32f5.5b00
             Cost        19
             Port        1 (FastEthernet0/1)
             Hello Time   2 sec  Max Age 20 sec  Forward Delay 15 sec

  Bridge ID  Priority    32769  (priority 32768 sys-id-ext 1)
             Address     000d.bd06.4100
             Hello Time   2 sec  Max Age 20 sec  Forward Delay 15 sec
             Aging Time 300

Interface        Role Sts Cost      Prio.Nbr Type
---------------- ---- --- --------- -------- --------------------------------
Fa0/1            Root FWD 19        128.1    P2p
Fa0/2            Altn BLK 19        128.2    P2p
Fa0/3            Desg FWD 19        128.3    P2p
```

The `show spanning-tree bridge` command prints out the switch status of each VLAN on the switch. This information includes the BID, priority values, and Spanning Tree timers as shown in the following output:

```
VTP-Switch-1#show spanning-tree bridge

                                                   Hello  Max  Fwd
Vlan                         Bridge ID              Time  Age  Dly  Protccol
---------------- --------------------------------- -----  ---  ---  --------
VLAN0001           32769 (32768,1) 000d.bd06.4100 2       20   15   ieee
VLAN0010          32778 (32768,10) 000d.bd06.4100 2       20   15   ieee
VLAN0020          32788 (32768,20) 000d.bd06.4100 2       20   15   ieee
VLAN0030          32798 (32768,30) 000d.bd06.4100 2       20   15   ieee
VLAN0040          32808 (32768,40) 000d.bd06.4100 2       20   15   ieee
VLAN0080                 80 (0,80) 000d.bd06.4100 2       20   15   ieee
VLAN4000        36768 (32768,4000) 000d.bd06.4100 2       20   15   ieee
```

This command has several sub-options that can also be used when troubleshooting STP. These sub-options are shown in the following output:

```
VTP-Switch-1#show spanning-tree bridge ?
  address        Mac address of this bridge
  detail         Details of the status and configuration
  forward-time   Forward delay interval
  hello-time     Hello time
  id             Spanning tree bridge identifier
  max-age        Max age
  priority       Bridge priority of this bridge
  protocol       Spanning tree protocol
  |              Output modifiers
  <cr>
```

The `show spanning-tree interface` command prints out the role of the interface as well as other Spanning Tree parameters, such as port cost, port priority, and operational state. This information is illustrated in the following output:

```
VTP-Switch-1#show spanning-tree interface fastethernet 0/1

Vlan             Role Sts Cost      Prio.Nbr Type
---------------- ---- --- --------- -------- --------------------------------
VLAN0001         Root FWD 19        128.1    P2p
VLAN0010         Root FWD 19        128.1    P2p
VLAN0020         Root FWD 19        128.1    P2p
VLAN0030         Root FWD 19        128.1    P2p
VLAN0040         Root FWD 19        128.1    P2p
VLAN0080         Desg FWD 19        128.1    P2p
VLAN4000         Desg FWD 19        128.1    P2p
```

The `show spanning-tree root` command prints information about the STP Root Bridge. This command has several sub-options, which are shown in the following output:

```
VTP-Switch-1#show spanning-tree root ?
  address       Mac address of the root bridge
  cost          Path cost from this bridge to the root
  detail        Details of the status and configuration
  forward-time  Forward delay interval for the spanning tree topology
  hello-time    Hello time for the spanning tree topology
  id            Spanning tree root bridge identifier
  max-age       Max age for the spanning tree topology
  port          Root port
  priority      Bridge priority of the root bridge
  |             Output modifiers
  <cr>
```

For example, the `show spanning-tree root address` command can be used to determine the MAC address of the Root Bridge for each particular VLAN. This is shown in the following output:

```
VTP-Switch-1#show spanning-tree root address
VLAN0001          0005.32f5.5b00
VLAN0010          0005.32f5.5b01
VLAN0020          0005.32f5.5b02
VLAN0030          0005.32f5.5b03
VLAN0040          0005.32f5.5b04
VLAN0080          000d.bd06.4100
VLAN4000          000d.bd06.4100
```

As an another example, the `show spanning-tree root detail` command prints out detailed information about the Root Bridge for each VLAN, the Root Port, the Root Path Cost, and the Bridge Priority value. This is illustrated in the following output:

```
VTP-Switch-1#show spanning-tree root detail
VLAN0001
  Root ID    Priority     32768
             Address      0005.32f5.5b00
             Cost         19
             Port         1 (FastEthernet0/1)
             Hello Time    2 sec  Max Age 20 sec  Forward Delay 15 sec
VLAN0010
  Root ID    Priority     0
             Address      0005.32f5.5b01
             Cost         19
             Port         1 (FastEthernet0/1)
             Hello Time    2 sec  Max Age 20 sec  Forward Delay 15 sec
VLAN0020
  Root ID    Priority     0
```

```
              Address     0005.32f5.5b02
              Cost        19
              Port        1 (FastEthernet0/1)
              Hello Time   2 sec  Max Age 20 sec  Forward Delay 15 sec
VLAN0030
  Root ID     Priority    0
              Address     0005.32f5.5b03
              Cost        19
              Port        1 (FastEthernet0/1)
```

Although advanced Spanning Tree troubleshooting will be tested in the TSHOOT exam, you should still have a basic understanding of how to verify and troubleshoot Spanning Tree networks using basic show commands. While the debugging of Spanning Tree is beyond the scope of this course, you can enable STP debugs using the `debug spanning-tree` command and selecting the appropriate option. These options are illustrated in the following output:

```
VTP-Switch-1#debug spanning-tree ?
  all             All Spanning Tree debugging messages
  backbonefast    BackboneFast events
  bpdu            Spanning tree BPDU
  bpdu-opt        Optimized BPDU handling
  config          Spanning tree config changes
  csuf            STP CSUF
  etherchannel    EtherChannel support
  events          Spanning tree topology events
  exceptions      Spanning tree exceptions
  general         Spanning tree general
  mstp            MSTP debug commands
  pvst+           PVST+ events
  root            Spanning tree root events
  snmp            Spanning Tree SNMP handling
  stp-sync        STP state sync support
  switch          Switch Shim debug commands
  uplinkfast      UplinkFast events
```

NOTE: Spanning Tree debugging is processor-intensive. Do not enable STP debugging in a production network unless you have exhausted all other troubleshooting mechanisms, or are instructed by the Cisco TAC.

Chapter Summary

The following section is a summary of the major points you should be aware of in this chapter.

An Introduction to the Spanning Tree Protocol

- The Spanning Tree Protocol (STP) is defined in the IEEE 802.1D standard
- The primary purpose of STP is to attempt to provide a loop free topology
- Spanning Tree Protocol operates by making the following assumptions about the network:
    1. All links are bidirectional and can both send and receive BPDUs
    2. The switch is able to regularly receive, process and send BPDUs

Spanning Tree Bridge Protocol Data Units

- Switches that reside in the STP domain communicate and exchange messages using BPDUs
- The exchange of BPDUs is used by STA to determine the network topology
- The topology of an active switched network is determined by the following three variables:
    1. The unique MAC address (switch identifier) that is associated with each switch
    2. The path cost to the Root Bridge associated with each switch port
    3. The port identifier (MAC address of the port) associated with each switch port

- BPDUs are sent to the STP Multicast destination address 01-80-C2-00-00-00
- By default, BPDUs are sent every 2 seconds
- There are two types of Spanning Tree BPDUs, which are:
    1. Configuration BPDUs
    2. Topology Change Notification BPDUs

- Switches determine the best Configuration BPDU based on the following:
    1. Lowest Root Bridge ID
    2. Lowest Root Path Cost to Root Bridge
    3. Lowest Sender Bridge ID
    4. Lowest Sender Port ID

- The completion of the Configuration BPDU exchange results in the following actions:
    1. A Root Switch is elected for the entire Spanning Tree domain
    2. A Root Port is elected on every Non-Root Switch in the Spanning Tree domain
    3. A Designated Switch is elected for every LAN segment
    4. A Designated Port is elected on the Designated Switch for every segment
    5. Loops in the network are eliminated by blocking redundant paths

- If the Root Bridge fails, Configuration BPDUs stop being sent throughout the network

- The TCN BPDU plays a key role in handling changes in the active topology
- TCN BPDUs are originated by any switch and are sent upstream toward the Root Bridge
- If the Least Significant Bit (LSB) is enabled, this indicates a TC BPDU
- If the Most Significant Bit (MSB) is enabled, then it indicates a TCA BPDU
- In the real world, most people often refer to Configuration BPDUs simply as BPDUs

Spanning Tree Port States

- The Spanning Tree Protocol transitions through several port states, which are:
  1. Blocking
  2. Listening
  3. Learning
  4. Forwarding
  5. Disabled

- A port moves through these states in the following manner:
  1. From initialization to blocking
  2. From blocking to either listening or disabled
  3. From listening to either listening or disabled
  4. From learning to either forwarding or disabled
  5. From forwarding to disabled

- When in a Blocking state, the port:
  1. Discards frames received on port from the attached segment
  2. Discards frames switched from another port
  3. Does not incorporate station location into its address database
  4. Receives BPDUs and directs them to the system module
  5. Does not transmit BPDUs received from the system module
  6. Receives and responds to network management messages

- When in a listening state, the port:
  1. Discards frames received on port from the attached segment
  2. Discards frames switched from another port
  3. Does not incorporate station location into its address database
  4. Receive BPDUs and directs them to the system module
  5. Receives, processes and transmits BPDUs received from the system module
  6. Receives and responds to network management messages

- A switch port that is in the learning state performs the following actions:
  1. Discards frames received from the attached segment
  2. Discards frames switched from another port
  3. Incorporates (installs) station location into its address database
  4. Receives BPDUs and directs them to the system module
  5. Receives, processes, and transmits BPDUs received from the system module
  6. Receives and responds to network management messages

- When in a listening state, the port:
  1. Discards frames received on port from the attached segment
  2. Discards frames switched from another port
  3. Does not incorporate station location into its address database
  4. Receive BPDUs and directs them to the system module
  5. Receives, processes and transmits BPDUs received from the system module
  6. Receives and responds to network management messages

- A switch port that is in the learning state performs the following actions:
  1. Discards frames received from the attached segment
  2. Discards frames switched from another port
  3. Incorporates (installs) station location into its address database
  4. Receives BPDUs and directs them to the system module
  5. Receives, processes, and transmits BPDUs received from the system module
  6. Receives and responds to network management messages

- A port in the forwarding state performs the following:
  1. Forwards frames received from the attached segment
  2. Forwards frames switched from another port
  3. Incorporates (installs) station location information into its address database
  4. Receives BPDUs and directs them to the system module
  5. Processes BPDUs received from the system module
  6. Receives and responds to network management messages

- A disabled port performs the following:
  1. Discards frames received from the attached segment
  2. Discards frames switched from another port
  3. Does not incorporate station location into its address database
  4. Receives BPDUs but does not direct them to the system module
  5. Does not receive BPDUs from the system module
  6. Receives and responds to network management messages

Understanding the Spanning Tree Bridge ID

- Switches in a STP domain have a BID which is used to uniquely identify the switch
- The Bridge ID is also used to assist in the election of an STP Root Bridge
- The BID is an 8-byte field composed from a 6-byte MAC and a 2-byte Bridge Priority
- The Bridge Priority is the priority of the switch in relation to all other switches
- The Bridge Priority values range from 0 through 65,535
- In the 802.1D standard, each VLAN requires a unique BID

IEEE 802.1t and the Extended System ID

- The 802.1t standard introduced the extended system ID to conserve MAC addresses
- 802.1t reduces the Bridge Priority to 4 bits and adds a 12-bit Extended System ID

Spanning Tree Root Bridge Election

- By default, following initialization, all switches initially assume that they are the Root
- By default, the switch with the highest Bridge Priority is elected the STP Root Bridge
- If Bridge Priority values are equal, the switch with the lowest order MAC is then elected
- During Root election, no traffic is forwarded over any switch in the same STP domain

Understanding Spanning Tree Cost and Priority

- Spanning Tree uses cost and priority values to determine the best path to the Root Bridge
- The 802.1D specification assigns 16-bit (short) default port cost values to each port
- The STP default port cost values for each type of port when using the short method are:

Bandwidth	Default Port Cost
4 Mbps	250
10 Mbps	100
16 Mbps	62
100 Mbps	19
1 Gbps	4
10 Gbps	2

- The 802.1t standard assigns 32-bit (long) default port cost values to each port
- The STP default port cost values for each type of port when using the long method are:

Bandwidth	Default Port Cost
4 Mbps	5000000
10 Mbps	2000000
16 Mbps	1250000
100 Mbps	200000
1 Gbps	20000
10 Gbps	2000

- By default, lower (numerically) costs are more preferred
- In the event that multiple ports have the same path cost, STP considers the port priority
- The valid port priority range is from 0 through 240 and the Cisco IOS default value is 128
- In traditional STP, the 8 bit Port Priority and 8 bit port number create the 16 bit port ID
- With 802.1t, the port priority is 4 bits, which allows 12 bits to be used for the port number
- The port priority is locally significant and is not included in STP BPDUs
- The port cost is globally significant and is included in all propagated STP BPDUs

Spanning Tree Root and Designated Ports

- Spanning Tree elects two types of ports that are used to forward BPDUs
- These two ports are:
    1. The Root Port, which points toward the Root Bridge
    2. The Designated Port, which points away from the Root Bridge

- In the event of a tie when selecting the Root Port, STP uses the following as tie-breakers:
    1. Lowest Root Bridge ID
    2. Lowest Root Path Cost to Root Bridge
    3. Lowest Sender Bridge ID
    4. Lowest Sender Port ID

- The Spanning Tree Root Port is the port that provides the best path to the Root Bridge
- The Root Port is the port that receives the best BPDU for the switch
- The Root Path Cost is calculated based on the cumulative cost (Path Cost) to the Root
- The Path Cost is the value that each port contributes to the Root Path Cost
- Unlike the Root Port, the Designated Port is a port that points away from the STP Root
- Some people refer to the Designated Port as the Designated Switch
- The primary purpose of the Designated Port is to prevent loops
- All ports on the Root are designated ports because the Root Path Cost will always be 0
- A non Designated Port is simply a port that STP places into the Blocking state

Spanning Tree Timers

- BPDUs include several timers that play an integral role in the operation of the protocol
- The Spanning Tree timer values are contained in the last three fields of a BPDU
- The default Spanning Tree timers are based on an STP network diameter of 7 hops
- The modification of any of STP timers should always be made at the Root Bridge
- There are 3 configurable Spanning Tree timer values, which are:
    1. The Hello Time
    2. The Forward Delay
    3. The Max Age

- In addition, Configuration BPDUs also include a Message Age timer
- The Message Age is modified by every switch that receives and propagates a BPDU
- The Hello Time is the time between each BPDU that is sent
- The Hello Time is set to 2 seconds by default
- The Forward Delay is the time that is spent in the Listening and Learning state
- The Forward Delay is set to 15 seconds by default
- The Forward Delay is calculated using the following formula:

Forward Delay = ((4 * hello) + (3 * Diameter)) / 2

- The Max Age time is set in the BPDU by the Root Bridge and defaults to 20 seconds
- The Max Age can be calculated using the following formula:

Max Age = (4 * Hello) + (2 * Diameter) – 2

- The Message Age timer displays the age of the Root Bridge BPDU
- The Message Age is incremented by 1 by every switch that receives and propagates a BPDU
- The Root Bridge sends BPDUs with a Message Age value of 0
- The Message Age timer can be used to determine the following:
  1. How far away the switch is from the Root Bridge
  2. The time before the received BPDU is aged out on the port

Understanding the Spanning Tree Diameter

- The default diameter is based on various timers being tuned to their default values
- Max Age and Forward Delay are used to calculate diameter using the formulas:

Diameter = (Max Age + 2 - (4 * Hello)) / 2

Diameter = ((2 * Forward Delay) - (4 * Hello)) / 3

- The network diameter may be higher than 7 although this is not recommended

Cisco Spanning Tree Enhancements

- Port Fast is a feature that is typically enabled only for a port that connects to a host
- The Port Fast feature does not disable Spanning Tree on the selected port
- Even with the Port Fast feature enabled, the port can still send and receive BPDUs
- This may create a loop if the port is connected to a device which send does BPDUs
- BPDU Guard feature is used to protect the STP domain from external influence
- Ports that have the BPDU Guard feature enabled still send out BPDUs
- Ports with BPDU Guard enabled transition to an errdisabled state when they receive BPDUs
- The BPDU Filter feature effectively disables Spanning Tree on the selected ports
- Ports with the BPDU Filter feature enabled do not send or receive any BPDUs

- The Loop Guard feature is used to prevent the formation of loops
- Loop Guard prevents non Designated Ports from becoming Designated due to no BPDUs
- Loop Guard restrictions and considerations include:
  1. You cannot enable Loop Guard on Port Fast or Dynamic VLAN ports
  2. You cannot enable Loop Guard on a Root Guard enabled switch
  3. Loop Guard does not affect Uplink Fast or Backbone Fast operation
  4. Loop Guard must be enabled on point to point links only
  5. Loop Guard operation is not affected by the Spanning Tree timers
  6. Loop Guard cannot actually detect a unidirectional link

- The Root Guard feature prevents a Designated Port from becoming a Root Port
- Root Guard must be manually enabled on all ports
- The Uplink Fast feature provides faster failover to a redundant link
- Uplink Fast is used on Access switches with redundant uplinks
- The Backbone Fast feature provides fast failover when an indirect link failure occurs
- Backbone Fast uses a new PDU named the Root Link Query (RLQ) PDU
- The RLQ PDU has the same packet format as a normal BPDU

Unidirectional Link Detection (UDLD)

- UDLD is a Layer 2 protocol designed to detect unidirectional link failures
- UDLD performs tasks that Layer 1 mechanisms, such as auto negotiation, cannot perform
- UDLD exchanges protocol packets between the neighboring switches
- Both devices on the link must support UDLD
- UDLD must be enabled on both sides of the link in order to work
- UDLD packets are sent out every 15 seconds
- The UDLD timeout value defaults to 45 seconds (3 times the message interval)
- UDLD operates in either normal mode or aggressive mode
- In normal mode, a unidirectional link is allowed to operate in the STP mode
- In aggressive mode, a unidirectional link is disabled

CHAPTER 4

Advanced Spanning Tree Protocols

In the previous chapter, we learned about the traditional IEEE 802.1D Spanning Tree Protocol (STP). This chapter describes two additional Spanning Tree Protocol variables: the IEEE 802.1w standard, or the Rapid Spanning Tree Protocol (RSTP), and the IEEE 802.1s standard, or the Multiple Spanning Tree Protocol (MST). The following core SWITCH exam objective is covered in this chapter:

- Implement VLAN-based solution, given a network design and a set of requirements

This chapter will be divided into the following sections:

- Rapid Spanning Tree Protocol Overview
- The Modified RSTP BPDU
- RSTP BPDU Handling
- RSTP Port States
- RSTP Port Roles
- RSTP Rapid Transition
- RSTP Synchronization
- RSTP Integrated Enhancements
- RSTP Topology Changes
- 802.1D and 802.1w Interoperability
- RSTP with PVST+
- Configuring Rapid Spanning Tree Protocol
- Understanding Multiple Spanning Tree Protocol
- MST BPDU Format
- Understanding MST Region Functionality
- MST Spanning Tree Instances
- Implementing and Verifying MST

SWITCH Exam Objective	Chapter Section(s) Covered
Configure loop prevention for the VLAN-based solution	• Rapid Spanning Tree Protocol Overview • The Modified RSTP BPDU • RSTP BPDU Handling • RSTP Port States • RSTP Port Roles • RSTP Rapid Transition • RSTP Synchronization • RSTP Integrated Enhancements • RSTP Topology Changes • 802.1D and 802.1w Interoperability • RSTP with PVST+ • Configuring Rapid Spanning Tree Protocol • Understanding Multiple Spanning Tree Protocol • MST BPDU Format • Understanding MST Region Functionality • MST Spanning Tree Instances • Implementing and Verifying MST

Rapid Spanning Tree Protocol Overview

The IEEE 802.1D standard was designed at a time when the recovery of connectivity after an outage within a minute or so was considered adequate performance. In the IEEE 802.1D Spanning Tree Protocol (STP) , recovery takes around 50 seconds, which includes 20 seconds for the Max Age timer to expire and then an additional 30 seconds for the port to transition from the Blocking state to the Forwarding state.

As computer technology evolved, and networks became more critical, it became apparent that more rapid network convergence was required. Cisco addressed this requirement by developing some proprietary enhancements to STP that included Backbone Fast and Uplink Fast.

With the continued evolution of technology and the amalgamation of routing and switching capabilities on the same physical platform, it soon became apparent that switched network convergence lagged behind that of routing protocols, such as OSPF and EIGRP, which are able to provide an alternate path in less time. The 802.1w standard was designed to address this.

The IEEE 802.1w standard, or Rapid Spanning Tree Protocol (RSTP), significantly reduces the time taken for STP to converge when a link failure occurs. With RSTP, network failover to an alternate path or link can occur in a sub-second timeframe. RSTP is an extension of 802.1D that performs similar functions to Uplink Fast and Backbone Fast. RSTP performs better than traditional STP, with no additional configuration. Additionally, RSTP is backward compatible with the original IEEE 802.1D STP standard.

The Modified RSTP BPDU

The Bridge Protocol Data Unit (BPDU) format used by RSTP is similar to that of the 802.1D BPDU. This ensures backward compatibility between RSTP and 802.1D. However, in the RSTP BPDU, the Protocol Version Identifier and the BPDU Type fields are now set to a value of 2, instead of the value 0, which indicates an IEEE 802.1D BPDU. These differences between the original IEEE 802.1D standard and RSTP BPDU are illustrated below in Figure 4-1:

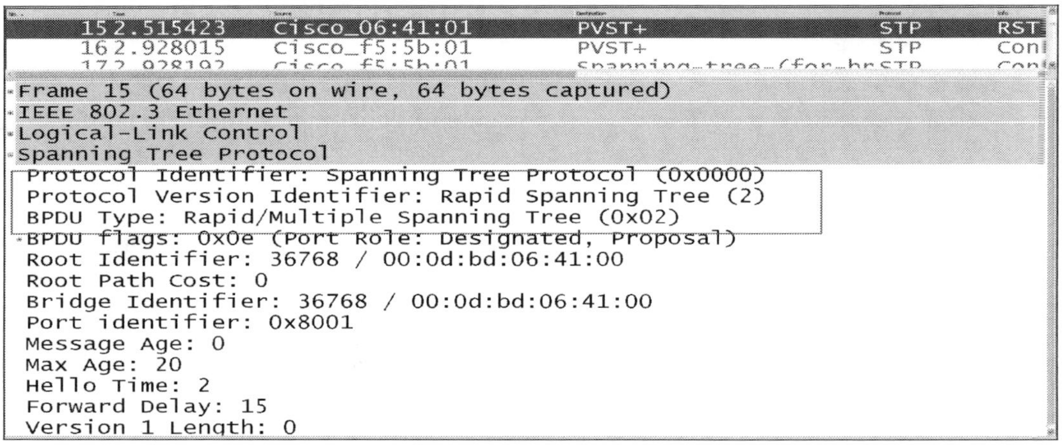

Fig. 4-1. RSTP BPDU Protocol Version Identifier and BPDU Type Fields

Only two Flags are defined in the IEEE 802.1D standard: the Topology Change (TC) and TC Acknowledgment (TCA) flags. Figure 4-2 below illustrates the layout of the Configuration BPDU Flag field as used in the original IEEE 802.1D standard:

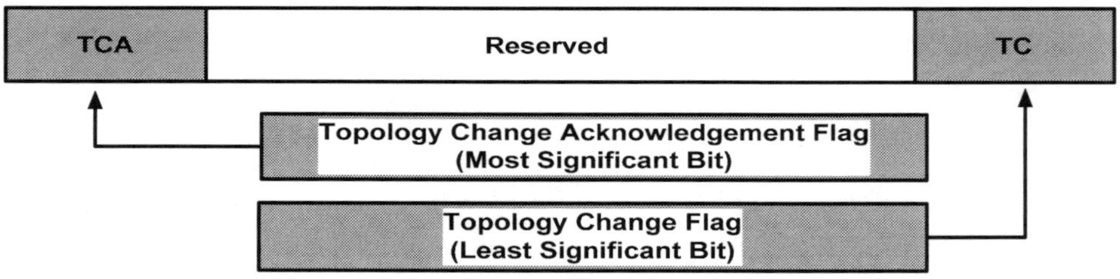

Fig. 4-2. 802.1D BPDU Flag Field Format

Unlike traditional Spanning Tree Protocol, RSTP uses all six bits of the Flag byte that remain in order to encode the role and the state of the port that originates the BPDU, as well as to handle the proposal and agreement mechanism. These fields are illustrated below in Figure 4-3:

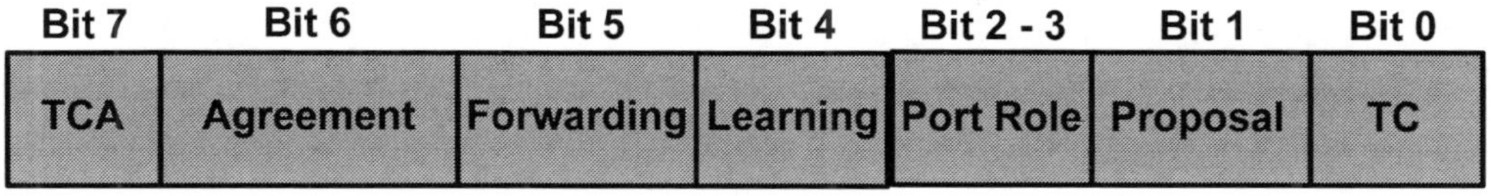

Fig. 4-3. 802.1w BPDU Flag Field Format

A detailed look at these additional fields that RSTP uses is provided below in Figure 4-4:

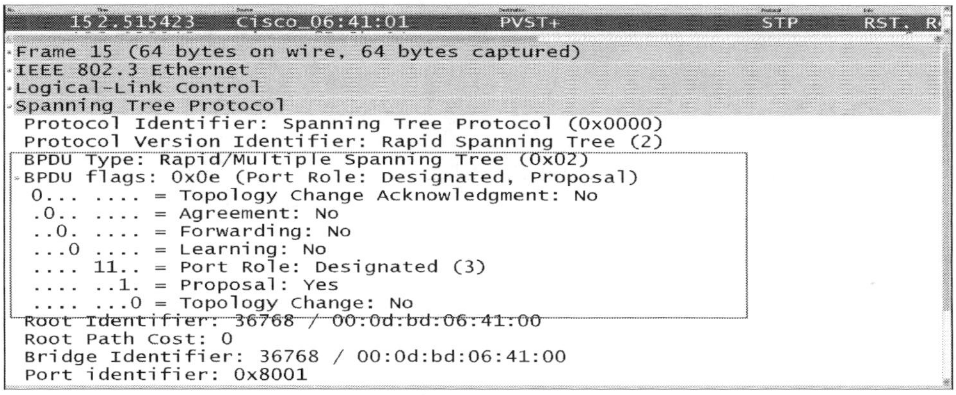

Fig. 4-4. A Detailed Look at the 802.1w BPDU Flag Field Format

The different fields that have been stated and are illustrated in the screenshot above will be described in detail as we progress through this chapter.

RSTP BPDU Handling

When using RSTP, BPDUs are sent every Hello Time interval (which is 2 seconds by default) and are not simply relayed anymore. With the 802.1D standard, Non-Root Bridges generate BPDUs when they receive one on the Root Port. This BPDU is then relayed to downstream switches. Topology Change Notification (TCN) BPDUs originated by a switch are also relayed up to the Root Bridge, which then propagates them to all other downstream switches.

With the 802.1w standard, switches now send a BPDU with their current information every Hello Time interval (2 seconds), even if they do not receive any BPDUs from the Root Bridge. In addition to this, port information is now invalidated (aged out) in 3 times the Hello Time interval (6 seconds) as opposed to using a Max Age timer-based invalidation (20 seconds), which is the default in the IEEE 802.1D standard.

Additionally, while the 802.1D standard used the Message Age in the calculation of the aging time for each port (i.e. Aging time = Max Age – Message Age), in RSTP the Message Age information is simply used as a hop count. The new method of handling BPDUs results in faster failure detection and faster convergence in RSTP networks. RSTP convergence will be described in detail later in this chapter.

RSTP Port States

Unlike the 802.1D standard, RSTP defines only three distinct port states for a port under STP control. Table 4-1 below lists these three states, compares them to the port states defined in the 802.1D standard, and provides a brief description of their behavior:

Table 4-1. Comparison between 802.1D and 802.1w Port States

802.1D State	802.1w State	Default Port Operational Status	Port in Active Topology?	Port Learning MAC Addresses?
Disabled	Discarding	Enabled	No	No
Blocking	Discarding	Enabled	No	No
Listening	Discarding	Enabled	Yes	No
Learning	Learning	Enabled	Yes	Yes
Forwarding	Forwarding	Enabled	Yes	Yes

As illustrated in Table 4-1, the 802.1D Disabled, Blocking, and Listening states are merged into a unique, single 802.1w Discarding state. In this state, all incoming frames are dropped and no MAC addresses are learned. RSTP also excludes the Listening state because unlike the 802.1D standard, RSTP can negotiate a state change without receiving any BPDUs.

RSTP Port Roles

Spanning Tree Protocol operates internally with port roles, which are determined by received BPDUs and on the ports via which those BPDUs are received. Ports change their STP port states based on their assigned roles.

For example, if a port that was previously a Non-Designated Port receives the best BPDU to the Root Bridge, and is elected Root Port, the STP topology is recalculated and the port transitions from a Blocking state to a Forwarding state. RSTP defines a set of port roles for Spanning Tree ports, and these port roles are defined as follows:

- Root Port (Forwarding state)
- Designated Port (Forwarding state)
- Alternate Port (Blocking state)
- Backup Port (Blocking state)

The Root Port is defined as the port that receives the best BPDU from the Root Bridge. This port provides the shortest path to the Root Bridge in terms of cost. The Root Port is always an active Forwarding port that points toward the STP Root Bridge. The Root Port is elected in the same manner for 802.1w as it is for 802.1D (i.e. based on the Path Cost value).

A Designated Port is an active forwarding port that points away from the Root Bridge and toward the edge of the network. This is the port sending the best BPDU on a segment. Again, the calculation of the Designated Port when using RTSP follows the same logic as that used when implementing traditional STP.

An Alternate Port is a non-forwarding (blocking) port that backs up a Root Port. In traditional STP, this would simply be referred to as a Blocking port. This port is blocked by BPDUs from a different bridge and therefore provides a redundant path to the Root Bridge. Figure 4-5 below illustrates an Alternate Port in an RSTP network:

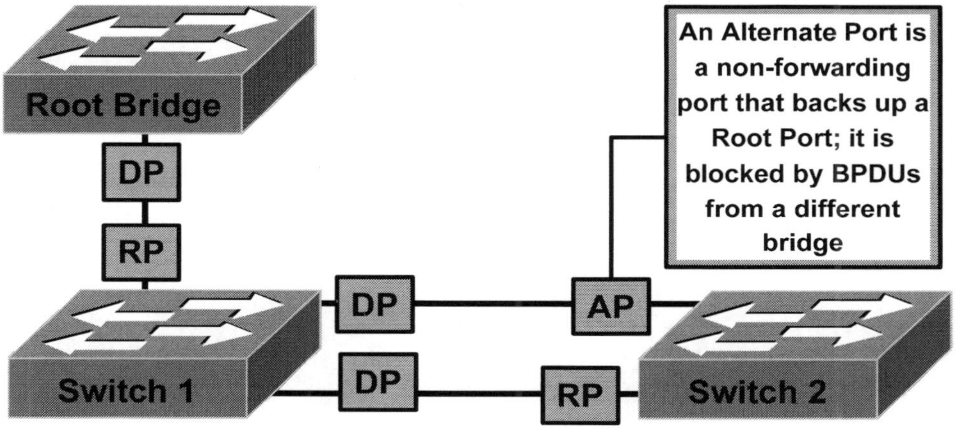

Fig. 4-5. The RSTP Alternate Port

A Backup Port receives better BPDUs from the same bridge rather than from a different bridge. Like an Alternate Port, a Backup Port is also a non-forwarding (blocking) port. Unlike the Alternate Port; however, a Backup Port backs up a Designated Port on the same segment, thus providing a redundant path to a network segment. Figure 4-6 illustrates a Backup Port in the Rapid Spanning Tree Protocol network:

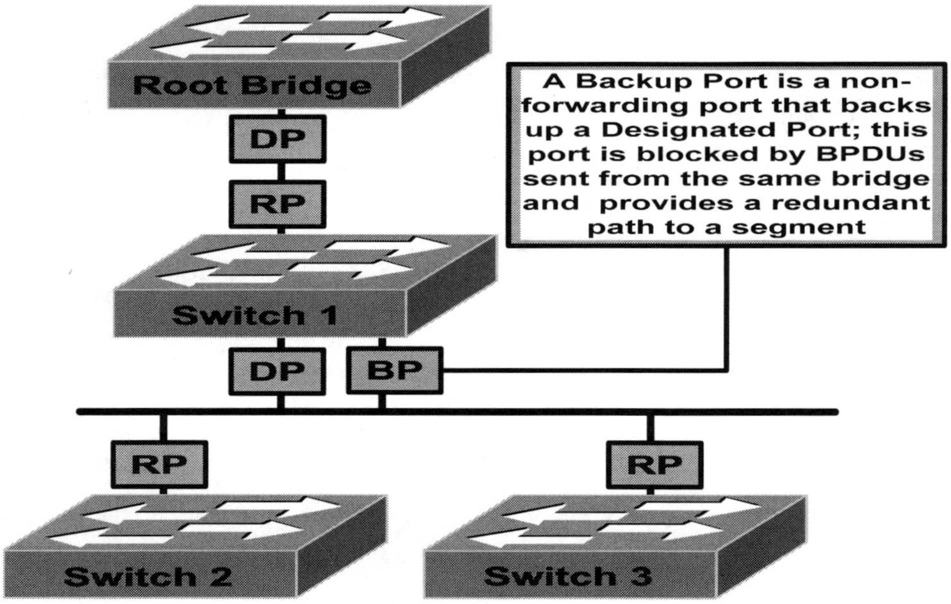

Fig. 4-6. The RSTP Backup Port

RSTP Rapid Transition

In traditional STP, convergence was very slow because of the default Forward Delay and Max Age timers. In order to speed up convergence in 802.1D networks, administrators manually decreased the default timers, allowing for faster transition into the Forwarding state.

The rapid transition feature allows RSTP to place ports into a Forwarding state without having to rely on any timer configuration, such as that used in traditional STP. In order to achieve fast convergence on a port, the protocol relies upon two new variables: edge ports and the link type. Both are described in detail in the following sub-sections.

Edge Ports

An edge port is simply a port at the edge of the Spanning Tree network. Edge ports are typically connected to network hosts and typically have the PortFast feature enabled. This feature is integrated into RSTP and so such ports are immediately placed into a Forwarding state. In the event that the port receives a BPDU, the edge port status is removed and the port becomes a normal Spanning Tree port type. The switch will also sends a TCN as this indicates that another switch is connected to the local switch and the Spanning Tree topology must be recalculated.

Link Type

Rapid Spanning Tree Protocol supports two different link types that are determined by the duplex setting on the specified port. These two link types are point-to-point and shared. By default, a port that operates in full-duplex mode is considered a point-to-point link, while a port that operates in half-duplex mode is considered a shared port. The following output shows an interface (port) that is operating in full-duplex mode:

```
VTP-Server-1#show interfaces fastethernet 0/23
FastEthernet0/23 is up, line protocol is up (connected)
  Hardware is Fast Ethernet, address is 000d.bd06.4117 (bia 000d.bd06.4117)
  MTU 1500 bytes, BW 100000 Kbit, DLY 1000 usec,
     reliability 255/255, txload 1/255, rxload 1/255
  Encapsulation ARPA, loopback not set
  Keepalive set (10 sec)
  Full-duplex, 100Mb/s
  input flow-control is off, output flow-control is off
  ARP type: ARPA, ARP Timeout 04:00:00
  Last input 01:03:21, output 00:00:00, output hang never
  Last clearing of 'show interface' counters never
  Input queue: 0/75/0/0 (size/max/drops/flushes); Total output drops: 0
  Queueing strategy: fifo
...
[Truncated Output]
```

The RSTP port type for this interface can be validated by using the `show spanning-tree interface [name] [detail]` command. This is illustrated in the following output:

```
VTP-Server-1#show spanning-tree interface fastethernet 0/23

Vlan             Role Sts Cost      Prio.Nbr Type
---------------- ---- --- --------- -------- --------------------------------
VLAN0010         Desg FWD 19        128.23   P2p
```

The detailed output of this command confirms the same, as seen in the following output:

```
VTP-Server-1#show spanning-tree interface fastethernet 0/23 detail
 Port 23 (FastEthernet0/23) of VLAN0010 is designated forwarding
...
[Truncated Output]
   Link type is point-to-point by default
   BPDU: sent 74, received 0
```

Despite the default settings, it is important to keep in mind that Cisco IOS software allows administrators to override this default selection via the `spanning-tree link-type [point-to-point|shared]` interface configuration command as illustrated in the following output:

```
VTP-Server-1#conf t
Enter configuration commands, one per line.  End with CNTL/Z.
VTP-Server-1(config)#interface fastethernet 0/23
VTP-Server-1(config-if)#spanning-tree link-type ?
  point-to-point  Consider the interface as point-to-point
  shared          Consider the interface as shared
```

RSTP considers half-duplex ports as ports that reside on shared medium, such as a network hub, and the segment contains two or more switches. Because of this, 802.1D traditional convergence is used on such ports, instead of the RSTP rapid transition mechanism.

REAL-WORLD OPERATION

It should be noted that most switches are connected using point-to-point links, and therefore it is very rare to ever see a shared link type. However, sometimes auto-negotiation may result in half-duplex operation for the point-to-point link between two switches. It is therefore good practice to always manually set the speed and duplex of FastEthernet links used for trunking in production networks; otherwise, this could affect RSTP operation and convergence.

RSTP Synchronization

RSTP uses an explicit handshake mechanism between switches via the use of the proposal and agreement flags. This handshake is performed as follows:

1. When a designated port is in a discarding or learning state, and only in either of these two states, it sets the proposal bit on the BPDUs it sends out. This is so that the switch can become a designated bridge for that segment. This proposal includes the BID and port role of the sending switch, which would be Switch 1. This is illustrated below in Figure 4-7:

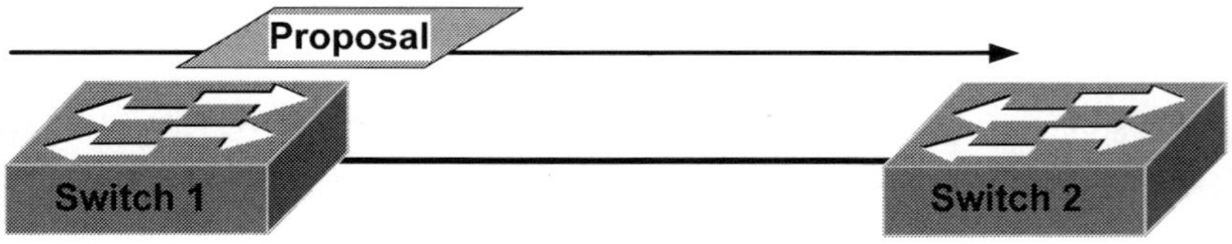

Fig. 4-7. The RSTP Proposal

Figure 4-8 below shows an RTSP BDPU with the proposal flag set:

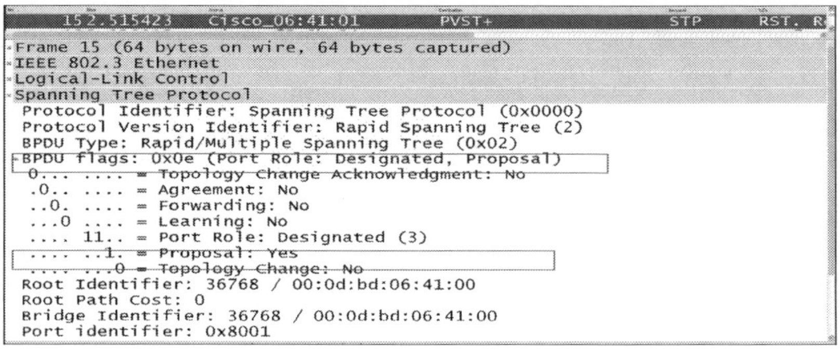

Fig. 4-8. The RSTP Proposal BPDU Format

2. Upon receiving the BPDU with the proposal flag set, the receiving switch (Switch 2) begins a sync to verify that all of its ports are in-sync with this new information. A port is in sync if it is either in a Blocking state or in an edge port. In other words, the sync mechanism places all other non-edge ports into the Blocking state and inspects the received BPDU with the proposal flag set to ensure that it does not conflict with the port roles on the local switch.

3. The receiving switch (Switch 2) places the port on which the BPDU with the proposal flag set was received into the Forwarding state and responds to the sender (Switch 1) with a BPDU with the agreement flag set. This is illustrated below in Figure 4-9:

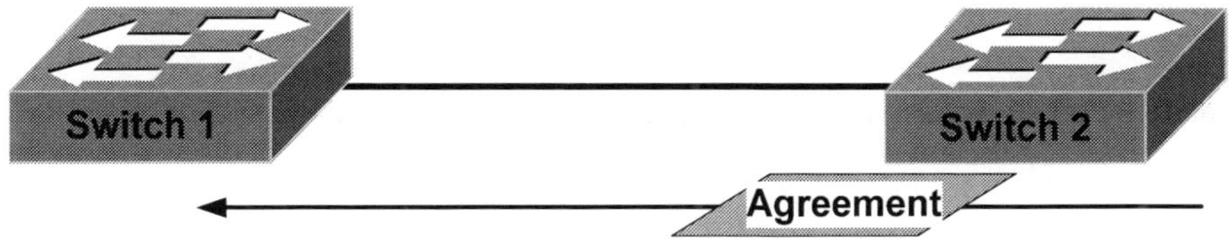

Fig. 4-9. The RSTP Agreement

4. When a BPDU with the agreement flag set is received by the switch that initially sent out the BPDU with the proposal flag set (Switch 1), it moves the designated port into the Forwarding state. Figure 4-10 below illustrates the port roles once the proposal and agreement exchange between the two switches is complete:

Fig. 4-10. RSTP Synchronization after the Proposal and Agreement Exchange

NOTE: It should be noted that if the switch port does not receive an agreement after it sends a proposal, it slowly transitions to the Forwarding state and falls back to traditional 802.1D operation. This typically happens when the neighboring switch does not understand RSTP BPDUs, or if its port is in the Blocking state.

Because of the fact that the proposal agreement mechanism is very fast, as it does not rely on any STP timers, these exchanges are propagated very quickly throughout the RSTP network, which allows for quick network convergence following a topology change.

Additionally, it is important to remember that the receiving switch must agree to the proposal prior to the port being placed into a Forwarding state. If the proposal is rejected, the receiving switch sends out its own proposal and the steps above are repeated.

Superior BPDUs and RSTP Synchronization

When running RSTP, if a port receives superior Root Bridge information, such as a lower Bridge ID, or a lower Path Cost than currently stored for the port, RSTP triggers a network reconfiguration. If the new port is selected as the new Root Port, then RSTP forces all the other ports to synchronize. If the BPDU received is an RSTP BPDU that has the proposal flag set, the switch sends a BPDU with the agreement flag set after all other ports have been synchronized.

However, if the BPDU is an 802.1D BPDU, the switch does not set the proposal flag. Instead, it defaults back to traditional STP operation and starts the Forward Delay timer for the port.

Finally, if the superior information received on the port causes the port to become a backup or alternate port, RSTP sets the port to the Blocking state but does not send the agreement message. Instead, the Designated Port continues sending BPDUs with the proposal flag set until the Forward Delay timer expires, at which time the port transitions to the Forwarding state.

Inferior BPDUs and RSTP Synchronization

If a Designated Port receives an inferior BPDU with a Designated Port role, it immediately replies with its own information in a proposal.

RSTP Integrated Enhancements

The Rapid Spanning Tree Protocol includes two integrated 802.1D enhancements, which are Uplink Fast and Backbone Fast. Although both of these enhancements are Cisco proprietary enhancement features designed for 802.1D, similar open-standard functionality has been integrated into RSTP based on these two features, allowing for faster convergence and failure restoration than traditional STP. These features will be described in this section.

RSTP Integrated Uplink Fast Functionality

Another form of immediate transition to the forwarding state included in RSTP is similar to the Uplink Fast Spanning Tree Protocol extension, with some notable differences. This operation is illustrated below in Figure 4-11:

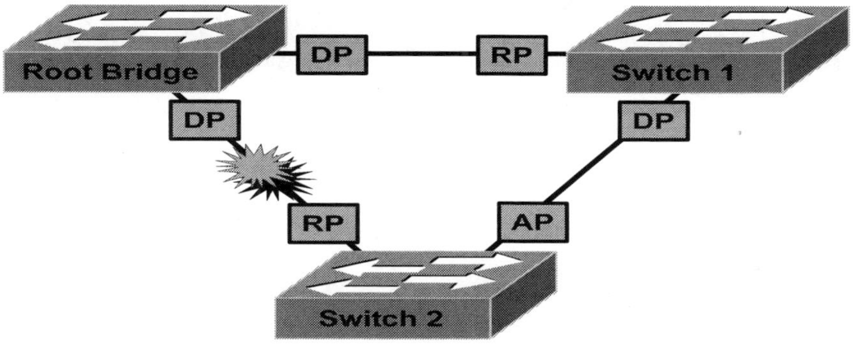

Fig. 4-11. RSTP Uplink Fast Operation

In Figure 4-11, Switch 2 has a Root Port and an Alternate Port, which backs up the Root Port based on the BPDUs received from Switch 1. By default, this port is in a Blocking state.

Upon detecting a direct Root link failure, Switch 2 is capable of immediately switching to a new Root Port by selecting the Alternate Port as the new Root Port.

The Alternate Port as the new Root Port generates a BPDU with the TC bit set. In traditional STP, when the Uplink Fast extension is employed, switches generate proxy Multicast frames, which appear to be originating from the MAC addresses currently in the switch CAM, so that upstream switches can relearn these addresses via the new path. In RTSP, the TC itself is used to advise the upstream devices of the new path for MAC addresses connected to it. This therefore negates the need for the generation of proxy Multicast frames by Switch 2, as upstream switches flush their CAM tables based on the BDPU with the TC bit set.

RSTP Integrated Backbone Fast Functionality

RSTP also includes a mechanism similar to the Backbone Fast enhancement used in traditional STP networks. This is illustrated in Figure 4-12 below:

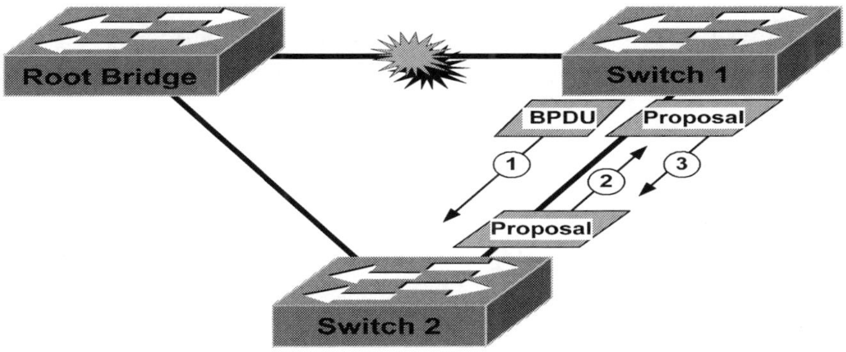

Fig. 4-12. RSTP Backbone Fast Operation

Referencing Figure 4-12, Switch 1 loses its Root link and sends a BPDU to Switch 2, claiming it is the Root Bridge. Upon receiving this inferior BPDU, Switch 2 immediately transitions the port on which the BPDU was received into a Designated Blocking state and sends a BDPU with the proposal flag set to Switch 1.

Switch 1 receives this proposal and transitions its port into the Forwarding state. Switch 1 then responds to Switch 2 with a BPDU that has the agreement flag set. Upon receipt of the agreement, Switch 2 transitions its port into the Forwarding state. Because the rapid transition is not STP timer-dependent, convergence is very fast, similar to Backbone Fast operation.

RSTP Topology Changes

The Topology Change (TC) detection and propagation mechanisms used in RSTP are different from those used in traditional STP. It is important to understand the differences between these two methods of TC detection and propagation.

IEEE 802.1D Topology Changes

Although described in detail in the previous chapter, this section summarizes the traditional Spanning Tree Protocol TC process. In traditional STP, when a port moves to the Forwarding or Blocking states, the switch originates a TCN BPDU. This TCN BPDU is sent out of the Root Port toward the Root Bridge.

The TCN BPDU is relayed until it reaches the Root Bridge. The Root Bridge then sets the TC flag in BPDUs that are then propagated to the rest of the STP domain, causing the MAC tables of domain switches to age out in 15 seconds.

IEEE 802.1w Topology Changes

In RSTP, a TC notification is sent when a non-edge port transitions to the Forwarding state, or as previously stated, when an edge port receives a BPDU. This differs from 802.1D where the transition of edge ports into the Forwarding state resulted in the origination and generation of BPDUs throughout the STP domain, even though the transition of such ports had no direct consequence to the STP domain as a whole.

Another significant difference between 802.1D and 802.1w is that RSTP no longer uses the specific TCN or TCA BPDUs, unless a legacy bridge needs to be notified. Interoperability between traditional STP and RSTP will be described later in this chapter. Instead, RSTP simply sends out BPDUs that have the TC bit set.

In RSTP, BPDUs with the TC bit set are sent out by the initiator and not just by the Root Bridge any more. The BPDUs are then propagated throughout the active topology by all neighboring switches. Figure 4-13 below shows an RSTP BPDU with the TC bit set:

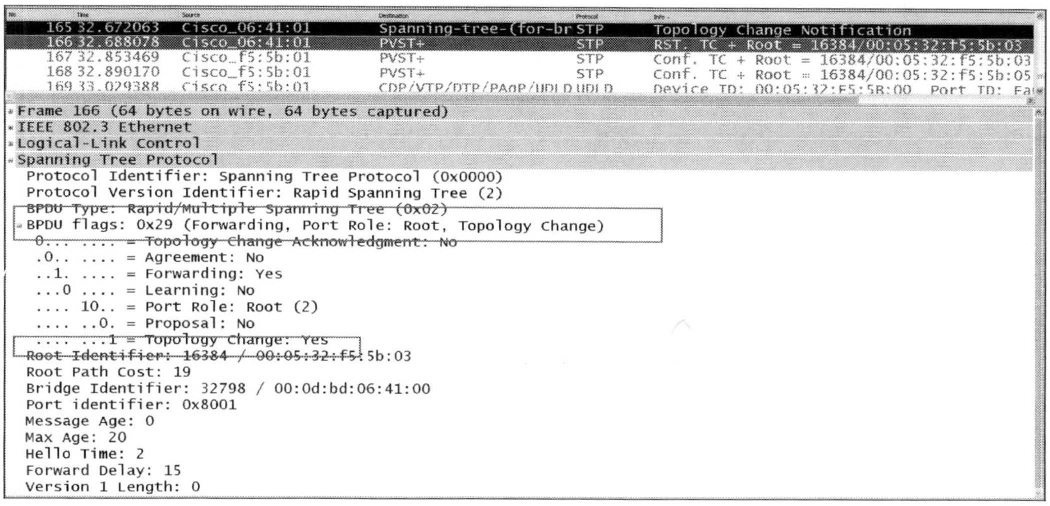

Fig. 4-13. RSTP BPDU with the TC Bit Set

When a switch running RSTP detects a topology change, it immediately sends BPDUs out of all non-edge ports with the TC bit set and begins the TC While timer, which is set to two times the Hello Time interval. The switch will continue to send these BPDUs out of these ports for the duration of the TC While timer.

This is because is no ACK used in RSTP, as would be the case in traditional Spanning Tree. In other words, RSTP BPDUs never have the TCA bit set. To prevent loops, the switch also flushes out MAC addresses that are known out of the ports on which the BPDUs are being sent.

When another switch running RSTP receives a BPDU with the TC bit set, it clears the MAC addresses learned on all its ports, except the one that receives the topology change. In addition, the switch also starts the TC While timer and sends BPDUs with TC set on all its designated ports and Root Port. This is continued throughout the entire RSTP domain.

802.1D and 802.1w Interoperability

RSTP is an IEEE standard and is therefore able to interoperate with traditional STP. However, it is important to realize that RSTP loses its ability to provide sub-second re-convergence when implemented in a network that also contains switches that are only 802.1D capable. This section describes the interaction of these two IEEE standards.

By default, 802.1D switches drop 802.1w BPDUs. This essentially means that in mixed 802.1D and 802.1w switched networks, 802.1D switches inevitably always end up initially sending BPDUs. In Figure 4-14 below, two switches, Switch 1 and Switch 2, reside in the same STP domain. Switch 1 is running RSTP and Switch 2 is running traditional STP.

Switch 1 sends out an RSTP BPDU and starts a Migration Delay timer, which is 3 seconds by default. The Migration Delay timer specifies the minimum time during which RSTP BPDUs are sent. As long as this timer continues to run, the port mode is locked and cannot be changed. In other words, the switch can only send out RSTP BPDUs. However, while this timer is running, the switch processes all BPDUs received on that port and ignores the protocol type.

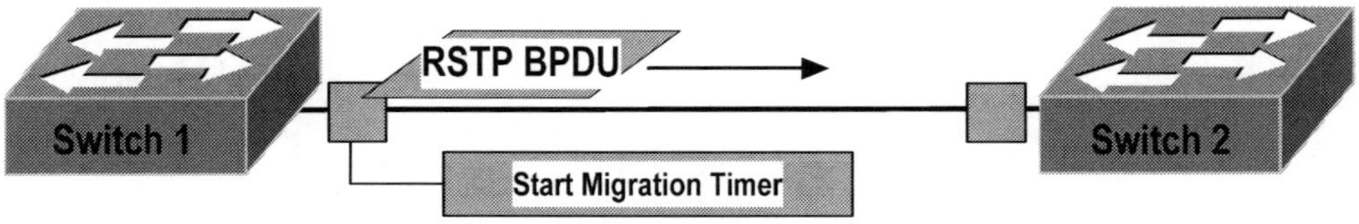

Fig. 4-14. RSTP BPDU Transmission and Migration Delay Timer Initialization

Switch 2 is running traditional STP, so when it receives the RSTP BPDU, it simply discards it. Switch 2 then sends out an STP BPDU and, assuming that the Migration Delay timer is still running on Switch 1, Switch 1 accepts and processes the received Spanning Tree BPDU. This is illustrated below in Figure 4-15:

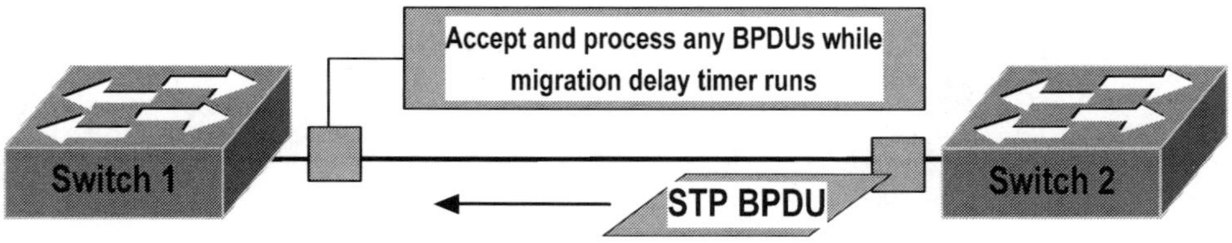

Fig. 4-15. RSTP BPDU Acceptance during Migration Delay Timer

Switch 1 receives the STP BPDU and, assuming that the Migration Delay timer has expired, adapts to the mode that corresponds to the next BPDU it receives, which is an 802.1D BPDU. Switch 1 then begins sending STP BPDUs and the switches begin to communicate using traditional STP.

This is illustrated below in Figure 4-16:

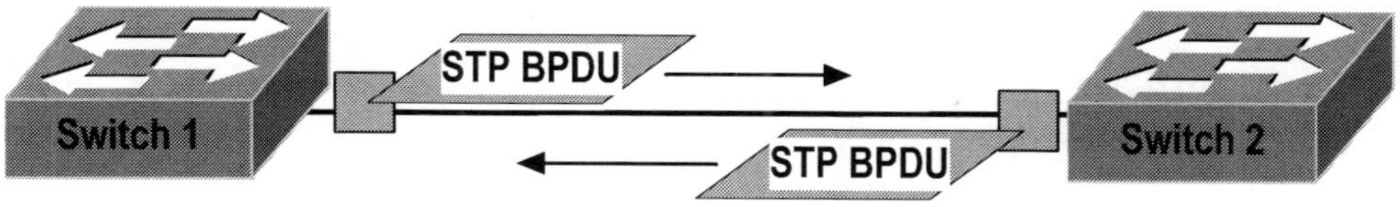

Fig. 4-16. RSTP Fallback to 802.1D Following Expiration of Migration Delay Timer

It is important to remember that when the port on Switch 1 is in 802.1D compatibility mode, it is also able to handle TCN BPDUs, as well as BPDUs with a TC or a TCA bit set. When an RSTP switch receives a TCN from an 802.1D switch, on a Designated Port, it replies with an 802.1D BPDU with the TCA bit set. However, if the TC While timer is active on a Root Port connected to an 802.1D switch and a BPDU with the TCA bit set is received, the TC While timer is reset.

RSTP with PVST+

Per VLAN Spanning Tree Plus (PVST+) allows for the definition of an individual STP instance per VLAN. Traditional or Normal PVST+ mode relies on the use of the older 802.1D STP for switched network convergence in the event of a link failure.

Rapid Per VLAN Spanning Tree Plus (R-PVST+) allows for the use of 802.1w with PVST+. This allows for the definition of an individual RSTP instance per VLAN, while providing for much faster convergence than would be attained with the traditional 802.1D STP. By default, when RSTP is enabled, R-PVST+ is enabled on the switch.

Configuring Rapid Spanning Tree Protocol

The only configuration command required to enable RSTP is the `spanning-tree mode rapid-pvst` global configuration command as illustrated in the following output:

```
VTP-Server-2#conf t
Enter configuration commands, one per line.  End with CNTL/Z.
VTP-Server-2(config)#spanning-tree mode rapid-pvst
VTP-Server-2(config)#exit
```

Once enabled, R-PVST+ configuration can be validated via the `show spanning-tree summary` command, the output of which is shown below :

```
VTP-Server-2#show spanning-tree summary
Switch is in rapid-pvst mode
Root bridge for: VLAN0050, VLAN0060, VLAN0070
```

```
EtherChannel misconfig guard is enabled
Extended system ID           is enabled
PortFast Default             is disabled
PortFast BPDU Guard Default  is disabled
PortFast BPDU Filter Default is disabled
LoopGuard Default            is disabled
UplinkFast                   is disabled
BackboneFast                 is disabled
PathCost method used         is short

Name                   Blocking Listening Learning Forwarding STP Active
---------------------- -------- --------- -------- ---------- ----------
VLAN0001               1        0         0        1          2
VLAN0050               0        0         0        2          2
VLAN0060               0        0         0        2          2
VLAN0070               0        0         0        2          2
---------------------- -------- --------- -------- ---------- ----------
4 vlans                1        0         0        7          8
```

NOTE: The `show spanning-tree bridge protocol` command may also be used to view the type of STP running on the switch, as shown in the following output:

```
VTP-Server-2#show spanning-tree bridge protocol
VLAN0001         rstp
VLAN0050         rstp
VLAN0060         rstp
VLAN0070         rstp
```

Understanding Multiple Spanning Tree Protocol

Traditional Spanning Tree Protocol, which is the IEEE 802.1D standard, supports two flavors of STP implementation, which are Common Spanning Tree Protocol (CST) and Per VLAN Spanning Tree Protocol Plus (PVST+).

CST, which is also referred to as 802.1Q, runs a single STP instance for all VLANs configured on the switch. The problem with running a single instance of STP is that any blocked link is unable to actively participate in the forwarding of data and thus the path becomes a wasted resource. This is illustrated below in Figure 4-17:

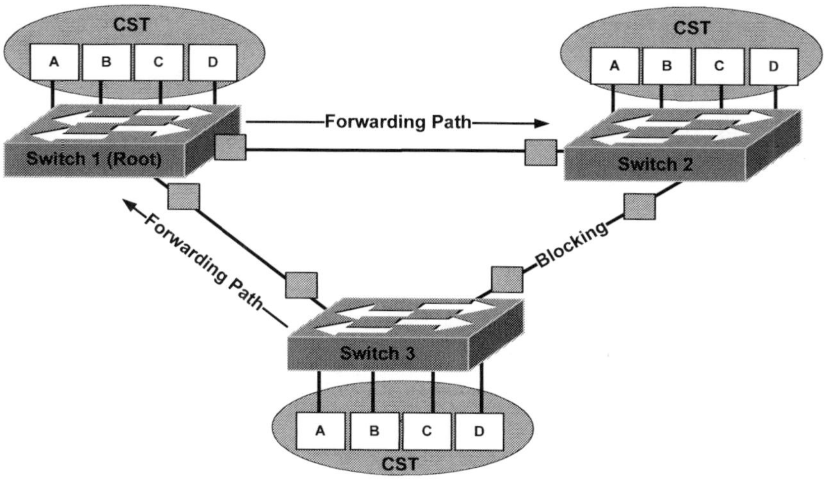

Fig. 4-17. Common STP Operation

In Figure 4-17, four VLANs—VLAN A, VLAN B, VLAN C, and VLAN D—are enabled and active within the STP domain. Assuming that CST is being used, a single STP instance is created for all VLANs. The advantage afforded by CST is that it reduces resource utilization (e.g. CPU) on the switches because only a single STP instance is running and active. The disadvantage with CST is that, assuming default STP behavior, the link between Switch 2 and Switch 3 becomes a wasted resource, as it is used only in the event that the primary link fails.

PVST+, on the other hand, allows for a single STP instance for each individual VLAN. On the plus side, this allows for flexible load balancing, as individual VLANs can be switched using different paths, based on STP topology. This is illustrated below in Figure 4-18:

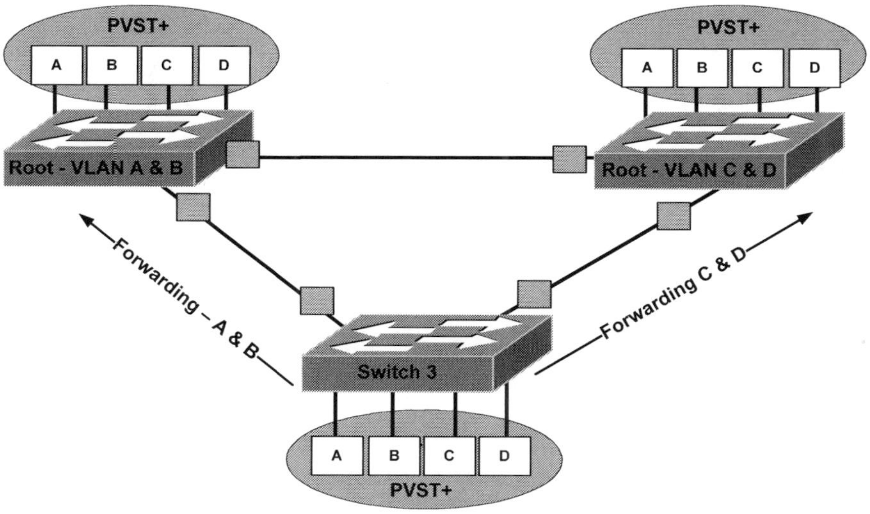

Fig.4-18. PVST+ Operation

In Figure 4-18, PVST+ is being used in the STP domain and one switch is configured as the Root Bridge for VLANs A and B, while another switch is configured as Root Bridge for VLANs C and D. This flexibility allows for load balancing from the perspective of Switch 3, as it can use both links to forward data for the respective VLANs.

The downside to PVST+ is that because each individual VLAN requires its own STP instance, if there are 4,000 VLANs, 4,000 STP instances are required. This is taxing on switch resources, such as CPU, and becomes an even greater issue in lower-end switch models.

Why MST?

Multiple Spanning Tree Protocol (MST), as defined in the IEEE 802.1s standard, provides the ability to group multiple VLANs into a single STP instance. Because multiple VLANs use a single instance, fewer switch resources, such as CPU and memory, are consumed.

Another advantage is that MST allows for flexible load balancing, as is possible with PVST+. Different instances, each supporting multiple VLANs, can be load balanced in a flexible yet efficient manner. These concepts are illustrated in Figure 4-19 below:

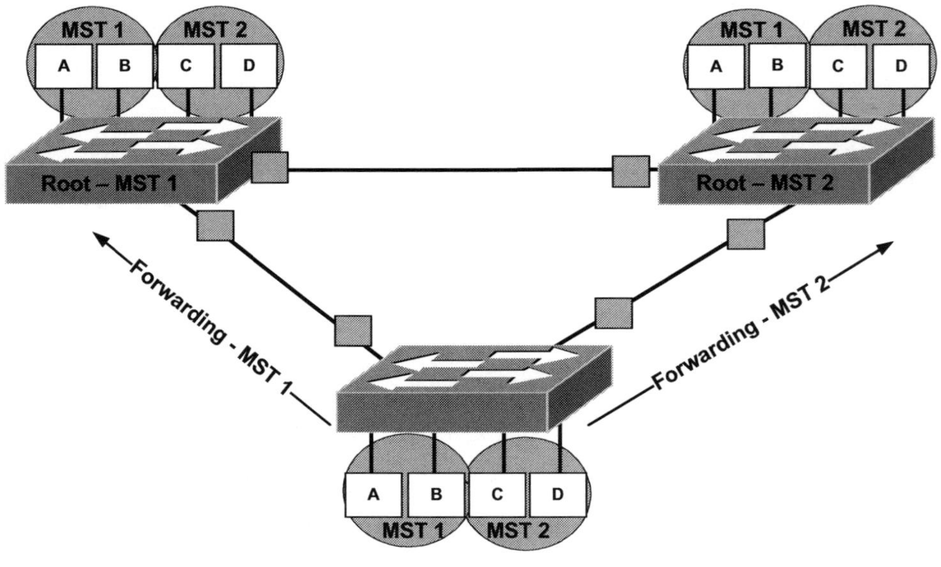

Fig. 4-19. MST Operation

In Figure 4-19, two MST instances are configured. Instance 1 carries VLANs A and B, while Instance 2 carries VLANs C and D. Two different switches are configured as the Root Bridge for the two different MST instances, which allows load balancing from Switch 3 in a manner similar to what is possible using PVST+. However, unlike PVST+, this time there are only two STP instances running instead of four if PVST+ was enabled.

MST uses RSTP for rapid convergence and appears as a single bridge to adjacent STP instances. The remainder of this chapter describes core MST elements and concludes with the configuration of MST on Cisco Catalyst switches.

MST BPDU Format

MST uses RSTP for rapid convergence; therefore, each switch must be capable of processing RSTP BPDUs in order to support MST. The MST BPDU format is similar to the BPDU used by Rapid Spanning Tree Protocol. The primary difference is that the Protocol Version Identifier Field is 3 and the MST BPDUs contain an MST extension field, the contents of which will be described in detail later in this chapter. Figure 4-20 illustrates these two different characteristics that are contained within the MST BPDU.

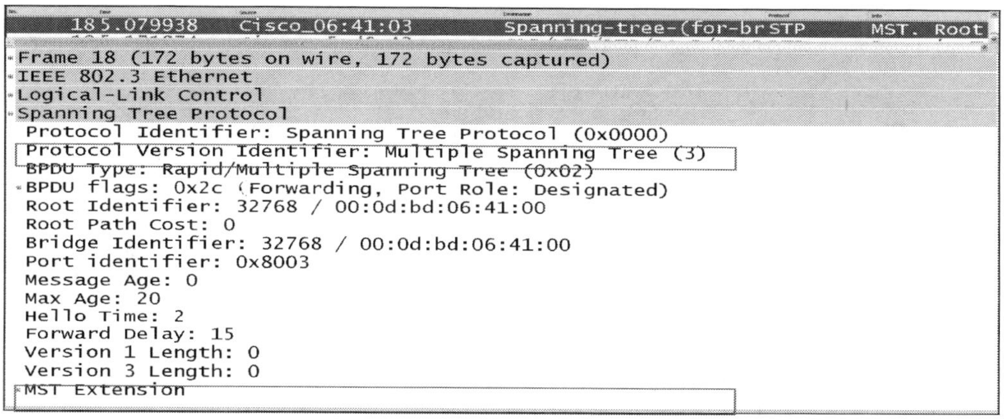

Fig. 4-20. MST BPDU Fields

The Flags field of the MST BPDU also uses the same fields (bit values) as those used in RSTP. This is illustrated below in Figure 4-21:

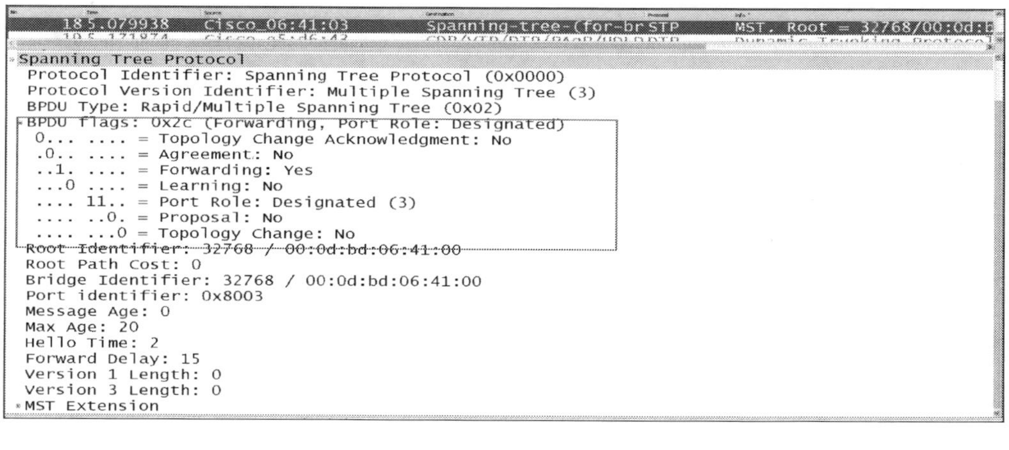

Fig. 4-21. MST BPDU Flags Field

Understanding MST Region Functionality

An MST Region defines a boundary within which a single instance of STP operates. MST employs the use of Regions because not all switches in the network might run or support MST; therefore, different kinds of STPs divide the network into STP regions.

A collection of interconnected switches that have the same MST configuration comprises an MST Region. MST configuration must be the same on all switches in the same MST region; this includes the following three user-configured parameters:

1. The MST Region Name (up to 32 bytes)
2. Configuration Revision Number (0 to 65,535)
3. VLAN-To-Instance Mapping (up to 4,096 entries)

Referencing the above, in order for two or more switches to be in the same MST Region, they must have the same VLAN-To-Instance Mapping, Configuration Revision Number, and MST Region Name. If not, the switches belong to two independent Regions. Figure 4-22 below illustrates multiple switches in a single MST Region:

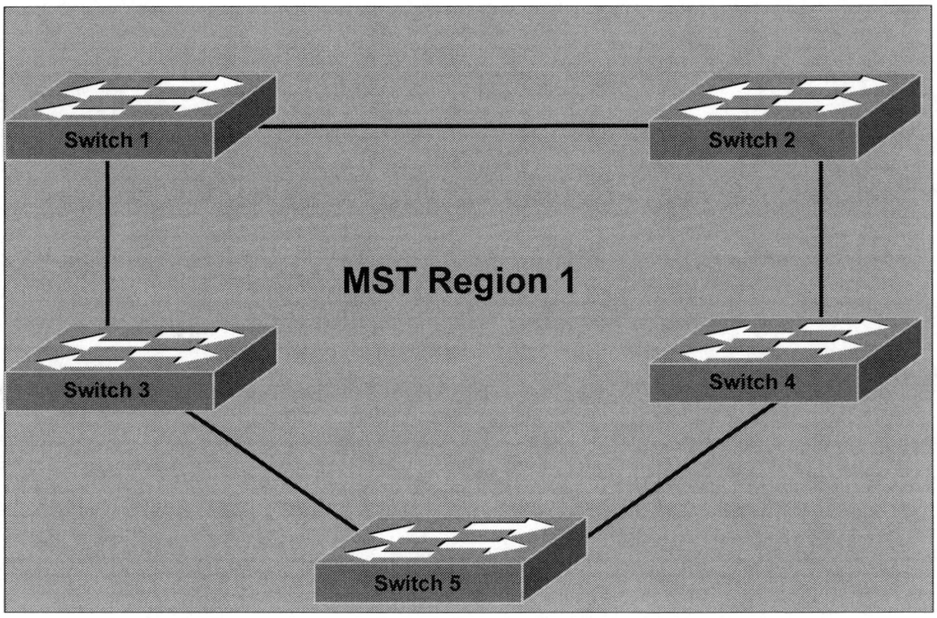

Fig.4-22. MST Region Illustration

Figure 4-23 below shows the MST BPDU MST Extension field. From the output below, we can determine that the Region name is MST-Region-A and that the MST Configuration Revision Number is 0. Additionally, two Multiple Instance STPs, Instance 1 and Instance 2, have also been configured within this Region:

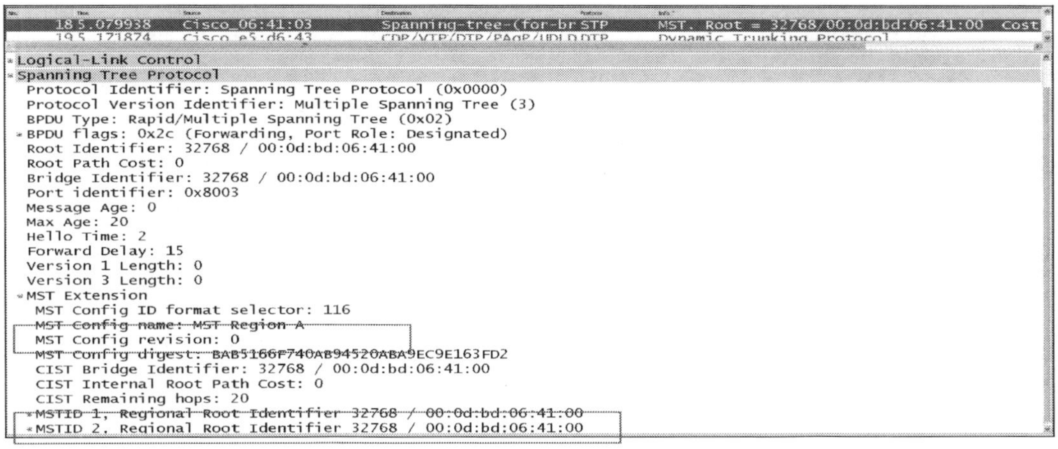

Fig. 4-23. MST BPDU Region, Configuration Revision, and Instance Fields

NOTE: Multiple Instance STP (MISTP) is described in detail later in this chapter.

While there is no limit to the number of MST Regions in a network, it is important to remember that a switch can belong to only a single MST Region.

MST Region Components

An MST Region consists of two different components: edge ports and boundary ports. An edge port is simply a port that connects to a non-bridging device, such as a network host. Additionally, a port that connects to a hub is also considered an edge port.

An MST boundary port connects an MST Region to a single STP Region running RSTP, 802.1D, or to another MST Region with a different MST configuration. An MST boundary port may also connect to a LAN, or to the Designated Switch that belongs to a single STP instance or another MST instance. These components are illustrated below in Figure 4-24:

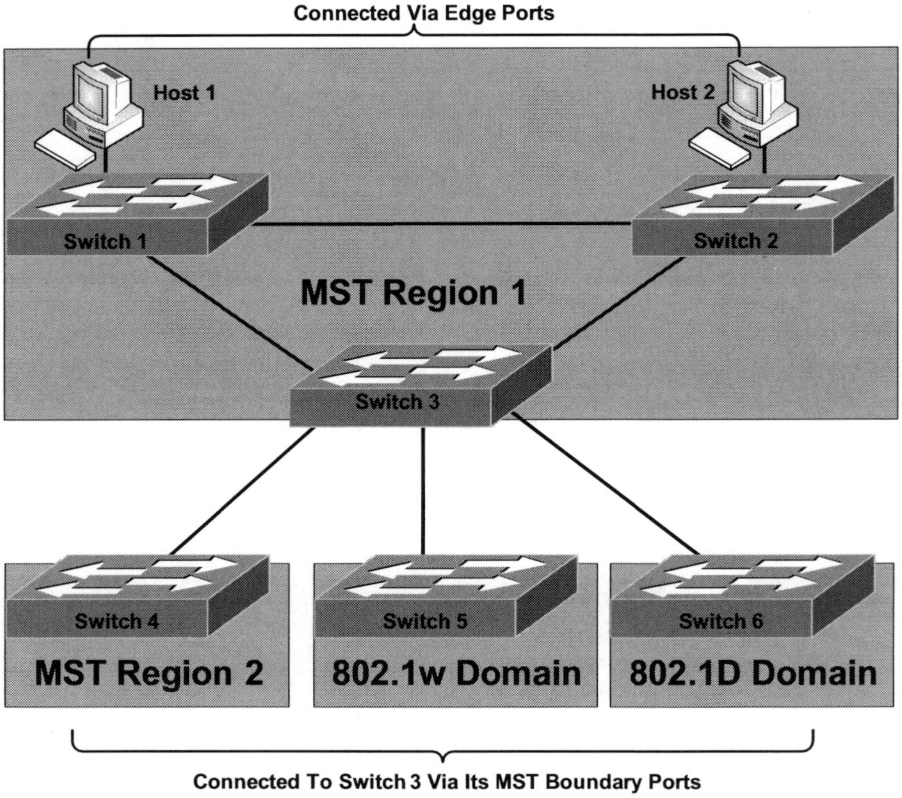

Fig. 4-24. MST Components

In Figure 4-24, Switch 1 is connected to Switches 4, 5, and 6, which are all Designated Bridges that belong to a different MST Region (Switch 4) or are running RSTP (Switch 5) or legacy STP (Switch 6). Network hosts (Host 1 and Host 2) connect to the edge MST ports.

NOTE: All other ports that do not fall into any one of these two categories are simply referred to as internal MST ports. They have no special name assigned to them.

MST Spanning Tree Instances

Unlike PVST+, in which all STP instances are independent, or CST, where only a single STP instance exists, MST establishes and maintains the following two types of STP instances:

- Internal Spanning Tree (IST)
- Multiple Instance Spanning Tree Protocol (MISTP)

These two instances are described in the following sub-sections.

Internal Spanning Tree (IST)

The MST Region sees the outside world via its Internal Spanning Tree (IST) interaction only; the IST presents the entire MST Region as a single virtual bridge to the outside world. Therefore, BPDUs are exchanged at the Region boundary only over the native VLAN of trunks, as if a single CST were in operation. IST is the only Instance that sends and receives BPDUs. All other STP instance information is contained in M-records, which are encapsulated within MST BPDUs. Because the MST BPDU carries information for all Instances, the number of BPDUs that need to be processed by a switch to support multiple Instances is significantly reduced. From a physical perspective, the MST Region looks as is illustrated below in Figure 4-25:

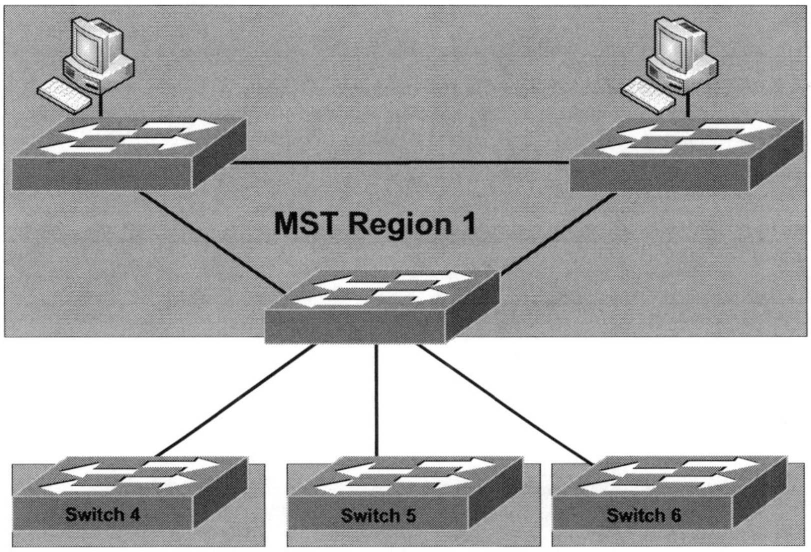

Fig. 4-25. MST Physical Topology

However, from a logical perspective, Switches 4, 5, and 6 would see the MST topology as illustrated below in Figure 4-26:

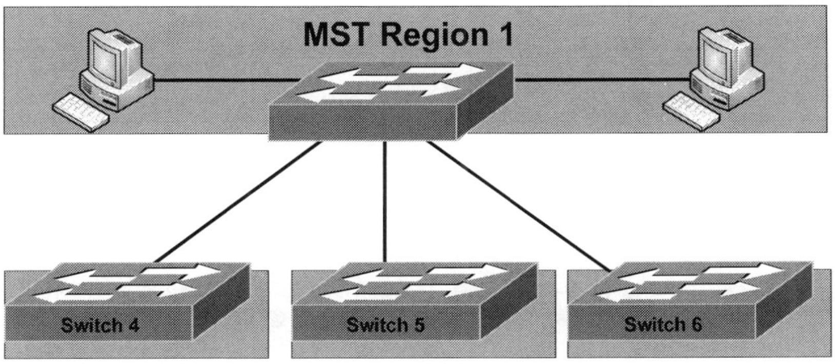

Fig. 4-26. MST Logical Topology

At the boundary of the MST Region, the Root Path Cost and Message Age values are incremented as though the BPDU had traversed only a single switch.

IST Master

The IST connects all the MST switches within a Region. When the IST converges, the Root of the IST becomes the IST master. The IST master election process is similar to traditional STP Root Bridge election. Initially, all switches in a region claim to be IST master. Switches within the Region then exchange BPDUs and eventually the switch within the region with the lowest BID and Path Cost to the CST Root is elected IST master.

If there is only a single Region, then the IST master will also be the CST Root. However, if the CST Root is outside of the Region, one of the MST switches at the boundary of the Region is selected as the IST master. In such cases, at the boundary, the MST switch adds the IST master ID as well as the IST master Path Cost to the BPDU, which is then propagated throughout the MST Region. This concept is illustrated in Figure 4-27 below:

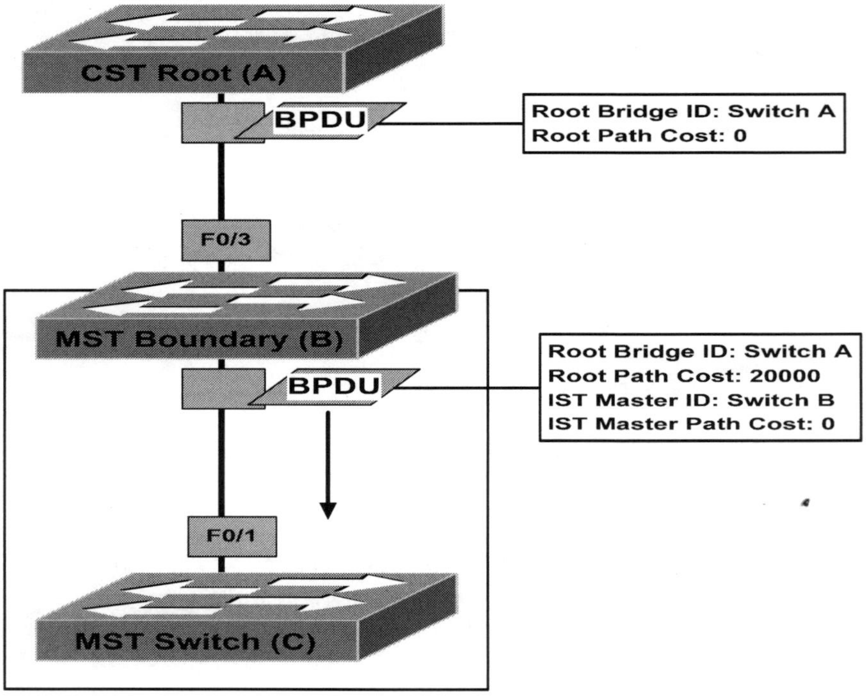

Fig. 4-27. IST Master Election and BPDU Propagation

In the following output, which shows the `show spanning-tree mst` command on Switch B (MST boundary), we can see that the Root Bridge is Switch A (CST Root). Switch A (CST Root) resides outside the MST Region; therefore, Switch B has been elected IST master for the Region:

```
Switch-B#show spanning-tree mst

###### MST00          vlans mapped:   1-9,11-19,21-29,31-39,41-49,51-59
                                       61-69,71-79,81-4094
Bridge        address 000d.bd06.4100  priority  32768 (32768 sysid 0)
Root          address 0005.32f5.5b00  priority  0     (0 sysid 0)
              port    Fa0/3           path cost 200000
IST master    this switch
Operational   hello time 2, forward delay 15, max age 20
Configured    hello time 2, forward delay 15, max age 20, max hops 20

Interface          Role Sts Cost      Prio.Nbr Type
----------------   ---- --- --------- -------- --------------------------------
Fa0/1              Desg FWD 200000    128.1    P2p
Fa0/2              Desg FWD 200000    128.2    P2p
Fa0/3              Root FWD 200000    128.3    P2p Bound(PVST)
...
[Truncated Output]
```

The BPDU that is propagated by Switch B to its downstream MST Region neighboring switches contains its own ID as the IST master and includes the Path Cost to this switch. This information is illustrated below in the following output:

```
Switch-C#show spanning-tree mst

###### MST00          vlans mapped:   1-9,11-19,21-29,31-39,41-49,51-59
                                       61-69,71-79,81-4094
Bridge        address 0014.a9e5.d640  priority  32768 (32768 sysid 0)
Root          address 0005.32f5.5b00  priority  0     (0 sysid 0)
              port    Fa0/1           path cost 200000
IST master    address 000d.bd06.4100  priority  32768 (32768 sysid 0)
                                      path cost 200000    rem hops 19
Operational   hello time 2, forward delay 15, max age 20
Configured    hello time 2, forward delay 15, max age 20, max hops 20

Interface          Role Sts Cost      Prio.Nbr Type
----------------   ---- --- --------- -------- --------------------------------
Fa0/1              Root FWD 200000    128.1    P2p
Fa0/2              Altn BLK 200000    128.2    P2p
...
[Truncated Output]
```

While going into any further detail on IST is beyond the requirements of the SWITCH exam, it is important to remember that the IST Root Path Cost is incremented as if the BPDU had traversed a single switch and that IST uses only the IST master ID and the IST master Path Cost.

Hop Count

IST and MISTP (which is described in the following sub-section) do not use the Message Age and Maximum Age information in the configuration BPDU to compute STP topology. Instead, they use the Path Cost to the Root and a hop-count mechanism, which is similar to the IP TTL mechanism.

The hop-count mechanism achieves the same result as the Message Age information and is used to determine when to trigger a reconfiguration. The Root Bridge of the Instance always sends a BPDU (or M-record) with a cost of 0 and the hop count set to the maximum value, which is 20 by default. When a switch receives this BPDU, it decrements the received remaining hop count by one and propagates this value as the remaining hop count in the BPDUs it generates. When the count reaches zero, the switch discards the BPDU and ages the information held for the port. The Message Age and Maximum Age information in the BPDU remain the same throughout the Region, and the same values are propagated by the Region's Designated Ports at the boundary.

Referencing the topology in Figure 4-27 above, we can see that Switch C, which is downstream from the IST master (Root) shows a hop count of 19 (20 – 1). This is illustrated in the following output:

```
Switch-C#show spanning-tree mst

###### MST00         vlans mapped:   1-9,11-19,21-29,31-39,41-49,51-59
                                      61-69,71-79,81-4094
Bridge        address 0014.a9e5.d640  priority  32768 (32768 sysid 0)
Root          address 0005.32f5.5b00  priority  0     (0 sysid 0)
              port    Fa0/1           path cost 200000
IST master    address 000d.bd06.4100  priority  32768 (32768 sysid 0)
                                      path cost 200000    rem hops 19
Operational   hello time 2, forward delay 15, max age 20
Configured    hello time 2, forward delay 15, max age 20, max hops 20

Interface        Role Sts Cost      Prio.Nbr Type
---------------- ---- --- --------- -------- --------------------------------
Fa0/1            Root FWD 200000    128.1    P2p
Fa0/2            Altn BLK 200000    128.2    P2p
...
[Truncated Output]
```

In the above output, notice that the Max Age timer is still at the default 20 seconds. When switch C sends this BPDU to a downstream switch, the hop count of 19 will be decremented by 1 and will show up on that switch with a value of 18.

REAL-WORLD OPERATION

Although adjusting the default hop count is beyond the scope of the SWITCH exam, the `spanning-tree mst max-hops [1-40]` global configuration command could be used to configure the maximum hops inside the Region and apply it to the IST and all MISTPs in that Region. This value can be changed (adjusted) to accommodate larger or smaller networks running MST. As always, it is important to be very careful when adjusting any default STP values in production networks.

Multiple Instance Spanning Tree Protocol (MISTP)

Multiple Instance Spanning Tree Protocol (MISTP) represents STP instances that exist only within the region. The IST presents the entire region as a single virtual bridge to the CST outside; however, MISTP does not interact directly with the CST outside of the region. Instead, MISTP conveys STP information for each instance within the Region.

Cisco Catalyst switches support up to 16 MISTPs on a single switch. These are identified by the numbers 0 through 15. However, it should be noted that MISTPs 0 through 64 are stated in the MST standard. MISTP 0 is mandatory and is always present; however, all other Instances are optional. Each MISTP typically maps to a VLAN or set of VLANs. By default, all VLANs are assigned to the IST, which is MISTP 0. This default behavior can be adjusted by manually configuring other MISTPs within the Region.

It is very important to know and remember that the IST exists on all ports within the MST Region, and only the IST has timer-related parameters. As previously stated, MST only sends one BPDU for all the Instances with one M-record per Instance. Additionally, unlike in traditional Spanning Tree Protocol, MST BPDUs are sent out of every port by all switches, versus being sent out only by the Designated Bridge. However, keep in mind, that MISTP does not send BPDUs out of boundary ports because only the IST interacts with external STP.

Implementing and Verifying MST

The configuration of MST is a straightforward task. The following steps are required to configure and implement MST:

1. Enter MST configuration mode by issuing the `spanning-tree mst configuration` configuration global configuration command on the switch.
2. Specify the MST Region name via the `name [name] MST` configuration mode command. The `[name]` string has a maximum length of 32 characters and is case sensitive.

3. Specify the Configuration Revision Number via the `revision [number]` MST configuration mode command. The range is 0 to 65,535.
4. Map VLANs to an MISTP via the `instance [number] id vlan [range]` MST configuration mode command. When specifying the Instance, the [number] range is 1 to 15 and for VLAN(s) mapped to an Instance, the [range] is 1 to 4,094.
5. Enable MST via the `spanning-tree mode mst` global configuration command. By default, RSTP is also enabled when this command is executed on the switch.

This section illustrates the configuration steps for MST on Cisco Catalyst Switches based on the switched network topology illustrated below in Figure 4-28:

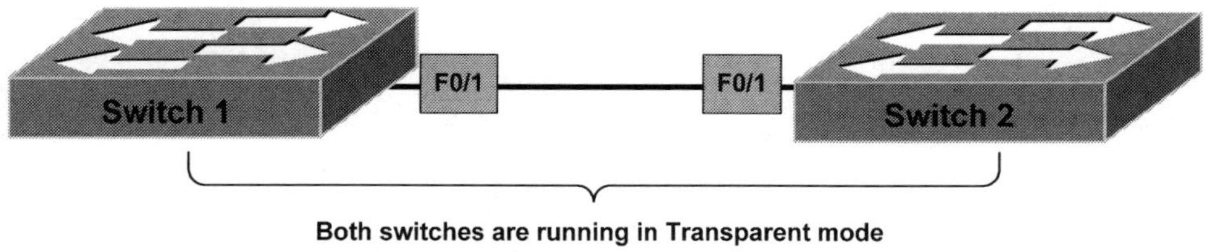

Fig. 4-28. MST Configuration Lab Topology

The VLANs configured on Switch 1 are illustrated below in the following output:

```
Switch-1#show vlan brief

VLAN Name                             Status    Ports
---- -------------------------------- --------- -------------------------------
1    default                          active    Fa0/3, Fa0/4, Fa0/5, Fa0/6
                                                Fa0/7, Fa0/8, Fa0/9, Fa0/10
                                                Fa0/11, Fa0/12, Fa0/13, Fa0/14
                                                Gi0/1, Gi0/2
10   Test-VLAN-10                     active    Fa0/24
20   Test-VLAN-20                     active
30   Test-VLAN-30                     active    Fa0/15, Fa0/16, Fa0/17, Fa0/18
                                                Fa0/19, Fa0/20, Fa0/21, Fa0/22
                                                Fa0/23
40   Test-VLAN-40                     active
50   Test-VLAN-50                     active
60   Test-VLAN-60                     active
70   Test-VLAN-70                     active
80   Test-VLAN-80                     active
1002 fddi-default                     active
1003 token-ring-default               active
1004 fddinet-default                  active
1005 trnet-default                    active
```

The VLANs configured on Switch 2 are illustrated below in the following output:

```
Switch-2#show vlan brief

VLAN Name                             Status    Ports
---- -------------------------------- --------- -------------------------------
1    default                          active    Fa0/3, Fa0/4, Fa0/5, Fa0/6
                                                Fa0/7, Fa0/8, Fa0/9, Fa0/10
                                                Fa0/11, Fa0/12, Fa0/13, Fa0/14
                                                Fa0/15, Fa0/16, Fa0/17, Fa0/18
                                                Fa0/19, Fa0/20, Fa0/21, Fa0/22
                                                Fa0/23, Fa0/24, Fa0/25, Fa0/26
                                                Fa0/27, Fa0/28, Fa0/29, Fa0/30
                                                Fa0/31, Fa0/32, Fa0/33, Fa0/34
                                                Fa0/35, Fa0/36, Fa0/37, Fa0/38
                                                Fa0/39, Fa0/40, Fa0/41, Fa0/42
                                                Fa0/43, Fa0/44, Fa0/45, Fa0/46
                                                Fa0/47, Fa0/48, Gi0/1, Gi0/2
10   Test-VLAN-10                     active
20   Test-VLAN-20                     active
30   Test-VLAN-30                     active
40   Test-VLAN-40                     active
50   Test-VLAN-50                     active
60   Test-VLAN-60                     active
70   Test-VLAN-70                     active
80   Test-VLAN-80                     active

VLAN Name                             Status    Ports
---- -------------------------------- --------- -------------------------------
1002 fddi-default                     act/unsup
1003 token-ring-default               act/unsup
1004 fddinet-default                  act/unsup
1005 trnet-default                    act/unsup
```

MST will be configured on both switches as follows:

- The MST Region Name will be SWITCH-Exam-MST-Region
- The Configuration Revision Number will be 0
- VLANs 10, 20, 30, and 40 will be mapped to MST Instance # 1
- VLANs 50, 60, 70, and 80 will be mapped to MST Instance # 2

The following output illustrates how to configure MST on Switch 1 based on the guidelines above:

```
Switch-1#conf t
Enter configuration commands, one per line.  End with CNTL/Z.
Switch-1(config)#spanning-tree mst configuration
Switch-1(config-mst)#name SWITCH-Exam-MST-Region
Switch-1(config-mst)#revision 0
Switch-1(config-mst)#instance 1 vlan 10, 20, 30, 40
Switch-1(config-mst)#instance 2 vlan 50, 60, 70, 80
Switch-1(config-mst)#exit
Switch-1(config)#spanning-tree mode mst
Switch-1(config)#exit
```

The following output illustrates how to configure MST on Switch 2 based on the guidelines above:

```
Switch-2#conf t
Enter configuration commands, one per line.  End with CNTL/Z.
Switch-2(config)#spanning-tree mst configuration
Switch-2(config-mst)#name SWITCH-Exam-MST-Region
Switch-2(config-mst)#revision 0
Switch-2(config-mst)#instance 1 vlan 10, 20, 30, 40
Switch-2(config-mst)#instance 2 vlan 50, 60, 70, 80
Switch-2(config-mst)#exit
Switch-2(config)#spanning-tree mode mst
Switch-2(config)#exit
```

The initial (first) step in verifying MST configuration is to issue the `show spanning-tree mst configuration` command. This command prints the Region Name, Configuration Revision Number, and the default MISTP (IST; Instance 0), as well as any manually configured Instances. This information is illustrated below in the following output:

```
Switch-1#show spanning-tree mst configuration
Name       [SWITCH-Exam-MST-Region]
Revision   0
Instance   Vlans mapped
--------   ----------------------------------------------------------------
0          1-9,11-19,21-29,31-39,41-49,51-59,61-69,71-79,81-4094
1          10,20,30,40
2          50,60,70,80
---------------------------------------------------------------------------
```

In the output above, any VLAN not explicitly mapped to an MISTP is automatically mapped to Instance 0 (CST). This is the default operation of MST.

REAL WORLD OPERATION

When implementing MST in production networks, it is always considered good practice to verify the changes before committing them to memory. This is performed using the `show [current|pending]` MST configuration mode commands.

NOTE: Even though you are in configuration command, you do not need to type in the `do` keyword to execute these show commands.

The show current MST configuration command shows the current MST configuration:

```
Switch-1(config)#spanning-tree mst configuration
Switch-1(config-mst)#show current
Current MST configuration
Name      [MST-Region-A]
```

```
Revision  0
Instance  Vlans mapped
--------  ---------------------------------------------------------------
0         1-9,11-19,21-29,31-39,41-49,51-59,61-69,71-79,81-4094
1         10,20,30,40
2         50,60,70,80
---------------------------------------------------------------------------
```

In the output above, two MSTIs are configured (MSTI 1 and MSTI 2) and are current active. The `show pending` configuration is used to view additional changes, which are not yet active and have yet to be committed, when configuring MST. The output that follows shows how to add three additional MSTIs and view the pending changes in Cisco IOS software:

```
Switch-1(config)#spanning-tree mst configuration
Switch-1(config-mst)#name MST-Region-A
Switch-1(config-mst)#instance 3 vlan 93
Switch-1(config-mst)#instance 4 vlan 94
Switch-1(config-mst)#instance 5 vlan 95
Switch-1(config-mst)#show pending
Pending MST configuration
Name      [MST-Region-A]
Revision  0
Instance  Vlans mapped
--------  ---------------------------------------------------------------
0         1-9,11-19,21-29,31-39,41-49,51-59,61-69,71-79,81-90,92,96-4094
1         10,20,30,40
2         50,60,70,80
3         91,93
4         94
5         95
---------------------------------------------------------------------------
```

Unfortunately, there is no way to differentiate between the current and pending configuration; therefore, you should always use the `show current` command to view what has already been implemented and then diff that against the `show pending` command to see the additional configuration that will be in place once your exit configuration mode. Make this a habit when implementing MST in production (or even lab) environments.

Additional MST Configuration Commands

All MST configuration commands are initiated by issuing the `spanning-tree mst` global configuration command. The following output shows the options available with this command:

```
Switch-1(config)#spanning-tree mst ?
  WORD            MST instance range, example: 0-3,5,7-9
  configuration   Enter MST configuration submode
  forward-time    Set the forward delay for the spanning tree
  hello-time      Set the hello interval for the spanning tree
  max-age         Set the max age interval for the spanning tree
  max-hops        Set the max hops value for the spanning tree
```

The same configuration logic used when configuring STP or RSTP is also applicable when configuring MST. For example, to configure a switch as the Root for an MISTP, the `spanning-tree mst [instance] [root|priority]` command is used. This is illustrated below in the following output:

```
Switch-1#conf t
Enter configuration commands, one per line.  End with CNTL/Z.
Switch-1(config)#spanning-tree mst 1 root primary
Switch-1(config)#spanning-tree mst 2 priority 4096
Switch-1(config)#exit
```

Verifying MST Operation

The `show spanning-tree mst` command is used to validate MST operation. The options available with this command are illustrated in the following output:

```
Switch-1#show spanning-tree mst ?
  WORD           MST instance list, example 0,2-4,6,8-12
  configuration  MST current region configuration
  detail         show detailed information
  interface      Spanning tree interface status and configuration
  |              Output modifiers
  <cr>
```

The `show spanning-tree mst [word]` command prints out information pertaining to a specific MISTP. The following output illustrates how to view information on Instance 1 using the `show spanning-tree mst [word]` command:

```
Switch-1#show spanning-tree mst 1

###### MST01         vlans mapped:   10,20,30,40
Bridge       address 000d.bd06.4100  priority  32769 (32768 sysid 1)
Root         this switch for MST01

Interface         Role Sts Cost      Prio.Nbr Type
----------------- ---- --- --------- -------- --------------------------------
Fa0/1             Desg FWD 200000    128.1    P2p
Fa0/2             Desg FWD 200000    128.2    P2p
```

This command can also be used with the `[detail]` and `[interface]` keywords, which print out detailed information or information pertaining to a specific interface, respectively. The following output shows the information printed by the `show spanning-tree mst [word] detail` command, which includes the number of M-records sent and received (in bold text):

```
Switch-1#show spanning-tree mst 1 detail

###### MST01          vlans mapped:   10,20,30,40
Bridge       address 000d.bd06.4100  priority  32769 (32768 sysid 1)
Root         this switch for MST01

FastEthernet0/1 of MST01 is designated forwarding
Port info            port id          128.1  priority    128  cost      200000
Designated root      address 000d.bd06.4100  priority  32769  cost           0
Designated bridge    address 000d.bd06.4100  priority  32769  port id    128.1
Timers: message expires in 0 sec, forward delay 0, forward transitions 1
Bpdus (MRecords) sent 699, received 4

FastEthernet0/2 of MST01 is designated forwarding
Port info            port id          128.2  priority    128  cost      200000
Designated root      address 000d.bd06.4100  priority  32769  cost           0
Designated bridge    address 000d.bd06.4100  priority  32769  port id    128.2
Timers: message expires in 0 sec, forward delay 0, forward transitions 1
Bpdus (MRecords) sent 700, received 1
```

NOTE: Keep in mind that you will not see M-records for Instance 0. This means that the output for this same command, if used to view information about Instance 0, would show only BPDUs sent and received, as illustrated in the following output:

```
Switch-1#show spanning-tree mst 0 detail

###### MST00          vlans mapped:   1-9,11-19,21-29,31-39,41-49,51-59
                                        61-69,71-79,81-4094
Bridge       address 000d.bd06.4100  priority  32768 (32768 sysid 0)
Root         this switch for CST and IST
Configured   hello time 2, forward delay 15, max age 20, max hops 20

FastEthernet0/1 of MST00 is designated forwarding
Port info              port id          128.1  priority    128  cost    200000
Designated root        address 000d.bd06.4100  priority  32768  cost         0
Designated ist master  address 000d.bd06.4100  priority  32768  cost         0
Designated bridge      address 000d.bd06.4100  priority  32768  port id  128.1
Timers: message expires in 0 sec, forward delay 0, forward transitions 1
Bpdus sent 781, received 86

FastEthernet0/2 of MST00 is designated forwarding
Port info              port id          128.2  priority    128  cost    200000
Designated root        address 000d.bd06.4100  priority  32768  cost         0
Designated ist master  address 000d.bd06.4100  priority  32768  cost         0
Designated bridge      address 000d.bd06.4100  priority  32768  port id  128.2
Timers: message expires in 0 sec, forward delay 0, forward transitions 1
Bpdus sent 782, received 43
```

The show spanning-tree mst interface [name] [detail] command prints information that pertains to the specified MST interface. This includes information on whether the port is an edge, boundary, or simply an internal port. This command also prints information about several STP features, such as BPDU Guard, Port Cost, Port ID, and BPDUs sent (Instance 0), or M-records sent and received (all other Instances). This is illustrated in the following output:

```
Switch-1#show spanning-tree mst interface fastethernet 0/1 detail
Edge port: no              (default)          port guard : none          (default)
Link type: point-to-point (auto)              bpdu filter: disable       (default)
Boundary : internal                           bpdu guard : disable       (default)

FastEthernet0/1 of MST00 is designated forwarding
Vlans mapped to MST00 1-9,11-19,21-29,31-39,41-49,51-59,61-69,71-79,81-4094
Port info             port id           128.1  priority    128  cost     200000
Designated root       address 000d.bd06.4100  priority  32768  cost          0
Designated ist master address 000d.bd06.4100  priority  32768  cost          0
Designated bridge     address 000d.bd06.4100  priority  32768  port id  128.1
Timers: message expires in 0 sec, forward delay 0, forward transitions 1
Bpdus sent 1026, received 86

FastEthernet0/1 of MST01 is designated forwarding
Vlans mapped to MST01 10,20,30,40
Port info             port id           128.1  priority    128  cost     200000
Designated root       address 000d.bd06.4100  priority  32769  cost          0
Designated bridge     address 000d.bd06.4100  priority  32769  port id  128.1
Timers: message expires in 0 sec, forward delay 0, forward transitions 1
Bpdus (MRecords) sent 1026, received 4

FastEthernet0/1 of MST02 is designated forwarding
Vlans mapped to MST02 50,60,70,80
Port info             port id           128.1  priority    128  cost     200000
Designated root       address 000d.bd06.4100  priority  32770  cost          0
Designated bridge     address 000d.bd06.4100  priority  32770  port id  128.1
Timers: message expires in 0 sec, forward delay 0, forward transitions 1
Bpdus (MRecords) sent 1027, received 4
```

Debugging MST

While debugging should always be considered a last-resort option, it is still important that you are familiar with the commands available to debug MST operation. In Cisco IOS, MST debugging is enabled via the debug spanning-tree mstp command. The options available with this command are printed in the following output:

```
Switch-1#debug spanning-tree mstp ?
  all            All MSTP Switch debugging messages
  boundary       boundary flag changes
  bpdu-rx        Received BPDUs
  bpdu-tx        Transmitted BPDUs
```

```
errors        MST Protocol errors
flush         Port flushing mechanism
init          MSTP Data Structures initializations
migration     protocol migration state machine
pm            MST Port manager debugging
proposals     designated<-->root handshakes
region        Region sync between SP and RP
roles         MST Protocol roles
sanity_check  Received BPDU sanity check messages
sync          Port sync
tc            Topology change notification
timers        MSTP timers start/stop/expire events
```

NOTE: Troubleshooting and debugging advanced STP will be covered in detail in the TSHOOT certification exam. It is not a requirement of the SWITCH exam and will not be described in any greater detail in this chapter or for the remainder of this guide.

Chapter Summary

The following section is a summary of the major points you should be aware of in this chapter.

Rapid Spanning Tree Protocol Overview

- RSTP significantly reduces the time taken for STP to converge when a link failure occurs
- With RSTP, failover to an alternate path or link can occur in the sub second timeframe
- RSTP is an extension of 802.1D
- RSTP performs better that the 802.1D with no additional configuration

The Modified RSTP BPDU

- The BPDU format used by RSTP is similar to that of the 802.1D BPDU
- In the RSTP BPDU, the Protocol Version ID and the BPDU Type fields are now set to 2
- Only 2 Flags are defined in the IEEE 802.1D standard
- RSTP uses all 6 bits of the Flag byte that remain to encode the role and state of the port

RSTP BPDU Handling

- RSTP BPDUs are sent every Hello Time (2 seconds) and are not simply relayed anymore
- Switches send BPDUs even if they do not receive any BPDUs from the Root Bridge
- Port information is now invalidated in 3 times the Hello Time interval (which is 6 seconds)
- In RSTP the Message Age information is simply used as a hop count

RSTP Port States

- RSTP defines only three distinct port states for a port under STP control
- These port states and their characteristics are listed in the following table:

802.1D State	802.1w State	Default Port Operational Status	Port in Active Topology?	Port Learning MAC Addresses?
Disabled	Discarding	Enabled	No	No
Blocking	Discarding	Enabled	No	No
Listening	Discarding	Enabled	Yes	No
Learning	Learning	Enabled	Yes	Yes
Forwarding	Forwarding	Enabled	Yes	Yes

- 802.1D Disabled, Blocking, and Listening states are merged into an 802.1w Discarding state
- RSTP also excludes the Listening state

RSTP Port Roles

- Spanning Tree Protocol operates internally with port roles
- Port roles are determined by received BPDUs and on the ports those BPDUs are received
- Ports change their Spanning Tree Protocol port states based on their assigned roles
- RSTP defines a set of port roles for Spanning Tree ports, which includes the following roles:
    1. Root Port (Forwarding state)
    2. Designated Port (Forwarding state)
    3. Alternate Port (Blocking state)
    4. Backup Port (Blocking state)

- The Root Port is defined as the port that receives the best BPDU from the Root Bridge
- A Designated Port is an active forwarding port that points away from the Root Bridge
- An Alternate Port is a non-forwarding (blocking) port that backs up a Root Port
- A Backup Port is a non-forwarding (blocking) port that backs up the Designated Port

RSTP Rapid Transition

- Rapid transition places ports into a Forwarding state without having to rely on timers
- Rapid transition is based on edge ports and the link type
- An edge port is simply a port at the edge of the Spanning Tree network
- By default, a port that operates in full-duplex mode is considered a point-to-point link
- A port that operates in half-duplex mode is considered a shared port

RSTP Synchronization

- RSTP uses an explicit handshake mechanism between switches RSTP switches
- RSTP switches exchange BPDUs with the proposal and agreement flags
- If a switch receives no response to its proposal, it falls back to 802.1D
- The receiving switch must agree to the proposal before the port begins Forwarding

RSTP Integrated Enhancements

- RSTP includes several integrated 802.1D enhancements:
    1. Operation similar to Uplink Fast
    2. Operation similar to Backbone Fast

RSTP Topology Changes

- In 802.1D, when a port moves to Forwarding or Blocking, a TCN BPDU is originated
- The TCN BPDU is propagated to the Root, which sends it to all other switches
- In RSTP, a TC is initiated only when a non-edge port transitions to the Forwarding state
- RSTP does not use TCN or TCA BPDUs, unless a legacy bridge needs to be notified

802.1D and 802.1w Interoperability

- By default, 802.11D switches drop 802.1w BPDUs
- RTSP begins a Migration Delay timer after sending out a BPDU
- The Migration Delay timer runs for 3 seconds
- The switch accepts and processes all BPDUs received during the Migration Timer
- The switch uses the format of the last BPDU received after the timer expires

RSTP with PVST+

- Rapid Per VLAN Spanning Tree allows for the use of 802.1w with PVST+
- By default, when RSTP is enabled, R-PVST+ is enabled on the switch

Understanding Multiple Spanning Tree Protocol

- 802.1D supports two flavors of Spanning Tree:
  1. Common Spanning Tree (802.1Q)
  2. Per VLAN Spanning Tree

- CST uses a single Spanning Tree instance for all VLANs configured on the switch
- PVST allows for a single Spanning Tree instance for each individual VLAN
- MST provides the ability to group multiple VLANs into a single Spanning Tree instance

MST BPDU Format

- MST uses RSTP for rapid convergence
- Each switch must be capable of processing RSTP BPDUs in order to support MST
- The MST BPDU is similar to the RSTP BPDU, with two differences:
  1. The Protocol Version Identifier Field is 0x03
  2. The MST BPDUs contain an MST extension field

Understanding MST Regions

- An MST Region defines a boundary in which a single instance of Spanning Tree operates
- A Region is a collection of interconnected switches that have the same MST configuration
- Switches in an MST Region must have the following values set the same:
  1. The MST Region Name (up to 32 bytes)
  2. Config Revision Number (0 to 65,535)
  3. VLAN-To-Instance Mapping (up to 4096 entries)

- An MST Region consists of a two different components:
  1. Edge ports
  2. Boundary ports

- An edge port is simply a port that connects to a non bridging device
- An MST boundary port connects an MST region to:
    1. A single Spanning Tree region running Rapid Spanning Tree (802.1w)
    2. A single Spanning Tree region running traditional Spanning Tree (802.1D)
    3. Another MST Region with a different MST configuration
    4. The Designated Switch that belongs to a single Spanning Tree Instance
    5. The Designated Switch that belongs to another MST instance

- All other ports are simply referred to as internal MST ports

MST Spanning Tree Instances

- MST establishes and maintains two types of Spanning Trees instances:
    1. Internal Spanning Tree (IST) Instances
    2. Multiple Spanning Tree (MST) Instances

- The MST Region sees the outside world via its IST interaction only
- IST presents the entire MST Region as a single virtual bridge to the outside world
- BPDUs are exchanged at the Region boundary over the native VLAN of trunks
- The IST is the only Instance that sends and receives BPDUs
- All other Spanning Tree Instance information is contained in M-records
- When the IST converges, the Root of the IST becomes the IST master
- The switch with the lowest BID and path cost to the CST Root is elected IST master
- If there is only a single Region, then the IST master will also be the CST Root
- If the CST Root is outside of the Region, a boundary switch is selected as the IST master
- IST and MST Instances do not use the Message Age and Maximum Age information
- IST and MST Instances use the Path Cost to the Root and a hop-count mechanism
- The Root Bridge of the Instance sends a BPDU (or M-record) with a cost of 0
- The Root Bridge of the Instance sends a BPDU (or M-record) with a hop count of 20
- MST Instances (MSTIs) are STP instances that exist only within the region
- MSTIs convey the Spanning Tree information for each instance within the Region
- Cisco Catalyst switches support up to 16 MSTIs on a single switch
- MST Instance 0 is mandatory and is always present; all other Instances are optional
- By default, all VLANs are assigned to the IST, which is MST Instance 0
- The IST Instance exists on all ports within the MST Region
- Only the IST Instance has timer-related parameters
- MST BPDUs are sent out of every port by all switches

CHAPTER 5

EtherChannels and Link Aggregation Protocols

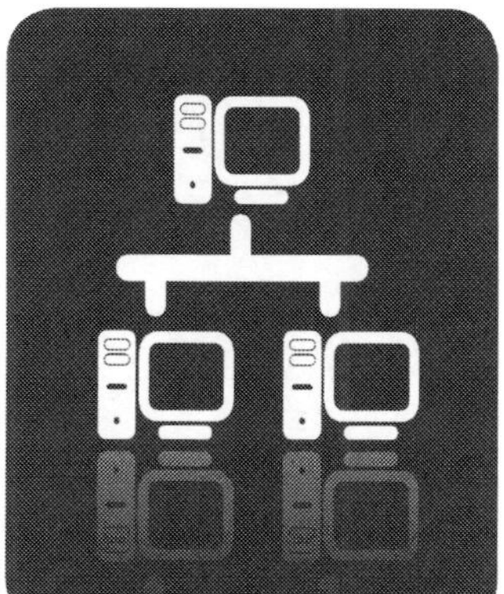

Cisco IOS software allows administrators to combine multiple physical links in the chassis into a single logical link. This provides an ideal solution for load sharing, as well as link redundancy, and can be used by both Layer 2 and Layer 3 sub-systems. The following core SWITCH exam objective is covered in this chapter:

- Implement VLAN-based solution, given a network design and a set of requirements

This chapter will be divided into the following sections:

- Understanding EtherChannels
- Port Aggregation Protocol Overview
- PAgP Port Modes
- PAgP Learn Method
- PAgP EtherChannel Protocol Packet Forwarding
- Link Aggregation Control Protocol Overview
- LACP Port Modes
- LACP Parameters
- LACP Redundancy
- EtherChannel Load-Distribution Methods
- EtherChannel Configuration Guidelines
- Configuring and Verifying Layer 2 EtherChannels
- Protecting STP When Using EtherChannels

SWITCH Exam Objective	Chapter Section(s) Covered
Configure switch-to-switch connectivity for the VLAN-based solution	• Understanding EtherChannels • Port Aggregation Protocol Overview • PAgP Port Modes • PAgP Learn Method • PAgP EtherChannel Protocol Packet Forwarding • Link Aggregation Control Protocol Overview • LACP Port Modes • LACP Parameters • LACP Redundancy • EtherChannel Load-Distribution Methods • EtherChannel Configuration Guidelines • Configuring and Verifying Layer 2 EtherChannels • Protecting STP When Using EtherChannels

Understanding EtherChannels

An EtherChannel is comprised of physical, individual FastEthernet, GigabitEthernet, or Ten-GigabitEthernet (10Gbps) links that are bundled together into a single logical link as illustrated in Figure 5-1 below. An EtherChannel comprised of FastEthernet links is referred to as a FastEtherChannel (FEC); an EtherChannel comprised of GigabitEthernet links is referred to as a GigabitEtherChannel (GEC); and finally, an EtherChannel comprised of Ten-GigabitEthernet links is referred to as a Ten-GigabitEtherChannel (10GEC):

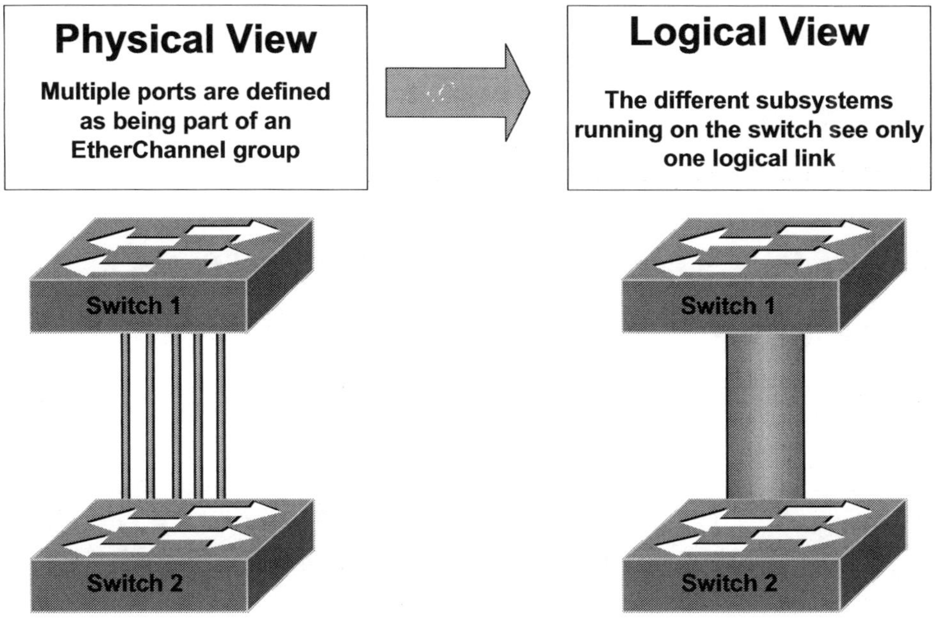

Fig. 5-1. EtherChannel Physical and Logical View

Each EtherChannel can consist of up to eight (8) ports. Physical links in an EtherChannel must share similar characteristics, such as be defined in the same VLAN or have the same speed and duplex settings, for example. When configuring EtherChannels on Cisco Catalyst switches, it is important to remember that the number of supported EtherChannels will vary between the different Catalyst switch models.

For example, on the Catalyst 3750 series switches, the range is 1 to 48; on the Catalyst 4500 series switches, the range is 1 to 64; and on the flagship Catalyst 6500 series switches, the number of valid values for *EtherChannel configuration* depends on the software release. For releases prior to Release 12.1(3a)E3, valid values are from 1 to 256; for Releases 12.1(3a)E3, 12.1(3a)E4, and 12.1(4)E1, valid values are from 1 to 64. Release 12.1(5c)EX and later support a maximum of 64 values ranging from 1 to 256.

NOTE: You are not expected to known the values supported in each different IOS version.

In addition to increasing the aggregate link bandwidth between two devices, Etherchannels also provide redundancy in the event of a single link failure within the bundle group. If for example, a single link fails, the traffic previously carried over the failed link is switched over to, or distributed across, the remaining links within the port channel. In addition to this, when you change the number of active bundled ports in a port channel, traffic patterns will reflect the rebalanced state of the port channel. This will be described later in this chapter when we learn about the different Etherchannel load-distribution methods.

There are two link aggregation protocol options that can be used to automate the creation of an EtherChannel group: Port Aggregation Protocol (PAgP) and Link Aggregation Control Protocol (LACP). PAgP is a Cisco proprietary protocol while LACP is part of the IEEE 802.3ad specification for creating a logical link from multiple physical links. These two protocols will be described in detail throughout this chapter.

Port Aggregation Protocol Overview

Port Aggregation Protocol (PAgP) is a Cisco proprietary link aggregation protocol that enables the automatic creation of EtherChannels. By default, PAgP packets are sent between EtherChannel-capable ports in order to negotiate the forming of an EtherChannel. These packets are sent to the destination Multicast MAC address 01-00-0C-CC-CC-CC, which is also the same Multicast address that is used by CDP, UDLD, VTP, and DTP. Figure 5-2 below shows the fields contained within a PAgP frame as seen on the wire:

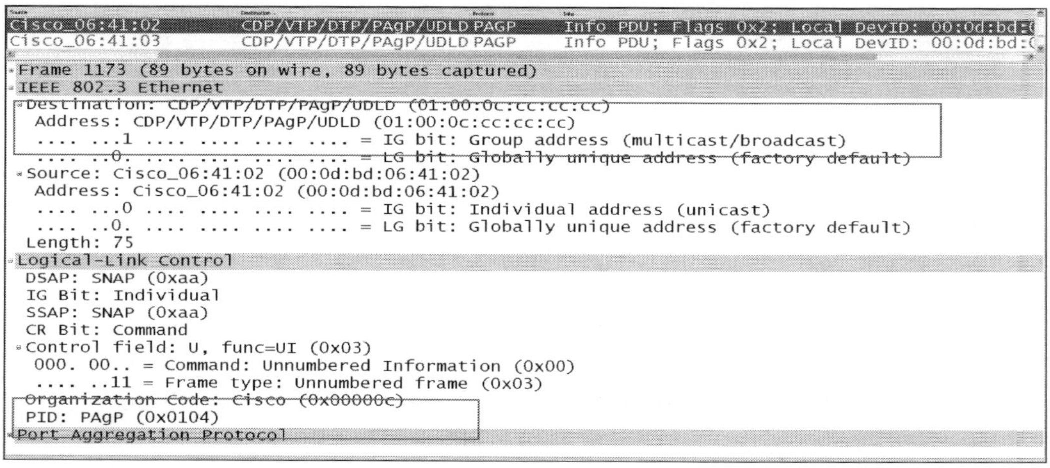

Fig. 5-2. PAgP Ethernet Header

Although going into detail on the PAgP packet format is beyond the scope of the SWITCH exam requirements, Figure 5-3 below shows the fields contained in a typical PAgP packet. Some of the fields contained within the PAgP packet are of relevance to the SWITCH exam and will be described in detail as we progress through this chapter:

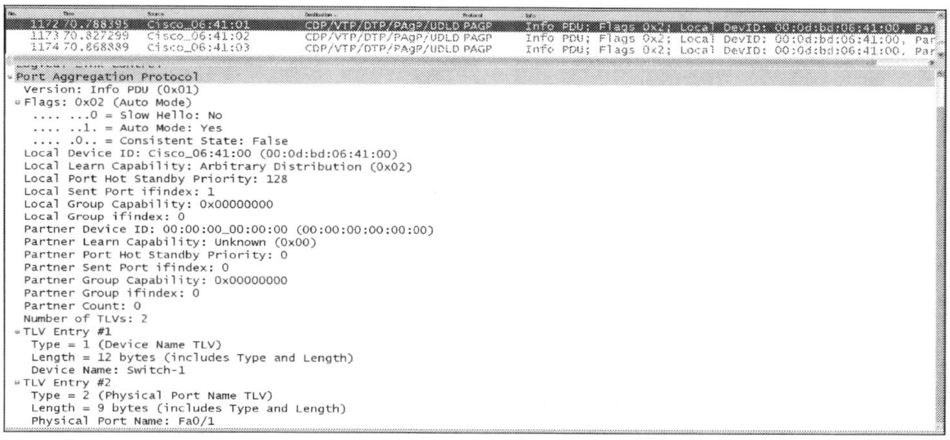

Fig. 5-3. The Port Aggregation Protocol Frame

PAgP Port Modes

PAgP supports different port modes that determine whether an EtherChannel will be formed between two PAgP-capable switches. Before we delve into the two PAgP port modes, one particular mode deserves special attention. This mode (the 'on' mode) is sometimes incorrectly referenced as a PAgP mode. The truth, however, is that it is not a PAgP port mode.

The on mode forces a port to be placed into a channel unconditionally. The channel will only be created if another switch port is connected and is configured in the on mode. When this mode is enabled, there is no negotiation of the channel performed by the local EtherChannel protocol. In other words, this effectively disables EtherChannel negotiation and forces the port to the channel. The operation of this mode is similar to the operation of the `switchport nonegotiate` command on trunk links. It is important to remember that switch interfaces that are configured in the on mode do not exchange PAgP packets.

Switch EtherChannels using PAgP may be configured to operate in one of two modes: auto or desirable. These two PAgP modes of operation are described in the following sub-sections.

Auto Mode

Auto mode is a PAgP mode that will negotiate with another PAgP port only if the port receives a PAgP packet. When this mode is enabled, the port(s) will never initiate PAgP communications but instead will listen passively for any received PAgP packets before creating an EtherChannel with the neighboring switch.

Desirable Mode

Desirable mode is a PAgP mode that causes the port to initiate PAgP negotiation for a channel with another PAgP port. In other words, in this mode, the port actively attempts to establish an EtherChannel with another switch running PAgP.

In summation, it is important to remember that switch interfaces configured in the on mode do not exchange PAgP packets but they do exchange PAgP packets with partner interfaces configured in the auto or desirable modes. Table 5-1 shows the different PAgP combinations and the result of their use in establishing an EtherChannel:

Table 5-1. EtherChannel Formation Using Different PAgP Modes

Switch 1 PAgP Mode	Switch 2 PAgP Mode	EtherChannel Result
Auto	Auto	No EtherChannel Formed
Auto	Desirable	EtherChannel Formed
Desirable	Auto	EtherChannel Formed
Desirable	Desirable	EtherChannel Formed

PAgP Learn Method

Switches running PAgP are classified as either physical learners or aggregate learners. These two device types are described in the following sub-sections.

PAgP Physical Learners

PAgP physical learners are switches that learn MAC addresses using the physical ports within the EtherChannel instead of via the logical EtherChannel link. Physical learners forward traffic to addresses based on the physical port via which the address was learned. In other words, the switch will send packets to the neighboring switch using the same port in the EtherChannel from which it learned the source address. Figure 5-4 below illustrates a switch using physical learning in a three-port EtherChannel:

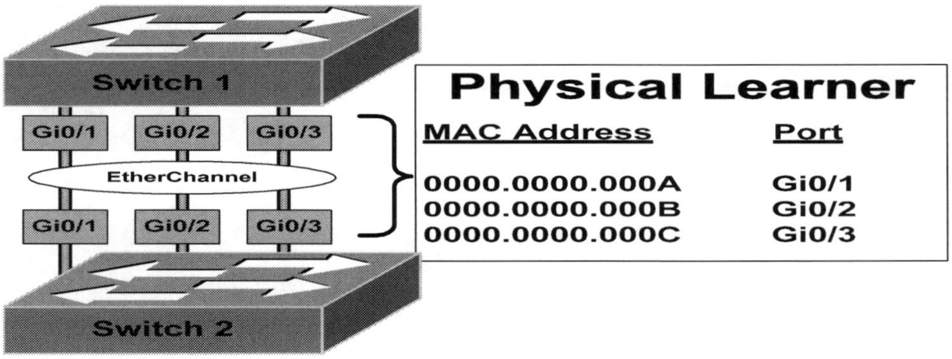

Fig. 5-4. PAgP Physical Learning

PAgP Aggregate (Logical) Learners

Unlike a physical learner, an aggregate learner learns addresses based on the aggregate or logical EtherChannel port. This allows the switch to transmit packets to the source by using any of the interfaces in the EtherChannel. Aggregate learning is the default in current Cisco IOS switches. However, it should be noted that legacy switches, such as the Catalyst 1900 series switches, support only physical learning.

By default, PAgP is not able to detect whether a neighboring switch is a physical learner. Therefore, when configuring PAgP EtherChannels on switches that support only physical learning, the learning method must be manually set to physical learning. In addition to this, it is important to set the load-distribution method to source-based distribution so that any given source MAC address is always sent on the same physical port. The different EtherChannel load-distribution methods will be described in detail later in this chapter. Figure 5-5 below illustrates logical learning:

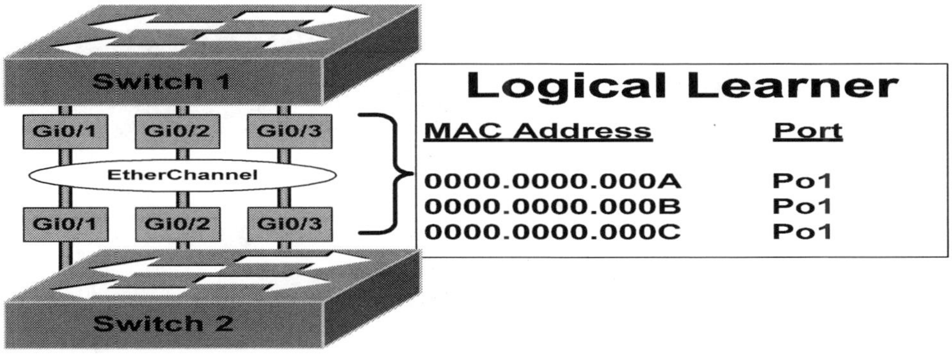

Fig. 5-5. PAgP Logical Learning

The following output shows the MAC entries in the CAM on a device performing aggregate learning:

```
Switch-1#show mac-address-table
          Mac Address Table
-------------------------------------------

Vlan    Mac Address       Type        Ports
----    -----------       --------    -----
...
[Truncated Output]
...
  10    0014.a9e5.d640    DYNAMIC     Po1
  10    001d.09d4.0238    DYNAMIC     Po1
  10    0014.a9e5.d641    DYNAMIC     Po1
  10    0014.a9e5.d642    DYNAMIC     Po1
  10    0014.a9e5.d643    DYNAMIC     Po1
Total Mac Addresses for this criterion: 9
```

PAgP EtherChannel Protocol Packet Forwarding

While PAgP allows for all links within the EtherChannel to be used to forward and receive user traffic, there are some restrictions that you should be familiar with regarding the forwarding of traffic from other protocols. DTP and CDP send and receive packets over all the physical interfaces in the EtherChannel. PAgP sends and receives PAgP Protocol Data Units only from interfaces that are up and have PAgP enabled for auto or desirable modes.

When an EtherChannel bundle is configured as a trunk port, the trunk sends and receives PAgP frames on the lowest numbered VLAN. Spanning Tree Protocol (STP) always chooses the first operational port in an EtherChannel bundle. The `show pagp [channel number] neighbor` command, which can also be used to validate the port that will be used by STP to send packets and receive packets, determines the port STP will use in an EtherChannel bundle, as shown in the following output:

```
Switch-1#show pagp neighbor
Flags:  S - Device is sending Slow hello. C - Device is in Consistent state.
        A - Device is in Auto mode.       P - Device learns on physical port.

Channel group 1 neighbors
          Partner              Partner         Partner         Partner Group
Port      Name                 Device ID       Port       Age  Flags   Cap.
Fa0/1     Switch-2             0014.a9e5.d640  Fa0/1      2s   SC      10001
Fa0/2     Switch-2             0014.a9e5.d640  Fa0/2      1s   SC      10001
Fa0/3     Switch-2             0014.a9e5.d640  Fa0/3      15s  SC      10001
```

Referencing the above output, STP will send packets only out of port FastEthernet0/1 because it is the first operational interface. If that port fails, STP will send packets out of FastEthernet0/2. The default port used by PAgP can be viewed in the `show EtherChannel summary` as illustrated in the following output:

```
Switch-1#show EtherChannel summary
Flags:  D - down        P - in port-channel
        I - stand-alone s - suspended
        H - Hot-standby (LACP only)
        R - Layer3      S - Layer2
        u - unsuitable for bundling
        U - in use      f - failed to allocate aggregator
        d - default port

Number of channel-groups in use: 1
Number of aggregators:           1

Group  Port-channel  Protocol    Ports
------+-------------+-----------+----------------------------------------
1      Po1(SU)       PAgP        Fa0/1(Pd)   Fa0/2(P)    Fa0/3(P)
```

When configuring additional STP features such as Loop Guard on an EtherChannel, it is very important to remember that if Loop Guard blocks the first port, no BPDUs will be sent over the channel, even if other ports in the channel bundle are operational. This is because PAgP will enforce uniform Loop Guard configuration on all of the ports that are part of the EtherChannel group.

REAL WORLD IMPLEMENTATION

In production networks, you may run across the Cisco Virtual Switching System (VSS), which is comprised of two physical Catalyst 6500 series switches acting as a single logical switch. In the VSS, one switch is selected as the active switch while the other is selected as the standby switch. The two switches are connected together via an EtherChannel, which allows for the sending and receiving of control packets between them.

Access switches are connected to the VSS using Multichassis EtherChannel (MEC). An MEC is simply an EtherChannel that spans the two physical Catalyst 6500 switches but terminates to the single logical VSS. Enhanced PAgP (PAgP+) can be used to allow the Catalyst 6500 switches to communicate via the MEC in the event that the EtherChannel between them fails, which would result in both switches assuming the active role (dual active), effectively affecting forwarding of traffic within the switched network. This is illustrated in the diagram below:

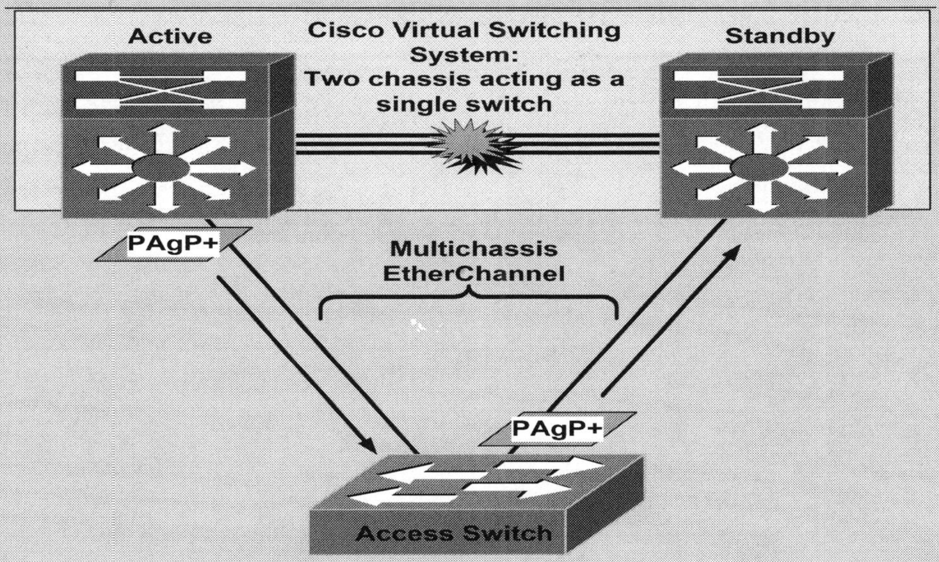

While VSS is beyond the scope of the SWITCH exam requirements, it is beneficial to know that only PAgP can be used to relay VSS control packets. Therefore, if implementing EtherChannels in a VSS environment, or an environment in which VSS may eventually be implemented, you may want to consider running PAgP instead of LACP, which is an open standard that does not support the proprietary VSS frames. VSS will not be described any further in this guide.

Link Aggregation Control Protocol Overview

Link Aggregation Control Protocol (LACP) is part of the IEEE 802.3ad specification for creating a logical link from multiple physical links. Because LACP and PAgP are incompatible, both ends of the link need to run LACP in order to automate the formation of EtherChannel groups.

As is the case with PAgP, when configuring LACP EtherChannels, all LAN ports must be the same speed and must all be configured as either Layer 2 or Layer 3 LAN ports. Unlike PAgP, LACP does not support half-duplex links. Half-duplex ports in an LACP Etherchannel are placed into the suspended state. If a link within a port channel fails, traffic previously carried over the failed link is distributed between the remaining links within the port channel. Additionally, when you change the number of active bundled ports in a port channel, traffic patterns will also reflect the rebalanced state of the port channel.

LACP supports the automatic creation of port channels by exchanging LACP packets between ports. It learns the capabilities of port groups dynamically and informs the other ports. Once LACP identifies correctly matched Ethernet links, it facilitates grouping the links into a Gigabit Ethernet port channel. Unlike PAgP, where ports are required to have the same speed and duplex settings, LACP mandates that ports be only full-duplex, as half-duplex is not supported. Half-duplex ports in an LACP EtherChannel are placed into the suspended state.

By default, all inbound Broadcast and Multicast packets on one link in a port channel are blocked from returning on any other link of the port channel. LACP packets are sent to the IEEE 802.3 Slow Protocols Multicast group address 01-80-C2-00-00-02. LACP frames are encoded with the EtherType value 0x8809. Figure 5-6 below illustrates these fields in an Ethernet frame:

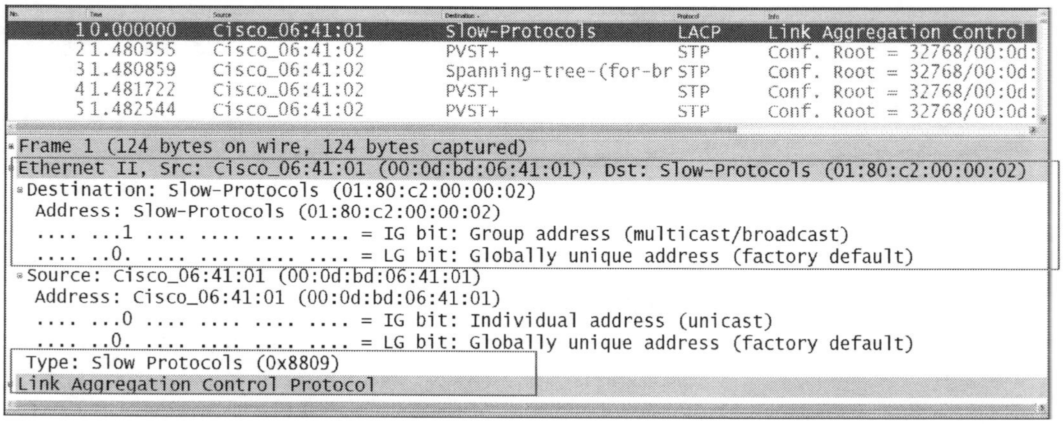

Fig. 5-6. IEEE 802.3 LACP Frame

LACP Architecture

Architecturally, the LACP application is a client to the MAC Sub-Layer. In other words, with LACP, link aggregation applies to the MAC Sub-Layer of the Data Link Layer. The Link Aggregation Sub-Layer binds multiple physical ports and presents them to upper Layers of the stack as a single logical port. The major LACP architectural components (or blocks) are illustrated in Figure 5-7 below:

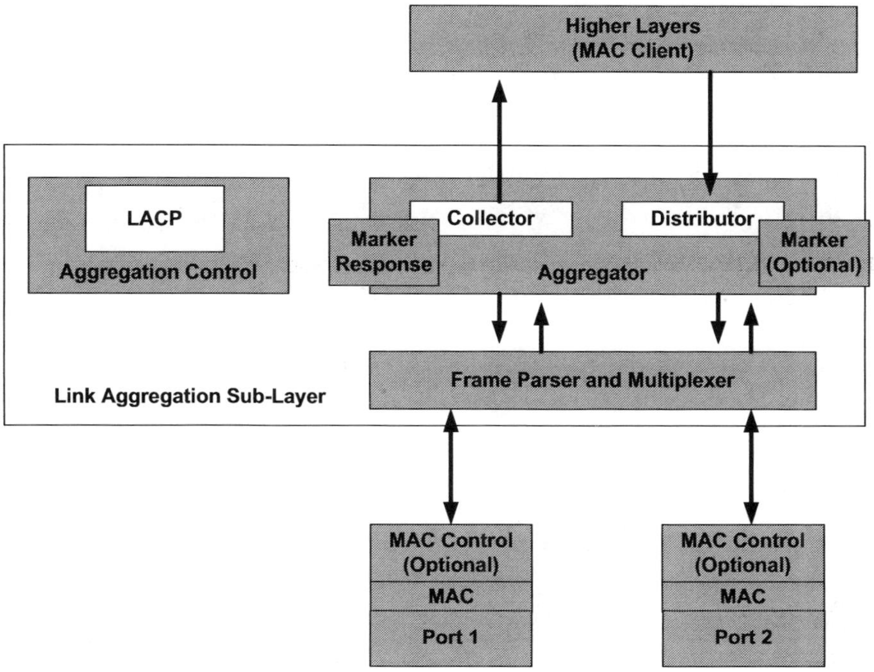

Fig. 5-7. LACP Architectural Blocks

Table 5-2 below lists and describes the core components illustrated in Figure 5-7:

Table 5-2. EtherChannel Formation Using Different LACP Modes

Component	Description
Collector	The Collector accepts frames from the physical link and passes them to upper layers. The Collector parses special marker packets from the incoming stream. These packets are then passed to the LACP agent. The LACP agent can also instruct the Distributor to generate marker response packets.
Distributor	The Distributor transmits outgoing frames from the MAC client to links in the aggregation group. This block also implements the distribution algorithm, which is used to redistribute traffic among links. To do so, the higher layer sends a special marker packet at the point where it wishes to re-distribute traffic and waits for the marker response packet. The marker response packet is generated by the receiving agent only after all frames have been passed to the higher layer applications.
Marker and Marker Response	These are used to maintain frame ordering when moving frames from one link in the group to another, such as when a physical link fails.

The LACP defines frame collection and distribution along with an LACP agent. The LACP defines two modes to re-distribute traffic among links. First is with the use of special packets called markers. The frame collector at either end of the link parses special marker packets from the incoming stream. These packets are then passed to the LACP agent. In addition to this, the LACP agent can also instruct the distributor to generate marker response packets.

LACP Port Modes

LACP supports the automatic creation of port channels by exchanging LACP packets between ports. LACP does this by learning the capabilities of port groups dynamically and informing the other ports. Once LACP identifies correctly matched Ethernet links, it facilitates grouping the links into a port channel. Once an LACP mode has been configured, it can only be changed if a single interface has been assigned to the specified channel group. LACP supports two modes: active and passive. These two modes of operation are described in the following sub-sections.

LACP Active Mode

LACP active mode places a switch port into an active negotiating state in which the switch port initiates negotiations with remote ports by sending LACP packets. Active mode is the LACP equivalent of PAgP desirable mode. In other words, in this mode, the switch port actively attempts to establish an EtherChannel with another switch that is also running LACP.

LACP Passive Mode

When a switch port is configured in passive mode, it will negotiate an LACP channel only if it receives another LACP packet. In passive mode, the port responds to LACP packets that the interface receives but does not start LACP packet negotiation. This setting minimizes the transmission of LACP packets. In this mode, the port channel group attaches the interface to the EtherChannel bundle. This mode is similar to the auto mode that is used with PAgP.

It is important to remember that the active and passive modes are valid on non-PAgP interfaces only. However, if you have a PAgP EtherChannel and want to convert it to LACP, then Cisco IOS software allows you to change the protocol at any time. The only caveat is that this change causes all existing EtherChannels to reset to the default channel mode for the new protocol. Table 5-3 below shows the different LACP combinations and the result of their use in establishing an EtherChannel between two switches:

Table 5-3. EtherChannel Formation Using Different LACP Modes

Switch 1 LACP Mode	Switch 2 LACP Mode	EtherChannel Result
Passive	Passive	No EtherChannel Formed
Passive	Active	EtherChannel Formed
Active	Active	EtherChannel Formed
Active	Passive	EtherChannel Formed

LACP Parameters

There are several LACP parameters that are contained in the LACP PDUs that are exchanged between switches. After exchanging LACP PDUs (also referred to as LACPDUs in some texts), the actor (local switch) and the partner (remote switch) come to agreement about each other's settings. The switches can now decide whether the ports at each end of the link can be added to an aggregation. LACP uses the following parameters:

- LACP System Priority
- LACP Port Priority
- LACP Administrative Key

These three LACP parameters, which are illustrated in Figure 5-8 below, will be described in detail in this section:

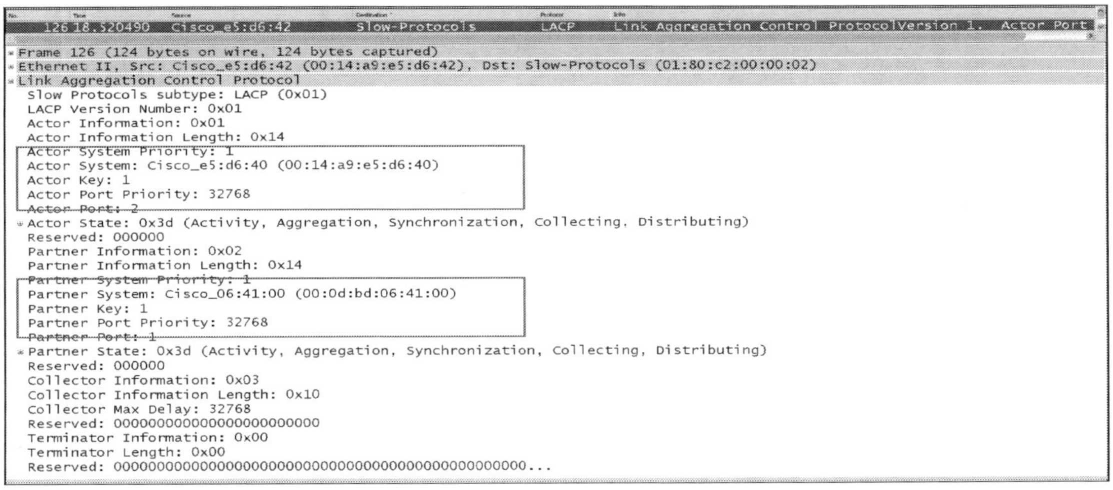

Fig. 5-8. LACP PDU (LACPDU) Parameters

LACP System Priority

An LACP System Priority must exist on each device running LACP. The LACP system priority can be configured automatically (default) or through the Command Line Interface (CLI). The LACP

System Priority must be configured at each end in order for LACP to successfully negotiate the Etherchannel group between the two end points. LACP uses the System Priority with the device MAC address to form the System ID and also during negotiation with other systems. This is illustrated in Figure 5-9:

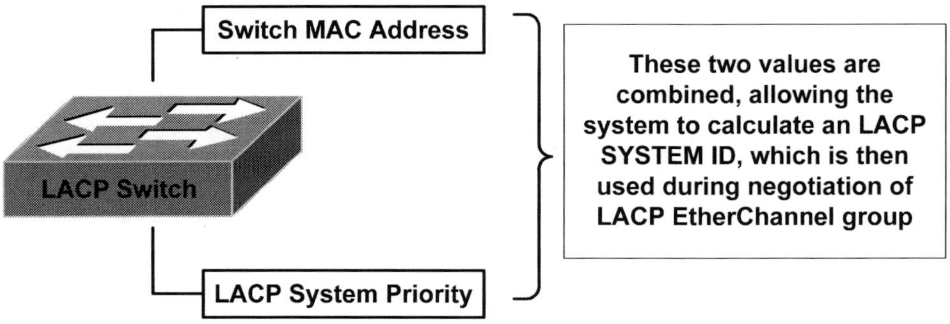

Fig. 5-9. Deriving the LACP System ID from the MAC Address and System Priority

LACP Port Priority

As is the case with the LACP System Priority, the LACP port priority must be defined on each port configured to use LACP. The Port Priority can be configured automatically (default) or through the CLI. LACP uses the Port Priority to decide which ports should be put into the bundle and which ports should be placed into LACP standby mode when there is a hardware limitation that prevents all compatible ports from aggregating.

In other words, if more than eight links are assigned to an Etherchannel bundle running LACP, the protocol uses the Port Priority to determine which ports are placed into a standby mode, i.e. will be placed into the Etherchannel if one or more of the current active LACP links fails. LACP also uses the port priority with the port number to form the port identifier. The higher the configured priority value (lower numerical value) the greater the chances of the port being used by LACP. The lower the value (higher numerical value) the lower the chances of the port being used by LACP. This concept is illustrated below in Figure 5-10:

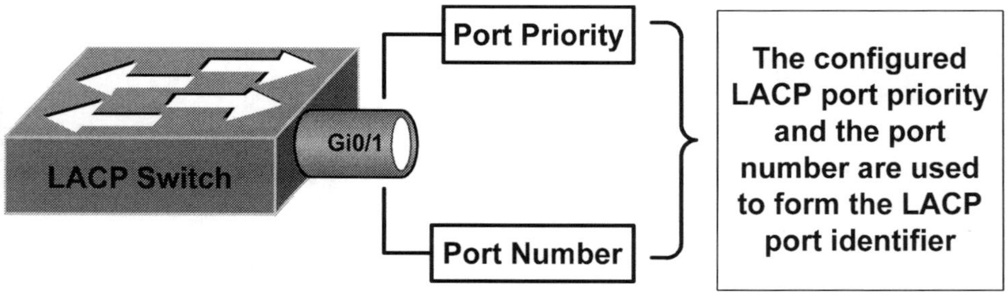

Fig. 5-10. Deriving the LACP Port ID from the Port Priority and Port Number

LACP Administrative Key

LACP automatically configures an administrative key value on each port configured to use LACP. The administrative key defines the ability of a port to aggregate with other ports. Only ports that have the same administrative key are allowed to be aggregated into the same port channel group. This is illustrated below in Figure 5-11:

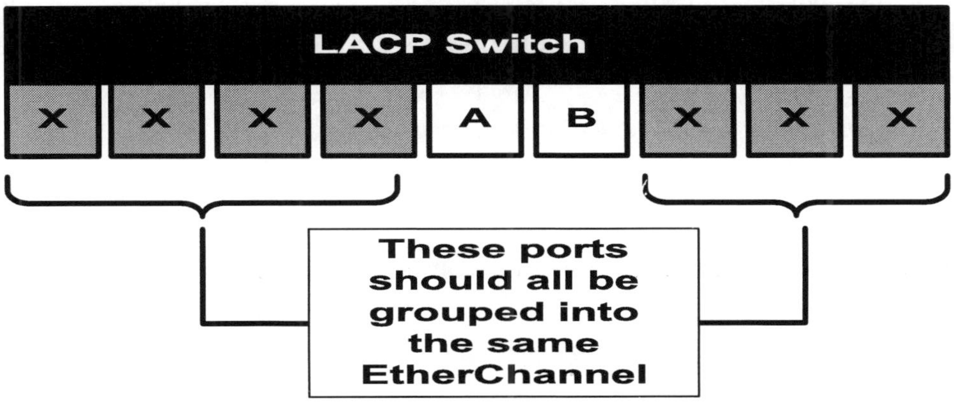

Fig. 5-11. Aggregating LACP Ports Based on the Administrative Key

A port's ability to aggregate with other ports is determined by physical characteristics, such as data rate, duplex capability, and point-to-point or shared medium, or by administrator-defined configuration restrictions or constraints.

LACP Redundancy

LACP provides two key features that afford redundancy for LACP EtherChannels. These two features are LACP hot-standby ports and LACP 1:1 redundancy with fast switchover.

LACP Hot-Standby Ports

By default, when LACP is configured on ports, it tries to configure the maximum number of compatible ports in a port channel, up to the maximum allowed by the hardware, which is typically eight ports.

However, if LACP is unable to aggregate all the ports that are compatible into an EtherChannel (e.g. if the neighboring switch has hardware limitations and can only support a fewer number of ports per EtherChannel), then all the ports that cannot be actively included in the channel are put in hot-standby state and are used only if one of the active ports in the EtherChannel fails.

Cisco IOS software allows administrators to restrict the maximum number of bundled ports allowed in the port channel using the `lacp max-bundle [number]` command in interface configuration mode. By default, up to eight ports may be bundled into a single channel. Inversely, a port channel must have a minimum of one port configured.

However, Cisco IOS software allows this value to be changed via the `port-channel min-links [number]` interface configuration command on the port channel interface. This command specifies the minimum number of member ports that must be in the link-up state and bundled in the EtherChannel for the port channel interface to transition to the link-up state.

LACP 1:1 Redundancy with Fast-Switchover

The LACP 1:1 redundancy feature provides an EtherChannel configuration with one active link and the ability to perform a fast switchover to a hot-standby link. To use LACP 1:1 redundancy, configure an LACP EtherChannel with two ports: one active and one standby. In the event that the active link goes down, the EtherChannel stays up and the switch performs fast switchover to the hot-standby link. Traffic is then subsequently forwarded using that interface.

When the failed link becomes operational again (i.e. is restored to its original state), the switch performs another fast switchover to revert to the original active link. The LACP 1:1 redundancy feature must be enabled on both ends of the link.

NOTE: The configuration of LACP redundancy is beyond the scope of the SWITCH exam requirements and will not be illustrated in this chapter or the remainder of this guide.

EtherChannel Load-Distribution Methods

For Etherchannel load distribution, Catalyst switches use a polymorphic or XOR algorithm which uses key fields from the header of the packet to generate a hash which is then matched to a physical link in the Etherchannel group. This XOR operation can be performed on MAC addresses or IP addresses and can be based solely on source or destination addresses. However, in some switching platforms, the operation is based on both source and destination addresses and is performed on the last two bits of the source MAC and the destination MAC.

NOTE: An XOR is an algorithm that basically means either one or the other, but not both.

While delving into detail on the actual computation of the hash used in Etherchannel load distribution is beyond the scope of the SWITCH requirements, it is important to know that the administrator can define what fields in the header can be used as input to the algorithm used to determine the physical link transport the packet.

The load distribution type is configured via the `port-channel load-balance [method]` global configuration command. Only a single method can be used at any given time. Table 5-4 lists and describes the different methods available in Cisco IOS Catalyst switches when configuring Etherchannel load distribution.

Table 5-4. EtherChannel Load Distribution (Load Balancing) Options

Method	Description
dst-ip	Performs load distribution based on the destination IP address
dst-mac	Performs load distribution based on the destination MAC address
dst-port	Performs load distribution based on the destination Layer 4 port
src-dst-ip	Performs load distribution based on the source or destination IP address
src-dst-mac	Performs load distribution based on the source or destination MAC address
src-dst-port	Performs load distribution based on the source or destination Layer 4 port
src-ip	Performs load distribution based on the source IP address
src-mac	Performs load distribution based on the source MAC address
src-port	Performs load distribution based on the source Layer 4 port

EtherChannel Configuration Guidelines

The following section lists and describes the steps that are required to configure Layer 2 PAgP EtherChannels. However, before we delve into these configuration steps, it is important that you are familiar with the following caveats when configuring Layer 2 EtherChannels:

- Each EtherChannel can have up to eight compatibly configured Ethernet interfaces. LACP allows you to have more than eight ports in an EtherChannel group. These additional ports are hot-standby ports. This was described in the previous section.
- All interfaces in the EtherChannel must operate at the same speed and duplex modes. Keep in mind, however, that unlike PAgP, LACP does not support half-duplex ports.
- Ensure all interfaces in the EtherChannel are enabled. In some cases, if the interfaces are not enabled, the logical port channel interface will not be created automatically.
- When first configuring an EtherChannel group, it is important to remember that ports follow the parameters set for the first group port added.
- If Switch Port Analyzer (SPAN) is configured for a member port in an EtherChannel, then the port will be removed from the EtherChannel group.
- It is important to assign all interfaces in the EtherChannel to the same VLAN or configure them as trunk links. If these parameters are different, the channel will not form.
- Keep in mind that similar interfaces with different STP Path Costs (manipulated by an administrator) can still be used to form an EtherChannel.

NOTE: SPAN is beyond the scope of the SWITCH exam requirements and will not be described in this guide.

Configuring and Verifying Layer 2 EtherChannels

This section describes the configuration of Layer 2 EtherChannels by unconditionally forcing the selected interfaces to establish an EtherChannel.

1. The first configuration step is to enter interface configuration mode for the desired EtherChannel interface(s) via the `interface [name]` or `interface range [range]` global configuration commands.
2. The second configuration step is to configure the interfaces as Layer 2 switch ports via the `switchport` interface configuration command.
3. The third configuration step is to configure the switch ports as either trunk or access links via the `switchport mode [access|trunk]` interface configuration command.
4. Optionally, if the interface or interfaces have been configured as access ports, assign them to the same VLAN using the `switchport access vlan [number]` command. If the interface or interfaces have been configured as a trunk port, select the VLANs allowed to traverse the trunk by issuing the `switchport trunk allowed vlan [range]` interface configuration command; if VLAN 1 will not be used as the native VLAN (for 802.1Q), enter the native VLAN by issuing the `switchport trunk native vlan [number]` interface configuration command. This configuration must be the same on all of the port channel member interfaces.
5. The next configuration step is to configure the interfaces to unconditionally trunk via the `channel-group [number] mode on` interface configuration command.

The configuration of unconditional EtherChannel using the steps described above will be based on the network topology illustrated in Figure 5-12 below:

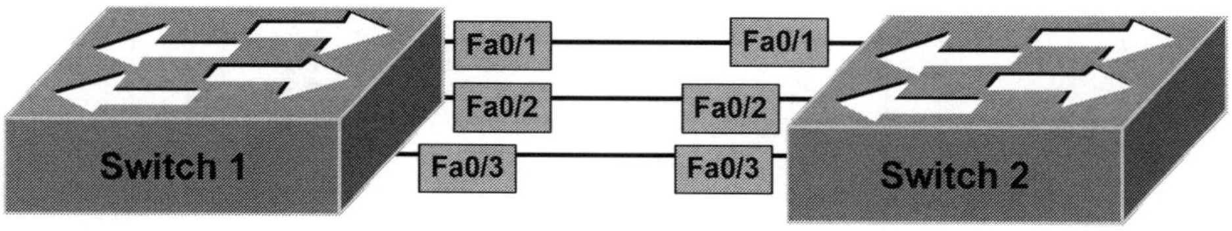

Fig. 5-12. Network Topology for EtherChannel Configuration Output Examples

The following output illustrates how to configure unconditional channeling on Switch 1 and Switch 2 based on the network topology depicted in Figure 5-12. The EtherChannel will be configured as a Layer 2 802.1Q trunk using default parameters:

```
Switch-1#conf t
Enter configuration commands, one per line.  End with CNTL/Z.
Switch-1(config)#interface range fa0/1 - 3
Switch-1(config-if-range)#no shutdown
Switch-1(config-if-range)#switchport
Switch-1(config-if-range)#switchport trunk encapsulation dot1q
Switch-1(config-if-range)#switchport mode trunk
Switch-1(config-if-range)#channel-group 1 mode on
Creating a port-channel interface Port-channel 1
Switch-1(config-if-range)#exit
Switch-1(config)#exit
```

NOTE: Notice that the switch automatically creates interface port-channel 1 by default. No explicit user configuration is required to configure this interface.

```
Switch-2#conf t
Enter configuration commands, one per line.  End with CNTL/Z.
Switch-2(config)#interface range fa0/1 - 3
Switch-2(config-if-range)#switchport
Switch-2(config-if-range)#switchport trunk encapsulation dot1q
Switch-2(config-if-range)#switchport mode trunk
Switch-2(config-if-range)#channel-group 1 mode on
Creating a port-channel interface Port-channel 1
Switch-2(config-if-range)#exit
Switch-2(config)#exit
```

The `show etherchannel [options]` command can then be used to verify the configuration of the EtherChannel. The available options (which may vary depending on platform) are printed in the following output:

```
Switch-2#show etherchannel ?
  <1-6>          Channel group number
  detail         Detail information
  load-balance   Load-balance/frame-distribution scheme among ports in port-
                 channel
  port           Port information
  port-channel   Port-channel information
  protocol       protocol enabled
  summary        One-line summary per channel-group
  |              Output modifiers
  <cr>
```

The following output illustrates the `show etherchannel summary` command:

```
Switch-2#show etherchannel summary
Flags:  D - down        P - in port-channel
        I - stand-alone s - suspended
```

```
        H - Hot-standby (LACP only)
        R - Layer3      S - Layer2
        u - unsuitable for bundling
        U - in use      f - failed to allocate aggregator
        d - default port

Number of channel-groups in use: 1
Number of aggregators:           1

Group  Port-channel  Protocol    Ports
------+-------------+-----------+-----------------------------------------
1      Po1(SU)          -        Fa0/1(Pd)   Fa0/2(P)    Fa0/3(P)
```

In the output above, we can determine that there are three links in channel group 1. Interface FastEthernet0/1 is the default port; this port will be used to send STP packets, for example. If this port fails, FastEthernet0/2 will be designated as the default port, and so forth. We can also determine that this is an active Layer 2 EtherChannel by looking at the SU flags next to Po1. The following output shows the information printed by the `show EtherChannel detail` command:

```
Switch-2#show etherchannel detail
                Channel-group listing:
                ----------------------

Group: 1
----------
Group state = L2
Ports: 3   Maxports = 8
Port-channels: 1 Max Port-channels = 1
Protocol:    -
                Ports in the group:
                -------------------
Port: Fa0/1
------------

Port state    = Up Mstr In-Bndl
Channel group = 1           Mode = On/FEC          Gcchange = -
Port-channel  = Po1         GC   =   -             Pseudo port-channel = Po1
Port index    = 0           Load = 0x00            Protocol =    -

Age of the port in the current state: 0d:00h:20m:20s

Port: Fa0/2
------------

Port state    = Up Mstr In-Bndl
Channel group = 1           Mode = On/FEC          Gcchange = -
Port-channel  = Po1         GC   =   -             Pseudo port-channel = Po1
Port index    = 0           Load = 0x00            Protocol =    -
```

```
Age of the port in the current state: 0d:00h:21m:20s

Port: Fa0/3
------------

Port state    = Up Mstr In-Bndl
Channel group = 1            Mode = On/FEC          Gcchange = -
Port-channel  = Po1          GC   =   -             Pseudo port-channel = Po1
Port index    = 0            Load = 0x00            Protocol =    -

Age of the port in the current state: 0d:00h:21m:20s

                Port-channels in the group:
                ---------------------------

Port-channel: Po1
------------

Age of the Port-channel   = 0d:00h:26m:23s
Logical slot/port   = 1/0          Number of ports = 3
GC                  = 0x00000000      HotStandBy port = null
Port state          = Port-channel Ag-Inuse
Protocol            =    -

Ports in the Port-channel:

Index   Load   Port     EC state        No of bits
------+------+------+------------------+-----------
0       00     Fa0/1    On/FEC          0
0       00     Fa0/2    On/FEC          0
0       00     Fa0/3    On/FEC          0

Time since last port bundled:    0d:00h:21m:20s    Fa0/3
```

In the output above, we can determine that this is a Layer 2 EtherChannel with three out of a maximum of eight possible ports in the channel group. We can also determine that the EtherChannel mode is on, based on the protocol being denoted by a dash (-). In addition to this, we can also determine that this is a FastEtherChannel (FEC).

Finally, we can also verify the Layer 2 operational status of the logical port-channel interface by issuing the `show interfaces port-channel [number] switchport` command. This is illustrated in the following output:

```
Switch-2#show interfaces port-channel 1 switchport
Name: Po1
Switchport: Enabled
Administrative Mode: trunk
Operational Mode: trunk
```

```
Administrative Trunking Encapsulation: dot1q
Operational Trunking Encapsulation: dot1q
Negotiation of Trunking: On
Access Mode VLAN: 1 (default)
Trunking Native Mode VLAN: 1 (default)
Voice VLAN: none
Administrative private-vlan host-association: none
Administrative private-vlan mapping: none
Administrative private-vlan trunk native VLAN: none
Administrative private-vlan trunk encapsulation: dot1q
Administrative private-vlan trunk normal VLANs: none
Administrative private-vlan trunk private VLANs: none
Operational private-vlan: none
Trunking VLANs Enabled: ALL
Pruning VLANs Enabled: 2-1001
Protected: false
Appliance trust: none
```

Configuring and Verifying PAgP EtherChannels

This section describes the configuration of PAgP Layer 2 EtherChannels. The following steps need to be executed in order to configure and establish a PAgP EtherChannel.

1. The first configuration step is to enter interface configuration mode for the desired EtherChannel interface(s) via the `interface [name] or interface range [range]` global configuration commands.
2. The second configuration step is to configure the interfaces as Layer 2 switch ports via the `switchport` interface configuration command.
3. The third configuration step is to configure the switch ports as either trunk or access links via the `switchport mode [access|trunk]` interface configuration command.
4. Optionally, if the interface or interfaces have been configured as access ports, assign them to the same VLAN using the `switchport access vlan [number]` command. If the interface or interfaces have been configured as a trunk port, select the VLANs allowed to traverse the trunk by issuing the `switchport trunk allowed vlan [range]` interface configuration command; if VLAN 1 will not be used as the native VLAN (for 802.1Q), enter the native VLAN by issuing the `switchport trunk native vlan [number]` interface configuration command. This configuration must be the same on all of the port channel member interfaces.
5. Optionally, configure PAgP as the EtherChannel protocol by issuing the `channel-protocol pagp` interface configuration command. Because EtherChannels default to PAgP, this command is considered optional and is not required. It is considered good practice to issue this command just to be absolutely sure of your configuration.
6. The next configuration step is to configure the interfaces to unconditionally trunk via the `channel-group [number] mode on` interface configuration command.

The following output illustrates how to configure PAgP channeling on Switch 1 and Switch 2 based on the network topology depicted in Figure 5-12 above. The EtherChannel will be configured as a Layer 2 802.1Q trunk using default parameters:

```
Switch-1#conf t
Enter configuration commands, one per line.  End with CNTL/Z.
Switch-1(config)#interface range fa0/1 - 3
Switch-1(config-if-range)#switchport
Switch-1(config-if-range)#switchport trunk encap dot1q
Switch-1(config-if-range)#switchport mode trunk
Switch-1(config-if-range)#channel-group 1 mode desirable
Creating a port-channel interface Port-channel 1
Switch-1(config-if-range)#exit
```

NOTE: In the above output, the port channel desirable mode has been selected. An additional keyword (`non-silent`) may also be appended to the end of this command. This is because, by default, PAgP auto and desirable modes default to a silent mode. The silent mode is used when the switch is connected to a device that is not PAgP-capable and seldom, if ever, transmits packets. An example of a silent partner is a file server or a packet analyzer that is not generating traffic. It is also used if a device will not be sending PAgP packets (such as in auto mode).

In this case, running PAgP on a physical port connected to a silent partner prevents that switch port from ever becoming operational; however, the silent setting allows PAgP to operate, to attach the interface to a channel group, and to use the interface for transmission. In this example, because Switch 2 will be configured for auto mode (passive mode), it is preferred that the port uses the default silent mode operation. This is illustrated in the PAgP EtherChannel configuration output below:

```
Switch-1#conf t
Enter configuration commands, one per line.  End with CNTL/Z.
Switch-1(config)#interface range fa0/1 - 3
Switch-1(config-if-range)#switchport
Switch-1(config-if-range)#switchport trunk encap dot1q
Switch-1(config-if-range)#switchport mode trunk
Switch-1(config-if-range)#channel-group 1 mode desirable ?
  non-silent  Start negotiation only after data packets received
  <cr>
Switch-1(config-if-range)#channel-group 1 mode desirable non-silent
Creating a port-channel interface Port-channel 1
Switch-1(config-if-range)#exit
```

Proceeding with PAgP EtherChannel configuration, Switch 2 is configured as follows:

```
Switch-2#conf t
Enter configuration commands, one per line.  End with CNTL/Z.
Switch-2(config)#int range fa0/1 - 3
Switch-2(config-if-range)#switchport
Switch-2(config-if-range)#switchport trunk encapsulation dot1q
Switch-2(config-if-range)#switchport mode trunk
Switch-2(config-if-range)#channel-group 1 mode auto
Creating a port-channel interface Port-channel 1
Switch-2(config-if-range)#exit
```

The following output illustrates how to verify the PAgP EtherChannel configuration by using the `show EtherChannel summary` command on Switch 1 and Switch 2:

```
Switch-1#show etherchannel summary
Flags:  D - down        P - in port-channel
        I - stand-alone s - suspended
        H - Hot-standby (LACP only)
        R - Layer3      S - Layer2
        u - unsuitable for bundling
        U - in use      f - failed to allocate aggregator
        d - default port

Number of channel-groups in use: 1
Number of aggregators:           1

Group  Port-channel  Protocol    Ports
------+-------------+-----------+-----------------------------------------
1      Po1(SU)         PAgP      Fa0/1(Pd)   Fa0/2(P)    Fa0/3(P)
```

PAgP EtherChannel configuration and statistics may also be viewed by issuing the `show pagp [options]` command. The options available with this command are illustrated in the following output:

```
Switch-1#show pagp ?
  <1-6>     Channel group number
  counters  Traffic information
  internal  Internal information
  neighbor  Neighbor information
```

NOTE: Entering the desired port channel number provides the same options as the last three options printed above. This is illustrated in the following output:

```
Switch-1#show pagp 1 ?
  counters  Traffic information
  internal  Internal information
  neighbor  Neighbor information
```

The `counters` keyword provides information on PAgP sent and received packets. The internal keyword provides information such as the port state, Hello Interval, PAgP port priority, and the port learning method, for example. Using the show `pagp internal` command, this is illustrated in the following output:

```
Switch-1#show pagp 1 internal
Flags:  S - Device is sending Slow hello.  C - Device is in Consistent state.
        A - Device is in Auto mode.        d - PAgP is down.
Timers: H - Hello timer is running.        Q - Quit timer is running.
        S - Switching timer is running.    I - Interface timer is running.

Channel group 1
                                Hello     Partner PAgP      Learning Group
Port      Flags State    Timers Interval  Count   Priority  Method   Ifindex
Fa0/1     SC    U6/S7    H      30s       1       128       Any      29
Fa0/2     SC    U6/S7    H      30s       1       128       Any      29
Fa0/3     SC    U6/S7    H      30s       1       128       Any      29
```

The `neighbor` keyword prints out the neighbor name, ID of the PAgP neighbor, the neighbor device ID (MAC) and the neighbor port. The flags also indicate the mode the neighbor is operating in as well as if it is a physical learner, for example. Using the `show pagp neighbor` command, this is illustrated in the following output:

```
Switch-1#show pagp 1 neighbor
Flags:  S - Device is sending Slow hello. C - Device is in Consistent state.
        A - Device is in Auto mode.       P - Device learns on physical port.

Channel group 1 neighbors
          Partner                   Partner          Partner         Partner Group
Port      Name                      Device ID        Port       Age  Flags   Cap.
Fa0/1     Switch-2                  0014.a9e5.d640   Fa0/1      19s  SAC     10001
Fa0/2     Switch-2                  0014.a9e5.d640   Fa0/2      24s  SAC     10001
Fa0/3     Switch-2                  0014.a9e5.d640   Fa0/3      18s  SAC     10001
```

Configuring and Verifying LACP EtherChannels

This section describes the configuration of LACP Layer 2 EtherChannels. The following steps need to be executed in order to configure and establish an LACP EtherChannel.

1. The first configuration step is to enter interface configuration mode for the desired EtherChannel interface(s) via the `interface [name] or interface range [range]` global configuration commands.
2. The second configuration step is to configure the interfaces as Layer 2 switch ports via the `switchport` interface configuration command.
3. The third configuration step is to configure the switch ports as either trunk or access links via the `switchport mode [access|trunk]` interface configuration command.

4. Optionally, if the interface or interfaces have been configured as access ports, assign them to the same VLAN using the `switchport access vlan [number]` command. If the interface or interfaces have been configured as a trunk port, select the VLANs allowed to traverse the trunk by issuing the `switchport trunk allowed vlan [range]` interface configuration command; if VLAN 1 will not be used as the native VLAN (for 802.1Q), enter the native VLAN by issuing the `switchport trunk native vlan [number]` interface configuration command. This configuration must be the same on all of the port channel member interfaces.
5. Configure LACP as the EtherChannel protocol by issuing the `channel-protocol lacp` interface configuration command. Because EtherChannels default to PAgP, this command is considered mandatory for LACP and is required.
6. The next configuration step is to configure the interfaces to unconditionally trunk via the `channel-group [number] mode on` interface configuration command.

In the above output illustrating how to configure PAgP channeling on Switch 1 and Switch 2 based on the network topology depicted in Figure 5-12, the EtherChannel will be configured as a Layer 2 802.1Q trunk using default parameters, as shown in the following outputs:

```
Switch-1#conf t
Enter configuration commands, one per line.  End with CNTL/Z.
Switch-1(config)#int range fastethernet 0/1 - 3
Switch-1(config-if-range)#switchport
Switch-1(config-if-range)#switchport trunk encapsulation dot1q
Switch-1(config-if-range)#switchport mode trunk
Switch-1(config-if-range)#channel-protocol lacp
Switch-1(config-if-range)#channel-group 1 mode active
Creating a port-channel interface Port-channel 1
Switch-1(config-if-range)#exit

Switch-2#conf t
Enter configuration commands, one per line.  End with CNTL/Z.
Switch-2(config)#interface ra fast 0/1 - 3
Switch-2(config-if-range)#switchport
Switch-2(config-if-range)#switchport trunk encap dot1q
Switch-2(config-if-range)#switchport mode trunk
Switch-2(config-if-range)#channel-protocol lacp
Switch-2(config-if-range)#channel-group 1 mode passive
Creating a port-channel interface Port-channel 1
Switch-2(config-if-range)#exit
```

The following output illustrates how to verify the LACP EtherChannel configuration by using the `show EtherChannel summary` command on Switch 1 and Switch 2:

```
Switch-1#show etherchannel summary
Flags:  D - down        P - in port-channel
        I - stand-alone s - suspended
```

```
        H - Hot-standby (LACP only)
        R - Layer3      S - Layer2
        u - unsuitable for bundling
        U - in use      f - failed to allocate aggregator
        d - default port

Number of channel-groups in use: 1
Number of aggregators:           1

Group  Port-channel  Protocol    Ports
------+-------------+-----------+-----------------------------------------
1      Po1(SU)       LACP        Fa0/1(Pd)   Fa0/2(P)    Fa0/3(P)
```

LACP allows up to 16 ports to be entered into a port channel group. The first eight operational interfaces will be used by LACP, while the remaining eight interfaces will be placed into the hot-standby state. The `show etherchannel detail` command shows the maximum number of supported links in an LACP EtherChannel, as illustrated in the following output:

```
Switch-1#show etherchannel 1 detail
Group state = L2
Ports: 3   Maxports = 16
Port-channels: 1 Max Port-channels = 16
Protocol:   LACP
                Ports in the group:
                -------------------
Port: Fa0/1
------------

Port state    = Up Mstr In-Bndl
Channel group = 1           Mode = Active      Gcchange = -
Port-channel  = Po1         GC   =   -         Pseudo port-channel = Po1
Port index    = 0           Load = 0x00        Protocol =   LACP

Flags:  S - Device is sending Slow LACPDUs.  F - Device is sending fast
                                                LACPDUs.
        A - Device is in active mode.        P - Device is in passive mode.

Local information:
                                LACP port     Admin     Oper    Port     Port
Port      Flags   State         Priority      Key       Key     Number   State
Fa0/1     SA      bndl          32768         0x1       0x1     0x0      0x3D

Partner's information:

          Partner               Partner                         Partner
Port      System ID             Port Number     Age             Flags
Fa0/1     00001,0014.a9e5.d640  0x1             4s              SP

          LACP Partner         Partner         Partner
          Port Priority        Oper Key        Port State
          32768                0x1             0x3C
```

```
Age of the port in the current state: 00d:00h:00m:35s

Port: Fa0/2
------------

Port state    = Up Mstr In-Bndl
Channel group = 1           Mode = Active      Gcchange = -
Port-channel  = Po1         GC   =   -         Pseudo port-channel = Po1
Port index    = 0           Load = 0x00        Protocol =   LACP

Flags:  S - Device is sending Slow LACPDUs.  F - Device is sending fast
                                                 LACPDUs.
        A - Device is in active mode.        P - Device is in passive mode.

Local information:
                            LACP port     Admin     Oper    Port     Port
Port      Flags   State     Priority      Key       Key     Number   State
Fa0/2     SA      bndl      32768         0x1       0x1     0x1      0x3D

Partner's information:

          Partner               Partner                     Partner
Port      System ID             Port Number     Age         Flags
Fa0/2     00001,0014.a9e5.d640  0x2             28s         SP

          LACP Partner         Partner         Partner
          Port Priority        Oper Key        Port State
          32768                0x1             0x3C

Age of the port in the current state: 00d:00h:00m:33s

Port: Fa0/3
------------

Port state    = Up Mstr In-Bndl
Channel group = 1           Mode = Active      Gcchange = -
Port-channel  = Po1         GC   =   -         Pseudo port-channel = Po1
Port index    = 0           Load = 0x00        Protocol =   LACP

Flags:  S - Device is sending Slow LACPDUs.  F - Device is sending fast
                                                 LACPDUs.
        A - Device is in active mode.        P - Device is in passive mode.

Local information:
                            LACP port     Admin     Oper    Port     Port
Port      Flags   State     Priority      Key       Key     Number   State
Fa0/3     SA      bndl      32768         0x1       0x1     0x2      0x3D

Partner's information:

          Partner               Partner                     Partner
Port      System ID             Port Number     Age         Flags
Fa0/3     00001,0014.a9e5.d640  0x3             5s          SP
```

```
          LACP Partner         Partner         Partner
          Port Priority        Oper Key        Port State
          32768                0x1             0x3C

Age of the port in the current state: 00d:00h:00m:29s

                Port-channels in the group:
                ----------------------

Port-channel: Po1    (Primary Aggregator)

------------

Age of the Port-channel   = 00d:00h:13m:50s
Logical slot/port   = 1/0          Number of ports = 3
HotStandBy port = null
Port state          = Port-channel Ag-Inuse
Protocol            =   LACP

Ports in the Port-channel:

Index   Load   Port    EC state
------+------+------+-----------
0       00     Fa0/1   Active
0       00     Fa0/2   Active
0       00     Fa0/3   Active

Time since last port bundled:    00d:00h:00m:32s    Fa0/3
Time since last port Un-bundled: 00d:00h:00m:49s    Fa0/1
```

LACP configuration and statistics may also be viewed by issuing the `show lacp [options]` command. The options available with this command are illustrated in the following output:

```
Switch-1#show lacp ?
  <1-6>      Channel group number
  counters   Traffic information
  internal   Internal information
  neighbor   Neighbor information
  sys-id     LACP System ID
```

The `counters` keyword provides information on LACP sent and received packets. The output printed by this command is illustrated below:

```
Switch-1#show lacp counters
             LACPDUs         Marker       Marker Response    LACPDUs
Port         Sent   Recv     Sent   Recv     Sent   Recv      Pkts Err
---------------------------------------------------------------------
Channel group: 1
Fa0/1        14     12       0      0        0      0         0
Fa0/2        21     18       0      0        0      0         0
Fa0/3        21     18       0      0        0      0         0
```

The `internal` keyword provides information such as the port state, administrative key, LACP port priority, and the port number, for example. This is illustrated in the following output:

```
Switch-1#show lacp internal
Flags:  S - Device is sending Slow LACPDUs. F - Device is sending Fast
                                                LACPDUs.
        A - Device is in Active mode.       P - Device is in Passive mode.

Channel group 1
                            LACP port     Admin     Oper    Port      Port
Port      Flags   State     Priority      Key       Key     Number    State
Fa0/1     SA      bndl      32768         0x1       0x1     0x0       0x3D
Fa0/2     SA      bndl      32768         0x1       0x1     0x1       0x3D
Fa0/3     SA      bndl      32768         0x1       0x1     0x2       0x3D
```

The `neighbor` keyword prints out the neighbor name, ID of the LACP neighbor, the neighbor device ID (MAC), and the neighbor port. The flags also indicate the mode the neighbor is operating in as well as whether it is a physical learner, for example. This is illustrated in the following output:

```
Switch-1#show lacp neighbor
Flags:  S - Device is sending Slow LACPDUs. F - Device is sending Fast
                                                LACPDUs.
        A - Device is in Active mode.       P - Device is in Passive mode.

Channel group 1 neighbors

Partner's information:

          Partner                  Partner                      Partner
Port      System ID                Port Number     Age          Flags
Fa0/1     00001,0014.a9e5.d640     0x1             11s          SP

          LACP Partner            Partner         Partner
          Port Priority           Oper Key        Port State
          32768                   0x1             0x3C

Partner's information:

          Partner                  Partner                      Partner
Port      System ID                Port Number     Age          Flags
Fa0/2     00001,0014.a9e5.d640     0x2             19s          SP

          LACP Partner            Partner         Partner
          Port Priority           Oper Key        Port State
          32768                   0x1             0x3C

Partner's information:

          Partner                  Partner                      Partner
```

```
Port      System ID              Port Number    Age      Flags
Fa0/3     00001,0014.a9e5.d640   0x3            24s      SP

          LACP Partner         Partner        Partner
          Port Priority        Oper Key       Port State
          32768                0x1            0x3C
```

And finally, the `sys-id` keyword provides the system ID of the local switch. This is a combination of the switch MAC and LACP priority as illustrated in the following output:

```
Switch-1#show lacp sys-id
1    ,000d.bd06.4100
```

Configuring and Verifying the LACP System Priority

The LACP system priority, which is used in conjunction with the switch MAC address to form the LACP system ID, may be manually changed via the `lacp system-priority [1-65535]` global configuration command. The following output illustrates how to configure a system priority of 255 and verify this configuration using the `show lacp sys-id` command:

```
Switch-1#conf t
Enter configuration commands, one per line.  End with CNTL/Z.
Switch-1(config)#lacp system-priority 255
Switch-1(config)#exit
Switch-1#
Switch-1#show lacp sys-id
255  ,000d.bd06.4100
```

Configuring and Verifying the LACP Port Priority

LACP uses the port priority to decide which ports should be put into standby mode when there is a hardware limitation that prevents all compatible ports from aggregating. The default port priority for all LACP ports is 32,768. However, this default value can be manually adjusted via the `lacp port-priority [1-65535]` interface configuration command. The lower the value, the more likely that the interface will be used for LACP transmission. The following output illustrates how to configure an interface with a port priority of 4000:

```
Switch-1#conf t
Enter configuration commands, one per line.  End with CNTL/Z.
Switch-1(config)#int fa0/1
Switch-1(config-if)#lacp port-priority 4000
Switch-1(config-if)#exit
Switch-1(config)#exit
Switch-1#
Switch-1#show lacp 1 internal
Flags:  S - Device is sending Slow LACPDUs. F - Device is sending Fast
                                                LACPDUs.
```

```
        A - Device is in Active mode.        P - Device is in Passive mode.

Channel group 1
                                 LACP port     Admin     Oper     Port      Port
Port        Flags    State       Priority      Key       Key      Number    State
Fa0/1       SA       bndl        4000          0x1       0x1      0x0       0x3D
Fa0/2       SA       bndl        32768         0x1       0x1      0x1       0x3D
Fa0/3       SA       bndl        32768         0x1       0x1      0x2       0x3D
```

Configuring and Verifying EtherChannel Load Balancing

EtherChannel load balancing, for both PAgP and LACP, is configured in global mode using the `port-channel load-balance [src-mac | dst-mac | src-dst-mac | src-ip | dst-ip | src-dst-ip | src-port | dst-port | src-dst-port]` command. The following output illustrates how to configure EtherChannel load distribution using the destination MAC address:

```
Switch-1#conf t
Enter configuration commands, one per line.  End with CNTL/Z.
Switch-1(config)#port-channel load-balance dst-mac
Switch-1(config)#exit
```

The `show etherchannel load-balance` command is used to verify the selected EtherChannel load-distribution method. This is illustrated in the following output:

```
Switch-1#show etherchannel load-balance
Destination MAC address
Switch-1#
```

Protecting STP When Using EtherChannels

The final section of this chapter describes the EtherChannel Guard feature, which is an optional Cisco STP feature designed to protect the Spanning Tree Protocol network when using Layer 2 EtherChannel trunks. The EtherChannel Guard feature is designed to detect an EtherChannel misconfiguration between the switch and another connected device.

For example, a misconfiguration can occur if the local switch interfaces are configured in an EtherChannel, but the interfaces on the other device are not. A misconfiguration can also occur if the channel parameters are not the same at both ends of the EtherChannel. If the switch detects a misconfiguration on the other device, EtherChannel Guard places the switch interfaces in the err-disabled state, and an error message is printed on the console.

By default, EtherChannel Guard Status is enabled and requires no further configuration. This default behavior is illustrated in the output shown below:

```
Switch-1#show spanning-tree summary
```

```
Switch is in mst mode
Root bridge for: MST00-MST02
EtherChannel misconfiguration guard is enabled
Extended system ID   is enabled
PortFast             is disabled by default
PortFast BPDU Guard  is disabled by default
PortFast BPDU Filter is disabled by default
LoopGuard            is disabled by default
UplinkFast           is disabled
BackboneFast         is disabled
PathCost method used is short

Name                   Blocking Listening Learning Forwarding STP Active
---------------------- -------- --------- -------- ---------- ----------
MST00                  0        0         0        1          1
MST01                  0        0         0        1          1
MST02                  0        0         0        1          1
---------------------- -------- --------- -------- ---------- ----------
3 msts                 0        0         0        3          3
```

If this feature is disabled, it can be re-enabled using the `spanning-tree etherchannel guard misconfig` global configuration command as illustrated in the following output:

```
Switch-1#conf t
Enter configuration commands, one per line.  End with CNTL/Z.
Switch-1(config)#spanning-tree EtherChannel guard misconfig
Switch-1(config)#exit
```

Chapter Summary

The following section is a summary of the major points you should be aware of in this chapter.

Understanding EtherChannels

- An EtherChannel is comprised of physical, individual Fast, Gigabit, or 10Gbps links
- The links in an EtherChannel appear as a single logical link
- Each EtherChannel can consist of up to eight (8) ports
- Physical links in an EtherChannel must share similar characteristics
- There are two aggregation protocol used to create EtherChannels:
    1. Port Aggregation Protocol (PAgP)
    2. Link Aggregation Control Protocol (LACP)

Port Aggregation Protocol Overview

- Port Aggregation Protocol (PAgP) is a Cisco proprietary link aggregation protocol
- PAgP packets are sent to the destination Multicast MAC address 01-00-0C-CC-CC-CC

PAgP Port Modes

- PAgP supports different ports modes which determine EtherChannel formation
- The on mode is commonly mistaken as a PAgP mode; but it is not
- The on mode forces a port to be placed into a channel unconditionally
- The on mode disables EtherChannel protocol negotiation
- Auto mode is a PAgP mode
- Auto mode will negotiate and EtherChannel only if the device receives PAgP packets
- Desirable mode is a PAgP mode
- Desirable mode causes a port to initiate PAgP negotiation for a channel
- PAgP EtherChannel combinations are illustrated in the table below:

Switch 1 PAgP Mode	Switch 2 PAgP Mode	EtherChannel Result
Auto	Auto	No EtherChannel Formed
Auto	Desirable	EtherChannel Formed
Desirable	Auto	EtherChannel Formed
Desirable	Desirable	EtherChannel Formed

PAgP Learn Method

Switches running PAgP are classified as either physical learners or aggregate learners

- PAgP physical learners are switches that learn MAC addresses using the physical ports
- Physical learners forward traffic to addresses based on the port the address was learned
- An aggregate learner learns addresses based on the aggregate (logical) EtherChannel

- With logical learning, the switch to transmit packets by using any of the channel interfaces
- Aggregate learning is the default in current Cisco IOS switches
- By default, PAgP is not able to detect whether a neighbor switch is a physical learner
- The learning method must be manually set to physical learning to physical learner switches

PAgP EtherChannel Protocol Packet Forwarding

- PAgP allows all links within the EtherChannel to be used to forward and receive user traffic
- DTP and CDP send and receive packets over all the physical interfaces in the EtherChannel
- PAgP sends and receives PAgP PDUs from interfaces that are up
- PAgP sends and received PAgP PDUs from interfaces enabled for auto or desirable modes
- An EtherChannel trunk sends and receives PAgP frames on the lowest numbered VLAN
- Spanning Tree always chooses first operational port in an EtherChannel bundle
- STP sends packets over a single physical interface in the EtherChannel

Link Aggregation Control Protocol Overview

- Link Aggregation Control Protocol (LACP) is part of the IEEE 802.3ad specification
- LACP and PAgP are incompatible
- LACP requires that channel ports only be full-duplex as half-duplex is not supported
- Half-duplex ports in an LACP EtherChannel are placed into the suspended state
- LACP packets are sent to the Slow Protocols Multicast group address 01-80-C2-00-00-02
- Architecturally, the LACP application is a client to the MAC Sub-Layer
- The Link Aggregation Sub-Layer binds multiple physical ports
- The Link Aggregation Sub-Layer presents ports to upper Layers as a single logical port
- The LACP defines frame collection and distribution along with an LACP agent

LACP Port Modes

- LACP supports the automatic creation of port channels by exchanging LACP packets
- LACP does this by learning the capabilities of port groups dynamically
- LACP supports two modes:
    1. Active Mode
    2. Passive Mode

- LACP active mode places a switch port into an active negotiating state
- Active mode is the LACP equivalent of PAgP desirable mode
- In passive mode, the port only responds to LACP packets that the interface receives

LACP Parameters

- LACP uses the following parameters:
    1. LACP System Priority
    2. LACP Port Priority
    3. LACP Administrative Key

- You must configure an LACP system priority on each device running the LACP protocol
- The LACP system priority can be configured automatically or through the CLI
- LACP uses the system priority with the device MAC address to form the system ID
- You must also configure an LACP port priority on each port configured to use LACP
- The port priority can be configured automatically or through the CLI
- LACP uses the port priority to decide which ports should be put in standby mode
- LACP automatically configures an administrative key value on each port
- The administrative key defines the ability of a port to aggregate with other ports
- A port's ability to aggregate is determined by its physical characteristics

LACP Redundancy

- LACP provides two key features which provide redundancy for LACP EtherChannels:
    1. LACP hot-standby ports
    2. LACP 1:1 redundancy with fast switchover

EtherChannel Load Distribution Methods

- EtherChannel load distribution (load balancing) is based on a polymorphic algorithm
- The different EtherChannel load distribution methods supported in Cisco IOS are:

Method	Description
dst-ip	Performs load distribution based on the destination IP address
dst-mac	Performs load distribution based on the destination MAC address
dst-port	Performs load distribution based on the destination Layer 4 port
src-dst-ip	Performs load distribution based on the source or destination IP address
src-dst-mac	Performs load distribution based on the source or destination MAC address
src-dst-port	Performs load distribution based on the source or destination Layer 4 port
src-ip	Performs load distribution based on the source IP address
src-mac	Performs load distribution based on the source MAC address
src-port	Performs load distribution based on the source Layer 4 port

EtherChannel Configuration Guidelines

- Each EtherChannel can have up to eight compatibly configured Ethernet interfaces
- All interfaces in the EtherChannel must operate at the same speeds and duplex modes
- Ensure all interfaces in the EtherChannel are enabled
- Ports follow the parameters set for the first group port added
- Ports configured for SPAN will be removed from the EtherChannel group
- Assign all interfaces to the same VLAN or configure them as trunks
- Similar interfaces with different STP path costs can still be used to form an EtherChannel

Protecting STP When Using EtherChannels

- EtherChannel Guard detects EtherChannel mis-configuration between devices
- EtherChannel Guard places mis-configured switch interfaces in the err-disabled state
- EtherChannel Guard also prints a message on the console advising of this state
- By default, EtherChannel Guard is enabled and requires no further configuration

CHAPTER 6

Understanding and Configuring LAN Security

In addition to being able to implement a switched internetwork, it is important to understand how to secure it. LAN security is a fundamental requirement when designing and implementing a network. This chapter describes common LAN security mechanisms and protocols. The following core SWITCH exam objective is covered in this chapter:

- Implement a Security Extension of a Layer 2 solution, given a network design and a set of requirements

This chapter will be divided into the following sections:

- Switch Port Security
- Dynamic ARP Inspection
- DHCP Snooping and IP Source Guard
- Securing Trunk Links
- Identity Based Networking Services
- Private VLANs
- Port ACLs and VLAN ACLs
- Other Security Features

SWITCH Exam Objective	Chapter Section(s) Covered
• Configure port security features	• Switch Port Security
• Configure general security features	• Dynamic ARP Inspection • DHCP Snooping and IP Source Guard • Securing Trunk Links • Identity Based Networking Services • Other Security Features
• Configure private VLANs	• Private VLANs
• Configure VACL and PACL	• Port ACLs and VLAN ACLs

Switch Port Security

The port security feature is a dynamic Catalyst switch feature that secures switch ports, and ultimately the CAM table, by limiting the number of MAC addresses that can be learned on a particular port or interface. With the port security feature, the switch maintains a table that is used to identify which MAC address (or addresses) can access which local switch port. Additionally, the switch can also be configured to allow only a certain number of MAC addresses to be learned on any given switch port. Port security is illustrated below in Figure 6-1:

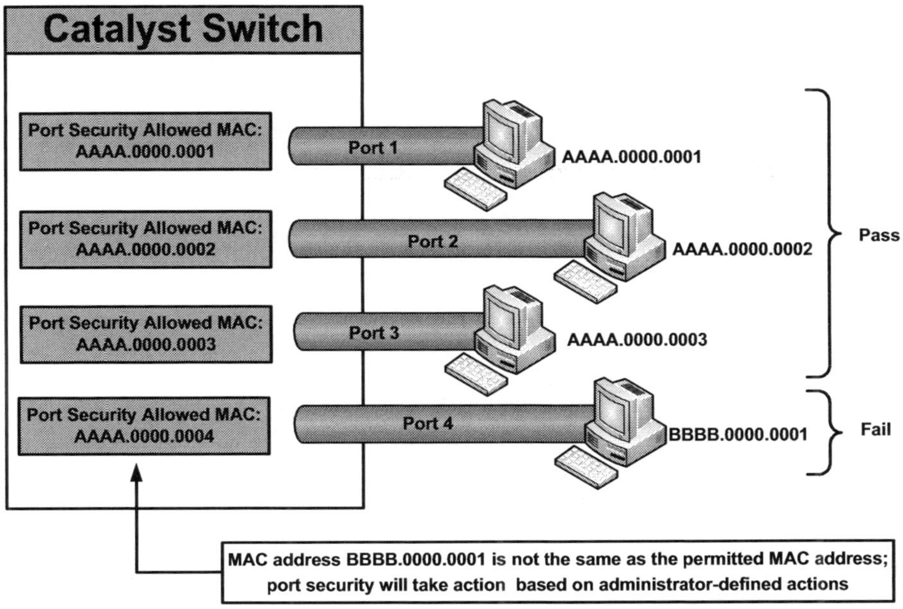

Fig. 6-1. Port Security Operation

Figure 6-1 shows four ports on a Catalyst switch configured to allow a single MAC address via the port security feature. Ports 1 through 3 are connected to hosts whose MAC address matches the address permitted by port security. Assuming no other filtering is in place, these hosts are able to forward frames through their respective switch ports. Port 4, however, has been configured to allow a host with MAC address AAAA.0000.0004, but instead a host with MAC address BBBB.0000.0001 has been connected to this port. Because the host MAC and the permitted MAC are not the same, port security will take appropriate action on the port as defined by the administrator. The valid port security actions will be described in detail later in this chapter.

The port security feature is designed to protect the switched LAN from two primary methods of attack. These attack methods, which will be described in the following section, are:

1. CAM Table Overflow Attacks
2. MAC Spoofing Attacks

CAM Table Overflow Attacks

Switch CAM tables are storage locations that contain lists of MAC addresses known on physical ports, as well as their VLAN parameters. Dynamically learned contents of the switch CAM table, or MAC address table, can be viewed by issuing the `show mac-address-table dynamic` command as illustrated in the following output:

```
VTP-Server-1#show mac-address-table dynamic
          Mac Address Table
-------------------------------------------

Vlan    Mac Address       Type        Ports
----    -----------       --------    -----
   2    000c.cea7.f3a0    DYNAMIC     Fa0/1
   2    0013.1986.0a20    DYNAMIC     Fa0/2
   6    0004.c16f.8741    DYNAMIC     Fa0/3
   6    0030.803f.ea81    DYNAMIC     Fa0/4
   8    0004.c16f.8742    DYNAMIC     Fa0/5
   8    0030.803f.ea82    DYNAMIC     Fa0/6
Total Mac Addresses for this criterion: 6
```

Switches, like all computing devices, have finite memory resources. This means that the CAM table has a fixed, allocated memory space. CAM table overflow attacks target this limitation by flooding the switch with a large number of randomly generated invalid source and destination MAC addresses until the CAM table fills up and the switch is no longer able to accept new entries. In such situations, the switch effectively turns into a hub and simply begins to broadcast all newly received frames to all ports (within the same VLAN) on the switch, essentially turning the VLAN into one big Broadcast domain.

CAM table attacks are easy to perform because common tools, such as MACOF and DSNIFF, are readily available to perform these activities. While increasing the number of VLANs, which reduces the size of Broadcast domains, can assist in reducing the effects of CAM table attacks, the recommended security solution is to configure the port security feature on the switch.

MAC Spoofing Attacks

MAC address spoofing is used to spoof a source MAC address in order to impersonate other hosts or devices in the network. Spoofing is simply a term that means masquerading or pretending to be someone you are not. The primary objective of MAC spoofing is to confuse the switch and cause it to believe that the same host is connected to two ports, which causes the switch to attempt to forward frames destined to the trusted host to the attacker as well. Figure 6-2 below shows the CAM table of a switch connected to four different network hosts:

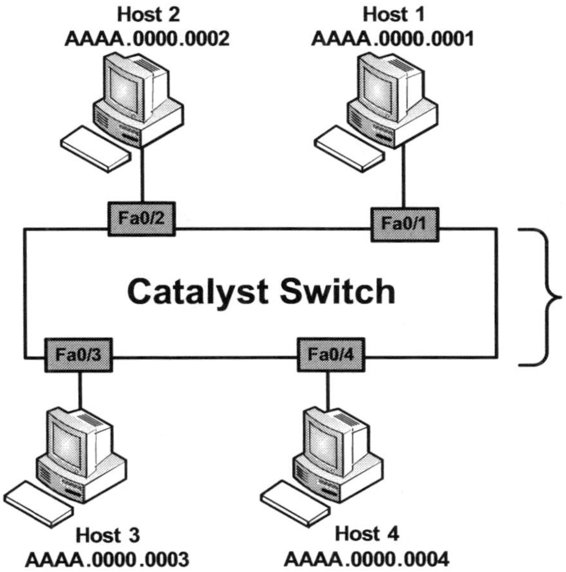

Switch CAM TABLE	
MAC ADDRESS	INTERFACE/ PORT
AAAA.0000.0001	FastEthernet0/1
AAAA.0000.0002	FastEthernet0/2
AAAA.0000.0003	FastEthernet0/3
AAAA.0000.0004	FastEthernet0/4

Fig. 6-2. Building the Switch CAM Table

In Figure 6-2, the switch is operating normally and, based on CAM table entries, knows the MAC addresses for all devices connected to its ports. Based on the current CAM table, if Host 4 wanted to send a frame to Host 2, the switch would simply forward the frame out of its FastEthernet0/2 interface toward Host 2, for example.

Now, assume that Host 1 has been compromised by an attacker who wants to receive all traffic destined for Host 2. By using MAC address spoofing, the attacker crafts an Ethernet frame using the source address of Host 2. When the switch receives this frame, it notes the source MAC address and overwrites the CAM table entry for the MAC address of Host 2, and points it to port FastEthernet0/1 instead of FastEthernet0/2, where the real Host 2 is connected. This concept is illustrated below in Figure 6-3:

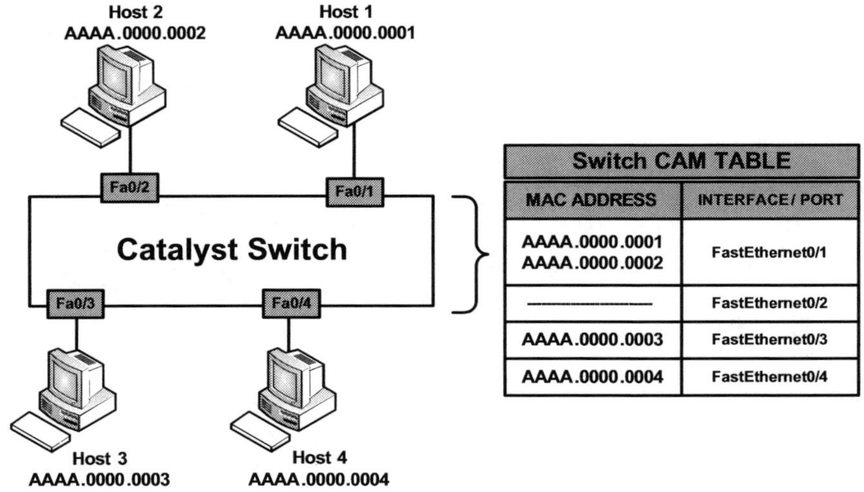

Fig. 6-3. MAC Address Spoofing

Referencing Figure 6-3, when Host 3 or Host 4 attempts to send frames to Host 2, the switch will forward them out of FastEthernet0/1 to Host 1 because the CAM table has been poisoned by a MAC spoofing attack. When Host 2 sends another frame, the switch relearns its MAC address from FastEthernet0/2 and rewrites the CAM table entry once again to reflect this change. The result is a tug-of-war between Host 2 and Host 1 as to which host owns this MAC address.

In addition, this confuses the switch and causes repetitive rewrites of MAC address table entries, causing a Denial of Service (DoS) attack on the legitimate host (i.e. Host 2). If the number of spoofed MAC addresses used is high, this attack could have serious performance consequences for the switch that is constantly rewriting its CAM table. MAC address spoofing attacks can be mitigated by implementing port security.

Port Security Secure Addresses

The port security feature can be used to specify what specific MAC address is permitted access to a switch port as well as to limit the number of MAC addresses that can be supported on a single switch port. The methods of port security implementation described in this section are as follows:

- Static secure MAC addresses
- Dynamic secure MAC addresses
- Sticky secure MAC addresses

Static secure MAC addresses are statically configured by network administrators and are stored in the MAC address table as well as in the switch configuration. When static secure MAC addresses are assigned to a secure port, the switch will not forward frames that do not have a source MAC address that matches the configured static secure MAC address or addresses.

Dynamic secure MAC addresses are dynamically learned by the switch and are stored in the MAC address table. However, unlike static secure MAC addresses, dynamic secure MAC address entries are removed from the switch when the switch is reloaded or powered down. These addresses must then be relearned by the switch when it boots up again.

Sticky secure MAC addresses are a mix of static secure MAC addresses and dynamic secure MAC addresses. These addresses can be learned dynamically or configured statically and are stored in the MAC address table as well as in the switch configuration (NVRAM). This means that when the switch is powered down or rebooted, it will not need to dynamically discover the MAC addresses again because they will already be saved in the configuration file.

Port Security Actions

Once port security has been enabled, administrators can define the actions the switch will take in the event of a port security violation. Cisco IOS software allows administrators to specify four different actions to take when a violation occurs, as follows:

1. Protect
2. Shutdown (default)
3. Restrict
4. Shutdown VLAN

The protect option forces the port into a protected port mode. In this mode, the switch will simply discard all Unicast or Multicast frames with unknown source MAC addresses. When the switch is configured to protect a port, it will not send out a notification when operating in protected port mode, meaning that administrators would never know when any traffic was prevented by the switch port operating in this mode.

The shutdown option places a port in an errdisabled state when a port security violation occurs. The corresponding port LED on the switch is also turned off when a port security violation occurs and this configured action mode is used. In shutdown mode, the switch sends out an SNMP trap and a Syslog message, and the violation counter is incremented. This is the default action taken when port security is enabled on an interface.

The restrict option is used to drop packets with unknown MAC addresses when the number of secure MAC addresses reaches the administrator-defined maximum limit for the port. In this mode, the switch will continue to restrict additional MAC addresses from sending frames until a sufficient number of secure MAC addresses is removed, or the number of maximum allowable addresses is increased. As is the case with the shutdown option, the switch sends out an SNMP trap and a Syslog message, and the violation counter is incremented.

The shutdown VLAN option is similar to the shutdown option; however, this option shuts down a VLAN instead of the entire switch port. This configuration could be applied to ports that have more than one single VLAN assigned to them, such as a voice VLAN and a data VLAN, for example, as well as to trunk links on the switches.

Configuring Port Security

Before configuring port security, it is recommended that the switch port be statically configured as a Layer 2 access port. This configuration is illustrated in the following output:

```
VTP-Server-1(config)#interface fastethernet 0/1
VTP-Server-1(config-if)#switchport
VTP-Server-1(config-if)#switchport mode access
```

NOTE: The `switchport` command is not required in Layer 2 switches, such as the Catalyst 2950 and Catalyst 2960 series switches. However, it must be used on Multilayer switches, such as the Catalyst 3750, Catalyst 4500, and Catalyst 6500 series switches.

By default, port security is disabled; however, this feature can be enabled using the `switchport port-security [mac-address {mac-address} [vlan {vlan-id | {access | voice}}] | mac-address {sticky} [mac-address | vlan {vlan-id | {access | voice}}]] [maximum {value} [vlan {vlan-list | {access | voice}}]]` interface configuration command. The options that are available with this command are described below in Table 6-1:

Table 6-1. Port Security Configuration Keywords

Keyword	Description
`mac-address {mac-address}`	This keyword is used to specify a static secure MAC address. You can add additional secure MAC addresses up to the maximum value configured.
`vlan {vlan id}`	This keyword should be used on a trunk port only to specify the VLAN ID and the MAC address. If no VLAN ID is specified, the native VLAN is used.
`vlan access`	This keyword should be used on an access port only to specify the VLAN as an access VLAN.
`vlan voice`	This keyword should be used on an access port only to specify the VLAN as a voice VLAN. This option is only available if a voice VLAN is configured on the specified port.
`mac-address {sticky} [mac-address]`	This keyword is used to enable dynamic or sticky learning on the specified interface or to configure a static secure MAC address.
`maximum {value}`	This keyword is used to specify the maximum number of secure addresses that can be learned on an interface. The default is 1.

Configuring Static Secure MAC Addresses

The following output illustrates how to enable port security on an interface and to configure a static secure MAC address of 001f:3c59:d63b on a switch access port:

```
VTP-Server-1(config)#interface gigabitethernet 0/2
VTP-Server-1(config-if)#switchport
VTP-Server-1(config-if)#switchport mode access
VTP-Server-1(config-if)#switchport port-security
VTP-Server-1(config-if)#switchport port-security mac-address 001f.3c59.d63b
```

The following output illustrates how to enable port security on an interface and to configure a static secure MAC address of 001f:3c59:d63b in VLAN 5 on a switch trunk port:

```
VTP-Server-1(config)#interface gigabitethernet 0/2
VTP-Server-1(config-if)#switchport
VTP-Server-1(config-if)#switchport trunk encapsulation dot1q
VTP-Server-1(config-if)#switchport mode trunk
VTP-Server-1(config-if)#switchport port-security
VTP-Server-1(config-if)#switchport port-security mac-address 001f.3c59.d63b
                        vlan 5
```

The following output illustrates how to enable port security on an interface and to configure a static secure MAC address of 001f:3c59:5555 for VLAN 5 (the data VLAN) and a static secure MAC address of 001f:3c59:7777 for VLAN 7 (the voice VLAN) on a switch access port:

```
VTP-Server-1(config)#interface gigabitethernet 0/2
VTP-Server-1(config-if)#switchport
VTP-Server-1(config-if)#switchport mode access
VTP-Server-1(config-if)#switchport access vlan 5
VTP-Server-1(config-if)#switchport voice vlan 7
VTP-Server-1(config-if)#switchport port-security
VTP-Server-1(config-if)#switchport port-security maximum 2
VTP-Server-1(config-if)#switchport port-security mac-address 001f.3c59.5555
                        vlan access
VTP-Server-1(config-if)#switchport port-security mac-address 001f.3c59.7777
                        vlan voice
```

While multi-VLAN access port configuration will be described in detail later in this guide, in the chapter pertaining to the configuration of Catalyst switches to support voice traffic, it is very important to remember that when enabling port security on an interface that is also configured with a voice VLAN in conjunction with the data VLAN, the maximum allowed secure addresses on the port should be set to 2. This is performed via the `switchport port-security maximum 2` interface configuration command, which is included in the output above.

One of the two MAC addresses is used by the IP phone and the switch learns about this address on the voice VLAN. The other MAC address is used by a host (such as a PC) that may be connected to the IP phone. This MAC address will be learned by the switch on the data VLAN.

Verifying Static Secure MAC Address Configuration

Global port security configuration parameters can be validated by issuing the `show port-security` command. The following shows the output printed by this command based on default values:

```
VTP-Server-1#show port-security
Secure Port      MaxSecureAddr  CurrentAddr  SecurityViolation  Security
Action
                    (Count)         (Count)       (Count)
---------------------------------------------------------------------------
     Gi0/2             1               1             0              Shutdown
---------------------------------------------------------------------------
Total Addresses in System : 1
Max Addresses limit in System : 1024
```

As seen in the output above, by default, only a single secure MAC address is permitted per port. In addition to this, the default action in the event of a violation is to shut down the port. The text in bold indicates that only a single secured address is known, which is the static address configured on the interface. The same can also be confirmed by issuing the `show port-security interface [name]` command as illustrated in the following output:

```
VTP-Server-1#show port-security interface gi 0/2
Port Security : Enabled
Port status : SecureUp
Violation mode : Shutdown
Maximum MAC Addresses : 1
Total MAC Addresses : 1
Configured MAC Addresses : 1
Sticky MAC Addresses : 0
Aging time : 0 mins
Aging type : Absolute
SecureStatic address aging : Disabled
Security Violation count : 0
```

NOTE: The modification of the other default parameters in the above output will be described in detail as we progress through this chapter.

To see the actual configured static secure MAC address on the port, the `show port-security address` or the `show running-config interface [name]` command must be used. The following output illustrates the show port-security address command:

```
VTP-Server-1#show port-security address
               Secure Mac Address Table
-------------------------------------------------------------------
Vlan    Mac Address       Type                 Ports   Remaining Age
                                                          (mins)
----    -----------       ----                 -----   -------------
   1    001f.3c59.d63b    SecureConfigured     Gi0/2        -
-------------------------------------------------------------------
Total Addresses in System : 1
Max Addresses limit in System : 1024
```

Configuring Dynamic Secure MAC Addresses

By default, when port security is enabled on a port, the port will dynamically learn and secure one MAC address without any further configuration from the administrator. To allow the port to learn and secure more than a single MAC address, the `switchport port-security maximum [number]` command must be used. Keep in mind that the `[number]` is platform-dependent and will vary on different Cisco Catalyst switch models.

REAL-WORLD IMPLEMENTATION

In production networks with Cisco Catalyst 3750 switches, it is always a good idea to determine what the switch will be used for and then select the appropriate Switch Database Management (SDM) template via the `sdm prefer {access | default | dual-ipv4-and-ipv6 {default | routing | vlan} | routing | vlan} [desktop]` global configuration command.

Each template allocates system resources to best support the features being used or that will be used. By default, the switch attempts to provide a balance to all features. However, this may impose a limit on the maximum possible values for other available features and functions in order to achieve balance between all features. An example would be the maximum possible number of secure MAC addresses that can be learned or configured when using port security.

The following output illustrates how to configure a switch port to dynamically learn and secure up to two MAC addresses on interface GigabitEthernet0/2:

```
VTP-Server-1(config)#interface gigabitethernet 0/2
VTP-Server-1(config-if)#switchport
VTP-Server-1(config-if)#switchport mode access
VTP-Server-1(config-if)#switchport port-security
VTP-Server-1(config-if)#switchport port-security maximum 2
```

Verifying Dynamic Secure MAC Addresses

Dynamic secure MAC address configuration can be verified using the same commands as those illustrated in the static secure address configuration examples, with the exception of the `show running-config` command. This is because, unlike static or sticky secure MAC addresses, all dynamically learned addresses are not saved in the switch configuration and are removed if the port is shut down. These same addresses must then be relearned when the port comes back up. The following output illustrates the `show port-security address` command, which shows an interface configured for secure dynamic MAC address learning:

```
VTP-Server-1#show port-security address
          Secure Mac Address Table
-------------------------------------------------------------------
Vlan    Mac Address       Type                Ports   Remaining Age
                                                          (mins)
----    -----------       ----                -----   -------------
   1    001d.09d4.0238    SecureDynamic       Gi0/2       -
   1    001f.3c59.d63b    SecureDynamic       Gi0/2       -
-------------------------------------------------------------------
Total Addresses in System : 2
Max Addresses limit in System : 1024
```

Configuring Sticky Secure MAC Addresses

The following output illustrates how to configure dynamic sticky learning on a port and restrict the port to dynamically learn up to a maximum of 10 MAC addresses:

```
VTP-Server-1(config)#interface gigabitethernet 0/2
VTP-Server-1(config-if)#switchport
VTP-Server-1(config-if)#switchport mode access
VTP-Server-1(config-if)#switchport port-security
VTP-Server-1(config-if)#switchport port-security mac-address sticky
VTP-Server-1(config-if)#switchport port-security maximum 10
```

Based on the configuration above, by default, up to 10 addresses will be dynamically learned on interface GigabitEthernet0/2 and will be added to the current switch configuration. When sticky address learning is enabled, MAC addresses learned on each port are automatically saved to the current switch configuration and added to the address table. The following output shows the dynamically learned MAC addresses (in bold font) on interface Gi0/2:

```
VTP-Server-1#show running-config interface gigabitethernet 0/2
Building configuration...

Current configuration : 550 bytes
!
interface GigabitEthernet0/2
 switchport
```

```
 switchport mode access
 switchport port-security
 switchport port-security maximum 10
 switchport port-security mac-address sticky
 switchport port-security mac-address sticky 0004.c16f.8741
 switchport port-security mac-address sticky 000c.cea7.f3a0
 switchport port-security mac-address sticky 0013.1986.0a20
 switchport port-security mac-address sticky 001d.09d4.0238
 switchport port-security mac-address sticky 0030.803f.ea81
...
```

The MAC addresses in bold text in the output above are dynamically learned and added to the current configuration. No manual administrator configuration is required to add these addresses to the configuration. By default, sticky secure MAC addresses are not automatically added to the startup configuration (NVRAM). To ensure that this information is saved to NVRAM, which means that these addresses are not relearned when the switch is restarted, it is important to remember to issue the `copy running-config startup-config` command, or the `copy system:running-config nvram:startup-config` command, depending on the IOS version of the switch on which this feature is implemented. The following output shows the `show port-security address` command on a port configured for sticky address learning:

```
VTP-Server-1#show port-security address
               Secure Mac Address Table
-------------------------------------------------------------------
Vlan    Mac Address       Type                Ports   Remaining Age
                                                          (mins)
----    -----------       ----                -----   -------------
   1    0004.c16f.8741    SecureSticky        Gi0/2         -
   1    000c.cea7.f3a0    SecureSticky        Gi0/2         -
   1    0013.1986.0a20    SecureSticky        Gi0/2         -
   1    001d.09d4.0238    SecureSticky        Gi0/2         -
   1    0030.803f.ea81    SecureSticky        Gi0/2         -
-------------------------------------------------------------------
Total Addresses in System : 5
Max Addresses limit in System : 1024
```

Configuring the Port Security Aging Time

By default, secure MAC addresses will not be aged out and will remain in the switch MAC table until the switch is powered off. This means that even if a host with a secured MAC address is removed from the switch port, the MAC address entry will be retained in the switch CAM table. This default behavior may be adjusted by configuring aging values for dynamic and secure static MAC addresses. The valid aging time range is 0 to 1440 minutes.

Port security aging for both static and dynamic secure addresses is configured using the `switchport port-security [aging {static|time {aging_time} |type {absolute|inactivity}}]` interface configuration command. The following output illustrates the command required to configure an aging time of 2 hours for dynamic secure addresses:

```
VTP-Server-1(config)#interface gigabitethernet 0/2
VTP-Server-1(config-if)#switchport
VTP-Server-1(config-if)#switchport mode access
VTP-Server-1(config-if)#switchport port-security
VTP-Server-1(config-if)# switchport port-security aging time 120
```

The following output illustrates how to configure aging for static secure MAC addresses:

```
VTP-Server-1(config)#interface gigabitethernet 0/2
VTP-Server-1(config-if)#switchport port-security aging static
```

Verifying the Port Security Aging Time

The port security aging time configuration can be validated using either the `show port-security interface [name]` command as illustrated in the following output, or the `show port-security address` command as illustrated in the output to follow:

```
VTP-Server-1#show port-security interface gi 0/2
Port Security : Enabled
Port status : SecureUp
Violation mode : Shutdown
Maximum MAC Addresses : 2
Total MAC Addresses : 2
Configured MAC Addresses : 1
Sticky MAC Addresses : 0
Aging time : 120 mins
Aging type : Absolute
SecureStatic address aging : Enabled
Security Violation count : 0
```

```
VTP-Server-1#show port-security address
          Secure Mac Address Table
-------------------------------------------------------------------
Vlan    Mac Address       Type                Ports   Remaining Age
                                                          (mins)
----    -----------       ----                -----   -------------
   1    0000.0000.aaaa    SecureConfigured    Gi0/2     117
   1    001d.09d4.0238    SecureDynamic       Gi0/2     109
-------------------------------------------------------------------
Total Addresses in System : 2
Max Addresses limit in System : 1024
```

NOTE: By default, the aging time is set to 0, which means that secure MAC addresses will never be aged out. Therefore, to enable secure address aging for a particular port, you must set the aging time to a value other than 0 for that particular port. Additionally, it is important to remember that configuring secure address aging parameters allows administrators to remove and add hosts on a secure port without manually deleting the existing secure MAC addresses, while at the same time still limiting the number of secure addresses on a port.

Configuring the Port Security Aging Type

In addition to allowing administrators to specify an aging time, Cisco IOS software also allows administrators to specify the following two aging types that can also be configured on ports configured with the port security feature:

1. Absolute
2. Inactivity

The absolute mechanism causes the secured MAC addresses on the port to age out after a fixed specified time. All references are flushed from the secure address list after the specified time and the address must then be relearned on the switch port. Once relearned, the timer begins again and the process is repeated as often as has been defined in the configured timer values. This is the default aging type for secure MAC addresses.

The inactivity time, also referred to as the idle time, causes secured MAC addresses on the port to age out if there is no activity (i.e. frames or data) received from the secure addresses learned on the port for the specified time period.

When configuring the port security aging type, it is important to remember that configuring an absolute timeout (default) allows all secured MAC addresses limited time access, which is determined by the value in the aging time. After this time expires, all entries are removed without prejudice.

Alternatively, configuring an aging type of inactivity allows continuous access to a limited number of secure addresses. The reason behind this is due to the fact that the switch flushes a secure address when the inactivity time expires, which allows other addresses to become secure. The following output illustrates how to configure an aging time of 2 hours for the inactivity aging type:

```
VTP-Server-1(config)#interface gigabitethernet 0/2
VTP-Server-1(config-if)#switchport
VTP-Server-1(config-if)#switchport mode access
VTP-Server-1(config-if)#switchport port-security
VTP-Server-1(config-if)# switchport port-security aging time 120
VTP-Server-1(config-if)#switchport port-security aging type inactivity
```

Verifying the Port Security Aging Type

Port security aging type configuration can be validated using either the `show port-security interface [name]` command as illustrated in the following output, or the `show port-security address` command as illustrated in the output that follows:

```
VTP-Server-1#show port-security interface gi 0/2
Port Security : Enabled
Port status : SecureUp
Violation mode : Shutdown
Maximum MAC Addresses : 2
Total MAC Addresses : 2
Configured MAC Addresses : 1
Sticky MAC Addresses : 0
Aging time : 120 mins
Aging type : Inactivity
SecureStatic address aging : Enabled
Security Violation count : 0

VTP-Server-1#show port-security address
          Secure Mac Address Table
-------------------------------------------------------------------
Vlan     Mac Address        Type                Ports   Remaining Age
                                                            (mins)
----     -----------        ----                -----   -------------
   1     0000.0000.aaaa     SecureConfigured    Gi0/2      117 (I)
   1     001d.09d4.0238     SecureDynamic       Gi0/2      109 (I)
-------------------------------------------------------------------
Total Addresses in System : 2
Max Addresses limit in System : 1024
```

NOTE: The (I) indicates the inactivity aging type. This would not be present if the absolute (default) aging type was configured on the port.

Configuring the Port Security Violation Action

As stated earlier in this chapter, Cisco IOS software allows administrators to specify four different actions to take when a violation occurs, as follows:

1. Protect
2. Shutdown (default)
3. Restrict
4. Shutdown VLAN

These options are configured using the `switchport port-security [violation {protect | restrict | shutdown | shutdown vlan}]` interface configuration command. The following output illustrates how to enable sticky learning on a port for a maximum of 10 MAC addresses. In the event that an unknown MAC address (e.g. an eleventh MAC address) is detected on the port, the port will be configured to drop the received frames:

```
VTP-Server-1(config)#interface gigabitethernet 0/2
VTP-Server-1(config-if)#switchport port-security
VTP-Server-1(config-if)#switchport port-security mac-address sticky
VTP-Server-1(config-if)#switchport port-security maximum 10
VTP-Server-1(config-if)#switchport port-security violation restrict
```

The following output illustrates how to configure a switch port to shutdown only the VLAN if a port security violation occurs:

```
VTP-Server-1(config)#interface gigabitethernet 0/2
VTP-Server-1(config-if)#switchport
VTP-Server-1(config-if)#switchport mode access
VTP-Server-1(config-if)#switchport access vlan 5
VTP-Server-1(config-if)#switchport voice vlan 7
VTP-Server-1(config-if)#switchport port-security
VTP-Server-1(config-if)#switchport port-security maximum 2
VTP-Server-1(config-if)#switchport port-security mac-address 001f.3c59.5555
                        vlan access
VTP-Server-1(config-if)#switchport port-security mac-address 001f.3c59.7777
                        vlan voice
VTP-Server-1(config-if)#switchport port-security violation shutdown vlan
```

Verifying the Port Security Violation Action

The configured port security violation action is validated via the `show port-security` command as shown in the following output:

```
VTP-Server-1#show port-security
Secure Port     MaxSecureAddr  CurrentAddr  SecurityViolation  Security
Action
                   (Count)        (Count)      (Count)

     Gi0/2           10              5            0                Restrict

Total Addresses in System : 5
Max Addresses limit in System : 1024
```

Additionally, if logging is enabled and either the restrict or shutdown violation modes are configured on the switch, messages similar to those shown in the following output will be printed on the switch console, logged into the local buffer, or sent to a Syslog server:

```
VTP-Server-1#show logging
...
[Truncated Output]
...
04:23:21: %PORT_SECURITY-2-PSECURE_VIOLATION: Security violation occurred,
caused by MAC address 0013.1986.0a20 on port Gi0/2.
04:23:31: %PORT_SECURITY-2-PSECURE_VIOLATION: Security violation occurred,
caused by MAC address 000c.cea7.f3a0 on port Gi0/2.
04:23:46: %PORT_SECURITY-2-PSECURE_VIOLATION: Security violation occurred,
caused by MAC address 0004.c16f.8741 on port Gi0/2.
```

Dynamic ARP Inspection

ARP is used to resolve IP addresses to MAC addresses. Routers and switches maintain ARP tables to show IP-to-MAC address mappings. ARP spoofing attacks are used to disguise a source MAC address via the impersonation of another host on the network. It is important to understand that an ARP spoofing attack is not the same thing as a MAC spoofing attack. In an ARP spoofing attack, the switch is misguided by poisoning the ARP cache.

In MAC spoofing, the switch is tricked into believing that the same MAC address is connected to two different ports, which effectively poisons the MAC address table. ARP spoofing occurs during the ARP request and reply message exchange between two or more hosts. It is during this exchange of messages that attackers can inject a fake reply message with their own MAC address masquerading as one of the legitimate hosts, as illustrated below in Figure 6-4:

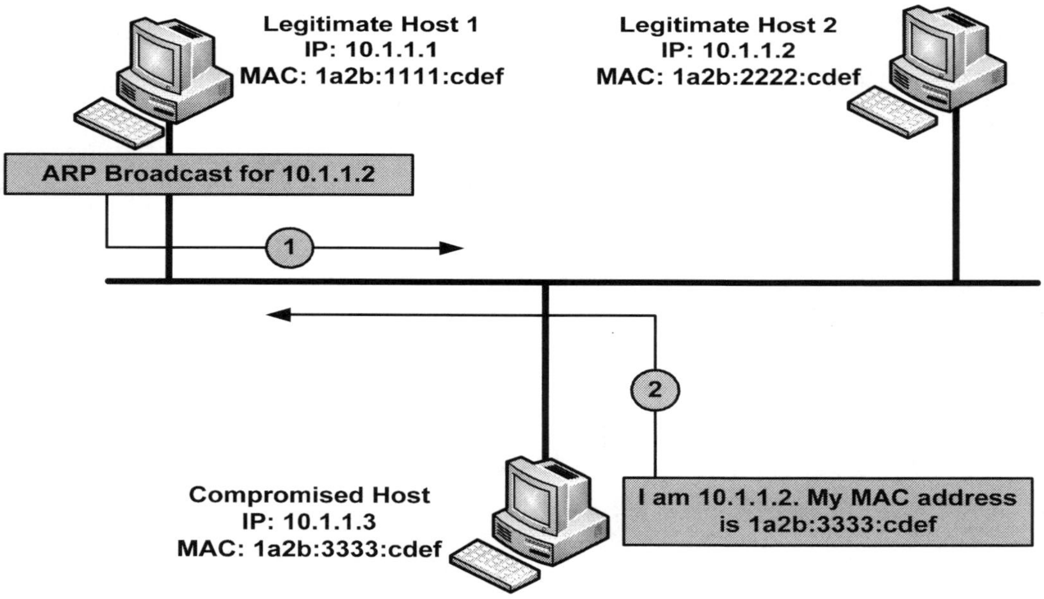

Fig. 6-4. Understanding ARP Spoofing Attacks

In Figure 6-4, three hosts reside on a shared LAN segment. There are two legitimate hosts, Host 1 and Host 2, and there is also a machine that has been compromised and is now being operated by the attacker. When Host 1 wants to send data to Host 2, it sends out an ARP broadcast to resolve the IP address of Host 2 to a MAC address. This process is illustrated in step number 1.

Before Host 2 can respond to the ARP request from Host 1, the attacker crafts a packet and responds to Host 1, providing Host 1 with the attacker's MAC address instead. The ARP table on Host 1 is updated and incorrectly reflects an IP-to-MAC address mapping of 10.1.1.2 with the MAC address 1a2b.3333.cdef. Host 1 sends all traffic that should be destined to Host 2 to the attacker's machine instead. The recommended solution to prevent such attacks in Cisco Catalyst switches is to implement Dynamic ARP Inspection (DAI).

Dynamic ARP Inspection Overview

Dynamic ARP Inspection is a Catalyst switch security feature that validates ARP packets in a network. DAI determines the validity of packets by performing an IP-to-MAC address binding inspection. Once this validity has been confirmed, packets are then forwarded to their destination; however, DAI will drop all packets with invalid IP-to-MAC address bindings that fail the inspection validation process. DAI ensures that only valid ARP requests and responses are relayed. When DAI is enabled, the switch performs the following three activities:

1. Intercepts all ARP requests and responses on untrusted ports. However, it is important to keep in mind that it inspects only inbound packets; it does not inspect outbound packets;
2. Verifies that each of these intercepted packets has a valid IP-to-MAC address binding before updating the local ARP cache or before forwarding the packet to its destination; and
3. Drops invalid ARP packets. These ARP packets contain invalid or incorrect IP-to-MAC address bindings.

Dynamic ARP Inspection can be used in both Dynamic Host Configuration Protocol (DHCP) and non-DHCP environments. In DHCP environments, DAI is typically implemented in conjunction with the DHCP snooping feature, which allows DAI to validate bindings based on the DHCP snooping Database. However, in non-DHCP environments, DAI can also validate ARP packets against a user-defined ARP ACL, which maps hosts with a statically configured IP address to their MAC address. The DHCP snooping feature will be described in detail later in this chapter.

Figure 6-5 below illustrates basic DAI operation in a DHCP environment, on a Cisco Catalyst switch enabled for DAI in conjunction with DHCP snooping:

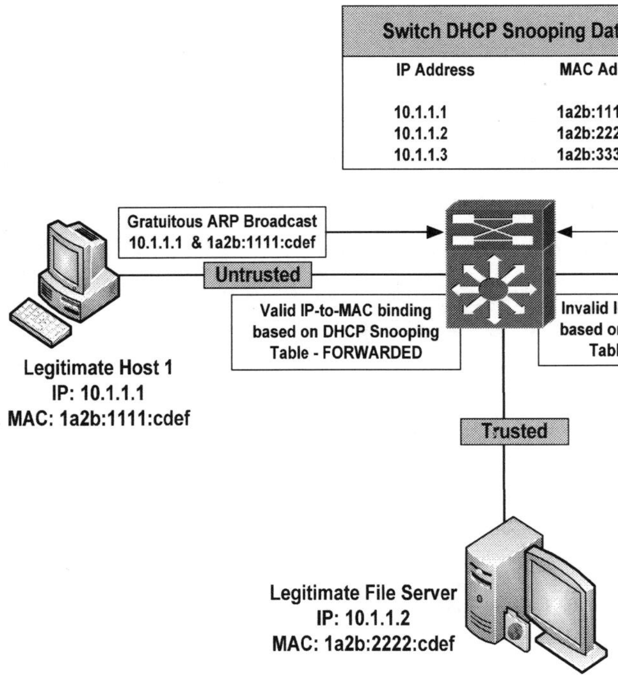

Fig. 6-5. DAI in Environments with DHCP Snooping

In Figure 6-5, DAI has been enabled on the switch to which Host 1, the compromised machine, and the file server are both connected. The switch is showing the IP-to-MAC bindings in the DHCP snooping database. Therefore, if the attacker attempts to send a GARP with a spoofed MAC address, DAI will intercept the packet, and because it has an invalid IP-to-MAC address binding, the packet will be discarded.

DAI associates a trust state with each interface on the switch. All packets that arrive on trusted interfaces bypass all DAI validation checks, and those arriving on untrusted interfaces undergo the DAI validation process. In a typical network configuration, all switch ports connected to hosts are configured as untrusted and all switch ports connected to switches (i.e. trunks) and servers are configured as trusted. With this configuration, all ARP packets entering the network from a given switch bypass the security check, but because they have been validated on the host port, they pose no security threats. No other validation is needed at any other place in the VLAN or in the network. This concept is illustrated below in Figure 6-6:

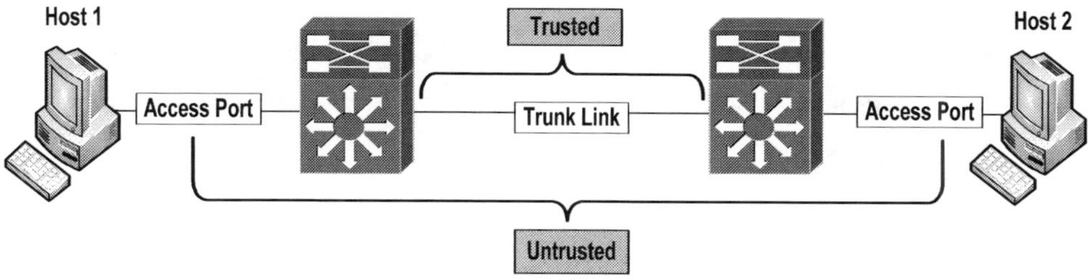

Fig. 6-6. DAI Trusted and Untrusted Interfaces

As shown in Figure 6-6, the trunk link between the two switches is trusted. This means that ARP packets that traverse this link will not be subject to DAI validation. However, the access ports that connect Host 1 and Host 2 to the switches are untrusted. This means that ARP packets that traverse these links will be subject to DAI validation. The respective switches will discard all packets with invalid bindings that are received on these interfaces.

Configuring Dynamic ARP Inspection in a DHCP Environment

Dynamic ARP Inspection is supported on access ports, trunk ports, EtherChannel ports, or private VLAN (PVLAN) ports. Globally, DAI is enabled on a per-VLAN basis using the `ip arp inspection vlan [vlan-range]` global configuration command.

Once DAI has been configured for a specific VLAN or range of VLANs, all ports are untrusted, by default. In this mode, the switch intercepts all ARP requests and responses. It verifies that the intercepted packets have valid IP-to-MAC address bindings before updating the local cache and before forwarding the packet to the appropriate destination. The switch drops invalid packets and logs them in the log buffer according to the logging configuration specified with the `ip arp inspection vlan logging` global configuration command.

When a switch port is configured as trusted, the switch does not check ARP packets that it receives on the trusted interface. Instead, it simply forwards the packets. To enable the trusted state for ports, the `ip arp inspection trust` interface configuration command must be configured on the trusted interface. The following output shows how to enable DAI for VLAN 5 and configure interface GigabitEthernet5/1 as a trusted interface:

```
VTP-Server-1(config)#ip arp inspection vlan 5
VTP-Server-1(config)#int gigabitethernet5/1
VTP-Server-1(config-if)#description 'Connected To DHCP Server'
VTP-Server-1(config-if)#switchport mode access
VTP-Server-1(config-if)#switchport access vlan 5
VTP-Server-1(config-if)#ip arp inspection trust
VTP-Server-1(config-if)#exit
```

Verifying Dynamic ARP Inspection in a DHCP Environment

Dynamic ARP Inspection configuration for a particular VLAN is validated using the `show ip arp inspection vlan [number]` command, as illustrated in the following output, while trusted interface configuration can be validated using the `show ip arp inspection interfaces [name]` command as illustrated in the output that follows:

```
VTP-Server-1#show ip arp inspection vlan 5
Source Mac Validation       : Disabled
Destination Mac Validation  : Disabled
IP Address Validation       : Disabled

 Vlan     Configuration     Operation    ACL Match            Static ACL
 ----     -------------     ---------    ---------            ----------
    5     Enabled           Active

 Vlan     ACL Logging       DHCP Logging
 ----     -----------       ------------
    5     Deny              Deny

VTP-Server-1#show ip arp inspection interfaces gigabitethernet5/1

Interface          Trust State      Rate (pps)
---------------    -----------      ----------
Gi5/1              Trusted                None
```

Configuring and Verifying DAI Validation

With DAI, by default, only the MAC and IP addresses contained within the ARP reply are validated. However, Cisco IOS software allows you to configure the switch to further inspect these ARP packets via the use of the `ip arp inspection validate {[src-mac] [dst-mac] [ip [allow zeros]]}` command. The options that are available with this command are listed and described below in Table 6-2:

Table 6-2. DAI Validation Keywords

Keyword	Description
`src-mac`	This keyword is used to compare the source MAC address in the Ethernet header against the sender MAC address in the ARP body. This check is performed on both ARP requests and responses. When enabled, packets with different MAC addresses are classified as invalid and are dropped.
`dst-mac`	This keyword is used to compare the destination MAC address in the Ethernet header against the target MAC address in the ARP body. This check is performed for ARP responses. When enabled, packets with different MAC addresses are classified as invalid and are dropped.

`ip`	This keyword is used to compare the ARP body for invalid and unexpected IP addresses, which includes 0.0.0.0, 255.255.255.255, and all IP Multicast addresses. Sender IP addresses are compared in all ARP requests and responses. Target IP addresses are checked only in ARP responses.
`allow zeros`	This keyword modifies the IP validation test so that ARPs with a sender address of 0.0.0.0 are not denied by the switch.

The following output shows how to configure DAI to compare the ARP body for invalid and unexpected IP addresses:

```
VTP-Server-1(config)#ip arp inspection vlan 5
VTP-Server-1(config)#ip arp inspection validate ip
VTP-Server-1(config)#exit
```

This configuration is validated using the `show ip arp inspection vlan [number]` command as illustrated in the following output:

```
VTP-Server-1#show ip arp inspection vlan 5
Source Mac Validation      : Disabled
Destination Mac Validation : Disabled
IP Address Validation      : Enabled

 Vlan     Configuration    Operation   ACL Match            Static ACL
 ----     -------------    ---------   ---------            ----------
    5     Enabled          Active

 Vlan     ACL Logging      DHCP Logging
 ----     -----------      ------------
    5     Deny             Deny
```

Configuring Dynamic ARP Inspection in a Non-DHCP Environment

In order to configure DAI in a non-DHCP environment, you must first configure ARP ACLs that DAI will use to validate ARP packets. ARP ACLs are configured using the `arp access-list [name]` global configuration command. Next, configure DAI to validate packets against the ARP ACL(s) via the `ip arp inspection filter [arp-acl-name] vlan [vlan-range]` global configuration command.

The following output illustrates how to configure an ARP ACL to permit ARP packets from host 10.1.1.1 with a MAC address of 1a2b.1111.cdef and how to configure and verify DAI of ARP packets in VLAN 5 based on this ACL:

```
VTP-Server-1(config)#arp access-list VLAN-5-ARP
VTP-Server-1(config-arp-nacl)#permit ip host 10.1.1.1 mac host 1a2b.1111.cdef
VTP-Server-1(config-arp-nacl)#exit
```

```
VTP-Server-1(config)#ip arp inspection filter VLAN-5-ARP vlan 5
VTP-Server-1(config)#exit
```

Verifying Dynamic ARP Inspection in a Non-DHCP Environment

The `show ip arp inspection` command is used to validate the DAI configuration. The output of this command based on the configuration above is illustrated in the following output:

```
VTP-Server-1#show ip arp inspection vlan 5

Source Mac Validation      : Disabled
Destination Mac Validation : Disabled
IP Address Validation      : Disabled

 Vlan     Configuration    Operation   ACL Match          Static ACL
 ----     -------------    ---------   ---------          ----------
    5     Enabled          Active      VLAN-5-ARP          No

 Vlan     ACL Logging      DHCP Logging
 ----     -----------      ------------
    5     Deny             Deny
```

NOTE: The `show arp access-list [name]` command can be used to view the configured ARP ACLs. This is illustrated in the following output:

```
VTP-Server-1#show arp access-list
ARP access list VLAN-5-ARP
    permit ip host 10.1.1.1 mac host 1a2b.1111.cdef
```

DHCP Snooping and IP Source Guard

DHCP spoofing and starvation attacks are methods used by intruders to exhaust the DHCP address pool on the DHCP sever, resulting in resource starvation where there are no DHCP addresses available to be assigned to legitimate users.

DHCP is used to dynamically assign hosts with IP addresses. A DHCP server can be configured to provide DHCP clients with a great deal of information, such as DNS servers, NTP servers, WINS information, and default gateway (router) information. DHCP uses UDP port 68. Cisco IOS routers and some switches can be configured as both DHCP clients and DHCP servers.

When using DHCP on a network, the DHCP client sends a DHCPDISCOVER message to locate a DHCP server. This is a Layer 2 broadcast because the client has no Layer 3 address, and so the message is directed to the Layer 2 broadcast address FFFF:FFFF:FFFF. If the DHCP server is on the same Layer 2 broadcast domain as the DHCP client, no explicit configuration is needed from a network configuration standpoint.

Upon receiving the DHCPDISCOVER message, the DHCP server offers network configuration settings to the client via the DHCPOFFER message. This is sent only to the requesting client.

The client then sends a DHCPREQUEST Broadcast message so that any other servers that had responded to its initial DHCPDISCOVER message, after the first issuing DHCP server, can reclaim the IP addresses they had offered to that client. Finally, the issuing DHCP server then confirms that the IP address has been allocated to the client by issuing a DHCPACK message to the requesting client. Figure 6-7 below illustrates the DHCP exchange between a client and a server:

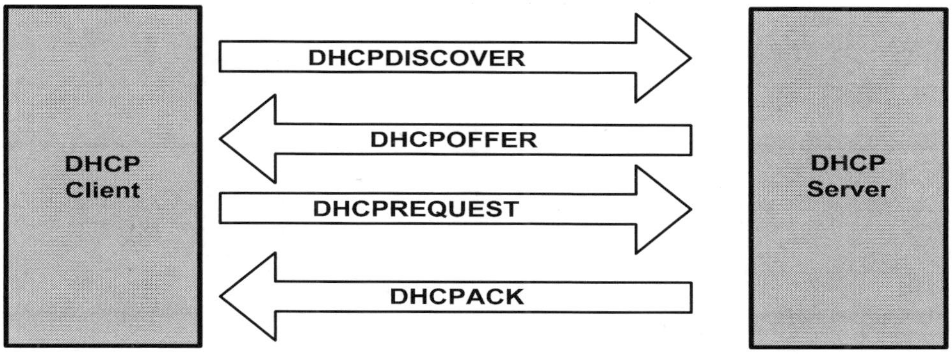

Fig. 6-7. The DHCP Client and Server Packet Exchange

DHCP starvation attacks work with MAC address spoofing by flooding a large number of DHCP requests with randomly generated spoofed MAC addresses to the target DHCP server, thereby exhausting the address space available for a period of time. This prevents legitimate DHCP clients from being serviced by the DHCP server.

Once the legitimate DHCP server has been successfully flooded and can no longer service the legitimate clients, the attacker introduces a rogue DHCP server, which then responds to the DHCP requests of legitimate clients with the intent of providing incorrect configuration information to the clients, such as default gateways and WINS or DNS servers. This forged information then allows the attacker to perform other types of attacks. Tools such as MACOF and GOBBLER can be used by attackers to perform starvation attacks.

There are several techniques that can be used to prevent such attacks from occurring. The first is port security, which can be used to limit the number of MAC addresses on a switch port and thus mitigate DHCP spoofing and starvation attacks. The second method is VLAN ACLs (VACLs), which are ACLs that are applied to entire VLANs and are used to control host communication within VLANs. VACLs are described later in this chapter. The third method, which is also the most recommended method, is to enable the DHCP snooping feature.

DHCP Snooping Overview

DHCP snooping provides network protection from rogue DHCP servers by creating a logical firewall between untrusted hosts and DHCP servers. When DHCP snooping is enabled, the switch builds and maintains a DHCP snooping table, which is also referred to as the DHCP binding table, and it is used to prevent and filter untrusted messages from the network.

DHCP snooping uses the concept of trusted and untrusted interfaces. This means that incoming packets received on untrusted ports are dropped if the source MAC address of those packets does not match the MAC address in the binding table. Figure 6-8 below illustrates the operation of the DHCP snooping feature:

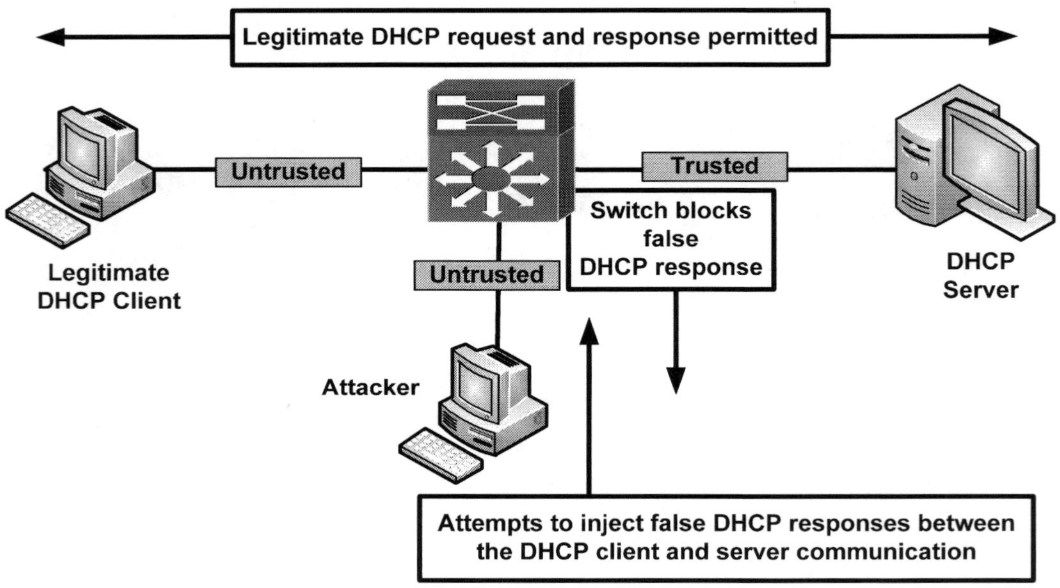

Fig. 6-8. DHCP Snooping Operation

As can be seen in Figure 6-8, an attacker attempts to inject false DHCP responses into the exchange of DHCP messages between the legitimate DHCP client and server. However, because DHCP snooping is enabled on the switch, these packets are dropped because they are originating from an untrusted interface and the source MAC address does not match the MAC address in the binding table.

The exchange between the legitimate client that is on an untrusted interface and the DHCP server is permitted because the source address does match the MAC address in the binding table entry.

Figure 6-9 below illustrates the use of the DHCP snooping table, which is used to filter untrusted DHCP messages from the network:

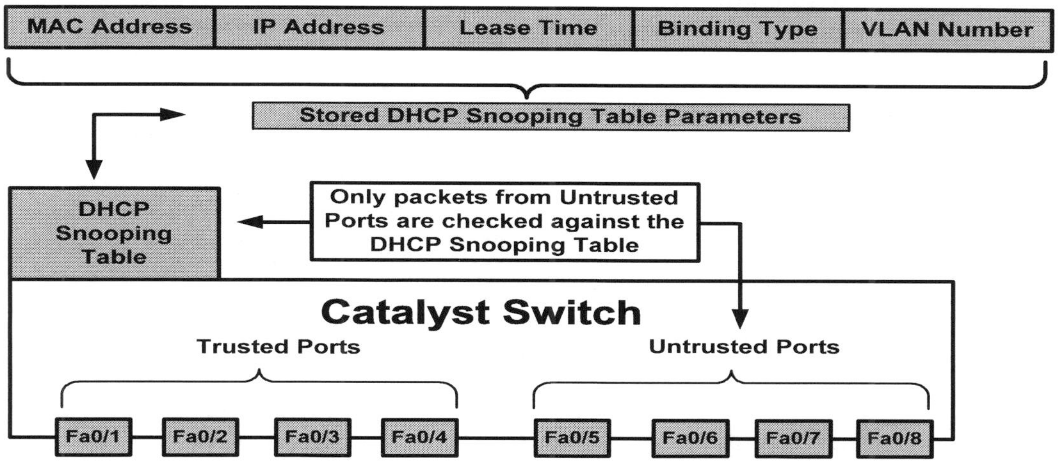

Fig. 6-9. The DHCP Snooping (Binding) Table

In Figure 6-9, packets sourced from trusted ports are not subject to DHCP snooping checks. Trusted interfaces for DHCP snooping would be configured for ports directly connected to DHCP servers. However, all packets from untrusted interfaces are checked against the entries in the DHCP snooping table.

This means that if an attacker attempts to use randomly generated MAC addresses to initiate a DHCP snooping and starvation attack, all packets will be checked against the DHCP snooping table, and because there will be no matches for those specific MAC addresses, all packets will be discarded by the switch, effectively preventing this type of attack from occurring.

Configuring DHCP Snooping

Configuring basic DHCP snooping involves three basic steps, as follows:

1. Globally enabling DHCP snooping on the switch by issuing the `ip dhcp snooping` global configuration command;
2. Enabling DHCP snooping for a VLAN or range of VLANs by issuing the `ip dhcp snooping vlan [vlan-number|vlan-range]` global configuration command; and
3. Configuring trusted interfaces for DHCP snooping by issuing the `ip dhcp snooping trust` interface configuration command. It is extremely important to remember that in order for DHCP snooping to function properly, all DHCP servers must be connected to the switch through trusted interfaces. All untrusted DHCP messages (i.e. messages from untrusted ports) will be forwarded only to trusted interfaces.

Optionally, network administrators can configure the switch to support the DHCP Relay Agent Information Option, which is DHCP Option 82, by issuing the `ip dhcp snooping information option` global configuration command when configuring DHCP snooping on the switch.

Once DHCP snooping has been enabled, administrators can use the `show ip dhcp snooping` configuration to validate their configuration. The following output shows how to configure DHCP snooping for VLAN 100 and also how to enable DHCP Option 82 insertion. Interface GigabitEthernet2/24 is connected to a DHCP server and is configured as a trusted interface:

```
VTP-Server-1(config)#ip dhcp snooping
VTP-Server-1(config)#ip dhcp snooping vlan 100
VTP-Server-1(config)#ip dhcp snooping information option
VTP-Server-1(config)#int gi 2/24
VTP-Server-1(config-if)#description 'Connected to Legitimate DHCP Server'
VTP-Server-1(config-if)#ip dhcp snooping trust
```

Cisco IOS software allows you to rate-limit, or specify, the number of DHCP messages an untrusted interface can receive per second via the `ip dhcp snooping limit rate [rate]` interface configuration command. The specified rate can be anywhere between 1 and 2048 DHCP packets per second. By default, this feature is disabled and there is no rate-limiting of DHCP packets on any interfaces when DHCP snooping is enabled. The following output demonstrates how to set a message rate limit of 150 messages per second on an untrusted interface connected to a host:

```
VTP-Server-1(config)#int gi 5/45
VTP-Server-1(config-if)#description 'Connected to Network Host'
VTP-Server-1(config-if)#ip dhcp snooping limit rate 150
```

Verifying DHCP Snooping

Once DHCP snooping has been enabled, the `show ip dhcp snooping` command can be used to validate DHCP snooping configuration, as illustrated in the following output:

```
VTP-Server-1#show ip dhcp snooping
Switch DHCP snooping is enabled.
DHCP Snooping is configured on the following VLANs:
100
Insertion of option 82 information is enabled.
Interface            Trusted        Rate limit (pps)
---------            -------        ----------------
GigabitEthernet2/24    yes              none
```

You can also use the `show ip dhcp snooping binding` command to view DHCP snooping binding entries that correspond to untrusted ports. This is illustrated in the following output:

```
VTP-Server-1#show ip dhcp snooping binding
MacAddress        IP Address        Lease (seconds)       Type          VLAN
Interface
-----------       -----------       ----------------      -----         -----

0021.8642.0b01  10.1.1.254        1600                  dynamic       100
GigabitEthernet5/1
```

IP Source Guard

The IP Source Guard feature is typically enabled in conjunction with DHCP snooping on untrusted Layer 2 ports. IP Source Guard is a feature that restricts IP traffic on untrusted Layer 2 ports by filtering the traffic based on the DHCP snooping binding database or manually configured IP source bindings. This feature is used to prevent IP spoofing attacks. Any traffic coming into the interface with a source IP address other than that assigned via DHCP or static configuration will be filtered out on the untrusted Layer 2 ports.

Initially, all IP traffic on the port is blocked except for DHCP packets that are captured by the DHCP snooping process. IP Source Guard builds and maintains an IP source binding table that is learned by DHCP snooping or manually configured bindings. Entries in the IP source binding table contain the IP address and the associated MAC and VLAN numbers. When a client receives a valid IP address from the DHCP server, or when a static IP source binding is configured by the user, a per-port and VLAN Access Control List (PVACL) is installed on the port. This filters out any IP traffic received on the interface that contains an IP address other than the address in the IP source binding table, thus preventing IP spoofing attacks.

The IP Source Guard feature is supported only on Layer 2 interfaces, which include access and trunk links. For each untrusted Layer 2 port, there are two modes of IP traffic security filtering, as follows:

1. Source IP address filter
2. Source IP and MAC address filter

In the source IP address filter mode, IP traffic is filtered based on its source IP address. Only IP traffic with a source IP address that matches the IP source binding entry is permitted. An IP source address filter is changed when a new IP source entry binding is created or deleted on the port. The port PVACL will be recalculated and reapplied in the switch hardware to reflect the IP source binding change. By default, if the IP filter is enabled without any IP source binding on the port, a default PVACL that denies all IP traffic is installed on the port. Similarly, when the IP filter is disabled, any IP source filter PVACL will be removed from the interface.

In source IP and MAC address filter mode, IP traffic is filtered based on its source IP address as well as its MAC address; only IP traffic with source IP and MAC addresses matching the IP source binding entry is permitted. When IP Source Guard is enabled in IP and MAC filtering mode, the DHCP snooping Option 82 must be enabled. Without Option 82 data, the switch cannot locate the client host port to forward the DHCP server reply, and the DHCP server reply is dropped and the client cannot obtain an IP address.

Configuring IP Source Guard

In lower-end switch models, such as the Catalyst 3750 series switch, IP Source Guard is enabled by issuing the `ip verify source [port-security]` interface configuration command. The `[port-security]` option is used to enable IP Source Guard with IP and MAC address filtering. If this option is omitted, then only IP Source Guard with IP address filtering is enabled. The following output illustrates how to enable basic IP Source Guard functionality on a Catalyst 3750 series switch:

```
VTP-Server-1(config)#ip dhcp snooping
VTP-Server-1(config)#ip dhcp snooping vlan 100
VTP-Server-1(config)#ip dhcp snooping information option
VTP-Server-1(config)#int gi 2/24
VTP-Server-1(config-if)#description 'Connected to Network Host'
VTP-Server-1(config-if)#ip verify source
```

In higher-end Catalyst switch models, such as the Catalyst 4500 and Catalyst 6500 series switches, IP Source Guard is enabled using the `ip verify source vlan dhcp-snooping [port-security]` interface configuration command. The `[port-security]` option may be used to enable IP and MAC mode filtering. The following output illustrates how to enable IP Source Guard on a Catalyst 4500 or Catalyst 6500 series switch:

```
VTP-Server-1(config)#ip dhcp snooping
VTP-Server-1(config)#ip dhcp snooping vlan 100
VTP-Server-1(config)#ip dhcp snooping information option
VTP-Server-1(config)#int gi 2/24
VTP-Server-1(config-if)#description 'Connected to Network Host'
VTP-Server-1(config-if)#ip verify source vlan dhcp-snooping
```

In environments that do not use DHCP, static bindings can be configured using the `ip source binding mac-address vlan [vlan-id] [ip-address] interface [name]` global configuration command in all Catalyst switch models that support the IP Source Guard feature. The following output illustrates how to configure a static source binding in a Catalyst switch:

```
VTP-Server-1(config)#ip source binding 1a2b.1111.cdef vlan 5 10.1.1.1 int gi
2/24
VTP-Server-1(config)#exit
```

Verifying IP Source Guard

The `show ip verify source` command is used to display all interfaces on the switch that have IP Source Guard enabled. The output of this command is illustrated as follows:

```
VTP-Server-1# show ip verify source
Interface  Filter-type  Filter-mode  IP-address       Mac-address      Vlan
---------  -----------  -----------  ---------------  ---------------  -------

gi2/24       ip           active       10.1.1.1                          5
```

IP Source Guard bindings can be viewed using the `show ip source binding` command as illustrated in the following output:

```
VTP-Server-1#show ip source binding
MacAddress          IpAddress          Lease(sec)  Type           VLAN
Interface
--------------      ---------------    ----------  -------------  ----

1A:2B:11:11:CD:EF   10.1.1.1           infinite    static         5
GigabitEthernet2/4
```

Securing Trunk Links

By default, in order for users in different VLANs to communicate, inter-VLAN routing must be employed. This can be done using a one-armed-router, also referred to as a router-on-a-stick, by using sub-interfaces on the router. Alternatively, and more commonly, Multilayer switches, such as the Cisco Catalyst 3750, 4500, and 6500 series switches, are used in the network. These switches have the capability to both route and switch. Inter-VLAN routing is a core concept and will be described in detail later in this guide.

VLAN hopping attacks are methods in which an attacker attempts to bypass a Layer 3 device to communicate directly between VLANs, with the main objective being to compromise a device residing on another VLAN. There are two primary methods used to perform VLAN hopping attacks, as follows:

1. Switch spoofing
2. Double-tagging

Switch Spoofing Attacks

In switch spoofing, the attacker impersonates a switch by emulating ISL or 802.1Q signaling, as well as Dynamic Trunking Protocol (DTP) signaling. DTP provides switches with the ability to negotiate the trunking method for the trunk link they will establish between themselves.

If an attacker can successfully emulate a trunk, the attacker's system becomes a member of all VLANs, since trunk links forward all VLAN information by default. Switch spoofing attacks attempt to exploit the default native VLAN (VLAN 1) that is used on Cisco Catalyst switches.

By default, when an access port sends a frame to a remote switch, and that packet is encapsulated into 802.1Q format with the native VLAN ID, it will be successfully forwarded to the remote switch without the need to cross a Layer 3 device. Network administrators can prevent switch spoofing attacks by performing the following actions:

- Disabling the DTP on trunk ports by issuing the `switchport nonegotiate` interface configuration command on trunk links;
- Disabling trunking capability on ports that should not be configured as trunk links by statically configuring them as access ports using the `switchport mode access` interface configuration command on all non-trunk links; and
- Preventing user data from traversing the native VLAN by specifying a VLAN other than VLAN 1, which does not span the entire Layer 2 network. For example, VLAN 5 could be configured as the native VLAN for a trunk using the `switchport trunk native vlan 5` and the `switchport trunk allowed vlan remove 5` interface configuration commands.

Double-Tagging Attacks

By default, traffic in the native VLAN using 802.1Q trunks is not tagged as frames travel between switches in the Layer 2 switched network. This default behavior means that if an attacker resides on the native VLAN used by the switches, the attacker could successfully launch a double-tagging network attack.

Double-tagging or double-encapsulated VLAN attacks involve tagging frames with two 802.1Q tags in order to forward the frames to a different VLAN. The embedded hidden 802.1Q tag inside the frame allows the frame to traverse a VLAN that the outer 802.1Q tag did not specify. This is a particularly dangerous attack because it will work even if the trunk port is set to off.

The first switch that encounters the double-tagged frame strips off the first tag and forwards the frame. This results in the frame being forwarded with the inner 802.1Q tag out of all ports on the switch, including the trunk ports configured with the native VLAN ID of the network attacker. The second switch then forwards the frame to the destination based on the VLAN identifier in the second 802.1Q header. This double-tagging concept is illustrated below in Figure 6-10:

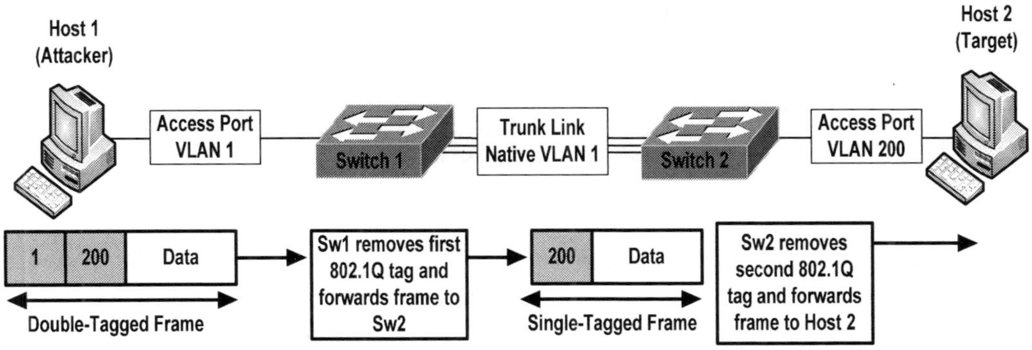

Fig. 6-10. Double-Tagging Attacks

As illustrated in Figure 6-10, an attacker has compromised Host 1 and is trying to access Host 2. The attacker sends a double-tagged frame to Switch 1, which includes the native VLAN (VLAN 1), and the VLAN Host 2 resides in, which is VLAN 200.

When Switch 1 receives the frame, it strips off the first tag and forwards the frame to Switch 2. When Switch 2 receives the frame, it contains only VLAN 200. The switch removes this tag and forwards the frame to Host 2, which resides in VLAN 200. The attacker has successfully managed to traverse the two different VLANs while bypassing any Layer 3 network devices.

To prevent double-tagging attacks, administrators should ensure that the native VLAN used on all the trunk ports is different from the VLAN ID of user access ports. It is best to use a dedicated VLAN that is specific for each pair of trunk ports and not the default VLAN. In addition to this, configuring the native VLAN to tag all traffic prevents the vulnerability of double-tagged 802.1Q frames hopping VLANs. This functionality can be enabled by issuing the `vlan dot1q tag native` global configuration command.

Identity Based Networking Services

Identity Based Networking Services (IBNS) provides identity-based network access control and policy enforcement at the switch port level. The IBNS solution extends network access security based on the 802.1x technology, Extensible Authentication Protocol (EAP) technologies, and the Remote Authentication Dial-In User (RADIUS) security server service.

Cisco IBNS offers scalable and flexible access control and policy enforcement services and capabilities at the network edge (i.e. at switch access ports) by providing the following:

- Per-user or per-service authentication services
- Policies mapped to network identity

- Port-based network access control based on authentication and authorization policies
- Additional policy enforcement based on access level

When the Cisco Access Control Server (ACS) is used as the authentication server in IBNS, the following features are available for network security administrators:

- Time and day restrictions
- NAS restrictions
- MAC address filtering
- Per-user and per-group VLAN assignments
- Per-user and per-group ACL assignments

IEEE 802.1x Overview

IEEE 802.1x is a protocol standard framework for both wired and wireless Local Area Networks that authenticates users or network devices and provides policy enforcement services at the port level in order to provide secure network access control. 802.1x is an IEEE standard for access control and authentication that provides a means for authenticating users who want to gain access to the network and placing them into a pre-determined VLAN, effectively granting them certain access rights to the network.

The 802.1x protocol provides the definition to encapsulate the transport of EAP messages at the Data Link Layer over any PPP or IEEE 802 media (e.g. Ethernet, FDDI, or Token Ring) through the implementation of a port-based network access control to a network device. EAP messages are communicated between an end device, referred to as a supplicant, and an authenticator, which can be either a switch or a wireless access point. The authenticator relays the EAP messages to the authentication server (e.g. a Cisco ACS server) via the RADIUS server protocol.

There are three primary components (or roles) in the 802.1x authentication process, as follows:

1. Supplicant or client
2. Authenticator
3. Authentication server

An IEEE 802.1x supplicant or client is simply an 802.1x-compliant device, such as a workstation, a laptop, or even an IP phone, with software that supports the 802.1x and EAP protocols. The supplicant sends an authentication request to the access LAN via the connected authenticator device (e.g. the access switch) using EAP.

An 802.1x authenticator is a device that enforces physical access control to the network based on the authentication status (i.e. permit or deny) of the supplicant. An example of an authenticator would be the switch illustrated in Figure 6-12 below. The authenticator acts as a proxy and relays information between the supplicant and the authentication server.

The authenticator receives the identity information from the supplicant via EAP over LAN (EAPOL) frames, which are verified and then encapsulated into RADIUS protocol format before being forwarded to the authentication server. It is important to remember that the EAP frames are not modified or examined during the encapsulation process, which means that the authentication server must support EAP within the native frame format. When the authenticator receives frames from the authentication server, the RADIUS header is removed, leaving only the EAP frame, which is then encapsulated in the 802.1x format. These frames are then sent back to the supplicant or client.

The authentication server is the database policy software, such as Cisco Secure ACS, that supports the RADIUS server protocol and performs authentication of the supplicant that is relayed by the authenticator via the RADIUS client-server model.

The authentication server validates the identity of the client and notifies the authenticator whether the client is allowed or denied access to the network. Based on the response from the authentication server, the authenticator relays this information back to the supplicant. It is important to remember that during the entire authentication process, the authentication server remains transparent to the client because the supplicant is communicating only to the authenticator. The RADIUS protocol with EAP extensions is the only supported authentication server; in other words, you cannot use TACACS+ or Kerberos as the authentication server.

NOTE: TACACS+ and Kerberos are authentication servers. Going into detail on the different types of authentication servers is beyond the scope of the SWITCH exam requirements.

Extensible Authentication Protocol Packet Format

802.1x authentication is initiated when the link transitions from a state of down to up. Either the switch or the client (supplicant) can initiate authentication. EAPOL is the encapsulation technique used to carry EAP frames between the supplicant and the authenticator. The frames have a destination MAC of 01-80-C3-00-00-03 whether the packet is to the supplicant or the switch. EAPOL is wrapped in an Ethernet frame as illustrated below in Figure 6-11:

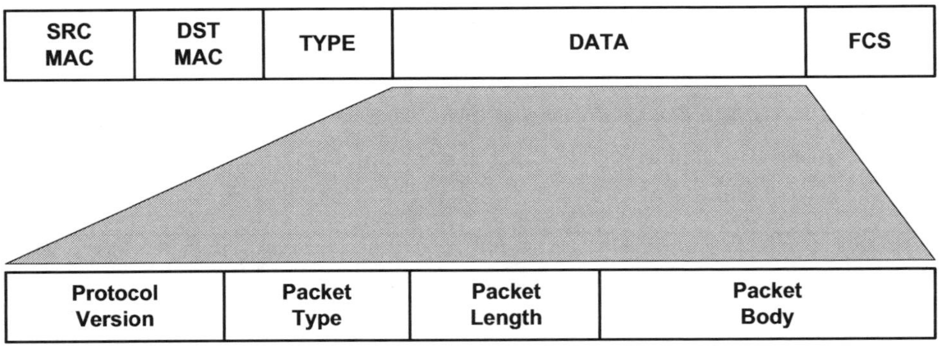

Fig. 6-11. EAPOL Frame Format

While delving into all the different fields illustrated in Figure 6-11 is beyond the scope of the SWITCH exam requirements, Table 6-3 below lists and describes common values that may be contained in the Packet Type field:

Table 6-3. EAP Packet Types

Keyword	Description
EAP Packet (0)	This packet is sent by both the supplicant and the authenticator. It is used during authentication and contains information required to complete the authentication process.
EAPOL Start (1)	This packet is sent by the supplicant when it starts authentication process.
EAPOL Logoff (2)	This packet is sent by the supplicant when it wants to terminate the 802.1x session.
EAPOL Key (3)	This packet is sent by the switch to the supplicant and contains a key used during Transport Layer Security (TLS) authentication.

The Extensible Authentication Protocol Message Exchange

The EAP message exchange is illustrated below in Figure 6-12:

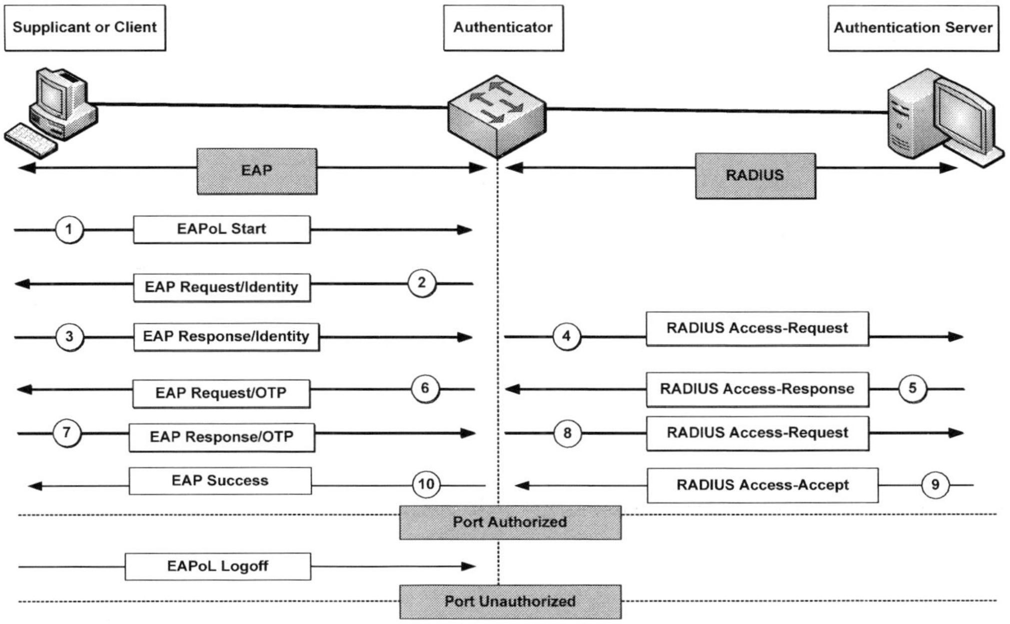

Fig. 6-12. EAP Message Exchange

The following sequence of steps reference the message exchange illustrated in Figure 6-12:

1. The client or supplicant sends the authenticator an EAPOL frame to start the authentication process.
2. The switch responds to the EAPOL frame by sending the supplicant a login request, asking for the correct credentials (e.g. username and password pair) to gain network access.
3. The supplicant provides the credentials to the authenticator.
4. The authentication encapsulates the received credentials in RADIUS format and relays them to the RADIUS authentication server.
5. When the RADIUS server receives the authentication request, it checks its database, which can be either internal or external, and then sends a response back.
6. This response is relayed by the authenticator to the supplicant.
7. The supplicant provides the requested information.
8. The authenticator relays this information to the RADIUS server.
9. Assuming that the check is successful, and the credentials match and have been validated, the supplicant receives a permit access message. VLAN assignment is added to the access-accept packet from the RADIUS server.
10. This information is relayed by the authenticator to the supplicant.

The port then transitions to an authorized state and the supplicant is allowed to send packets on to the network. When the supplicant logs off the network, the port transitions to the unauthorized state and the login and authentication process will start over when the supplicant logs back on. If the credentials are incorrect, the supplicant can also receive a deny message and will not be allowed access to the LAN, and will be blocked at the port level. The authorized and unauthorized port states are described later in this chapter.

Configuring 802.1x Port-Based Authentication

Configuring basic 802.1x port-based authentication is a relatively straightforward process that is comprised of the following five basic steps:

1. Globally enable AAA services on the switch by issuing the `aaa new-model` global configuration command. AAA must be enabled before a switch can be configured for 802.1x port-based authentication services;
2. Create or use the default 802.1x authentication method list and specify RADIUS server information by issuing the `aaa authentication dot1x [method-list|default] group [name|radius]` global configuration command;
3. Configure RADIUS server parameters (e.g. keys and ports) via the radius-server host global configuration command for an individual server or the `aaa group server radius` global configuration command for a RADIUS server group;
4. Globally enable IEEE 802.1x authentication on the switch using the `dot1x system-auth-control` global configuration command; and
5. Enable 802.1x port-based authentication on desired switch ports by issuing the dot1x port-control {auto|force-authorized |force-unauthorized} interface configuration command.

When 802.1x is enabled on the authenticator, there are two port states in which the physical ports on the authenticator may be: authorized or unauthorized. Initially, all 802.1x-enabled ports start in an unauthorized state. In this state, no traffic is allowed through the port except for 802.1x message exchange packets.

If a non-802.1x connects to an unauthorized port, the authenticator has no way of knowing that the client does not support 802.1x and so it sends the client a login request asking it for identity credentials. However, because the client does not support 802.1x, it is unable to interpret the received packet and so it does not respond to the authenticator's request.

Based on this, the authenticator denies all packets on that port and the switch port remains in the unauthorized state. Administrators control the port authorization state by using the `dot1x port-control` interface configuration command and one of the following keywords:

- The `force-authorized` keyword—disables 802.1x and causes the port to transition to the authorized state without any authentication exchange required. The port transmits and receives normal traffic without 802.1x-based authentication of the client. This is the default option.
- The `force-unauthorized` keyword—causes the port to remain in the unauthorized state, ignoring all attempts by the client to authenticate. In other words, the switch cannot provide authentication services to the client through the interface.
- The `auto` keyword—enables 802.1x authentication and forces the switch port to begin in the unauthorized state, allowing only EAPOL frames to be sent and received. The authentication process begins when the link state of the port transitions from down to up, or when an EAPOL-start frame is received. The switch requests the identity of the client and begins relaying authentication messages between the client and the authentication server. Each client attempting to access the network is uniquely identified by the switch by using the client's MAC address. This is the recommended mode when enabling 802.1x security.

The following output demonstrates the configuration of 802.1x port-based authentication on the FastEthernet0/23 and FastEthernet0/24 interfaces of a Cisco Catalyst switch. A RADIUS server with the IP address 10.1.1.254 and secret key *switchauth* will be configured to authentication 802.1x users. This RADIUS server will use UDP port 1812 for authentication services:

```
VTP-Server-1(config)#aaa new-model
VTP-Server-1(config)#aaa authentication dot1x default group radius
VTP-Server-1(config)#radius-server host 10.1.1.254 auth-port 1812 key
                     switchauth
VTP-Server-1(config)#dot1x system-auth-control
VTP-Server-1(config)#interface range fastethernet0/23 - 24
VTP-Server-1(config-if-range)#switchport mode access
VTP-Server-1(config-if-range)#dot1x port-control auto
VTP-Server-1(config-if-range)#exit
```

NOTE: It is important to remember to configure the switch port as a static access port before enabling 802.1x port-based authentication; otherwise, the error message illustrated in the following output will be printed on the switch console:

```
VTP-Server-1(config)#int f0/15
VTP-Server-1(config-if)#dot1x port-control auto
% Error: 802.1X cannot be configured on a dynamic port
```

Verifying 802.1x Port-Based Authentication

To view the 802.1x configuration of an interface, administrators should issue the `show dot1x interface [name]` command. The output of this command is shown as follows:

```
VTP-Server-1#show dot1x interface fastethernet 0/1
802.1X is enabled on FastEthernet0/1
  Status                Unauthorized
  Port-control          Auto
  Supplicant            Not set
  Multiple Hosts        Disallowed
  Current Identifier    2

  Authenticator State Machine
    State               CONNECTING
    Reauth Count        2

  Backend State Machine
    State               IDLE
    Request Count       0
    Identifier (Server) 0

  Reauthentication State Machine
    State               INITIALIZE
```

For troubleshooting, you can use the `show dot1x statistics interface [name]` command to view 802.1x statistics on a per-interface basis as shown in the following output:

```
VTP-Server-1#show dot1x statistics interface fastethernet 0/1

FastEthernet0/1

    Rx: EAPOL     EAPOL     EAPOL     EAPOL     EAP       EAP       EAP
        Start     Logoff    Invalid   Total     Resp/Id   Resp/Oth  LenError
        0         0         0         0         0         0         0

        Last      Last
        EAPOLVer  EAPOLSrc
        0         0000.0000.0000

    Tx: EAPOL     EAP       EAP
        Total     Req/Id    Req/Oth
        23        13        0
```

802.1x Multiple Hosts Authentication

In most implementations, a single network host is connected to each individual switch port. This allows 802.1x to be configured on each switch port to support that individual host. However, in some networks, it is possible that multiple hosts may be connected to the same switch port, such as via a hub, for example.

To allow for 802.1x authentication in such situations, the 802.1x multiple hosts feature allows multiple users to gain access to a single authenticated 802.1x port. An initial user is required to go through normal authentication to 'open' up the link. Once authenticated, other users on the same link can gain access to the network without going through authentication.

Multiple hosts mode is enabled using the `dot1x host-mode multi-host` interface configuration command in addition to the five configuration steps listed at the beginning of this section. The following output illustrates how to enable this feature:

```
VTP-Server-1(config)#aaa new-model
VTP-Server-1(config)#aaa authentication dot1x default group radius
VTP-Server-1(config)#radius-server host 10.1.1.254 auth-port 1812 key
                        switchauth
VTP-Server-1(config)#dot1x system-auth-control
VTP-Server-1(config)#interface range fastethernet0/23 - 24
VTP-Server-1(config-if-range)#switchport mode access
VTP-Server-1(config-if-range)#dot1x port-control auto
VTP-Server-1(config-if-range)#dot1x host-mode multi-host
VTP-Server-1(config-if-range)#exit
```

Private VLANs

Private VLANs (PVLANs) prevent inter-host communication by providing port-specific security between adjacent ports within a VLAN across one or more switches. Access ports within PVLANs are allowed to communicate only with the certain designated router ports, which are typically those connected to the default gateway for the VLAN. Both normal VLANs and PVLANs can co-exist on the same switch; however, unlike normal VLANs, PVLANs allow for the segregation of traffic at Layer 2. This effectively transforms a traditional Broadcast segment into a non-Broadcast multi-access segment.

Private VLAN Port Types

The PVLAN feature uses three different types of ports, as follows:

1. Community
2. Isolated
3. Promiscuous

Community PVLAN ports are logically combined groups of ports in a common community that can pass traffic amongst themselves and with promiscuous ports. Ports are separated at Layer 2 from all other interfaces in other communities or isolated ports within their PVLAN.

Isolated PVLAN ports cannot communicate with any other ports within the PVLAN. However, isolated ports can communicate with promiscuous ports. Traffic from an isolated port can be forwarded only to a promiscuous port and no other port.

Promiscuous PVLAN ports can communicate with any other ports, including community and isolated PVLAN ports. The function of the promiscuous port is to allow traffic between ports in a community of isolated VLANs. Promiscuous ports can be configured with switch ACLs to define what traffic can pass between these VLANs. It is important to know that only one (1) promiscuous port is allowed per PVLAN, and that port serves the community and isolated VLANs within that PVLAN. Because promiscuous ports can communicate with all other ports, this is the recommended location to place switch ACLs to control traffic between the different types of ports and VLANs.

Isolated and community port traffic can enter or leave switches via trunk links because trunks support VLANs carrying traffic among isolated community and promiscuous ports. Hence, PVLANs are associated with a separate set of VLANs that are used to enable PVLAN functionality in Cisco Catalyst switches. The three types of VLANs used in PVLANs are as follows:

1. Primary VLAN
2. Isolated VLAN
3. Community VLAN

Primary VLANs carry traffic from a promiscuous port to isolated, community, and other promiscuous ports within the same primary VLAN. Isolated VLANs carry traffic from isolated ports to a promiscuous port. Ports in isolated VLANs cannot communicate with any other port in the private VLAN without going through the promiscuous port.

Community VLANs carry traffic between community ports within the same PVLAN, as well as to promiscuous ports. Ports within the same community VLAN can communicate with each other at Layer 2; however, they cannot communicate with ports in other community or isolated VLANs without going through a promiscuous port. Isolated and community VLANs are typically referred to as secondary VLANs. A private VLAN, therefore, actually contains three elements, as follows:

1. The PVLAN itself
2. The secondary VLANs (community and isolated)
3. The promiscuous port

PVLAN operation is illustrated below in Figure 6-13:

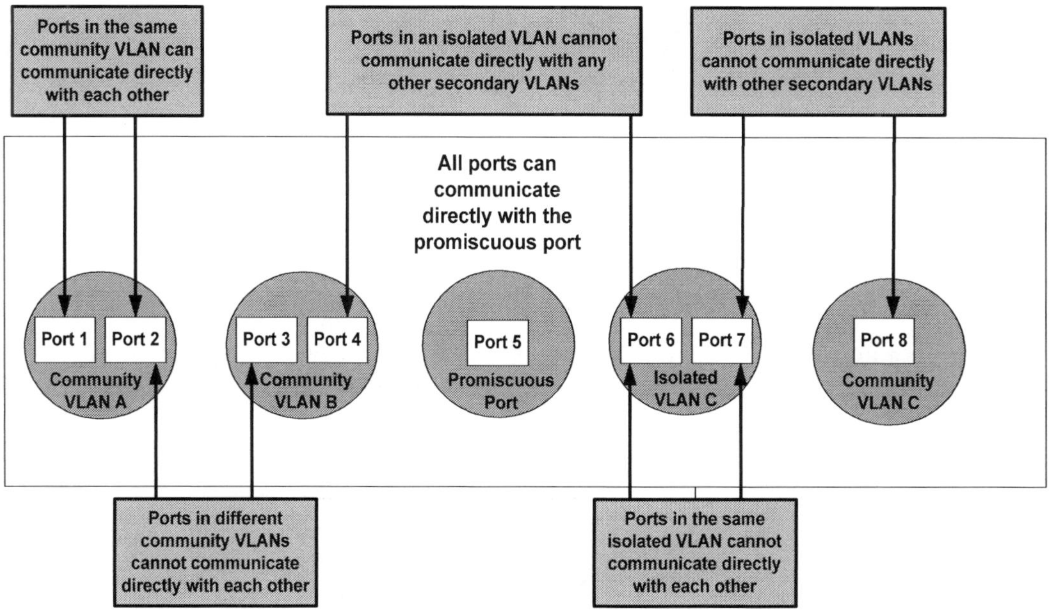

Fig. 6-13. PVLAN Operation

Referencing Figure 6-13, the Community VLAN defines a set of ports that can communicate with each other at Layer 2, as long as they belong to the same community VLAN, but cannot communicate with ports in other community VLANs or isolated VLANs without first going through the promiscuous port.

The isolated VLAN defines a set of ports that cannot communicate with any other port within the PVLAN, either another community VLAN port or even a port in the same isolated VLAN, at Layer 2. In order to communicate with ports in either of these VLANs, isolated ports must go through the promiscuous port. Only a single isolated VLAN per PVLAN is allowed.

The promiscuous port forwards traffic between ports in community and/or isolated VLANs. Only one promiscuous port can exist within a single PVLAN; however, this port can serve all the community and isolated VLANs in the PVLAN. ACLs may be applied to the promiscuous port to define the traffic that is allowed to pass between these different VLANs.

Configuring Private VLANs

Before configuring PVLANs, it is important to remember that VTP does not support carrying PVLAN information in its updates within its VTP domain. Therefore, switches should be configured in Transparent and should never be changed to either VTP Server or VTP Client mode once PVLANs have been configured and are used in the VTP domain. In addition to this, it is also important to know that certain VLANs cannot be added to a PVLAN. These VLANs include VLAN 1 and VLANs 1002 through 1005. The following configuration steps are required to configure Private VLANs:

1. Configure the primary VLAN by issuing the `private-vlan primary` VLAN configuration mode command for the desired VLAN;
2. Associate the secondary VLAN(s) to the primary VLAN via the `private-vlan association` VLAN configuration command under the primary VLAN created in step 1;
3. Configure the secondary VLAN(s) by issuing the `private-vlan [community|isolated]` VLAN configuration mode command for the desired VLAN(s);
4. Map secondary VLANs to the Switch Virtual Interface (Layer 3 VLAN interface) of the primary VLAN via the `private-vlan mapping` interface configuration command;
5. Configure Layer 2 interfaces as isolated or community ports, and associate the Layer 2 interface with the primary VLAN and selected secondary VLAN pair via the `switchport mode private-vlan host` and the `switchport private-vlan host association [primary vlan] [secondary vlan]` interface configuration commands; and
6. Configure a Layer 2 interface as a promiscuous port and map the PVLAN promiscuous port to the PVLAN and to the selected VLAN pair via the `switchport mode private-vlan promiscuous` and the `switchport private-vlan mapping [primary vlan] [secondary vlans]` interface configuration commands.

These configuration steps are illustrated in the following output:

```
VTP-Server-1(config)#vlan 111
VTP-Server-1(config-vlan)#name 'My-Primary-VLAN'
VTP-Server-1(config-vlan)#private-vlan primary
VTP-Server-1(config)#vlan 111
VTP-Server-1(config-vlan)#private-vlan association 222,333
VTP-Server-1(config-vlan)#exit
VTP-Server-1(config)#vlan 222
VTP-Server-1(config-vlan)#name 'My-Community-VLAN'
VTP-Server-1(config-vlan)#private-vlan community
VTP-Server-1(config-vlan)#exit
VTP-Server-1(config)#vlan 333
VTP-Server-1(config-vlan)#name 'My-Isolated-VLAN'
VTP-Server-1(config-vlan)#private-vlan isolated
VTP-Server-1(config-vlan)#exit
VTP-Server-1(config-if)#int vlan 111
VTP-Server-1(config-if)#ip address 10.1.1.1 255.255.255.0
VTP-Server-1(config-if)#private-vlan mapping add 222,333
VTP-Server-1(config-if)#exit
VTP-Server-1(config)#int fa0/2
VTP-Server-1(config-if)#switchport mode private-vlan host
VTP-Server-1(config-if)#switchport private-vlan host-association 111 222
VTP-Server-1(config-if)#exit
```

```
VTP-Server-1(config)#int fa0/3
VTP-Server-1(config-if)#switchport mode private-vlan host
VTP-Server-1(config-if)#switchport private-vlan host-association 111 333
VTP-Server-1(config-if)#exit
VTP-Server-1(config)#int fast0/1
VTP-Server-1(config-if)#switchport mode private-vlan promiscuous
VTP-Server-1(config-if)#switchport private-vlan mapping 111 222 333
VTP-Server-1(config-if)#exit
```

Verifying PVLAN Configuration

The `show vlan private-vlan` command can be used to verify the PVLAN configuration. This command prints information on the primary VLAN, secondary VLANs, and the ports assigned to those respective VLANs. This output is illustrated as follows:

```
VTP-Server-1#show vlan private-vlan
Primary Secondary Type              Ports
------- --------- ----------------- ------------------------------------------
111     222       community         Fa0/1, Fa0/2, Fa0/3
111     333       isolated          Fa0/1, Fa0/1, Fa0/3
```

The `show interface [name] switchport` command can be used to verify a host port configured in a PVLAN. This is illustrated in the following output:

```
VTP-Server-1# show interface fast 0/2 switchport
Name: Fa0/2
Switchport: Enabled
Administrative Mode: private-vlan host
Operational Mode: up
Administrative Trunking Encapsulation: dot1q
Negotiation of Trunking: Off
Access Mode VLAN: 1 (default)
Trunking Native Mode VLAN: 1 (default)
Voice VLAN: none
Administrative private-vlan host-association: 111 (My-Primary-VLAN) 222 (My-
Community-VLAN)
Administrative private-vlan mapping: none
Operational private-vlan: none
Trunking VLANs Enabled: ALL
Pruning VLANs Enabled: 2-1001
...
[Truncated Output]
```

The output for a promiscuous port would differ slightly as illustrated in the following output:

```
VTP-Server-1#show interface fast 0/1 switchport
Name: Fa0/1
Switchport: Enabled
Administrative Mode: promiscuous
```

```
Operational Mode: up
Administrative Trunking Encapsulation: dot1q
Negotiation of Trunking: Off
Access Mode VLAN: 1 (default)
Trunking Native Mode VLAN: 1 (default)
Voice VLAN: none
Administrative private-vlan host-association: none
Administrative private-vlan mapping: 111 (My-Primary-VLAN) 222 (My-Community-
VLAN) 333 (My-Isolated-VLAN)
Operational private-vlan: none
Trunking VLANs Enabled: ALL
Pruning VLANs Enabled: 2-1001
...
[Truncated Output]
```

Port ACLs and VLAN ACLs

Understanding PACLs

Port ACLs (PACLs) are similar to Router ACLs (RACLs) but are supported and configured on Layer 2 interfaces on a switch. PACLs are supported on physical interfaces as well as on EtherChannel interfaces. PACLs are not supported on PVLANs. In addition to this, keep in mind that PACLs do not support the router access list keywords `log` or `reflexive`.

Port ACLs perform access control on all traffic entering the specified Layer 2 port and apply only to ingress traffic on the port. However, it is important to remember that the PACL feature does not affect Layer 2 control packets (e.g. CDP) that are received on the port.

PACLs are supported in hardware only and do not apply to packets that are processed in software. When you create a PACL, an entry is created in the ACL TCAM. PACLs can be configured as either standard or extended IP ACLs or MAC ACLs. This allows you to filter IP traffic by using IP access lists and non-IP traffic by using MAC addresses.

Configuring and Applying PACLs

MAC ACLs are configured using the `mac access-list extended [name]` global configuration command, and then individual permit and deny statements can be used within MAC ACL configuration mode to permit or deny defined MAC addresses. If you are unable to remember how to configure standard and extended ACLs, please refer to the CCNA guide for a refresher.

These ACLs are then applied to Layer 2 ports using the `[ip|mac] access-group [name|number] in` interface configuration command. The following output illustrates the configuration of a PACL based on a configured IP Extended ACL on a Layer 2 port on the switch:

```
VTP-Server-1(config)#ip access-list extended MY-SWITCH-PACL
VTP-Server-1(config-ext-nacl)#permit udp any any
VTP-Server-1(config-ext-nacl)#permit tcp any any
VTP-Server-1(config-ext-nacl)#deny ip any any
VTP-Server-1(config-ext-nacl)#exit
VTP-Server-1(config)#interface gigabitethernet 3/1
VTP-Server-1(config-if)#switchport
VTP-Server-1(config-if)#switchport mode access
VTP-Server-1(config-if)#switchport access vlan 15
VTP-Server-1(config-if)#ip access-group MY-SWITCH-PACL in
```

The following output illustrates how to configure a MAC ACL and apply it inbound to a Layer 2 port:

```
VTP-Server-1(config)#mac access-list extended MY-MAC-PACL
VTP-Server-1(config-ext-macl)#permit host 1a2b.1111.cdef any
VTP-Server-1(config-ext-macl)#exit
VTP-Server-1(config)#interface gigabitethernet 3/1
VTP-Server-1(config)#switchport mode access
VTP-Server-1(config)#switchport access vlan 7
VTP-Server-1config-if)#mac access-group MY-MAC-PACL in
```

NOTE: You cannot apply more than one IP access list and one MAC access list to a Layer 2 interface. If an IP access list or MAC access list is already configured on a Layer 2 interface and you apply a new IP access list or MAC access list to the interface, the new ACL replaces the previously configured one.

Configuring the PACL Access Group Mode

Cisco IOS software allows administrators to use the `access-group mode` interface configuration command to change the way PACLs interact with other ACLs, such as VLAN ACLs (VACLs), that may be configured for the VLAN that the Layer 2 interface is also configured for. In a per-interface fashion, the `access-group mode` command can be implemented with one of the following keywords in Catalyst 4500 series switches:

- The `prefer port` keyword—if a PACL is configured on a Layer 2 interface, then the PACL takes effect and overrides other ACLs configured on the interface or for the VLAN. If no PACL is configured on the Layer 2 interface, other features applicable to the interface are merged and applied on the interface. This is the default option.
- The `prefer vlan` keyword—when used, VLAN-based ACL features take effect on the port provided they have been applied on the port and no PACLs are in effect. If no VLAN-based ACL features are applicable to the Layer 2 interface, then the PACL feature already on the interface is applied.
- The `merge` keyword—this option merges applicable ACL features before they are programmed into the switch hardware. The PACL, VACL, and Cisco IOS ACLs are merged in the ingress direction.

In Catalyst 6500 series switches, the following modes are supported:

- The `prefer port` keyword—if a PACL is configured on a Layer 2 interface, then the PACL takes effect and overrides other ACLs configured on the interface or for the VLAN. If no PACL is configured on the Layer 2 interface, other features applicable to the interface are merged and applied on the interface.
- The `merge` keyword—this option merges applicable ACL features before they are programmed into the switch hardware. The PACL, VACL, and Cisco IOS ACLs are merged in the ingress direction. This is the default option.

The following output illustrates how to configure an interface to use prefer port mode:

```
VTP-Server-1(config)#interface gigabitethernet 3/1
VTP-Server-1(config)#description 'Switchport Configured with PACL'
VTP-Server-1(config-if)#access-group mode prefer port
```

Understanding VACLs

VLAN Access Control Lists (VACLs) operate in a similar manner to Router ACLs (RACLs) but are a means to apply access control to packets bridged within a VLAN or routed between VLANs. Unlike RACLs, which are applied on an inbound or outbound basis, VACLs have no sense of direction and therefore apply to traffic at both ingress and egress. Within a VLAN, packets arriving on the Layer 2 interface have the VACL processed on ingress and egress. This concept is illustrated below in Figure 6-14:

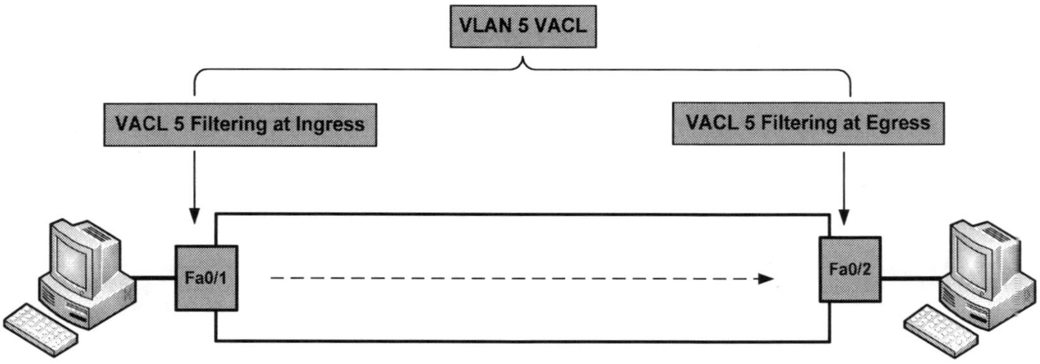

Fig. 6-14. VACL Processing within the VLAN

VACLs may be used in conjunction with RACLs. In such situations, you need to understand the order in which the VACLs and the RACLs are processed in order to ensure that the implemented configuration works in the manner expected. Figure 6-15 below illustrates the processing order of a packet when both RACLs and VACLs are configured on the switch:

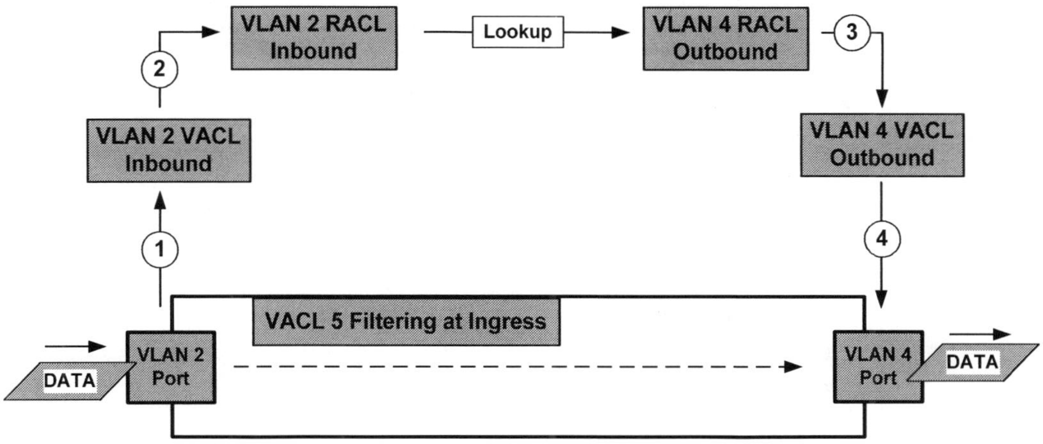

Fig. 6-15. Processing RACLs and VACLs

Referencing Figure 6-15, the following sequence of steps is performed:

1. Data is received on the Layer 2 port in VLAN 2. This is matched against the configured VACL for VLAN 2 in the inbound direction.
2. The data is destined to another VLAN and must be routed. It is forwarded to the route processor and matched against the ingress RACL configured on VLAN interface 2.
3. After packet lookup has determined interface VLAN 4 as the outbound interface, the data is matched against the outbound RACL configured on interface VLAN 4.
4. The data is then matched against the VACL applied to VLAN 4 in the egress direction. The data is forwarded out of the port in VLAN 4.

Configuring and Applying VACLs

VACLs are processed in switch hardware and therefore do not cause any performance impact when implemented on switches. VACL configuration is straightforward and is performed in four simple steps, as follows:

1. Create the extended IP ACL that matches the desired packets using either the IP or MAC address against one or more standard or extended access lists;
2. Configure the VLAN access map, which is an ordered list of entries, that will be used to match against configured ACLs. This is performed via the `vlan access-map [name] [number]` global configuration command. The `[name]` is a user-defined string and can be any value. The `[number]` represents the sequence number of the map entry. This can range from 0 to 65,535. If you are creating a VLAN map and the sequence number is not specified, it is automatically assigned in increments of 10, starting from 10. This number is the sequence to insert into, or delete from, a VLAN access map entry;

3. Configure the VLAN access map to drop or forward the packets matched in the ACL by using the `action [drop|forward]` VLAN access map configuration command; and
4. Apply a VLAN map to one or more VLANs by using the `vlan filter [map-name] vlan-list [list-of-vlans]` global configuration command.

The following output illustrates how to configure a VACL that matches an ACL that permits all TCP traffic and apply the VACL to VLAN 22:

```
VTP-Server-1(config)#ip access-list extended ALLOW-TCP
VTP-Server-1(config-ext-nacl)#permit tcp any any
VTP-Server-1(config-ext-nacl)#exit
VTP-Server-1(config)#vlan access-map MY-VACL-MAP
VTP-Server-1(config-access-map)#match ip address ALLOW-TCP
VTP-Server-1(config-access-map)#action forward
VTP-Server-1(config-access-map)#exit
VTP-Server-1(config)#vlan filter map MY-VACL-MAP vlan-list 22
```

The following output illustrates how to configure a VACL that matches three different ACLs. The first ACL allows all TCP traffic, the second ACL denies all UDP traffic, and the third ACL permits all IP traffic. This VACL is then applied to VLAN 22:

```
VTP-Server-1(config)#ip access-list extended ALLOW-TCP
VTP-Server-1(config-ext-nacl)#permit tcp any any
VTP-Server-1(config-ext-nacl)#exit
VTP-Server-1(config)#ip access-list extended ALLOW-UDP
VTP-Server-1(config-ext-nacl)#permit udp any any
VTP-Server-1(config-ext-nacl)#exit
VTP-Server-1(config)#ip access-list extended ALLOW-IP
VTP-Server-1(config-ext-nacl)#permit ip any any
VTP-Server-1(config-ext-nacl)#exit
VTP-Server-1(config)#vlan access-map MY-VACL-MAP 10
VTP-Server-1(config-access-map)#match ip address ALLOW-TCP
VTP-Server-1(config-access-map)#action forward
VTP-Server-1(config-access-map)#exit
VTP-Server-1(config)#vlan access-map MY-VACL-MAP 20
VTP-Server-1(config-access-map)#match ip address ALLOW-UDP
VTP-Server-1(config-access-map)#action drop
VTP-Server-1(config-access-map)#exit
VTP-Server-1(config)#vlan access-map MY-VACL-MAP 30
VTP-Server-1(config-access-map)#match ip address ALLOW-IP
VTP-Server-1(config-access-map)#action forward
VTP-Server-1(config-access-map)#exit
VTP-Server-1(config)#vlan filter map MY-VACL-MAP vlan-list 22
```

NOTE: The same filtering illustrated above could be configured in the manner illustrated in the following output:

```
VTP-Server-1(config)#ip access-list extended ALLOW-UDP
VTP-Server-1(config-ext-nacl)#permit udp any any
VTP-Server-1(config-ext-nacl)#exit
VTP-Server-1(config)#vlan access-map MY-VACL-MAP 10
VTP-Server-1(config-access-map)#match ip address ALLOW-UDP
VTP-Server-1(config-access-map)#action drop
VTP-Server-1(config-access-map)#exit
VTP-Server-1(config)#vlan access-map MY-VACL-MAP 20
VTP-Server-1(config-access-map)#action forward
VTP-Server-1(config-access-map)#exit
VTP-Server-1(config)#vlan filter map MY-VACL-MAP vlan-list 22
```

Because no ACL is specifically matched in sequence 20, all traffic that is not dropped in sequence 10 is effectively forwarded.

Verifying VACL Configuration

The `show vlan access-map` command is used to view VACL configuration. The information printed by this command is illustrated in the following output:

```
VTP-Server-1#show vlan access-map

Vlan access-map " MY-VACL-MAP " 10
  Match clauses:
    ip address: ALLOW-TCP
  Action:
    forward

Vlan access-map " MY-VACL-MAP " 20
  Match clauses:
    ip address: ALLOW-UDP
  Action:
    drop
```

Other Security Features

The final section in this chapter describes some additional Cisco Catalyst switch security features. The following features are described in this section:

- Storm Control
- Protected Ports
- Port Blocking

Storm Control

The storm control feature, also referred to as the traffic suppression feature, prevents network traffic from being disrupted by Broadcast, Multicast, or Unicast packet storms (i.e. floods) on any of the physical interfaces on the Cisco Catalyst switch. This feature monitors inbound packets on a physical interface over a 1-second interval and compares them to a configured storm control suppression level by using one of the following methods to measure the packet activity:

1. The percentage of total bandwidth available of the port allocated for Broadcast, Multicast, or Unicast traffic; or
2. The traffic rate over a 1-second interval in packets-per-second (pps) at which Broadcast, Multicast, or Unicast packets are received on the interface.

Regardless of the method used, packets are blocked until the traffic rate drops below the configured suppression level, at which point the port resumes normal forwarding. The storm control feature is enabled by issuing the `storm-control` interface configuration command. The options available with this command are illustrated in the following output:

```
VTP-Server-1(config)#int fastethernet0/1
VTP-Server-1(config-if)#storm-control ?
  action      Action to take for storm-control
  broadcast   Broadcast address storm control
  multicast   Multicast address storm control
  unicast     Unicast address storm control
```

The `action` keyword is used to specify the action that the port will enforce in the event of a violation against the configured policy. The actions that can be defined are either to shutdown the port or to generate and send an SNMP trap, as illustrated below in the following output:

```
VTP-Server-1(config)#int fastethernet0/1
VTP-Server-1(config-if)#storm-control action ?
  shutdown  Shutdown this interface if a storm occurs
  trap      Send SNMP trap if a storm occurs
```

The `broadcast`, `multicast`, and `unicast` keywords are used to define storm control parameters for Broadcast, Multicast, and Unicast traffic, respectively. For example, to block Broadcast traffic if it exceeds 50% of the physical port bandwidth, the configuration would be implemented on a switch port as shown in the following output:

```
VTP-Server-1(config)#int fast 0/2
VTP-Server-1(config-if)#storm-control broadcast level 50
```

The following output illustrates how to block all Multicast traffic if it exceeds 80% of the physical port bandwidth, but resume all normal forwarding when it falls below 40%:

```
VTP-Server-1(config)#int fastethernet 0/2
VTP-Server-1(config-if)#storm-control multicast level 80 40
```

Storm control configuration can be validated by issuing the `show storm-control [options]` command. The following output illustrates how to view configured storm control parameters for FastEthernet0/2 on a Cisco Catalyst switch:

```
VTP-Server-1#show storm-control fastethernet 0/2 broadcast
Interface  Filter State   Trap State    Upper    Lower    Current  Traps Sent
---------  -------------  ------------- -------  -------  -------  ----------
Fa0/2      Forwarding     inactive      50.00%   50.00%    0.00%   0

VTP-Server-1#
VTP-Server-1#show storm-control fastethernet 0/2 multicast
Interface  Filter State   Trap State    Upper    Lower    Current  Traps Sent
---------  -------------  ------------- -------  -------  -------  ----------
Fa0/2      Forwarding     inactive      80.00%   40.00%    0.00%   0

VTP-Server-1#
VTP-Server-1#show storm-control fastethernet 0/2 unicast
Interface  Filter State   Trap State    Upper    Lower    Current  Traps Sent
---------  -------------  ------------- -------  -------  -------  ----------
Fa0/2      inactive       inactive      100.00%  100.00%  N/A      0
```

Protected Ports

Protected ports operate in a similar manner to PVLANs and are supported on lower-end switch models, such as the Catalyst 2950 series switch. These ports have the following characteristics when enabled on Catalyst switches:

- The switch will not forward any traffic between ports that are configured as protected; any data must be routed via a Layer 3 device between the protected ports.
- Control traffic, such as routing protocol traffic, is considered an exception and will be forwarded between protected ports.
- Forwarding between protected and non-protected ports proceeds normally; that is, protected ports can communicate with non-protected ports without using a Layer 3 device.

By default, no ports are protected. However, administrators can enable this feature by issuing the `switchport protected` interface configuration command on all interfaces that they want to become protected ports. The following output illustrates how to configure a protected port:

```
VTP-Server-1(config)#int fastethernet 0/4
VTP-Server-1(config-if)#switchport protected
```

Once configured, you can validate protected port status by issuing the `show interfaces [name] switchport` command as illustrated in the following output:

```
VTP-Server-1#show interfaces fastethernet 0/4 switchport
Name: Fa0/4
Switchport: Enabled
Administrative Mode: dynamic desirable
...
[Truncated Output]

Protected: true

Voice VLAN: none (Inactive)
Appliance trust: none
```

Port Blocking

Port blocking is supported only in Cisco Catalyst 3750 series switches and above. It is not supported on lower-end switches, such as the Cisco Catalyst 2950 series switch.

When a packet arrives at a switch port, the switch performs a CAM table lookup to determine the port that it will use to send the packet to its destination. If no entry is found for the destination MAC address, the switch will flood the packet out of all interfaces, except for the interface on which the packet was received, and wait for a response. While this default behavior is generally acceptable, it is important to understand that from a security perspective, the forwarding of unknown traffic to a protected port could raise security concerns.

Switches can be configured to block unknown Unicast and Multicast traffic from being forwarded on a per-interface basis. This is performed by using the `switchport block [multicast|unicast]` interface configuration command. The following output illustrates how to block unknown Unicast and Multicast packets on a particular port:

```
VTP-Server-1(config)#int fast 0/6
VTP-Server-1(config-if)#switchport block multicast
VTP-Server-1(config-if)#switchport block unicast
```

This configuration can be validated by issuing the `show interfaces [name] switchport` command as shown in the following output:

```
VTP-Server-1#show interfaces fastethernet 0/6 switchport
Name: Fa0/6
Switchport: Enabled
Administrative Mode: dynamic auto
...
[Truncated Output]

Protected: false
Unknown unicast blocked: enabled
Unknown multicast blocked: enabled
```

Chapter Summary

The following section is a summary of the major points you should be aware of in this chapter.

Switch Port Security

- The port security feature is a dynamic Catalyst switch feature that secures switch ports
- Port security also protects the CAM by limiting the number of addresses learned on a port
- Port security protect the switched LAN from two primary methods of attack:
  1. CAM Table Overflow Attacks
  2. MAC Spoofing Attacks

- CAM overflow attacks target the CAM fixed, allocated memory space
- CAM overflow attacks flood the switch with invalid, randomly generated packets
- CAM table attacks are easy to perform
- MAC address spoofing is used to spoof a source MAC address
- MAC spoofing causes the switch to believe that the same host is connected to two ports
- MAC spoofing causes repetitive rewrites of MAC address table entries
- MAC spoofing also results in a Denial of Service (DoS) attack on the legitimate host(s)
- The methods of port security implementation supported in switches are:
  1. Static Secure MAC Addresses
  2. Dynamic Secure MAC Addresses
  3. Sticky Secure MAC Addresses

- Static secure MAC addresses are statically configured by network administrators
- Static secure MAC addresses are stored in the MAC table and the switch configuration
- Dynamic secure MAC addresses are dynamically learned by the switch
- Dynamic secure MAC addresses are stored in the MAC table, but not the configuration
- Sticky secure MAC addresses are a mix of static and dynamic secure MAC addresses
- Sticky addresses can be learned dynamically or configured statically
- Sticky addresses are stored in the MAC table as well as the switch configuration
- The port security feature can perform the following in the event of a security violation:
  1. Protect
  2. Shutdown (default)
  3. Restrict
  4. Shutdown VLAN

- The protect option forces the port into a protected port mode
- In protected mode, frames with unknown source addresses are simply discarded
- The shutdown option places a port in an err-disabled state if a violation is detected

- Shutdown sends an SNMP trap, a Syslog message, and increments the violation counter
- Restrict drops frames from unknown MACs when the address limit is reached
- Restrict also sends an SNMP trap, a Syslog message, and increments the violation counter
- The shutdown VLAN option shuts down the VLAN on multi-VLAN access ports

Dynamic ARP Inspection

- DAI is a security feature that validates Address Resolution Protocol packets in a network
- ARP spoofing occurs during the ARP request and reply message exchange between hosts
- DAI determines the validity of packets via an IP-to-MAC address binding inspection
- DAI will drop all packets with invalid IP-to-MAC address bindings that fail the inspection
- Dynamic ARP Inspection can be used in both DHCP and non-DHCP environments
- DAI associates a trust state with each interface on the switch
- All packets that arrive on trusted interfaces bypass all DAI validation checks
- All packets that arrive on untrusted interfaces undergo the DAI validation process

DHCP Snooping and IP Source Guard

- DHCP spoofing and starvation attacks are used to exhaust the DHCP address pool
- DHCP Snooping uses the concept of trusted and untrusted interfaces
- Packets received on untrusted ports are dropped if they have invalid bindings
- The IP Source Guard feature is typically enabled in conjunction with DHCP Snooping
- IP Source Guard is a feature that restricts IP traffic on untrusted Layer 2 ports
- IP Source Guard filters traffic based on the DHCP Snooping Binding Database
- IP Source Guard also filters traffic based on configured IP source bindings
- The IP Source Guard feature is primary used to prevent IP address spoofing attacks
- For each untrusted Layer 2 port, there are two modes of IP traffic filtering:
  1. Source IP address filter
  2. Source IP and MAC address filter

Securing Trunk Links

- VLAN hopping attacks attempt to bypass Layer 3 communication between VLANs
- The two primary methods used to perform VLAN hopping attacks are:
  1. Switch spoofing
  2. Double-tagging

- In switch spoofing, the attacker impersonates a switch by emulating a trunk
- Switch spoofing attacks attempt to exploit the default native VLAN
- Switch spoofing attacks can be prevented by performing the following:
  1. Disabling the Dynamic Trunking Protocol on trunk ports

2. Disabling trunking capability on ports that should not be configured as trunk
3. Preventing user data from traversing the native VLAN

- Double-tagging VLAN attacks involve tagging frames with two 802.1Q tags
- Double-tagging VLAN attacks can be prevented by performing the following:
  1. Ensuring the native VLAN on trunk ports is different from user access VLANs
  2. Configuring the native VLAN to tag all traffic

Identity Based Networking Services

- IBNS provides identity-based access control and policy enforcement at the switch port level
- IBNS incorporates 802.1x, EAP, and the RADIUS security protocols
- IBNS offers scalable and flexible access control and policy enforcement services and allows:
  1. Per-user or per-service authentication services
  2. Policies mapped to network identity
  3. Port-based network access control based on authentication and authorization policies
  4. Additional policy enforcement based on access level

- IEEE 802.1x is an open protocol standard framework for both wired and wireless LANs
- 802.1x is an IEEE standard for access control and authentication
- 802.1x provides the definition to encapsulate the transport of EAP messages at Layer 2
- There are three primary components in the 802.1x authentication process:
  1. Supplicant or Client
  2. Authenticator
  3. Authentication Server

- An 802.1x supplicant or client is simply an 802.1x-compliant device, such as a workstation
- An 802.1x authenticator is a device that enforces physical access control to the network
- The authentication server validates the identity of the client and authorizes the client access
- EAPOL frames have a destination MAC of 01-80-C3-00-00-03
- Either the Switch or the Client (Supplicant) can initiate 802.1x authentication
- 802.1x authentication is initiated when the link transitions from a state of down to up

Private VLANs

- Private VLANs allow for the segregation of traffic at Layer 2
- PVLANs transform a Broadcast segment into a non-Broadcast multi-access segment
- The private VLAN feature uses three different types of ports:
  1. Community
  2. Isolated
  3. Promiscuous

- The three types of VLANs used in PVLANs are:
  1. The Primary VLAN
  2. Isolated VLANs
  3. Community VLAN

- A private VLAN therefore actually contains three elements:
  1. The PVLAN itself
  2. The secondary VLANs (Community and Isolated)
  3. The promiscuous port

Port ACLs and VLAN ACLs

- PACLs are similar to RACLs but are supported and configured on Layer 2 interfaces
- Port ACLs are supported on both physical and Etherchannel interfaces
- Port ACLs perform access control on all traffic entering the specified Layer 2 port
- Port ACLs apply only to ingress traffic on the port
- PACLs are supported only in hardware only and do not affect packets routed in software
- When you create a Port ACL, an entry is created in the ACL TCAM
- VACLs operate similar to RACLs
- VACLs apply access control to packets bridged within a VLAN or routed between VLANs
- VACLs have no sense of direction and apply to traffic at both ingress and egress

Other Security Features

- Storm control prevents network traffic from being disrupted by traffic storms or floods
- Protected ports operate in a similar manner to private VLANs
- Traffic between protected ports cannot be switched and must therefore be routed
- Port blocking blocks unknown Unicast and Multicast traffic

CHAPTER 7

Cisco Catalyst Multilayer Switching

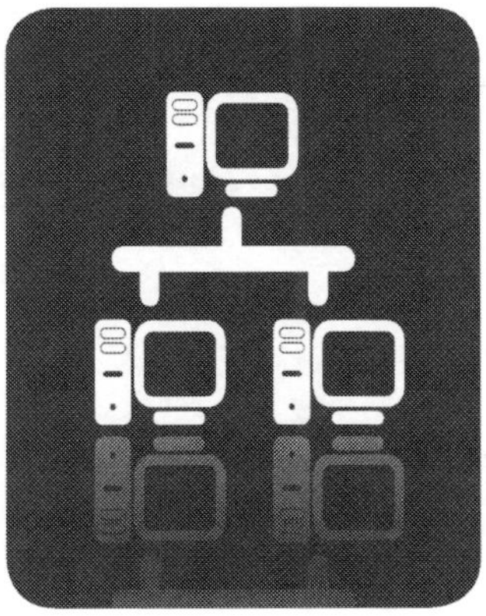

Multilayer switching is an integral part of any LAN in present-day internetworks. Unlike the networks of yesteryear that were designed around the 80/20 rule, modern networks are designed around the 20/80 rule. This requires a lot of interVLAN communication. Because routing is invariably slower than switching, Cisco Catalyst switches support Multilayer switching functionality, which allows the switching of packets at Layers 3 and 4 of the OSI Model. The following core SWITCH exam objective is covered in this chapter:

- Implement switch-based Layer 3 services, given a network design and a set of requirements

This chapter will be divided into the following sections:

- InterVLAN Routing
- Multilayer Switching Components
- Demand-Based Switching
- Topology-Based (CEF) Switching
- Verifying MLS Operation
- Protecting the Route Processor
- Fallback Bridging

SWITCH Exam Objective	Chapter Section(s) Covered
• Configure routing interfaces	• InterVLAN Routing
• Verify the switch-based Layer 3 solution	• Verifying MLS Operation
• Related topics	• Multilayer Switching Components • Demand-Based Switching • Topology-Based (CEF) Switching • Protecting the Route Processor • Fallback Bridging

InterVLAN Routing

By default, although VLANs can span the entire Layer 2 switched network, hosts in one VLAN cannot communicate directly with hosts in another VLAN. In order to do so, traffic must be routed between the different VLANs. This is referred to as interVLAN routing. The three methods of implementing interVLAN routing in switched LANs, including their advantages and disadvantages, will be described in the following sections:

- InterVLAN Routing Using Physical Router Interfaces
- InterVLAN Routing Using Router Subinterfaces
- InterVLAN Routing Using Switched Virtual Interfaces

InterVLAN Routing Using Physical Router Interfaces

The first method of implementing interVLAN routing for communication entails using a router with multiple physical interfaces as the default gateway for each individually configured VLAN. The router can then route packets received from one VLAN to another using these physical LAN interfaces. This method is illustrated below in Figure 7-1:

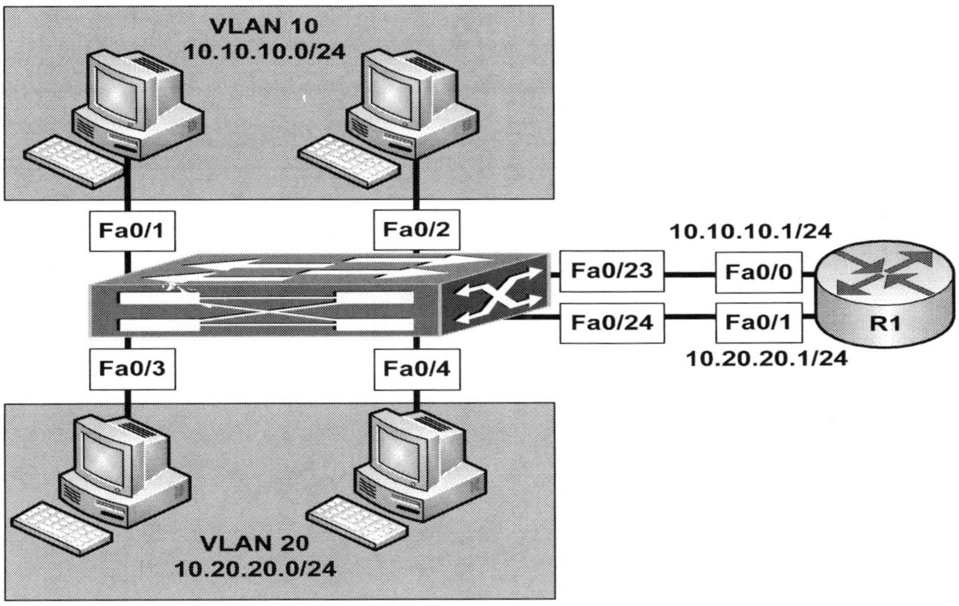

Fig. 7-1. InterVLAN Routing Using Multiple Physical Router Interfaces

Fig. 7-1. InterVLAN Routing Using Multiple Physical Router Interfaces

Figure 7-1 illustrates a single LAN using two different VLANs, each with an assigned IP subnet. Although the network hosts depicted in Figure 7-1 are connected to the same physical switch, because they reside in different VLANs, packets between hosts in VLAN 10 and those in VLAN 20 must be routed, while packets within the same VLAN are simply switched.

The primary advantage of using this solution is that it is simple and easy to implement. The primary disadvantage, however, is that it is not scalable. For example, if 5, 10, or even 20 additional VLANs were configured on the switch, the same number of physical interfaces as VLANs would also be needed on the router. In most cases, this is technically not feasible.

When using multiple physical router interfaces, each switch link connected to the router is configured as an access link in the desired VLAN. The physical interfaces on the router are then configured with the appropriate IP addresses and the network hosts are either statically configured with IP addresses in the appropriate VLAN, using the physical router interface as the default gateway, or dynamically configured using DHCP. The configuration of the switch illustrated in Figure 7-1 is illustrated in the following output:

```
VTP-Server-1(config)#vlan 10
VTP-Server-1(config-vlan)#name Example-VLAN-10
VTP-Server-1(config-vlan)#exit
VTP-Server-1(config)#vlan 20
VTP-Server-1(config-vlan)#name Example-VLAN-20
VTP-Server-1(config-vlan)#exit
VTP-Server-1(config)#interface range fastethernet 0/1 - 2, 23
VTP-Server-1(config-if-range)#switchport
VTP-Server-1(config-if-range)#switchport access vlan 10
VTP-Server-1(config-if-range)#switchport mode access
VTP-Server-1(config-if-range)#exit
VTP-Server-1(config)#interface range fastethernet 0/3 - 4, 24
VTP-Server-1(config-if-range)#switchport
VTP-Server-1(config-if-range)#switchport access vlan 20
VTP-Server-1(config-if-range)#switchport mode access
VTP-Server-1(config-if-range)#exit
```

The router illustrated in Figure 7-1 is configured as shown in the following output:

```
R1(config)#interface fast 0/0
R1(config-if)#ip add 10.10.10.1 255.255.255.0
R1(config-if)#exit
R1(config)#interface fast 0/1
R1(config-if)#ip add 10.20.20.1 255.255.255.0
R1(config-if)#exit
```

InterVLAN Routing Using Router Subinterfaces

Implementing interVLAN routing using subinterfaces addresses the scalability issues that are possible when using multiple physical router interfaces. With subinterfaces, only a single physical interface is required on the router and subsequent subinterfaces are configured off that physical interface. This is illustrated below in Figure 7-2:

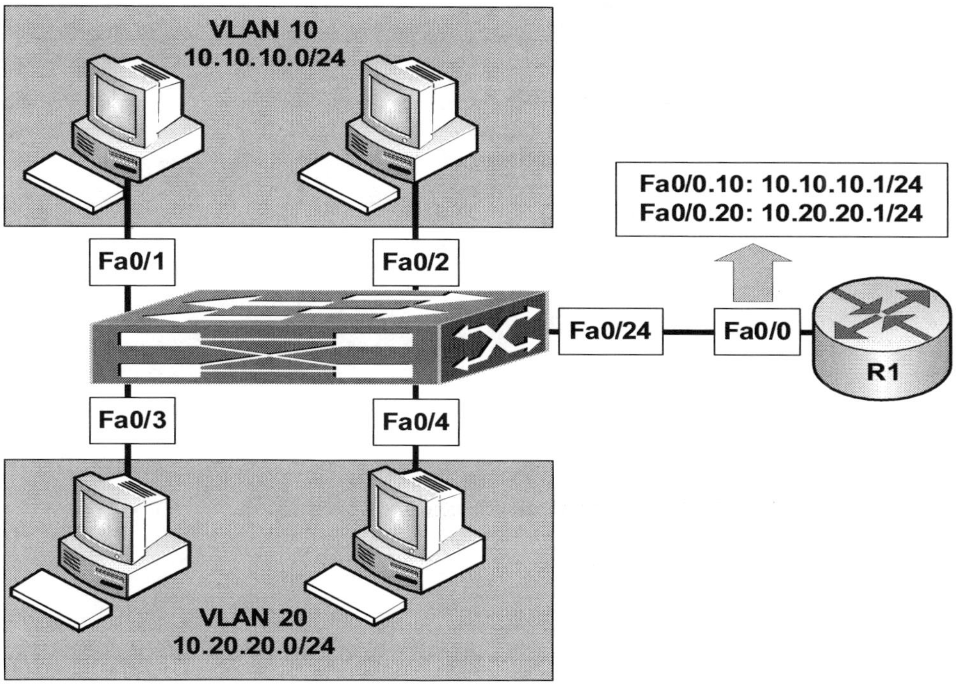

Fig. 7-2. InterVLAN Routing Using Router Subinterfaces

Figure 7-2 depicts the same LAN illustrated in Figure 7-1. In Figure 7-2, however, only a single physical router interface is being used. In order to implement an interVLAN routing solution, subinterfaces are configured off the main physical router interface using the interface `[name].[subinterface number]` global configuration command. Each subinterface is associated with a particular VLAN using the `encapsulation [isl|dot1Q] [vlan]` subinterface configuration command. The final step is to configure the desired IP address on the interface.

On the switch, the single link connected to the router must be configured as a trunk link. If the trunk is configured as an 802.1Q trunk, a native VLAN must be defined, if a VLAN other than the default will be used as the native VLAN. This native VLAN must also be configured on the respective router subinterface using the `encapsulation dot1Q [vlan] native` subinterface configuration command. The following output illustrates the configuration of interVLAN routing using a single physical interface (also referred to as 'router-on-a-stick'). The two VLANs depicted in Figure 7-2 are illustrated in the following output, as is an additional VLAN used for Management; this VLAN will be configured as the native VLAN:

```
VTP-Server-1(config)#vlan 10
VTP-Server-1(config-vlan)#name Example-VLAN-10
VTP-Server-1(config-vlan)#exit
VTP-Server-1(config)#vlan 20
VTP-Server-1(config-vlan)#name Example-VLAN-20
VTP-Server-1(config-vlan)#exit
```

```
VTP-Server-1(config)#vlan 30
VTP-Server-1(config-vlan)#name Management-VLAN
VTP-Server-1(config-vlan)#exit
VTP-Server-1(config)#interface range fastethernet 0/1 - 2
VTP-Server-1(config-if-range)#switchport
VTP-Server-1(config-if-range)#switchport access vlan 10
VTP-Server-1(config-if-range)#switchport mode access
VTP-Server-1(config-if-range)#exit
VTP-Server-1(config)#interface range fastethernet 0/3 - 4
VTP-Server-1(config-if-range)#switchport
VTP-Server-1(config-if-range)#switchport access vlan 20
VTP-Server-1(config-if-range)#switchport mode access
VTP-Server-1(config-if-range)#exit
VTP-Server-1(config)#interface fastethernet 0/24
VTP-Server-1(config-if)#switchport
VTP-Server-1(config-if)#switchport trunk encapsulation dot1q
VTP-Server-1(config-if)#switchport mode trunk
VTP-Server-1(config-if)#switchport trunk native vlan 30
VTP-Server-1(config-if)#exit
VTP-Server-1(config)#interface vlan 30
VTP-Server-1(config-if)#description 'This is the Management Subnet'
VTP-Server-1(config-if)#ip address 10.30.30.2 255.255.255.0
VTP-Server-1(config-if)#no shutdown
VTP-Server-1(config-if)#exit
VTP-Server-1(config)#ip default-gateway 10.30.30.1
```

The router illustrated in Figure 7-2 is configured as shown in the following output:

```
R1(config)#interface fastethernet 0/0
R1(config-if)#no ip address
R1(config-if)#exit
R1(config)#interface fast 0/0.10
R1(config-subitf)#description 'Subinterface For VLAN 10'
R1(config-subif)#encapsulation dot1Q 10
R1(config-subif)#ip add 10.10.10.1 255.255.255.0
R1(config-subif)#exit
R1(config)#interface fast 0/0.20
R1(config-subitf)#description 'Subinterface For VLAN 20'
R1(config-subif)#encapsulation dot1Q 20
R1(config-subif)#ip add 10.20.20.1 255.255.255.0
R1(config-subif)#exit
R1(config)#interface fast 0/0.30
R1(config-subitf)#description 'Subinterface For Management'
R1(config-subif)#encapsulation dot1Q 30 native
R1(config-subif)#ip add 10.30.30.1 255.255.255.0
R1(config-subif)#exit
```

The primary advantage of this solution is that only a single physical interface is required on the router. The primary disadvantage is that the bandwidth of the physical interface is shared between the various configured subinterfaces. Therefore, if there is a lot of interVLAN traffic, the router can quickly become a bottleneck in the network.

InterVLAN Routing Using Switched Virtual Interfaces

Multilayer switches support the configuration of IP addressing on physical interfaces. These interfaces, however, must be configured with the `no switchport` interface configuration command to allow administrators to configure IP addressing on them. In addition to using physical interfaces, Multilayer switches also support Switched Virtual Interfaces (SVIs).

SVIs are logical interfaces that represent a VLAN. Although the SVI represents a VLAN, it is not automatically configured when a Layer 2 VLAN is configured on the switch and must be manually configured by the administrator using the `interface vlan [number]` global configuration command. The Layer 3 configuration parameters, such as IP addressing, are then configured on the SVI in the same manner as they would be on a physical interface.

The following output illustrates the configuration of SVIs to allow interVLAN routing on a single switch. This output references the VLANs used in previous configuration outputs in this section:

```
VTP-Server-1(config)#vlan 10
VTP-Server-1(config-vlan)#name Example-VLAN-10
VTP-Server-1(config-vlan)#exit
VTP-Server-1(config)#vlan 20
VTP-Server-1(config-vlan)#name Example-VLAN-20
VTP-Server-1(config-vlan)#exit
VTP-Server-1(config)#interface range fastethernet 0/1 - 2
VTP-Server-1(config-if-range)#switchport
VTP-Server-1(config-if-range)#switchport mode access
VTP-Server-1(config-if-range)#switchport access vlan 10
VTP-Server-1(config-if-range)#exit
VTP-Server-1(config)#interface range fastethernet 0/3 - 4
VTP-Server-1(config-if-range)#switchport
VTP-Server-1(config-if-range)#switchport mode access
VTP-Server-1(config-if-range)#switchport access vlan 20
VTP-Server-1(config-if-range)#exit
VTP-Server-1(config)#interface vlan 10
VTP-Server-1(config-if)#description 'SVI for VLAN 10'
VTP-Server-1(config-if)#ip address 10.10.10.1 255.255.255.0
VTP-Server-1(config-if)#no shutdown
VTP-Server-1(config-if)#exit
VTP-Server-1(config)#interface vlan 20
VTP-Server-1(config-if)#description 'SVI for VLAN 10'
VTP-Server-1(config-if)#ip address 10.20.20.1 255.255.255.0
VTP-Server-1(config-if)#no shutdown
VTP-Server-1(config-if)#exit
```

When using Multilayer switches, SVIs are the recommended method for configuring and implementing an interVLAN routing solution.

Multilayer Switching Components

In order to understand Multilayer Switching (MLS), it is important to have some understanding of the components used in Multilayer switches, such as the Catalyst 6500 series switches.

The Control and Data Planes

It is important to have a solid understanding of the terms 'control plane' and 'data plane' in order to completely understand MLS and how it operates. Collectively, these two planes are responsible for the building of routing tables and the actual forwarding of packets.

The control plane is where routing information, routing protocol updates, and other control information is stored and exchanged. Using routing protocols, the control plane is responsible for updating the routing table as changes in the network topology occur.

The data plane is responsible for the actual forwarding of data. The data plane is typically populated using information derived from the control plane. This plane is used to determine the physical next hop egress interface for received packets or frames and then forwards the packets or frames using the correct egress interface.

Catalyst 6500 Supervisor Module Components

The Supervisor engine is the 'brains' of the Catalyst 6500 series switches. Although going into detail on all components on the Supervisor 720 module is beyond the scope of the SWITCH exam, a basic understanding of the Supervisor module is required in order to understand the terminology used in Multilayer switching. The Supervisor Engine 720 module is comprised of the following three integrated core components:

1. The Multilayer Switch Feature Card 3
2. The Policy Feature Card 3
3. The Switch or Switching Fabric

The location of the Multilayer Switch Feature Card (MSFC) 3 on the Supervisor Engine 720 module is illustrated below in Figure 7-3:

Fig. 7-3. Supervisor Engine 720 Module Multilayer Switch Feature Card 3

The Multilayer Switch Feature Card 3 (MSFC 3) is a standard daughter card on the Supervisor 720 engine. The Multilayer Switch Feature Card (MSFC) 3 runs all software processes and supports both the Switch Processor (SP) and the Route Processor (RP).

The MSFC 3 builds the Cisco Express Forwarding (CEF) Forwarding Information Base (FIB) table in the software and then downloads this table to the hardware Application Specific Integrated Circuits (ASICs) on the PFC 3 and the Distributed Forwarding Engine switch (if present) that make the forwarding decisions for IP Unicast and Multicast traffic. While the Distributed Forwarding Engine switch is beyond the scope of the SWITCH exam requirements, CEF and FIB are requirements and will therefore be described in detail later in this chapter.

The RP supports Layer 3 features and functionality such as routing protocols, address resolution, ICMP, the management of virtual interfaces, and IOS configuration, among many other things. The SP supports Layer 2 features and functionality such as the Spanning Tree Protocol, VLAN Trunking Protocol, and Cisco Discovery Protocol.

The Policy Feature Card (PFC) 3 is equipped with a high-performance ASIC complex that supports a wide range of hardware-based features. The PFC 3 makes forwarding decisions in the hardware and supports routing and bridging, Quality of Service (QoS), IP Multicast packet replication, and processes security policies such as Access Control Lists (ACLs).

The PFC 3 requires the route processor to populate the route cache or optimized route table structure used by the Layer 3 switching ASIC. If no route processor is present, the PFC can perform only Layer 3 and Layer 4 QoS classification and ACL filtering but will not be able to perform Layer 3 switching. The location of the PFC 3 is illustrated below in Figure 7-4:

Fig. 7-4. Supervisor Engine 720 Module Policy Feature Card 3

The switch fabric is the connection between multiple ports or slots within a switch. It is used for data transport. Going into detail on the switch fabric is beyond the scope of the SWITCH exam requirements. This will not be described any further in this chapter or remainder of the guide. Figure 7-5 below illustrates the location of the switch fabric on the Supervisor Engine 720 module:

Fig. 7-5. Supervisor Engine 720 Module Switch Fabric

NOTE: The number '3' at the end of MSFC and PFC represents the current revision number for these components. As of the time of the writing of this guide, the MSFC revision 3 (MSFC 3) as well as the PFC revision 3 (PFC 3) are the latest MSFC and PFC components on the Supervisor.

Demand-Based Switching

Demand-based switching is also referred to as flow-based switching and is a legacy method of implementing MLS in Cisco Catalyst switches. In Unicast transmission, a flow is a unidirectional sequence of packets between a particular source and destination that share the same protocol and Transport Layer information.

In MLS switching, a Layer 3 switching table, referred to as an MLS cache, is maintained for the Layer 3-switched flows. The MLS cache maintains flow information for all active flows and includes entries for traffic statistics that are updated in tandem with the switching of packets. After the MLS cache is created, any packets identified as belonging to an existing flow can be Layer 3-switched based on the cached information. Demand-based switching requires the following components:

- Multilayer Switching Engine (MLS-SE)
- Multilayer Switching Route Processor (MLS-RP)
- Multilayer Switching Protocol (MLSP)

The MLS-SE is responsible for the packet switching and rewrite functions in ASICs. The MLS-SE is also capable of identifying Layer 3 flows. The MLS-SE represents the data plane and is responsible for determining the next hop and egress interface information for each frame received that requires routing, and then rewriting the frame as required and forwarding the frame to the correct egress interface.

The MLS-RP informs the MLS-SE of MLS configuration, and runs routing protocols, which are used for route calculation. The MLS-RP represents the control plane and maintains the route table, and is responsible for updating the route table as changes in the network topology occur.

The MLSP is a Multicast protocol that is used by the MLS-RP to communicate information, such as routing changes, to the MLS-SE, which then uses that information to reprogram the hardware dynamically with the current Layer 3 routing information. This is what allows for faster packet processing. Figure 7-6 below illustrates the operation of demand-based or flow-based switching:

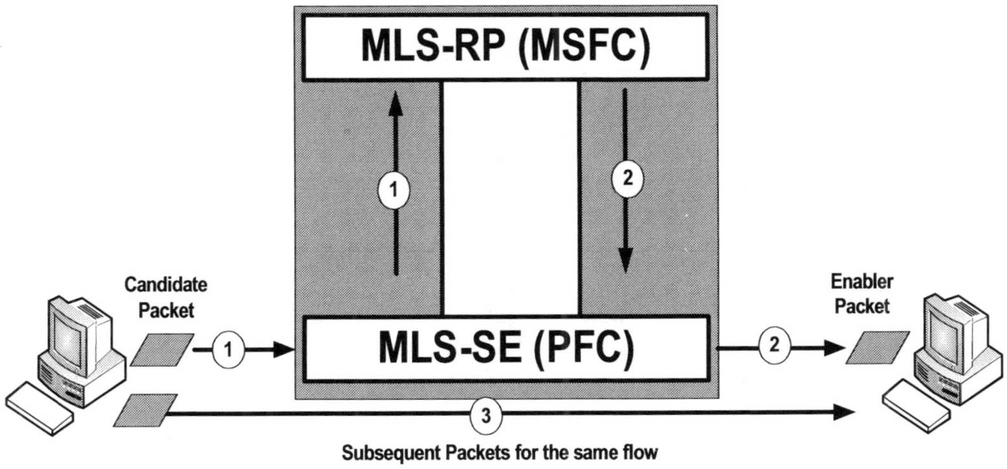

Fig. 7-6. Demand-Based or Flow-Based Switching Operation

The following sequence of steps is in reference to the diagram illustrated in Figure 7-6.

1. The MLS-SE (PFC) receives a candidate packet for a new flow. This packet is forwarded to the MLS-RP (MSFC) for a route lookup and is processed in software
2. The MLS-RP (MSFC) determines the destination of the packet and forwards it, via the MLS-SE (PFC) to the correct destination. This is referred to as the enabler packet
3. Given that both the candidate packet and the enabler packet have passed through the MLS-SE (PFC), the next packet in the flow is not sent to the MLS-RP (MSFC) but is instead switched in hardware using ASICs. It is important that both the candidate and the enabler packets for a single flow pass through the same switch; otherwise, flow-based switching will not be used. The same is applicable to all new flows that traverse the switch.

With the introduction of the Supervisor 720 engine, flow-based switching is considered a legacy MLS method. This method of MLS has been replaced by topology-based (CEF-based) MLS.

Topology-Based (CEF) Switching

The Supervisor Engine 720 module supports the Cisco Express Forwarding (CEF) architecture for forwarding packets. The MSFC performs control plane functions, such as learning about the networks, and builds routing tables. It then builds a Forwarding Information Base (FIB) and pushes this to the PFC, which forwards packets to their respective destinations based on the next-hop entries that are located in the FIB. This concept is illustrated below in Figure 7-7:

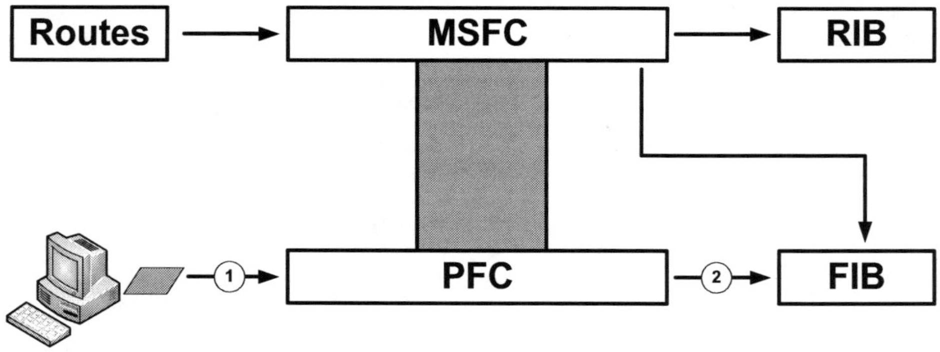

Fig. 7-7. Topology-Based or CEF-Based Switching Operation

Referencing Figure 7-7, the MSFC receives routing information via routing protocols and populates the Routing Information Base (RIB). The MSFC also builds an FIB and pushes this down to the PFC.

When the PFC receives a packet (step 1), it will perform a lookup in the FIB to determine where to switch the packet (i.e. the egress interface). This allows the majority of switching to be performed using hardware, although there are some exception packets, such as Telnet packets to the switch, that are sent to the MSFC for processing. The following sections describe the technologies referenced in this section.

Cisco Express Forwarding (CEF)

CEF operates at the data plane and is a topology-driven proprietary switching mechanism that creates a forwarding table that is tied to the routing table (i.e. the control plane). CEF was developed to eliminate the performance penalty experienced due to the first-packet process-switched lookup method used by flow-based switching.

CEF eliminates this by allowing the route cache used by the hardware-based Layer 3 routing engine to contain all the necessary information to the Layer 3 switch in the hardware before any packets associated with a flow are even received. Information that is conventionally stored in a route cache is stored in two data structures for CEF switching. These data structures provide optimized lookup for efficient packet forwarding and are referred to as the FIB and the adjacency table. Both will be described in detail in this chapter.

NOTE: It is important to remember that even with CEF, whenever there are routing table changes, the CEF forwarding table is also updated. While new CEF entries are being created, packets are switched in a slower switching path, using process switching, for example.

Forwarding Information Base (FIB)

CEF uses an FIB to make IP destination prefix-based switching decisions. The FIB is conceptually similar to a routing table or information base. It maintains a mirror image of the forwarding information contained in the IP routing table. In other words, the FIB contains all IP prefixes from the routing table.

When routing or topology changes occur in the network, the IP routing table is updated, and those changes are also reflected in the FIB. The FIB maintains next-hop address information based on the information in the IP routing table. Because there is a one-to-one correlation between FIB entries and routing table entries, the FIB contains all known routes and eliminates the need for route cache maintenance that is associated with switching paths, such as fast switching and optimum switching.

Additionally, because the FIB lookup table contains all known routes that exist in the routing table, it eliminates route cache maintenance and the fast-switching and process-switching forwarding scenarios. This allows CEF to switch traffic more efficiently than typical demand-caching schemes.

The Adjacency Table

The adjacency table is created to contain all connected next hops. An adjacent node is a node that is one hop away (i.e. directly connected). The adjacency table is populated as adjacencies are discovered. As soon as a neighbor becomes adjacent, a Data Link Layer header, called a MAC string or a MAC rewrite, which will be used to reach that neighbor, is created and stored in the table. On Ethernet segments, the header information is the destination MAC address, the source MAC address, and the EtherType, in that specific order.

As soon as a route is resolved, it points to an adjacent next hop. If an adjacency is found in the adjacency table, a pointer to the appropriate adjacency is cached in the FIB element. If multiple paths exist for the same destination, a pointer to each adjacency is added to the load-sharing structure, which allows for load balancing. When prefixes are added to the FIB, prefixes that require exception handling are cached with special adjacencies. These components, and their interaction, are illustrated below in Figure 7-8:

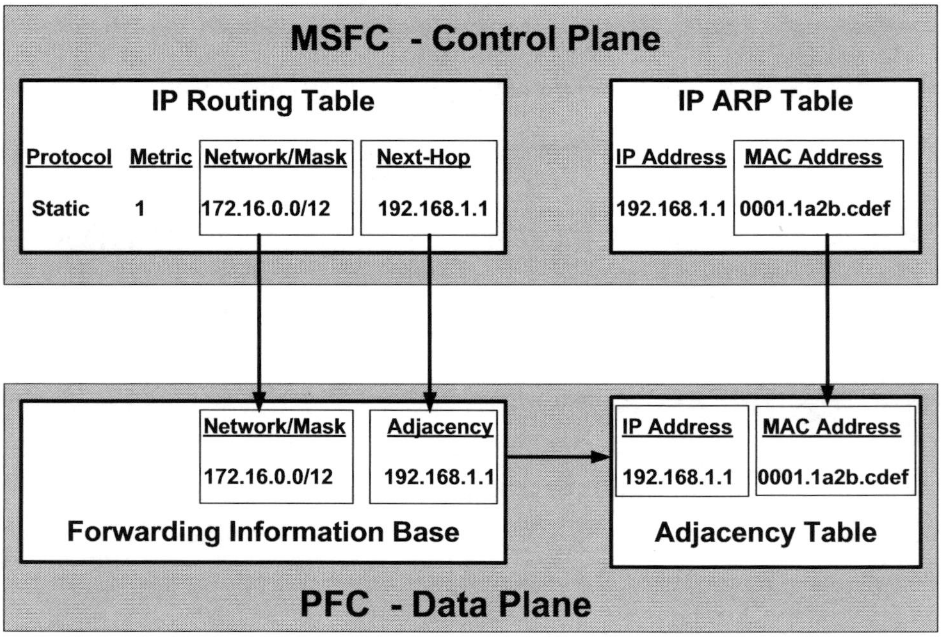

Fig. 7-8. Cisco Express Forwarding Components

Accelerated and Distributed CEF

By default, all CEF-based Cisco Catalyst switches use a central Layer 3 switching engine where a single processor makes all Layer 3 switching decisions for traffic received on all ports in the switch. Even though the Layer 3 switching engines used in Cisco Catalyst switches provide high performance, in some networks, having a single Layer 3 switching engine to all the Layer 3 switching does not provide sufficient performance. To address this issue, Cisco Catalyst 6500 series switches allow for CEF optimization through the use of specialized forwarding hardware. This is performed using either Accelerated CEF (aCEF) or Distributed CEF (dCEF).

Accelerated CEF allows a portion of the FIB to be distributed to capable line card modules in the Catalyst 6500 switch. This allows the forwarding decision to be made on the local line card using the locally stored scaled-down CEF table. In the event that FIB entries are not found in the cache, requests are sent to the Layer 3 engine for more FIB information.

Distributed CEF refers to the use of multiple CEF tables distributed across multiple line cards installed in the chassis. When using dCEF, the Layer 3 engine (MSFC) maintains the routing table and generates the FIB, which is then dynamically downloaded in full to each of the line cards, allowing for multiple Layer 3 data plane operations to be performed simultaneously.

In summation, dCEF and aCEF are technologies that implement multiple Layer 3 switching engines so that simultaneous Layer 3 switching operations can occur in parallel, boosting overall system performance. CEF technology offers the following benefits:

- Improved performance—CEF is less CPU-intensive than fast-switching route caching. More CPU processing power can be dedicated to Layer 3 services, such as Quality of Service (QoS) and encryption, for example.
- Scalability—CEF offers full switching capacity at each line card, in high-end platforms such as the Catalyst 6500 series switches, when dCEF mode is active.
- Resilience—CEF offers an unprecedented level of switching consistency and stability in large dynamic networks. In dynamic networks, fast-switching cache entries are frequently invalidated due to routing changes. These changes can cause traffic to be process-switched using the routing table rather than fast-switched using the route cache.

Configuring Cisco Express Forwarding

Enabling CEF requires the use of a single command, which is the `ip cef [distributed]` global configuration command. The `[distributed]` keyword is only applicable to high-end switches, such as the Catalyst 6500 series switches, that support dCEF. The following output shows how to configure CEF on a lower-end platform, such as the Catalyst 3750 series switch:

```
VTP-Server-1(config)#ip cef
VTP-Server-1(config)#exit
```

The following output illustrates how to enable dCEF on the Catalyst 6500 series switches:

```
VTP-Server-1(config)#ip cef distributed
VTP-Server-1(config)#exit
```

NOTE: There is no explicit command to configure or enable aCEF.

Verifying MLS Operation

MLS verification primarily entails verifying and validating correct CEF operation. This section guides you through the configuration commands required to verify MLS.

Verifying the Control Plane

The `show ip route and show arp` commands are used to verify that the correct information is present at the control plane. Additionally, an ICMP PING can also be used to verify connectivity with the IP address. The following output shows the `show ip route` command for the specified prefix:

```
VTP-Server-1#show ip route 150.254.1.2
Routing entry for 150.254.1.2/32
  Known via "ospf 1", distance 110, metric 2, type inter area
  Last update from 150.254.0.6 on FastEthernet0/1, 00:00:24 ago
  Routing Descriptor Blocks:
  * 150.254.0.6, from 150.254.0.6, 00:00:24 ago, via FastEthernet0/0
      Route metric is 2, traffic share count is 1
```

In the output above, the route is learned via OSPF and has a next hop interface and IP address of FastEthernet0/1 and 150.254.0.6, respectively.

The next step is to verify the ARP table and ensure that a valid Data Link Entry exists for the next hop IP address. This is illustrated in the following output:

```
VTP-Server-1#show arp
Protocol  Address          Age (min)  Hardware Addr   Type   Interface
Internet  150.254.0.5              -  000c.cea7.f3a0  ARPA   FastEthernet0/1
Internet  150.254.0.6              4  0013.1986.0a20  ARPA   FastEthernet0/1
```

Optionally, a simple PING can be sent to the destination address 150.254.1.2 to verify IP connectivity and complete the control plane check. This is illustrated in the following output:

```
VTP-Server-1#ping 150.254.1.2

Type escape sequence to abort.
Sending 5, 100-byte ICMP Echos to 150.254.1.2, timeout is 2 seconds:
!!!!!
Success rate is 100 percent (5/5), round-trip min/avg/max = 1/2/4 ms
```

Verifying the Data Plane

At a high level, the `show ip cef [distributed]` command is used to view the contents of the FIB. The output of this command is illustrated in the following output:

```
VTP-Server-1#show ip cef
Prefix              Next Hop             Interface
0.0.0.0/0           drop                 Null0 (default route handler entry)
0.0.0.0/8           drop
0.0.0.0/32          receive
127.0.0.0/8         drop
150.254.0.4/30      attached             FastEthernet0/1
150.254.0.4/32      receive
150.254.0.5/32      receive
150.254.0.6/32      150.254.0.6          FastEthernet0/1
150.254.0.7/32      receive
150.254.1.2/32      150.254.0.6          FastEthernet0/1
224.0.0.0/4         drop
224.0.0.0/24        receive
240.0.0.0/4         drop
255.255.255.255/32  receive
```

The values contained in the Next Hop field mean different things, all of which you should be familiar with. Table 7-1 below lists and describes the values that may be contained in this field:

Table 7-1. The Possible CEF Next Hop Field Values

Next Hop Field Values	Description
`drop`	This indicates that any packet that matches the indicated destination IP address or IP subnet should be dropped.
`receive`	This indicates that any packet that matches the indicated destination IP address or IP subnet should be sent to the MSFC for processing.
`attached`	This indicates an entry that represents a locally connected IP subnet.
`resolved`	This indicates an entry that represents the route to a host on the local subnet or remote destination subnet derived from the routing table on the MSFC. Every resolved FIB entry includes a next hop IP address.
`wildcard`	This indicates the entry that matches any packets that do not match other FIB entries. The action for this entry is to drop the traffic.

More granular and detailed verification of the data plane may be performed via the `show ip cef [network [mask]] [longer-prefixes] [checksum | detail | internal [checksum]]` to view specific FIB entries based on IP address information, or the `show ip cef [interface-type interface-number [checksum | [detail | internal [checksum] | platform]]` to view FIB entries based on interface information. The following output shows how to view a specific FIB entry based on IP address information:

```
VTP-Server-1#show ip cef 150.254.1.2 detail
150.254.1.2/32, version 25, epoch 0, cached adjacency 150.254.0.6
0 packets, 0 bytes
  via 150.254.0.6, FastEthernet0/1, 0 dependencies
    next hop 150.254.0.6, FastEthernet0/1
    valid cached adjacency
```

The following output illustrates how to view a specific FIB entry based on interface information:

```
VTP-Server-1#show ip cef fastethernet 0/1 detail
IP CEF with switching (Table Version 26), flags=0x0
  14 routes, 0 reresolve, 0 unresolved (0 old, 0 new), peak 0
  14 leaves, 12 nodes, 14608 bytes, 39 inserts, 25 invalidations
  0 load sharing elements, 0 bytes, 0 references
  universal per-destination load sharing algorithm, id E6B80BFB
  3(0) CEF resets, 0 revisions of existing leaves
  Resolution Timer: Exponential (currently 1s, peak 1s)
  0 in-place/0 aborted modifications
  refcounts:  3364 leaf, 3328 node

  Table epoch: 0 (14 entries at this epoch)

Adjacency Table has 1 adjacency
150.254.0.4/30, version 22, epoch 0, attached, connected
0 packets, 0 bytes
  via FastEthernet0/0, 0 dependencies
    valid glean adjacency
150.254.0.6/32, version 23, epoch 0, connected, cached adjacency 150.254.0.6
0 packets, 0 bytes
  via 150.254.0.6, FastEthernet0/1, 0 dependencies
    next hop 150.254.0.6, FastEthernet0/0
    valid cached adjacency
150.254.1.2/32, version 25, epoch 0, cached adjacency 150.254.0.6
0 packets, 0 bytes
  via 150.254.0.6, FastEthernet0/0, 0 dependencies
    next hop 150.254.0.6, FastEthernet0/1
    valid cached adjacency
```

The CEF adjacency table can be viewed via the `show adjacency [ip-address] [interface-type interface-number | null number | port-channel number | sysclock number | vlan number | ipv6-address | fcpa number | serial number] [connectionid number] [link {ipv4 | ipv6 | mpls}] [detail | encapsulation]` and the `show ip cef adjacency [interface-type] [interface-number] [ip-prefix] [checksum | detail | epoch epoch-number | internal | platform | source]` commands. The following output shows how to verify the CEF adjacency table:

```
VTP-Server-1#show adjacency detail
Protocol Interface                Address
IP       FastEthernet0/1          150.254.0.6(7)
```

```
                                    0 packets, 0 bytes
                                    001319860A20000CCEA7F3A00800
                                    ARP          03:33:44
                                    Epoch: 0
```

The `show ip cef adjacency` command allows administrators to view specific information on the different types of CEF adjacencies. Table 7-2 below lists and describes some of the following special adjacencies that may be found when CEF is enabled in Cisco IOS software:

Table 7-2. CEF Adjacency Types

Entry	Description
Null	This adjacency state is for packets destined for the Null 0 interface that are to be dropped or silently discarded by the switch.
Glean	This adjacency state is for destinations that are attached via a broadcast network but for which no MAC rewrite strings are available. Consider this route directly connected to a subnet with several hosts. The FIB table on the router maintains a prefix for the subnet instead of individual host prefixes. This subnet prefix points to a glean adjacency. When packets need to be forwarded to a specific host, the adjacency database is gleaned for the specific prefix. This incurs the cost of an additional lookup on the switch.
Punt	This adjacency state is for packets that are forwarded to the Layer 3 engine for handling and processing. This is typically performed for exception packets (e.g. packets with IP options) or if CEF switching is not supported for those packets. Punted packet statistics may be viewed using the show cef not-cef-switched command.
Drop	This adjacency state drops packets because they cannot be CEF-switched or cannot be punted to the Layer 3 engine. Packets may be dropped due to an encapsulation failure, an unresolved address, an unsupported protocol, no valid route present, no valid adjacency, or a checksum error, for example.
Discard	This adjacency state is similar to drop; however, it is applicable when packets must be discarded because of an access list or other policy.

The following output illustrates how to verify CEF Glean adjacencies:

```
VTP-Server-1#show ip cef adjacency glean detail
IP CEF with switching (Table Version 26), flags=0x0
  14 routes, 0 reresolve, 0 unresolved (0 old, 0 new), peak 0
  14 leaves, 12 nodes, 14608 bytes, 39 inserts, 25 invalidations
  0 load sharing elements, 0 bytes, 0 references
  universal per-destination load sharing algorithm, id E6B80BFB
  3(0) CEF resets, 0 revisions of existing leaves
  Resolution Timer: Exponential (currently 1s, peak 1s)
  0 in-place/0 aborted modifications
  refcounts:  3364 leaf, 3328 node

  Table epoch: 0 (14 entries at this epoch)
```

```
Adjacency Table has 1 adjacency
150.254.0.4/30, version 22, epoch 0, attached, connected
0 packets, 0 bytes
  via FastEthernet0/1, 0 dependencies
    valid glean adjacency
```

In the output above, notice that the entry is for the 150.254.0.4/30 subnet, to which the switch FastEthernet0/1 interface is directly connected. This is a valid glean adjacency.

The following output illustrates how to view punted packet statistics, which includes the number of packets punted to the Layer 3 engine for processing and the reason they were punted:

```
VTP-Server-1#show cef not-cef-switched
CEF Packets passed on to next switching layer
Slot  No_adj No_encap Unsupp'ted Redirect  Receive  Options   Access    Frag
RP         0        0          0        0     1124        0        0       0
```

In the output printed above, we can see that 1124 receive packets have been punted to the Layer 3 engine. These are packets that are destined directly to the switch and are therefore not CEF-switched. Such packets include PING or Telnet packets destined for a switch interface.

The following output illustrates how to view information on the prefixes that will be dropped by CEF:

```
VTP-Server-1#show ip cef adjacency drop detail
IP CEF with switching (Table Version 27), flags=0x0
  15 routes, 0 reresolve, 0 unresolved (0 old, 0 new), peak 0
  15 leaves, 12 nodes, 14760 bytes, 40 inserts, 25 invalidations
  0 load sharing elements, 0 bytes, 0 references
  universal per-destination load sharing algorithm, id E6B80BFB
  3(0) CEF resets, 0 revisions of existing leaves
  Resolution Timer: Exponential (currently 1s, peak 1s)
  0 in-place/0 aborted modifications
  refcounts:  3368 leaf, 3328 node

  Table epoch: 0 (15 entries at this epoch)

Adjacency Table has 1 adjacency
0.0.0.0/8, version 7, epoch 0
0 packets, 0 bytes
  via 0.0.0.0, 0 dependencies
    next hop 0.0.0.0
    valid drop adjacency
127.0.0.0/8, version 8, epoch 0
0 packets, 0 bytes
  via 0.0.0.0, 0 dependencies
    next hop 0.0.0.0
```

```
    valid drop adjacency
224.0.0.0/4, version 5, epoch 0
0 packets, 0 bytes
  via 0.0.0.0, 0 dependencies
    next hop 0.0.0.0
    valid drop adjacency
240.0.0.0/4, version 6, epoch 0
0 packets, 0 bytes
  via 0.0.0.0, 0 dependencies
    next hop 0.0.0.0
    valid drop adjacency
```

The `show ip cef adjacency drop detail` command simply lists the prefixes for which packets will be dropped. In order to view the actual statistics (i.e. the number of packets that have actually been dropped and the reason the packets were dropped), the `show cef drop` command is used as illustrated in the following output:

```
VTP-Server-1#show cef drop
CEF Drop Statistics
Slot  Encap_fail  Unresolved Unsupported    No_route      No_adj  ChkSum_Err
RP             6           0           0           0           0           0
```

In the output above, only six packets have been dropped, the reason being failed encapsulation.

Protecting the Route Processor

As stated earlier in this chapter, when using CEF, the majority of packets are forwarded by the PFC, referencing the entries contained in the FIB, which is populated by the MSFC. However, there are certain exception packets, such as packets with IP options, that must be punted to the Route Processor (MSFC) for further processing.

While the PFC can forward up to 30 million packets per second (pps), the MSFC is typically capable of forwarding only up to 500,000 pps. This significant difference in the forwarding capabilities means that it is possible for the MSFC to be oversubscribed or overutilized if the PFC punts a large number of packets to it. This may result in the following:

- Routing protocols getting out of sync with the rest of the network. This may result in network flaps and major network-wide transitions;
- The console on the switch may lock up. This results in the switch becoming unreachable and unmanageable, leaving administrators no avenues to troubleshoot; or
- Other Route Processor (RP)-based processes may cease operation altogether. This may result in the switch running with unpredictable results, or crashing.

To prevent such situations, IOS software allows administrators to configure MLS rate limiters. Rate limiters throttle the pps rate of certain packets that are punted to the MSFC by the PFC, which effectively ensures that the MSFC is never overwhelmed by the much faster PFC, allowing the switch to continue normal operations. Because the rate limiting functionality is performed in hardware, MLS rate limiters are typically referred to as hardware rate limiters (HWRLs) in various texts. These terms are interchangeable. Cisco Catalyst 6500 series switches support the following two types of CEF rate limiters:

1. CEF Receive
2. CEF Glean

CEF Receive is used for interfaces that belong to the switch. CEF Receive rate limiters are used to limit packets destined to the RP for interfaces that belong to the switch itself. CEF Glean occurs when a directly connected host does not have an entry in the ARP table and the RP has to ARP for the next hop MAC. CEF Glean rate limiters are used to limit these types of packets.

Configuring CEF Rate Limiters

The Glean and Receive CEF rate limiters are configured using the `mls rate-limit unicast cef` global configuration command. The following output illustrates the two options available with this global configuration command:

```
VTP-Server-1(config)# mls rate-limit unicast cef ?
  glean     Packets requiring ARP resolution
  receive   Packets falling in the Receive case
```

In addition to CEF rate limiters, the Catalyst 6500 series PFC 3 also supports the following HWRLs:

- Ingress-Egress ACL Bridged Packets (Unicast Only)
- uRPF Check Failure
- TTL Failure
- ICMP Unreachable (Unicast Only)
- Layer 3 Security Features (Unicast Only)
- ICMP Redirect (Unicast Only)
- VACL Log (Unicast Only)
- MTU Failure
- Layer 2 PDU
- Layer 2 Protocol Tunneling
- IP Errors
- Layer 2 Multicast IGMP Snooping

- IPv4 Multicast
- IPv6 Multicast

The following output illustrates how to rate limit ICMP unreachable and redirect packets:

```
VTP-Server-1(config)#mls rate-limit unicast ip icmp ?
  redirect     packets requiring ICMP redirect (same VLAN)
  unreachable  packets requiring ICMP unreachable message
```

The following output illustrates how to configure rate limiters for ACLs on the switch:

```
VTP-Server-1(config)#mls rate-limit unicast acl ?
  input     Input ACL lookups requiring punt to RP
  output    Output ACL lookups requiring punt to RP
  vacl-log  Vlan ACL logging requiring punt to RP
```

The following output illustrates how to rate limit IP packets, IP features, and RPF failure checks:

```
VTP-Server-1(config)#mls rate-limit unicast ip ?
  errors       packets with IP Checksum and length errors
  features     packets to layer3 software security features (Auth.Proxy,
               IPSEC, Inspection)
  icmp         packets requiring ICMP messages from the RP
  rpf-failure  packets failing the RPF check
```

NOTE: You are not expected to perform any MLS rate-limiting configuration; however, you should be familiar with the capability to rate limit various types of traffic when using MLS.

Fallback Bridging

By default, Multilayer switching does not work for all routed protocols. For example, routed protocols such as Novell's Internetwork Packet Exchange (IPX) and Apple's AppleTalk are routed only in software, not in hardware.

In addition to this, there are some protocols, such as DECnet, that are simply not routable. These protocols, however, may be bridged between different VLANs and routed interfaces using fallback bridging, which allows the switch to forward traffic that cannot be routed.

Fallback bridging allows two or more VLANs or routed ports to forward non-routable traffic between them by assigning them to the same bridge group. Each bridge group that is configured on the switch functions in the same manner as a unique bridge. Bridge Protocol Data Units (BPDUs) are exchanged only within a unique bridge group, not between bridge groups. Figure 7-9 below illustrates a LAN that is using fallback bridging to support non-routable protocols:

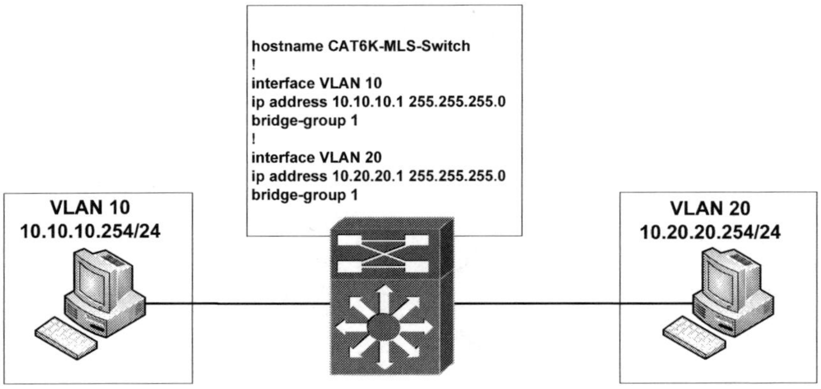

Fig. 7-9. Understanding Fallback Bridging

The diagram illustrated in Figure 7-9 shows two hosts connected to the CAT6K-MLS-Switch Multilayer switch. This switch is the default gateway for both VLANs, which allows interVLAN communication (routing) between the two subnets. In addition to this, the SVIs on the switch are also configured as part of the same bridge group. This allows non-routable traffic to be bridged between the two different subnets in a manner that is transparent to end hosts.

By default, fallback bridging is disabled. This feature is enabled by assigning two or more switch interfaces to a bridge group. Once the interfaces have been assigned to a bridge group, the interfaces are able to bridge all non-routed traffic between them and other member interfaces. This process happens regardless of the IP subnet the interfaces are configured on.

Fallback Bridging Configuration Guidelines

The following are guidelines and restrictions that you should be aware of when implementing fallback bridging on a Catalyst switch:

- Up to a maximum of thirty two (32) bridge groups can be configured on the switch
- An interface (an SVI or routed port) can be a member of only one bridge group
- Use a different bridge group for each separately bridged network connected to the switch
- Do not configure fallback bridging on a switch configured with private VLANs
- When enabled, all protocols are bridged, except for the following:
  - IP Version 4
  - IP Version 6
  - Address Resolution Protocol (ARP)
  - Reverse ARP (RARP)

- Frame Relay ARP
- Shared STP packets are fallback bridged

Configuring Fallback Bridging

The following sequence of steps should be taken when configuring fallback bridging:

1. Configure one or more bridge groups using the `bridge [1-255] bridge-group protocol vlan-bridge` global configuration command. Keep in mind that although any number between 1 and 255 is allowed, the switch only supports up to 32 unique groups.
2. Assign either a Layer 3 (routed) switch port or SVI to the configured bridge group using the `bridge-group [number]` interface configuration command. It is important to know that this command is not supported on Layer 2 ports.

The following output illustrates the configuration of fallback bridging on a switch:

```
VTP-Server-1(config)#bridge 1 protocol vlan-bridge
VTP-Server-1(config)#int f4/1
VTP-Server-1(config-if)#description 'Routed Layer 3 Interface'
VTP-Server-1(config-if)#no switchport
VTP-Server-1(config-if)#ip address 192.168.1.1 255.255.255.0
VTP-Server-1(config-if)#bridge-group 1
VTP-Server-1(config-if)#exit
VTP-Server-1(config)#int vlan 20
VTP-Server-1(config-if)#description 'SVI For VLAN 20'
VTP-Server-1(config-if)#ip address 172.16.20.1 255.255.255.0
VTP-Server-1(config-if)#bridge-group 1
VTP-Server-1(config-if)#exit
```

Verifying Fallback Bridging Configuration

The `show bridge [number] [group] [verbose]` command is used to view information, such as learned MAC addresses, pertaining to the bridge group. The following output shows the `show bridge` command:

```
VTP-Server-1#show bridge

Total of 300 station blocks, 299 free
Codes: P - permanent, S - self

Bridge Group 1:

    Address       Action    Interface         Age   RX count   TX count
000c.cea7.f3a0   forward   Vlan20             3          4          2
0013.1986.0a20   forward   FastEthernet4/1    3          1          1
```

In the output above, the `show bridge` command prints the bridge group number (1), the addresses learned within the bridge group, the interfaces on which these addresses are learned, their age, and both transmitted and received packet statistics.

Chapter Summary

The following section is a summary of the major points you should be aware of in this chapter.

InterVLAN Routing

- By default, hosts in one VLAN cannot directly communicate with hosts in another VLAN
- Routing is required to allow interVLAN communication between hosts
- Three solutions may be used to allow and enable interVLAN routing on switches
  1. InterVLAN Routing Using Physical Router Interfaces
  2. InterVLAN Routing Using Router Subinterfaces
  3. InterVLAN Routing Using Switched Virtual Interfaces

- Using physical router interfaces for interVLAN routing is simple but not scalable
- Using subinterfaces for interVLAN routing means shared bandwidth
- Using Switched Virtual Interfaces for interVLAN routing is the recommended solution

Multilayer Switching Components

- The control plane is responsible for updating and populating the routing table
- The data plane is responsible for the actual forwarding of packets
- The Supervisor 720 module is comprised of three integrated core components:
  1. The Multilayer Switch Feature Card 3
  2. The Policy Feature Card 3
  3. The Switch or Switching Fabric

- The MSFC 3 runs all software processes
- The MSFC 3 supports both the Switch Processor (SP) and Route Processor (RP)
- The RP supports Layer 3 features and functionality such as routing protocols
- The SP supports Layer 2 features and functionality such as the Spanning Tree Protocol
- The MSFC 3 builds the CEF FIB table in software
- The MSFC downloads the FIB to the hardware ASICs on the PFC 3
- The PFC makes forwarding decisions in hardware
- The PFC supports routing and bridging, QoS, IP Multicast packet replication, and ACLs
- The switch fabric is the connection between multiple ports or slots within a switch

Demand-Based Switching

- Demand-based switching is also referred to as flow-based switching
- Demand-based switching is a legacy method of implementing MLS in Catalyst switches
- A flow is a unidirectional sequence of packets between a source and destination
- Demand-based switching requires the following components:

1. Multilayer Switching Engine (MLS-SE)
2. Multilayer Switching Route Processor (MLS-RP)
3. Multilayer Switching Protocol (MLSP)

- The MLS-SE is responsible for the packet switching and rewrite functions in the ASICs
- The MLS-SE represents the data plane
- The MLS-RP informs the MLS-SE of MLS configuration, and runs routing protocols
- The MLS-RP represents the control plane
- MLSP is a Multicast protocol used by the MLS-RP to communicate with the MLS-SE

Topology-Based (CEF) Switching

- The Supervisor 720 supports the CEF architecture for forwarding packets
- CEF operates at the data plane and is a topology-driven proprietary switching mechanism
- CEF uses two data structures for switching:
  1. Forwarding Information Base (FIB)
  2. Adjacency Table

- CEF uses a FIB to make IP destination prefix-based switching decisions
- The FIB is conceptually similar to a routing table or information base
- The FIB maintains a mirror image of the forwarding information contained in the RIB
- The adjacency table is created to contain all connected next hops
- An adjacent node is a node that is one hop away, i.e. directly connected
- The adjacency table is populated as adjacencies are discovered
- By default, all CEF-based Cisco Catalyst switches use a central Layer 3 switching engine
- Cisco Catalyst switches allow for the optimization of CEF using two methods:
  1. Accelerated CEF (aCEF)
  2. Distributed CEF (dCEF)

- Accelerated CEF allows only a portion of the FIB to be distributed to capable line cards
- With aCEF, if FIB entries are not found in the cache, requests are sent to the Layer 3 engine
- Distributed CEF refers to the use of multiple CEF tables distributed across line cards
- With dCEF, the entire FIB contents are downloaded to all line cards with dCEF support
- CEF technology offers the following benefits:
  1. Improved performance
  2. Scalability
  3. Resilience

Protecting the Route Processor

- The PFC can forward up forwarding rates to 30 Million Packets per Second (pps)
- The MSFC is typically capable of forwarding only up to 500,000 pps
- This may result in the MSFC being oversubscribed, which could lead to:
    1. Routing protocols getting out of sync with the rest of the network
    2. The console on the switch may lock up
    3. Other Route Processor (RP) based processes may cease operation altogether

- MLS rate limiters limit the PPS rate of certain packets that are punted to the MSFC
- Catalyst 6500 series switches support the following CEF rate limiters:
    1. CEF Receive
    2. CEF Glean

- The Catalyst 6500 series PFC 3also supports the following hardware rate limiters (HWRLs):
    1. Ingress-Egress ACL Bridged Packets (Unicast Only)
    2. uRPF Check Failure
    3. TTL Failure
    4. ICMP Unreachable (Unicast Only)
    5. Layer 3 Security Features (Unicast Only)
    6. ICMP Redirect (Unicast Only)
    7. VACL Log (Unicast Only)
    8. MTU Failure
    9. Layer 2 PDU
    10. Layer 2 Protocol Tunneling
    11. IP Errors
    12. Layer 2 Multicast IGMP Snooping

Fallback Bridging

- MLS does not working for all routed protocols
- Non-IP protocols, such as IPX and AppleTalk, are forwarded using software
- Fallback bridging is used to bridge non-routable protocols
- Fallback bridging creating an STP instance for each bridge group
- Only 32 bridge groups can be configured on the switch
- Fallback bridging is configured on physical Layer 3 or SVI interfaces only

CHAPTER 8

High Availability and LAN Redundancy

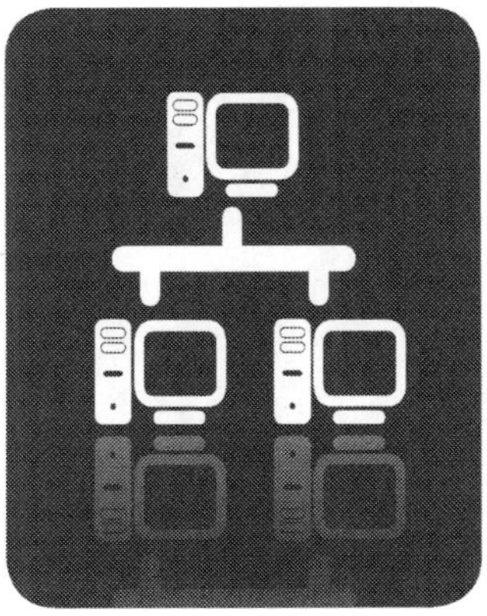

High Availability (HA) is an integral component when designing and implementing switched networks. HA is technology delivered in Cisco IOS software that enables network-wide resilience to increase IP network availability. All network segments must be resilient to recover quickly enough for faults to be transparent to users and network applications. First Hop Redundancy Protocols (FHRPs) provide redundancy in switched LAN environments. In addition to this, medium-end and high-end Cisco Catalyst switches, such as the Catalyst 4500 and 6500 series switches, support redundant Supervisor modules, which provide additional redundancy. The following core SWITCH exam objective is covered in this chapter:

- Implement High Availability, given a network design and a set of requirements

This chapter will be divided into the following sections:

- Hot Standby Router Protocol
- Virtual Router Redundancy Protocol
- Gateway Load Balancing Protocol
- ICMP Router Discovery Protocol
- Supervisor Engine Redundancy
- StackWise Technology
- Catalyst Switch Power Redundancy
- Non-Stop Forwarding

SWITCH Exam Objective	Chapter Section(s) Covered
• Implement first hop redundancy protocols • Verify High Availability solution	• Hot Standby Router Protocol • Virtual Router Redundancy Protocol • Gateway Load Balancing Protocol • ICMP Router Discovery Protocol
• Implement switch supervisor redundancy • Verify High Availability solution	• Supervisor Engine Redundancy • StackWise Technology • Catalyst Switch Power Redundancy • Non-Stop Forwarding

Hot Standby Router Protocol

Hot Standby Router Protocol (HSRP) is a Cisco-proprietary First Hop Redundancy Protocol (FHRP). HSRP allows two physical gateways that are configured as part of the same HSRP group to share the same virtual gateway address. Network hosts residing on the same subnet as the gateways are configured with the virtual gateway IP address as their default gateway.

While operational, the primary gateway forwards packets destined to the virtual gateway IP address of the HSRP group. In the event that the primary gateway fails, the secondary gateway assumes the role of primary and forwards all packets sent to the virtual gateway IP address. Figure 8-1 below illustrates the operation of HSRP in a network:

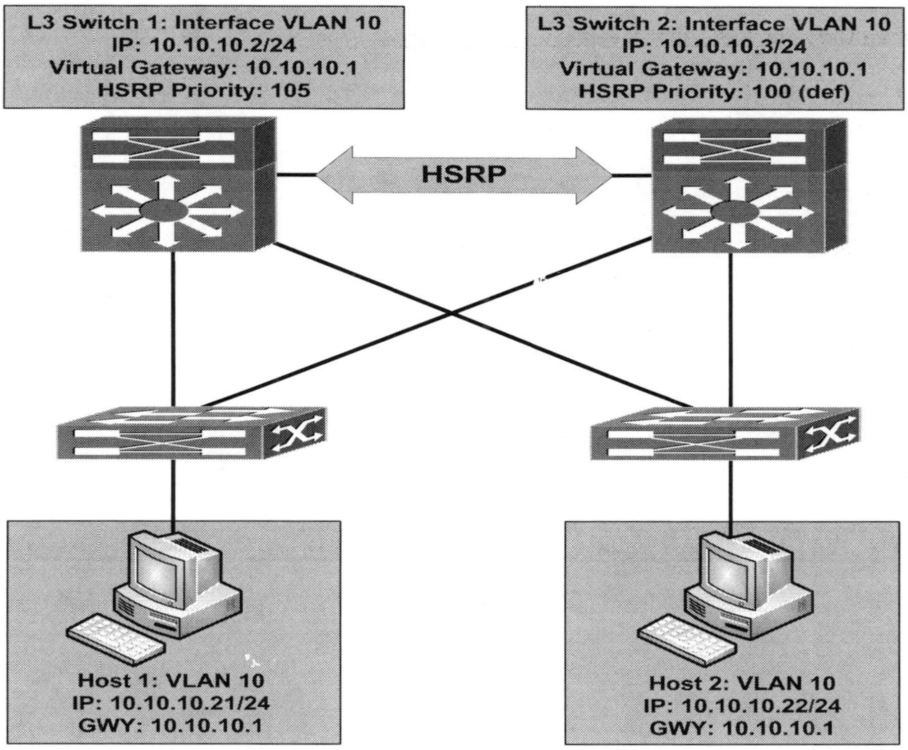

Fig. 8-1. Hot Standby Router Protocol (HSRP) Operation

Referencing Figure 8-1, HSRP is configured between the Layer 3 (Distribution Layer) switches, providing gateway redundancy for VLAN 10. The IP address assigned to the Switch Virtual Interface (SVI) on Layer 3 Switch 1 is 10.10.10.2/24, and the IP address assigned to the SVI on Layer 3 Switch 2 is 10.10.10.3/24. Both switches are configured as part of the same HSRP group and share the IP address of the virtual gateway, which is 10.10.10.1.

Switch 1 has been configured with a priority of 105, while Switch 2 is using the default priority of 100. Because of the higher priority, Layer 3 Switch 1 is elected as the primary switch and Layer 3

Switch 2 is elected as the secondary switch. All hosts on VLAN 10 are configured with a default gateway address of 10.10.10.1. Based on this solution, Switch 1 will forward all packets sent to the 10.10.10.1 address. However, in the event that Switch 1 fails, then Switch 2 will assume this responsibility. This process is entirely transparent to the network hosts.

REAL WORLD IMPLEMENTATION

In production networks, when configuring FHRPs, it is considered good practice to ensure that the active (primary) gateway is also the Spanning Tree Root Bridge for the particular VLAN. Referencing the diagram in Figure 8-1, for example, Switch 1 would be configured as the Root Bridge for VLAN 10 in tandem with being the HSRP primary gateway for the same VLAN.

This results in a deterministic network and avoids suboptimal forwarding at Layer 2 or Layer 3. For example, if Switch 2 was the Root Bridge for VLAN 10, while Switch 1 was the primary gateway for VLAN 10, packets from the network hosts to the default gateway IP address would be forwarded as shown in Figure 8-2 below:

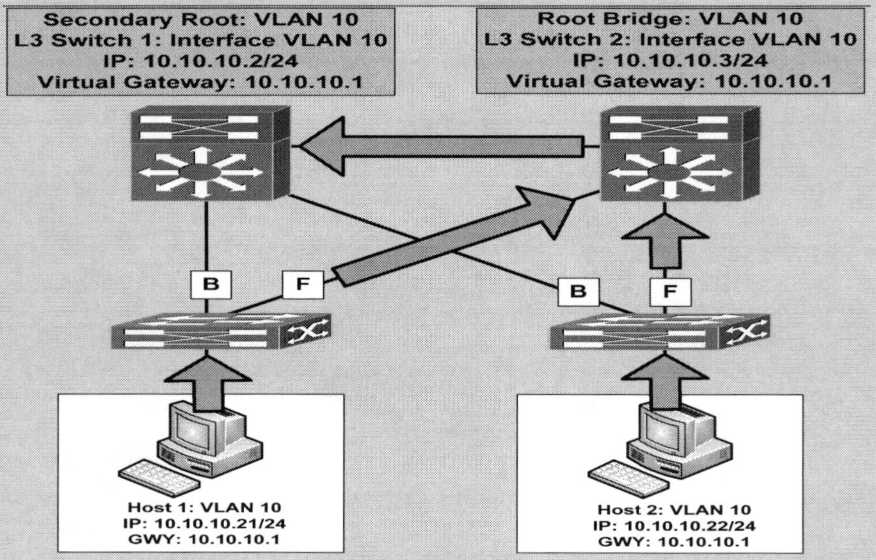

Fig. 8-2. Synchronizing the STP Topology with HSRP

In the network above, packets from Host 1 to 10.10.10.1 are forwarded as follows:

1. The access layer switch receives a frame destined to the MAC address of the virtual gateway IP address from Host 1. This frame is received in VLAN 10 and the MAC address for the virtual gateway has been learned by the switch via its Root Port.
2. Because the Root Bridge for VLAN 10 is Switch 2, the uplink toward Switch 1, the HSRP primary router, is placed into a Blocking state. The access layer switch forwards the frame via the uplink to Switch 2.
3. Switch 2 forwards the frame via the designated port connected to Switch 1. The same suboptimal forwarding path is used for frames received from Host 2.

Currently, two versions of HSRP are supported in Cisco IOS software: versions 1 and 2. The similarities and differences between the versions will be described in the sections that follow.

Hot Standby Router Protocol Version 1

By default, when Hot Standby Router Protocol is enabled in Cisco IOS software, version 1 is enabled. HSRP version 1 restricts the number of configurable HSRP groups to 255. HSRP version 1 routers communicate by sending messages to Multicast group address 224.0.0.2 using UDP port 1985. This is shown in Figure 8-3 below:

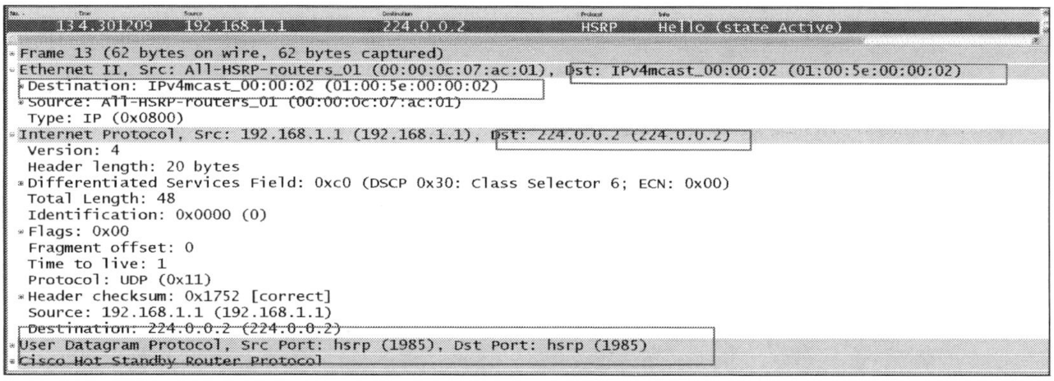

Fig. 8-3. HSRP Version 1 Multicast Group Address

While going into detail on the HSRP packet format is beyond the scope of the SWITCH exam requirements, Figure 8-4 below illustrates the information contained in the HSRP version 1 packet:

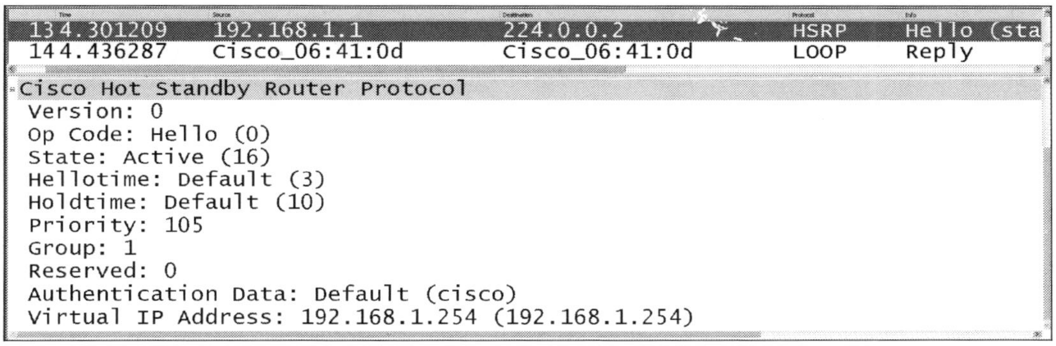

Fig. 8-4. The HSRP Version 1 Packet Fields

In Figure 8-4, notice that the Version field shows a value of 0. This is the default value for this field when version 1 is enabled; however, remember that this implies HSRP version 1.

Hot Standby Router Protocol Version 2

HSRP version 2 uses the new Multicast address 224.0.0.102 to send Hello packets instead of the Multicast address of 224.0.0.2, which is used by version 1. The UDP port number, however, remains the same. This new address is also encoded in both the IP packet and the Ethernet frame as shown below in Figure 8-5:

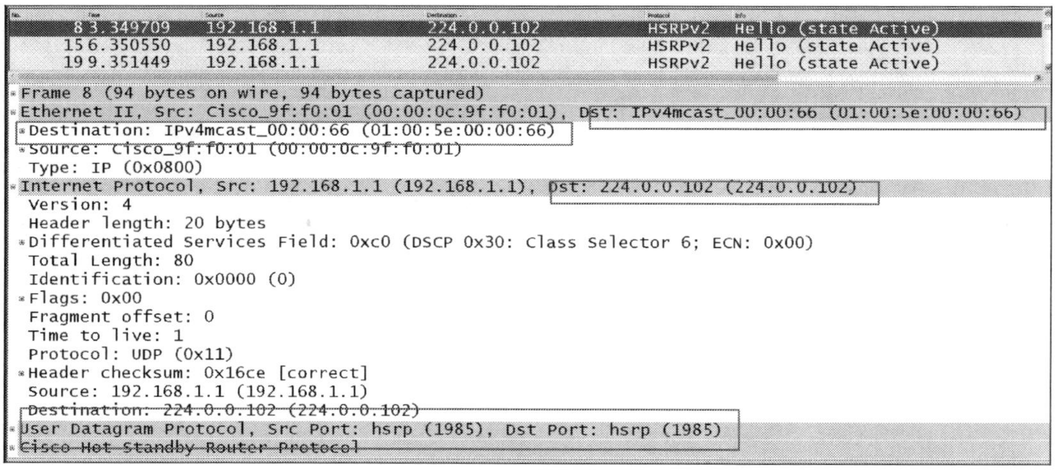

Fig. 8-5. HSRP Version 2 Multicast Group Address

While going into detail on the HSRP version 2 packet format is beyond the scope of the SWITCH exam requirements, it is important to remember that HSRP version 2 does not use the same packet format as HSRP version 1.

The version 2 packet format uses a Type/Length/Value (TLV) format. HSRP version 2 packets received by an HSRP version 1 router will have the Type field mapped to the Version field by HSRP version 1 and will be subsequently ignored. Figure 8-6 illustrates the information contained in the HSRP version 2 packet:

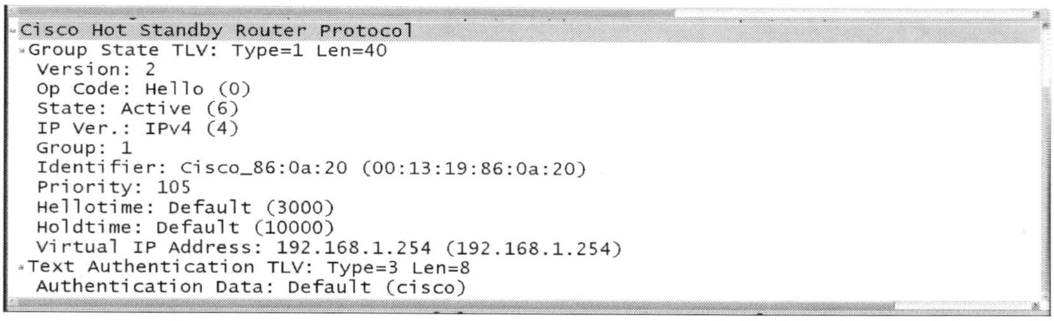

Fig. 8-6. The HSRP Version 2 Packet Fields

Hot Standby Router Protocol Version 1 and Version 2 Comparison

HSRP version 2 includes enhancements to HSRP version 1. The version 2 enhancements and differences from version 1 are described in the following section.

Although HSRP version 1 advertises timer values, these values are always to the whole second, as it is not capable of advertising or learning millisecond timer values. Version 2 is capable of both advertising and learning millisecond timer values. Figures 8-7 and 8-8 below highlight the differences between the Timer fields for both HSRP version 1 and HSRP version 2, respectively:

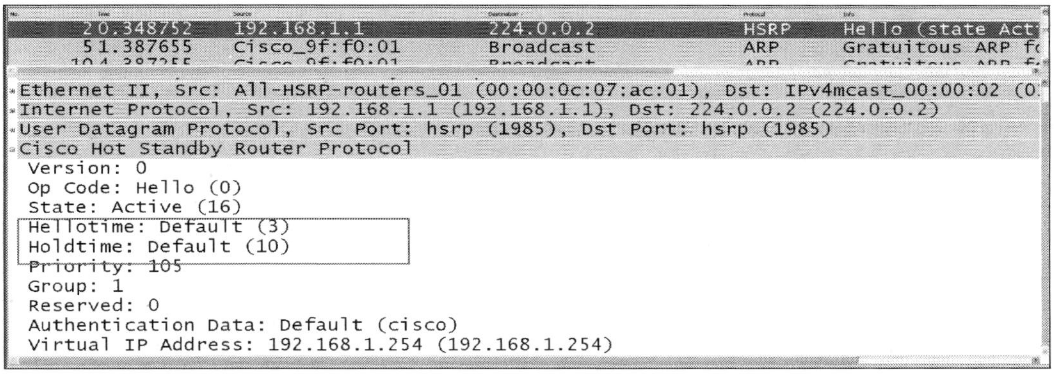

Fig. 8-7. HSRP Version 1 Timer Fields

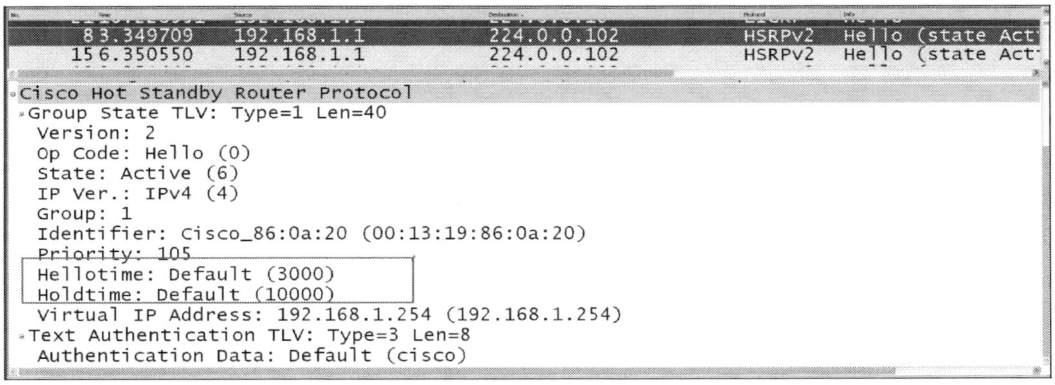

Fig. 8-8. HSRP Version 2 Timer Fields

HSRP version 1 group numbers are restricted to the range of 0 to 255, whereas the version 2 group numbers have been extended from 0 to 4095. This difference will be illustrated in the HSRP configuration examples that will be provided and documented later in this chapter.

Version 2 provides improved management and troubleshooting by including a 6-byte Identifier field that is populated with the physical router interface MAC address and is used to uniquely identify the source of HSRP active Hello messages. In version 1, these messages contain the virtual

MAC address as the source MAC, which means it is not possible to determine which HSRP router actually sent the HSRP Hello message. Figure 8-9 below shows the Identifier field that is present in the version 2 packet but not in the HSRP version 1 packet:

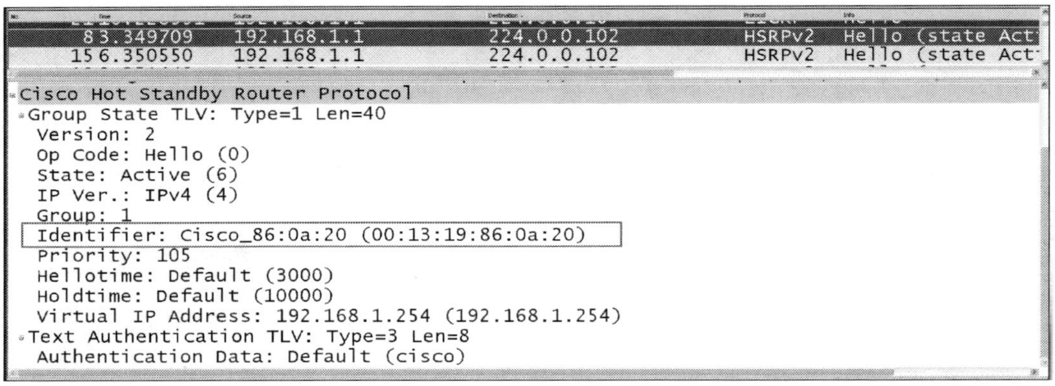

Fig. 8-9. HSRP Version 2 Identifier Field

In HSRP version 1, the Layer 2 address that is used by the virtual IP address will be a virtual MAC address composed of 0000.0C07.AC*xx*, where '*xx*' is the HSRP group number in Hexadecimal value and is based on the respective interface. HSRP version 2, however, uses a new MAC address range of 0000.0C9F.F000 to 0000.0C9F.FFFF for the virtual gateway IP address. These differences are illustrated below in Figure 8-10, which shows the version 1 virtual MAC address for HSRP Group 1, as well as in Figure 8-11, which shows the version 2 virtual MAC address, also for HSRP Group 1:

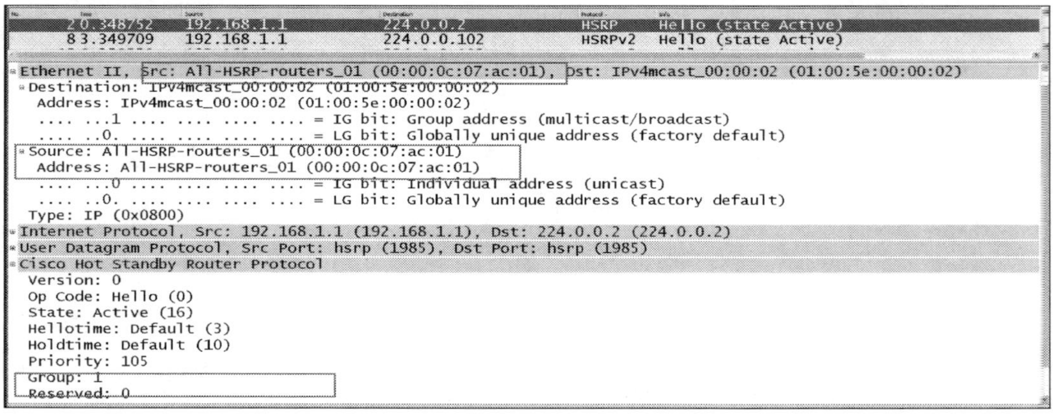

Fig. 8-10. HSRP Version 1 Virtual MAC Address Format

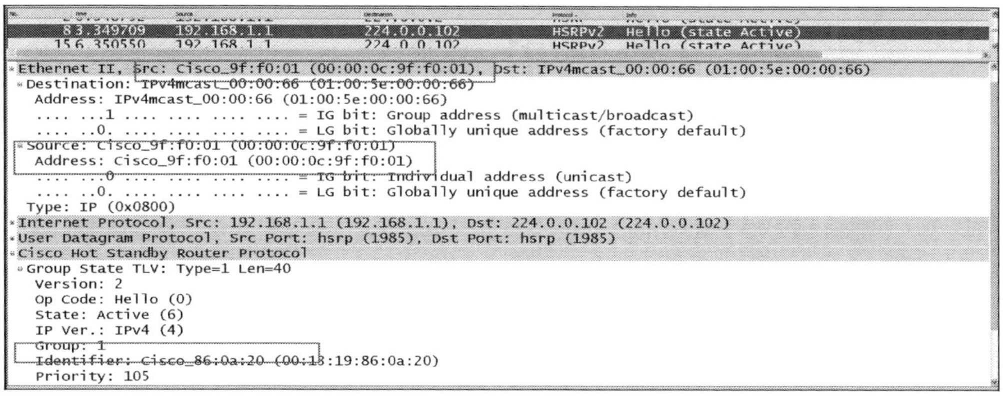

Fig. 8-11. HSRP Version 2 Virtual MAC Address Format

Hot Standby Router Protocol Primary Gateway Election

HSRP primary gateway election can be influenced by adjusting the default HSRP priority of 100 to any value between 1 and 255. The router with the highest priority will be elected as the primary gateway for the HSRP group.

If two gateways are using the default priority values, or if the priority values on two gateways are manually configured as equal, the router with the highest IP address will be elected as the primary gateway. The HSRP priority value is carried in the HSRP frame, as is the current state of the router (e.g. primary or standby). Figure 8-12 below illustrates the Priority and State fields of a gateway configured with a non-default priority value of 105, which resulted in it being elected as the active gateway for the HSRP group:

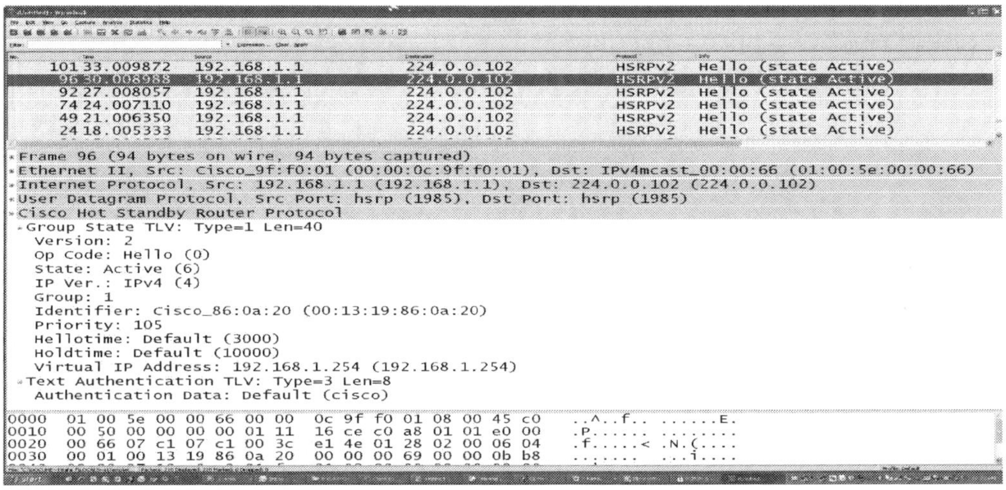

Fig. 8-12. HSRP Priority and State Fields

Hot Standby Router Protocol Messages

HSRP routers exchange the following three types of messages:

1. Hello messages
2. Coup messages
3. Resign messages

Hello messages are exchanged via Multicast and tell the other gateway the HSRP state and priority values of the local router. Hello messages also include the Group ID, HSRP timer values, version, and authentication information. All of the messages shown in the previous messages are HSRP Hello messages.

HSRP Coup messages are sent when the current standby router wants to assume the role of active gateway for the HSRP group. This is similar to a coup d'état in real life.

HSRP Resign messages are sent by the active router when it is about to shut down or when a gateway that has a higher priority sends a Hello or Coup message. In other words, this message is sent when the active gateway concedes its role as primary gateway.

HSRP Preemption

If a gateway has been elected as the active gateway and another gateway that is part of the HSRP group is reconfigured with a higher priority value, the current active gateway retains the primary forwarding role. This is the default behavior of HSRP.

In order for a gateway with a higher priority to assume active gateway functionality when a primary gateway is already present for an HSRP group, the router must be configured for preemption. This allows the gateway to initiate a coup and assume the role of the active gateway for the HSRP group. HSRP preemption is illustrated in the configuration examples to follow.

NOTE: Preemption does not necessarily mean that the Spanning Tree topology changes also.

Hot Standby Router Protocol States

In a manner similar to Open Shortest Path First (OSPF), when HSRP is enabled on an interface, the gateway interface goes through the following series of states:

1. Disabled
2. Init

3. Listen
4. Speak
5. Standby
6. Active

NOTE: There are no set time values for these interface transitions.

In either the disabled or the init states, the gateway is not yet ready or is unable to participate in HSRP, possibly because the associated interface is not up.

The listen state is applicable to the standby gateway. Only the standby gateway monitors Hello messages from the active gateway. If the standby gateway does not receive Hellos within 10 seconds, it assumes that the active gateway is down and takes on this role itself. If other gateways exist on the same segment, they also listen to Hellos and will be elected as the group active gateway if they have the next highest priority value or IP address.

During the speak phase, the standby gateway exchanges messages with the active gateway. Upon completion of this phase, the primary gateway transitions to the active state and the backup gateway transitions to the standby state. The standby state indicates that the gateway is ready to assume the role of active gateway if the primary gateway fails, and the active state indicates that the gateway is ready to actively forward packets.

The following output shows the state transitions displayed in the `debug standby` command on a gateway for which HSRP has just been enabled:

```
R2#debug standby
HSRP debugging is on
R2#
R2#
R2#
R2#conf
Configuring from terminal, memory, or network [terminal]?
Enter configuration commands, one per line.  End with CNTL/Z.
R2(config)#logging con
R2(config)#int f0/0
R2(config-if)#stand 1 ip 192.168.1.254
R2(config-if)#
R2(config-if)#
R2(config-if)#
R2(config-if)#
*Mar  1 01:21:55.471: HSRP: Fa0/0 API 192.168.1.254 is not an HSRP address
*Mar  1 01:21:55.471: HSRP: Fa0/0 Grp 1 Disabled -> Init
```

```
*Mar  1 01:21:55.471: HSRP: Fa0/0 Grp 1 Redundancy "hsrp-Fa0/0-1" state
Disabled -> Init
*Mar  1 01:22:05.475: HSRP: Fa0/0 Interface up
...
[Truncated Output]
...
*Mar  1 01:22:06.477: HSRP: Fa0/0 Interface min delay expired
*Mar  1 01:22:06.477: HSRP: Fa0/0 Grp 1 Init: a/HSRP enabled
*Mar  1 01:22:06.477: HSRP: Fa0/0 Grp 1 Init -> Listen
*Mar  1 01:22:06.477: HSRP: Fa0/0 Redirect adv out, Passive, active 0 passive
1
...
[Truncated Output]
...
*Mar  1 01:22:16.477: HSRP: Fa0/0 Grp 1 Listen: d/Standby timer expired
(unknown)
*Mar  1 01:22:16.477: HSRP: Fa0/0 Grp 1 Listen -> Speak
...
[Truncated Output]
...
*Mar  1 01:22:26.478: HSRP: Fa0/0 Grp 1 Standby router is local
*Mar  1 01:22:26.478: HSRP: Fa0/0 Grp 1 Speak -> Standby
*Mar  1 01:22:26.478: %HSRP-5-STATECHANGE: FastEthernet0/0 Grp 1 state Speak
-> Standby
*Mar  1 01:22:26.478: HSRP: Fa0/0 Grp 1 Redundancy "hsrp-Fa0/0-1" state Speak
-> Standby
```

HSRP Addressing

Earlier in this chapter, we learned that in HSRP version 1, the Layer 2 address that is used by the virtual IP address will be a virtual MAC address composed of 0000.0C07.AC*xx*, where '*xx*' is the HSRP group number in Hexadecimal value and is based on the respective interface. HSRP version 2, however, uses a new MAC address range of 0000.0C9F.F000 to 0000.0C9F.FFFF for the virtual gateway IP address.

In some cases, it may not be desirable to use these default address ranges. An example would be a situation where several HSRP groups were configured on a router interface connected to a switch port that was configured for port security. In such a case, the router would use a different MAC address for each HSRP group, the result being multiple MAC addresses that would all need to be accommodated in the port security configuration. This configuration would have to be modified each time an HSRP group was added to the interface; otherwise, a port security violation would occur.

To address this issue, Cisco IOS software allows administrators to configure HSRP to use the actual MAC address of the physical interface on which it is configured. The result is that a single MAC address is used by all groups (the MAC address of the active gateway is used) and the port security configuration need not be modified each time an HSRP group is configured between the routers connected to the switches. This is performed via the `standby use-bia` interface configuration command. The following output illustrates the `show standby` command, which shows a gateway interface that is configured with two different HSRP groups:

```
Gateway-1#show standby
FastEthernet0/0 - Group 1
  State is Active
    8 state changes, last state change 00:13:07
  Virtual IP address is 192.168.1.254
  Active virtual MAC address is 0000.0c07.ac01
    Local virtual MAC address is 0000.0c07.ac01 (v1 default)
  Hello time 3 sec, hold time 10 sec
    Next hello sent in 2.002 secs
  Preemption disabled
  Active router is local
  Standby router is 192.168.1.2, priority 100 (expires in 9.019 sec)
  Priority 105 (configured 105)
  IP redundancy name is "hsrp-Fa0/0-1" (default)
FastEthernet0/0 - Group 2
  State is Active
    2 state changes, last state change 00:09:45
  Virtual IP address is 172.16.1.254
  Active virtual MAC address is 0000.0c07.ac02
    Local virtual MAC address is 0000.0c07.ac02 (v1 default)
  Hello time 3 sec, hold time 10 sec
    Next hello sent in 2.423 secs
  Preemption disabled
  Active router is local
```

In the output above, based on the default HSRP version, the virtual MAC address for HSRP Group 1 is 0000.0c07.ac01, while that for HSRP Group 2 is 0000.0c07.ac02. This means that the switch port that this gateway is connected to learns three different addresses: the actual or burnt-in MAC address assigned to the actual physical FastEthernet0/0 interface, the virtual MAC address for HSRP Group 1, and the virtual MAC address for HSRP Group 2.

The following output illustrates how to configure HSRP to use the actual MAC address of the gateway interface as the virtual MAC address of the different HSRP groups:

```
Gateway-1#conf
Configuring from terminal, memory, or network [terminal]?
Enter configuration commands, one per line.  End with CNTL/Z.
Gateway-1(config)#int f0/0
Gateway-1(config-if)#standby use-bia
Gateway-1(config-if)#exit
```

Based on the configuration in the above output, the `show standby` command reflects the new MAC address for the HSRP group as illustrated in the following output:

```
Gateway-1#show standby
FastEthernet0/0 - Group 1
  State is Active
    8 state changes, last state change 00:13:30
  Virtual IP address is 192.168.1.254
  Active virtual MAC address is 0013.1986.0a20
    Local virtual MAC address is 0013.1986.0a20 (bia)
  Hello time 3 sec, hold time 10 sec
    Next hello sent in 2.756 secs
  Preemption disabled
  Active router is local
  Standby router is 192.168.1.2, priority 100 (expires in 9.796 sec)
  Priority 105 (configured 105)
  IP redundancy name is "hsrp-Fa0/0-1" (default)
FastEthernet0/0 - Group 2
  State is Active
    2 state changes, last state change 00:10:09
  Virtual IP address is 172.16.1.254
  Active virtual MAC address is 0013.1986.0a20
    Local virtual MAC address is 0013.1986.0a20 (bia)
  Hello time 3 sec, hold time 10 sec
    Next hello sent in 0.188 secs
  Preemption disabled
  Active router is local
  Standby router is unknown
  Priority 105 (configured 105)
  IP redundancy name is "hsrp-Fa0/0-2" (default)
```

The MAC address used by both groups, 0013.1986.0a20, is the MAC address assigned to the physical gateway interface. This is illustrated in the following output:

```
Gateway-1#show interface fastethernet 0/0
FastEthernet0/0 is up, line protocol is up
  Hardware is AmdFE, address is 0013.1986.0a20 (bia 0013.1986.0a20)
  Internet address is 192.168.1.1/24
  MTU 1500 bytes, BW 100000 Kbit/sec, DLY 100 usec,
     reliability 255/255, txload 1/255, rxload 1/255
  Encapsulation ARPA, loopback not set
...
[Truncated Output]
```

NOTE: In addition to configuring HSRP to use the burnt-in address (BIA), administrators also have the option of statically specifying the MAC address that the virtual gateway should use via the `standby [number] mac-address [mac]` interface configuration command. This option is typically avoided as it can result in duplicate MAC addresses in the switched network, which can cause severe network issues and possibly even an outage.

HSRP Plain Text Authentication

By default, HSRP messages are sent with the plain-text key string 'cisco' as a simple method to authenticate HSRP peers. If the key string in a message matches the key configured on an HSRP peer, the message is accepted. If not, HSRP ignores the unauthenticated message(s).

Plain text keys provide very little security because they can be 'captured on the wire' using simple packet capture tools, such as Wireshark and Ethereal. Figure 8-13 below shows the default plain-text authentication key used in HSRP messages:

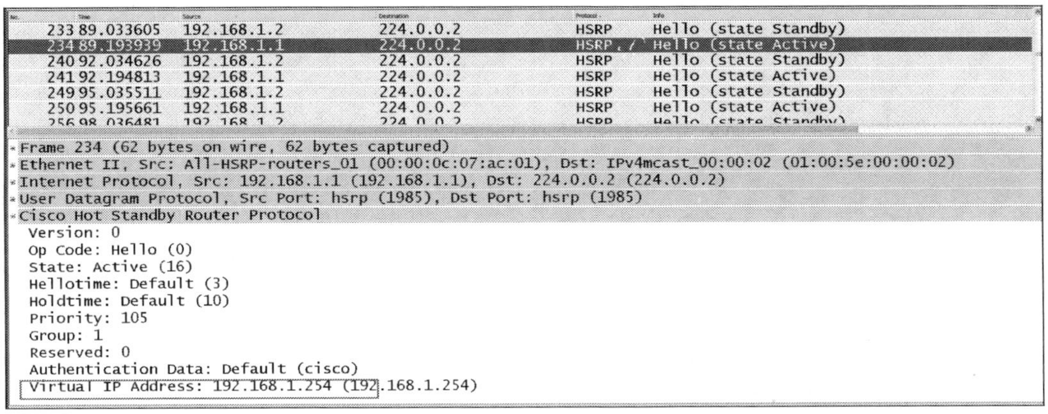

Fig. 8-13. Viewing the Default HSRP Plain-Text Key

Because plain-text authentication provides very little security, Message Digest 5 (MD5) authentication, which is described in the following section, is the recommended authentication method for HSRP.

HSRP MD5 Authentication

Message Digest 5 authentication provides greater security for HSRP than that provided by plain text authentication by generating an MD5 digest for the HSRP portion of the Multicast HSRP protocol packet. Using MD5 authentication allows each HSRP group member to use a secret key to generate a keyed MD5 hash that is part of the outgoing packet. A keyed hash of the incoming HSRP packet is generated and if the hash within the incoming packet does not match the MD5-generated hash, the packet is simply ignored by the receiving router.

The key for the MD5 hash either can be given directly in the configuration using a key string or can be supplied indirectly through a key chain. Both configuration options will be described in detail later in this chapter. When using plain-text or MD5 authentication, the gateway will reject HSRP packets if any of the following is true:

- The authentication schemes differ on the router and in the incoming packets
- The MD5 digests differ on the router and in the incoming packets
- The text authentication strings differ on the router and in the incoming packets

HSRP Interface Tracking

HSRP allows administrators to track the status of interfaces on the current active gateway so that when that interface fails, the gateway decrements its priority by a specified value, the default being 10, allowing another gateway to assume the role of active gateway for the HSRP group. This concept is illustrated below in Figure 8-14:

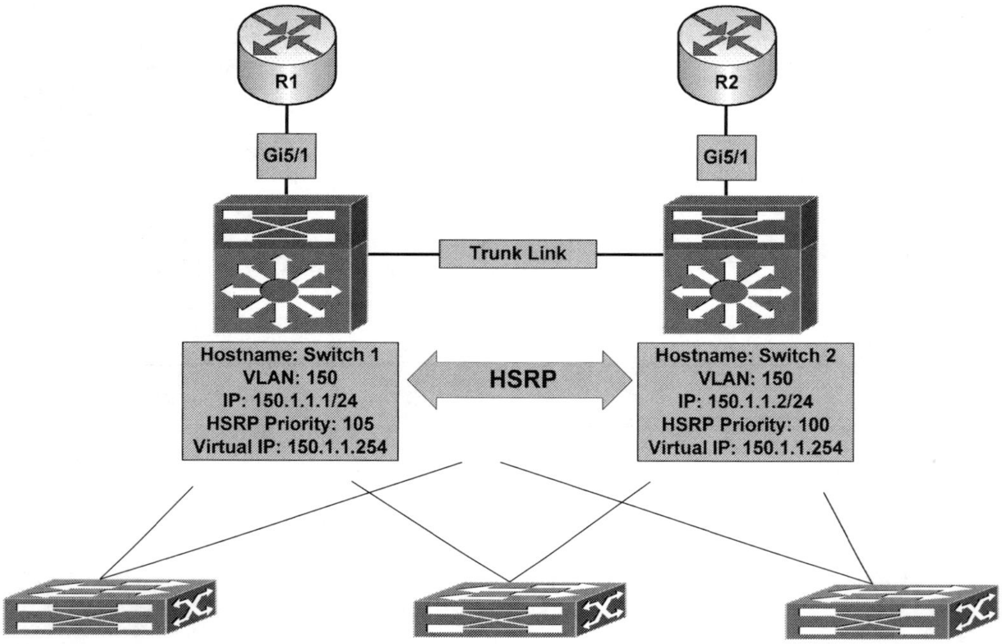

Fig. 8-14. HSRP Interface Tracking

Referencing Figure 8-14, HSRP has been enabled on Switch 1 and Switch 2 for VLAN 150. Based on the current priority configuration, Switch 1, with a priority value of 105, has been elected as the primary switch for this VLAN. Both Switch 1 and Switch 2 are connected to two routers via their GigabitEthernet5/1 interfaces. It is assumed that these two routers peer with other external networks, such as the Internet.

Without HSRP interface tracking, if the GigabitEthernet0/1 interface between Switch 1 and R1 failed, Switch 1 would retain its primary gateway status. It would then have to forward any received packets destined for the Internet, for example, over to Switch 2 using the connection between itself and Switch 2. The packets would be forwarded out via R2 toward their intended destination. This results in a suboptimal traffic path within the network.

HSRP interface tracking allows the administrators to configure HSRP to track the status of an interface and decrement the active gateway priority by either a default value of 10 or a value specified by the administrators. Referencing Figure 8-14, if HSRP interface tracking was configured using the default values on Switch 1, allowing it to track the status of interface GigabitEthernet5/1, and that interface failed, Switch 1 would decrement its priority for the HSRP group by 10, resulting in a priority of 95.

Assuming that Switch 2 was configured to preempt, which is mandatory in this situation, it would realize that it had the higher priority (100 versus 95) and perform a coup, assuming the role of active gateway for this HSRP group.

REAL WORLD IMPLEMENTATION

In production networks, Cisco Catalyst switches also support Enhanced Object Tracking (EOT), which can be used with any FHRP (i.e. HSRP, VRRP, and GLBP). Enhanced Object Tracking allows administrators to configure the switch to track the following parameters:

- The IP routing state of an interface
- IP route reachability
- The threshold of IP-Route metrics
- IP SLAs operations

FHRPs, such as HSRP, can be configured to track these enhanced objects, allowing for greater flexibility when implementing FHRP failover situations. For example, using EOT, the active HSRP router could be configured to decrement its priority value by a certain amount if a network or host route was not reachable (i.e. present in the routing table). EOT is beyond the scope of the SWITCH exam requirements and will not be illustrated in the configuration examples.

HSRP Load Balancing

HSRP allows administrators to configure multiple HSRP groups on physical interfaces to allow for load balancing. By default, when HSRP is configured between two gateways, only one gateway actively forwards traffic for that group at any given time. This can result in wasted bandwidth for the standby gateway link. This is illustrated below in Figure 8-15:

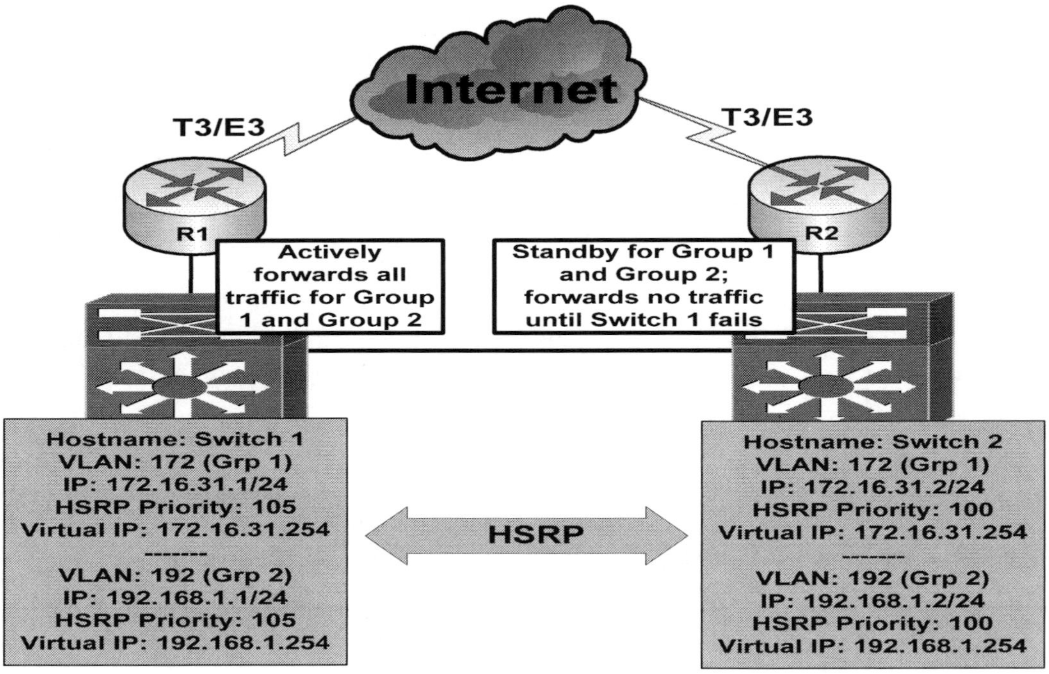

Fig. 8-15. A Network without HSRP Load Balancing

In Figure 8-15, two HSRP groups are configured between Switch 1 and Switch 2. Switch 1 has been configured as the active (primary) gateway for both groups – based on the higher priority value. Switch 1 and Switch 2 are connected to R1 and R2, respectively. These routers are both connected to the Internet via T3/E3 dedicated lines. Because Switch 1 is the active gateway for both groups, it will forward traffic for both groups until such time that it fails and Switch 2 assumes the role of active (primary) gateway.

While this does satisfy the redundancy needs of the network, it also results in the expensive T3/E3 link on R2 remaining idle until Switch 2 becomes the active gateway and begins to forward traffic through it. Naturally, this represents a wasted amount of bandwidth.

By configuring multiple HSRP groups, each using a different active gateway, administrators can effectively prevent the unnecessary waste of resources and load balance between Switch 1 and Switch 2. This is illustrated below in Figure 8-16:

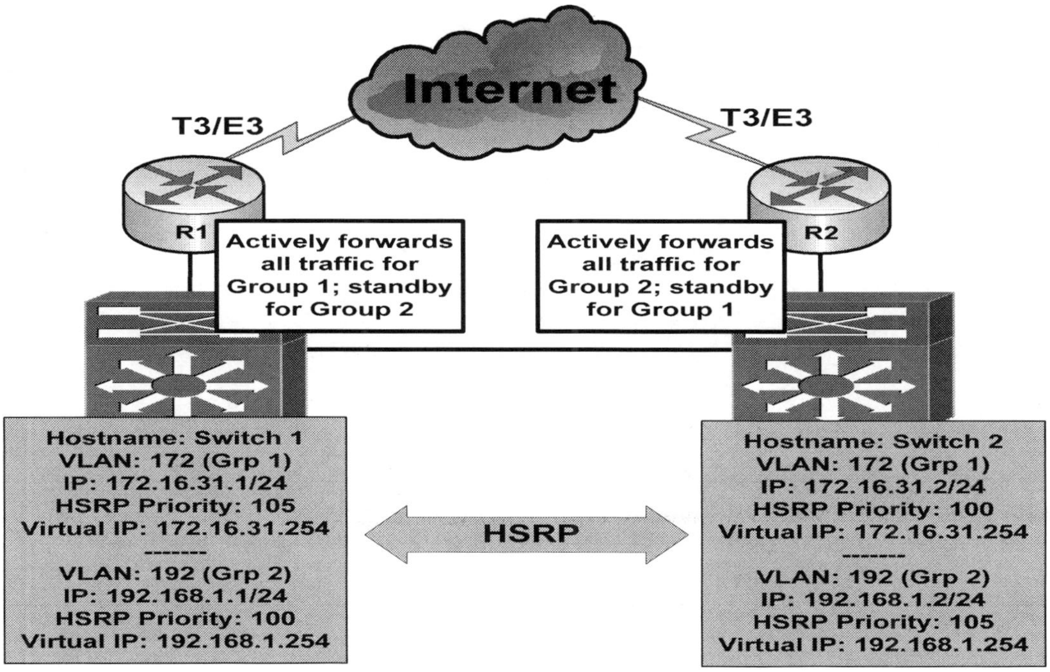

Fig. 8-16. A Network Using HSRP for Load Balancing

By configuring Switch 1 as the active gateway for HSRP Group 1 and Switch 2 as the active gateway for HSRP Group 2, administrators can allow traffic from these two groups to be load balanced between Switch 1 and Switch 2, and ultimately across the two dedicated T3/E3 WAN connections. Each switch then backs up the other's group. For example, Switch 1 will assume the role of active gateway for Group 2 if Switch 2 fails, and vice versa.

REAL WORLD IMPLEMENTATION

In production networks, it is important to remember that creating multiple HSRP groups may result in increased gateway CPU utilization, as well as increased network utilization due to HSRP message exchanges. Cisco Catalyst switches, such as the Catalyst 4500 and 6500 series switches, support the implementation of HSRP client groups.

In the previous section, we learned that HSRP allows for the configuration of multiple groups on a single gateway interface. The primary issue with running many different HSRP groups on the gateway interface is that it increases CPU utilization on the gateway and may potentially also increase the amount of network traffic, given the 3-second Hello interval used by HSRP.

To address this potential issue, HSRP also allows for the configuration of client or slave groups. These are simply HSRP groups that are configured to follow a master HSRP group and that do not participate in the HSRP election. These client or slave groups follow the operation and

HSRP status of the master group and, therefore, do not need to exchange periodic Hello packets themselves. This reduces CPU and network utilization when using multiple HSRP groups.

However, it should be noted that client groups send periodic messages in order to refresh their virtual MAC addresses in switches. The refresh message may be sent at a much lower frequency compared with the protocol election messages sent by the master group. While the configuration of client groups is beyond the scope of the SWITCH exam requirements, the following output illustrates the configuration of two client groups, which are configured to follow master group HSRP Group 1, also named the SWITCH-HSRP group:

```
Gateway-1(config)#interface vlan 100
Gateway-1(config-if)#ip address 192.168.1.1 255.255.255.0
Gateway-1(config-if)#ip address 172.16.31.1 255.255.255.0 secondary
Gateway-1(config-if)#ip address 10.100.10.1 255.255.255.0 secondary
Gateway-1(config-if)#standby 1 ip 192.168.1.254
Gateway-1(config-if)#standby 1 name SWITCH-HSRP
Gateway-1(config-if)#standby 2 ip 172.16.31.254
Gateway-1(config-if)#standby 2 follow SWITCH-HSRP
Gateway-1(config-if)#standby 3 ip 10.100.10.254
Gateway-1(config-if)#standby 3 follow SWITCH-HSRP
Gateway-1(config-if)#exit
```

In the configuration in the above output, Group 1 is configured as the master HSRP group and Groups 2 and 3 are configured as client or slave HSRP groups.

Configuring HSRP on the Gateway

The following steps are required to configure HSRP on the gateway:

1. Configure the correct IP address and mask for the gateway interface using the `ip address [address] [mask] [secondary]` interface configuration command.
2. Create an HSRP group on the gateway interface and assign the group the virtual IP address via the `standby [number] ip [virtual address][secondary]` interface configuration command. The `[secondary]` keyword specifies the IP address as a secondary gateway IP address for the specified group.
3. Optionally, assign the HSRP group a name using the `standby [number] name [name]` interface configuration command.
4. Optionally, if you want to control the election of the active gateway, configure the group priority via the `standby [number] priority [value]` interface configuration command.

The following HSRP configuration outputs in this section will be based on the network below in Figure 8-17:

Fig. 8-17. HSRP Configuration Examples Topology

NOTE: It is assumed that the VLAN and trunking configuration between VTP-Server-1 and VTP-Server-2 is already in place and the switches are successfully able to ping each other across VLAN 172. For brevity, this configuration output will be omitted from the configuration examples.

```
VTP-Server-1(config)#interface vlan 172
VTP-Server-1(config-if)#ip address 172.16.31.1 255.255.255.0
VTP-Server-1(config-if)#standby 1 ip 172.16.31.254
VTP-Server-1(config-if)#standby 1 priority 105
VTP-Server-1(config-if)#exit

VTP-Server-2(config)#interface vlan 172
VTP-Server-2(config-if)#ip address 172.16.31.2 255.255.255.0
VTP-Server-2(config-if)#standby 1 ip 172.16.31.254
VTP-Server-2(config-if)#exit
```

NOTE: No priority value is manually assigned for the HSRP configuration applied to VTP-Server-2. By default, HSRP will use a priority value of 100, allowing VTP-Server-1, with a priority value of 105, to win the election and to be elected the primary gateway for the HSRP group.

Once implemented, HSRP configuration may be validated using the `show standby [interface brief]` command. The `show standby brief` command is shown in the following outputs:

```
VTP-Server-1#show standby brief
                     P indicates configured to preempt.
                     |
Interface   Grp  Pri P State   Active          Standby         Virtual IP
Vl172       1    105   Active  local           172.16.31.2     172.16.31.254

VTP-Server-2#show standby brief
                     P indicates configured to preempt.
                     |
Interface   Grp  Pri P State   Active          Standby         Virtual IP
Vl172       1    100   Standby 172.16.31.1     local           172.16.31.254
```

Based on this configuration, VTP-Server-2 will become the active gateway for this group only if VTP-Server-1 fails. Additionally, because preemption is not configured, when VTP-Server-1 comes back online, it will not be able to assume forcefully the role of active gateway, even though it has a higher priority for the HSRP group than that being used on VTP-Server-2.

Configuring HSRP Preemption

Preemption allows a gateway to assume forcefully the role of active gateway if it has a higher priority than the current active gateway. HSRP preemption is configured using the `standby [number] preempt` command. This configuration is illustrated on VTP-Server-1 in the following output:

```
VTP-Server-1(config)#interface vlan 172
VTP-Server-1(config-if)#standby 1 preempt
```

The `show standby [interface [name]|brief]` command is also used to verify that preemption has been configured on a gateway. This is illustrated by the 'P' shown in the output of the `show standby brief` command below:

```
VTP-Server-1#show standby brief
                     P indicates configured to preempt.
                     |
Interface   Grp  Pri P State   Active          Standby         Virtual IP
Vl172       1    105 P Active  local           172.16.31.2     172.16.31.254
```

Based on this modification, if VTP-Server-1 did fail and VTP-Server-2 assumed the role of active gateway for VLAN 172, VTP-Server-1 could forcibly reassume that role once it reinitializes. When configuring preemption, Cisco IOS software allows you to specify the duration the switch must wait before it preempts and forcibly reassumes the role of active gateway.

By default, this happens immediately. However, it may be adjusted using the `standby [number] preempt delay [minimum|reload|sync]` interface configuration command. The `[minimum]` keyword is used to specify the minimum amount of time to wait (seconds) before preemption. The following output shows how to configure the gateway to wait 30 seconds before preemption:

```
VTP-Server-1(config)#interface vlan 172
VTP-Server-1(config-if)#standby 1 preempt delay minimum 30
```

This configuration may be validated using the `show standby [interface]` command. This is illustrated in the following output:

```
VTP-Server-1#show standby vlan 172
Vlan172 - Group 1
  State is Active
    5 state changes, last state change 00:00:32
```

```
  Virtual IP address is 172.16.31.254
  Active virtual MAC address is 0000.0c07.ac01
    Local virtual MAC address is 0000.0c07.ac01 (v1 default)
  Hello time 3 sec, hold time 10 sec
    Next hello sent in 0.636 secs
  Preemption enabled, delay min 30 secs
  Active router is local
  Standby router is 172.16.31.2, priority 100 (expires in 8.629 sec)
  Priority 105 (configured 105)
  IP redundancy name is "hsrp-Vl172-1" (default)
```

The `[reload]` keyword is used to specify the amount of time the gateway should wait after it initializes following a reload. The `[sync]` keyword is used in conjunction with IP redundancy clients. This configuration is beyond the scope of the SWITCH exam requirements.

Configuring HSRP Interface Tracking

HSRP interface tracking allows administrators to configure HSRP in order to track the state of interfaces and decrement the current priority value by the default value (10) or a preconfigured value, allowing another gateway to assume the role of primary gateway for the specified HSRP group.

In the following output, VTP-Server-1 is configured to track the state of interface GigabitEthernet5/1, which is connected to an imaginary WAN router. In the event that the state of that interface transitions to 'down,' the gateway will decrement its priority value by 10 (which is the default):

```
VTP-Server-1(config)#interface vlan 172
VTP-Server-1(config-if)#standby 1 track gigabitethernet 5/1
```

This configuration may be validated using the `show standby [interface]` command. This is illustrated in the following output:

```
VTP-Server-1#show standby vlan 172
Vlan172 - Group 1
  State is Active
    5 state changes, last state change 00:33:22
  Virtual IP address is 172.16.31.254
  Active virtual MAC address is 0000.0c07.ac01
    Local virtual MAC address is 0000.0c07.ac01 (v1 default)
  Hello time 3 sec, hold time 10 sec
    Next hello sent in 1.085 secs
  Preemption enabled
  Active router is local
  Standby router is 172.16.31.2, priority 100 (expires in 7.616 sec)
  Priority 105 (configured 105)
  IP redundancy name is "hsrp-Vl172-1" (default)
  Priority tracking 1 interfaces or objects, 1 up:
  Interface or object          Decrement  State
  GigabitEthernet5/1           10         Up
```

To configure the gateway to decrement its priority value by 50, for example, the `standby [name] track [interface] [decrement value]` command can be issued as shown in the following output:

```
VTP-Server-1(config)#interface vlan 172
VTP-Server-1(config-if)#standby 1 track gigabitethernet 5/1 50
```

This configuration may be validated using the `show standby [interface]` command. This is illustrated in the following output:

```
VTP-Server-1#show standby vlan 172
Vlan172 - Group 1
  State is Active
    5 state changes, last state change 00:33:22
  Virtual IP address is 172.16.31.254
  Active virtual MAC address is 0000.0c07.ac01
    Local virtual MAC address is 0000.0c07.ac01 (v1 default)
  Hello time 3 sec, hold time 10 sec
    Next hello sent in 1.085 secs
  Preemption enabled
  Active router is local
  Standby router is 172.16.31.2, priority 100 (expires in 7.616 sec)
  Priority 105 (configured 105)
  IP redundancy name is "hsrp-Vl172-1" (default)
  Priority tracking 1 interfaces or objects, 1 up:
  Interface or object          Decrement  State
  GigabitEthernet5/1           50         Up
```

Configuring the HSRP Version

As stated previously in this chapter, by default, when HSRP is enabled, version 1 is enabled. HSRP version 2 can be manually enabled using the `standby version [1|2]` interface configuration command. HSRP version 2 configuration is illustrated in the following output:

```
VTP-Server-1(config)#interface vlan 172
VTP-Server-1(config-if)#standby version 2
```

This configuration may be validated using the `show standby [interface]` command. This is illustrated in the following output:

```
VTP-Server-1#show stand vlan 172
Vlan172 - Group 1 (version 2)
  State is Active
    5 state changes, last state change 00:43:42
  Virtual IP address is 172.16.31.254
  Active virtual MAC address is 0000.0c9f.f001
    Local virtual MAC address is 0000.0c9f.f001 (v2 default)
  Hello time 3 sec, hold time 10 sec
    Next hello sent in 2.419 secs
```

```
  Preemption enabled
  Active router is local
  Standby router is 172.16.31.2, priority 100 (expires in 4.402 sec)
  Priority 105 (configured 105)
  IP redundancy name is "hsrp-Vl172-1" (default)
```

Enabling HSRP automatically changes the MAC address range used by HSRP from an address in the 0000.0C07.ACxx range to one in the 0000.0C9F.F000 to 0000.0C9F.FFFF range. It is therefore important to understand that this may cause some packet loss in a production network, as devices must learn the new MAC address of the gateway. Such changes are always recommended during a maintenance window or planned outage window.

Configuring the HSRP Timers

HSRP timers are configured using the `standby [number] timers [[hello-time][hold-time]|msec [hello-time][hold-time]|msec[hold-time]]` interface configuration command. The [msec] keyword allows administrators to configure timer values in milliseconds (ms).

If the timer values are not configured using this keyword, they will be configured in seconds. The following output illustrates how to configure a Hello time of 5 seconds and a Hold time of 15 seconds for HSRP Group 1:

```
VTP-Server-1(config)#interface vlan 172
VTP-Server-1(config-if)#standby 1 timers 5 15
```

This configuration may be validated using the `show standby [interface]` command. This is illustrated in the following output:

```
VTP-Server-1#show standby vlan 172
Vlan172 - Group 1
  State is Active
    5 state changes, last state change 00:54:12
  Virtual IP address is 172.16.31.254
  Active virtual MAC address is 0000.0c07.ac01
    Local virtual MAC address is 0000.0c07.ac01 (v1 default)
  Hello time 5 sec, hold time 15 sec
    Next hello sent in 1.463 secs
  Preemption enabled
  Active router is local
  Standby router is 172.16.31.2, priority 100 (expires in 11.599 sec)
  Priority 105 (configured 105)
  IP redundancy name is "hsrp-Vl172-1" (default)
```

The following output illustrates how to configure Hello and Hold timers of 15 and 60 ms, respectively, for HSRP Group 1:

```
VTP-Server-1(config)#interface vlan 172
VTP-Server-1(config-if)#standby 1 timers msec 15 msec 60
```

This configuration may be validated using the `show standby [interface]` command. The output of this command based on this configuration is illustrated as follows:

```
VTP-Server-1#show standby vlan 172
Vlan172 - Group 1
  State is Active
    5 state changes, last state change 00:56:34
  Virtual IP address is 172.16.31.254
  Active virtual MAC address is 0000.0c07.ac01
    Local virtual MAC address is 0000.0c07.ac01 (v1 default)
  Hello time 15 msec, hold time 60 msec
    Next hello sent in 0.007 secs
  Preemption enabled
  Active router is local
  Standby router is 172.16.31.2, priority 100 (expires in 0.048 sec)
  Priority 105 (configured 105)
  IP redundancy name is "hsrp-Vl172-1" (default)
```

Configuring HSRP Plain Text Authentication

By default, plain-text authentication is enabled for HSRP using the default password 'cisco.' Cisco IOS software allows administrators to configure a different plain-text password using the `standby authentication text [password]` or `standby [number] authentication text [password]` interface configuration commands.

> **NOTE:** If you do not issue the HSRP group number, authentication will be configured for all configured HSRP groups on the interface using the password specified. The group number allows you to configure a different text password for each HSRP group.

The following outputs illustrate how to configure a plain text password of SWITCH for HSRP Group 1:

```
VTP-Server-1(config)#interface vlan 172
VTP-Server-1(config-if)#standby 1 authentication text SWITCH

VTP-Server-2(config)#interface vlan 172
VTP-Server-2(config-if)#standby 1 authentication text SWITCH
```

This configuration may be validated using the `show standby [interface]` command. The output of this command based on this configuration is illustrated as follows:

```
VTP-Server-1#show standby
Vlan172 - Group 1
  State is Active
    2 state changes, last state change 01:54:48
  Virtual IP address is 172.16.31.254
  Active virtual MAC address is 0000.0c07.ac01
    Local virtual MAC address is 0000.0c07.ac01 (v1 default)
  Hello time 15 msec, hold time 60 msec
    Next hello sent in 0.000 secs
  Authentication text, string "SWITCH"
  Preemption enabled
  Active router is local
  Standby router is 172.16.31.2, priority 100 (expires in 0.052 sec)
  Priority 105 (configured 105)
  IP redundancy name is "hsrp-Vl172-1" (default)
```

Configuring HSRP MD5 Authentication

Cisco IOS software allows administrators to configure MD5 authentication for HSRP with or without a key chain. The `standby authentication md5 key-string [password]` or `standby [number] authentication md5 key-string [password]` interface configuration commands are used to configure HSRP MD5 authentication without configuring a key chain.

NOTE: If you do not issue the HSRP group number, authentication will be configured for all configured HSRP groups on the interface using the password specified. The group number allows you to configure a different text password for each HSRP group.

The following outputs illustrate how to configure an MD5 password of SWITCH for HSRP Group 1:

```
VTP-Server-1(config)#interface vlan 172
VTP-Server-1(config-if)# standby 1 authentication md5 key-string SWITCH

VTP-Server-2(config)#interface vlan 172
VTP-Server-2(config-if)#standby 1 authentication md5 key-string SWITCH
```

This configuration may be validated using the `show standby [interface]` command. The output of this command based on this configuration is illustrated as follows:

```
VTP-Server-1#show standby
Vlan172 - Group 1
  State is Active
    2 state changes, last state change 01:59:41
  Virtual IP address is 192.168.1.254
  Active virtual MAC address is 0000.0c07.ac01
    Local virtual MAC address is 0000.0c07.ac01 (v1 default)
  Hello time 15 msec, hold time 60 msec
    Next hello sent in 0.007 secs
  Authentication MD5, key-string
```

```
Preemption enabled
Active router is local
Standby router is 172.16.31.2, priority 100 (expires in 0.040 sec)
Priority 105 (configured 105)
IP redundancy name is "hsrp-Vl172-1" (default)
```

NOTE: Notice that when MD5 authentication is enabled, the password string is not displayed in the output of the `show standby [interface]` command. The only way to view the configured password is to issue the `show running-config [interface][name]` command on the switch.

The configuration of HSRP using key chains requires the use of additional global configuration commands to create the key chain, which are then associated with the HSRP authentication. Key chains contain the keys that are configured with the actual password to be used for authentication. Think of a key chain as something of an authentication route-map. The route-map itself does nothing, but it is required in order to be able to create match and set clauses that perform the required actions.

Similarly, the key chain is required to be able to configure the keys, which contain the actual passwords that are used for routing protocol authentication. The keys do not have to be the same on the gateways on which authentication is being configured; however, the password in the keys (the key-string) must be the same in order for authentication to be successful. The following steps describe the configuration commands required to configure key chains in Cisco IOS software:

1. Configure and name the key chain to be used for authentication using the `key chain [name]` global configuration command.
2. Configure a key for the key chain. Multiple keys may be configured for each key chain. The key is configured using the `key [number]` key-chain key configuration command. The valid `[number]` range is 0 to 2147483647, though this may vary depending on IOS image or platform.
3. Configure a password (secret) for the key using the `key-string [password]` key-chain key configuration command.
4. Optionally, configure advanced key lifetime parameters using the `send-lifetime` and `accept-lifetime` key-chain key configuration commands.

NOTE: You are not expected to perform advanced key chain configuration using the `send-lifetime` and `accept-lifetime` key-chain key configuration commands. More information on these commands can be found in the ROUTE certification guide on www.howtonetwork.net, under the EIGRP configuration section, as well as in the current SWITCH exam labs available online.

The following outputs illustrate how to configure an MD5 password of SWITCH for HSRP Group 1 using key chains on VTP-Server-1 and VTP-Server-2:

```
VTP-Server-1(config)#key chain VTP-Server-1-HSRP-Key-Chain
VTP-Server-1(config-keychain)#key 1
VTP-Server-1(config-keychain-key)#key-string SWITCH
VTP-Server-1(config-keychain-key)#exit
VTP-Server-1(config-keychain)#exit
VTP-Server-1(config)#interface vlan 172
VTP-Server-1(config-if)#standby 1 authentication md5 key-chain VTP-Server-1-
                        HSRP-Key-Chain
VTP-Server-1(config-if)#exit


VTP-Server-2(config)#key chain VTP-Server-2-HSRP-Key-Chain
VTP-Server-2(config-keychain)#key 1
VTP-Server-2(config-keychain-key)#key-string SWITCH
VTP-Server-2(config-keychain-key)#exit
VTP-Server-2(config-keychain)#exit
VTP-Server-2(config)#interface vlan 172
VTP-Server-2(config-if)#standby 1 authentication md5 key-chain VTP-Server-2-
                        HSRP-Key-Chain
VTP-Server-2(config-if)#exit
```

NOTE: Notice that although the key chain names on both switches are different, both keys are using the same key number and the same key string (password).

This configuration may be validated using the `show standby [interface]` command. The output of this command based on this configuration is illustrated as follows:

```
VTP-Server-2#show standby
Vlan172 - Group 1
  State is Standby
    79 state changes, last state change 00:02:00
  Virtual IP address is 192.168.1.254
  Active virtual MAC address is 0000.0c07.ac01
    Local virtual MAC address is 0000.0c07.ac01 (v1 default)
  Hello time 15 msec, hold time 60 msec
    Next hello sent in 0.000 secs
  Authentication MD5, key-chain "VTP-Server-2-HSRP-Key-Chain"
  Preemption enabled, delay min 30 secs
  Active router is 192.168.1.1, priority 105 (expires in 0.012 sec)
  Standby router is local
  Priority 100 (default 100)
  IP redundancy name is "hsrp-Vl172-1" (default)
```

In the output above, on the standby router, we can see that HSRP is using a key chain named for authentication. However, the password in that key chain is not included, for security purposes. To view the configured key or keys, use the `show key chain [name]` command as illustrated in the following output:

```
VTP-Server-2#show key chain
Key-chain VTP-Server-2-HSRP-Key-Chain:
    key 1 -- text "SWITCH"
        accept lifetime (always valid) - (always valid) [valid now]
        send lifetime (always valid) - (always valid) [valid now]
```

NOTE: Once a key chain has been configured and applied, all keys are immediately activated and the passwords used in those keys are used for authentication. This default behavior can be adjusted using the `accept-lifetime` and `send-lifetime` commands.

Debugging Hot Standby Router Protocol

Although FHRP debugging and troubleshooting will be covered in detail in the TSHOOT guide, the `debug standby` command can be used to debug HSRP operation. The options that are available with this command are shown in the following output:

```
VTP-Server-1#debug standby ?
  errors    HSRP errors
  events    HSRP events
  packets   HSRP packets
  terse     Display limited range of HSRP errors, events and packets
  <cr>
```

Virtual Router Redundancy Protocol

Virtual Router Redundancy Protocol (VRRP) is a gateway election protocol that dynamically assigns responsibility for one or more virtual gateways to the VRRP routers on a LAN, which allows several routers on a multi-access segment, such as Ethernet, to use the same virtual IP address as their default gateway.

VRRP operates in a similar manner to HSRP; however, unlike HSRP, VRRP is an open standard that is defined in RFC 2338, which was made obsolete by RFC 3768. VRRP sends advertisements to the Multicast destination address 224.0.0.18 (VRRP), using IP protocol number 112. At the Data Link layer, advertisements are sent from the master virtual router MAC address 00-00-5e-00-01xx, where 'xx' represents the two-digit Hexadecimal group number. This is illustrated below in Figure 8-18:

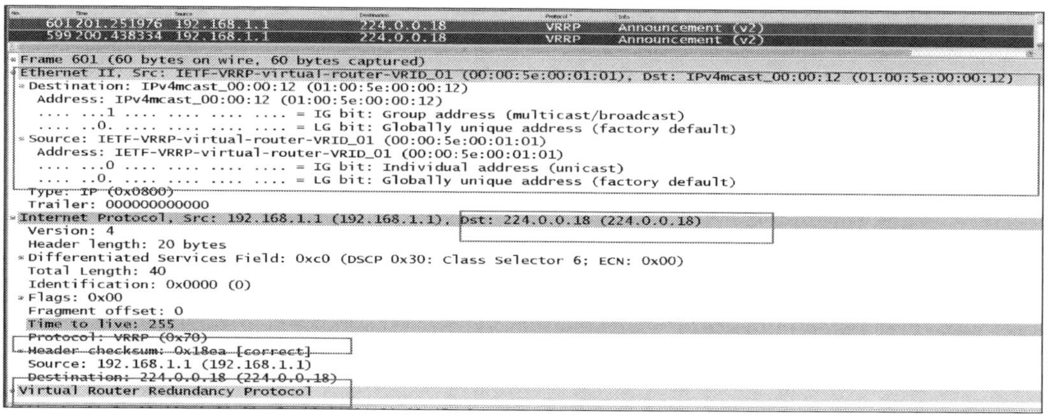

Fig. 8-18. VRRP Multicast Addresses

NOTE: The protocol number is in Hexadecimal value. The Hexadecimal value 0x70 is the equivalent of the Decimal value 112. Similarly, the 12 in the destination Data Link layer address 01-00-5e-00-00-12 is the Hexadecimal value of 18 in Decimal value (i.e. 224.0.0.18). If you are unable to determine how these values are reached, Hexadecimal to Decimal conversion is covered in detail in the current CCNA guide that is available online.

REAL WORLD IMPLEMENTATION

Unlike HSRP, VRRP does not have the option of allowing the gateway to use the BIA or a statically configured address as the MAC address for VRRP groups. Therefore, in production networks with more than one VRRP group, it is important to understand the implications of multiple MAC addresses on a particular interface, especially when features such as port security have been implemented. Remember to look at the overall picture; otherwise, you may find that, even though correctly configured, certain features and protocol are not working as they should.

A VRRP gateway is configured to run the VRRP protocol in conjunction with one or more other routers attached to a LAN. In a VRRP configuration, one gateway is elected as the master virtual router, with the other gateways acting as backup virtual routers in case the master virtual router fails. This concept is illustrated below in Figure 8-19:

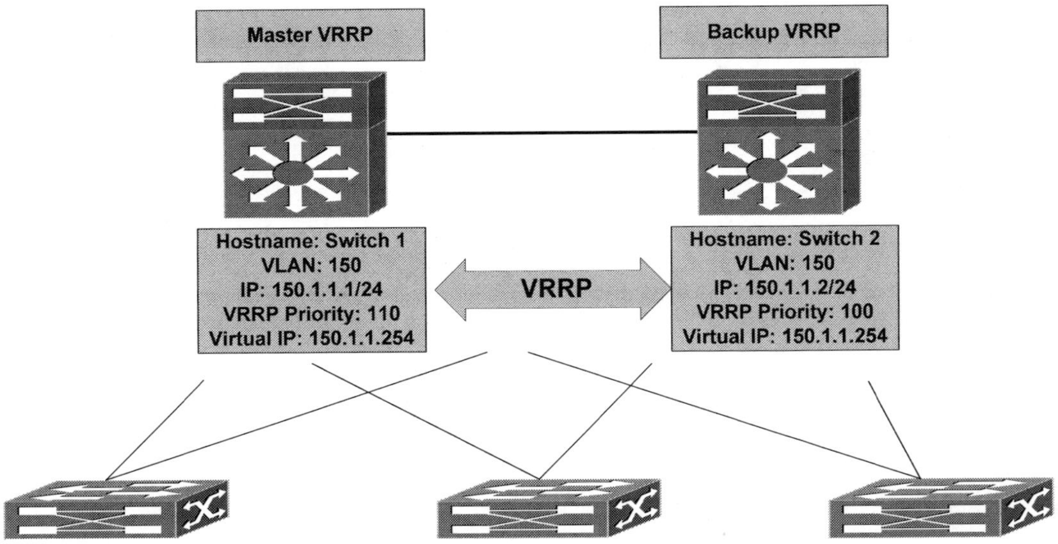

Fig. 8-19. Virtual Router Redundancy Protocol Basic Operation

VRRP Multiple Virtual Router Support

You can configure up to 255 virtual routers on an interface. The actual number of virtual routers that a router interface can support depends on the following factors:

- Router processing capability
- Router memory capability
- Router interface support of multiple MAC addresses

VRRP Master Router Election

By default, VRRP uses priority values to determine which router will be elected as the master virtual router. The default VRRP priority value is 100; however, this value can be manually adjusted to a value between 1 and 254. If gateways have the same priority values, the gateway with the highest IP address will be elected as the master virtual router, while the one with the lower IP address becomes the backup virtual router.

If more than two routers are configured as part of the VRRP group, the backup virtual router with the second-highest priority is elected as the master virtual router if the current master virtual router fails or becomes unavailable. If the backup virtual routers have the same priority value, the backup virtual router with the highest IP address is elected as the master virtual router. This concept is illustrated below in Figure 8-20:

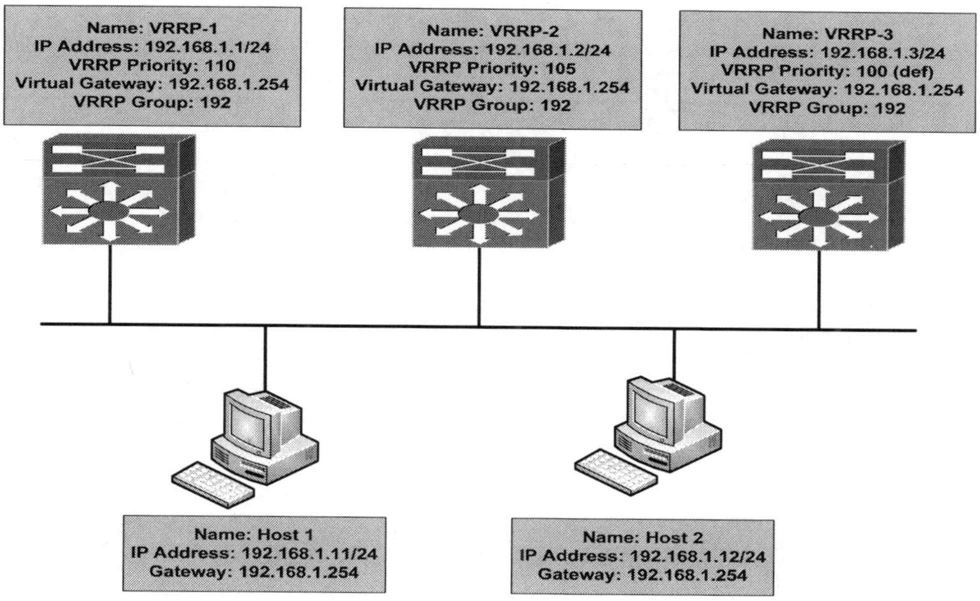

Fig. 8-20. VRRP Master Virtual Router and Backup Virtual Router Election

Figure 8-20 illustrates a network using VRRP for gateway redundancy. Hosts 1 and 2 are configured with a default gateway of 192.168.1.254, which is the virtual IP address configured for VRRP group 192 defined on Switches VRRP-1, VRRP-2, and VRRP-3.

VRRP-1 has a configured priority value of 110, VRRP-2 has a configured priority value of 105, and VRRP-3 is using the default VRRP priority of 100. Based on this configuration, VRRP-1 is elected as the master virtual router and VRRP-2 and VRRP-3 become backup virtual routers.

In the event that VRRP-1 fails, VRRP-2 becomes the master virtual router because it has a higher priority value than VRRP-3. However, if both switches had the same priority value, VRRP-3 would be elected as the master virtual router because it has the higher IP address.

VRRP Preemption

By default, unlike HSRP, preemption is enabled for VRRP and no explicit configuration is required by the administrator to enable this functionality. However, this functionality can be disabled by using the `no vrrp [number] preempt` interface configuration command.

VRRP Load Balancing

VRRP allows for load balancing in a manner similar to HSRP. For example, in a network where multiple virtual routers are configured on a gateway, the interface can act as a master for one virtual router and as a backup for one or more virtual routers. This is illustrated below in Figure 8-21:

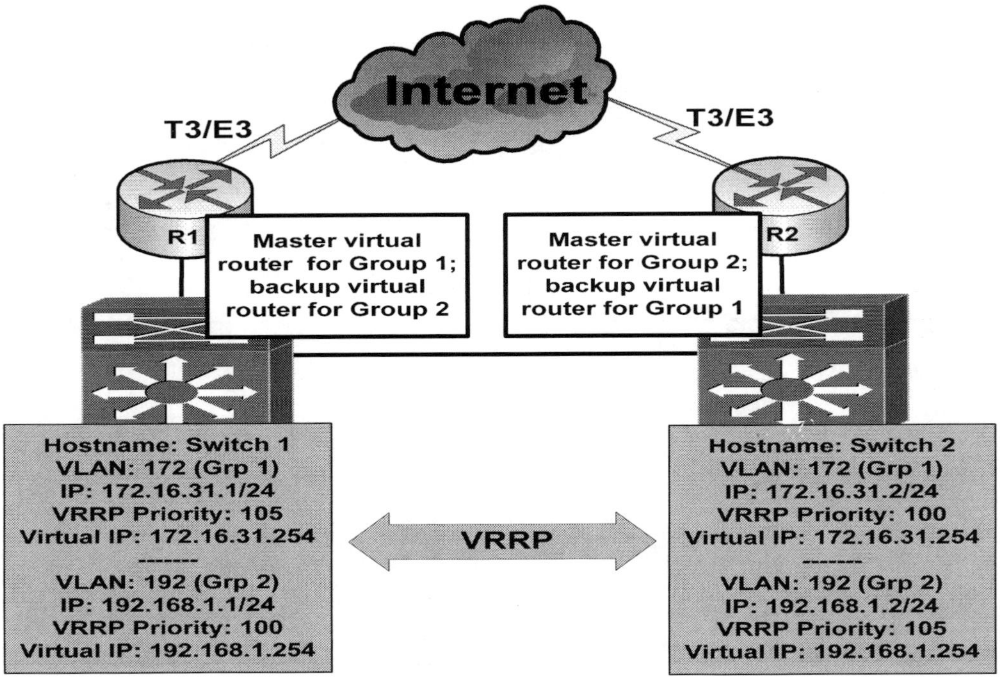

Fig. 8-21. Virtual Router Redundancy Protocol Load Balancing

VRRP Versions

By default, VRRP version 2 is enabled when VRRP is configured on a gateway in Cisco IOS software. Version 2 is the default and current VRRP version. It is not possible to change the version as is the case with HSRP. There is no VRRP version 1 standard.

NOTE: As of the time of the writing of this guide, VRRP version 3, which defines the VRRP for IPv4 and IPv6, is in draft form and has not yet been standardized.

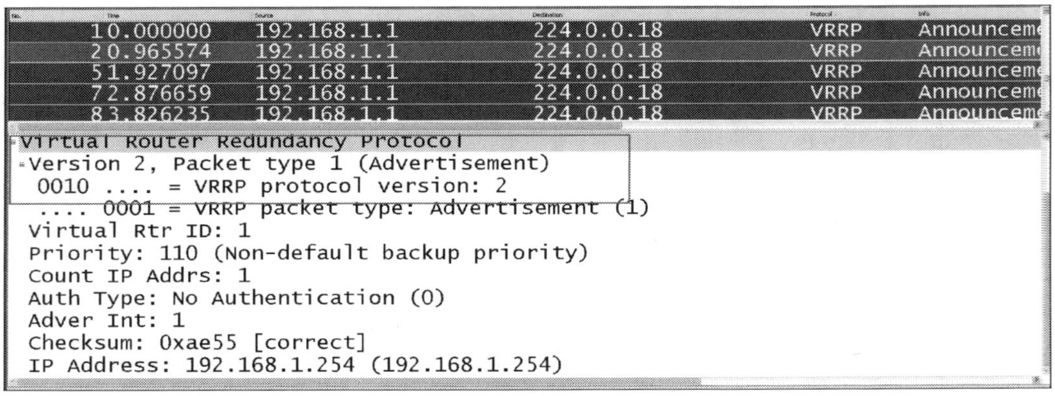

Fig. 8-22. Virtual Router Redundancy Protocol Version 2 Packet

VRRP Advertisements

The master virtual router sends advertisements to other VRRP routers in the same group. The advertisements communicate the priority and the state of the master virtual router. The VRRP advertisements are encapsulated in IP packets and are sent to the IP Version 4 Multicast address assigned to the VRRP group, which was illustrated in Figure 8-18. The advertisements are sent every second by default; however, this interval is user-configurable and may be changed. Backup virtual routers also optionally learn the advertisement interval from the master virtual router.

VRRP Authentication

Like HSRP, VRRP supports both plain-text and MD5 authentication. MD5 authentication may be configured with or without a key chain. Unlike HSRP, however, it is important to remember that authentication is not enabled by default for VRRP. This is illustrated below in Figure 8-23:

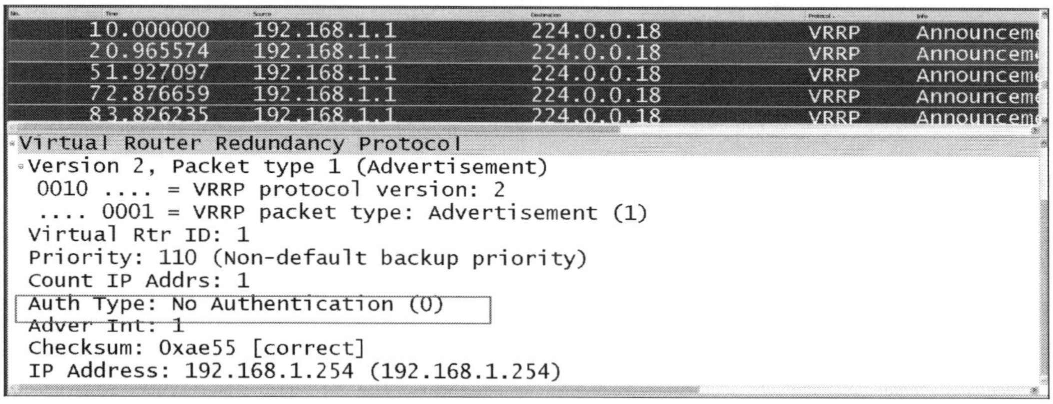

Fig. 8-23. Virtual Router Redundancy Protocol Authentication

Configuring VRRP on the Gateway

The following steps are required to configure HSRP on the gateway:

1. Configure the correct IP address and mask for the gateway interface using the `ip address [address] [mask] [secondary]` interface configuration command.
2. Create a VRRP group on the gateway interface and assign the group the virtual IP address via the `vrrp [number] ip [virtual address][secondary]` interface configuration command. The `[secondary]` keyword configures the virtual IP address as a secondary gateway address for the specified group.
3. Optionally, assign the VRRP group a description using the `vrrp [number] description [name]` interface configuration command.
4. Optionally, if you want to control the elections of the master virtual router and the backup virtual routers, configure the group priority via the `vrrp [number] priority [value]` interface configuration command.

The VRRP configuration outputs in this section will be based on Figure 8-24 below:

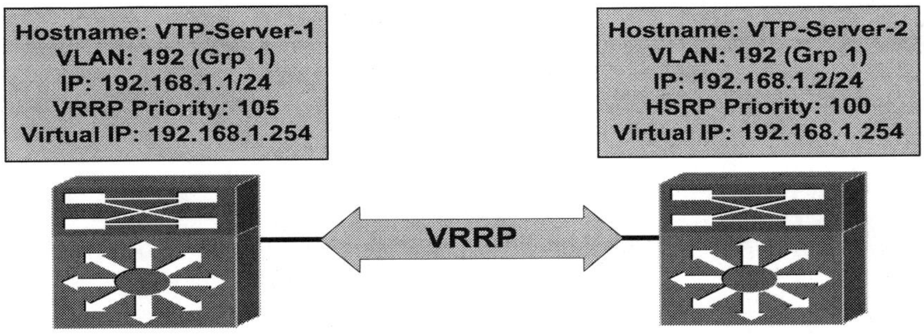

Fig. 8-24. VRRP Configuration Examples Topology

NOTE: It is assumed that the VLAN and trunking configuration between VTP-Server-1 and VTP-Server-2 is already in place and the switches are successfully able to ping each other across VLAN 172. For brevity, this configuration output will be omitted from the configuration examples.

```
VTP-Server-1(config)#interface vlan 192
VTP-Server-1(config-if)#ip address 192.168.1.1 255.255.255.0
VTP-Server-1(config-if)#vrrp 1 ip 192.168.1.254
VTP-Server-1(config-if)#vrrp 1 priority 105
VTP-Server-1(config-if)#vrrp 1 description 'SWITCH-VRRP-Example'
VTP-Server-1(config-if)#exit
```

```
VTP-Server-2(config)#interface vlan 192
VTP-Server-2(config-if)#ip address 192.168.1.2 255.255.255.0
VTP-Server-2(config-if)#vrrp 1 ip 192.168.1.254
VTP-Server-2(config-if)#vrrp 1 description 'SWITCH-VRRP-Example'
VTP-Server-2(config-if)#exit
```

NOTE: No priority value is manually assigned for the VRRP configuration applied to VTP-Server-2. By default, VRRP will use a priority value of 100, allowing VTP-Server-1, with a priority value of 105, to win the election and to be elected as the master virtual router for the VRRP group. In addition to this, a description has also optionally been configured for the group.

This configuration is validated using the `show vrrp [all|brief|interface]` command. The `[all]` keyword shows all information pertaining to the VRRP configuration, which includes the group state, description (if configured), local gateway priority, and master virtual router, among other things. The `[brief]` keyword prints a summary of the VRRP configuration. The `[interface]` keyword prints VRRP information for the specified interface. The following outputs show the `show vrrp all` command:

```
VTP-Server-1#show vrrp all
Vlan192 - Group 1
'SWITCH-VRRP-Example'
  State is Master
  Virtual IP address is 192.168.1.254
  Virtual MAC address is 0000.5e00.0101
  Advertisement interval is 1.000 sec
  Preemption enabled
  Priority is 105
  Master Router is 192.168.1.1 (local), priority is 105
  Master Advertisement interval is 1.000 sec
  Master Down interval is 3.589 sec

VTP-Server-2#show vrrp all
Vlan192 - Group 1
'SWITCH-VRRP-Example'
  State is Backup
  Virtual IP address is 192.168.1.254
  Virtual MAC address is 0000.5e00.0101
  Advertisement interval is 1.000 sec
  Preemption enabled
  Priority is 100
  Master Router is 192.168.1.1, priority is 105
  Master Advertisement interval is 1.000 sec
  Master Down interval is 3.609 sec (expires in 3.328 sec)
```

The following outputs show the information printed by the `show vrrp brief` command:

```
VTP-Server-1#show vrrp brief
Interface          Grp Pri Time  Own Pre State   Master addr     Group addr
Vl192              1   105 3589       Y  Master  192.168.1.1
192.168.1.254

VTP-Server-2#show vrrp brief
Interface          Grp Pri Time  Own Pre State   Master addr     Group addr
Vl192              1   100 3609       Y  Backup  192.168.1.1
192.168.1.254
```

Configuring VRRP Timers

The interval for advertisement updates sent by the VRRP master virtual router is configured using the `vrrp [number] timers [[seconds] [msec][milliseconds]]` interface configuration command. The following output illustrates how to configure an advertisement interval of 5 seconds:

```
VTP-Server-1(config)#interface vlan  192
VTP-Server-1(config-if)#vrrp 1 timers advertise 5
```

The following output illustrates how to configure an advertisement interval of 100 milliseconds:

```
VTP-Server-1(config)#interface vlan  192
VTP-Server-1(config-if)#vrrp 1 timers advertise msec 100
```

VRRP timer configuration can be validated using the `show vrrp interface [name]` command, the output of which is illustrated as follows:

```
VTP-Server-1#show vrrp interface vlan 192
Vlan192 - Group 1
'SWITCH-VRRP-Example'
  State is Master
  Virtual IP address is 192.168.1.254
  Virtual MAC address is 0000.5e00.0101
  Advertisement interval is 0.100 sec
  Preemption enabled
  Priority is 105
  Master Router is 192.168.1.1 (local), priority is 105
  Master Advertisement interval is 0.100 sec
  Master Down interval is 0.889 sec
```

Configuring VRRP Timer Learning

As previously stated in this chapter, backup virtual routers can be optionally configured to learn timer values from the master virtual router. This is configured using the `vrrp 1 timers learn` interface configuration command on the backup virtual router. The following output shows how to configure a backup virtual router to learn about timers from the master virtual router:

```
VTP-Server-2(config)#interface vlan 192
VTP-Server-2(config-if)#vrrp 1 timers learn
VTP-Server-2(config-if)#exit
```

Again, the `show vrrp interface [name]` command can be used to validate this configuration. The output of this command is shown as follows:

```
VTP-Server-2#show vrrp interface vlan 192
Vlan192 - Group 1
'SWITCH-VRRP-Example'
  State is Backup
  Virtual IP address is 192.168.1.254
  Virtual MAC address is 0000.5e00.0101
  Advertisement interval is 1.000 sec
  Preemption enabled
  Priority is 100
  Master Router is 192.168.1.1, priority is 105
  Master Advertisement interval is 1.000 sec
  Master Down interval is 3.609 sec (expires in 3.572 sec) Learning
```

Configuring VRRP Plain Text Authentication

VRRP plain-text authentication is configured using the `vrrp [number authentication text [password]` interface configuration command. As is the case with plain-text authentication when using HSRP, the password is sent unencrypted and can be viewed 'on-the-wire' as well as in the output of the `show vrrp interface [name]` command. The following outputs illustrate the configuration of plain-text authentication for VRRP using the password SWITCH:

```
VTP-Server-1(config)#interface vlan 192
VTP-Server-1(config-if)#vrrp 1 authentication text SWITCH
VTP-Server-1(config-if)#exit

VTP-Server-2(config)#interface vlan 192
VTP-Server-2(config-if)#vrrp 1 authentication text SWITCH
VTP-Server-2(config-if)#exit
```

The plain text password is present in the output of the `show vrrp interface [name]` command as shown as follows:

```
VTP-Server-1#show vrrp interface vlan 192
Vlan192 - Group 1
'SWITCH-VRRP-Example'
  State is Master
  Virtual IP address is 192.168.1.254
  Virtual MAC address is 0000.5e00.0101
  Advertisement interval is 0.100 sec
  Preemption enabled
  Priority is 105
  Authentication text, string "SWITCH"
  Master Router is 192.168.1.1 (local), priority is 105
  Master Advertisement interval is 0.100 sec
  Master Down interval is 0.889 sec
```

Configuring VRRP MD5 Authentication

Cisco IOS software supports two methods for configuring MD5 authentication for VRRP. The first method does not require key chains and is configured using the `vrrp [number] authentication md5 key-string [password]` interface configuration command. The second method, which requires key chain configuration, is applied using the `vrrp [number] authentication md5 key-chain [name]` interface configuration command.

Key chain configuration is illustrated in HSRP configuration and will not be illustrated in this section. Refer to that section if you are unable to remember how to configure key chains. The following outputs illustrate how to configure MD5 authentication for VRRP without a key chain:

```
VTP-Server-1(config)#interface vlan 192
VTP-Server-1(config-if)#vrrp 1 authentication md5 key-string SWITCH
```

```
VTP-Server-1(config-if)#exit

VTP-Server-2(config)#interface vlan 192
VTP-Server-2(config-if)# vrrp 1 authentication md5 key-string SWITCH
VTP-Server-2(config-if)#exit
```

MD5 authentication for VRRP is verified using the `show vrrp interface [name]` command as shown in the following output:

```
VTP-Server-2#show vrrp interface vlan 192
Vlan192 - Group 1
'SWITCH-VRRP-Example'
  State is Backup
  Virtual IP address is 192.168.1.254
  Virtual MAC address is 0000.5e00.0101
  Advertisement interval is 1.000 sec
  Preemption enabled
  Priority is 100
  Authentication MD5, key-string
  Master Router is 192.168.1.1, priority is 105
  Master Advertisement interval is 1.000 sec
  Master Down interval is 3.609 sec (expires in 3.516 sec) Learning
```

As is the case with MD5 authentication for HSRP, notice that the password is not displayed in the output of the show command. It can be validated by viewing the switch configuration.

Configuring VRRP Interface Tracking

In order to configure VRRP to track an interface, for example, a tracked object must be created in global configuration mode using the `track [object number] interface][line-protocol|ip routing]` global configuration command for interface tracking or the track `[object number] ip route [address/prefix] {reachability | metric threshold}` command for IP prefix tracking. Up to 500 track objects may be tracked on the switch, depending on the software and platform. Tracked objects are then tracked by VRRP using the `vrrp [number] track [object]` interface configuration command.

NOTE: You are not expected to perform any advanced object tracking configurations.

The following output shows how to configure tracking for VRRP, referencing object 1, which tracks the line protocol of the Loopback0 interface:

```
VTP-Server-1(config)#track 1 interface loopback 0 line-protocol
VTP-Server-1(config-track)#exit
VTP-Server-1(config)#interface vlan 192
VTP-Server-1(config-if)#vrrp 1 track 1
VTP-Server-1(config-if)#exit
```

The following output shows how to configure tracking for VRRP, referencing object 2, which tracks the reachability of the 1.1.1.1/32 prefix. A tracked IP route object is considered to be up and reachable when a routing table entry exists for the route and the route is not inaccessible (i.e. has a route metric of 255), in which case the route is removed from the Routing Information Base (RIB) anyway:

```
VTP-Server-1(config)#track 2 ip route 1.1.1.1/32 reachability
VTP-Server-1(config-track)#exit
VTP-Server-1(config)#interface vlan 192
VTP-Server-1(config-if)#vrrp 1 track 2
```

VRRP tracking configuration is verified using the `show vrrp interface [name]` command. This is illustrated in the following output:

```
VTP-Server-1#show vrrp interface vlan 192
Vlan192 - Group 1
'SWITCH-VRRP-Example'
  State is Master
  Virtual IP address is 192.168.1.254
  Virtual MAC address is 0000.5e00.0101
  Advertisement interval is 0.100 sec
  Preemption enabled
  Priority is 105
    Track object 1 state Up decrement 10
    Track object 2 state Up decrement 10
  Authentication MD5, key-string
  Master Router is 192.168.1.1 (local), priority is 105
  Master Advertisement interval is 0.100 sec
  Master Down interval is 0.889 sec
```

To view the parameters of the tracked objects, use the `show track [number][brief] [interface] [ip] [resolution][timers]` command. The output of the `show track` command is illustrated as follows:

```
VTP-Server-1#show track
Track 1
  Interface Loopback0 line-protocol
  Line protocol is Up
    1 change, last change 00:11:36
  Tracked by:
    VRRP Vlan192 1
Track 2
  IP route 1.1.1.1 255.255.255.255 reachability
  Reachability is Up (connected)
    1 change, last change 00:08:48
  First-hop interface is Loopback0
  Tracked by:
    VRRP Vlan192 1
```

NOTE: Tracked objects can also be used in conjunction with HSRP and GLBP. GLBP is described in a section to follow.

Debugging the Virtual Router Redundancy Protocol

The `debug vrrp` command provides several options that the administrator can use to view real-time information on VRRP operation. These options are illustrated in the following output:

```
VTP-Server-1#debug vrrp ?
  all       Debug all VRRP information
  auth      VRRP authentication reporting
  errors    VRRP error reporting
  events    Protocol and Interface events
  packets   VRRP packet details
  state     VRRP state reporting
  track     Monitor tracking
  <cr>
```

Gateway Load Balancing Protocol

Like HSRP, Gateway Load Balancing Protocol (GLBP) is a Cisco proprietary protocol. GLBP provides high network availability in a manner similar to HSRP and VRRP. However, unlike HSRP and VRRP, in which only a single gateway actively forwards traffic for a particular group at any given time, GLBP allows multiple gateways within the same GLBP group to actively forward network traffic at the same time.

GLBP gateways communicate through Hello messages that are sent every 3 seconds to the Multicast address 224.0.0.102, using UDP port 3222. This is illustrated below in Figure 8-25:

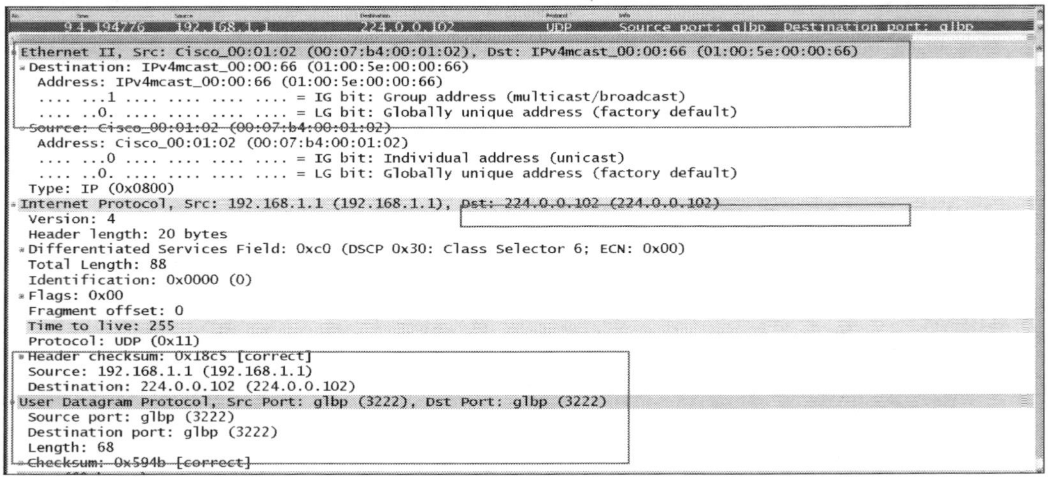

Fig. 8-25. GLBP Layer 3 and Layer 4 Protocols and Addresses

Gateway Load Balancing Protocol Operation

When GLBP is enabled, the GLBP group members elect one gateway to be the active virtual gateway (AVG) for that group. The AVG is the gateway that has the highest priority value. In the event that the priority values are equal, the AVG with the highest IP address in the group will be elected as the gateway. The other gateways in the GLBP group provide backup for the AVG in the event that the AVG becomes unavailable.

The AVG answers all Address Resolution Protocol (ARP) requests for the virtual router address. In addition to this, the AVG assigns a virtual MAC address to each member of the GLBP group. Each gateway is therefore responsible for forwarding packets that are sent to the virtual MAC address it has been assigned by the AVG. These gateways are referred to as active virtual forwarders (AVFs) for their assigned MAC addresses. This allows GLBP to provide load sharing. This concept is illustrated below in Figure 8-26:

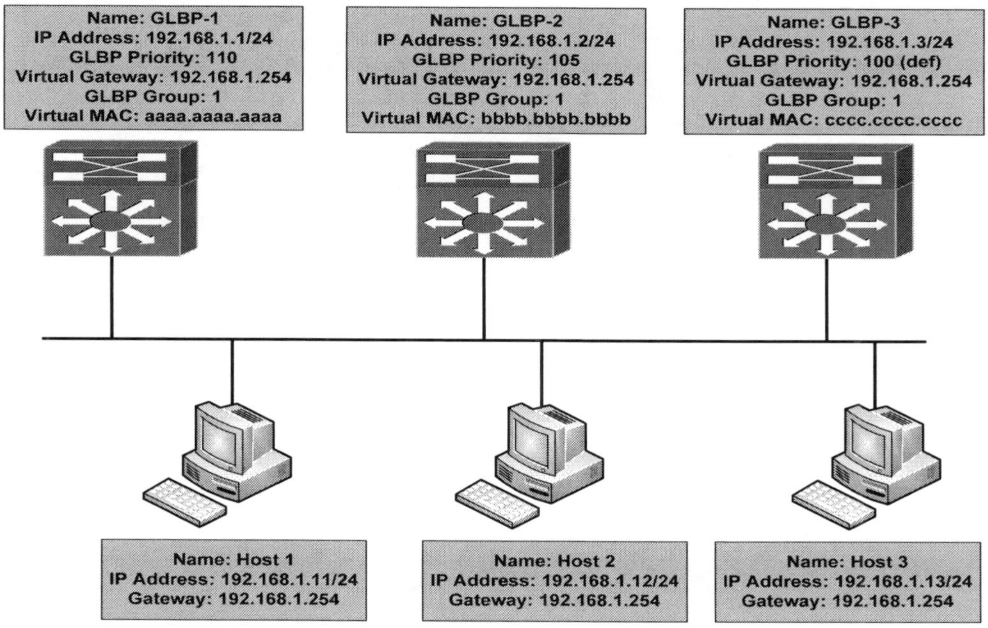

Fig. 8-26. GLBP Active Virtual Gateway and Active Virtual Forwarders

Figure 8-26 shows a network using GLBP as the FHRP. The three gateways are all configured in GLBP Group 1. Gateway GLBP-1 is configured with a priority of 110, gateway GLBP-2 is configured with a priority of 105, and gateway GLBP-3 is using the default priority of 100. GLBP-1 is elected AVG, and GLBP-2 and GLBP-3 are assigned virtual MAC addresses bbbb.bbbb.bbbb and cccc.cccc.cccc, respectively, and become AVFs for those virtual MAC addresses. GLBP-1 is also AVF for its own virtual MAC address, aaaa.aaaa.aaaa.

Hosts 1, 2, and 3 are all configured with the default gateway address 192.168.1.254, which is the virtual IP address assigned to the GLBP group. Host 1 sends out an ARP Broadcast for its gateway IP address. This is received by the AVG (GLBP-1), which responds with its own virtual MAC address aaaa.aaaa.aaaa. Host 1 forwards traffic to 192.168.1.254 to this MAC address.

Host 2 sends out an ARP Broadcast for its gateway IP address. This is received by the AVG (GLBP-1), which responds with the virtual MAC address of bbbb.bbbb.bbbb (GLBP-2). Host 2 forwards traffic to 192.168.1.254 to this MAC address and GLBP-2 forwards this traffic.

Host 3 sends out an ARP Broadcast for its gateway IP address. This is received by the AVG (GLBP-1), which responds with the virtual MAC address of cccc.cccc.cccc (GLBP-3). Host 3 forwards traffic to 192.168.1.254 to this MAC address and GLBP-3 forwards this traffic.

By using all gateways in the group, GLBP allows for load sharing without having to configure multiple groups as would be required if either HSRP or VRRP was being used as the FHRP.

GLBP Virtual MAC Address Assignment

A GLBP group allows up to four virtual MAC addresses per group. The AVG is responsible for assigning the virtual MAC addresses to each member of the group. Other group members request a virtual MAC address after they discover the AVG through Hello messages.

Gateways are assigned the next virtual MAC address in sequence. A gateway that is assigned a virtual MAC address by the AVG is known as a primary virtual forwarder, while a gateway that has learned the virtual MAC address is referred to as a secondary virtual forwarder.

GLBP Redundancy

Within the GLBP group, a single gateway is elected as the AVG, and another gateway is elected as the standby virtual gateway. All other remaining gateways in the group are placed in a listen state. If an AVG fails, the standby virtual gateway will assume responsibility for the virtual IP address. At the same time, an election is held and a new standby virtual gateway is then elected from the gateways currently in the listen state.

In the event the AVF fails, one of the secondary virtual forwarders in the listen state assumes responsibility for the virtual MAC address. However, because the new AVF is already a forwarder using another virtual MAC address, GLBP needs to ensure that the old forwarder MAC address ceases being used and hosts are migrated away from this address. This is achieved using the following two timers:

1. The redirect timer
2. The timeout timer

The redirect time is the interval during which the AVG continues to redirect hosts to the old virtual forwarder MAC address. When this timer expires, the AVG stops using the old virtual forwarder MAC address in ARP replies, although the virtual forwarder will continue to forward packets that were sent to the old virtual forwarder MAC address.

When the timeout timer expires, the virtual forwarder is removed from all gateways in the GLBP group. Any clients still using the old MAC address in their ARP caches must refresh the entry to obtain the new virtual MAC address. GLBP uses the Hello messages to communicate the current state of these two timers.

GLBP Load Preemption

By default, GLBP preemption is disabled, which means that a backup virtual gateway can become the AVG only if the current AVG fails, regardless of the priorities assigned to the virtual gateways. This method of operation is similar to that used by HSRP.

Cisco IOS software allows administrators to enable preemption, which allows a backup virtual gateway to become the AVG if the backup virtual gateway is assigned a higher priority than the current AVG. By default, the GLBP virtual forwarder preemptive scheme is enabled with a delay of 30 seconds. However, this value can be manually adjusted by administrators.

GLBP Weighting

GLBP uses a weighting scheme to determine the forwarding capacity of each gateway that is in the GLBP group. The weighting assigned to a gateway in the GLBP group can be used to determine whether it will forward packets and, if so, the proportion of hosts in the LAN for which it will forward packets.

By default, each gateway is assigned a weight of 100. Administrators can additionally configure the gateways to make dynamic weighting adjustments by configuring object tracking, such as for interfaces and IP prefixes, in conjunction with GLBP. If an interface fails, the weighting is dynamically decreased by the specified value, allowing gateways with higher weighting values to be used to forward more traffic than those with lower weighting values.

In addition to this, thresholds can be set to disable forwarding when the weighting for a GLBP group falls below a certain value and then when it rises above another threshold, forwarding is automatically re-enabled. A backup virtual forwarder can become the AVF if the current AVF weighting falls below the low weighting threshold for 30 seconds.

GLBP Load Sharing

GLBP supports the following three load sharing methods:

1. Host-dependent
2. Round-robin
3. Weighted

With host-dependent load sharing, each client that generates an ARP request for the virtual router address always receives the same virtual MAC address in reply. This method provides clients with a consistent gateway MAC address.

The round-robin load-sharing mechanism distributes the traffic evenly across all gateways participating as AVFs in the group. This is the default load-sharing mechanism.

The weighted load-sharing mechanism using the weighting value determines the proportion of traffic that should be sent to a particular AVF. A higher weighting value results in more frequent ARP replies containing the virtual MAC address of that gateway.

GLBP Client Cache

The GLBP client cache contains information about network hosts that are using a GLBP group as the default gateway. The cache entry contains information about the host that sent the IPv4 ARP or IPv6 Neighbor Discovery (ND) request and which forwarder the AVG has assigned to it, the number of the GLBP forwarder that each network host has been assigned to, and the total number of network hosts currently assigned to each forwarder in a GLBP group.

The AVG for a GLBP group can be enabled to store a client cache database of all the LAN clients using this group. The maximum number of entries that may be stored can be up to 2000, but it is recommended that this number never exceed 1000. While GLBP cache configuration is beyond the scope of the SWITCH exam requirements, this feature can be configured using the `glbp client-cache` command and then verified using the `show glbp detail` command.

GLBP Authentication

By default, GLBP authentication is disabled. However, authentication can be configured using either a plain-text password or MD5 with, or without, a key chain. MD5 authentication provides greater security than plain-text authentication and is the recommended method for enabling GLBP authentication.

Configuring GLBP on the Gateway

The following steps are required to configure GLBP on the gateway:

1. Configure the correct IP address and mask for the gateway interface using the `ip address [address] [mask] [secondary]` interface configuration command.
2. Create a GLBP group on the gateway interface and assign the group the virtual IP address via the `glbp [number] ip [virtual address][secondary]` interface configuration command. The `[secondary]` keyword configures the virtual IP address as a secondary gateway address for the specified group.
3. Optionally, assign the VRRP group a name using the `glbp [number] name [name]` interface configuration command.
4. Optionally, if you want to control the election of the AVG, configure the group priority via the `glbp [number] priority [value]` interface configuration command.

The GLBP configuration examples in this section will be based on Figure 8-27 below:

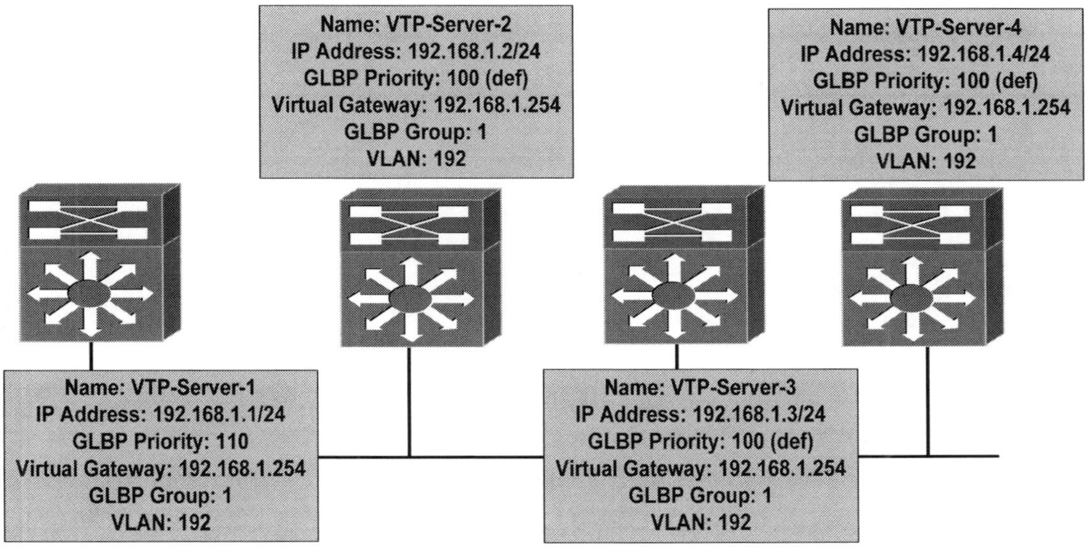

Fig. 8-27. GLBP Configuration Examples Topology

NOTE: It is assumed that VLAN and trunking configuration between the switches is already in place and the switches are successfully able to ping each other across VLAN 192. For the sake of brevity, this configuration output will be omitted from the configuration examples.

```
VTP-Server-1(config)#interface vlan 192
VTP-Server-1(config-if)#glbp 1 ip 192.168.1.254
VTP-Server-1(config-if)#glbp 1 priority 110
VTP-Server-1(config-if)#exit
```

```
VTP-Server-2(config)#interface vlan 192
VTP-Server-2(config-if)#glbp 1 ip 192.168.1.254
VTP-Server-2(config-if)#exit

VTP-Server-3(config)#interface vlan 192
VTP-Server-3(config-if)#glbp 1 ip 192.168.1.254
VTP-Server-3(config-if)#exit

VTP-Server-4(config)#interface vlan 192
VTP-Server-4(config-if)#glbp 1 ip 192.168.1.254
VTP-Server-4(config-if)#exit
```

Once the GLBP group has been configured, the `show glbp brief` command can be used to view a summary of the GLBP configuration as shown in the following outputs:

```
VTP-Server-1#show glbp brief
Interface    Grp  Fwd Pri State    Address         Active router   Standby
router
Vl192        1    -   110 Active   192.168.1.254   local           192.168.1.
Vl192        1    1   -   Active   0007.b400.0101  local           -
Vl192        1    2   -   Listen   0007.b400.0102  192.168.1.2     -
Vl192        1    3   -   Listen   0007.b400.0103  192.168.1.3     -
Vl192        1    4   -   Listen   0007.b400.0104  192.168.1.4     -


VTP-Server-2#show glbp brief
Interface    Grp  Fwd Pri State    Address         Active router   Standby
router
Vl192        1    -   100 Listen   192.168.1.254   192.168.1.1     192.168.1.4
Vl192        1    1   -   Listen   0007.b400.0101  192.168.1.1     -
Vl192        1    2   -   Active   0007.b400.0102  local           -
Vl192        1    3   -   Listen   0007.b400.0103  192.168.1.3     -
Vl192        1    4   -   Listen   0007.b400.0104  192.168.1.4     -

VTP-Server-3#show glbp brief
Interface    Grp  Fwd Pri State    Address         Active router   Standby
router
Vl192        1    -   100 Listen   192.168.1.254   192.168.1.1     192.168.1.4
Vl192        1    1   -   Listen   0007.b400.0101  192.168.1.1     -
Vl192        1    2   -   Listen   0007.b400.0102  192.168.1.2     -
Vl192        1    3   -   Active   0007.b400.0103  local           -
Vl192        1    4   -   Listen   0007.b400.0104  192.168.1.4     -

VTP-Server-4#show glbp brief
Interface    Grp  Fwd Pri State    Address         Active router   Standby
router
Vl192        1    -   100 Standby  192.168.1.254   192.168.1.1     local
Vl192        1    1   -   Listen   0007.b400.0101  192.168.1.1     -
Vl192        1    2   -   Listen   0007.b400.0102  192.168.1.2     -
Vl192        1    3   -   Listen   0007.b400.0103  192.168.1.3     -
Vl192        1    4   -   Active   0007.b400.0104  local           -
```

From the output above, we can determine that VTP-Server-1 (192.168.1.1) has been elected as the AVG based on its priority value of 110, which is higher than that of all the other gateways. Gateway VTP-Server-4 (192.168.1.4) has been elected as the standby virtual gateway because it has the highest IP address of the remaining three gateways, even though they all share the same priority value. Gateways VTP-Server-2 and VTP-Server-3 are therefore placed in the listen state.

The `show glbp` command prints detailed information on the status of the GLBP group. The output of this command is illustrated as follows:

```
VTP-Server-1#show glbp
Vlan192 - Group 1
  State is Active
    2 state changes, last state change 02:52:22
  Virtual IP address is 192.168.1.254
  Hello time 3 sec, hold time 10 sec
    Next hello sent in 1.465 secs
  Redirect time 600 sec, forwarder time-out 14400 sec
  Preemption disabled
  Active is local
  Standby is 192.168.1.4, priority 100 (expires in 9.619 sec)
  Priority 110 (configured)
  Weighting 100 (default 100), thresholds: lower 1, upper 100
  Load balancing: round-robin
  Group members:
    0004.c16f.8741 (192.168.1.3)
    000c.cea7.f3a0 (192.168.1.2)
    0013.1986.0a20 (192.168.1.1) local
    0030.803f.ea81 (192.168.1.4)
  There are 4 forwarders (1 active)
  Forwarder 1
    State is Active
      1 state change, last state change 02:52:12
    MAC address is 0007.b400.0101 (default)
    Owner ID is 0013.1986.0a20
    Redirection enabled
    Preemption enabled, min delay 30 sec
    Active is local, weighting 100
  Forwarder 2
    State is Listen
    MAC address is 0007.b400.0102 (learnt)
    Owner ID is 000c.cea7.f3a0
    Redirection enabled, 599.299 sec remaining (maximum 600 sec)
    Time to live: 14399.299 sec (maximum 14400 sec)
    Preemption enabled, min delay 30 sec
    Active is 192.168.1.2 (primary), weighting 100 (expires in 9.295 sec)
  Forwarder 3
    State is Listen
    MAC address is 0007.b400.0103 (learnt)
    Owner ID is 0004.c16f.8741
    Redirection enabled, 599.519 sec remaining (maximum 600 sec)
    Time to live: 14399.519 sec (maximum 14400 sec)
```

```
    Preemption enabled, min delay 30 sec
    Active is 192.168.1.3 (primary), weighting 100 (expires in 9.515 sec)
  Forwarder 4
    State is Listen
    MAC address is 0007.b400.0104 (learnt)
    Owner ID is 0030.803f.ea81
    Redirection enabled, 598.514 sec remaining (maximum 600 sec)
    Time to live: 14398.514 sec (maximum 14400 sec)
    Preemption enabled, min delay 30 sec
    Active is 192.168.1.4 (primary), weighting 100 (expires in 8.510 sec)
```

When executed on the AVG, the `show glbp` command shows, among other things, the address of the standby virtual gateway and the number of AVFs in the group, as well as the states that it has assigned to them. The virtual MAC addresses for each AVF are also displayed.

Configuring GLBP Load Sharing

The `glbp [number] load-balancing [host-dependent| round-robin|weighted]` command is used to configure the GLBP load-sharing method. The default is round-robin, which can be verified in the output of the `show glbp` command as follows:

```
VTP-Server-1#show glbp
Vlan192 - Group 1
  State is Active
    2 state changes, last state change 02:52:22
  Virtual IP address is 192.168.1.254
  Hello time 3 sec, hold time 10 sec
    Next hello sent in 1.465 secs
  Redirect time 600 sec, forwarder time-out 14400 sec
  Preemption disabled
  Active is local
  Standby is 192.168.1.4, priority 100 (expires in 9.619 sec)
  Priority 110 (configured)
  Weighting 100 (default 100), thresholds: lower 1, upper 100
  Load balancing: round-robin
  Group members:
    0004.c16f.8741 (192.168.1.3)
    000c.cea7.f3a0 (192.168.1.2)
    0013.1986.0a20 (192.168.1.1) local
    0030.803f.ea81 (192.168.1.4)
  There are 4 forwarders (1 active)
...
[Truncated Output]
```

The following output shows how to change the load-sharing method on the AVG to host-dependent:

```
VTP-Server-1(config)#interface vlan 192
VTP-Server-1(config-if)#glbp 1 load-balancing host-dependent
VTP-Server-1(config-if)#exit
```

The `show glbp` command is again used to verify this configuration as shown in the following output:

```
VTP-Server-1#show glbp
Vlan192 - Group 1
  State is Active
    2 state changes, last state change 03:52:19
  Virtual IP address is 192.168.1.254
  Hello time 3 sec, hold time 10 sec
    Next hello sent in 2.503 secs
  Redirect time 600 sec, forwarder time-out 14400 sec
  Preemption disabled
  Active is local
  Standby is 192.168.1.4, priority 100 (expires in 9.495 sec)
  Priority 110 (configured)
  Weighting 100 (default 100), thresholds: lower 1, upper 100
  Load balancing: host-dependent
  Group members:
    0004.c16f.8741 (192.168.1.3)
    000c.cea7.f3a0 (192.168.1.2)
    0013.1986.0a20 (192.168.1.1) local
    0030.803f.ea81 (192.168.1.4)
  There are 4 forwarders (1 active)
...
[Truncated Output]
...
```

Configuring GLBP Plain Text and MD5 Authentication

The `glbp [number] authentication text [password]` interface configuration command is used to enable GLBP plain-text authentication for group members. This command must be configured on all members of the group as illustrated in the following outputs:

```
VTP-Server-1(config)#interface vlan 192
VTP-Server-1(config-if)# glbp 1 authentication text SWITCH
VTP-Server-1(config-if)#exit

VTP-Server-2(config)#interface vlan 192
VTP-Server-2(config-if)# glbp 1 authentication text SWITCH
VTP-Server-2(config-if)#exit

VTP-Server-3(config)#interface vlan 192
VTP-Server-3(config-if)# glbp 1 authentication text SWITCH
VTP-Server-3(config-if)#exit

VTP-Server-4(config)#interface vlan 192
VTP-Server-4(config-if)# glbp 1 authentication text SWITCH
VTP-Server-4(config-if)#exit
```

The `glbp [number] authentication md5 key-string [password]` interface configuration command is used to enable MD5 authentication for GLBP without using a key chain. The `glbp` [number] authentication md5 key-chain [name] interface configuration command is used to enable MD5 authentication for GLBP referencing a configured key chain. The following outputs show how to enable MD5 authentication, without a key chain, for GLBP:

```
VTP-Server-1(config)#interface vlan 192
VTP-Server-1(config-if)# glbp 1 authentication md5 key-string SWITCH
VTP-Server-1(config-if)#exit

VTP-Server-2(config)#interface vlan 192
VTP-Server-2(config-if)# glbp 1 authentication md5 key-string SWITCH
VTP-Server-2(config-if)#exit

VTP-Server-3(config)#interface vlan 192
VTP-Server-3(config-if)# glbp 1 authentication md5 key-string SWITCH
VTP-Server-3(config-if)#exit

VTP-Server-4(config)#interface vlan 192
VTP-Server-4(config-if)# glbp 1 authentication md5 key-string SWITCH
VTP-Server-4(config-if)#exit
```

This configuration is verified using the show glbp command as shown in the following output:

```
VTP-Server-1#show glbp
Vlan192 - Group 1
  State is Active
    2 state changes, last state change 04:06:10
  Virtual IP address is 192.168.1.254
  Hello time 3 sec, hold time 10 sec
    Next hello sent in 0.840 secs
  Redirect time 600 sec, forwarder time-out 14400 sec
  Authentication MD5, key-string
  Preemption disabled
  Active is local
  Standby is 192.168.1.4, priority 100 (expires in 8.721 sec)
  Priority 110 (configured)
  Weighting 100 (default 100), thresholds: lower 1, upper 100
  Load balancing: host-dependent
  Group members:
    0004.c16f.8741 (192.168.1.3)
    000c.cea7.f3a0 (192.168.1.2)
    0013.1986.0a20 (192.168.1.1) local
    0030.803f.ea81 (192.168.1.4)
  There are 4 forwarders (1 active)
...
[Truncated Output]
...
```

ICMP Router Discovery Protocol

The ICMP Router Discovery Protocol (IRDP) uses Internet Control Message Protocol (ICMP) router advertisements and router solicitation messages to allow a network host to discover the addresses of operational gateways on the subnet. IRDP is an alternative gateway discovery method that eliminates the need for manual configuration of gateway addresses on network hosts and is independent of any specific routing protocol.

It is important to remember that ICMP router discovery messages do not constitute a routing protocol. Instead, they enable hosts to discover the existence of neighboring gateways but do not determine which gateway is best to reach a particular destination.

On networks with more than one gateway, if a host chooses a poor gateway for a particular destination, it should receive an ICMP Redirect from that router, identifying a better gateway to reach the required destination host. This concept is illustrated below in Figure 8-28:

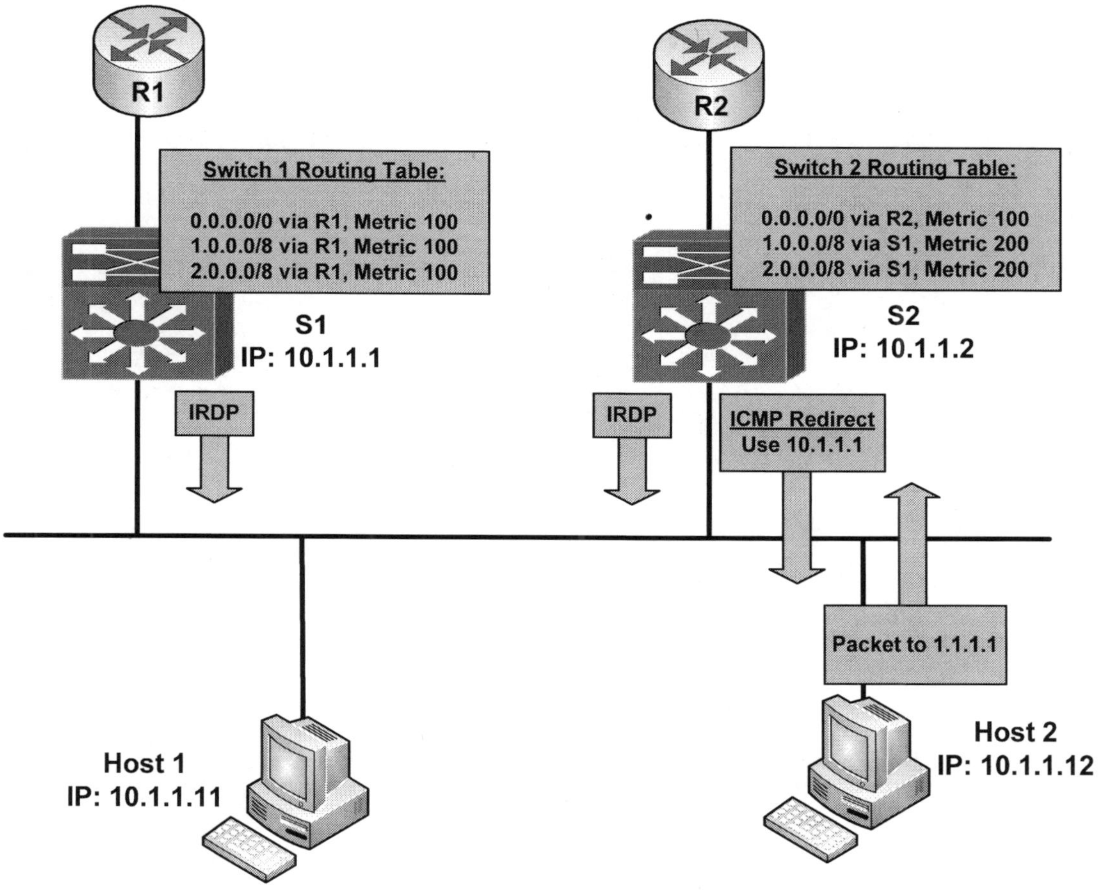

Fig. 8-28. IRDP and ICMP Redirects

Referencing Figure 8-28, Multilayer Switch 1 is connected to router R1 and is receiving the default route, as well as routing entries for the 1.0.0.0/8 and 2.0.0.0/8 networks. Multilayer Switch 2 is connected to router R2 and is receiving only the default route from this router. However, it is receiving the 1.0.0.0/8 and 2.0.0.0/8 networks from Switch 1.

The LAN has been configured to run IRDP, and Host 1 and Host 2 are running an ICMP router discovery client, which allows them to listen to the ICMP router advertisements being sent by Switch 1 and Switch 2.

Host 2 selects Switch 2 as its gateway and decides it wants to send a packet to 1.1.1.1. Switch 2 receives this request but knows that Switch 1 has a better path to the destination, and so it sends an ICMP Redirect to Host 2, telling it to use Switch 1instead. Host 2 receives the ICMP Redirect and forwards the packet to Switch 1, which forwards it to R1.

By default, ICMP router advertisements are sent out as Broadcast packets to the destination address 255.255.255.255., as shown below in Figure 8-29:

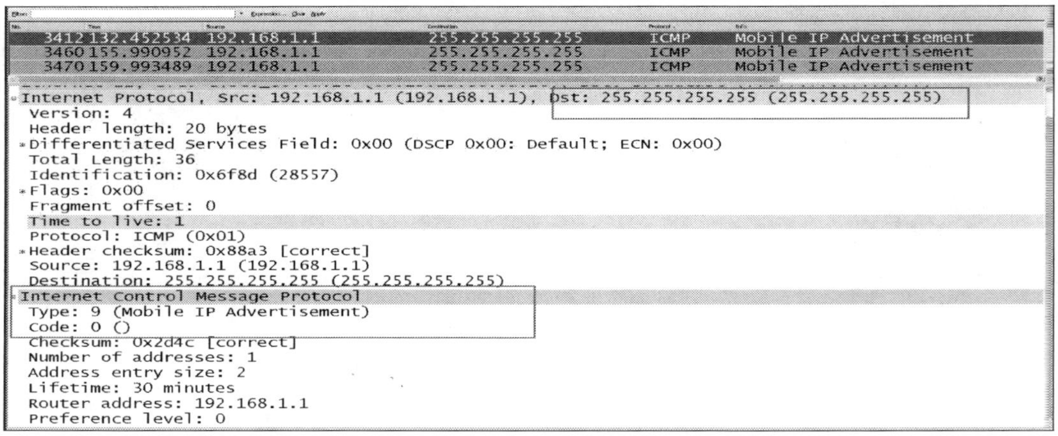

Fig. 8-29. IRDP Broadcast Router Advertisements

However, Cisco IOS software allows administrators to configure the gateways to send IRDP messages using IP Multicast to the destination address 224.0.0.1, as shown below in Figure 8-30:

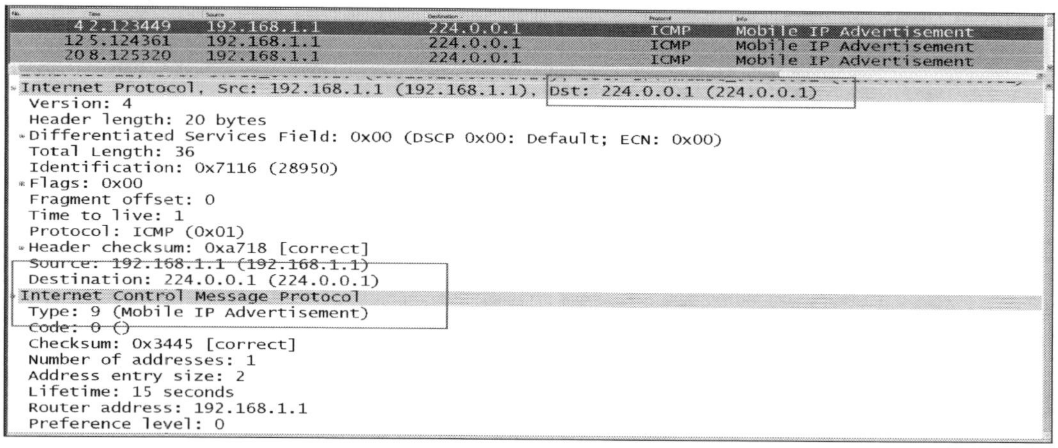

Fig. 8-30. IRDP Multicast Router Advertisements

NOTE: Going into detail on the IRDP packet format is beyond the scope of the SWITCH exam requirements.

IRDP is enabled on a router interface using the `ip irdp` interface configuration command. This configures the router to Broadcast router advertisement messages. To configure the router to Multicast messages instead, the `ip irdp multicast` interface configuration command must be added to the configuration. The following output illustrates how to enable IRDP using Multicast:

```
Gateway-R1(config)#interface fastethernet 0/0
Gateway-R1(config-if)#ip irdp
Gateway-R1(config-if)#ip irdp multicast
Gateway-R1(config-if)#exit
```

IRDP configuration can be validated using the `show ip irdp [interface]` command as illustrated in the following output:

```
Gateway-R1#show ip irdp
FastEthernet0/0 has router discovery enabled

Advertisements will occur between every 450 and 600 seconds.
Advertisements are sent with multicasts.
Advertisements are valid for 1800 seconds.
Default preference will be 0.
```

By default, Cisco IOS software sends out IRDP advertisements between every 450 and 600 seconds. This default message interval time can be modified using the `ip irdp minadvertinterval [3-1800]` interface configuration command to specify the minimum interval between advertisements and the `ip irdp maxadvertinterval [0, 4-1800]` interface configuration command to specify the maximum interval between advertisements.

NOTE: Issuing the `ip irdp maxadvertinterval 0` interface configuration command causes the router to advertise only when solicited by clients.

The following output illustrates how to configure the router to send IRDP router advertisement messages between every 3 and 5 seconds:

```
Gateway-R1(config)#interface fastethernet 0/0
Gateway-R1(config-if)#ip irdp minadvertinterval 3
Gateway-R1(config-if)#ip irdp maxadvertinterval 5
Gateway-R1(config-if)#exit
```

This is verified using the `show ip irdp [interface]` command as shown in the following output:

```
Gateway-R1#show ip irdp
FastEthernet0/0 has router discovery enabled

Advertisements will occur between every 3 and 5 seconds.
Advertisements are sent with multicasts.
Advertisements are valid for 15 seconds.
Default preference will be 0.
```

Supervisor Engine Redundancy

Cisco Catalyst 4500 and 6500 series switches support two Supervisor modules within the switch chassis to allow for HA of the switch. When the switch boots up, the first Supervisor that boots up is referred to as the Primary or Active Supervisor Engine and the second Supervisor module is referred to as the Standby or Redundant Supervisor Engine. The Standby Supervisor Engine assumes Primary Supervisor Engine status when one of the following events occurs:

- The Primary Supervisor Engine fails or crashes
- The Primary Supervisor Engine is rebooted
- The administrator forces a manual failover
- The Primary Supervisor Engine is physically removed

Cisco IOS software supports the following three redundancy modes for Redundant Supervisor Engines:

1. Route Processor Redundancy (RPR)
2. Route Processor Redundancy Plus (RPR+)
3. Stateful Switchover (SSO)

Route Processor Redundancy (RPR)

With RPR, when the switch boots up, RPR runs between the two Supervisor Engines and the first Supervisor to complete the boot process becomes the Active Supervisor Engine. The Standby Supervisor Engine is only partially booted and initialized and therefore not all switch subsystems become operational (e.g. the MSFC and PFC are not active).

Clock synchronization occurs between Primary and Backup every 60 seconds, and the startup configuration and configuration registers are synchronized between Supervisors. When the Primary Supervisor Engine fails, the Standby Supervisor Engine becomes operational and the following occurs within the switch:

- All switching modules are reloaded and powered up again
- Remaining subsystems on the MSFC are brought up
- ACLs are reprogrammed into Supervisor Engine hardware

Because the Standby Supervisor Engine is not fully initialized, failover from the Primary to the Secondary Supervisor Engine results in a disruption of network traffic, as the Standby Supervisor Engine goes through the steps listed above and assumes the Primary Supervisor Engine role. This entire process generally takes 2 to 4 minutes.

Route Processor Redundancy Plus (RPR+)

RPR+ improves on RPR and provides failover generally within 30 to 60 seconds. When RPR+ mode is used, the Redundant Supervisor Engine is fully initialized and configured but is not fully operational. When the Redundant Supervisor Engine first initializes, the startup-configuration file is copied from the Active Supervisor Engine to the Redundant Supervisor Engine, which overrides any existing startup-configuration file on the Redundant Supervisor Engine, allowing the Supervisor Engines to become synchronized.

When configuration changes occur during normal operation, redundancy performs an incremental synchronization from the Active Supervisor Engine to the Redundant Supervisor Engine. RPR+ synchronizes user-entered CLI commands incrementally line-by-line from the Active Supervisor Engine to the Redundant Supervisor Engine.

Even though the Redundant Supervisor Engine is fully initialized, it only interacts with the Active Supervisor Engine to receive incremental changes to the configuration files. The console on the Redundant Supervisor Engine is locked and CLI commands cannot be entered on the Redundant Supervisor Engine.

When the Active Supervisor Engine fails, the Redundant Supervisor Engine finishes initializing without reloading other switch modules and the following occurs:

- Traffic is disrupted until the Redundant Supervisor Engine takes over
- The switch maintains any static routes across the switchover
- The switch does not maintain any dynamic routing protocol information
- The switch clears the FIB tables on switchover
- The switch clears the CAM tables on switchover
- State information, such as active TCP sessions, is not maintained on switchover

When implementing RPR+, it is important to ensure the following:

- The Supervisor modules are similar (i.e. the same model)—memory and version, for example
- The Supervisor engines are running the same Cisco IOS software

If any of these is not the same, then the switch will revert to RPR mode instead of RPR+.

Stateful Switchover (SSO)

SSO is the preferred redundancy mode for Supervisor Engines. Similar to RPR and RPR+, SSO establishes one of the Supervisor Engines as Active while the other Supervisor Engine is designated as Standby. Unlike RPR and RPR+ however, with SSO, the Redundant Supervisor Engine is fully booted and initialized and then SSO synchronizes the two Supervisors.

With SSO, both Supervisor Engines must be running the same configuration so that the Redundant Supervisor Engine is always ready to assume control in the event that the Active Supervisor Engine fails. Configuration information and data structures are synchronized between the Supervisor Engines at startup and whenever changes to the Active Supervisor Engine configuration occur.

Unlike RPR and RPR+ redundancy, SSO maintains state information between the Redundant Supervisor Engines. This includes forwarding information in the Forwarding Information Base (FIB), as well as adjacency entries, which ensures that Layer 2 traffic is not interrupted and the switch can still forward Layer 3 traffic after a switchover from the Active to the Redundant Supervisor Engine.

During SSO switchover, all system control and routing protocol execution is transferred from the Active Supervisor Engine to the Redundant Supervisor Engine within 0 to 3 seconds.

Configuring Supervisor Engine Redundancy

Supervisor redundancy is configured in redundancy configuration mode, which is entered by issuing the `redundancy` global configuration command as illustrated in the following output:

```
Catalyst-6500-1(config)#redundancy
Catalyst-6500-1(config-red)#
```

The next configuration step is to specify the redundancy mode via the `mode {rpr | rpr-plus | sso}` redundancy-mode configuration command. The following output illustrates how to configure RPR+ redundancy for the Supervisor Engines:

```
Catalyst-6500-1(config)#redundancy
Catalyst-6500-1(config-red)#mode rpr-plus
```

This configuration is validated using the `show redundancy states` command as illustrated in the following output:

```
Catalyst-6500-1#show redundancy states
my state = 13 -ACTIVE
     peer state = 8  -STANDBY HOT
           Mode = Duplex
           Unit = Primary
        Unit ID = 1

Redundancy Mode (Operational) = Route Processor Redundancy Plus
Redundancy Mode (Configured)  = Route Processor Redundancy Plus
     Split Mode = Disabled
   Manual Swact = Enabled
 Communications = Up

   client count = 11
 client_notification_TMR = 30000 milliseconds
          keep_alive TMR = 9000 milliseconds
        keep_alive count = 0
    keep_alive threshold = 18
           RF debug mask = 0x0
```

The following output illustrates how to configure SSO (preferred) redundancy:

```
Catalyst-4500-1(config)#redundancy
Catalyst-4500-1(config-red)#mode sso
```

This configuration is validated using the `show redundancy states` command as illustrated in the following output:

```
Catalyst-4500-1#show redundancy states
       my state = 13 -ACTIVE
     peer state = 8  -STANDBY HOT
```

```
           Mode = Duplex
           Unit = Secondary
        Unit ID = 1
Redundancy Mode (Operational) = Stateful Switchover
Redundancy Mode (Configured)  = Stateful Switchover
Redundancy State              = Stateful Switchover
     Maintenance Mode = Disabled
    Manual Swact = enabled
 Communications = Up
   client count = 54
 client_notification_TMR = 240000 milliseconds
          keep_alive TMR = 9000 milliseconds
        keep_alive count = 0
    keep_alive threshold = 18
           RF debug mask = 0x0
```

The `show redundancy` command can also be used to provide detailed redundancy information, such as the uptime of the Supervisor Engines, the IOS version the Supervisor Engines are running, the number of switchovers, the reason for the last (most recent) switchover, and failure statistics. The output of this command is illustrated as follows:

```
Catalyst-4500-1#show redundancy
Redundant System Information :
------------------------------
       Available system uptime = 1 year, 4 days, 2 hours, 45 minutes
Switchovers system experienced = 2
              Standby failures = 1
        Last switchover reason = user forced

                 Hardware Mode = Duplex
    Configured Redundancy Mode = Stateful Switchover
     Operating Redundancy Mode = Stateful Switchover
              Maintenance Mode = Disabled
                Communications = Up

Current Processor Information :
-------------------------------
               Active Location = slot 1
        Current Software state = ACTIVE
       Uptime in current state = 1 year, 4 days, 1 hour, 2 minutes
                 Image Version = Cisco IOS Software, Catalyst 4500 L3 Switch
Software (cat4500-ENTSERVICESK9-M), Version 12.2(50)SG1, RELEASE SOFTWARE
(fc2)
Technical Support: http://www.cisco.com/techsupport
Copyright (c) 1986-2009 by Cisco Systems, Inc.
Compiled Mon 09-Feb-09 19:21 by prod_rel_team
                          BOOT = bootflash:cat4500-entservicesk9-mz.122-
                                 50.SG1.bin,1;bootflash:cat4000-i5k91s-
                                 mz.122-20.EW4.bin,1;
        Configuration register = 0x2102
```

```
Peer Processor Information :
----------------------------
              Standby Location = slot 2
        Current Software state = STANDBY HOT
       Uptime in current state = 1 year, 4 days, 58 minutes
                 Image Version = Cisco IOS Software, Catalyst 4500 L3 Switch
Software (cat4500-ENTSERVICESK9-M), Version 12.2(50)SG1, RELEASE SOFTWARE
(fc2)
Technical Support: http://www.cisco.com/techsupport
Copyright (c) 1986-2009 by Cisco Systems, Inc.
Compiled Mon 09-Feb-09 19:21 by
                          BOOT = bootflash:cat4500-entservicesk9-mz.122-
                                 50.SG1.bin,1;bootflash:cat4000-i5k91s-
                                 mz.122-20.EW4.bin,1;
        Configuration register = 0x2102
```

Configuring Manual Supervisor Synchronization

By default, during normal redundancy operation, the Primary Supervisor will synchronize its start-up configuration and configuration registers with the Redundant Supervisor. However, Cisco IOS software also allows administrators to manually configure synchronization between the two Supervisor Engines. The following sequence of steps is required to perform this action:

1. Enter redundancy configuration mode by issuing the `redundancy` global configuration command on the Active Supervisor Engine.
2. Enter main CPU configuration mode, within redundancy configuration mode, by entering the `main-cpu` redundancy configuration command.
3. Specify the variables that you want synchronized between the Supervisor Engines by issuing the `auto-sync [startup-config | config-register | bootvar |standard]` main CPU redundancy configuration command. Repeat this command as needed for each variable to synchronize between the Supervisor Engines.
   The `[startup-config]` keyword is used to synchronize the startup-configuration files on the redundant Supervisor Engines. The `[config-register]` keyword is used to synchronize the configuration registers on the Redundant Supervisor Engines. The `[bootvar]` keyword is used to synchronize the boot variables on the Redundant Supervisor Engines. Finally, the `[standard]` keyword is used to configure the Redundant Supervisor Engines to use default automatic synchronization.
4. Save the switch configuration to NVRAM using the copy `running-config startup-config` or `copy system:running-config nvram:startup-config` commands.

The following output illustrates how to manually disable the default automatic synchronization and manually configure only the synchronization of the startup configuration between the Redundant Supervisor Engines. Once configured, the bootvar and configuration register will not be synchronized:

```
Catalyst-6500-1(config)#redundancy
Catalyst-6500-1(config-red)#main-cpu
Catalyst-6500-1(config-r-mc)#no auto-sync standard
Catalyst-6500-1(config-r-mc)#auto-sync startup-config
Catalyst-6500-1(config-r-mc)#exit
Catalyst-6500-1(config-red)#exit
Catalyst-6500-1(config)#exit
Catalyst-6500-1#copy running-config startup-config
```

The following output illustrates how to re-enable default automatic synchronization on the Supervisor Engines:

```
Catalyst-6500-1(config)#redundancy
Catalyst-6500-1(config-red)#main-cpu
Catalyst-6500-1(config-r-mc)#auto-sync standard
Catalyst-6500-1(config-r-mc)#end
Catalyst-6500-1#copy system:running-config nvram:startup-config
```

NOTE: Manual synchronization configuration is validated in the running configuration of the switch.

Manually Forcing a Switchover or Failover to the Standby Supervisor

Cisco IOS software allows administrators to manually force a switchover or failover from the Active or Primary Supervisor Engine to the Standby Supervisor Engine. This is typically performed when the Active Supervisor Engine is experiencing issues and needs to be removed or replaced, or needs to have the software upgraded, for example. A manual failover may be initiated by issuing the `redundancy force-switchover` privileged EXEC command.

StackWise Technology

Cisco Catalyst 3750 series switches support Cisco StackWise technology, which allows network administrators to combine up to nine (9) physical Catalyst 3750 series switch chassis and create a single switching unit with a 32-Gbps switching stack interconnect.

This single logical chassis is commonly simply referred to as a switch stack. All stack members have full access to the stack interconnect bandwidth. The stack is managed as a single unit from the master switch, which is elected from one of the stack member switches. Master switch election is described in the following section.

Stack Master Election

As previously stated, up to nine physical chassis can be combined into a single logical switch unit, referred to as a stack. This stack elects a master switch, from which the entire stack is managed and configured by administrators. The stack master is also responsible for creating and updating the CAM and routing tables (if applicable) for the stack. The stack master is typically elected within 20 seconds of the stack being initialized.

Upon initialization, or reboot of the entire stack, an election process occurs among the switches in the stack to elect the master switch. While any member of the stack can become the master switch, there is a hierarchy of selection criteria for the election. The stack master will be chosen based on the following rules, in the order specified:

1. The switch with the highest stack member priority value is elected. The priority value can be manually configured by administrators.
2. The switch with the highest hardware and software priority will be elected. This defaults to the unit with the most extensive feature set. The Cisco Catalyst 3750 Advanced IP Services IPv6 (AIPv6) image has the highest priority, followed by Cisco Catalyst 3750 switches with Enhanced Multilayer Software Image (EMI) and then the Standard Multilayer Software Image (SMI) versions.
3. The switch with non-default configuration is elected. In other words, if a switch has a pre-existing configuration, it will be preferred over one that has no configuration.
4. The switch with the longest system uptime is elected.
5. The switch with the lowest MAC address will be elected.

The stack master election is held when one of the following events occurs:

- When the whole switch stack is reset or rebooted
- When the stack master is reset or powered off
- When the stack master is removed from the stack
- When the stack master switch has failed
- When switches are added to the existing stack

REAL WORLD IMPLEMENTATION

Although the stack master election process seems very straightforward, it is important to also understand that sometimes the election process does not necessarily result in the 'best' switch being elected stack master.

For example, switches that run a Cryptographic image will sometimes take a longer time to boot up than those running a non-Cryptographic image. This may result in those switches taking longer than 20 seconds to boot up completely.

Because the stack master election occurs within the 20-second timeframe, these switches may not be able to participate in the election, allowing lower priority switches to be elected stack master. Because they missed the initial election, these switches become regular stack members. It may therefore be necessary for manual administrator intervention to ensure that the desired or 'best' switch is elected stack master.

During stack master election, it is important to remember that data forwarding will not be affected. When a new master is elected, the entire stack continues to function and Layer 2 connectivity is unaffected because the remaining switches within the stack continue to forward traffic based on the tables that they last received from the master.

Layer 3 resiliency is protected with Non-Stop Forwarding (NSF), which gracefully and rapidly transitions Layer 3 forwarding from the old master switch to the new stack master. However, in a manner similar to RPR+ operation, the routing tables are flushed and rebuilt again when a new master has been elected.

NOTE: NSF will be described later in this chapter.

StackWise High Availability

Cisco StackWise technology supports several mechanisms that can be used to ensure switch stack HA. These mechanisms are listed and described below in Table 8-1:

Table 8-1. StackWise High Availability Mechanisms

Mechanism	Description
CrossStack EtherChannel Technology	This allows multiple switches in a stack to create an EtherChannel connection between them. This prevents the loss of an individual switch from affecting connectivity for other switches in the stack.
Equal Cost Paths	The switch stack can be dual-homed to multiple Distribution Layer switches or multiple routers for redundancy.
1:N Master Redundancy	Each switch in the stack participates in the master election and is therefore eligible to be elected master in the event that the master fails.
Stacking Cable Resiliency	When a break in the stacking cable is detected, switches begin sending data using the alternate path that is currently operational.
Online Insertion and Removal (OIR)	OIR allows switches to be added and removed from the switch stack while it is operational.

Distributed Layer 2 Forwarding	If the master switch fails, stack members continue Layer 2 forwarding using the most recent tables received from the master.
RPR+ for Layer 3 Resiliency	As is the case with RPR+, each stack member is initialized and is ready to assume the role of master if the current master fails.

NOTE: Stacking configuration is beyond the requirements of the current SWITCH exam requirements and will not be illustrated in this chapter.

Catalyst Switch Power Redundancy

Different Catalyst switches support different power redundancy capabilities. This section describes the power redundancy capabilities of the medium-end and high-end Catalyst switches, such as the Catalyst 4500 and Catalyst 6500 series switches, and low-end switches, such as the Catalyst 3750 series switches.

Catalyst 4500 and Catalyst 6500 Power Redundancy

In addition to supporting Redundant Supervisor Engines, Catalyst 4500 and 6500 series switches also support redundant power supplies. The redundant power supplies must be identical and must possess the same power input and output ratings. Cisco IOS software supports the following two power redundancy modes in Catalyst 4500 and Catalyst 6500 series switches:

1. Combined
2. Redundant

In combined mode, both power supplies are used at the same time by the switch. This means that the total power load required can exceed the maximum power output rating of one power supply but cannot exceed the sum of both power supplies.

When combined mode is used, the switch will power up as many modules as the combined capacity allows. However, in the event that one of the power supplies should fail and there is not enough power for all previously powered-up modules, the system powers down the modules for which there is not enough power.

NOTE: Combined mode is typically used when the switch has a large amount of Power over Ethernet (PoE) modules, which may be used to provide power to IP phones or other devices, such as wireless access points. PoE will be described in detail in the following chapter.

In redundant mode, by default, the switch will draw its full power from both power supplies. Unlike combined mode, however, both power supplies provide only half of the required power each, meaning that the switch uses no more combined power than the maximum power capability of one of the single power supplies.

When one power supply fails, the other immediately takes over the full load, preventing the modules from being powered down or disabled due to insufficient power.

Configuring Catalyst 4500 and Catalyst 6500 Power Redundancy

The power redundancy mode is configured using the `power redundancy-mode [combined | redundant]` global configuration command. The following output illustrates how to configure power redundant mode:

```
Catalyst-6500-1(config)# power redundancy-mode redundant
Catalyst-6500-1(config)#exit
```

This configuration is validated using the `show power` command and any applicable keywords, which are illustrated in the following output:

```
Catalyst-6500-1#show power ?
  available      System power available (margin)
  capabilities   Show individual power supply capabilities
  detail         Show detailed information on power resources
  inline         Show inline power status
  module         Show power consumed by modules
  status         Show all power status
  supplies       Show power supplies needed
  |              Output modifiers
  <cr>
```

The following output shows the `show power` command, which is used to verify the configured power redundancy method on the switch:

```
Catalyst-6500-1#show power
system power redundancy mode = redundant
system power total =     1153.32 Watts (27.46 Amps @ 42V)
system power used =       397.74 Watts ( 9.47 Amps @ 42V)
system power available =  755.58 Watts (17.99 Amps @ 42V)
                        Power-Capacity PS-Fan Output Oper
PS   Type               Watts   A @42V Status Status State
---- ------------------ ------- ------ ------ ------ -----
1    WS-CAC-2500W       1153.32 27.46  OK     OK     on
1    WS-CAC-2500W       1153.32 27.46  OK     OK     on

...
[Truncated Output]
```

If mismatched or different capability power supplies are detected, the switch will disable one of them as shown in the following output:

```
Catalyst-4500-1#show power

Power                                                     Fan      Inline
Supply  Model No            Type       Status             Sensor   Status
------  ----------------   ---------  -----------        ------   ------
PS1     PWR-C45-2800AC     AC 2800W   good               good     good
PS2     PWR-C45-1000AC     AC 1000W   err-disable        good     n.a.

...
[Truncated Output]
...
```

Catalyst 3750 Power Redundancy

Unlike the Catalyst 4500 and Catalyst 6500 series switches, Catalyst 3750 power redundancy is provided by an external power supply unit: the Cisco Redundant Power System (RPS) 2300.

The RPS 2300 contains two power supply bays and can provide complete internal power supply redundancy for up to two attached networking devices. The RPS 2300 can be combined with the Cisco Catalyst 3750-E and 3560-E PoE switches and any uninterruptible power supply (UPS) systems to provide protection against any one of the following:

- Internal power supply failures in network devices
- Failure of an AC circuit (a circuit breaker tripping, for example)
- Interruption of utility power

Non-Stop Forwarding

In Catalyst 4500 and 6500 series switches, Cisco Non-Stop Forwarding (NSF) works in conjunction with SSO to minimize the amount of time a network is unavailable to its users following a switchover while continuing to forward IP packets. NSF is primarily used to ensure the continued forwarding of IP packets following a Supervisor Engine switchover.

NSF is supported by BGP, OSPF, EIGRP, IS-IS, and CEF. Non-Stop Forwarding allows the routing protocols to detect a switchover and take the necessary action to continue forwarding network traffic. NSF allows routing protocols to recover route information from the NSF-capable peer devices instead of waiting for the FIB to be rebuilt before the switch can actually begin forwarding traffic. This allows for high availability and resiliency during Supervisor Engine switchover.

When NSF is implemented, routing protocols depend on CEF to continue forwarding packets during switchover while they build the Routing Information Base (RIB) tables. After the routing protocols have converged, CEF updates the FIB table and removes stale route entries.

CEF then updates the switch modules with the new FIB information. Cisco NSF is configured on a per-routing protocol basis. While the configuration of routing protocols is beyond the scope of the SWITCH exam requirements, the following outputs show the commands required to enable NSF for OSPF, IS-IS, EIGRP, and BGP, respectively, in Cisco IOS software:

```
Catalyst-6500-Switch(config)#router ospf [process id]
Catalyst-6500-Switch(config-router)#nsf

Catalyst-6500-Switch(config)#router isis [tag]
Catalyst-6500-Switch(config-router)#nsf [cisco|ietf]
```

NOTE: IS-IS supports both Cisco NSF and IETF NSF. The IETF NSF implementation is based on a proposed standard while the Cisco NSF implementation is based on Cisco-proprietary operation. You are not expected to go into detail on the differences between the two standards.

```
Catalyst-6500-Switch(config)#router eigrp [autonomous system number]
Catalyst-6500-Switch(config-router)#nsf

Catalyst-6500-Switch(config)#router bgp [autonomous system number]
Catalyst-6500-Switch(config-router)#bgp graceful-restart
```

NOTE: By default, CEF NSF is enabled when SSO redundancy mode is enabled and no further configuration is necessary. NSF operation can be verified in the output of the `show ip protocols` command for OSPF, IS-IS, and EIGRP. For BGP, the `show ip bgp neighbors [address]` command can be used to verify NSF configuration as illustrated in the following output.

```
Catalyst-6500-Switch#show ip bgp neighbors 150.1.1.1
BGP neighbor is 150.1.1.1,  remote AS 1, external link
  BGP version 4, remote router ID 1.1.1.1
  BGP state = Established, up for 00:00:21
  Last read 00:00:21, last write 00:00:21, hold time is 180, keepalive
interval is 60 seconds
  Neighbor capabilities:
    Route refresh: advertised and received(old & new)
    Address family IPv4 Unicast: advertised and received
    Graceful Restart Capability: advertised and received
      Remote Restart timer is 120 seconds
      Address families preserved by peer:
        none
```

```
  Message statistics:
    InQ depth is 0
    OutQ depth is 0
                         Sent       Rcvd
    Opens:                  1          1
    Notifications:          0          0
    Updates:                2          2
    Keepalives:             3          3
    Route Refresh:          0          0
    Total:                  6          6
  Default minimum time between advertisement runs is 30 seconds
...
[Truncated Output]
...
```

Chapter Summary

The following section is a summary of the major points you should be aware of in this chapter.

Hot Standby Router Protocol

- HSRP is a Cisco-proprietary First Hop Redundancy Protocol (FHRP)
- Two versions are HSRP are supported in Cisco IOS software: versions 1 and 2
- HRSP version 1 is the default HSRP version
- HSRP version 1 restricts the number of configurable HSRP groups to 255
- HSRP version 1 sends updates to Multicast group address 224.0.0.2 using UDP port 1985
- HSRP version 2 uses the new Multicast address 224.0.0.102
- The version 2 packet format uses a Type/Length/Value (TLV) format
- HSRP version 2 packets are ignored by gateways running version 1
- HSRP version 1 is not capable of advertising or learning millisecond timers; version 2 is
- HSRP version 2 numbers have been extended from 0 to 4095
- HSRP version 2 includes a 6-byte Identifier field that contains the router MAC address
- HSRP version 1 uses the MAC range 0000.0C07.ACxx
- HSRP version 2 uses the MAC range 0000.0C9F.F000 to 0000.0C9F.FFFF
- The default HSRP gateway priority is 100; the range is 1 – 255
- HSRP routers exchange three types of messages:
  1. Hello Messages
  2. Coup Messages
  3. Resign Messages

By default, preemption is disabled for HSRP

- HSRP interfaces transition through several states, which are:
  1. Disabled
  2. Init
  3. Listen
  4. Speak
  5. Standby
  6. Active

- HSRP uses a default plain-text authentication password of 'cisco'
- HSRP supports plain text and MD5 authentication
- MD5 authentication can be configured with or without key chains
- HSRP supports interface tracking configuration
- Multiple HSRP groups can be configured on the gateway for load balancing

Virtual Router Redundancy Protocol

- VRRP is an open standard First Hop Redundancy Protocol, similar to HSRP
- VRRP is defined in RFC 2338, which was made obsolete by RFC 3768
- VRRP sends advertisements to the Multicast destination address 224.0.0.18
- VRRP uses IP protocol number 112
- VRRP uses MAC addresses in the range 00-00-5e-00-01xx
- VRRP elects a virtual router master and virtual router backup
- You configure up to 255 virtual routers on an interface
- The number of supported virtual routers that can be configured depends on:
    1. Router processing capability
    2. Router memory capability
    3. Router interface support of multiple MAC addresses

- The default VRRP priority value is 100; the valid range is 1 – 254
- By default, preemption is enabled for VRRP
- The default VRRP version is version 2; there is no version 1
- VRRP version 3 is still in the draft stage
- The virtual router master sends advertisements to other routers in the same group
- Like HSRP, VRRP supports both plain text and MD5 authentication

Gateway Load Balancing Protocol

- GLBP allows multiple gateways in the same GLBP group to actively forward traffic
- GLBP gateways communicate via Hello messages that are sent every 3 seconds
- GLBP Hello messages are sent to the Multicast address 224.0.0.102, using UDP port 3222
- GLBP group members elect one gateway to be the AVG for that group
- The other gateways in the GLBP group provide backup for the AVG in case it fails
- The AVG answers all ARP requests for the virtual router address
- In addition, the AVG assigns a virtual MAC address to each member of the GLBP group
- Each gateway is an AVF for the virtual MAC address it has been assigned
- A GLBP group allows up to four virtual MAC addresses to be used per group
- A primary virtual forwarder is assigned a virtual MAC address by the AVG
- A secondary virtual forwarder is one that has learned the virtual MAC address
- GLBP uses two timers to migrate away from an old forwarder address:
    1. The redirect timer
    2. The timeout timer

- By default, GLBP preemption is disabled; however, this feature can be manually enabled
- GLBP uses a weighting scheme to determine the forwarding capacity of each gateway

- By default, each gateway is assigned a default weight of 100
- GLBP supports three different load sharing methods:
  1. Host-dependent
  2. Round Robin
  3. Weighted

- The client cache contains information about hosts using a GLBP group as default gateway
- The maximum number of cache entries that may be stored can be up to 2000
- In production environments, is recommended that this number never exceed 1000
- GLBP supports plain-text and MD5 authentication

ICMP Router Discovery Protocol

- IRDP uses ICMP router advertisements and ICMP router solicitation messages
- IRDP is an alternative gateway discovery method
- IDRP eliminates the need for manual configuration of gateway addresses on network
- IRDP is independent of any specific routing protocol
- By default, ICMP router advertisements are sent out as Broadcast packets
- ICMP router advertisements can also be sent as Multicasts
- Cisco IOS software sends out IRDP advertisements between every 450 and 600 seconds

Supervisor Engine Redundancy

- Cisco Catalyst 4500 and 6500 series switches support redundant Supervisor modules
- The first Supervisor that boots up is referred to as the Primary or Active Supervisor Engine
- The second Supervisor is referred to as the Standby or Redundant Supervisor Engine
- A failover or switchover to the Standby or Redundant Supervisor Engines happens when:
  1. The Primary Supervisor Engine fails or crashes
  2. The Primary Supervisor Engine is rebooted
  3. The administrator forces a manual failover
  4. The Primary Supervisor Engine is physically removed

- Cisco IOS software supports three redundancy modes for redundant Supervisor Engines:
  1. Route Processor Redundancy (RPR)
  2. Route Processor Redundancy Plus (RPR+)
  3. Stateful Switchover (SSO)

- With RPR, the Standby Supervisor Engine is only partially booted and initialized
- With RPR, not all switch subsystems on The Redundant Supervisor become operational
- With RPR, clock synchronization occurs between Primary and Backup every 60 seconds

- With RPR, when the Standby Supervisor becomes operational, the following occurs
  1. All switching modules are reloaded and powered up again
  2. Remaining subsystems on the MSFC are brought up
  3. ACLs are reprogrammed into Supervisor Engine hardware

- The RPR failover or switchover process takes generally takes between 2 to 4 minutes
- RPR+ improves on RPR and provides failover generally within 30 to 60 seconds
- With RPR+, the Redundant Supervisor is fully initialized and configured
- With RPR+, although initialized, the Redundant Supervisor is not fully operational
- RPR+ synchronizes user-entered CLI commands incrementally line-by-line
- When failover or switchover occurs with RPR+, the following events occur on the switch:
  1. Traffic is disrupted until the Redundant Supervisor Engine completes the takes over
  2. The switch maintains any static routes across the switchover
  3. The switch does not maintain any dynamic routing protocol information
  4. The switch clears the FIB Tables on switchover
  5. The switch clears the CAM Tables on switchover
  6. State information, such as active TCP sessions, is not maintained on switchover

- SSO is the preferred redundancy mode for Supervisor Engines
- With SSO, the Redundant or Standby Supervisor Engine is fully booted and initialized
- With SSO, Configuration information and data structures are synchronized
- SSO maintains state information between the redundant Supervisor Engines
- Failover or switchover with SSO redundancy generally happens within 0 to 3 seconds
- Administrators can initiate a manual failover to the Standby Supervisor Engine

StackWise Technology

- Cisco Catalyst 3750 series switches support Cisco StackWise technology
- This allows up to nine (9) switches to be combined into a single logical unit
- The switch stack is managed and configured from the master switch
- The stack master is elected upon initialization based on the following criteria:
  1. The switch with the highest stack member priority value is elected
  2. The switch with the highest hardware and software priority will be elected
  3. The switch with non-default configuration is elected
  4. The switch with the longest system uptime is elected
  5. The switch with the lowest MAC will be elected

- The stack master election is held when one of the following events occurs:
  1. When the whole switch stack is reset or rebooted
  2. When the stack master is reset or powered off

3. When the stack master is removed from the stack
4. When the stack master switch has failed
5. When switches are added to the existing stack

- Cisco StackWise Technology supports the following High Availability mechanisms:
  1. CrossStack Etherchannel technology
  2. Equal Cost Paths
  3. 1:N Master Redundancy
  4. Stacking Cable Resiliency
  5. Online Insertion and Removal (OIR)
  6. Distributed Layer 2 Forwarding
  7. RPR+ for Layer 3 Resiliency

Catalyst Switch Power Redundancy

- Cisco Catalyst 4500 and 6500 series switches support redundant power supplies
- Two power redundancy modes are supported:
  1. Combined
  2. Redundant

- In combined mode, both switch power supplies are used at the same time by the switch
- In combined mode, the total power load cannot exceed the sum of both supplies
- Combined mode is typically used when the switch has a large amount of PoE modules
- In redundant mode, the switch draws power from both power supplies
- In redundant mode, the switch uses no more power than the capacity of a single supply
- Catalyst 3750 switches do not support internal redundant power supplies
- The RPS 2300 is used, with a UPS, to provide the following for Catalyst 3750 series switches:
  1. Internal power supply failures in network devices
  2. Failure of an AC circuit (a circuit breaker tripping, for example)
  3. Interruption of utility power

Non-Stop Forwarding

- Cisco Non-Stop Forwarding (NSF) works with in conjunction with SSO
- NSF minimizes the amount of time a network is unavailable following a switchover
- NSF is used to ensure the continued forwarding IP packets after switchover
- NSF is supported by BGP, OSPF, EIGRP, IS-IS, and CEF
- NSF allows routing protocols to detect a switchover
- NSF allows routing protocols to recover route information from the NSF-capable peers
- With NSF, routing protocols depend on CEF to continue forwarding packets
- NSF is configured on a per-routing protocol basis

CHAPTER 9

Extending the LAN with Wireless Solutions

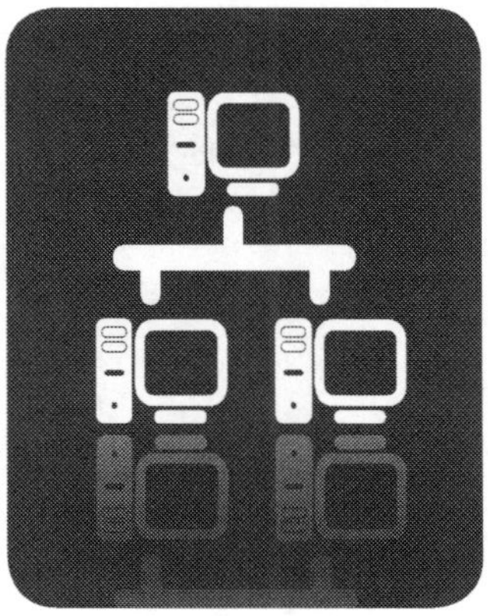

Traditional LANs are based on the IEEE 802.3 standards, which define the Physical Layer and the Data Link Layer's Media Access Control (MAC) sublayer of wired Ethernet. Wireless network solutions, defined in the IEEE 802.11 standards, can be used to extend the wired network, at a much lower cost than a wired infrastructure. The following core SWITCH exam objective is covered in this chapter:

- Prepare infrastructure to support advanced services by implementing a wireless extension of a Layer 2 solution

This chapter will be divided into the following sections:

- Wireless Local Area Network Overview
- IEEE 802.11 Components
- IEEE 802.11 and the OSI Reference Model
- Collision Avoidance: CSMA/CA
- MAC Sublayer Coordination Functions
- The Wireless Network Hidden Node Problem
- IEEE 802.11 Frame Types
- Wireless LAN Standards
- The Cisco Unified Wireless Network
- The Cisco Wireless LAN Solution
- Configuring Switches for WLAN Solutions

SWITCH Exam Objective	Chapter Section(s) Covered
• Implement a wireless extension of a Layer 2 solution	• Wireless Local Area Network Overview • IEEE 802.11 Components • IEEE 802.11 and the OSI Reference Model • Collision Avoidance: CSMA/CA • MAC Sublayer Coordination Functions • The Wireless Network Hidden Node Problem • IEEE 802.11 Frame Types • Wireless LAN Standards • The Cisco Unified Wireless Network • The Cisco Wireless LAN Solution • Configuring Switches for WLAN Solutions

Wireless Local Area Network Overview

Wireless Local Area Networks (WLANs) provide network connectivity almost anywhere and at much less cost than traditional wired LANs. A traditional wired network connects devices to the Internet or other networks using physical network cables. The wired infrastructure, based on IEEE 802.3 standards, supports the IEEE 802.1 network architecture, which is concerned with LAN and MAN standards, such as 802.1D and 802.1Q, as well as network security standards, such as 802.1x, for example.

A wireless network, on the other hand, uses radio waves to transmit data and connect devices to the Internet, as well as to other networks and applications, which minimizes the need for wired connections. WLANs are defined in the IEEE 802.11 standards, which will be described later in this chapter. Although a wireless network allows users to access network resources 'over-the-air,' it is important keep in mind that wireless traffic also traverses the physical wired infrastructure. Therefore, it is imperative to remember that WLANs are meant to augment, rather than replace, the wired LAN campus infrastructure. This augmentation allows for a flexible data communication system within the enterprise network.

Although traditional wired network solutions do have their advantages, such as greater throughput speeds, it is also important to know that current wireless network solutions do have some advantages over wired networks, which include the following:

- Monetary cost
- Flexibility
- Load distribution
- Redundancy

In terms of monetary cost, a wireless infrastructure requires less physical connections because the primary medium, the air, is free. This can mean significant cost savings not only in cabling terms but also in the number of switch ports required to provide connectivity for users.

Wireless network solutions provide greater flexibility than wired connections in that users are not restricted to a single physical location, such as a cubicle, to gain access to the network. Instead, users are able gain network access from just about anywhere, which could include the break room, a coffee shop, or even outside the physical office building.

Wireless solutions can provide load distribution by dynamically redirecting additional users to other Base Stations or Access Points (APs) if the local AP is overloaded. This capability allows for the load to be distributed among the APs, which results in an improvement in network performance. Users connected to wired networks, for example, cannot dynamically be handed off to an underutilized, available switch because they are physically 'bound' to their present location until a manual change to another switch or port is performed.

Wireless solutions provide physical redundancy in that if an AP fails, another one can simply accept and connect wireless users to the network. This is unlike wired networks where, for example, if a switch fails, physical cabling moves are required to reconnect the disconnected users to the network via a replacement switch.

IEEE 802.11 Components

The 802.11 architecture is comprised of several logical and physical components. The following 802.11 components will be described in this section:

- Client or Station (STA)
- Access Point (AP)
- Independent Basic Service Set (IBSS)
- Basic Service Set (BSS)
- Extended Service Set (ESS)
- Distribution System (DS)

Client or Station (STA)

The client or station (STA) refers to any appliance that interfaces with the wireless medium and operates as an end-user device. The STA contains an adapter card, a PC Card, or an embedded device to provide wireless connectivity. Some common examples of STAs include laptop computers, desktop computers, and PDAs with wireless network interface cards.

Access Point (AP)

The wireless Access Point (AP) functions as a bridge between the wireless STAs and the existing network backbone for network access. APs serve as the central points in an all-wireless network, or as the connection point between wired and wireless networks. When APs are used in a wireless network, any STA attempting to use the wireless network must first establish membership, or an association, with the AP.

Independent Basic Service Set (IBSS)

An Independent Basic Service Set (IBSS) is a wireless network consisting of at least two STAs, used where no access to a Distribution System (DS) is available. DS will be described later in this section. An IBSS is sometimes referred to as an independent configuration or as an ad hoc wireless network.

From a logical perspective, an IBSS is very similar to a peer-to-peer network in which no one node performs any server functions. Figure 9-1 below illustrates an IBSS:

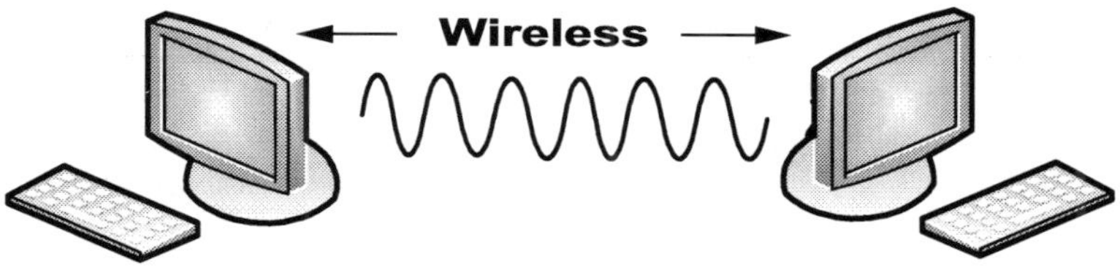

Fig. 9-1. Independent Basic Service Set

Basic Service Set (BSS)

The 802.11 WLAN infrastructure architecture is based on a cellular architecture that divides the system into cells, referred to as a Basic Service Set (BSS). The BSS is controlled by a Base Station or, more commonly, an AP. The cell is restricted to the AP's coverage area. Clients, or STAs, within the cell can then associate themselves with the AP, allowing them to use the WLAN. The BSS is depicted below in Figure 9-2:

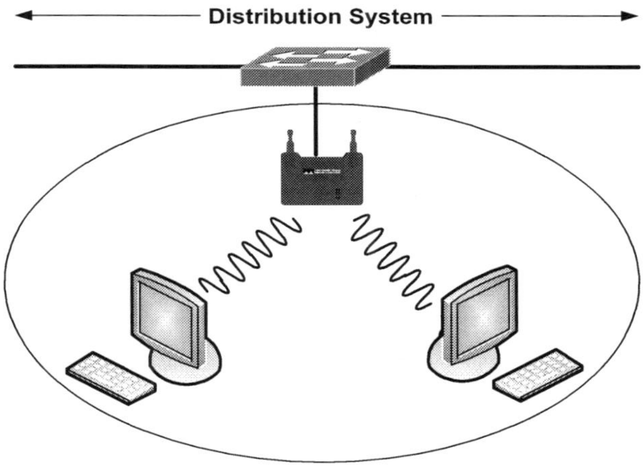

Fig. 9-2. Basic Service Set

Figure 9-2 illustrates a single cell, referred to as a BSS. The AP serves as the logical server for the cell and communications between the two STAs, flowing from one STA through the AP, and then from the AP to the other STA. The AP is also typically connected to a distribution system, such as Ethernet, that allows STAs to communicate with another node on the DS.

When an STA wants to access an existing BSS, it needs to get synchronization information from the AP. This information is derived using one of the following two methods:

1. Passive scanning
2. Active scanning

When using passive scanning, the STA waits to receive a beacon frame from the AP, which is simply a periodic frame sent by the AP that contains synchronization information. When using active scanning, the STA attempts to locate an AP by sending out Probe Request frames, and then waiting for a Probe Response from the AP.

Once the AP has been discovered, the client must establish an association. The AP may have some specific requirements that must be satisfied before allowing the STA to join the cell. For example, the AP may request a matching Service Set Identifier (SSID), a supported 802.11 standard, or some form of authentication.

NOTE: An SSID uniquely identifies an 802.11 WLAN. The SSID can be up to 32 characters long. This may be received by the STA via Broadcast messages from the AP (i.e. using passive scanning) or an STA may be manually configured to join a particular WLAN, in which case it will actively seek out an AP (i.e. active scanning).

If authentication is enabled, the station must first go through the authentication process. After the STA has been successfully authenticated, the STA can then initiate the association process. The association process is the exchange of information about the STAs capabilities and those of the BSS. Association also allows other nodes to know the current location of the STA. An STA is capable of transmitting and receiving frames only after the association process is complete.

Extended Service Set (ESS)

Access Points may be interconnected using the switched network, creating what is referred to as an Extended Service Set (ESS). The ESS is comprised of overlapping BSS sets (cells) that are usually connected together by some wired medium (Distribution System). In most cases, the ESS allowsSTAs to roam. Roaming is the process of moving from one cell (BSS) to another without losing the wireless connection. Figure 9-3 below illustrates an ESS:

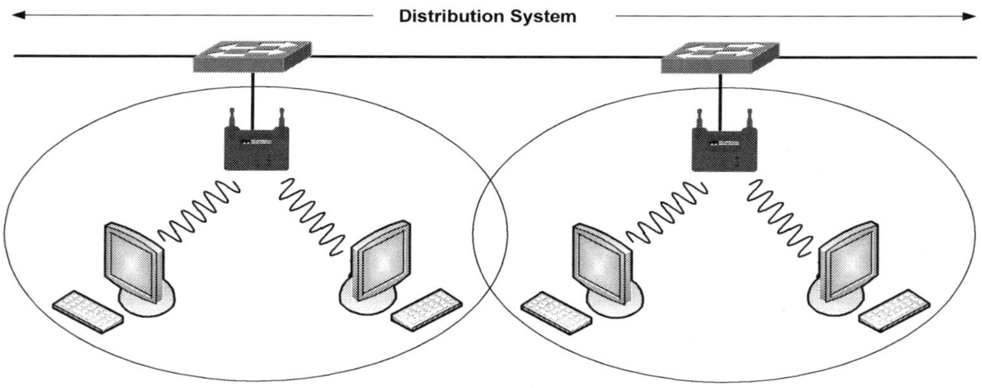

Fig. 9-3. Extended Service Set

Figure 9-3 illustrates a basic ESS that contains two cells (BSSs) connected together via the DS, which will be described next.

Distribution System (DS)

The Distribution System (DS) allows for the interconnection of the APs of multiple cells (BSSs). This allows for mobility because STAs can move from one BSS to another BSS. Although the DS could be any type of network, it is almost always a wired Ethernet LAN. However, it should be noted that it is also possible for APs to be interconnected without using wires. The DS includes the following three types of connections:

1. Integrated
2. Wired
3. Wireless

The integrated DS is comprised of a single AP in a standalone network. The wired DS, which is the most common, uses physical cabling to interconnect multiple APs. Finally, the wireless DS uses wireless connections to interconnect the APs.

IEEE 802.11 and the OSI Reference Model

The IEEE 802 standards define two separate layers for the Data Link layer (Layer 2) of the OSI Reference Model. These two layers are the Logical Link Control (LLC) and the Media Access Control (MAC) sublayers. The IEEE 802.11 standards cover the operation of the MAC sublayer and the Physical layer of the OSI Model. This is illustrated below in Figure 9-4:

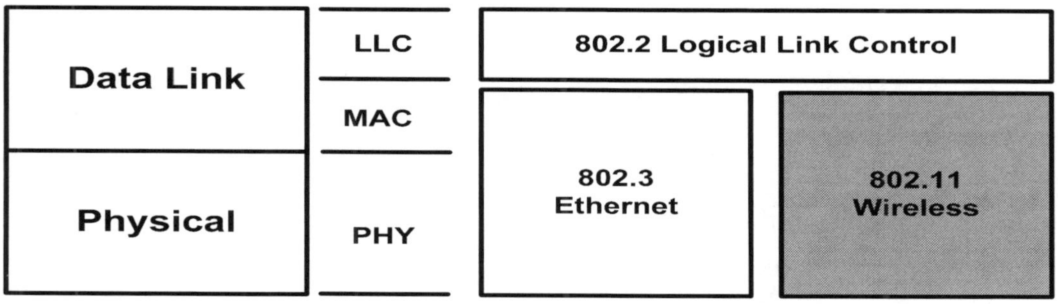

Fig. 9-4. IEEE 802.11 and the OSI Reference Model

The 802.11 frame consists of a 32-byte MAC header, a variable length body (0 to 2312 bytes), and 4-byte Frame Check Sequence (FCS). Although going into detail on the contents of the MAC frame format is beyond the scope of the SWITCH exam requirements, it is important to have a basic understanding of the fields contained in the MAC header, which include the following:

- The Frame Control field (2 bytes in length)
- The Duration / ID field (2 bytes in length)
- The Sequence Control field (2 bytes in length)
- The Four Address fields (6 bytes each)
- The Quality of Service field (2 bytes in length)

The Frame Control field contains control information that is used to define the type of 802.11 MAC frame. This field also provides information that is necessary for the following fields to understand how to process the frame. This information includes, but is not limited to, the frame type, whether the frame is fragmented, whether encryption and authentication are being used, or even whether the sending STA is in active mode or power-saving mode. The different 802.11 frames will be described in detail later in this chapter.

The Duration / ID field is used to indicate the remaining duration needed to receive the next frame transmission. Other STAs must look at the duration value contained in this field and wait that length of time before considering their own transmissions. The information that is contained is essentially used to avoid collisions in the wireless network. This will be described in detail later in this chapter.

The Sequence Control field contains the sequence number of each frame, as well as the number of each fragmented frame sent. This information is stored in the Sequence Number and Fragment Number subfields of the Sequence Control field.

802.11 uses 48-bit addresses, similar to the 802.3 standard. The MAC frame can include up to four addresses. The addresses used will depend on the frame type and include the following:

- The BSS Identifier (BSSID)
- The Destination Address (DA)
- The Source Address (SA)
- The Receiver Address (RA)
- The Transmitter Address (TA)

The BSS Identifier (BSSID) uniquely identifies each BSS. The BSSID is simply the MAC address of the AP. The Destination Address (DA) field contains the MAC address of the final destination for the frame. The Source Address (SA) field contains the source MAC address of the original source that initially originated and transmitted the frame. The Receiver Address (RA) field contains the MAC address of the next immediate STA on the wireless medium to receive the frame. Finally, the Transmitter Address (TA) field contains the MAC address of the STA that transmitted the frame onto the wireless medium.

The Quality of Service (QoS) field is based on the IEEE 802.11e amendment to the original 802.11 standard. The 802.11e amendment has since been incorporated into the published 802.11-2007 standard. While going into detail on WLAN QoS is beyond the scope of the SWITCH exam requirements, it is important to remember that Cisco Unified Wireless products support Wi-Fi MultiMedia (WMM), which is a QoS system based on IEEE 802.11e that has been published by the Wi-Fi Alliance.

Collision Avoidance: CSMA/CA

The IEEE defines different access methods for 802.3 and 802.11 standards. On wired Ethernet LANs, Carrier Sense Multiple Access/Collision Detection (CSMA/CD) is used to detect collisions. Collision detection is used to improve performance by terminating transmission as soon as a collision is detected and reducing the probability of a second collision on retry.

Unlike the 802.3 standards, the 802.11 standards seek to avoid, rather than to detect, collisions and thus employ Carrier Sense Multiple Access/Collision Avoidance (CSMA/CA). The basic premise behind collision avoidance is that any STA wishing to transmit a frame must first sense the medium, and if the medium is busy (e.g. because another STA is transmitting at that time), the STA must defer its transmission. However, if the medium is free, the STA is allowed to transmit the frame or frames as desired.

Collision avoidance works well when the medium is not heavily loaded (i.e. there are not a lot of STAs using the medium) because it allows STAs to transmit with minimal delay. However, there is still the possibility that collisions will occur because different STAs may sense the medium as free at the same time and decide to transmit at the same time. While such issues could be avoided by using collision detection mechanisms in conjunction with an exponential random backoff algorithm, collision detection mechanisms cannot be applied to WLANs.

This is because WLANs operate in half-duplex mode, since a single frequency is used to transmit and receive data. Because a single channel is used, it cannot always be assumed that all wireless STAs will be able to hear each other. For example, this might be because the transmitting station may have its receiver turned off when it is sending data. In CSMA/CD, the device would simply send a jam signal. However, if the receiver is off, the STA will never be able to tell when another STA is sending data at the same time as it, which would result in collisions. To overcome these issues, the IEEE 802.11 standard defines different MAC coordination functions. These are described in detail in the following sections.

MAC Sublayer Coordination Functions

Two types of coordination functions are used to ensure collision-free access to the wireless medium: the Distributed Coordination Function (DCF) and the Point Coordination Function (PCF). These two methods will be described in the following sections.

The Distributed Coordination Function (DCF)

The Distributed Coordination Function (DCF) is a MAC sublayer technique that employs CSMA/CA and an exponential random backoff algorithm to avoid collisions in IEEE 802.11-based standards. The DCF is used in IEEE 802.11 networks to manage access to the RF medium. The DCF is composed of the following two main components:

1. Interframe spaces
2. Random backoff

The interframe spaces (IFS) allow 802.11 to control which traffic gets first access to the channel after the carrier declares the channel to be free. In most cases, 802.11 management frames use SIFS and data frames use DIFS. 802.11 frame types are described in the following section. The following two interframe spaces will be described in this section:

- Short Interframe Space (SIFS)
- DCF Interframe Space (DIFS)

The Short Interframe Space (SIFS) is used to separate transmissions belonging to a single dialog. In other words, the SIFS is the time interval between the data frame and its acknowledgment. The DCF Interframe Space (DIFS) is used by an STA that is ready to start a new transmission.

DCF requires all IEEE 802.11 STAs to sense the status of the medium and wait a short amount of time before transmitting. Wireless stations provide an estimate of the amount of time that is required to send a frame by including a duration value within the IEEE 802.11 header. Other STAs using the medium must look at the duration value contained in this field and wait that length of time before initiating their own transmissions.

If the medium is busy during the DIFS interval, STAs will defer their transmission. If the medium is idle for the DIFS duration, then STAs are allowed to transmit a frame. The potential issue here, though, is that all of the other STAs might decide to transmit at the same time once the duration time has elapsed, which would result in a collision, or multiple collisions, on the wireless network. This issue is addressed with the random backoff algorithm.

The Duration / ID field contains time slots, which indicate the amount of time needed to send a frame of a particular size. The time slot is defined in such a way that ensures that all STAs are capable of determining whether another STA has accessed the media before. Each STA selects a random number of time slots that it will wait before transmitting a frame. However, even though STAs select random integers, it is still possible that a collision might occur. If that does indeed happen, the station will increase the maximum number for the random integer exponentially. The DCF is illustrated below in Figure 9-5:

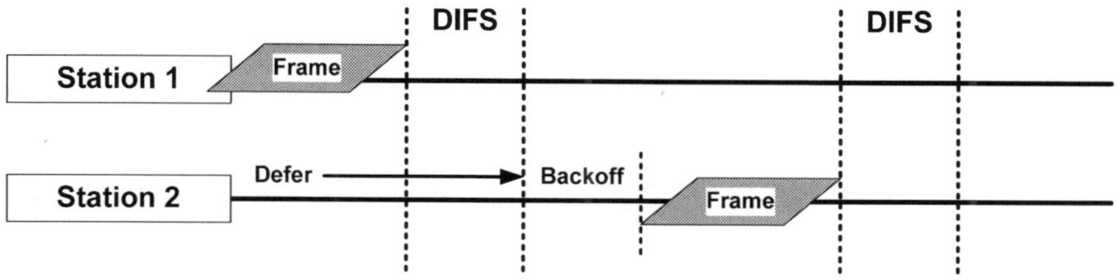

Fig. 9-5. The Distributed Coordination Function

Figure 9-5 provides a very basic illustration of the DCF. Referencing this diagram, Station 1 successfully sends a frame. Although Station 2 also wants to send a frame, it must defer to Station 1 since it is already using the medium.

After Station 1 has completed sending the frame, Station 2 must still defer to the DIFS and cannot immediately begin transmitting. When the DIFS is complete, Station 2 decrements the backoff counter and, when it reaches 0, it can send the frame.

If there were more STAs using the medium that wanted to send frames, they would all have to wait for Station 1 to complete sending the frame and then defer to the DIFS. Once the DIFS was complete, the STAs would begin to decrement the backoff counter, once every time slot. The first STA to decrement its backoff counter to zero can then begin to transmit. The other remaining STAs must stop decrementing their backoff counters and defer until the frame is transmitted and a DIFS has passed, and then the entire process is repeated over and over again.

The Point Coordination Function (PCF)

The Point Coordination Function (PCF) is used by the AP, or Point Coordinator, to coordinate communication within the wireless network. The AP issues polling requests to the STAs about data transmissions and sends Contention Free-Poll (CF-Poll) packets to each station, one at a time, to give them the right to send a packet. It is important to remember that this mode is optional and only very few APs or Wi-Fi adapters actually implement it. However, it should also be noted that a device that is able to use PCF is one that is able to participate in a method to provide limited QoS (for time-sensitive data) within the network.

If the PCF is employed, the PCF Interframe Space (PIFS) is used by the AP to gain access to the medium before any other STA. The PCF-enabled AP waits for PIFS duration rather than DIFS duration before it occupies the wireless medium. The PIFS duration is less than DIFS but greater than SIFS (i.e. DIFS > PIFS > SIFS). Channel access in PCF mode is centralized while it is distributed between STAs in DCF mode. The PCF is located directly above the Distributed Coordinate Function (DCF) in the IEEE 802.11 MAC sublayer architecture, as illustrated below in Figure 9-6:

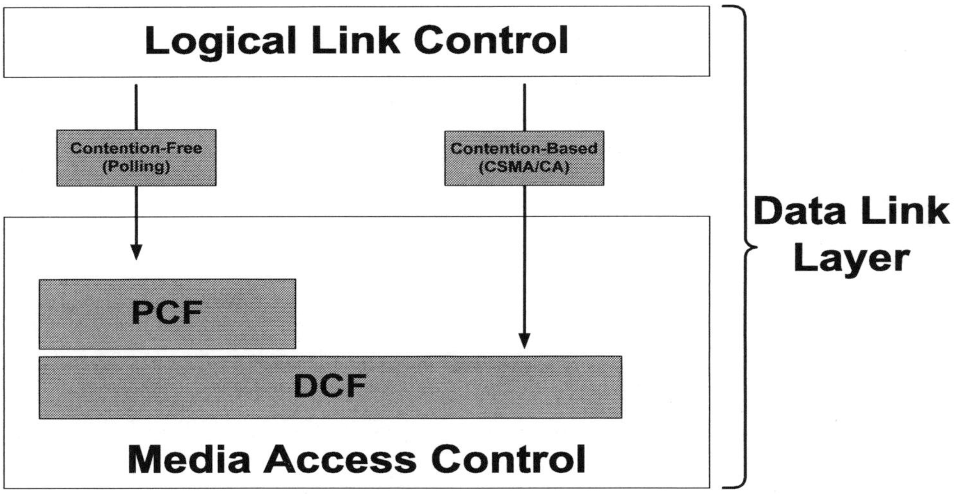

Fig. 9-6. The PCF and DCF MAC Sublayer Hierarchy

The Wireless Network Hidden Node Problem

Wireless networking is susceptible to the hidden node problem, which occurs when an STA is visible from the AP, but not from other STAs that are also communicating with the AP. This typically occurs with STAs that are at the far end of the AP's range. This leads to difficulties in media access control because the STAs cannot sense the carrier and both send packets to the AP at the same time, which results in collisions. This concept is illustrated below in Figure 9-7:

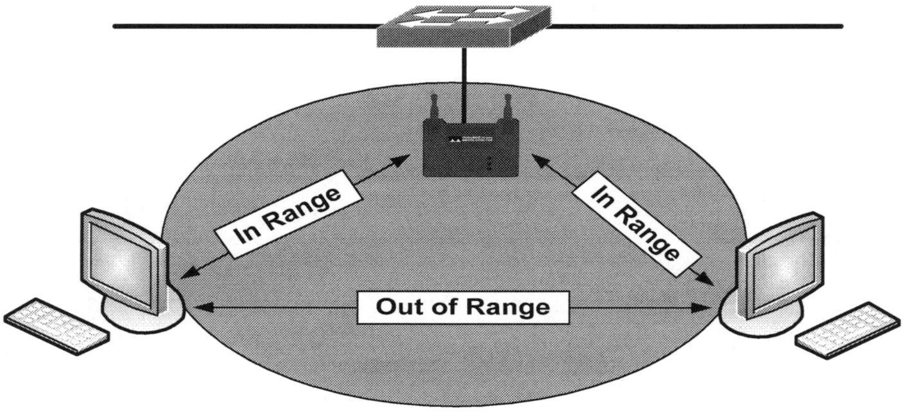

Fig. 9-7. The Hidden Node Problem

Referencing Figure 9-7, the two STAs can see the AP but are unable to see each other because they reside at the very end of the AP's range. Because the nodes cannot see each other, they may send frames to the AP at the same time. Because the STAs are hidden, CSMA/CA will not work because the STAs are unable to sense the carrier and collisions will occur.

To address this issue, and reduce the probability of STAs colliding because they cannot hear each other, the IEEE defines a Virtual Carrier Sense mechanism. This mechanism uses the Ready To Send (RTS) and Clear To Send (CTS) acknowledgment and handshake packets to partly overcome the hidden node problem.

With the RTS and CTS exchange, STAs must first request access to the medium from the AP with an RTS message. The RTS packet includes the source, destination, and duration information. The STA will refrain from accessing the medium and transmitting its data packets until it receives the CTS from the AP. The CTS is a response control packet from the AP that also includes duration information. The RTS originator then proceeds and sends frames.

All other stations that receive the CTS set their Virtual Carrier Sense indicator, commonly referred to as the Network Allocation Vector (NAV), for the given duration and will use that information along with the physical carrier sense when sensing the medium.

IEEE 802.11 Frame Types

The 802.11 standard uses the following three main types of frames:

1. Control frames
2. Management frames
3. Data frames

Control Frames

The IEEE 802.11 standard uses control frames to control access to the medium. The following are the most common control frames:

- Ready (Request) To Send (RTS)
- Clear To Send (CTS)
- Acknowledgement (ACK)

The RTS/CTS function is optional and is employed to prevent frame collisions when hidden STAs have associations with the same AP. The RTS/CTS frame exchange is part of the two-way handshake necessary before an STA can send a data frame. The STA sends an RTS frame to the AP requesting access to the medium. The AP responds to an RTS with a CTS frame, providing clearance for the requesting STA to send a data frame. Other STAs that receive the CTS will not send any frames for the duration within the CTS.

After receiving a data frame, the receiving STA will utilize an error-checking process to detect the presence of errors. The receiving STA will send an ACK frame to the sending STA if no errors are found. Receipt of the acknowledgment tells the original sender STA of the frame that no collisions occurred. However, if the sending STA doesn't receive an ACK after a period of time it assumes a collision has occurred and will retransmit the frame.

Management Frames

802.11 management frames enable stations to establish and maintain communications. There are several management frame subtypes, including the following:

- The Beacon Frame (Beacons)
- The Probe Request Frame
- The Probe Response Frame
- The Association Request Frame
- The Association Response Frame
- The Disassociation Request Frame
- The Re-association Request Frame
- The Re-association Response Frame
- The Authentication Request Frame
- The Authentication Response Frame
- The De-authentication Frame

A beacon frame is periodically sent out by an Access Point (AP) to announce its presence and relay information, such as timestamp, SSID, and other parameters regarding the AP to STAs that are within range. STAs continually scan all 802.11 radio channels and listen to beacons as the basis for choosing with which access point is best to associate. In IBSS networks, beacon generation is distributed among the stations.

A client sends a probe request frame when he or she needs to obtain information from another station or to seek out an available AP. Another station will respond with a probe response frame containing capability information, supported data rates, etc. after it receives a probe request frame. Alternatively, an AP can also respond with a probe response frame that it sends to advertise its existence to the client.

The association request and response frames are sent by the STA and the AP, respectively, following the probe request and probe response messages, or after a passive STA discovers an AP by listening to beacon frames. The STA sends an association request to the AP and the AP responds with either an acceptance or rejection association frame. If the association request from the STA is accepted, the STA and the AP are associated and the STA is then able to transmit and receive frames. A station sends a disassociation frame to another station if it wishes to terminate the association with the AP.

If a station roams away from the currently associated AP and finds another AP with a stronger beacon signal, it will send a re-association frame to the new AP. The AP responds with a re-association response frame containing an acceptance or rejection notice to the requesting STA.

Following association, IEEE 802.11 authentication occurs at the AP. This happens before any upper layer authentication, such as 802.1x (dot1x). Authentication requires that a station establish its identity before sending frames. This process occurs every time a station connects to a network but does not provide any measure of network security. In other words, 802.11 authentication is simply the first step in a handshake process for network attachment that is not mutual, meaning only the AP authenticates the station and not vice versa. There is no user data encryption at this level.

The STA initiates authentication via the authentication request frame to the AP. The AP then responds with an authentication response frame accepting or rejecting the STA. A de-authentication request frame is sent by the STA when it wishes to terminate secure communication or by the AP. Once a station receives a de-authentication frame from the AP it is disconnected from the network. Figure 9-8 below shows the exchange of management frames between the Access Point and an STA using passive scanning to synchronize with the AP:

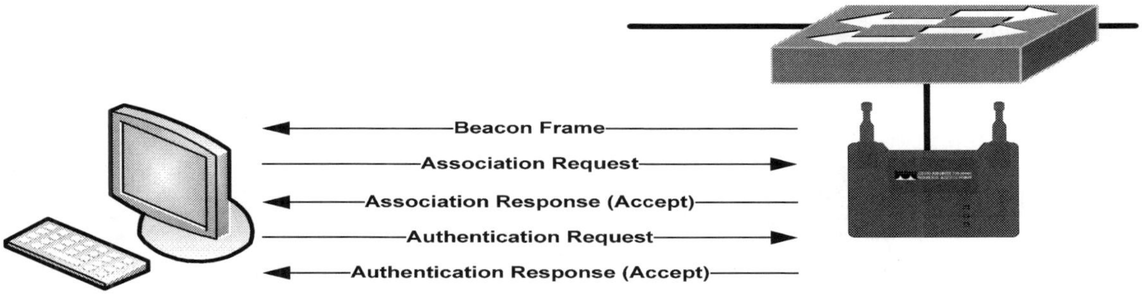

Fig. 9-8: Passive Scanning

Figure 9-9 below shows the exchange of management frames between the AP and an STA using active scanning to synchronize with the AP:

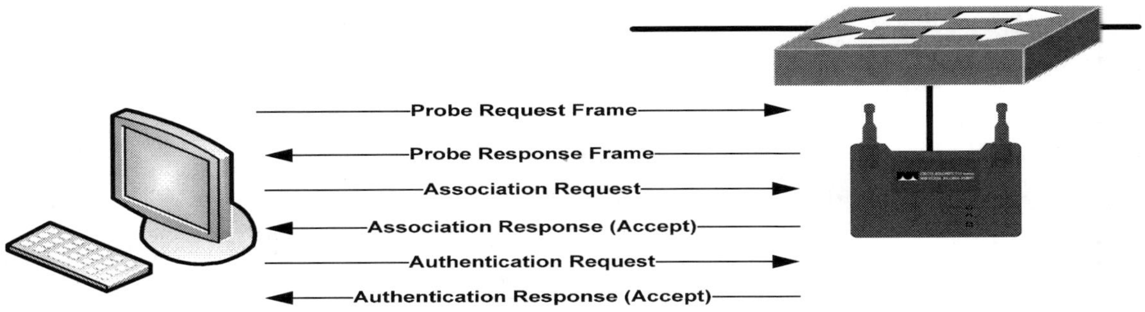

Fig. 9-9: Active Scanning

Data Frames

Data frames are sent by any STA and contain higher layer protocol information or data. There are several types of Data frames. While going into the different types of frames is beyond the scope of the SWITCH exam requirements, Table 9-1 below shows the Data frames used in Contention-free (i.e. Polling and Point Coordination Function) and Contention-based (i.e. Distributed Coordination Function and CSMA/CA) environments and whether the frames have data.

Table 9-1. IEEE 802.11 Data Frame Types and Subtypes

Type	Subtype	Contention-Free	Contention-Based	Contains Data
Data	Data		Yes	Yes
Data	Data + CF-Ack	Yes		Yes
Data	Data + CF-Poll	Yes		Yes
Data	Data + CF-Ack + CF-Poll	Yes		Yes
Data	Null Function		Yes	No
Data	CF-Ack	Yes		No
Data	CF-Poll	Yes		No
Data	CF-Ack + CF-Poll	Yes		No

Wireless LAN Standards

At the physical (PHY) layer, IEEE 802.11 defines a series of encoding and transmission schemes for wireless communications, the most common of which are the Frequency Hopping Spread Spectrum (FHSS), Direct Sequence Spread Spectrum (DSSS), and Orthogonal Frequency Division Multiplexing (OFDM) transmission schemes. Although Infra Red (IR) also exists at this layer, very little development of this standard has occurred due to line-of-sight limitations. The 802.11 standards described in this section are as follows:

- IEEE 802.11 (original)
- IEEE 802.11b
- IEEE 802.11a
- IEEE 802.11g
- IEEE 802.11n

NOTE: Going into detail on FHSS, DSSS, and OFDM is beyond the scope of the SWITCH exam requirements. Also, keep in mind that you are not required to go into detail on the different 802.11 standards; however, you are expected to demonstrate basic familiarity with the standards and understand the differences between them.

IEEE 802.11 (Original)

The original IEEE 802.11 standard was released in 1997 and clarified in 1999. This standard defined wireless LANs that provided up to 2 Mbps of throughput. The original standard specified the FHSS and DHSS transmission schemes and the S-Band Industrial, Scientific, and Medical (ISM) frequency band, which operates in the frequency range of 2.4 to 2.5 GHz. This standard is now considered obsolete because this throughput rate is too slow for the majority of modern applications. The original 802.11 standard is also sometimes referred to as IEEE 802.11 legacy.

IEEE 802.11b

The 802.11b standard is an extension to 802.11 that operates in the same unregulated 2.4-GHz band as the original 802.11 standard. While this reduces the overall cost of the WLAN, it also means that this standard is susceptible to interference from other devices, which include microwave ovens, cordless telephones, and baby monitors, for example. Devices operating on 802.11b use DSSS modulation for higher speeds. The data rates on a channel can vary according to client capabilities and conditions. However, the only possible data rates are 1, 2, 5.5, and 11 Mbps. The 5.5 Mbps and 11 Mbps are two new speeds added to the original specification.

The 2.4-GHz band consists of 14 channels, each 22-MHz wide. In North America, the Federal Communications Commission (FCC) allows channels 1 through 11. Most of Europe can use channels 1 through 13. In Japan, only channel 14 is used. APs or clients use a spectral mask or a template to filter out a single channel based around a center frequency.

While going into specific detail on 802.11b channel separation is beyond the scope of the SWITCH exam requirements, it is important to know that even though 11 channels are supported in the U.S., there are only three non-overlapping channels available: Channels 1, 6, and 11. It is therefore recommended that APs that are located near each use one of these three non-overlapping channels to minimize the effects of interference.

IEEE 802.11a

The IEEE 802.11a standard is an extension to 802.11 that applies to WLANs and provides up to 54 Mbps. This standard uses OFDM and does away with the spread spectrum. As a result, it is not compatible with 802.11b or 802.11g and therefore this standard is seldom used any more.

802.11a equipment operates at 5 GHz. This higher frequency range means that 802.11 signals are absorbed more readily by walls and other solid objects in their path due to their smaller wavelength, and, as a result, they cannot penetrate as far as 802.11b signals. The FCC has allocated 300 MHz of RF spectrum for unlicensed operation in the 5 GHz block referred to as the Unlicensed National Information Infrastructure (U-NII) band. This is broken down into three smaller working bands, which are described below.

The first 100-MHz band (5.15 to 5.25 GHz) in the lower section is primarily for indoor use. This band is restricted to a maximum power output of 50 milliwatts (mW). The second 100-MHz band (5.25 to 5.35 GHz) in the middle section is for both indoor and outdoor use. This band has a maximum power output of 250 mW. The top 100-MHz band is delegated for outdoor usage and has a maximum power output of 1 watt.

IEEE 802.11g

The 802.11g standard also works in the same 2.4 GHz range as 802.11b. IEEE 802.11g operates at a bit rate as high as 54 Mbps but uses the S-Band ISM and OFDM. However, unlike 802.11a, 802.11g is backward compatible with 802.11b and can operate at the 802.11b bit rates and use DSSS.

Like 802.11a, 802.11g uses 54 Mbps in ideal conditions and the slower speeds of 48 Mbps, 36 Mbps, 24 Mbps, 18 Mbps, 12 Mbps, and 6 Mbps in less-than-ideal conditions.

IEEE 802.11n

IEEE 802.11n improves on 802.11a and 802.11g maximum data rate with a significant increase in the rate from 54 Mbps to approximately 600 Mbps. The 802.11n standard includes several enhancements to the previously described 802.11 standards. These new enhancements include the following:

- Multiple-Input Multiple-Output (MIMO) uses the diversity and duplication of signals using the multiple transmit and receive antennas, which allows it to resolve more information than possible using a single antenna.

- 40-MHz operation bonds adjacent channels combined with some of the reserved channel space between the two to more than double the data rate. This allows for a doubling of the PHY data rate over a single 20-MHz channel.

- Frame aggregation at the MAC sublayer reduces the overhead of 802.11 by aggregating multiple packets together. Frame aggregation may be performed by aggregating MAC Service Data Units (MSDUs) or MAC Protocol Data Units (PDUs). The former method is referred to as A-MSDU while the latter is referred to as A-MPDU.

- Backward compatibility, which makes it possible for 802.11 a/b/g and 802.11n devices to co-exist, thereby allowing customers to phase in their AP or client migrations over time.

The Cisco Unified Wireless Network

Having learned about the different physical and logical components pertaining to the IEEE 802.11 wireless standards, it is important to understand how all these various components, and more, are integrated into the Cisco Unified Wireless Network, which combines the best elements of wireless and wired networking to deliver scalable, manageable, and secure WLANs.

The Cisco Unified Wireless Network provides an integrated end-to-end solution that addresses all layers of the WLAN, from client devices and APs to the network infrastructure. It also includes network management and the delivery of wireless mobility services integration, as well as world-wide, 24-hour product support. The Cisco Unified Wireless Network described in this section is composed of the following five interconnected elements that work together to deliver a unified, enterprise-class WLAN solution:

1. Client Devices
2. Access Points and Wireless Bridges
3. Network Unification
4. Network Management
5. Mobility Services

Client Devices

Client devices are secure devices that work right out of the box. These include Cisco-compatible client devices and Wi-Fi tags, Cisco Secure Services Client, and Cisco Aironet client devices. Compatible-client devices are simply devices that have been verified to be interoperable with a Cisco wireless LAN (WLAN) infrastructure.

NOTE: Wi-Fi tags are small devices that are attached to key assets and resources to allow their location to be determined on the system. The Wi-Fi tags broadcast out a signal which is picked up directly by the wireless LAN and used to calculate the location. This allows the asset to be identified and the location displayed on the system.

The Cisco Compatible Extensions program ensures the widespread availability of client devices that are interoperable with a Cisco WLAN infrastructure and take advantage of Cisco innovations for enhanced security, mobility, QoS, and network management. Cisco Compatible client devices are sold and supported by their manufacturers, not by Cisco.

The Cisco Secure Services Client (SSC) is a software supplicant that helps the user to deploy a single authentication framework to access both wired and wireless networks. It provides 802.1x user and device authentication, and manages user and device identity and the network-access protocols required for secure access.

Cisco Aironet Wireless LAN Client Adapters quickly connect desktop and mobile computing devices to the wireless LAN in 802.11a-, 802.11b-, or 802.11g-compliant networks. These wireless adapters are available in CardBus, PCMCIA, and PCI form factors.

Access Points and Wireless Bridges

The Cisco Aironet family offers a range of enterprise-class robust and high performance Access Points and Wireless Bridges designed to fit the needs of a variety of installation environments and requirements. A Wireless Bridge can connect another Wireless Bridge and transparently bridge two networks, in the same manner that is performed by a transparent bridge in a wired Ethernet network. A Wireless Bridge can also connect wireless clients at the same time. However, an AP connects wireless clients. Although another AP may be connected, it simply acts only as a repeater for wireless client connections.

Cisco Aironet APs provide network access for both indoor and outdoor environments. Although Cisco Aironet APs can operate in Autonomous mode, which will be described later in this chapter, it is required that they operate in Lightweight mode when incorporated in the Cisco Unified Wireless Network. Lightweight APs are dynamically configured and managed via the Lightweight Access Point Protocol (LWAPP).

Cisco Aironet LAPs connect to Cisco Wireless LAN Controllers (WLCs) and provide RF access via a unique split-MAC architecture, wherein some timing-critical functions are managed within the AP and other functions are managed at the controller. In addition to this, all Cisco Aironet LAPs support mobility services, such as fast secure roaming for voice and location services for real-time network visibility. Location and management services are supported by the Cisco Wireless Location Appliance and the Cisco Wireless Control System (WCS). These devices and terms will be described later in this chapter.

Network Unification

Network unification involves the integration of the Cisco Unified Wireless Network into all major Cisco switching and routing platforms through secure, innovative WLCs. The following WLCs are available from Cisco and can be used to meet different requirements:

- The Cisco 4400 and 2000 Series Wireless LAN Controllers
- The Cisco Catalyst 6500 Series Wireless Services Module (WiSM)
- The Cisco Catalyst 3750 Series Integrated Wireless LAN Controllers
- The Cisco Wireless LAN Controller Module (WLCM) for ISRs

The WLC details in this guide will be restricted to 4400 series controllers. A WiSM is a WLC module that is designed specifically for Cisco's Catalyst 6500 series switches that can support up to 300 APs per module. The Catalyst 3750 and WLCMs are integrated controllers that are supported by Catalyst 3750 series switches and Cisco ISRs, such as the 3800 series switches.

Network Management

Network management ensures that the same level of security, scalability, reliability, ease of deployment, and management that is available for wired LANs is also available for wireless LANs. The Cisco Wireless Control System (WCS) allows for comprehensive lifecycle management of 802.11n and 802.11a/b/g enterprise-class wireless networks. WCS enables administrators to successfully plan, deploy, monitor, troubleshoot, and report on indoor and outdoor wireless networks.

Mobility Services

Mobility services provide support for unified cellular and voice over WLAN services, as well as advanced threat detection, identity networking, location-based security, asset tracking, and guest access. These services are enabled by the Cisco Unified Wireless Network as part of the Cisco Service-Oriented Network Architecture (SONA). SONA is an open framework for network-based services used by enterprise applications to drive business results. This framework includes the following three interconnected layers:

1. Applications layer
2. Core common services
3. Physical infrastructure

The applications layer includes enterprise software the addresses the needs of organizational processes and data flow. This includes commercial, composite, and internally developed applications, as well as Software as a Service (SaaS), which is simply externally hosted software that is provided as a licensed service to customers.

Core common services are a network-based functionality that creates a common quality, ability, or feature that can be used by higher-level applications. Common core services include application delivery, real-time communication, management, mobility, security, transportation, and virtualization services.

The physical infrastructure is comprised of the network, servers, clients, and storage hardware devices or systems that are deployed throughout the enterprise.

The Cisco Wireless LAN Solution

The Cisco Wireless LAN solution is designed to provide 802.11 wireless networking solutions for enterprises and service providers. It consists of WLCs and their associated LAPs.

Wireless LAN Controllers are responsible for system-wide wireless LAN functions, such as security policies, intrusion prevention, RF management, QoS, and mobility. They work in conjunction with Cisco APs and the WCS to support business-critical wireless applications. WLCs are responsible for system-wide WLAN functions, such as the following:

- Integrated Intrusion Prevention System (IPS)
- Zero-Touch Deployment of Lightweight Access Points (LAPs)
- Real-time Radio Frequency (RF) management
- Wireless LAN Redundancy
- Dynamic Channel Assignment for each LAP
- Dynamic Client Load Balancing across LAPs
- Dynamic LAP Transmit Power Optimization
- Wireless LAN Security Management

NOTE: While going into detail on all of these functions is beyond the scope of the SWITCH exam requirements, you should still be familiar with the functions listed above.

WLCs communicate with controller-based APs over any Layer 2 (Ethernet) or Layer 3 (IP) infrastructure using the LWAPP, which is an IETF draft protocol. A LAP discovers a controller with the use of LWAPP discovery mechanisms. The LAP sends an LWAPP Join Request to the WLC and the controller sends the LAP an LWAPP Join Response, which allows the AP to join the controller.

When using LWAPP, although the LAP is under the control of the centralized WLC, the actual processing of data and management protocols and Access Point capabilities is divided between the LAP and the centralized WLC (the split-MAC architecture).

NOTE: In controller software release 5.2 or later, Cisco LAPs use the IETF standard Control and Provisioning of Wireless Access Points protocol (CAPWAP) in order to communicate between the controller and other LAPs on the network. Controller software releases prior to 5.2 use the LWAPP for these communications.

CAPWAP, which is based on LWAPP, is a standard, interoperable protocol that enables a controller to manage a collection of wireless APs. LAPs can discover and join a CAPWAP controller. The one exception is for Layer 2 deployments, which are not supported by CAPWAP. Additionally, CAPWAP and LWAPP controllers may be deployed in the same network. The CAPWAP-enabled software allows APs to join a controller that runs either CAPWAP or LWAPP.

When the LAP joins to the controller, it downloads the controller software if the revisions on the LAP and controller do not match. Following that, the LAP is completely under the control of the controller and is unable to function independently of the controller.

LWAPP secures the control communication between the LAP and the controller by means of a secure key distribution, which requires already provisioned X.509 digital certificates on both the LAP and the controller. Factory-installed certificates are referenced with the term 'MIC,' which is an acronym for Manufacturing Installed Certificate.

REAL WORLD IMPLEMENTATION

Cisco Aironet APs that shipped before July 18, 2005, do not have a MIC, so these APs create a self-signed certificate (SSC) when they are upgraded in order to operate in Lightweight mode. Controllers are programmed to accept SSCs for the authentication of specific APs.

The LWAPP Discovery Process

Despite the split-MAC architecture, it is important to remember that Lightweight Access Points (LAPs) cannot act independently of the WLC. The WLC manages the LAP configurations and firmware. The LAPs are zero-touch deployed; meaning that there is no individual configuration of LAPs required when they are deployed into the WLAN.

In order for the WLC to manage the LAP, the LAP should discover the controller and register with the WLC. After the LAP has registered to the WLC, LWAPP messages are exchanged and the AP initiates a firmware download from the WLC if there is a version mismatch between the AP and the WLC. This allows the LAP to sync with the WLC.

Following the sync, the WLC provisions the LAP with the configurations that are specific to the WLANs so that the LAP can accept client associations. These WLAN-specific configurations include the Service Set Identifier (SSID), any additional required security parameters, and 802.11 parameters, such as the data rate, radio channels to use, and the power levels. The following sequence of events must occur in order for an LAP to register to a WLC:

1. The LAPs issue a DHCP Discovery Request to get an IP address. This only happens if the LAP has not been configured with a static IP address.

2. The LAP sends LWAPP discovery request messages to the WLCs. If Layer 2 LWAPP mode is supported on the LAP, the LAP broadcasts an LWAPP discovery message in a Layer 2 LWAPP frame. However, if the LAP or the WLC does not support Layer 2 LWAPP mode, the LAP attempts a Layer 3 LWAPP WLC discovery. The LAPs use the Layer 3 discovery algorithm only if the Layer 2 discovery method is not supported or if the Layer 2 discovery method fails. The LWAPP Layer 3 WLC discovery algorithm repeats until at least one WLC is found and joined. It is important to remember this order of processing.

3. Any available WLC that receives the LWAPP DHCP Discovery Request responds with an LWAPP Discovery Response.

4. If the LAP receives more than one LWAPP Discovery Response, it selects the WLC to join, which is typically the first WLC to respond to the LAP.

5. The LAP then sends an LWAPP Join Request to the WLC and the WLC validates the LAP, and then sends an LWAPP Join Response to the LAP.

6. The LAP validates the WLC, which completes the Discovery and Join process. The LWAPP Join process includes mutual authentication and encryption key derivation, which is used to secure both the join process and LWAPP control messages between the LAP and WLC.

7. The LAP registers with the WLC and can begin accepting client associations.

Wireless LAN Roaming

One of the most significant advantages of WLANs over wired LANs is roaming, or mobility. Roaming is a wireless LAN client's ability to maintain its association seamlessly from one AP to another securely and with as little latency as possible.

When a wireless client associates and authenticates to an AP, the APs controller places an entry for that client in its client database. This entry includes the client's MAC and IP addresses, security context and associations, QoS contexts, the WLAN, and the associated AP. The controller uses this information to forward frames and manage traffic to and from the wireless client. The Cisco WLAN supports the following three types of roaming:

1. Intra-controller roaming
2. Inter-controller roaming
3. Inter-subnet roaming

Intra-controller roaming occurs when a wireless client roams from one AP to another while both APs are joined to the same controller. This is illustrated below in Figure 9-10:

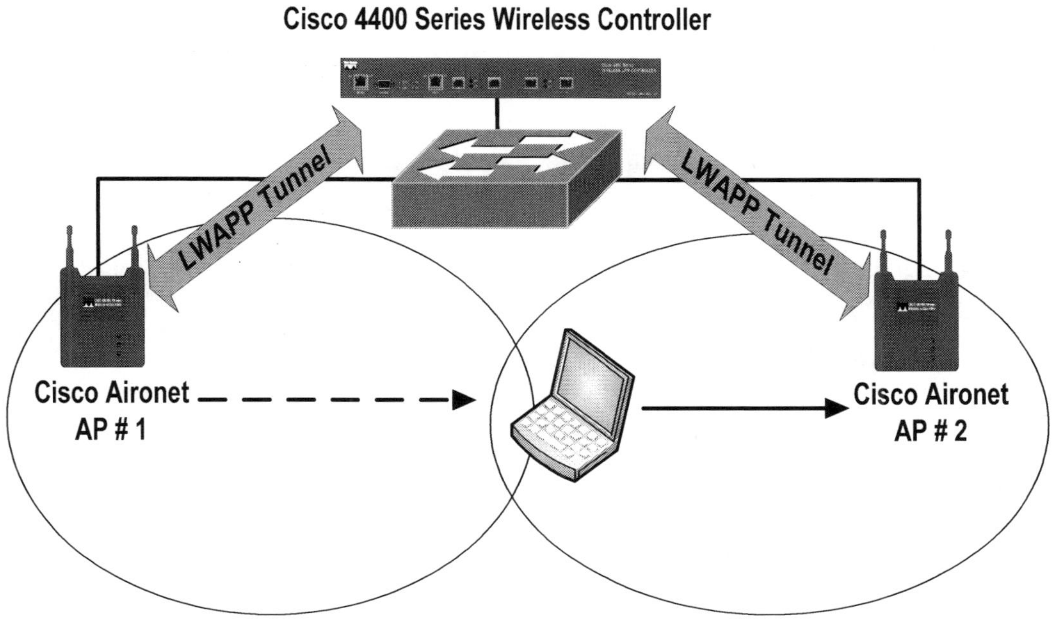

Fig. 9-10. Intra-Controller Roaming

Figure 9-10 illustrates a wireless client that has just moved from AP # 1 to AP # 2. Because both APs are under the administration of the same controller, when the wireless client is associated with AP # 2, the controller simply updates the client database with the newly associated AP. If necessary, new security context and associations are established as well.

Inter-controller roaming occurs when the client roams from an AP joined to one controller to an AP joined to a different controller. When the client associates to an AP joined to a new controller, the new controller exchanges mobility messages with the original controller, and the client database entry is moved to the new controller. New security context and associations are established if necessary, and the client database entry is updated for the new AP. This process is transparent or invisible to the user. This is illustrated below in Figure 9-11:

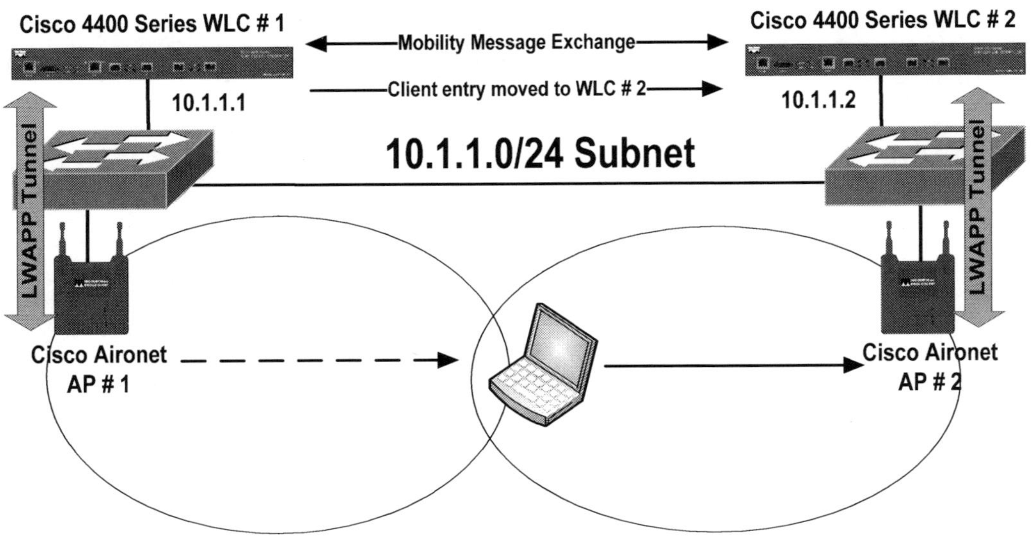

Fig. 9-11. Inter-Controller Roaming

Referencing Figure 9-11, the client roams from AP # 1, which is joined to WLC # 1, to AP # 2, which is joined to WLC # 2. Given that the WLAN interfaces of the WLCs are on the same subnet, as illustrated in the diagram, inter-controller roaming is permitted.

This is performed by the exchange of mobility and packets between the WLCs. These packets are exchanged through EtherIP packets (which are IP protocol 97). The client entry is then moved from the client database of WLC # 1 and added to the client database of WLC # 2.

Inter-subnet roaming is somewhat similar to inter-controller roaming, with some differences. With inter-subnet roaming, the WLAN interfaces of the WLCs are on different subnets. In addition to this, inter-subnet roaming does not move the client database entry to the new controller. Instead, the original controller marks the client with an anchor entry in its local database, and this is then copied to the new controller client database and marked as a foreign entry. The client keeps the IP address and the entire process is transparent. Inter-subnet roaming is illustrated below in Figure 9-12:

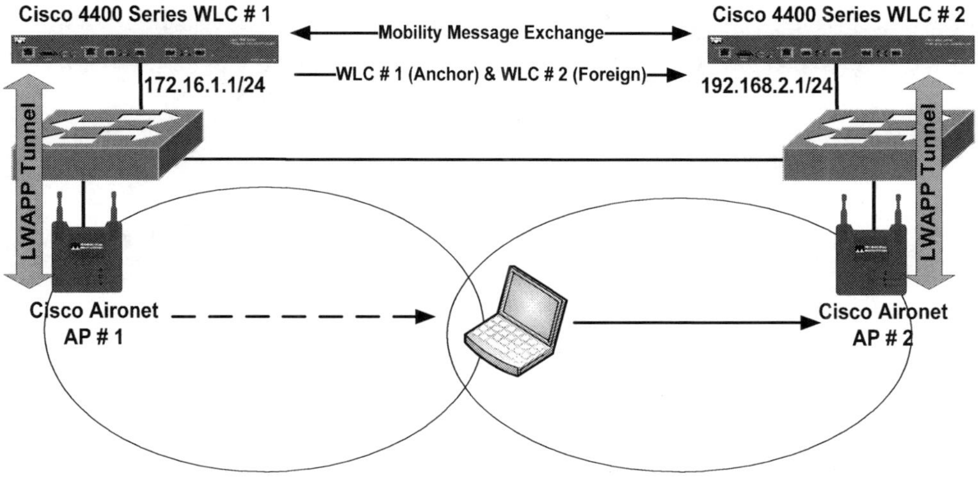

Fig. 9-12. Inter-Subnet Roaming

One very important aspect to remember regarding inter-subnet roaming is that it results in asynchronous routing for the client. When traffic is sent to the client, it is received by the anchor controller, which then forwards the traffic to the foreign controller in an Ethernet-over-IP (EtherIP) tunnel. When the foreign controller receives this traffic, it forwards it to the client. This is shown below in Figure 9-13:

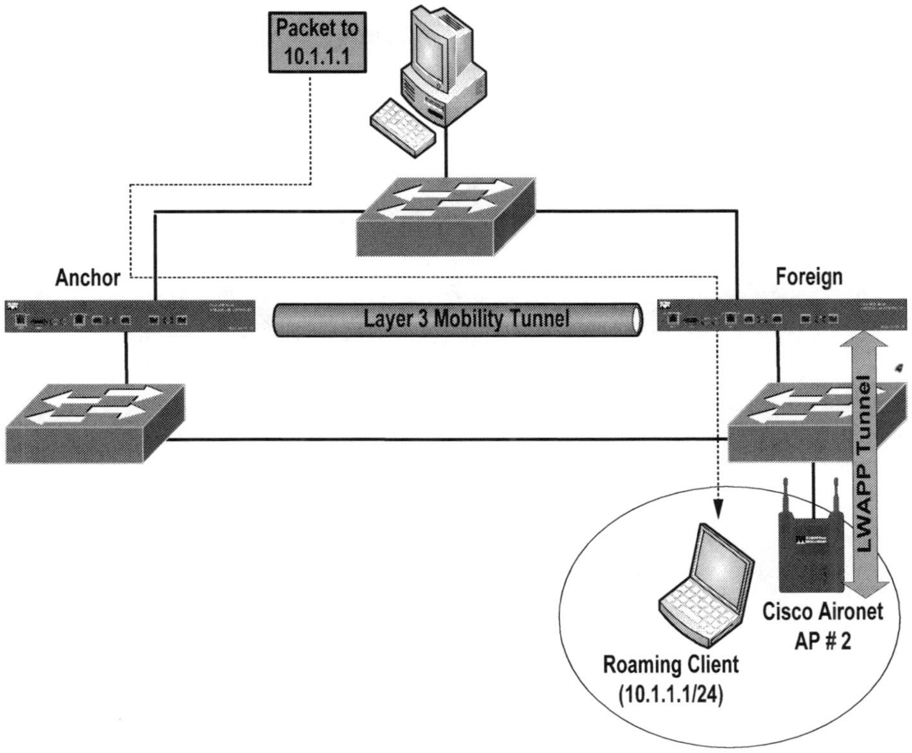

Fig. 9-13. Sending Data to an Inter-Subnet Roaming Client

However, when the client sends traffic, it is sent to the foreign controller, which forwards it to the destination through the distribution network. This is illustrated below in Figure 9-14:

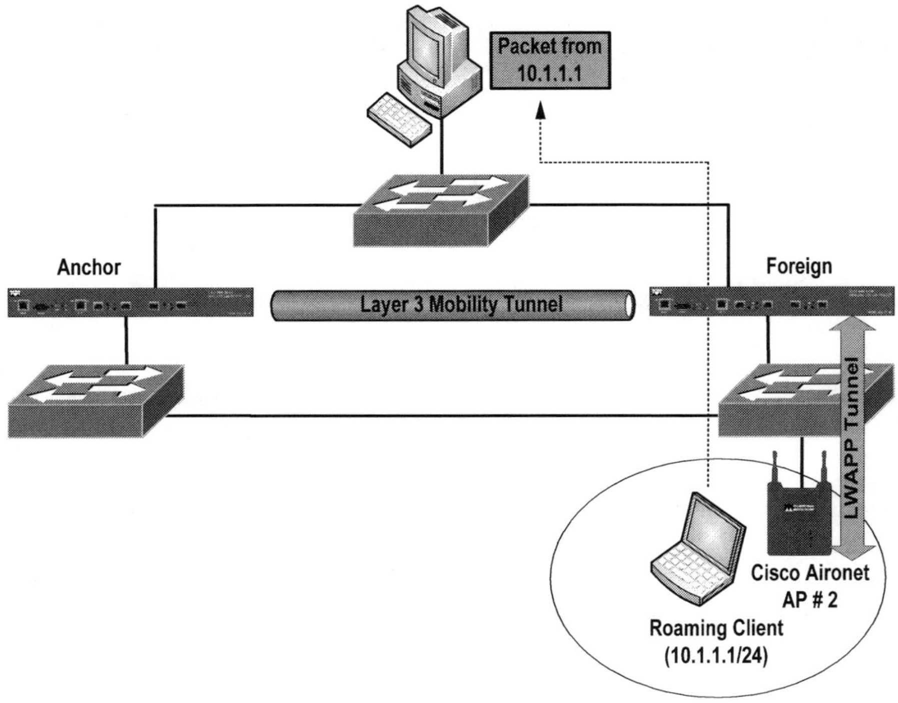

Fig. 9-14. Forwarding Data from an Inter-Subnet Roaming Client

If the client again roams to a new foreign controller, the client database entry is moved from the original foreign controller to the new foreign controller, but the original anchor controller is always maintained, as is the asynchronous routing. When the client moves back to the original controller, it becomes local again and there is no longer any asynchronous routing.

When implementing inter-subnet roaming, ensure that the WLANs on both anchor and foreign controllers have the same network access privileges. Additionally, disable source-based routing and avoid firewalls, as these may cause client network connectivity issues.

Mobility Groups

In order to support roaming, Mobility Groups must be configured. A Mobility Group is a group of WLCs in a network with the same Mobility Group name. These WLCs can dynamically share context and state of client devices, WLC loading information, and can also forward data traffic among them, which enables inter-controller wireless LAN roaming and controller redundancy.

Mobility Groups must be manually (statically) defined by the administrators. The IP and the MAC addresses of the WLCs that belong to the same Mobility Group can be configured on each of the

WLCs individually or via the WCS. Irrespective of the method used, keep in mind that WLCs can only be configured in one Mobility Group.

Although the configuration of Mobility Groups is beyond the scope of the SWITCH exam requirements, the following is a list of prerequisites required to configure Mobility Groups:

- All WLCs must be configured for the same LWAPP Layer 2 or Layer 3 transport mode
- All devices must have IP connectivity with each other via their management interfaces
- All WLCs must be configured with the same Mobility Group name
- All WLCs must be configured with the same virtual interface IP address
- Each WLC must be configured with the MAC and IP addresses of the other WLCs

Lightweight Access Point Operating Modes

Lightweight Access Points can operate in the following modes, which will be described in this section:

- Local mode
- Monitor mode
- REAP mode
- Rogue detector mode
- Sniffer mode

Local mode is the default mode of operation for an LAP. When an LAP is placed into local mode, it spends 60 milliseconds (ms) on channels that it does not operate on every 180 seconds. During this time, the AP performs noise floor and interference measurements, and intrusion detection (IDS).

REAP (Remote Edge Access Point) mode enables an LAP to reside across a WAN link and still be able to communicate with the WLC and provide the functionality of a regular LAP.

Monitor mode allows specified LWAPP-enabled APs to exclude themselves from handling data traffic between clients and the infrastructure. They instead act as dedicated sensors for location-based services (LBS), rogue access point detection, and IDS. When APs are in monitor mode they cannot serve clients and continuously cycle through all configured channels, listening to each channel for approximately 60 ms.

Rogue detector mode allows LAPs to monitor rogue APs. These APs should be able to see all the VLANs in the network since rogue APs can be connected to any of the VLANs in the network. The switch sends all rogue AP and client MAC address lists to the Rogue Detector (RD), which then forwards those up to the WLC in order to compare with the MACs of clients that the WLC APs have heard over the air. If MAC addresses match, then the WLC knows the rogue AP to which those clients are connected is on the wired network.

Sniffer mode allows an AP to function as a sniffer. In this mode, the AP captures and forwards all the packets on a particular channel to a remote machine that runs Airopeek. These packets contain information on timestamp, signal strength, packet size, and so on. The sniffer feature can be enabled only if you run Airopeek, which is a third-party network analyzer software that supports decoding of data packets.

Configuring Switches for WLAN Solutions

This section describes the Catalyst switch configurations required to support APs and WLCs. It is important to remember that you are not expected to perform any AP or WLC configurations. AP and WLC configurations will not be included in this chapter, or the remainder of this guide. The following configurations will be illustrated in this section:

- Configuring Switch Ports for Autonomous Access Points
- Configuring Switch Ports for Lightweight Access Points
- Configuring Cisco IOS DHCP for Lightweight Access Points
- Configuring Switch Ports for Wireless LAN Controllers

Configuring Switch Ports for Autonomous Access Points

An Autonomous AP is a standalone AP that is not controlled by a Wireless LAN Controller. While the configuration of the actual AP itself is beyond the scope of the SWITCH exam requirements, configuring the switch port to support the Autonomous AP is not. This configuration example will be based on the wireless LAN network illustrated below in Figure 9-15:

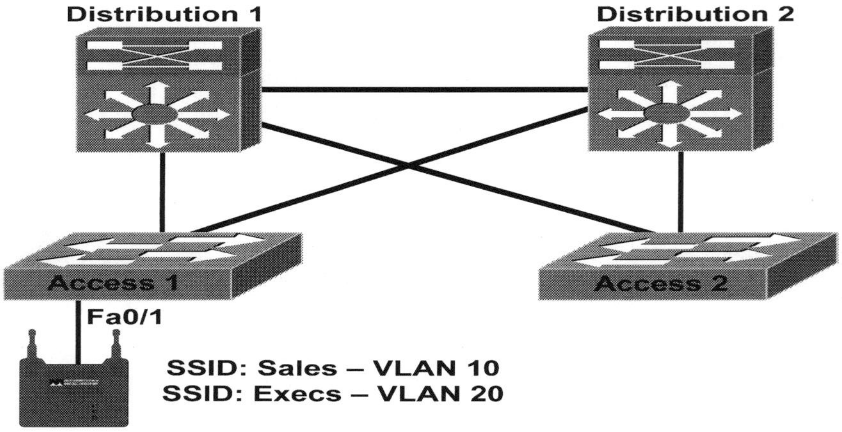

Fig. 9-15. Autonomous Access Point Wireless Network Topology

NOTE: It should be assumed that VLAN 10 and VLAN 20 have already been configured on the Distribution Layer switches, as are the corresponding SVIs for those VLANs. The SSIDs are configured on the AP itself and not on the switch. Also, assume that all trunking between the Distribution and Access Layer switches is in place. This section focuses exclusively on the configuration of the FastEthernet0/1 interface on switch Access 1. The steps to configure the Access Layer switch to support the autonomous AP are as follows:

1. Select the desired interface and configure it as a Layer 2 port using the `switchport` interface configuration command.
2. Configure the trunking encapsulation for the switch port using the `switchport trunk encapsulation` interface configuration command.
3. Configure the switch as a trunk port using the `switchport mode trunk` interface configuration command.
4. Explicitly only allow the configured VLANs using the `switchport trunk allowed vlan` interface configuration command.
5. Optionally, enable PortFast for the trunk port using the `spanning-tree portfast trunk` interface configuration command.

The following output illustrates how to configure the Fa0/1 interface on switch Access 1 to support the connected autonomous Access Point:

```
Access-1(config)#interface fastethernet 0/1
Access-1(config-if)#description 'Connected to Autonomous AP # 1'
Access-1(config-if)#switchport
Access-1(config-if)#switchport trunk encapsulation dot1q
Access-1(config-if)#switchport mode trunk
Access-1(config-if)#switchport trunk allowed vlan 10,20
Access-1(config-if)#spanning-tree portfast trunk
%Warning: portfast should only be enabled on ports connected to a single
 host. Connecting hubs, concentrators, switches, bridges, etc... to this
 interface when portfast is enabled can cause temporary bridging loops.
 Use with CAUTION

Access-1(config-if)#exit
```

This configuration can be validated using the `show interfaces [name] switchport` command as illustrated in the following output:

```
Access-1#show interfaces fastethernet 0/1 switchport
Name: Fa0/1
Switchport: Enabled
Administrative Mode: trunk
Operational Mode: trunk
Administrative Trunking Encapsulation: dot1q
```

```
Operational Trunking Encapsulation: dot1q
Negotiation of Trunking: On
Access Mode VLAN: 1 (default)
Trunking Native Mode VLAN: 1 (default)
Voice VLAN: none
Administrative private-vlan host-association: none
Administrative private-vlan mapping: none
Operational private-vlan: none
Trunking VLANs Enabled: 10,20
Pruning VLANs Enabled: 2-1001
Capture Mode Disabled
Capture VLANs Allowed: ALL

Protected: false

Voice VLAN: none (Inactive)
Appliance trust: none
```

It is important to always use the `switchport trunk allowed vlan [range]` command on the trunk link connected to an Autonomous AP. This command should always be used to permit only the VLANs that exist on the AP. If not, this may result in unexpected issues.

Enabling the PortFast feature on a trunk port can result in loops, as seen in the warning above. While this allows the port to transition to the forwarding state much faster, it is important to understand the topology before this is applied.

Configuring Switch Ports for Lightweight Access Points

Unlike Autonomous APs, Lightweight APs are completely controlled by the WLC. Because of this, the switch port that the LAP is connected to must always be configured as an access port. The switch access port can be assigned to any particular VLAN, though it is common practice to assign it to a designated 'network management' VLAN.

This is because, unlike an Autonomous AP, which must be manually configured, LAPs receive their configuration from the WLC. Therefore, information about VLANs mapped to any SSID is transported between the LAP and the WLC using either an LWAPP or a CAPWAP tunnel. This configuration example will be based on the wireless LAN network illustrated in Figure 9-16.

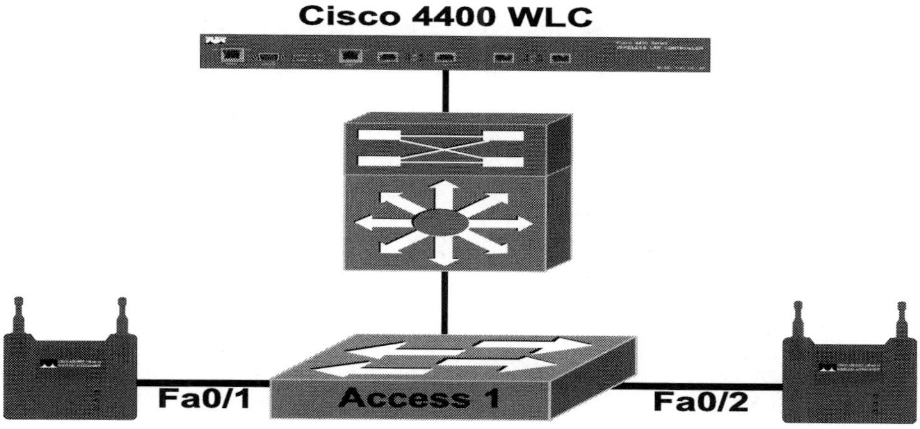

Fig. 9-16. Lightweight Access Point Wireless Network Topology

NOTE: It should be assumed that connectivity between the Access and Distribution switches is already in place, as is connectivity between the Distribution switch and the WLC.

The following sequence of steps is required to configure a switch port to support an LAP:

1. Select the desired interface and configure it as a Layer 2 port using the `switchport` interface configuration command.
2. Assign the switch port to the desired VLAN using the `switchport access vlan` interface configuration command.
3. Configure the switch as a static access port using the `switchport mode access` interface configuration command.
4. Optionally, enable PortFast for the access port using the `spanning-tree portfast` interface configuration command.

The following output illustrates how to configure the Fa0/1 interface on switch Access 1 to support the connected LAP:

```
Access-1(config)#interface range fastethernet 0/1 - 2
Access-1(config-if-range)#description 'Connected to Lightweight Access
                         Points'
Access-1(config-if-range)#switchport
Access-1(config-if-range)#switchport access vlan 10
Access-1(config-if-range)#switchport mode access
Access-1(config-if-range)#spanning-tree portfast
%Warning: portfast should only be enabled on ports connected to a single
 host. Connecting hubs, concentrators, switches, bridges, etc... to this
 interface when portfast is enabled can cause temporary bridging loops.
 Use with CAUTION

Access-1(config-if-range)#exit
```

This configuration can be validated using the `show interfaces [name] switchport` command as illustrated in the following output:

```
Access-1#show interfaces fastethernet 0/2 switchport
Name: Fa0/2
Switchport: Enabled
Administrative Mode: static access
Operational Mode: static access
Administrative Trunking Encapsulation: dot1q
Negotiation of Trunking: Off
Access Mode VLAN: 10 (Wireless-AP-VLAN)
Trunking Native Mode VLAN: 1 (default)
Voice VLAN: none
Administrative private-vlan host-association: none
Administrative private-vlan mapping: none
Operational private-vlan: none
Trunking VLANs Enabled: ALL
Pruning VLANs Enabled: 2-1001
Capture Mode Disabled
Capture VLANs Allowed: ALL

Protected: false

Voice VLAN: none (Inactive)
Appliance trust: none
```

Configuring Cisco IOS DHCP for Lightweight Access Points

LAPs require IP addressing information from a DHCP server. This includes not only their IP address and default gateway but also the IP address of the WLC controller that they will contact to derive their configuration. The LAP takes the following sequence of steps when it boots up:

1. The LAP obtains IP addressing information from the DHCP server. This information also contains the IP address of one or more WLCs.
2. The LAP sends a Join Request to the first WLC in the list (if more than one is available). If no response is received from the first WLC, the next is attempted, and so forth.
3. The WLC compares the images stored on the LAP to its local release. If these images are not the same, the LAP downloads and installs the updated image and reboots.
4. The WLC and the LAP build either a secure LWAPP or CAPWAP tunnel for management traffic and an unsecure LWAPP or CAPWAP tunnel for wireless clients.

In most networks, a dedicated DHCP server provides IP addressing information to all network hosts, which may include workstations, laptops, IP phones, and LAPs. However, it is also possible to configure the Cisco IOS DHCP server to perform the same functionality. Although basic IOS DHCP configuration is described in detail in the CCNA course, additional configuration is required to provide the LAPs with the IP address, or addresses, of one or more WLCs. This address must be provided using DHCP Option 43, which returns vendor-specific information to the LAPs.

RFC 2132 defines that DHCP servers must return vendor-specific information as DHCP Option 43. The RFC allows vendors to define encapsulated vendor-specific sub-option codes between 0 and 255. The sub-options are included in the DHCP offer as Type/Length/Value (TLV) blocks embedded within Option 43. The definition of the sub-option codes and their related message format is left to the different vendors.

When configuring a Cisco IOS DHCP server to provide IP addressing information to LAPs, the IP address, or addresses, or the WLC are defined within the DHCP using the `option 43 [ascii|hex] [string]` DHCP pool configuration command. The [ascii] keyword allows you to specify the IP address of the WLC using dotted-decimal notation, while the [hex] keyword allows you to specify the IP address of the WLC in Hexadecimal format. However, this option is beyond the scope of the SWITCH exam requirements and is not described in this section. The following output illustrates how to configure a Cisco IOS DHCP server for network 192.168.5.0/24, with a default gateway of 192.168.5.1, and specify three WLC IP addresses to be used by the LAPs:

```
Distribution-Switch-1(config)#ip dhcp pool SWITCH-LAP-DHCP-Pool
Distribution-Switch-1(dhcp-config)#network 192.168.5.0/24
Distribution-Switch-1(dhcp-config)#default-router 192.168.5.1
Distribution-Switch-1(dhcp-config)# option 43 ascii
                                    "172.16.1.1,172.16.1.2,172.16.1.3"
Distribution-Switch-1(dhcp-config)#exit
```

Although this configuration cannot be validated using the `show ip dhcp pool [name]` command, it can be viewed by looking at the configuration as illustrated below:

```
Distribution-1#show running-config | begin ip dhcp pool
ip dhcp pool SWITCH-LAP-DHCP-Pool
   network 192.168.5.0 255.255.255.0
   default-router 192.168.5.1
   option 43 ascii "172.16.1.1,172.16.1.2,172.16.1.3"
```

NOTE: DHCP is required only if the LAP and the WLC are not in the same VLAN. If they are, the LAP simply Broadcasts out a Join Request and a WLC will respond to this request.

Configuring Switch Ports for Wireless LAN Controllers

As is the case with switch ports connected to Autonomous APs, switch ports connected to WLCs should always be configured as trunk links. However, unlike Autonomous APs, WLCs may have more than one physical interface and therefore an EtherChannel can be configured between the

WLC and the switch; however, keep in mind that it will also still be a trunk port. The switch configuration required to support a WLC will be based on Figure 9-17 below:

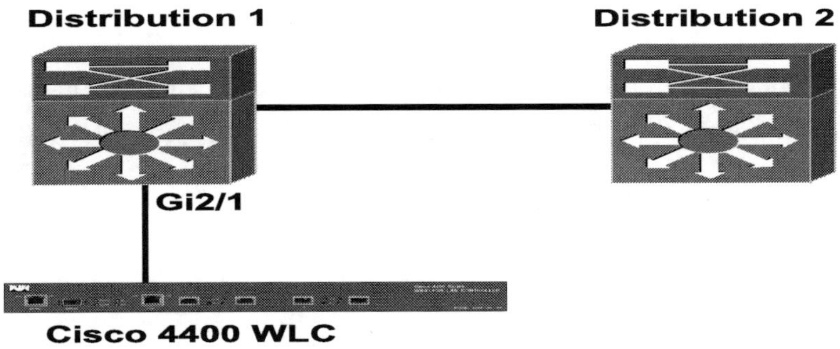

Fig. 9-17. Wireless LAN Controller Wireless Network Topology

NOTE: The topology above assumes that all pertinent configurations on the WLC have already been applied and the VLANs are already configured on the Distribution switches. In addition to this, the WLC is connected to only a single Distribution Layer switch (for simplicity) using a single interface. The steps required to configure the Distribution Layer switch to support the WLC are as follows:

1. Select the desired interface and configure it as a Layer 2 port using the `switchport` interface configuration command.
2. Configure the trunking encapsulation for the switch port using the `switchport trunk encapsulation` interface configuration command.
3. Configure the switch as a trunk port using the `switchport mode trunk` interface configuration command.
4. Optionally, enable PortFast for the trunk port using the `spanning-tree portfast trunk` interface configuration command.

The following output illustrates how to configure the Gi2/1 interface on switch Distribution 1 to support the connected WLC:

```
Access-1(config)#interface gigabitethernet 2/1
Access-1(config-if)#description 'Connected to Cisco 4400 WLC'
Access-1(config-if)#switchport
Access-1(config-if)#switchport trunk encapsulation dot1q
Access-1(config-if)#switchport trunk allowed vlan 10,20
Access-1(config-if)#spanning-tree portfast trunk
%Warning: portfast should only be enabled on ports connected to a single
 host. Connecting hubs, concentrators, switches, bridges, etc... to this
 interface when portfast is enabled can cause temporary bridging loops.
 Use with CAUTION

Access-1(config-if)#exit
```

This configuration can be validated using the `show interfaces [name] switchport` command as illustrated in the following output:

```
Access-1#show interfaces gigabitethernet 0/1 switchport
Name: Gi2/1
Switchport: Enabled
Administrative Mode: trunk
Operational Mode: trunk
Administrative Trunking Encapsulation: dot1q
Operational Trunking Encapsulation: dot1q
Negotiation of Trunking: On
Access Mode VLAN: 1 (default)
Trunking Native Mode VLAN: 1 (default)
Voice VLAN: none
Administrative private-vlan host-association: none
Administrative private-vlan mapping: none
Operational private-vlan: none
Trunking VLANs Enabled: 10,20
Pruning VLANs Enabled: 2-1001
Capture Mode Disabled
Capture VLANs Allowed: ALL

Protected: false

Voice VLAN: none (Inactive)
Appliance trust: none
```

As is the case when you are configuring switch ports connected to support LAPs, it is important to always use the `switchport trunk allowed vlan [range]` command on the trunk link connected to the WLC. This command should always be used to permit only the VLANs that exist on the WLC.

In addition, always remember that enabling the PortFast feature on a trunk port can result in loops, as seen in the warning above. While this allows the port to transition to the forwarding state much faster, it is important to understand the topology before this is applied to the port.

Chapter Summary

The following section is a summary of the major points you should be aware of in this chapter.

Wireless Local Area Network Overview

- WLANs provide network connectivity almost anywhere
- WLANs can typically be implemented at much less cost than traditional wired LANs
- The wired infrastructure is based on the IEEE 802.3 standards
- A wireless network uses radio waves to transmit data and connect devices
- WLANs are defined in the IEEE 802.11 standards
- The advantages of WLANs over wired LANs include the following:
  1. Monetary Cost
  2. Flexibility
  3. Load Distribution
  4. Redundancy

IEEE 802.11 Components

- The 802.11 components are:
  1. Client or Station (STA)
  2. Access Point (AP)
  3. Independent Basic Service Set (IBSS)
  4. Basic Service Set (BSS)
  5. Extended Service Set (ESS)
  6. Distribution System (DS)

- The wireless client or station (STA) is an appliance that interfaces with the wireless medium
- The STA operates as an end user device
- The wireless AP functions as a bridge between the STAs and the existing network backbone
- An IBSS is a wireless network, consisting of at least two STAs and no DS
- The WLAN infrastructure architecture is based on a cellular architecture
- The WLAN architecture divides the system into cells, referred to as a Basic Service Set (BSS)
- The BSS is controlled by a Base Station, or more commonly, an Access Point
- Access Points may be interconnected using the switched network, creating an ESS
- The DS allows for the interconnection of the APs of multiple cells (BSSs)
- Three types of Distribution System are:
  1. Integrated
  2. Wired
  3. Wireless

IEEE 802.11 and the OSI Reference Model

- The IEEE 802 standards define two separate layers for the Data Link layer of the OSI Model
- These two layers are the LLC and MAC sublayers
- The IEEE 802.11 standards cover the operation of the MAC sublayer and the Physical layer
- The 802.11 frame consists of a 32-byte MAC header, a variable length, and an FCS
- The fields contained in the MAC header are:
  1. The Frame Control Field (2 bytes in length)
  2. The Duration / ID Field (2 bytes in length)
  3. The Sequence Control Field (2 bytes in length)
  4. The Four Address Fields (6 bytes each)
  5. The Quality of Service Field (2 bytes in length)

Collision Avoidance: CSMA/CA

- On wired Ethernet LANs, CSMA/CD is used to detect collisions
- The 802.11 standards seek to avoid, rather than to detect, collisions and thus use CSMA/CA
- Collision avoidance works well when the medium is not heavily loaded
- Collision avoidance requires STAs to sense the medium before sending any traffic

MAC Sublayer Coordination Functions

- There are two types of coordination functions used to ensure collision free access:
  1. The Distributed Coordination Function (DCF)
  2. The Point Coordination Function (PCF)

- The DCF is a MAC sublayer technique that employs CSMA/CA to avoid collisions
- The DCF also uses an exponential random backoff algorithm to avoid collisions
- The DCF is used in IEEE 802.11 networks to manage access to the Radio Frequency medium
- The DCF is composed of the following two main components:
  1. Interframe spaces
  2. Random backoff

- The IFS allow 802.11 to control which traffic gets first access to the channel
- In DCF, there are two types of interframe spaces that are used. These are:
  1. Short Interframe Space (SIFS)
  2. DCF Interframe Space (DIFS)

- The SIFS is used to separate transmissions belonging to a single dialog
- The DIFS is used by a station that is ready to start a new transmission
- The PCF is used by the AP to coordinate communication within the wireless network

The Wireless Network Hidden Node Problem

- Wireless networking is susceptible to the hidden node problem
- This leads to difficulties in media access control
- To address this issue the IEEE defines a Virtual Carrier Sense mechanism

IEEE 802.11 Frame Types

- The 802.11 standard uses three main types of frames:
  1. Control Frames
  2. Management Frames
  3. Data Frames

- The IEEE 802.11 standard uses control frames to control access to the medium
- The most common control frames are:
  1. Ready (Request) To Send (RTS)
  2. Clear To Send (CTS)
  3. Acknowledgement (ACK)

- 802.11 management frames enable stations to establish and maintain communications
- There are several management frame subtypes, which are:
  1. Association request frame
  2. Association response frame
  3. Disassociation frame
  4. Reassociation request frame
  5. Reassociation response frame
  6. Probe request frame
  7. Probe response frame
  8. Beacon frame
  9. Authentication frame
  10. Deauthentication frame

- Data frames are sent by any STA and contain higher layer protocol information or data

Wireless LAN Standards

- At the PHY layer, IEEE 802.11 defines a series of encoding and transmission schemes
- The most common of which are the FHSS, DSSS, and OFDM
- Although IR also exists at this layer, very little development of this standard has occurred
- The 802.11 standards are:
  1. IEEE 802.11 (original)

2. IEEE 802.11b
3. IEEE 802.11a
4. IEEE 802.11g
5. IEEE 802.11n

The Cisco Unified Wireless Network

- The Cisco Unified Wireless Network is composed of 5 interconnected elements, which are:
    1. Client Devices
    2. Access Points and Wireless Bridges
    3. Network Unification
    4. Network Management
    5. Mobility Services

- Client devices are secure devices that work right out of the box
- Client device examples include Cisco Secure Services Client and Cisco Aironet client devices
- Cisco Aironet APs provide network access for both indoor and outdoor environments
- A Wireless Bridge can connect another Wireless Bridge
- A Wireless Bridge can also transparently bridge two networks and connect wireless clients
- Network unification integrates the CUWN into all major switching and routing platforms
- Network management is used to manage the WLAN in a manner similar to the wired LAN
- Mobility services provide support for unified cellular and voice over WLAN services

The Cisco Wireless LAN Solution

- The Cisco Wireless LAN solution of WLCs and their associated LAPs
- WLCs are responsible for system wide wireless LAN functions, such as:
    1. Integrated Intrusion Prevention System (IPS)
    2. Zero-Touch Deployment of Lightweight Access Points (LAPs)
    3. Real-time Radio Frequency (RF) management
    4. Wireless LAN Redundancy
    5. Dynamic Channel Assignment for each LAP
    6. Dynamic Client Load Balancing across LAPs
    7. Dynamic LAP Transmit Power Optimization
    8. Wireless LAN Security Management

- WLCs communicate with Controller-based APs over any Layer 2 or Layer 3 infrastructure
- WLCs communicate with LAPs using LWAPP or CAPWAP
- LWAPP is an IETF draft protocol
- CAPWAP, which is based on LWAPP, is a standard, interoperable protocol

- The Cisco WLAN supports three types of roaming:
  1. Intra-controller Roaming
  2. Inter-controller Roaming
  3. Inter-Subnet Roaming

- In order to support roaming, Mobility Groups must be configured
- A Mobility Group is a group of WLCs in a network with the same Mobility Group name
- Lightweight Access Points (LAPs) can operate in several modes. These modes are:
  1. Local Mode
  2. Monitor Mode
  3. REAP Mode
  4. Rogue Detector Mode
  5. Sniffer Mode

CHAPTER 10

QoS and Advanced Catalyst Services

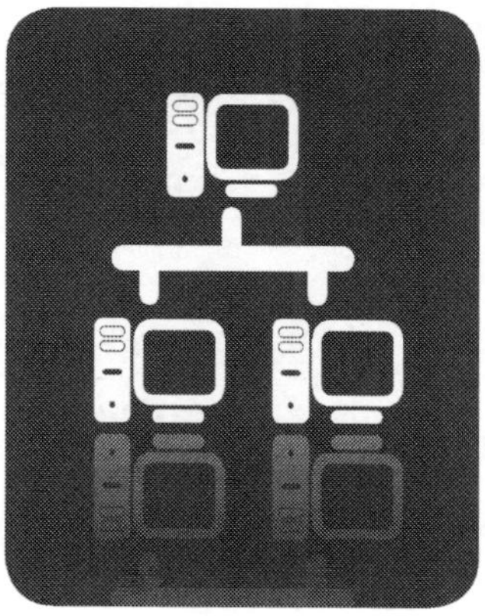

In most cases, present-day networks support integrated voice, video, and data traffic. These types of networks are referred to as converged networks because the voice, video and data traffic travels over a single transport infrastructure. Carrying voice, video, and data traffic over a single transport infrastructure requires properly designed Quality of Service (QoS) implementation to ensure the required level of service for all three traffic types. The following core SWITCH exam objective is covered in this chapter:

- Prepare infrastructure to support advanced services by implementing a VoIP support solution and a video support solution

This chapter will be divided into the following sections:

- Integrating Voice, Video, and Data Traffic
- Configuring Switches to Support Cisco IP Phones
- The Three QoS Models
- Quality of Service Overview
- Understanding LAN QoS
- Catalyst QoS Basics
- Catalyst Ingress QoS Mechanisms
- Catalyst Egress QoS Mechanisms
- Understanding Power over Ethernet

SWITCH Exam Objective	Chapter Section(s) Covered
• Implement a VoIP support solution	• Integrating Voice, Video, and Data Traffic • Configuring Switches to Support Cisco IP Phones • The Three QoS Models • Quality of Service Overview • Understanding LAN QoS • Catalyst QoS Basics • Catalyst Ingress QoS Features • Catalyst Egress QoS Features • Understanding Power over Ethernet
• Implement video support solution	• Integrating Voice, Video, and Data Traffic • The Three QoS Models

Integrating Voice, Video, and Data Traffic

IP Telephony (IPT) solutions make use of packet-switched connections from the Internet for the exchange of communications services, which include voice, facsimile, and voice-messaging applications, instead of using the traditional dedicated circuit-switched connections from PSTNs.

Cisco IPT solutions are an integral part of Cisco Unified Communications, which allows for the integration of voice, video, data, and mobile applications on fixed and mobile networks. Cisco IPT solutions are comprised of call processing solutions, such as Cisco Unified Communications Manager, formerly Cisco CallManager, and IP phones.

Cisco Unified Video Advantage enhances the Cisco IPT solution by providing video telephony functionality to Cisco Unified IP phones. The Cisco Unified Videoconferencing solution, which is based on the H.323 standard, allows for a wide range of customized and fully converged voice, video, and data solutions. Integrating voice, video, and data traffic requires an understanding of the different characteristics of these traffic types.

NOTE: H.323 is beyond the scope of the SWITCH exam requirements and is not described in this chapter.

Voice calls create traffic flows with fixed data rates. Voice traffic flows are considered isochronous, which means that packets arrive either at the same time or in equal time intervals. Isochronous traffic does not tolerate delay or packet loss very well. Excessive delay and packet loss, which may be due to several reasons as will be described in the section that follows, can severely affect voice quality, typically resulting in choppy or even dropped calls.

Packet video can be divided into two categories: interactive video and non-interactive video. Interactive video includes solutions such as videoconferencing, where participants can communicate with each other on the video call, while non-interactive video includes solutions such as Cisco IP/TV, which allows users to view the video stream passively. Unlike packet voice traffic, packet video traffic comes in different packet sizes and traffic rates. However, like packet voice traffic, packet video quality is also impacted by delay and packet loss, which can result in freezing images and the loss of synchronization between the audio and the video, for example.

Traditional data traffic is completely different from both packet voice and video traffic in that, for the most part, it tolerates both delay and packet loss quite well. Some applications have the capability to retransmit or re-send lost packets while others are not affected at all. Because of these characteristics, and the greater amount of bandwidth available on LANs, LAN Quality of Service (QoS) is typically overlooked as unnecessary. However, the integration of real-time applications, such as voice and video, on the LAN requires QoS implementation to ensure optimum and predictable performance.

Configuring Switches to Support Cisco IP Phones

Cisco IP phones are part of the Cisco IPT solution. Cisco IP phones typically have two or three Ethernet ports that allow the phone to be connected to the switch and that allow users to be connected to the switch via the phone. This is illustrated below in Figure 10-1:

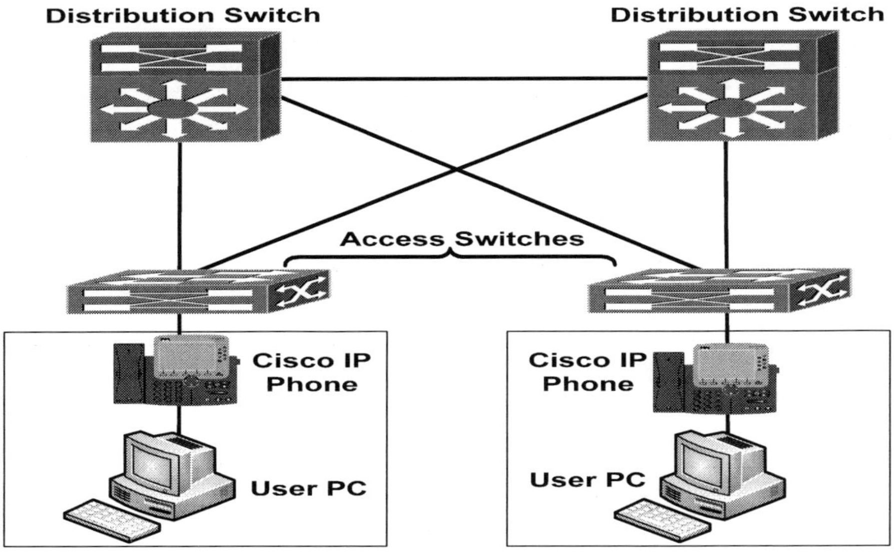

Fig. 10-1. Integrating Cisco IP Phones into the LAN

Referencing Figure 10-1, two different Cisco IP phones are connected to two different access switches. These phones use one port (designated as the uplink) to connect to the switches. The IP phones also have another port that users can use to connect to the network. This port functions as an access port. In this manner, the Cisco IP phone behaves somewhat like a typical access switch and can even control how packets are presented to the Catalyst switch. This concept will be described later in this chapter.

Cisco IP phones can be connected to the Catalyst switch using either a trunk port or an access port. The configuration implemented on the switch is used to instruct the phone about the mode. This is performed via the exchange of Cisco Discovery Protocol (CDP) packets. No explicit trunk port or access port configuration is required on the phone itself.

Configuring a trunk to the Cisco IP phone allows voice traffic to be isolated from user traffic, which provides security. In addition to this, trunking allows for QoS using the User Priority bits (802.1p) contained in the VLAN tag of 802.1Q and ISL-encapsulated frames. These fields will be described in detail later in this chapter; the emphasis at this point is simply to understand how to configure the Catalyst switch to support Cisco IP phones.

One major disadvantage to configuring the switch port as a trunk port is that it can cause high CPU utilization in the switch. This is because all the VLANs trunked to the IP phone require a single Spanning Tree Protocol instance that must be managed by the switch.

Configuring a trunk also results in unnecessary Broadcast, Multicast, and unknown Unicast traffic being sent to the IP phone. The recommended method of configuring the switch port is to configure it as an access port and then designating a voice VLAN and a data VLAN. This configuration is referred to as a Multi-VLAN Access Port (MVAP). This is not a trunk port!

On an MVAP, the port VLAN identifier (PVID) identifies a native VLAN for data traffic for the workstation connected to the IP phone, and the voice VLAN identifier (VVID) identifies an auxiliary VLAN for voice service. The switch communicates the VVID to the IP phone using the CDP.

Frames sent by the PC connected to the Cisco IP phone will be sent in the native VLAN (PVID). These frames will be untagged. Frames or packets sent by the Cisco IP phone will use the auxiliary VLAN (VVID). These frames will include the 802.1Q tag. Within this tag, the User Priority field contains the Quality of Service Information.

The voice VLAN (VVID) is configured using the `switchport voice vlan [vlan-id | dot1p |none| untagged]` interface configuration command. The `[vlan-id]` keyword specifies the VVID. The configuration of a VVID configures the switch to send CDP packets to the Cisco IP phone, instructing the phone to send voice traffic in 802.1Q frames tagged with the specified VVID and a Layer 2 Class of Service (CoS) value of 5. CoS will be described in detail later in this chapter. The switch then places the 802.1Q voice traffic into the specified voice VLAN. The following output illustrates how to configure a switch port as an MVAP with a PVID of 100 and a VVID of 200:

```
Catalyst-Switch-1(config)#interface fastethernet 0/1
Catalyst-Switch-1(config-if)#description 'Connected to Cisco IP Phone'
Catalyst-Switch-1(config-if)#switchport
Catalyst-Switch-1(config-if)#switchport access vlan 100
Catalyst-Switch-1(config-if)#switchport voice vlan 200
Catalyst-Switch-1(config-if)#switchport mode access
Catalyst-Switch-1(config-if)#spanning-tree portfast
%Warning: portfast should only be enabled on ports connected to a single
 host. Connecting hubs, concentrators, switches, bridges, etc... to this
 interface when portfast is enabled can cause temporary bridging loops.
 Use with CAUTION
```

```
%Portfast has been configured on FastEthernet0/1 but will only
 have effect when the interface is in a non-trunking mode.
Catalyst-Switch-1(config-if)#exit
```

Based on the above configuration output, voice packets are tagged with the specified VVID, which is 200. However, data traffic is untagged. This traffic is sent in the native VLAN, which is identified by the PVID (100). This configuration is validated using the `show interfaces [name] switch-port` command. The output of this command based on the previous configuration example is illustrated as follows:

```
Catalyst-Switch-1#show interfaces fastethernet 0/1 switchport
Name: Fa0/1
Switchport: Enabled
Administrative Mode: static access
Operational Mode: static access
Administrative Trunking Encapsulation: dot1q
Operational Trunking Encapsulation: native
Negotiation of Trunking: Off
Access Mode VLAN: 100 (User-Data-VLAN)
Trunking Native Mode VLAN: 1 (default)
Voice VLAN: 200 (User-Voice-VLAN)
Administrative private-vlan host-association: none
Administrative private-vlan mapping: none
Operational private-vlan: none
Trunking VLANs Enabled: ALL
Pruning VLANs Enabled: 2-1001
Capture Mode Disabled
Capture VLANs Allowed: ALL

Protected: false

Voice VLAN: 200 (User-Voice-VLAN)
Appliance trust: none
```

The `[dot1p]` tags the voice packets with a VLAN ID of 0. If you recall, earlier in Chapter 2 we learned that VLAN 0 is a reserved system VLAN that is not configurable. This VLAN is for IEEE 802.1p (dot1p) priority tagging for voice traffic.

This keyword configures the switch to send CDP packets instructing the Cisco IP phone to send voice traffic in 802.1Q/p frames, tagged with a VLAN ID of 0 and the default Layer 2 CoS value of 5. This keyword allows voice packets to be tagged without the need to configure a unique voice VLAN manually. Instead, the switch puts the 802.1p voice traffic into the access VLAN. The different 802.1Q/p priority values are described in detail later in this chapter. The following output illustrates how to configure a switch port to instruct the connected Cisco IP phone to use IEEE 802.1Q/p priority tagging for voice traffic:

```
Catalyst-Switch-1(config)#interface fastethernet 0/1
Catalyst-Switch-1(config-if)#description 'Connected to Cisco IP Phone'
Catalyst-Switch-1(config-if)#switchport
Catalyst-Switch-1(config-if)#switchport access vlan 100
Catalyst-Switch-1(config-if)#switchport voice vlan dot1p
Catalyst-Switch-1(config-if)#switchport mode access
Catalyst-Switch-1(config-if)#spanning-tree portfast
%Warning: portfast should only be enabled on ports connected to a single
 host. Connecting hubs, concentrators, switches, bridges, etc... to this
 interface when portfast is enabled can cause temporary bridging loops.
 Use with CAUTION

%Portfast has been configured on FastEthernet0/1 but will only
 have effect when the interface is in a non-trunking mode.
Catalyst-Switch-1(config-if)#exit
```

This above configuration output can be validated using the `show interfaces [name] switchport` command as illustrated in the following output:

```
Catalyst-Switch-1#show interfaces fastethernet 0/1 switchport
Name: Fa0/1
Switchport: Enabled
Administrative Mode: static access
Operational Mode: static access
Administrative Trunking Encapsulation: dot1q
Operational Trunking Encapsulation: native
Negotiation of Trunking: Off
Access Mode VLAN: 100 (User-Data-VLAN)
Trunking Native Mode VLAN: 1 (default)
Voice VLAN: dot1p
Administrative private-vlan host-association: none
Administrative private-vlan mapping: none
Operational private-vlan: none
Trunking VLANs Enabled: ALL
Pruning VLANs Enabled: 2-1001
Capture Mode Disabled
Capture VLANs Allowed: ALL

Protected: false

Voice VLAN: dot1p (Inactive)
Appliance trust: none
```

The `[none]` keyword allows the IP phone to use its own configuration and transmit untagged voice traffic. The switch puts the untagged voice traffic into the access VLAN. By default, CDP is used to communicate the VVID information to the Cisco IP phone. The use of this keyword prevents the switch from communicating this information to the Cisco IP phone using CDP. In other words, the switch does not configure the Cisco IP phone and all traffic from the IP phone and connected workstation is sent in the access VLAN. This is the default mode of operation.

The [untagged] keyword is used to instruct the switch to tell the Cisco IP phone, using CDP, to send untagged voice packets. Both voice and data traffic will be carried in the access VLAN. The configuration of this keyword does not require a unique voice VVID or even a VLAN ID.

Because this is a core SWITCH exam concept, Table 10-1 below lists and summarizes the usage of the keywords that can be used in the `switchport voice vlan` interface configuration command:

Table 10-1. The `switchport voice vlan` **Command Keywords**

Command Keyword	Description
`vlan-id`	This is used to specify the VVID. Voice traffic is placed into the voice VLAN specified by this command.
`dot1p`	This keyword instructs the IP phone to place voice traffic into an 802.1Q/p (priority) tagged frame with the VLAN ID set to 0. Voice traffic is placed into the access VLAN.
`none`	This keyword is the default and it allows the IP phone to use its own configuration. Voice traffic is placed into the access VLAN.
`untagged`	This keyword instructs the IP phone to place voice traffic into an untagged frame. Voice traffic is placed into the access VLAN.

The Three QoS Models

In order to understand QoS implementation, it is important to have an understanding of the three different QoS models and how they are applicable when designing and implementing a QoS solution. The three QoS models are as follows:

1. Best-Effort Delivery (Default)
2. Integrated Services
3. Differentiated Services

Best Effort Delivery (Default)

As the name implies, the Best-Effort Delivery (BE) model does not guarantee any level of service; instead, internetwork devices simply make their 'best effort' to deliver packets as quickly as possible. The BE model scales well but provides no difference in service for different traffic classes. In other words, when this model is used (which is the default), voice, video, and data traffic are all treated as one and the same. This model requires no QoS implementation within the internetwork.

Integrated Services

The Integrated Services (IntServ) model performs admission control for each flow request. The IntServ architecture model, defined in RFC 1633, was motivated by the needs of real-time applications, such as voice and video. IntServ provides a way to deliver end-to-end QoS for real-time applications by explicitly managing network resources in order to provide QoS to specific user packet streams (flows). RFC 1633 defines two components to provide guarantees per flow: resource reservation and admission control.

IntServ uses Resource Reservation Protocol (RSVP) to signal the internetworking devices about how much bandwidth and delay a particular flow requires. Admission control is used to decide when a reservation request should be rejected. The primary issue with IntServ is that it scales very poorly, especially when many sources are attempting to reserve end-to-end bandwidth for each of their particular flows. An alternative approach would be to use Differentiated Services. Going into detail on IntServ QoS mechanisms is beyond the scope of the SWITCH exam requirements. These concepts will not be described in any further detail in this chapter.

Differentiated Services

Unlike IntServ, the Differentiated Services (DiffServ) model requires no advance reservations and therefore scales very well. DiffServ defines the concept of service classes. DiffServ also allows each internetwork device to handle these packets on an individual (per hop) basis. This is referred to as per-hop behavior (PHB). DiffServs are applicable to Layer 3. Layer 2 frames use CoS bits that are contained within the 802.1Q or ISL-encapsulated frame. CoS will be described in detail later in this chapter. The IPv4 header contains an 8-bit Type of Service (ToS) field, which specifies the parameters for the type of service requested.

Networks may use these settings to define the handling of the datagram during transport. This is typically performed using the IP Precedence, which is contained in the first three bits of the ToS field. The IPv4 header ToS field IP Precedence bits are illustrated below in Figure 10-2:

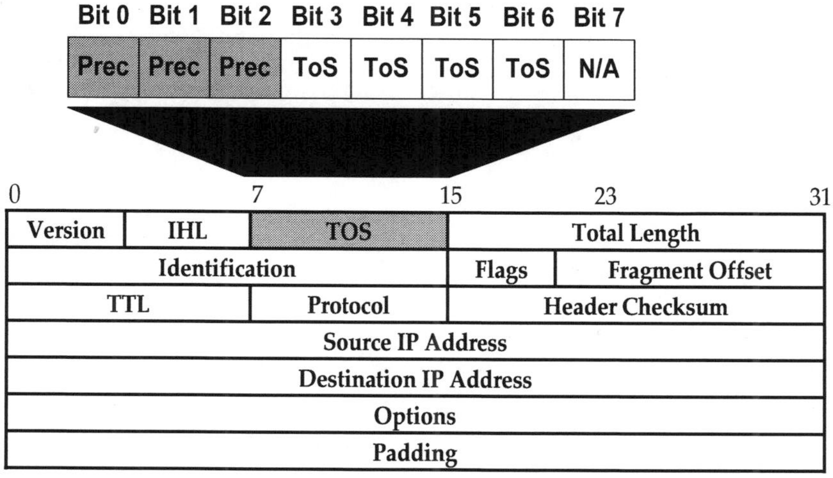

Fig. 10-2. Type of Service IP Precedence Bits

Figure 10-2 illustrates the IPv4 packet header and highlights the 8-bit ToS field. The first three bits, bits 0 to 2, of this field are used for IP Precedence, which allows for up to eight (2^3) IP Precedence values. The next four bits, bits 3 to 6, comprise the ToS field inside the ToS byte and are used as flags for throughput, delay, reliability, and cost. These bits, however, are beyond the scope of the SWITCH exam requirements. The last bit, bit 7, is unused.

The IP Precedence field values are used to imply a particular CoS. In essence, the higher the IP Precedence value (numerically), the more important the traffic. Table 10-2 below lists and describes the different IP Precedence values:

Table 10-2. Type of Service IP Precedence Values

IP Precedence Value	Bits	Description / Name
0	000 000	Routine
1	001 000	Priority
2	010 000	Immediate
3	011 000	Flash
4	100 000	Flash Override
5	101 000	Critical
6	110 000	Internetwork Control
7	111 000	Network Control

NOTE: The highest IP Precedence value that should be assigned to data traffic (e.g. voice packets) should always be 5. IP Prec 6 and 7 should never be assigned to user traffic, as these are used by network control traffic, such as routing protocol updates.

DiffServ defines a new Differentiated Services Code Point (DSCP) field in the IP packet header by redefining the ToS byte and creating a replacement for the IP Precedence field with a new 6-bit field called the Differentiated Services (DS) field. In addition to this, the last 2 bits of the ToS byte can now be used to perform flow control and are referred to as the Explicit Congestion Notification (ECN) bits. This is illustrated below in Figure 10-3:

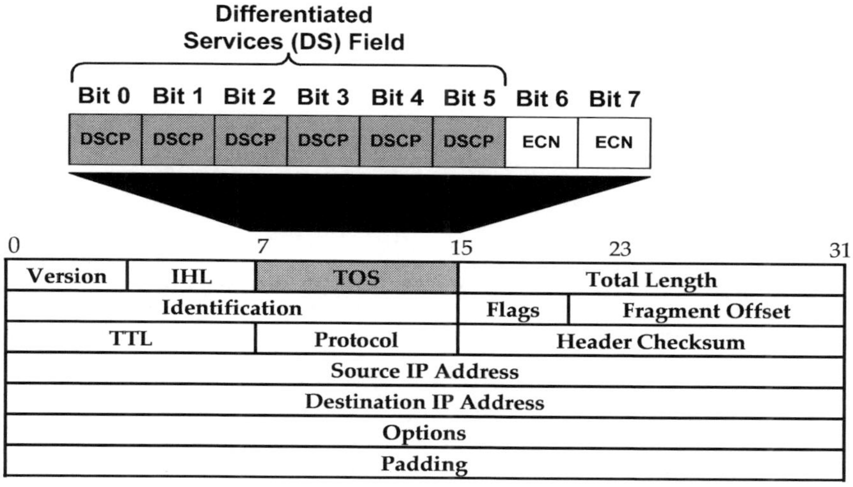

Fig. 10-3. Type of Service Differentiated Services Code Point Bits

Figure 10-3 illustrates the IPv4 packet header and highlights the 8-bit ToS field. The first six bits, bits 0 to 5, of this field are used for DSCP, which allows for up to 64 (2^6) DSCP values. The decimal DSCP range is from 0 to 63. The next two bits are the Explicit Congestion Notification bits. Explicit Congestion Notification (ECN) is beyond the scope of the SWITCH exam requirements and will not be described in this chapter. The 64 DSCP values are backward compatible with IP Precedence values. This compatibility is based on the first three bits, bits 0 through 2, which both IP Precedence and DSCP share in common. Table 10-3 below shows how the decimal DSCP values are mapped to IP Precedence:

Table 10-3. Mapping Decimal DSCP Values to IP Precedence

IP Precedence Value	Decimal DSCP
0	0
1	8
2	16
3	24
4	32
5	40
6	48
7	56

NOTE: You are not expected to go into detail on how these values are derived. Instead, simply ensure that you are familiar with the DSCP ranges that correspond to an IP Precedence value.

DiffServ defines the following three sets of PHBs:

- Class Selector (CS)
- Assured Forwarding (AF)
- Expedited Forwarding (EF)

The CSs are DSCP values that are compatible with IP Precedence values. Although referred to as DSCP values, the CSs use only the first three bits of the DS field, which is the same three bits used by IP Precedence. Table 10-4 below illustrates how the DSCP CS values match the IP Precedence:

Table 10-4. DSCP Class Selector Values

DSCP Class Selector	IP Precedence	Description
Default	0	Routine
CS 1	1	Priority
CS 2	2	Immediate
CS 3	3	Flash
CS 4	4	Flash Override
CS 5	5	Critical
CS 6	6	Internetwork Control
CS 7	7	Network Control

NOTE: The highest DSCP CS value that should be assigned to user traffic (e.g. voice packets) should always be CS 5 – CS 6 and CS 7 should never be assigned to user traffic.

The Assured Forwarding (AF) PHB set is used for two functions: queuing and congestion avoidance. Queuing places the packets into the different software queues based on the QoS labels. Queuing will be described in detail later in this chapter.

Congestion avoidance is used to avoid congestion by randomly discarding packets. Congestion avoidance will also be described in detail later in this chapter. Four AF classes, 1 through 4, are defined. Class 1 is the lowest class, while Class 4 is the highest class. Therefore, packets with AF Class 4 will be de-queued before packets with AF Class 1, for example. Each class has three levels of drop precedence, 1 through 3. Drop precedence 1 is the lowest, while drop precedence 3 is the highest. This is used for congestion avoidance.

For example, if two packets, both in AF Class 2, are received, and one has a drop precedence of 1 while the other has a drop precedence of 2, the packet with the drop precedence of 2 will be discarded first (if congestion is experienced) because it has a higher drop precedence. Table 10-5 lists the four AF classes and their respective drop precedence values.

Table 10-5. Assured Forwarding DSCP Values

Class	Low Drop Probability	Medium Drop Probability	High Drop Probability
1	AF 11	AF 12	AF 13
2	AF 21	AF 22	AF 23
3	AF 31	AF 32	AF 33
4	AF 41	AF 42	AF 43

To determine the decimal DSCP value for each AF class, you can use the formula $8x + 2y$, where x references the first number in the AF class and y represents the second number in the AF class (i.e. AFxy). For example, to determine the decimal DSCP value of AF 42, do the following:

- If DSCP = AF42, then x = 4 and y = 2
- Therefore 8x + 2y = 8(4) + 2(2) = 32 + 4
- 32 + 4 = 36 (This is the decimal DSCP value for AF 42)

As a final example, we will use the same formula to calculate the decimal value for AF 22, as follows:

- If DSCP = AF22, then x = 2 and y = 2
- Therefore 8x + 2y = 8(2) + 2(2) = 16 + 4
- 16 + 4 = 20 (This is the decimal DSCP value for AF 22)

The last PHB set is the Expedited Forwarding (EF) set. This uses a single DSCP value (EF) to represent it. The Binary notation of the DSCP value is 101 110, which is 46 in decimal. EF packets are given premium service (above all other classes). This is the default value assigned to voice media packets in Cisco IPT solutions. It is important to remember that even though the DSCP decimal range for both CS 5 and IP Precedence 5 is 40 – 47, DSCP value EF is designated as only 46. CS 5 is not the same as EF. Make sure you commit that to memory.

Quality of Service Overview

Converged networks are networks with the capacity to transport a multitude of applications and data, including high-quality video and delay-sensitive data such as real-time voice. Although bandwidth-intensive applications stretch network capabilities and resources, they also complement, add value, and enhance every business process.

Converged networks must provide secure, predictable, measurable, and sometimes guaranteed services. In order to ensure successful end-to-end business solutions, Quality of Service (QoS) is required to manage network resources. Most networks experience the following:

- Delay issues
- Bandwidth issues
- Jitter issues
- Packet loss issues

All packets in a network experience some kind of delay from the time the packet is first sent to when it arrives at its intended destination. This total delay, from start to finish, is referred to as latency. Packets or frames may experience several types of delay. While delving into the specifics on each one of them is beyond the scope of the SWITCH exam requirements, some common causes of delay include the following:

- Serialization delay—the time it takes to send bits, one-at-a-time, across the wire
- Queuing delay—the delay experienced when packets wait for other packets to be sent
- Forwarding delay—the processing time from when a frame is sent and when the packet has been placed in the output queue

Generally speaking, bandwidth refers to the number of bits per second (bps) that are expected to be delivered successfully across some medium. Based on this definition, bandwidth is equal to the physical link speed or clock rate of the interface. In switching terms, however, the term bandwidth refers to the capacity of the switch fabric. Therefore, the bandwidth considerations for WAN connections, for example, are not necessarily the same for LAN connections.

Jitter is the variation in delay between consecutive packets. Jitter is often referred to as variation delay. While such variations may be acceptable for applications and data traffic, they can severely impact isochronous traffic, such as digitized voice, which requires that packets are transmitted in a consistent, uniform manner.

Packet loss occurs when one or more packets traversing the network fail to reach their intended destination. This may occur for several reasons, such as bit errors or lack of space in queues, for example. While this does not generally affect connection-oriented protocols, such as TCP, packet loss can cause major issues for real-time traffic, such as voice and streaming video traffic.

Understanding LAN QoS

One of the primary reasons for implementing a QoS solution is to manage scarce bandwidth, which must be shared by voice, data, and even video traffic. WAN connections are relatively expensive and the more bandwidth capability they have, the greater the financial cost. For example, a T1 (1.544 Mbps) would cost more than a T3 (45 Mbps). In such situations, it becomes important to allocate the different types of traffic that will traverse that link a certain percentage or portion of the available total bandwidth. In addition to this, it is also important to ensure that critical and delay-sensitive traffic, such as voice and video, is sent before data.

In LAN switching, however, bandwidth refers to the capacity of the switch fabric. LAN QoS does not pertain to bandwidth management. Instead, LAN QoS is used for buffer management. Switches require buffering to avoid buffer overflows, which occur when multiple ingress ports are contending for the same egress port, as shown below in Figure 10-4:

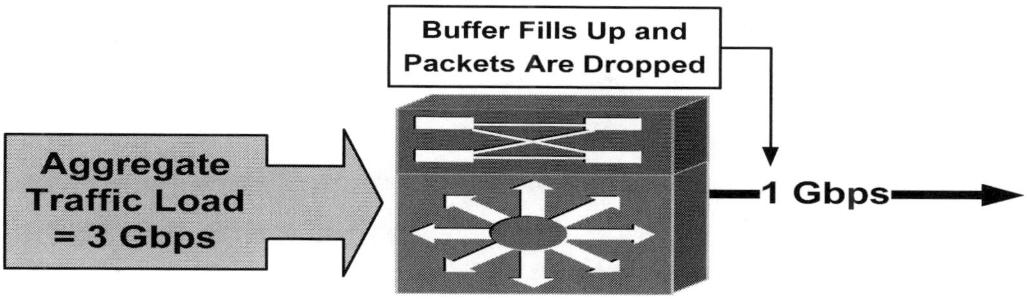

Fig. 10-4. Buffer Overflows

In Figure 10-4, multiple ingress ports are all contending for the same egress port. The aggregate traffic load from these ports is 3 Gbps. However, the egress port is only 1 Gbps. The egress port is therefore oversubscribed and its buffers begin to fill up, which may result in packet loss. This may result in head of line blocking (HOLB). The HOLB concept is shown below in Figure 10-5:

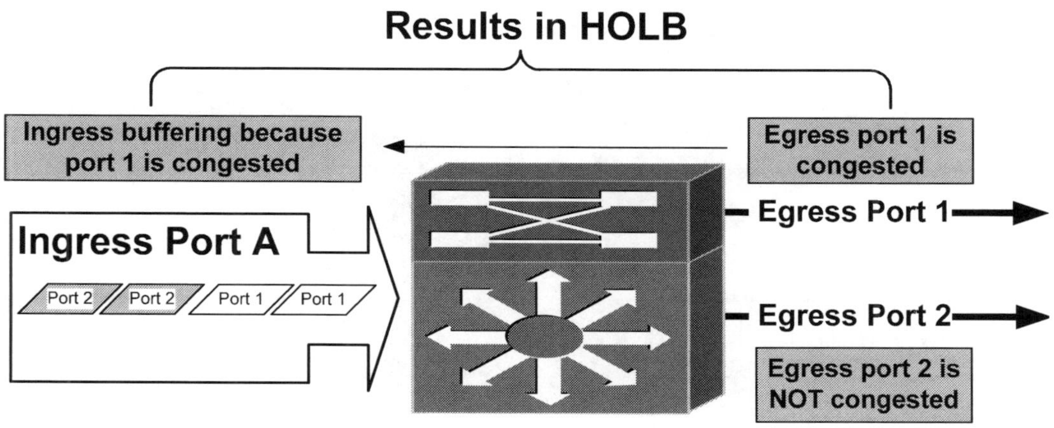

Fig. 10-5. Head of Line Blocking (HOLB)

Referencing the diagram illustrated in Figure 10-5, Ingress Port A has frames to send via Egress Port 1 and Egress Port 2. Egress Port 1 is currently congested but Egress Port 2 is not. The congestion on Egress Port 1 results in ingress buffering on Ingress Port A. By default, the frames destined to both

Egress Port 1 and Egress Port 2 are buffered in the same input First-In First-Out (FIFO) queue. This means that frames destined to Egress Port 2 are blocked by the head of the line (frames destined to Egress Port 1), even though Egress Port 2 is not congested.

If, for example, the traffic destined to Egress Port 2 were real-time traffic, such as voice or video, this would severely impact the quality of these applications. These issues cannot simply be resolved by increasing the bandwidth. Instead, Catalyst QoS features must be implemented to ensure adequate queue management for the queues serving different traffic classes.

Catalyst QoS Basics

Catalyst switch QoS is primarily based on the Layer 2 markings that are contained within a frame (i.e. the CoS value). However, it can also be based on the Layer 3 markings contained within a packet (i.e. the IP Precedence or DSCP values). IP Precedence and DSCP were described in the preceding sections. The CoS value is contained in the VLAN field for 802.1Q and ISL-encapsulated frames.

IEEE 802.1Q inserts a 4-byte field into the original frame. The first 2 bytes are the Tag Protocol Identifier field, which is used to indicate an IEEE 802.1Q tag. The second 2 bytes are the Tag Control Information field. The TCI field contains a 3-bit User Priority field, referred to as the 802.1p User Priority field, which is used to implement CoS. This field is illustrated below in Figure 10-6:

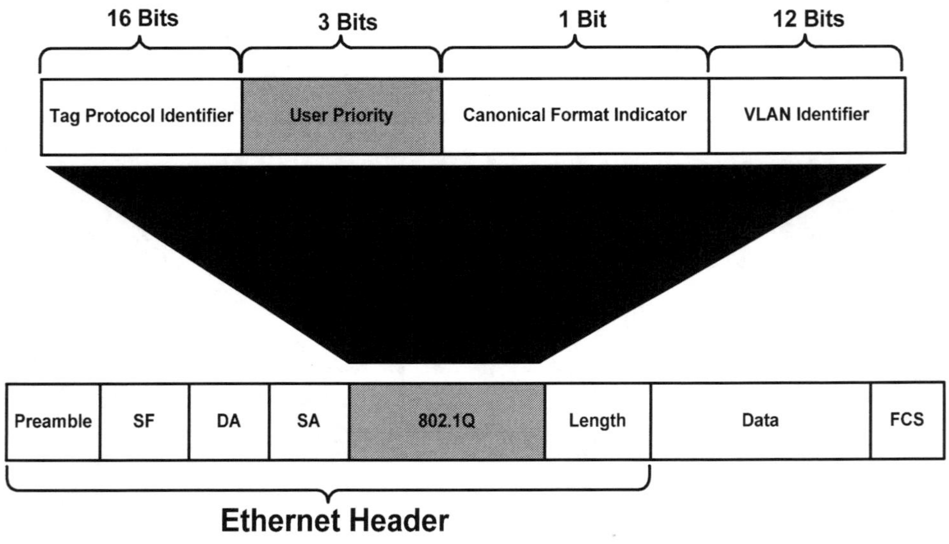

Fig. 10-6. IEEE 802.1Q Class of Service Bits

Referencing Figure 10-6, the 3-bit User Priority (802.1p) field can be used to set eight (2^3) different binary values. These values are illustrated below in Table 10-6, which also illustrates how these values are mapped to the decimal DSCP values and the DSCP PHB sets.

Table 10-6. The Default CoS-to-DSCP Mappings

Layer 2 CoS	Binary	Layer 3 DSCP (Decimal)	Layer 3 DSCP (PHB Set)
0	000	0	Default
1	001	8	CS 1, AF 11, AF 12, AF 13
2	010	16	CS 2, AF 21, AF 22, AF 23
3	011	24	CS 3, AF 31, AF 32, AF 33
4	100	32	CS 4, AF 41, AF 42, AF 43
5	101	40	CS 5
6	110	48	CS 6
7	111	56	CS 7

There is also a CoS value contained in the ISL frame. Unlike 802.1Q, ISL prepends an ISL header to the Ethernet header. This is contained within the VLAN field as shown below in Figure 10-7:

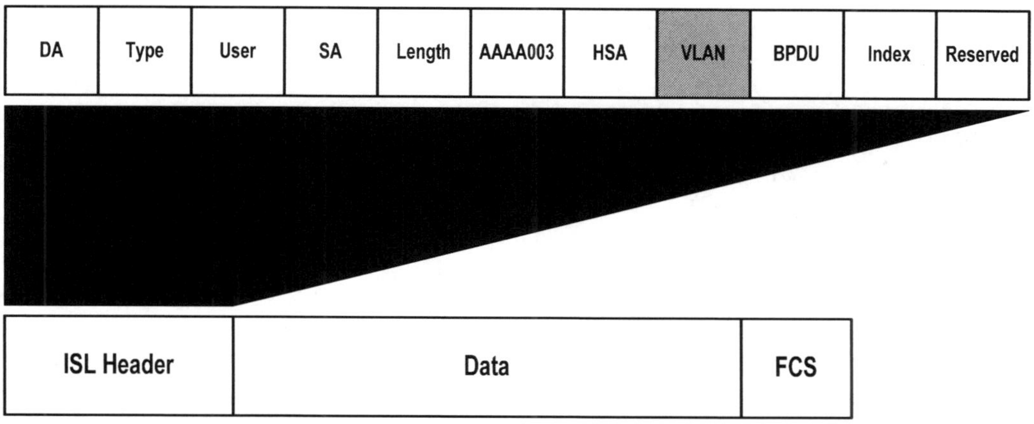

Fig. 10-7. ISL Class of Service Bits

When using ISL, 3 bits within the VLAN field contain the priority bit setting. This allows for the same eight priority levels (2^3) supported by the 802.1Q standard and listed in Table 10-6 above.

NOTE: Newer Catalyst switches no longer support ISL and default to 802.1Q. These switches will ignore ISL because IEEE 802.1Q is the default. Therefore, you will almost always find documentation referring to 802.1Q/p, which indicates the User Priority bit in the 802.1Q frame. However, because ISL is still supported in some Cisco Catalyst switches, you should know it.

By default, QoS is disabled on Catalyst switches. In this default mode, all frames and packets received by the switch are passed through unaltered. For example, if a Catalyst switch receives a frame with a particular CoS value and an IP packet with a particular DSCP value, these received values are in no way modified by the switch, and the frame and packet are transmitted with the same values.

However, in this default mode, it is important to know that all traffic, including real-time traffic such as voice, will be delivered on a best-effort basis, and all traffic will use a single queue on the switch. The different queues will be described later in this chapter. This default behavior is verified using the `show mls qos` command as shown in the following output:

```
Catalyst-Switch-1#show mls qos
QoS is disabled
QoS ip packet dscp rewrite is enabled
```

NOTE: Although the second statement states that DSCP rewrite is enabled, it is not. In other words, when QoS is enabled, the switch will not rewrite the DSCP value of received frames. QoS is enabled on the switch by issuing the `mls qos` global configuration command. This configuration is illustrated in the following output:

```
Catalyst-Switch-1(config)#mls qos
```

Once enabled, the `show mls qos` command can be used to verify this configuration. The output of this configuration once QoS is enabled is illustrated as follows:

```
Catalyst-3750-1#show mls qos
QoS is enabled
QoS ip packet dscp rewrite is enabled
```

When QoS is enabled on the switch, all switch ports are considered untrusted. In this mode, the switch port will assign the incoming frame a CoS value based on a configured default CoS for the port or based on the internal mapping tables within the switch. The switch mapping tables are beyond the scope of the SWITCH exam requirements.

In Catalyst switches, the default CoS value assigned to an untrusted interface is 0; however, it can be set to any value manually defined by the administration. The packet DSCP value is also set based on the internal CoS-to-DSCP mapping table on the switch. The default CoS-to-DSCP mapping values are illustrated in Table 10-6 above.

For example, if the switch receives a frame from an untrusted access port with a CoS value of 3, it will reset the three 802.1Q/p priority bits contained in the frame to 0. The switch will use this value to derive the DSCP value based on the CoS-to-DSCP map that resides internally within the switch. Given that CoS 0 maps to DSCP 0, the DSCP of the packet is also set to 0. The following output shows the default CoS value on an untrusted port when QoS is enabled globally and the port trust state is untrusted.

```
Catalyst-Switch-1#show mls qos interface gigabitethernet 0/1
GigabitEthernet0/1
trust state: not trusted
trust mode: not trusted
COS override: dis
default COS: 0
pass-through: none
trust device: none
```

Catalyst Ingress QoS Mechanisms

Ingress QoS mechanisms are applied to frames and packets received by the switch in the inbound direction. The following Catalyst switch ingress QoS mechanisms are described:

- Traffic Classification
- Traffic Policing
- Marking
- Congestion Management and Avoidance

NOTE: Only the QoS configurations that are relevant to the SWITCH exam will be illustrated in the configuration examples in this chapter.

Traffic Classification

Classification is used to differentiate one stream of traffic from another so that different service levels can be applied to different streams of traffic. Frames can be classified based on the incoming CoS or DSCP values or even based on Access Control List (ACL) configuration.

Frames contain CoS bits that are used to differentiate different classes of traffic. Classification in the Layer 3 header takes place in the ToS field. The QoS labels used in the Layer 3 IP header are IP Precedence and DSCP.

When the switch receives a frame or packet with an already existing QoS value, it must decide whether to trust the received QoS value. This is determined using the port trust setting. As stated earlier in this chapter, when QoS is enabled, by default, all switch interfaces are untrusted. Untrusted ports do not trust any of the QoS markings sent by the connected device and the switch will re-mark all inbound Ethernet frames to a CoS value of 0.

Trust settings are configured at the trust boundary, which is the perimeter of the network, such as the access port to which a user PC or IP phone is connected. The traffic received from beyond the perimeter is considered untrusted. The concept of the trust boundary is illustrated below in Figure 10-8:

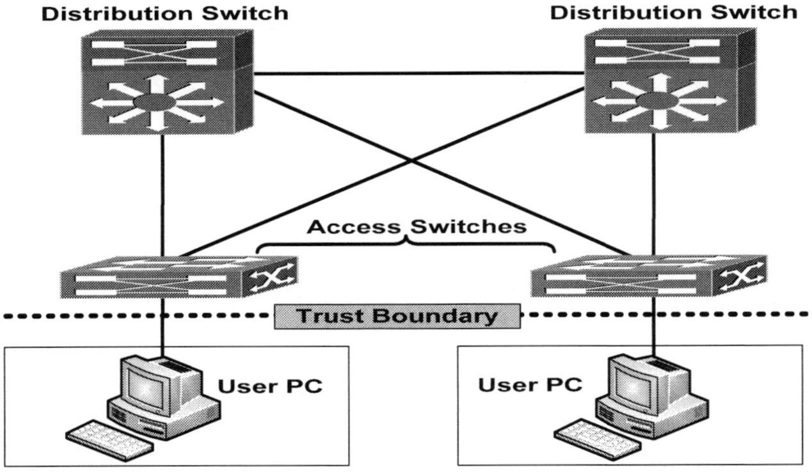

Fig. 10-8. Understanding the Trust Boundary

Referencing Figure 10-8, the trust boundary, which is the perimeter at which switches do not trust incoming QoS labels, resides between the switch ports and the connected workstations. By default, the access layer switches will not trust the QoS settings set by either workstation. In Cisco IPT solutions, when IP phones are integrated into the LAN, the trust boundary is typically extended to the region between the phone and the connected device.

The IP phone should be trusted; however, the QoS settings from the device connected to the IP phone should not. By default, when a Cisco IP phone is connected to a Catalyst switch, the switch instructs the phone to consider the port connected to the attached device as untrusted. The packets of frames received from that device are therefore rewritten to the default value. Figure 10-9 below illustrates the trust boundary when Cisco IP phones are connected to the switches:

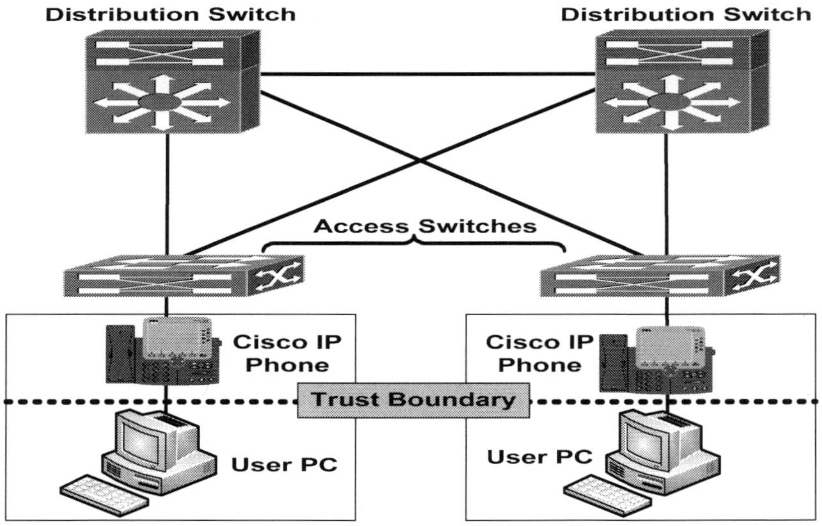

Fig. 10-9. Understanding the Trust Boundary with Cisco IP Phones

Referencing Figure 10-9, the IP phone is basically looked at as another switch, which is trusted. The IP phone port to which the end user connects becomes the perimeter. Any packets or frames with QoS settings received by the connected workstations are untrusted. The phone rewrites these to the default value.

The trust boundary is configured using the `mls qos trust [cos|device cisco-phone|dscp|ip-precedence]` interface configuration command. The `[cos]` keyword configures the switch port to trust the received CoS value on ingress (inbound) frames.

The CoS bits are only present in the 802.1Q or ISL-encapsulated frame, which means that the `[cos]` keyword should only be used on trunk ports or on ports connected to Cisco IP phones. While ports connected to Cisco IP phones are MVAPs, the switch uses CDP to instruct the IP phone to tag the voice packets with the specified VVID. The 802.1Q tag contains the User Priority bits (802.1p), which allow for classification of the voice traffic.

Normal data from the PC connected to the Cisco IP phone is sent untagged and is placed into the normal queue. The following output illustrates how to configure a Layer 2 access port that is connected to a Cisco IP phone to trust the CoS values in traffic sent by the phone:

```
Catalyst-Switch-1(config)#mls qos
Catalyst-Switch-1(config)#interface fastethernet 0/1
Catalyst-Switch-1(config-if)#description 'Layer 2 Access Port To Cisco IP
                             Phone'
Catalyst-Switch-1(config-if)#switchport
Catalyst-Switch-1(config-if)#switchport access vlan 100
Catalyst-Switch-1(config-if)#switchport voice vlan 200
Catalyst-Switch-1(config-if)#switchport mode access
Catalyst-Switch-1(config-if)#mls qos trust cos
Catalyst-Switch-1(config-if)#exit
```

The following output illustrates how to configure an 802.1Q trunk port to trust the incoming CoS settings on received frames:

```
Catalyst-Switch-1(config)#mls qos
Catalyst-Switch-1(config)#interface gigabitethernet 0/1
Catalyst-Switch-1(config-if)#description 'Trunk Port To Catalyst-Switch-2'
Catalyst-Switch-1(config-if)#switchport
Catalyst-Switch-1(config-if)#switchport trunk encapsulation dot1q
Catalyst-Switch-1(config-if)#switchport mode trunk
Catalyst-Switch-1(config-if)#mls qos trust cos
Catalyst-Switch-1(config-if)#exit
```

These configurations can be validated using the `show mls qos interface [name]` command. The output of this command is illustrated as follows:

```
Catalyst-Switch-1#show mls qos interface gigabitethernet 0/1
GigabitEthernet0/1
trust state: trust cos
trust mode: trust cos
COS override: dis
default COS: 0
pass-through: none
trust device: none
```

The `[device cisco-phone]` keywords configure the switch port to trust the specified QoS setting only if it is received from a Cisco IP phone. This configuration must be used in conjunction with either the `mls qos trust cos`, the `mls qos trust dscp`, or the `mls qos trust ip-precedence` interface configuration commands.

The switch will only trust the CoS or DSCP value sent from the Cisco IP phone. If a Cisco IP phone is not detected, the specified QoS parameter is not trusted. The following output illustrates how to configure the switch to trust the CoS value on ingress packets sent by a Cisco IP phone:

```
Catalyst-Switch-1(config)#mls qos
Catalyst-Switch-1(config)#interface fastethernet 0/1
Catalyst-Switch-1(config-if)#description 'Layer 2 Access Port To Cisco IP
                             Phone'
Catalyst-Switch-1(config-if)#switchport
Catalyst-Switch-1(config-if)#switchport access vlan 100
Catalyst-Switch-1(config-if)#switchport voice vlan 200
Catalyst-Switch-1(config-if)#switchport mode access
Catalyst-Switch-1(config-if)#mls qos trust cos
Catalyst-Switch-1(config-if)#mls qos trust device cisco-phone
Catalyst-Switch-1(config-if)#exit
```

Again, the `show mls qos interface [name]` command can be used to verify this configuration. The output of this command is illustrated as follows:

```
Catalyst-Switch-1#show mls qos interface fastethernet 0/1
FastEthernet0/1
trust state: not trusted
trust mode: trust cos
COS override: dis
default COS: 0
pass-through: none
trust device: cisco-phone
```

NOTE: In the output above, the CoS value is not trusted because the switch has discovered that a Cisco IP phone is not connected to the port. However, once a Cisco IP phone is connected, the trust state will revert to 'trusted.'

The `[dscp]` keyword configures the switch to classify an ingress packet by using the packet DSCP value. This keyword should be on the port if it is an access port that is NOT connected to a Cisco IP phone (e.g. is connected to a regular workstation) or Layer 3 port.

To understand the reasoning behind this, you have to remember once again that by default, frames or packets received from access ports are untagged, with the exception of Cisco IP phones, which tag frames, as we learned earlier in this chapter. Therefore, traffic sent in from access ports, such as from workstations, is untagged.

This means that there will be no 802.1Q/p bits in such frames, so it is not possible for the switch to classify traffic based on the CoS value. Instead, the switch must be configured to classify ingress packets by looking at the Layer 3 DSCP value of the ingress packet. Once the switch has determined the DSCP value, it maps it to a corresponding Layer 2 CoS value. These values, which are shown in Table 10-6, are again printed below in Table 10-7 for easier reference:

Table 10-7. The Default CoS-to-DSCP Mappings

Layer 2 CoS	Binary	Layer 3 DSCP (Decimal)	Layer 3 DSCP (PHB Set)
0	000	0	Default
1	001	8	CS 1, AF 11, AF 12, AF 13
2	010	16	CS 2, AF 21, AF 22, AF 23
3	011	24	CS 3, AF 31, AF 32, AF 33
4	100	32	CS 4, AF 41, AF 42, AF 43
5	101	40	CS 5
6	110	48	CS 6
7	111	56	CS 7

The same tables are automatically created in the switch when QoS is enabled. While going into the different internal QoS table maps in the switch is beyond the requirements of the SWITCH exam requirements, you can view these on your own using the `show mls qos maps` command. The following output illustrates the configuration of a Layer 2 access port connected to a regular workstation. Ingress packets will be classified based on the DSCP value:

```
Catalyst-Switch-1(config)#mls qos
Catalyst-Switch-1(config)#interface fastethernet 0/1
Catalyst-Switch-1(config-if)#description 'Layer 2 Access Port To Workstation'
Catalyst-Switch-1(config-if)#switchport
Catalyst-Switch-1(config-if)#switchport access vlan 100
Catalyst-Switch-1(config-if)#switchport mode access
Catalyst-Switch-1(config-if)#mls qos trust dscp
Catalyst-Switch-1(config-if)#exit
```

This configuration is verified using the `show mls qos interface [name]` command as illustrated below:

```
Catalyst-Switch-1#show mls qos interface fastethernet 0/1
FastEthernet0/1
trust state: trust dscp
trust mode: trust dscp
COS override: dis
default COS: 0
pass-through: none
trust device: none
```

The `[ip-precedence]` keyword configures the switch to classify an ingress packet by using the packet IP Precedence value. As is the case with the `[dscp]` keyword, the switch will use an internal mapping table to set the appropriate CoS value. The same configuration rule that was stated for the `[dscp]` keyword is also applicable when using the `[ip-precedence]` keyword.

The switch can be configured to instruct the IP phone to trust the IEEE 802.1p priority values received from the PC or the attached device. This may be applicable in situations where the device connected to the IP phone has an application that legitimately sets QoS values, which should be honored by the network.

In addition to this, the switch can also be used to instruct the IP phone to override the IEEE 802.1p values in frames received from the attached workstation to either 0, which is the default, or to another administrator-defined value between 1 and 7. These two functions can be enabled using the `switchport priority extend [cos <value> | trust]` interface configuration command.

The `switchport priority extend cos <value>` interface configuration command configures the switch to instruct the Cisco IP phone to override the 802.1p values from the attached device with the CoS value specified in this command.

By default, the Cisco IP phone sets the 802.1p values from any attached device to 0 and does not trust tagged traffic received from a device connected to its access port. The following output illustrates how to configure the switch to instruct the IP phone to mark tagged ingress traffic received from a device connected to the access port on the IP phone to a CoS value of 3:

```
Catalyst-Switch-1(config)#mls qos
Catalyst-Switch-1(config)#interface fastethernet 0/1
Catalyst-Switch-1(config-if)#description 'Layer 2 Access Port To Cisco IP
                                Phone'
Catalyst-Switch-1(config-if)#switchport
Catalyst-Switch-1(config-if)#switchport access vlan 100
Catalyst-Switch-1(config-if)#switchport voice vlan 200
```

```
Catalyst-Switch-1(config-if)#switchport mode access
Catalyst-Switch-1(config-if)#mls qos trust cos
Catalyst-Switch-1(config-if)#switchport priority extend cos 3
Catalyst-Switch-1(config-if)#exit
```

This configuration can be verified using the `show interfaces [name] switchport` command, which shows the configured appliance trust value. This is illustrated below in the following output:

```
Catalyst-Switch-1#show interfaces fastethernet 0/1 switchport
Name: Fa0/1
Switchport: Enabled
Administrative Mode: static access
Operational Mode: static access
Administrative Trunking Encapsulation: dot1q
Operational Trunking Encapsulation: native
Negotiation of Trunking: Off
Access Mode VLAN: 100 (User-Data-VLAN)
Trunking Native Mode VLAN: 1 (default)
Voice VLAN: 200 (User-Voice-VLAN)
Administrative private-vlan host-association: none
Administrative private-vlan mapping: none
Operational private-vlan: none
Trunking VLANs Enabled: ALL
Pruning VLANs Enabled: 2-1001
Capture Mode Disabled
Capture VLANs Allowed: ALL

Protected: false

Voice VLAN: 200 (User-Voice-VLAN)
Appliance trust: 3
```

The following output illustrates how to configure the switch to instruct the Cisco IP phone to trust tagged traffic received from a device connected to the access port of the Cisco IP phone:

```
Catalyst-Switch-1(config)#mls qos
Catalyst-Switch-1(config)#interface fastethernet 0/1
Catalyst-Switch-1(config-if)#description 'Layer 2 Access Port To Cisco IP
                             Phone'
Catalyst-Switch-1(config-if)#switchport
Catalyst-Switch-1(config-if)#switchport access vlan 100
Catalyst-Switch-1(config-if)#switchport voice vlan 200
Catalyst-Switch-1(config-if)#switchport mode access
Catalyst-Switch-1(config-if)#mls qos trust cos
Catalyst-Switch-1(config-if)#switchport priority extend trust
Catalyst-Switch-1(config-if)#exit
```

This configuration is verified using the `show interfaces [name] switchport` command as illustrated below in the following output:

```
Catalyst-Switch-1#show interfaces fastethernet 0/1 switchport
Name: Fa0/1
Switchport: Enabled
Administrative Mode: static access
Operational Mode: static access
Administrative Trunking Encapsulation: dot1q
Operational Trunking Encapsulation: native
Negotiation of Trunking: Off
Access Mode VLAN: 100 (User-Data-VLAN)
Trunking Native Mode VLAN: 1 (default)
Voice VLAN: 200 (User-Voice-VLAN)
Administrative private-vlan host-association: none
Administrative private-vlan mapping: none
Operational private-vlan: none
Trunking VLANs Enabled: ALL
Pruning VLANs Enabled: 2-1001
Capture Mode Disabled
Capture VLANs Allowed: ALL

Protected: false

Voice VLAN: 200 (User-Voice-VLAN)
Appliance trust: trusted
```

In addition to manual configuration, Cisco IOS software allows administrators to use Auto-QoS to simplify QoS implementation. Auto-QoS is implemented by a macro that makes assumptions about the network. As a result, the switch can prioritize different traffic flows and appropriately use the egress queues instead of using the default QoS behavior. The switch egress queues will be described later in this chapter.

Auto-QoS configures QoS classification and configures egress queues. Auto-QoS should never be used in conjunction with manual QoS configuration. Either Auto-QoS or manual QoS configuration should be implemented, never both. Therefore, before implementing Auto-QoS, it is important to ensure that you remove any previously implemented QoS configuration on the switch.

When Auto-QoS is enabled, Cisco IOS software automatically enables QoS globally if it has not already been enabled. In other words, you do not need to issue the `mls qos` global configuration command before enabling Auto-QoS. Enabling Auto-QoS does the following on the switch:

- It enables QoS in the global configuration (i.e. issues the mls qos command)
- It configures the switch port to trust the incoming CoS parameters
- It configures queues and thresholds in the global configuration
- It configures the traffic-shaping parameters for the port on which it is enabled

After these initial changes, every time you configure any port with Auto-QoS, it configures only the switch port with QoS parameters. Auto-QoS is enabled using the `auto qos voip [cisco-phone | cisco-softphone | trust]` interface configuration command.

The `[cisco-phone]` keyword should be used to enable Auto-QoS if the switch port is connected to a Cisco IP phone. The CoS values will be trusted only if the port is indeed connected to an IP phone; otherwise, the port will be considered untrusted if a phone is not detected. The following output illustrates how to enable Auto-QoS on a switch port so that it trusts the received QoS labels if the port is connected to a Cisco IP phone:

```
Catalyst-Switch-1(config)#mls qos
Catalyst-Switch-1(config)#interface fastethernet 0/1
Catalyst-Switch-1(config-if)#description 'Layer 2 Access Port To Cisco IP
                                 Phone'
Catalyst-Switch-1(config-if)#switchport
Catalyst-Switch-1(config-if)#switchport access vlan 100
Catalyst-Switch-1(config-if)#switchport voice vlan 200
Catalyst-Switch-1(config-if)#switchport mode access
Catalyst-Switch-1(config-if)# auto qos voip cisco-phone
Catalyst-Switch-1(config-if)#exit
```

This configuration is verified using the `show mls qos interface [name]` command as illustrated below in the following output:

```
Catalyst-Switch-1#show mls qos interface fastethernet 0/1
FastEthernet0/1
trust state: not trusted
trust mode: trust cos
COS override: dis
default COS: 0
pass-through: none
trust device: cisco-phone
```

The `show auto qos [interface [name]]` command can also be used to verify Auto-QoS implementation for all interfaces, or on a per-interface basis. The output of this command is illustrated as follows:

```
Catalyst-Switch-1#show auto qos interface fastethernet 0/1
Initial configuration applied by AutoQoS:
!
interface FastEthernet0/1
 mls qos trust device cisco-phone
 mls qos trust cos
```

The commands implemented by Auto-QoS can also be viewed in the `running-config` command of the switch as shown in the following output:

```
Catalyst-Switch-1#show running-config interface fastethernet 0/1
Building configuration...

Current configuration : 129 bytes
!
interface FastEthernet0/1
 no ip address
 mls qos trust device cisco-phone
 mls qos trust cos
 auto qos voip cisco-phone
end
```

The [cisco-softphone] keyword should be used on an access port that is connected to a workstation, laptop, etc., that is running the Cisco SoftPhone. When this command is enabled, the switch uses policing, which will be described later in this chapter, to decide whether a packet is in-profile or out-of-profile and to specify the action on the packet.

If the packet does not have a DSCP value of 24, 26, or 46, or is out-of-profile, the switch changes the DSCP value to 0. In addition to this, the switch configures ingress and egress queues on the port. While the configuration of the ingress and egress queues is beyond the scope of the SWITCH exam requirements, the debug autoqos command can be used to see the various queue parameters that are automatically configured by the switch when Auto-QoS is enabled. The output of the debug autoqos command on a Catalyst 2950 switch is shown in the following output:

```
Catalyst-2950-1-#debug autoqos
AutoQoS debugging is on
Catalyst-Switch-1#
Catalyst-Switch-1#conf t
Enter configuration commands, one per line.  End with CNTL/Z.
Catalyst-Switch-1(config)#int f0/1
Catalyst-Switch-1(config-if)#auto qos voip cisco-phone

00:53:39: wrr-queue bandwidth 20 1 80 0
00:53:40: no wrr-queue cos-map
00:53:41: wrr-queue cos-map 1 0 1 2 4
Catalyst-Switch-1(config-if)#
00:53:42: wrr-queue cos-map 3 3 6 7
00:53:43: wrr-queue cos-map 4 5
00:53:44: mls qos map cos-dscp 0 8 16 26 32 46 48 56
00:53:46: interface FastEthernet0/1
00:53:46:  mls qos trust device cisco-phone
00:53:46:  mls qos trust cos
```

NOTE: In newer switch models, the command is debug auto qos, not debug autoqos. The [trust] keyword should be issued on a switch port that is connected to the interior of the network. This could be a trunk to another switch or router, for example. When this keyword is used, the switch trusts the CoS value for Layer 2 ports or the DSCP value for Layer 3 ports in ingress packets. This is based on the assumption that traffic has already been classified by other edge devices. The switch also configures the ingress and egress queues on the switch port. The following output illustrates how to configure the switch port to trust QoS values in incoming packets and frames on an uplink (trunk) to another switch:

```
Catalyst-Switch-1(config)#mls qos
Catalyst-Switch-1(config)#interface gigabitethernet 0/1
Catalyst-Switch-1(config-if)#description 'Trunk Port To Distribution Switch'
Catalyst-Switch-1(config-if)#switchport
Catalyst-Switch-1(config-if)#switchport trunk encapsulation dotlq
Catalyst-Switch-1(config-if)#switchport mode trunk
Catalyst-Switch-1(config-if)# auto qos voip trust
Catalyst-Switch-1(config-if)#exit
```

These configurations can be validated using the `show auto qos interface [name]` command. The output of this command is illustrated as follows:

```
Catalyst-Switch-1#show auto qos interface gigabitethernet 0/1
Initial configuration applied by AutoQoS:
!
interface GigabitEthernet0/1
 mls qos trust cos
Catalyst-Switch-1#
```

In the configuration above, the `mls qos trust cos` interface configuration command has been automatically enabled on the uplink based on the Auto-QoS configuration. The switch will trust incoming QoS settings for all frames received via this interface. It is assumed that classification has already been performed and the QoS settings from the Distribution switch can be trusted.

NOTE: The configuration of the remaining ingress QoS mechanisms is beyond the scope of the SWITCH exam requirements; however, they are briefly described to give you an understanding of what the terms mean and how they are implemented.

Traffic Policing

Policing is a process that is used to limit traffic to a prescribed rate. Policing is used to compare the ingress traffic rate to a configured policer. The policer is configured with a rate and a burst. The rate defines the amount of traffic that is sent per given interval. When that specified amount has been sent, no more traffic is sent for that given interval. The burst defines the amount of traffic that can be held in readiness for being sent. Traffic in excess of the burst either can be dropped or have its priority setting reduced.

Traffic that conforms to the policing configuration is considered in-profile and will be forward, as configured, by the switch. However, traffic that does not conform to the policing configuration is considered out-of-profile, which either can be dropped or marked down (i.e. re-marked with a lower QoS value).

Marking

Marking involves setting QoS bits inside the Layer 2 or Layer 3 headers, which allows the other internetwork devices to classify based on the marked values. Marking is typically used in conjunction with traffic policing. For example, if the traffic is in-profile, the switch will typically allow the packets to be passed through (i.e. it will not change or reset the QoS settings in the packets). However, if the traffic is out-of-profile, the switch may be configured to mark down this traffic with a lower QoS value. This concept is illustrated below in Figure 10-10:

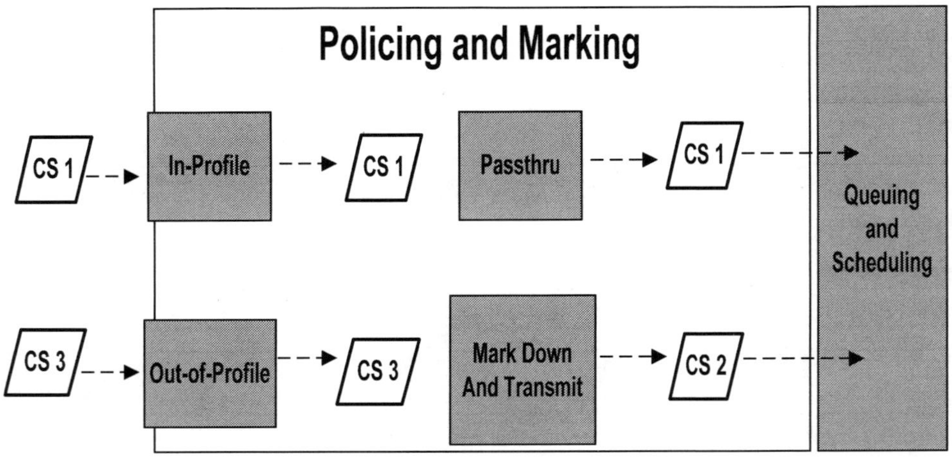

Fig. 10-10. Understanding Policing and Marking

Figure 10-10 shows two packets arriving at the policer. It is assumed that these packets have already been classified based on the port trust state configuration. The incoming packets are then compared against the configured policer rate. The packet with DSCP value CS 1 is in-profile (i.e. in conformance with the policing rate configuration). Based on the policing configuration, this packet is passed through the switch with the QoS setting unchanged.

The packet with DSCP CS 3 is out of policer profile configuration. This traffic is in excess of the burst configuration. This traffic either can be dropped or marked down. In Figure 10-10, assume that the policing configuration has been implemented so that this traffic is marked down and transmitted with the marked down DSCP value. The value is set to CS 2 and the packet is transmitted. The packet is then sent to the congestion management and avoidance mechanisms, which will determine the ingress queue to place the packet based on the QoS label.

Congestion Management and Avoidance

Congestion management and avoidance is comprised of the following three elements:

- Queuing
- Dropping
- Scheduling

Queuing is used to place packets into different software queues based on the QoS labels. After the traffic is classified and marked with QoS labels, it is assigned into different queues based on the QoS labels.

NOTE: Queuing is also spelled as queueing in some parts of the world. It means the same.

Catalyst switches typically have two ingress queues, one of which either is a priority queue or can be configured as a priority queue. The ingress frames and packets received by the switch are placed in a queue based on the ingress (received) CoS value. Voice traffic, for example, that is received with CoS 5 or DSCP EF will be placed into the priority queue, while regular data traffic will be placed into the normal queue. This queue concept is illustrated below in Figure 10-11:

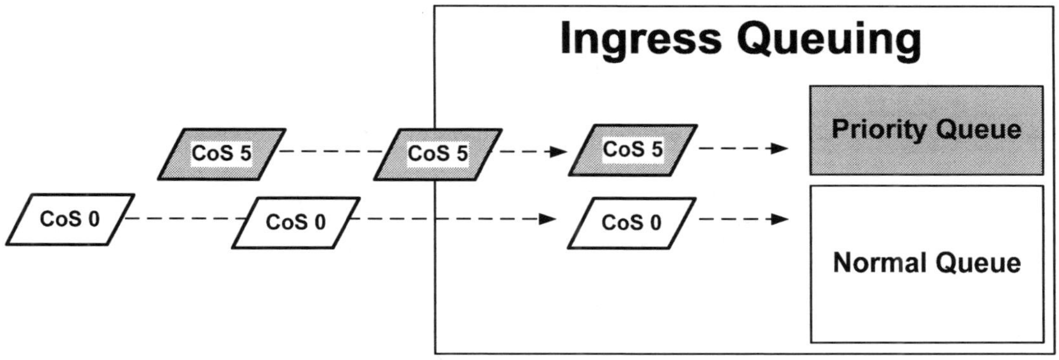

Fig. 10-11. Catalyst Switch Ingress Queue Operation

Once the packets have been placed into the appropriate queue based on their QoS values, dropping is used to manage queues. Dropping provides drop priorities for different classes of traffic. Queues have drop thresholds that are used to indicate which packets can be dropped once the queue has been filled beyond a certain threshold.

After ingress packets are placed into the queue, a congestion avoidance mechanism will use a CoS-to-threshold map to determine what frames are eligible to be dropped when a threshold is breached. This prevents the queues from filling up. The different congestion avoidance mechanisms that can be used are beyond the scope of the SWITCH exam requirements and will not be described in this chapter.

Scheduling refers to how the queues are serviced or emptied. If a priority queue is configured, it only makes sense that this be serviced (emptied) before the normal queue.

In other words, the packets in the priority queue should be sent before the packets in the normal queue. Catalyst switches use Strict Round Robin (SRR) for ingress scheduling. However, going into any detail on SRR is beyond the scope of the SWITCH exam requirements. SRR will not be described in any greater detail in this chapter. Figure 10-12 below illustrates the order of processing of the ingress QoS mechanisms described in this section:

Fig. 10-12. Ingress Quality of Service Mechanisms

Referencing Figure 10-12, we can see that the packet or frame is classified, policed, and marked and then it is sent to the ingress queue(s).

Catalyst Egress QoS Mechanisms

Egress QoS mechanisms are applied to frames and packets received by the switch in the outbound direction. The following Catalyst switch egress QoS mechanism is described:

- Congestion Management and Avoidance

Congestion Management and Avoidance

Congestion management and avoidance in the egress direction is also comprised of the same three elements used in ingress congestion management and avoidance, which are queuing, dropping, and scheduling. Queuing is used to place packets into different software queues based on the received packet QoS labels. Catalyst switches typically have more egress queues than ingress queues. Depending on the platform and other variables, this number may range from two queues to four queues.

Once the packets have been placed into the appropriate queue based on their QoS values, dropping is used to manage queues. Dropping is a congestion avoidance mechanism that uses drop priorities for different classes of traffic. Queues have drop thresholds that are used to indicate which packets can be dropped once the queue has filled beyond a certain threshold. The same congestion avoidance mechanism may be used for both ingress and egress queue congestion avoidance.

Scheduling refers to how the queues are serviced or emptied. As is the case with ingress QoS operation, if a priority queue is configured, it will be serviced before the normal queue. Strict Round Robin (SRR) is also used for egress scheduling. You are not required to implement any egress QoS configurations, as they are beyond the scope of the SWITCH exam requirements.

Understanding Power over Ethernet (PoE)

In converged internetworks, Cisco Catalyst switches interact with Cisco IP phones in the following three different ways:

1. VLAN tagging
2. Extended trust settings
3. Inline power delivery

VLAN tagging is based on the `switchport voice vlan` interface configuration command, which is described in detail in the 'Configuring Switches to Support Cisco IP Phones' section of this chapter. Extended trust settings are based on the `switchport priority extend` interface configuration command, which is described in the 'Catalyst Switch Ingress QoS Mechanisms' section of this chapter. This section describes inline power (ILP).

Cisco IP phones can use an external power cube to draw their power, or they can draw their power from the switch to which they are connected. This power is sent within the Ethernet cable connecting the switch and the IP phone. The following are two methods for providing ILP:

- IEEE 802.3af-2003
- Cisco Inline Power

IEEE 802.3af-2003 and Cisco Inline Power Overview

IEEE 802.3af-2003 is a ratified version of the original IEEE 802.3af standard. This was ratified in 2003, hence the name 802.3af-2003. The IEEE 802.3af-2003 Power over Ethernet (PoE) standard defines terminology to describe a port that acts as a power source (PSE) to a powered device (PD), defines how a powered device is detected, and defines two (2) methods of PoE to the discovered powered device.

IEEE 802.3af-2003 power may be delivered using a PoE-capable Ethernet port, which is referred to as an End-Point PSE, or by a mid-span PSE that can be used to deliver PoE in the event an existing non-PoE-capable Ethernet switch is used. The mid-span PSE is described later in this section.

IEEE 802.3af-2003 is an open standard that describes five power classes to which a device can belong. The default power classification within IEEE 802.3af-2003 delivers 15.4 W per power device. The five 802.3af-2003 power classes are listed below in Table 10-8:

Table 10-8. IEEE 802.3af-2003 Power Classes

	Min. Power Levels Output at PSE	Max. Power Levels at the PD	Usage
0	15.4 W	0.44 to 12.95 W	Default
1	4.0 W	0.44 to 3.84 W	Optional
2	7.0 W	3.84 to 6.49 W	Optional
3	15.4 W	6.49 to 12.95 W	Optional
4	N/A	N/A	Reserved

Cisco ILP is a proprietary approach. The IEEE 802.3af standard is actually based on this method of PoE, which was available before PoE was standardized. Cisco has also extended power management extensions using CDP negotiation to Cisco IEEE 802.3af-2003-compliant devices to further optimize PSE power management. Cisco Catalyst switches support both ILP and IEEE 802.3af-2003.

Discovering Powered Devices

Before providing power, the switch needs to determine whether the port is connected to a power-capable device. Cisco ILP and the IEEE 802.3af-2003 standard use different power detection methods, both of which are supported by the switch.

IEEE 802.3af-2003 uses a Direct Current (DC)-powered device detection method. The DC detection method applies a DC current and detects the presence of a PD by measuring the load applied by the PD. The switch (PSE) will expect to see a 25 kΩ (Kilo Ohm) resistance between the pairs in order for the device to be considered a valid PD. If the PSE does not detect a valid 25 kΩ resistor, power is not applied to the port.

Unlike the IEEE 802.3af-2003 standard, Cisco ILP uses Alternating Current (AC) for PD detection in conjunction with a low-pass filter that allows the phone discovery signal to loop back to the switch but prevents 10/100 or 1000 Mbps frames from passing between the receive and transmit pairs. PD discovery operates in the following manner for Cisco ILP:

1. The switch (PSE) sends a special tone, called a Fast Link Pulse (FLP), out of the port
2. The FLP goes to the PD, such as the Cisco IP phone

3. The PD connects the transmit line to the receive line using a low-pass filter
4. The FLP is looped back to the switch, indicating it is ILP-capable
5. When the switch receives the returning FLP, it applies power to the line
6. The switch port comes up within 5 seconds and the PD boots

NOTE: The FLP will only be looped back when the PD is unpowered (i.e. has not received power). This allows the switch (PSE) to know that the device requires power.

ILP device discovery is illustrated below in Figure 10-13:

Fig. 10-13. Inline Power Device Discovery

Using either the Cisco ILP or IEEE 802.3af-2003 method, if the PD is a Cisco IP phone, it uses CDP to tell the switch (PSE) how much power it wants. The CDP message contains an ILP Type/Length/Value (TLV) field that informs the Cisco Catalyst switch (PSE) of the actual power required by the device.

If the power is less than the default 15.4 W, the PSE acknowledges the request with its available power and modifies the PSE's power budget. If the requesting PD exceeds the power budget for the line card or switch, the port either is powered down or remains in low-power mode.

DC detection differs from AC detection in that AC detection transmits a low-frequency AC signal (a low-pass filter) and expects the same signal to be received back on the receive pair. DC detection applies a DC and detects the presence of a PD by measuring the load applied by the PD.

Supplying Power to Power-Capable Devices

Once the powered device has been detected, the PSE needs to supply power. The IEEE 802.3af-2003 standard states that power may be delivered by an end-point PSE, using either the active data wires of an Ethernet port or the spare wires, to a PD. An end-point PSE, such as a PoE-capable switch, may implement either scheme. It should be noted that even if a device supports both methods of providing power, only one mechanism may be used to deliver power to a PD.

With the IEEE 802.3af-2003 standard, there are two modes that can be used: mode A and mode B. In mode A, pins 1 and 2 form one side of the 48 VDC and pins 3 and 6 form the other side. These are the same pairs used for data transmission. In mode B, pins 4 and 5 form one side of the DC supply and pins 7 and 8 provide the return. These are the unused pairs.

Cisco ILP is provided over the data pairs, as is the case with IEEE 802.3af-2003 mode A. The default ILP allocation is 10 W. However, once the inline device is enabled, it will use CDP to adjust its power to the actual requirement. This enables the PD and PSE to negotiate their respective capabilities in order to explicitly manage how much power is required for the device and how the PSE-capable switch manages the allocation of power to individual PDs.

Disconnecting Power

The PSE is required to detect when the PD has been disconnected in order to ensure that power is withdrawn from a port before a non-powered device, such as a workstation or laptop, is connected to the switch port.

The IEEE 802.3af-2003 standard defines two mechanisms for disconnecting power once a device has failed: DC disconnect and AC disconnect. The DC disconnect method detects when PD current falls below a given threshold (5 to 10 mA) for a given time (300 msec to 400 msec). The AC Disconnect superimposes a small AC voltage on the power and measures the resulting AC current. If the impedance is above 26.25 kΩ (Kilo Ohms), power is shut off. With Cisco ILP, the PoE ports have a power disconnect mechanism that will remove power from the port if the Ethernet link status is down.

ADDITIONAL REAL-WORLD IMPLEMENTATION

The IEEE 802.3at-2009 PoE standard, sometimes called 'POE+,' provides up to 25.5 W of power, although some vendors have announced products that claim to comply with the new IEEE 802.3at-2009 standard and offer up to 50 W of power over a single cable by utilizing all four pairs in the cable.

The IEEE 802.3at-2009 standard also specifies two types of PSEs: endspans and midspans. Endspans are simply PoE-capable Ethernet switches, such as Cisco Catalyst 3750, 4500, and 6500 series switches. Midspans are power injectors that stand between a regular switch and the PD, injecting power without affecting the data. Endspans use pairs 2 and 3 (i.e pins 1, 2, 3, and 6) to send power to the PD. These are the data pairs. Midspans use pairs 1 and 4 (i.e. pins 4, 5, 7, and 8) to send power to the PD. These are the spare pairs.

While Cisco Catalyst switches support both the IEEE 802.3af-2003 and ILP PoE methods, it is important to remember the differences between these two in order to differentiate between them. These differences, which are described in the previous section, include the following:

- The amount of power that is available to the connected device
- The method used for device discovery
- The way that power is removed from the wire when a PD is removed

Configuring Power over Ethernet

Cisco PoE-capable Catalyst switches are configured to supply power on a per-interface or per-port basis using the power inline [auto [max <max-wattage>] | never | static [max <max-wattage>]] interface configuration command. By default, in PoE-capable switches, the default is auto (enabled) and the maximum wattage is 15400 milliwatts.

The [max <max-wattage>] allows the administrator to limit the power allowed on the port. The range is 4000 to 15400 milliwatts. If no value is specified, the maximum is allowed. The [never] keyword is used to disable device detection and disable power to the port.

The [static] keyword is used to enable PD detection and to pre-allocate or reserve power for a switch port before the switch discovers the PD. This is used when connecting to PDs that cannot communicate with the PSE using any of the discovery methods that are described earlier in this section. These advanced PoE configuration options are beyond the scope of the SWITCH exam requirements and will not be described or illustrated in this chapter.

Verifying Power over Ethernet

The show power inline [interface | consumption default | module switch-number] command is used to display the PoE status for the specified PoE port or for all PoE ports.

The [consumption default] option is used to display the power allocated to devices connected to PoE ports. The [module switch-number] keywords are applicable when the switches are stacked together. These keywords can be used to limit the display of ports on the specified stack member. This is beyond the scope of the SWITCH exam requirements. The following output illustrates how to verify PoE status using the show power inline command:

```
Catalyst-Switch-1#show power inline

Module   Available     Used     Remaining
          (Watts)     (Watts)    (Watts)
```

```
------    ---------    --------    ---------
1         370.0        114.9       255.1
2         370.0         34.3       335.0

Interface Admin  Oper       Power   Device              Class Max
                            (Watts)
--------- ------ ---------- ------- ------------------- ----- ----
Fa1/0/1   auto   on         6.3     IP Phone 7910       n/a   15.4
Fa1/0/2   auto   on         6.3     IP Phone 7910       n/a   15.4
...
[Truncated Output]
...
```

Chapter Summary

The following section is a summary of the major points you should be aware of in this chapter.

Integrating Voice, Video, and Data Traffic

- Converged networks carry voice, video and data traffic over the same infrastructure
- IPT makes use of packet-switched connections to exchange of communications services
- The Cisco Unified Videoconferencing solution is based on the H.323 standard
- Voice calls create traffic flows with fixed data rates
- Voice traffic flows are considered isochronous
- Isochronous traffic does not tolerate delay or packet loss very well
- Packet video can be divided into two categories: interactive video and non-interactive video

Configuring Switches to Support Cisco IP Phones

- Cisco IP phones can be connected to the switch either using a trunk port or an access port
- Configuring a trunk to the IP phone allows voice traffic to be isolated from user traffic
- Trunking allows for Quality of Service (QoS) using the User Priority bits (802.1p)
- The primary disadvantage to trunk port configuration is high CPU utilization on the switch
- The recommend method of configuring the switch port is to configure it as an MVAP
- On an MVAP, a native VLAN for data traffic is identified by the PVID
- An Auxiliary VLAN for voice service is identified by the voice VLAN identified (VVID)
- Frames sent by the PC connected to the Cisco IP phones are sent in the native VLAN
- Frames or packets sent by the Cisco IP phone will use the auxiliary VLAN (VVID)
- The `switchport voice vlan` configuration options are listed and described below:

Command Keyword	Description
`vlan-id`	This is used to specify the VVID. Voice traffic is placed into the voice VLAN specified by this command.
`dot1p`	This keyword instructs the IP phone to place voice traffic into an 802.1Q/p (priority) tagged frame with the VLAN ID set to 0. Voice traffic is placed into the access VLAN.
`none`	This keyword is the default and it allows the IP phone to use its own configuration. Voice traffic is placed into the access VLAN.
`untagged`	This keyword instructs the IP phone to place voice traffic into an untagged frame. Voice traffic is placed into the access VLAN.

The Three QoS Models

- The three Quality of Service models are:
    1. Best Effort Delivery (Default)
    2. Integrated Services
    3. Differentiated Services

- The Best-Effort (BE) model does not guarantee any level of service
- The Integrated Services (IntServ) performs admission control for each flow request
- The DiffServ model defines the concept of service classes

Quality of Service Overview

- Quality of Service (QoS) is required to manage network resources
- All networks experience the following:
  1. Delay
  2. Bandwidth
  3. Jitter
  4. Packet Loss

- The total delay, from start to finish, is referred to as latency
- Bandwidth is the bps that are expected to be delivered successfully across some medium
- Jitter is the variation in delay between consecutive packets
- Packet loss occurs when one or more packets fail to reach their intended destination

Understanding LAN QoS

- LAN Quality of Service does not pertain to bandwidth management
- LAN QoS is used for buffer management
- Switches require buffering to avoid buffer overflows

Catalyst QoS Basics

- Catalyst switch QoS is based on the Layer 2 markings that are contained within a frame
- The CoS value is contained in the VLAN field for 802.1Q and ISL-encapsulated frames
- IEEE 802.1Q inserts a 4 byte field into the original frame
- The TCI field contains a 3-bit User Priority field, referred to as the 802.1p priority field
- The 3-bit User Priority (802.1p) field can be used to set eight (2^3) different binary values
- By default, QoS is disabled on Catalyst switches
- In this default mode, all frames or packets are passed through unaltered
- With QoS disabled, traffic is delivered on a best-effort basis
- With QoS disabled, all traffic (including voice packets) use the same queue
- When Quality of Service is enabled on the switch, all switch ports are considered untrusted
- In Catalyst switches, the default CoS value assigned to an untrusted interface is 0

Catalyst Ingress QoS Mechanisms

- Catalyst switches use the following ingress QoS mechanisms:
  1. Traffic Classification

2. Traffic Policing
3. Marking
4. Congestion Management and Avoidance

- Classification is used to differentiate one stream of traffic from another
- Frames can be classified based on the incoming CoS or DSCP values
- Frames can also be classified based on ACL configuration
- With classification, trust settings are configured at the trust boundary
- Enabling Auto-QoS does the following on the switch:
  1. It enables Quality of Service in the global configuration (i.e. issues the `mls qos` command)
  2. It configures the switch port to trust the incoming CoS parameters
  3. It configures queues and thresholds in the global configuration
  4. It configures the traffic-shaping parameters for the port on which it is enabled

- Traffic policing is a process that is used to limit traffic to a prescribed rate
- Policing is used to compare the ingress traffic rate to a configured policer
- The policer is configured with a rate and a burst
- The rate defines the amount of traffic that is sent per given interval
- The burst defines the amount of traffic that can be held in readiness for being sent
- Marking involves setting QoS bits inside the Layer 2 or Layer 3 headers
- Congestion management and avoidance is comprised of three elements:
  1. Queuing (Queueing)
  2. Dropping
  3. Scheduling

- Queuing is used to place packets into different software queues based on the QoS labels
- Dropping provides drop priorities for different classes of traffic
- Scheduling refers to how the different queues are serviced or emptied

Catalyst Egress QoS Mechanisms

Catalyst switches use the following egress QoS mechanisms:

- Congestion Management and Avoidance
- Congestion management and avoidance is comprised of three elements:
  1. Queuing (Queueing)
  2. Dropping
  3. Scheduling

Understanding Power over Ethernet (PoE)

- Cisco Catalyst switches interact with Cisco IP phones in three different ways:
  1. VLAN Tagging
  2. Extended Trust Settings
  3. Inline Power Delivery

- There are 2 methods for providing inline power:
  1. IEEE 802.3af-2003
  2. Cisco Inline Power

IEEE 802.3af-2003 is a ratified version of the original IEEE 802.3af standard
IEEE 802.3af-2003 is an open standard that describes five power classes:

	Min. Power Levels Output at PSE	Max. Power Levels at the PD	Usage
0	15.4 W	0.44 to 12.95 W	Default
1	4.0 W	0.44 to 3.84 W	Optional
2	7.0 W	3.84 to 6.49 W	Optional
3	15.4 W	6.49 to 12.95 W	Optional
4	N/A	N/A	Reserved

- Cisco inline power (PoE) is a proprietary approach (802.3af is based on this method)
- IEEE 802.3af uses a Direct Current (DC) powered device detection method
- Cisco ILP uses Alternating Current (AC) for powered device detection
- The IEEE 802.3af-2003 standard uses either mode A or mode B to send power to the PD
- Mode A uses pins 1, 2, 3, and 6
- Mode B uses pins 4, 5, 7, and 8
- Cisco ILP uses pins 1, 2, 3, and 6
- If the PD is a Cisco IP phone, it uses CDP to tell the switch (PSE) how much power it wants
- The IEEE 802.3af-2003 standard uses DC disconnect and AC disconnect
- With Cisco ILP, power is removed if the Ethernet link status transitions to the down state
- The differences between IEEE 802.3af and Cisco Inline Power (ILP) are:
  1. The amount of power that is available to the connected device
  2. The method used for device discovery
  3. The way that power is removed from the wire when a powered device is removed

PART 2

Labs

LAB 1

Advanced Catalyst Security Configuration

Lab Objective:

The objective of this lab exercise is for you to learn and understand how to implement advanced Catalyst switch security solutions via DHCP Snooping and Dynamic ARP Inspection.

Lab Topology:

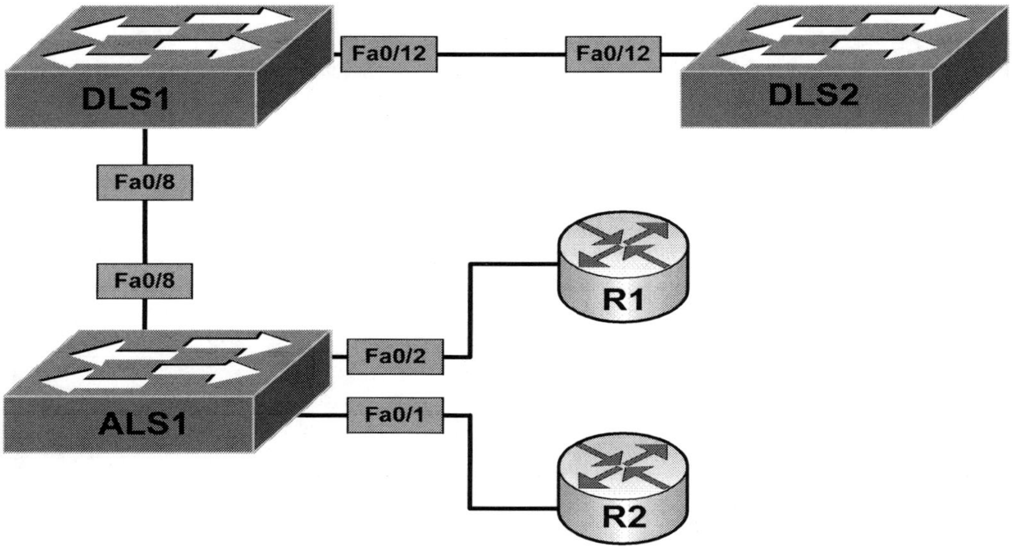

IMPORTANT NOTE

If you are using the www.howtonetwork.net racks, please begin each and every lab by shutting down all interfaces on all switches and then manually re-enabling the interfaces that are illustrated in this topology.

LAB-SPECIFIC NOTE

If you are using the www.howtonetwork.net racks, the diagram is based on the physical cabling of the CCNP Rack. This is seen in the CDP output:

```
ALS1#show cdp neighbors
Capability Codes: R - Router, T - Trans Bridge, B - Source Route Bridge
                  S - Switch, H - Host, I - IGMP, r - Repeater, P - Phone

Device ID        Local Intrfce     Holdtme    Capability  Platform  Port ID
R2               Fas 0/1            169          R S I    2620XM    Fas 0/0
R1               Fas 0/2            172          R S I    2620XM    Fas 0/0
```

If using a home lab, you can substitute the routers for any other devices, such as workstations. No explicit configuration is required other than that the device port or NIC is up so as to bring up the switch port and the device or router will need to be configured as a DHCP Client.

Task 1

Enable interfaces FastEthernet0/1 and FastEthernet0/2 on switch ALS1 and verify the connected devices using or by looking at the switch CAM table entry for the specific port or ports.

Task 2

Configure Cisco IOS DHCP Server functionality on DLS2 as follows:

- DHCP Subnet: 192.168.1.0/24
- DHCP Subnet Lease Range: 192.168.1.100 – 192.168.1.200
- Default Gateway: 192.168.1.254
- DNS Name: Howtonetwork.net
- Lease Duration: 4 Hours

Task 3

Configure VTP Domain SECURE on all switches. Use VTP version 2 with a password of CAT-SEC on all switches in the VTP domain. Disable VTP on all switches.

Task 4

Configure VLAN 192 on all switches. This VLAN should be named SECURE-VLAN.

Task 5

Configure an 802.1Q trunk between switches DLS1 and ALS1. You may use the default native VLAN for this trunk link or you can configure your own native VLAN. Either is acceptable.

Task 6

Configure the link between switches DLS1 and DLS2 as an access port. This port should be assigned to VLAN 192.

Task 7

Configure SVI 192 on switches DLS1 and DLS2. DLS1 SVI 192 should be assigned the IP address 192.168.1.1/24 and DLS2 SVI 192 should be assigned IP address 192.168.1.2/24. Configure Cisco IOS DHCP Relay Agent on SVI 192 on DLS1. This should point to the DHCP server 192.168.1.2. Verify that DLS1 and DLS2 can ping each other across the switch access link between them.

Task 8

Enable DHCP Snooping and DAI for VLAN 192. Configure the appropriate trusted port(s) for both of these features. Configure DHCP Snooping support for the DHCP Relay Agent.

Configure DAI to log all packets that match DHCP bindings. Up to 500 entries should be stored in the buffer. DAI should validate IP addresses.

Task 9

Configure FastEthernet0/1 and FastEthernet0/2 on ALS1 as access ports in VLAN 192. Configure R1 and R2 to receive their IP addressing information via DHCP. Verify your configuration.

Task 10

Verify that DHCP Snooping and Dynamic ARP Inspection are working as expected.

Lab Validation

Task 1

```
ALS1(config)#interface range fastethernet 0/1 - 2
ALS1(config-if-range)#no shutdown
ALS1(config-if-range)#exit
```

Verify this configuration as follows:

```
ALS1#show cdp neighbors
Capability Codes: R - Router, T - Trans Bridge, B - Source Route Bridge
                  S - Switch, H - Host, I - IGMP, r - Repeater, P - Phone

Device ID        Local Intrfce     Holdtme    Capability  Platform   Port ID
R2               Fas 0/1            130         R S I     2620XM     Fas 0/0
R1               Fas 0/2            130         R S I     2620XM     Fas 0/0

ALS1#show mac-address-table dynamic
          Mac Address Table
-------------------------------------------

Vlan    Mac Address       Type        Ports
----    -----------       --------    -----
   1    000c.85f8.1640    DYNAMIC     Fa0/1
   1    0013.c3bc.b720    DYNAMIC     Fa0/2
Total Mac Addresses for this criterion: 2
```

Task 2

```
DLS2(config)#ip dhcp excluded-address 192.168.1.1 192.168.1.99
DLS2(config)#ip dhcp excluded-address 192.168.1.201 192.168.1.254
DLS2(config)#ip dhcp pool DHCP-SNPNG-POOL
DLS2(dhcp-config)#network 192.168.1.0 /24
```

```
DLS2(dhcp-config)#default-router 192.168.1.254
DLS2(dhcp-config)#domain-name howtonetwork.net
DLS2(dhcp-config)#lease 0 4
DLS2(dhcp-config)#exit
```

Task 3

```
DLS1(config)#vtp domain SECURE
DLS1(config)#vtp password CAT-SEC
DLS1(config)#vtp version 2
DLS1(config)#vtp mode transparent

DLS2(config)#vtp domain SECURE
DLS2(config)#vtp pass CAT-SEC
DLS2(config)#vtp version 2
DLS2(config)#vtp mode transparent
ALS1(config)#vtp domain SECURE
ALS1(config)#vtp password CAT-SEC
ALS1(config)#vtp version 2
ALS1(config)#vtp mode transparent
```

Task 4

```
DLS1(config)#vlan 192
DLS1(config-vlan)#name SECURE-VLAN
DLS1(config-vlan)#exit

DLS2(config)#vlan 192
DLS2(config-vlan)#name SECURE-VLAN
DLS2(config-vlan)#exit

ALS1(config)#vlan 192
ALS1(config-vlan)#name SECURE-VLAN
ALS1(config-vlan)#exit
```

Task 5

```
DLS1(config)#interface fastethernet 0/8
DLS1(config-if)#switchport
DLS1(config-if)#switchport trunk encapsulation dot1q
DLS1(config-if)#switchport mode trunk
DLS1(config-if)#no shutdown
DLS1(config-if)#exit

ALS1(config)#interface fastethernet 0/8
ALS1(config-if)#no shutdown
ALS1(config-if)#switchport mode trunk
ALS1(config-if)#exit
```

Task 6

```
DLS1(config)#interface fastethernet 0/12
DLS1(config-if)#switchport
DLS1(config-if)#switchport access vlan 192
DLS1(config-if)#switchport mode access
DLS1(config-if)#no shutdown
DLS1(config-if)#exit

DLS2(config)#interface fastethernet 0/12
DLS2(config-if)#switchport
DLS2(config-if)#switchport access vlan 192
DLS2(config-if)#switchport mode access
DLS2(config-if)#no shutdown
DLS2(config-if)#exit
```

Task 7

```
DLS1(config)#ip routing
DLS1(config)#interface vlan 192
DLS1(config-if)#ip address 192.168.1.1 255.255.255.0
DLS1(config-if)#ip helper-address 192.168.1.2
DLS1(config-if)#no shutdown
DLS1(config-if)#exit

DLS2(config)#ip routing
DLS2(config)#interface vlan 192
DLS2(config-if)#ip address 192.168.1.2 255.255.255.0
DLS2(config-if)#no shutdown
DLS2(config-if)#exit
```

NOTE: Enabling IP routing is optional. It is not a mandatory requirement for this task.

Task 8

Complete the DHCP Snooping configuration as follows:

```
DLS1(config)#ip dhcp snooping
DLS1(config)#ip dhcp snooping vlan 192
DLS1(config)#ip dhcp snooping information option
DLS1(config)#interface fastethernet 0/12
DLS1(config-if)#ip dhcp snooping trust
DLS1(config-if)#exit
```

NOTE: Remember, DLS2 is the DHCP server, so Fa0/12 should be trusted.

Complete the Dynamic ARP Inspection configuration as follows:

```
DLS1(config)#ip arp inspection vlan 192
DLS1(config)#ip arp inspection vlan 192 logging dhcp-bindings all
DLS1(config)#ip arp inspection validate ip
DLS1(config)#ip arp inspection log-buffer entries 500
DLS1(config)#logging buffered informational
DLS1(config)#interface fastethernet 0/12
DLS1(config-if)#ip arp inspection trust
DLS1(config-if)#exit
```

NOTE: Remember, DLS2 is the DHCP server, so Fa0/12 should be trusted.

Verify your DHCP Snooping configuration as follows:

```
DLS1#show ip dhcp snooping
Switch DHCP snooping is enabled
DHCP snooping is configured on following VLANs:
192
Insertion of option 82 is enabled
Option 82 on untrusted port is not allowed
Verification of hwaddr field is enabled
Interface                    Trusted     Rate limit (pps)
------------------------     -------     ----------------
FastEthernet0/12             yes         unlimited
```

Verify your Dynamic ARP Inspection configuration as follows:

```
DLS1#show ip arp inspection vlan 192

Source Mac Validation      : Disabled
Destination Mac Validation : Disabled
IP Address Validation      : Enabled

 Vlan     Configuration    Operation   ACL Match          Static ACL
 ----     -------------    ---------   ---------          ----------
  192     Enabled          Active

 Vlan     ACL Logging      DHCP Logging
 ----     -----------      ------------
  192     Deny             All
```

Task 9

```
ALS1(config)#interface range fastethernet 0/1 - 2
ALS1(config-if-range)#switchport access vlan 192
ALS1(config-if-range)#switchport mode access
```

```
ALS1(config-if-range)#spanning-tree portfast
%Warning: portfast should only be enabled on ports connected to a single
 host. Connecting hubs, concentrators, switches, bridges, etc... to this
 interface  when portfast is enabled, can cause temporary bridging loops.
 Use with CAUTION

%Portfast will be configured in 2 interfaces due to the range command
 but will only have effect when the interfaces are in a non-trunking mode.
ALS1(config-if-range)#exit

R1(config)#int f0/0
R1(config-if)#ip address dhcp
R1(config-if)#exit
R1(config)#exit

R2(config)#int f0/0
R2(config-if)#ip address dhcp
R2(config-if)#exit
R2(config)#exit
```

Verify your configuration on the routers (DHCP Clients) as follows:

```
R1#show ip interface fastethernet 0/0
FastEthernet0/0 is up, line protocol is up
  Internet address is 192.168.1.100/24
  Broadcast address is 255.255.255.255
  Address determined by DHCP
  MTU is 1500 bytes
  Helper address is not set

R2#show ip interface fastethernet 0/0
FastEthernet0/0 is up, line protocol is up
  Internet address is 192.168.1.101/24
  Broadcast address is 255.255.255.255
  Address determined by DHCP
  MTU is 1500 bytes
```

Verify your configuration on the DHCP Server (DLS2) as follows:

```
DLS2#show ip dhcp binding
IP address       Client-ID/              Lease expiration        Type
                 Hardware address
192.168.1.100    0063.6973.636f.2d30.    Mar 01 1993 09:31 AM    Automatic
                 3031.332e.6333.6263.
                 2e62.3732.302d.4661.
                 302f.30
192.168.1.101    0063.6973.636f.2d30.    Mar 01 1993 09:31 AM    Automatic
                 3030.632e.3835.6638.
                 2e31.3634.302d.4661.
                 302f.30
```

Task 10

Verify DHCP Snooping operation as follows:

```
DLS1#show ip dhcp snooping binding vlan 192
MacAddress          IpAddress        Lease(sec)  Type           VLAN
Interface
------------------  ---------------  ----------  -------------  ----  -------
-------------
00:13:C3:BC:B7:20   192.168.1.100    13681       dhcp-snooping  192
FastEthernet0/8
00:0C:85:F8:16:40   192.168.1.101    13685       dhcp-snooping  192
FastEthernet0/8
Total number of bindings: 2
```

Verify Dynamic ARP Inspection configuration as follows:

```
DLS1#show ip arp inspection statistics

 Vlan      Forwarded        Dropped     DHCP Drops      ACL Drops
 ----      ---------        -------     ----------      ---------
  192              6              0              0              0

 Vlan   DHCP Permits    ACL Permits   Source MAC Failures
 ----   ------------    -----------   -------------------
  192              3              0                     0

 Vlan   Dest MAC Failures   IP Validation Failures   Invalid Protocol Data
 ----   -----------------   ----------------------   ---------------------
  192                   0                        0                       0
```

Finally, look at the switch log. Here, several shuts and no shuts have been performed on the routers (DHCP Clients) to generate more log messages for you to look at.

```
DLS1#show logging
Syslog logging: enabled (0 messages dropped, 78 messages rate-limited, 0
flushes, 0 overruns, xml disabled, filtering disabled)
    Console logging: level debugging, 251 messages logged, xml disabled,
                     filtering disabled
    Monitor logging: level debugging, 0 messages logged, xml disabled,
                     filtering disabled
    Buffer logging: level informational, 127 messages logged, xml disabled,
                    filtering disabled
    Exception Logging: size (4096 bytes)
    Count and timestamp logging messages: disabled
    File logging: disabled
    Trap logging: level informational, 128 message lines logged

Log Buffer (4096 bytes):
```

```
05:16:55: %SYS-5-CONFIG_I: Configured from console by console
05:18:04: %SYS-5-CONFIG_I: Configured from console by console
05:18:35: %SYS-5-CONFIG_I: Configured from console by console
05:19:46: %SYS-5-CONFIG_I: Configured from console by console
05:28:21: %SYS-5-CONFIG_I: Configured from console by console
05:31:30: %SYS-5-CONFIG_I: Configured from console by console
05:31:53: %SW_DAI-6-DHCP_SNOOPING_PERMIT: 1 ARPs (Res) on Fa0/8, vlan
192.([0013.c3bc.b720/192.168.1.100/ffff.ffff.ffff/192.168.1.100/05:31:53 UTC
Mon Mar 1 1993])
05:31:56: %SW_DAI-6-DHCP_SNOOPING_PERMIT: 1 ARPs (Res) on Fa0/8, vlan 192.([0
00c.85f8.1640/192.168.1.101/ffff.ffff.ffff/192.168.1.101/05:31:56 UTC Mon Mar
1 1993])
05:31:59: %SW_DAI-6-DHCP_SNOOPING_PERMIT: 1 ARPs (Req) on Fa0/8, vlan
192.([0013.c3bc.b720/192.168.1.100/0000.0000.0000/192.168.1.101/05:31:59 UTC
Mon Mar 1 1993])
05:52:29: %SW_DAI-6-DHCP_SNOOPING_PERMIT: 1 ARPs (Req) on Fa0/8, vlan
192.([0013.c3bc.b720/192.168.1.100/0000.0000.0000/192.168.1.2/05:52:28 UTC
Mon Mar 1 1993])
05:52:43: %SW_DAI-6-DHCP_SNOOPING_PERMIT: 1 ARPs (Res) on Fa0/8, vlan
192.([0013.c3bc.b720/192.168.1.100/ffff.ffff.ffff/192.168.1.100/05:52:43 UTC
Mon Mar 1 1993])
05:52:46: %SW_DAI-6-DHCP_SNOOPING_PERMIT: 1 ARPs (Req) on Fa0/8, vlan
192.([0013.c3bc.b720/192.168.1.100/0000.0000.0000/192.168.1.101/05:52:46 UTC
Mon Mar 1 1993])
05:53:56: %SW_DAI-6-DHCP_SNOOPING_PERMIT: 1 ARPs (Req) on Fa0/8, vlan 192.([0
00c.85f8.1640/192.168.1.101/0000.0000.0000/192.168.1.2/05:53:56 UTC Mon Mar 1
1993])
05:54:09: %SW_DAI-6-DHCP_SNOOPING_PERMIT: 1 ARPs (Res) on Fa0/8, vlan 192.([0
00c.85f8.1640/192.168.1.101/ffff.ffff.ffff/192.168.1.101/05:54:08 UTC Mon Mar
1 1993])
05:54:12: %SW_DAI-6-DHCP_SNOOPING_PERMIT: 1 ARPs (Req) on Fa0/8, vlan 192.([0
00c.85f8.1640/192.168.1.101/0000.0000.0000/192.168.1.100/05:54:12 UTC Mon Mar
1 1993])
```

Final Switch Configurations

DLS1

```
DLS1#show running-config
Building configuration...

Current configuration : 4635 bytes
!
version 12.2
no service pad
service timestamps debug uptime
service timestamps log uptime
no service password-encryption
!
```

```
hostname DLS1
!
logging buffered informational
!
no aaa new-model
ip subnet-zero
ip routing
!
ip dhcp snooping vlan 192
ip dhcp snooping
ip arp inspection vlan 192
ip arp inspection vlan 192 logging dhcp-bindings all
ip arp inspection validate ip
ip arp inspection log-buffer entries 500
vtp domain SECURE
vtp mode transparent
!
no file verify auto
spanning-tree mode pvst
spanning-tree extend system-id
!
vlan internal allocation policy ascending
!
vlan 192
 name SECURE-VLAN
!
!
interface FastEthernet0/1
 switchport mode dynamic desirable
 shutdown
!
interface FastEthernet0/2
 switchport mode dynamic desirable
 shutdown
!
interface FastEthernet0/3
 switchport mode dynamic desirable
 shutdown
!
interface FastEthernet0/4
 switchport mode dynamic desirable
 shutdown
!
interface FastEthernet0/5
 switchport mode dynamic desirable
 shutdown
!
interface FastEthernet0/6
 switchport mode dynamic desirable
 shutdown
!
interface FastEthernet0/7
```

```
 switchport mode dynamic desirable
 shutdown
!
interface FastEthernet0/8
 switchport trunk encapsulation dot1q
 switchport mode trunk
!
interface FastEthernet0/9
 switchport mode dynamic desirable
 shutdown
!
interface FastEthernet0/10
 switchport mode dynamic desirable
 shutdown
!
interface FastEthernet0/11
 switchport mode dynamic desirable
 shutdown
!
interface FastEthernet0/12
 switchport access vlan 192
 switchport mode access
 ip arp inspection trust
 ip dhcp snooping trust
!
interface FastEthernet0/13
 switchport mode dynamic desirable
 shutdown
!
interface FastEthernet0/14
 switchport mode dynamic desirable
 shutdown
!
interface FastEthernet0/15
 switchport mode dynamic desirable
 shutdown
!
interface FastEthernet0/16
 switchport mode dynamic desirable
 shutdown
!
interface FastEthernet0/17
 switchport mode dynamic desirable
 shutdown
!
interface FastEthernet0/18
 switchport mode dynamic desirable
 shutdown
!
interface FastEthernet0/19
 switchport mode dynamic desirable
 shutdown
```

```
!
interface FastEthernet0/20
 switchport mode dynamic desirable
 shutdown
!
interface FastEthernet0/21
 switchport mode dynamic desirable
 shutdown
!
interface FastEthernet0/22
 switchport mode dynamic desirable
 shutdown
!
interface FastEthernet0/23
 switchport mode dynamic desirable
 shutdown
!
interface FastEthernet0/24
 switchport mode dynamic desirable
 shutdown
!
interface FastEthernet0/25
 switchport mode dynamic desirable
 shutdown
!
interface FastEthernet0/26
 switchport mode dynamic desirable
 shutdown
!
interface FastEthernet0/27
 switchport mode dynamic desirable
 shutdown
!
interface FastEthernet0/28
 switchport mode dynamic desirable
 shutdown
!
interface FastEthernet0/29
 switchport mode dynamic desirable
 shutdown
!
interface FastEthernet0/30
 switchport mode dynamic desirable
 shutdown
!
interface FastEthernet0/31
 switchport mode dynamic desirable
 shutdown
!
interface FastEthernet0/32
 switchport mode dynamic desirable
 shutdown
```

```
!
interface FastEthernet0/33
 switchport mode dynamic desirable
 shutdown
!
interface FastEthernet0/34
 switchport mode dynamic desirable
 shutdown
!
interface FastEthernet0/35
 switchport mode dynamic desirable
 shutdown
!
interface FastEthernet0/36
 switchport mode dynamic desirable
 shutdown
!
interface FastEthernet0/37
 switchport mode dynamic desirable
 shutdown
!
interface FastEthernet0/38
 switchport mode dynamic desirable
 shutdown
!
interface FastEthernet0/39
 switchport mode dynamic desirable
 shutdown
!
interface FastEthernet0/40
 switchport mode dynamic desirable
 shutdown
!
interface FastEthernet0/41
 switchport mode dynamic desirable
 shutdown
!
interface FastEthernet0/42
 switchport mode dynamic desirable
 shutdown
!
interface FastEthernet0/43
 switchport mode dynamic desirable
 shutdown
!
interface FastEthernet0/44
 switchport mode dynamic desirable
 shutdown
!
interface FastEthernet0/45
 switchport mode dynamic desirable
 shutdown
```

```
!
interface FastEthernet0/46
 switchport mode dynamic desirable
 shutdown
!
interface FastEthernet0/47
 switchport mode dynamic desirable
 shutdown
!
interface FastEthernet0/48
 switchport mode dynamic desirable
 shutdown
!
interface GigabitEthernet0/1
 switchport mode dynamic desirable
!
interface GigabitEthernet0/2
 switchport mode dynamic desirable
!
interface Vlan1
 no ip address
 shutdown
!
interface Vlan192
 ip address 192.168.1.1 255.255.255.0
 ip helper-address 192.168.1.2
!
ip classless
ip http server
ip http secure-server
!
control-plane
!
line con 0
line vty 0 4
 no login
line vty 5 15
 no login
!
end
DLS1#
```

DLS2

```
DLS2#show running-config
Building configuration...

Current configuration : 4543 bytes
!
version 12.2
no service pad
```

```
service timestamps debug uptime
service timestamps log uptime
no service password-encryption
!
hostname DLS2
!
no aaa new-model
ip subnet-zero
ip routing
ip dhcp excluded-address 192.168.1.1 192.168.1.99
ip dhcp excluded-address 192.168.1.201 192.168.1.254
!
ip dhcp pool DHCP-SNPNG-POOL
   network 192.168.1.0 255.255.255.0
   default-router 192.168.1.254
   domain-name howtonetwork.net
   lease 0 4
!
vtp domain SECURE
vtp mode transparent
!
spanning-tree mode pvst
spanning-tree extend system-id
!
vlan internal allocation policy ascending
!
vlan 192
 name SECURE-VLAN
!
interface FastEthernet0/1
 switchport mode dynamic desirable
 shutdown
!
interface FastEthernet0/2
 switchport mode dynamic desirable
 shutdown
!
interface FastEthernet0/3
 switchport mode dynamic desirable
 shutdown
!
interface FastEthernet0/4
 switchport mode dynamic desirable
 shutdown
!
interface FastEthernet0/5
 switchport mode dynamic desirable
 shutdown
!
interface FastEthernet0/6
 switchport mode dynamic desirable
 shutdown
!
interface FastEthernet0/7
```

```
 switchport mode dynamic desirable
 shutdown
!
interface FastEthernet0/8
 switchport mode dynamic desirable
 shutdown
!
interface FastEthernet0/9
 switchport mode dynamic desirable
 shutdown
!
interface FastEthernet0/10
 switchport mode dynamic desirable
 shutdown
!
interface FastEthernet0/11
 switchport mode dynamic desirable
 shutdown
!
interface FastEthernet0/12
 switchport access vlan 192
 switchport mode access
!
interface FastEthernet0/13
 switchport mode dynamic desirable
 shutdown
!
interface FastEthernet0/14
 switchport mode dynamic desirable
 shutdown
!
interface FastEthernet0/15
 switchport mode dynamic desirable
 shutdown
!
interface FastEthernet0/16
 switchport mode dynamic desirable
 shutdown
!
interface FastEthernet0/17
 switchport mode dynamic desirable
 shutdown
!
interface FastEthernet0/18
 switchport mode dynamic desirable
 shutdown
!
interface FastEthernet0/19
 switchport mode dynamic desirable
 shutdown
!
interface FastEthernet0/20
 switchport mode dynamic desirable
 shutdown
```

```
!
interface FastEthernet0/21
 switchport mode dynamic desirable
 shutdown
!
interface FastEthernet0/22
 switchport mode dynamic desirable
 shutdown
!
interface FastEthernet0/23
 switchport mode dynamic desirable
 shutdown
!
interface FastEthernet0/24
 switchport mode dynamic desirable
 shutdown
!
interface FastEthernet0/25
 switchport mode dynamic desirable
 shutdown
!
interface FastEthernet0/26
 switchport mode dynamic desirable
 shutdown
!
interface FastEthernet0/27
 switchport mode dynamic desirable
 shutdown
!
interface FastEthernet0/28
 switchport mode dynamic desirable
 shutdown
!
interface FastEthernet0/29
 switchport mode dynamic desirable
 shutdown
!
interface FastEthernet0/30
 switchport mode dynamic desirable
 shutdown
!
interface FastEthernet0/31
 switchport mode dynamic desirable
 shutdown
!
interface FastEthernet0/32
 switchport mode dynamic desirable
 shutdown
!
interface FastEthernet0/33
 switchport mode dynamic desirable
 shutdown
!
interface FastEthernet0/34
```

```
 switchport mode dynamic desirable
 shutdown
!
interface FastEthernet0/35
 switchport mode dynamic desirable
 shutdown
!
interface FastEthernet0/36
 switchport mode dynamic desirable
 shutdown
!
interface FastEthernet0/37
 switchport mode dynamic desirable
 shutdown
!
interface FastEthernet0/38
 switchport mode dynamic desirable
 shutdown
!
interface FastEthernet0/39
 switchport mode dynamic desirable
 shutdown
!
interface FastEthernet0/40
 switchport mode dynamic desirable
 shutdown
!
interface FastEthernet0/41
 switchport mode dynamic desirable
 shutdown
!
interface FastEthernet0/42
 switchport mode dynamic desirable
 shutdown
!
interface FastEthernet0/43
 switchport mode dynamic desirable
 shutdown
!
interface FastEthernet0/44
 switchport mode dynamic desirable
 shutdown
!
interface FastEthernet0/45
 switchport mode dynamic desirable
 shutdown
!
interface FastEthernet0/46
 switchport mode dynamic desirable
 shutdown
!
interface FastEthernet0/47
 switchport mode dynamic desirable
 shutdown
```

```
!
interface FastEthernet0/48
 switchport mode dynamic desirable
 shutdown
!
interface GigabitEthernet0/1
 switchport mode dynamic desirable
!
interface GigabitEthernet0/2
 switchport mode dynamic desirable
!
interface Vlan1
 no ip address
 shutdown
!
interface Vlan192
 ip address 192.168.1.2 255.255.255.0
!
ip classless
ip http server
ip http secure-server
!
control-plane
!
line con 0
line vty 0 4
 login
line vty 5 15
 login
!
end

DLS2#
```

ALS1

```
ALS1#show running-config
Building configuration...

Current configuration : 1682 bytes
!
version 12.1
no service pad
service timestamps debug uptime
service timestamps log uptime
no service password-encryption
!
hostname ALS1
!
no logging console
!
ip subnet-zero
!
```

```
ip ssh time-out 120
ip ssh authentication-retries 3
vtp domain SECURE
vtp mode transparent
!
spanning-tree mode pvst
no spanning-tree optimize bpdu transmission
spanning-tree extend system-id
!
vlan 192
 name SECURE-VLAN
!
interface FastEthernet0/1
 switchport access vlan 192
 switchport mode access
 spanning-tree portfast
!
interface FastEthernet0/2
 switchport access vlan 192
 switchport mode access
 spanning-tree portfast
!
interface FastEthernet0/3
 shutdown
!
interface FastEthernet0/4
 shutdown
!
interface FastEthernet0/5
 shutdown
!
interface FastEthernet0/6
 shutdown
!
interface FastEthernet0/7
 shutdown
!
interface FastEthernet0/8
 switchport mode trunk
!
interface FastEthernet0/9
 shutdown
!
interface FastEthernet0/10
 shutdown
!
interface FastEthernet0/11
 shutdown
!
interface FastEthernet0/12
 shutdown
!
interface FastEthernet0/13
 shutdown
!
```

```
interface FastEthernet0/14
 shutdown
!
interface FastEthernet0/15
 shutdown
!
interface FastEthernet0/16
 shutdown
!
interface FastEthernet0/17
 shutdown
!
interface FastEthernet0/18
 shutdown
!
interface FastEthernet0/19
 shutdown
!
interface FastEthernet0/20
 shutdown
!
interface FastEthernet0/21
 shutdown
!
interface FastEthernet0/22
 shutdown
!
interface FastEthernet0/23
 shutdown
!
interface FastEthernet0/24
 shutdown
!
interface GigabitEthernet0/1
!
interface GigabitEthernet0/2
!
interface Vlan1
 no ip address
 no ip route-cache
 shutdown
!
ip http server
!
line con 0
line vty 0 4
 login
line vty 5 15
 login
!
!
end

ALS1#
```

LAB 2

Advanced Spanning Tree Configuration

Lab Objective:

The objective of this lab exercise is for you to learn and understand how implement Multiple Spanning Tree Protocol (MSTP) in conjunction with other Spanning Tree protocols.

Lab Topology:

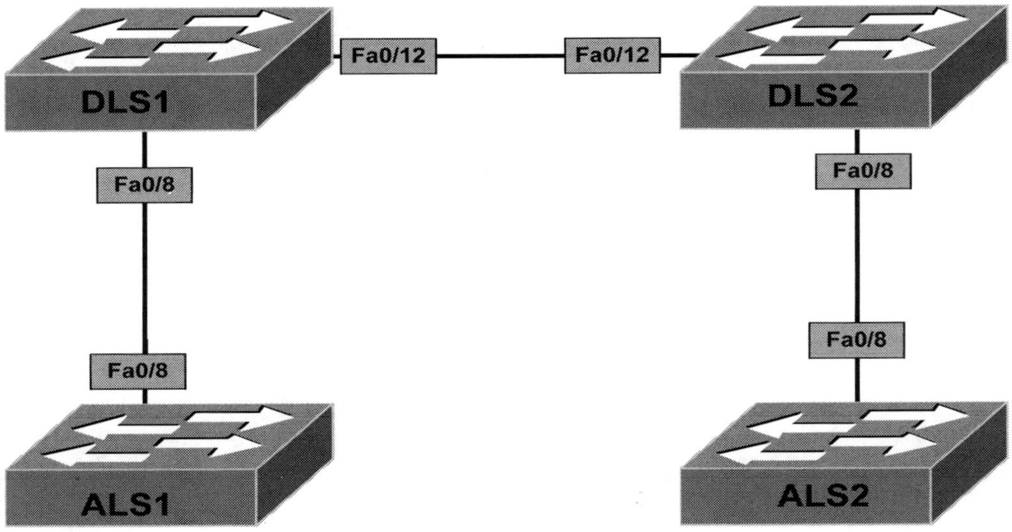

IMPORTANT NOTE

If you are using the www.howtonetwork.net racks, please begin each and every lab by shutting down all interfaces on all switches and then manually re-enabling the interfaces that are illustrated in this topology.

Task 1

Configure a VTP domain name of HARD for all switches. Configure a VTP password of STP on all switches within the VTP domain. All switches should be in VTP Transparent mode. Configure trunking between the switches using 802.1Q.

Task 2

Configure VLANs 100 and 200 on DLS1 and DSL2; VLAN 100 on ALS1 and VLAN 200 on ALS2.

Task 3

Configure MST on switch DLS1. The MST Region name should be DLS1-REGION. However, you may configure the other MST parameters as you would like and ensure that configured

VLANs 100 and 200 are mapped to the MST instance of you configure. Configure SVI 100 and assign in the IP address 192.168.100.1/24 and SVI 200 with the IP address 192.168.200.1/24.

Task 4

Configure MST on switch DLS2. The MST Region name should be DLS2-REGION. However, you may configure the other MST parameters as you would like and ensure that configured VLANs 100 and 200 are mapped to the MST instance of you configure. Configure SVI 100 and assign in the IP address 192.168.100.2/24 and SVI 200 with the IP address 192.168.200.2/24.

Task 5

Configure DLS1 as Root Bridge for the VLANs 100 and 200. This state should be applicable not only to the Region, but also to all other switches in the network.

Task 6

Configure 802.1w PVST on ALS1. Configure SVI 100 with the IP address 192.168.100.254/24.

Task 7

Configure 802.1D PVST on ALS2. Configure SVI 200 with the IP address 192.168.200.254/24.

Task 8

Verify your STP configuration and then verify that you can ping successfully end-to-end between switches ALS1 and ALS2.

Lab Validation

Task 1

```
DLS1(config)#vtp domain HARD
DLS1(config)#vtp password STP
DLS1(config)#int range f0/8 , f0/12
DLS1(config-if-range)#switchport
DLS1(config-if-range)#switchport trunk encapsulation dot1q
DLS1(config-if-range)#switchport mode trunk
DLS1(config-if-range)#no shut

DLS2(config)#vtp domain HARD
DLS2(config)#vtp password STP
DLS2(config)#int range f0/8 , f0/12
DLS2(config-if-range)#switchport
DLS2(config-if-range)#switchport trunk encap dot1q
DLS2(config-if-range)#switchport mode trunk
DLS2(config-if-range)#no shutdown
```

```
ALS1(config)#vtp domain HARD
ALS1(config)#vtp password STP
ALS1(config)#int f0/8
ALS1(config-if)#switchport mode trunk
ALS1(config-if)#no shut

ALS2(config)#vtp domain HARD
ALS2(config)#vtp password STP
ALS2(config)#int f0/8
ALS2(config-if)#switchport mode trunk
ALS2(config-if)#no shut
```

Task 2

```
DLS1(config)#vlan 100
DLS1(config-vlan)#exit
DLS1(config)#vlan 200
DLS1(config-vlan)#exit

DLS2(config)#vlan 100
DLS2(config-vlan)#exit
DLS2(config)#vlan 200
DLS2(config-vlan)#exit

ALS1(config)#vlan 100
ALS1(config-vlan)#exit

ALS2(config)#vlan 200
ALS2(config-vlan)#exit
```

Task 3

```
DLS1(config)#spanning-tree mst configuration
DLS1(config-mst)#revision 0
DLS1(config-mst)#instance 1 vlan 100,200
DLS1(config-mst)#name DLS1-REGION
DLS1(config-mst)#show pending
Pending MST configuration
Name      [DLS1-REGION]
Revision  0     Instances configured 2

Instance  Vlans mapped
--------  ---------------------------------------------------------------------
0         1-99,101-199,201-4094
1         100,200
-------------------------------------------------------------------------------
DLS1(config-mst)#exit
DLS1(config)#spanning-tree mode mst
DLS1(config)#int vlan 100
DLS1(config-if)#ip address 192.168.100.1 255.255.255.0
DLS1(config-if)#no shut
```

```
DLS1(config-if)#exit
DLS1(config)#int vlan 200
DLS1(config-if)#ip add 192.168.200.1 255.255.255.0
DLS1(config-if)#no shut
DLS1(config-if)#exit
```

Task 4

```
DLS2(config)#spanning-tree mst configuration
DLS2(config-mst)#revision 5
DLS2(config-mst)#name DLS2-REGION
DLS2(config-mst)#instance 3 vlan 100,200
DLS2(config-mst)#show pending
Pending MST configuration
Name       [DLS2-REGION]
Revision   5     Instances configured 2

Instance   Vlans mapped
--------   -------------------------------------------------------------
0          1-99,101-199,201-4094
3          100,200
------------------------------------------------------------------------
DLS2(config-mst)#exit
DLS2(config)#spanning-tree mode mst
DLS2(config)#interface vlan 100
DLS2(config-if)#ip address 192.168.100.2 255.255.255.0
DLS2(config-if)#no shut
DLS2(config-if)#exit
DLS2(config)#int vlan 200
DLS2(config-if)#ip address 192.168.200.2 255.255.255.0
DLS2(config-if)#no shutdown
DLS2(config-if)#exit
```

Task 5

```
DLS1(config)#spanning-tree mst 0 priority 0
```

This is where understanding the CST is important. Remember, the MST Region sees the outside world via its Internal Spanning Tree (IST) interaction only; the IST presents the entire MST Region as a single virtual bridge to the outside world.

Therefore, BPDUs are exchanged at the Region boundary only over the native VLAN of trunks, as if a single CST were in operation. IST is the only Instance that sends and receives BPDUs. MISTP does not interact directly with the CST outside of the region. To ensure that DLS1 is seen as the Root Bridge by all other switches in the network, i.e. switches that are outside of the Region, you must configure the priority value of instance 0.

For example, based on this configuration, ALS1 and DLS 2 show the following:

```
ALS1#show spanning-tree vlan 100

VLAN0100
  Spanning tree enabled protocol rstp
  Root ID    Priority    0
             Address     000d.291e.7f00

[Truncated]

DLS2#show spanning-tree mst

##### MST0     vlans mapped:   1-99,101-199,201-4094
Bridge         address 000f.24ce.0d80  priority      32768 (32768 sysid 0)
Root           address 000d.291e.7f00  priority      0     (0 sysid 0)
               port    Fa0/12          path cost     200000
Regional Root this switch

Truncated]
```

However, if you issued the `spanning-tree vlan [num] priority` or the `spanning-tree mst [MSTI] priority` commands, the parameters will only be locally significant to the Region and will not be reflected by any of the switches outside the Region as follows:

```
DLS1(config)#no spanning-tree mst 0 priority 0
DLS1(config)#spanning-tree vlan 100 priority 0
DLS1(config)#spanning-tree vlan 200 priority 0
DLS1(config)#spanning-tree mst 1 priority 0
DLS1(config)#exit
DLS1#show spanning-tree vlan 100

MST1
  Spanning tree enabled protocol mstp
  Root ID    Priority    1
             Address     000d.291e.7f00
             This bridge is the root

[Truncated]

DLS1#show spanning-tree vlan 200

MST1
  Spanning tree enabled protocol mstp
  Root ID    Priority    1
             Address     000d.291e.7f00
             This bridge is the root

[Truncated]
```

```
DLS1#show spanning-tree mst

##### MST0    vlans mapped:   1-99,101-199,201-4094
Bridge        address 000d.291e.7f00  priority      32768 (32768 sysid 0)
Root          this switch for the CIST

[Truncated]
```

Both ALS1 and DLS1 will show the default priority of 32,768 for the CIST Root Bridge:

```
ALS1#show spanning-tree vlan 100

VLAN0100
  Spanning tree enabled protocol rstp
  Root ID    Priority    32768
             Address     000d.291e.7f00
[Truncated]
```

```
DLS2#show spanning-tree mst

##### MST0    vlans mapped:   1-99,101-199,201-4094
Bridge        address 000f.24ce.0d80  priority      32768 (32768 sysid 0)
Root          address 000d.291e.7f00  priority      32768 (32768 sysid 0)
              port    Fa0/12          path cost     200000
Regional Root this switch

[Truncated]
```

Task 6

```
ALS1(config)#spanning-tree mode rapid-pvst
ALS1(config)#int vlan 100
ALS1(config-if)#ip address 192.168.100.254 255.255.255.0
ALS1(config-if)#no shut
ALS1(config-if)#exit
```

Task 7

NOTE: By default 802.1D PVST is enabled so no explicit configuration is required to enable it.

```
ALS2(config)#int vlan 200
ALS2(config-if)#ip address 192.168.200.254 255.255.255.0
ALS2(config-if)#no shutdown
ALS2(config-if)#exit
```

Task 8

Use the `show spanning-tree mst` commands on the MST switches DLS1 and DSL2 and the `show spanning-tree vlan` commands on ALS1 and ALS2 to verify your configuration.

```
DLS1#show spanning-tree mst

##### MST0     vlans mapped:   1-99,101-199,201-4094
Bridge         address 000d.291e.7f00  priority      0     (0 sysid 0)
Root           this switch for the CIST
Operational    hello time 2 , forward delay 15, max age 20, txholdcount 6
Configured     hello time 2 , forward delay 15, max age 20, max hops    20

Interface        Role Sts Cost      Prio.Nbr Type
---------------- ---- --- --------- -------- --------------------------------
Fa0/8            Desg FWD 200000    128.8    P2p Bound(PVST)
Fa0/12           Desg FWD 200000    128.12   P2p

##### MST1     vlans mapped:   100,200
Bridge         address 000d.291e.7f00  priority      32769 (32768 sysid 1)
Root           this switch for MST1

Interface        Role Sts Cost      Prio.Nbr Type
---------------- ---- --- --------- -------- --------------------------------
Fa0/8            Desg FWD 200000    128.8    P2p Bound(PVST)
Fa0/12           Desg FWD 200000    128.12   P2p

DLS2#show spanning-tree mst

##### MST0     vlans mapped:   1-99,101-199,201-4094
Bridge         address 000f.24ce.0d80  priority      32768 (32768 sysid 0)
Root           address 000d.291e.7f00  priority      0     (0 sysid 0)
               port    Fa0/12          path cost     200000
Regional Root this switch
Operational    hello time 2 , forward delay 15, max age 20, txholdcount 6
Configured     hello time 2 , forward delay 15, max age 20, max hops    20

Interface        Role Sts Cost      Prio.Nbr Type
---------------- ---- --- --------- -------- --------------------------------
Fa0/8            Desg FWD 200000    128.8    P2p Bound(PVST)
Fa0/12           Root FWD 200000    128.12   P2p Bound(RSTP)

##### MST3     vlans mapped:   100,200
Bridge         address 000f.24ce.0d80  priority      32771 (32768 sysid 3)
Root           this switch for MST3

Interface        Role Sts Cost      Prio.Nbr Type
---------------- ---- --- --------- -------- --------------------------------
Fa0/8            Desg FWD 200000    128.8    P2p Bound(PVST)
Fa0/12           Mstr FWD 200000    128.12   P2p Bound(RSTP)
```

NOTE: Notice that DLS1 is Root Bridge for the CST, but DLS2 is Root Bridge within its own Region and is also Root Bridge for the MSTI configured.

```
ALS1#show spanning-tree vlan 100

VLAN0100
  Spanning tree enabled protocol rstp
  Root ID    Priority    0
             Address     000d.291e.7f00
             Cost        19
             Port        8 (FastEthernet0/8)
             Hello Time   2 sec  Max Age 20 sec  Forward Delay 15 sec

[Truncated]

ALS2#show spanning-tree vlan 200

VLAN0200
  Spanning tree enabled protocol ieee
  Root ID    Priority    0
             Address     000d.291e.7f00
             Cost        200019
             Port        8 (FastEthernet0/8)
             Hello Time   2 sec  Max Age 20 sec  Forward Delay 15 sec
[Truncated]
```

To complete the final section of this task, you need to configure a default gateway on ALS1 and ALS2, which will allow them to ping each other as they reside on different subnets.

```
ALS1(config)#ip default-gateway 192.168.100.1

ALS2(config)#ip default-gateway 192.168.200.2
```

Next, IP routing must be enabled on the Layer 3 switches DLS1 and DLS2.

```
DLS1#show ip route
Default gateway is not set

Host               Gateway           Last Use    Total Uses  Interface
ICMP redirect cache is empty
DLS1#
DLS1#conf t
Enter configuration commands, one per line.  End with CNTL/Z.
DLS1(config)#ip routing
DLS1(config)#end
DLS1#
DLS1#show ip route
```

```
Codes: C - connected, S - static, R - RIP, M - mobile, B - BGP
       D - EIGRP, EX - EIGRP external, O - OSPF, IA - OSPF inter area
       N1 - OSPF NSSA external type 1, N2 - OSPF NSSA external type 2
       E1 - OSPF external type 1, E2 - OSPF external type 2, E - EGP
       i - IS-IS, su - IS-IS summary, L1 - IS-IS level-1, L2 - IS-IS level-2
       ia - IS-IS inter area, * - candidate default, U - per-user static
route
       o - ODR, P - periodic downloaded static route

Gateway of last resort is not set

C    192.168.200.0/24 is directly connected, Vlan200
C    192.168.100.0/24 is directly connected, Vlan100


DLS2#show ip route
Default gateway is not set

Host               Gateway           Last Use    Total Uses  Interface
ICMP redirect cache is empty
DLS2#
DLS2#conf t
Enter configuration commands, one per line.  End with CNTL/Z.
DLS2(config)#ip routing
DLS2(config)#end
DLS2#
DLS2#show ip route
Codes: C - connected, S - static, R - RIP, M - mobile, B - BGP
       D - EIGRP, EX - EIGRP external, O - OSPF, IA - OSPF inter area
       N1 - OSPF NSSA external type 1, N2 - OSPF NSSA external type 2
       E1 - OSPF external type 1, E2 - OSPF external type 2
       i - IS-IS, su - IS-IS summary, L1 - IS-IS level-1, L2 - IS-IS level-2
       ia - IS-IS inter area, * - candidate default, U - per-user static
route
       o - ODR, P - periodic downloaded static route

Gateway of last resort is not set

C    192.168.200.0/24 is directly connected, Vlan200
C    192.168.100.0/24 is directly connected, Vlan100
```

Complete the lab by pinging end-to-end between switches ALS1 and ALS2.

```
ALS1#ping 192.168.200.254

Type escape sequence to abort.
Sending 5, 100-byte ICMP Echos to 192.168.200.254, timeout is 2 seconds:
!!!!!
Success rate is 100 percent (5/5), round-trip min/avg/max = 1/5/16 ms
```

```
ALS2#ping 192.168.100.254

Type escape sequence to abort.
Sending 5, 100-byte ICMP Echos to 192.168.100.254, timeout is 2 seconds:
!!!!!
Success rate is 100 percent (5/5), round-trip min/avg/max = 1/5/12 ms
```

Final Switch Configurations

DLS1

```
DLS1#show running-config
Building configuration...

Current configuration : 4516 bytes
!
version 12.2
no service pad
service timestamps debug uptime
service timestamps log uptime
no service password-encryption
!
hostname DLS1
!
no logging console
!
no aaa new-model
ip subnet-zero
ip routing
!
vtp domain HARD
vtp mode transparent
!
no file verify auto
!
spanning-tree mode mst
spanning-tree extend system-id
!
spanning-tree mst configuration
 name DLS1-REGION
 instance 1 vlan 100, 200
!
spanning-tree mst 0 priority 0
!
vlan internal allocation policy ascending
!
vlan 100,200
!

interface FastEthernet0/1
```

```
 switchport mode dynamic desirable
 shutdown
!
interface FastEthernet0/2
 switchport mode dynamic desirable
 shutdown
!
interface FastEthernet0/3
 switchport mode dynamic desirable
 shutdown
!
interface FastEthernet0/4
 switchport mode dynamic desirable
 shutdown
!
interface FastEthernet0/5
 switchport mode dynamic desirable
 shutdown
!
interface FastEthernet0/6
 switchport mode dynamic desirable
 shutdown
!
interface FastEthernet0/7
 switchport mode dynamic desirable
 shutdown
!
interface FastEthernet0/8
 switchport trunk encapsulation dot1q
 switchport mode trunk
!
interface FastEthernet0/9
 switchport mode dynamic desirable
 shutdown
!
interface FastEthernet0/10
 switchport mode dynamic desirable
 shutdown
!
interface FastEthernet0/11
 switchport mode dynamic desirable
 shutdown
!
interface FastEthernet0/12
 switchport trunk encapsulation dot1q
 switchport mode trunk
!
interface FastEthernet0/13
 switchport mode dynamic desirable
 shutdown
!
interface FastEthernet0/14
 switchport mode dynamic desirable
 shutdown
```

```
!
interface FastEthernet0/15
 switchport mode dynamic desirable
 shutdown
!
interface FastEthernet0/16
 switchport mode dynamic desirable
 shutdown
!
interface FastEthernet0/17
 switchport mode dynamic desirable
 shutdown
!
interface FastEthernet0/18
 switchport mode dynamic desirable
 shutdown
!
interface FastEthernet0/19
 switchport mode dynamic desirable
 shutdown
!
interface FastEthernet0/20
 switchport mode dynamic desirable
 shutdown
!
interface FastEthernet0/21
 switchport mode dynamic desirable
 shutdown
!
interface FastEthernet0/22
 switchport mode dynamic desirable
 shutdown
!
interface FastEthernet0/23
 switchport mode dynamic desirable
 shutdown
!
interface FastEthernet0/24
 switchport mode dynamic desirable
 shutdown
!
interface FastEthernet0/25
 switchport mode dynamic desirable
 shutdown
!
interface FastEthernet0/26
 switchport mode dynamic desirable
 shutdown
!
interface FastEthernet0/27
 switchport mode dynamic desirable
 shutdown
!
interface FastEthernet0/28
```

```
 switchport mode dynamic desirable
 shutdown
!
interface FastEthernet0/29
 switchport mode dynamic desirable
 shutdown
!
interface FastEthernet0/30
 switchport mode dynamic desirable
 shutdown
!
interface FastEthernet0/31
 switchport mode dynamic desirable
 shutdown
!
interface FastEthernet0/32
 switchport mode dynamic desirable
 shutdown
!
interface FastEthernet0/33
 switchport mode dynamic desirable
 shutdown
!
interface FastEthernet0/34
 switchport mode dynamic desirable
 shutdown
!
interface FastEthernet0/35
 switchport mode dynamic desirable
 shutdown
!
interface FastEthernet0/36
 switchport mode dynamic desirable
 shutdown
!
interface FastEthernet0/37
 switchport mode dynamic desirable
 shutdown
!
interface FastEthernet0/38
 switchport mode dynamic desirable
 shutdown
!
interface FastEthernet0/39
 switchport mode dynamic desirable
 shutdown
!
interface FastEthernet0/40
 switchport mode dynamic desirable
 shutdown
!
interface FastEthernet0/41
 switchport mode dynamic desirable
 shutdown
```

```
!
interface FastEthernet0/42
 switchport mode dynamic desirable
 shutdown
!
interface FastEthernet0/43
 switchport mode dynamic desirable
 shutdown
!
interface FastEthernet0/44
 switchport mode dynamic desirable
 shutdown
!
interface FastEthernet0/45
 switchport mode dynamic desirable
 shutdown
!
interface FastEthernet0/46
 switchport mode dynamic desirable
 shutdown
!
interface FastEthernet0/47
 switchport mode dynamic desirable
 shutdown
!
interface FastEthernet0/48
 switchport mode dynamic desirable
 shutdown
!
interface GigabitEthernet0/1
 switchport mode dynamic desirable
!
interface GigabitEthernet0/2
 switchport mode dynamic desirable
!
interface Vlan1
 no ip address
 shutdown
!
interface Vlan100
 ip address 192.168.100.1 255.255.255.0
!
interface Vlan200
 ip address 192.168.200.1 255.255.255.0
!
ip classless
ip http server
ip http secure-server
!
control-plane
!
line con 0
line vty 0 4
 no login
```

```
line vty 5 15
 no login
!
end

DLS1#
```

DLS2

```
DLS2#show running-config
Building configuration...

Current configuration : 4478 bytes
!
version 12.2
no service pad
service timestamps debug uptime
service timestamps log uptime
no service password-encryption
!
hostname DLS2
!
no logging console
!
no aaa new-model
ip subnet-zero
ip routing
!
vtp domain HARD
vtp mode transparent
!
spanning-tree mode mst
spanning-tree extend system-id
!
spanning-tree mst configuration
 name DLS2-REGION
 revision 5
 instance 3 vlan 100, 200
!
vlan internal allocation policy ascending
!
vlan 100,200
!
interface FastEthernet0/1
 switchport mode dynamic desirable
 shutdown
!
interface FastEthernet0/2
 switchport mode dynamic desirable
 shutdown
!
interface FastEthernet0/3
```

```
 switchport mode dynamic desirable
 shutdown
!
interface FastEthernet0/4
 switchport mode dynamic desirable
 shutdown
!
interface FastEthernet0/5
 switchport mode dynamic desirable
 shutdown
!
interface FastEthernet0/6
 switchport mode dynamic desirable
 shutdown
!
interface FastEthernet0/7
 switchport mode dynamic desirable
 shutdown
!
interface FastEthernet0/8
 switchport trunk encapsulation dot1q
 switchport mode trunk
!
interface FastEthernet0/9
 switchport mode dynamic desirable
 shutdown
!
interface FastEthernet0/10
 switchport mode dynamic desirable
 shutdown
!
interface FastEthernet0/11
 switchport mode dynamic desirable
 shutdown
!
interface FastEthernet0/12
 switchport trunk encapsulation dot1q
 switchport mode trunk
!
interface FastEthernet0/13
 switchport mode dynamic desirable
 shutdown
!
interface FastEthernet0/14
 switchport mode dynamic desirable
 shutdown
!
interface FastEthernet0/15
 switchport mode dynamic desirable
 shutdown
!
interface FastEthernet0/16
 switchport mode dynamic desirable
 shutdown
```

```
!
interface FastEthernet0/17
 switchport mode dynamic desirable
 shutdown
!
interface FastEthernet0/18
 switchport mode dynamic desirable
 shutdown
!
interface FastEthernet0/19
 switchport mode dynamic desirable
 shutdown
!
interface FastEthernet0/20
 switchport mode dynamic desirable
 shutdown
!
interface FastEthernet0/21
 switchport mode dynamic desirable
 shutdown
!
interface FastEthernet0/22
 switchport mode dynamic desirable
 shutdown
!
interface FastEthernet0/23
 switchport mode dynamic desirable
 shutdown
!
interface FastEthernet0/24
 switchport mode dynamic desirable
 shutdown
!
interface FastEthernet0/25
 switchport mode dynamic desirable
 shutdown
!
interface FastEthernet0/26
 switchport mode dynamic desirable
 shutdown
!
interface FastEthernet0/27
 switchport mode dynamic desirable
 shutdown
!
interface FastEthernet0/28
 switchport mode dynamic desirable
 shutdown
!
interface FastEthernet0/29
 switchport mode dynamic desirable
 shutdown
!
interface FastEthernet0/30
 switchport mode dynamic desirable
```

```
 shutdown
!
interface FastEthernet0/31
 switchport mode dynamic desirable
 shutdown
!
interface FastEthernet0/32
 switchport mode dynamic desirable
 shutdown
!
interface FastEthernet0/33
 switchport mode dynamic desirable
 shutdown
!
interface FastEthernet0/34
 switchport mode dynamic desirable
 shutdown
!
interface FastEthernet0/35
 switchport mode dynamic desirable
 shutdown
!
interface FastEthernet0/36
 switchport mode dynamic desirable
 shutdown
!
interface FastEthernet0/37
 switchport mode dynamic desirable
 shutdown
!
interface FastEthernet0/38
 switchport mode dynamic desirable
 shutdown
!
interface FastEthernet0/39
 switchport mode dynamic desirable
 shutdown
!
interface FastEthernet0/40
 switchport mode dynamic desirable
 shutdown
!
interface FastEthernet0/41
 switchport mode dynamic desirable
 shutdown
!
interface FastEthernet0/42
 switchport mode dynamic desirable
 shutdown
!
interface FastEthernet0/43
 switchport mode dynamic desirable
 shutdown
!
interface FastEthernet0/44
```

```
 switchport mode dynamic desirable
 shutdown
!
interface FastEthernet0/45
 switchport mode dynamic desirable
 shutdown
!
interface FastEthernet0/46
 switchport mode dynamic desirable
 shutdown
!
interface FastEthernet0/47
 switchport mode dynamic desirable
 shutdown
!
interface FastEthernet0/48
 switchport mode dynamic desirable
 shutdown
!
interface GigabitEthernet0/1
 switchport mode dynamic desirable
!
interface GigabitEthernet0/2
 switchport mode dynamic desirable
!
interface Vlan1
 no ip address
 shutdown
!
interface Vlan100
 ip address 192.168.100.2 255.255.255.0
!
interface Vlan200
 ip address 192.168.200.2 255.255.255.0
!
ip classless
ip http server
ip http secure-server
!
control-plane
!

line con 0
line vty 0 4
 login
line vty 5 15
 login
!
end

DLS2#
```

ALS1

```
ALS1#show running-config
Building configuration...

Current configuration : 1670 bytes
!
version 12.1
no service pad
service timestamps debug uptime
service timestamps log uptime
no service password-encryption
!
hostname ALS1
!
no logging console
!
ip subnet-zero
!
ip ssh time-out 120
ip ssh authentication-retries 3
vtp domain HARD
vtp mode transparent
!
!
spanning-tree mode rapid-pvst
no spanning-tree optimize bpdu transmission
spanning-tree extend system-id
!
vlan 100
!
interface FastEthernet0/1
 shutdown
!
interface FastEthernet0/2
 shutdown
!
interface FastEthernet0/3
 shutdown
!
interface FastEthernet0/4
 shutdown
!
interface FastEthernet0/5
 shutdown
!
interface FastEthernet0/6
 shutdown
!
interface FastEthernet0/7
 shutdown
!
interface FastEthernet0/8
 switchport mode trunk
```

```
!
interface FastEthernet0/9
 shutdown
!
interface FastEthernet0/10
 switchport mode trunk
!
interface FastEthernet0/11
 shutdown
!
interface FastEthernet0/12
 shutdown
!
interface FastEthernet0/13
 shutdown
!
interface FastEthernet0/14
 shutdown
!
interface FastEthernet0/15
 shutdown
!
interface FastEthernet0/16
 shutdown
!
interface FastEthernet0/17
 shutdown
!
interface FastEthernet0/18
 shutdown
!
interface FastEthernet0/19
 shutdown
!
interface FastEthernet0/20
 shutdown
!
interface FastEthernet0/21
 shutdown
!
interface FastEthernet0/22
 shutdown
!
interface FastEthernet0/23
 shutdown
!
interface FastEthernet0/24
 shutdown
!
interface GigabitEthernet0/1
!
interface GigabitEthernet0/2
!
interface Vlan1
 no ip address
```

```
 no ip route-cache
 shutdown
!
interface Vlan100
 ip address 192.168.100.254 255.255.255.0
 no ip route-cache
!
ip default-gateway 192.168.100.1
ip http server
!
line con 0
line vty 0 4
 login
line vty 5 15
 login
!
end

ALS1#
```

ALS2

```
ALS2#show running-config
Building configuration...

Current configuration : 2598 bytes
!
version 12.1
no service pad
service timestamps debug uptime
service timestamps log uptime
no service password-encryption
!
hostname ALS2
!
no logging console
!
ip subnet-zero
!
ip ssh time-out 120
ip ssh authentication-retries 3
vtp domain HARD
vtp mode transparent
!
spanning-tree mode pvst
no spanning-tree optimize bpdu transmission
spanning-tree extend system-id
!
vlan 100
!
interface FastEthernet0/1
 shutdown
!
interface FastEthernet0/2
```

```
 shutdown
!
interface FastEthernet0/3
 shutdown
!
interface FastEthernet0/4
 shutdown
!
interface FastEthernet0/5
 shutdown
!
interface FastEthernet0/6
 shutdown
!
interface FastEthernet0/7
 shutdown
!
interface FastEthernet0/8
 switchport mode trunk
!
interface FastEthernet0/9
 shutdown
!
interface FastEthernet0/10
 switchport mode trunk
!
interface FastEthernet0/11
 shutdown
!
interface FastEthernet0/12
 shutdown
!
interface FastEthernet0/13
 shutdown
!
interface FastEthernet0/14
 shutdown
!
interface FastEthernet0/15
 shutdown
!
interface FastEthernet0/16
 shutdown
!
interface FastEthernet0/17
 shutdown
!
interface FastEthernet0/18
 shutdown
!
interface FastEthernet0/19
 shutdown
!
interface FastEthernet0/20
 shutdown
```

```
!
interface FastEthernet0/21
 shutdown
!
interface FastEthernet0/22
 shutdown
!
interface FastEthernet0/23
 shutdown
!
interface FastEthernet0/24
 shutdown
!
interface FastEthernet0/25
 shutdown
!
interface FastEthernet0/26
 shutdown
!
interface FastEthernet0/27
 shutdown
!
interface FastEthernet0/28
 shutdown
!
interface FastEthernet0/29
 shutdown
!
interface FastEthernet0/30
 shutdown
!
interface FastEthernet0/31
 shutdown
!
interface FastEthernet0/32
 shutdown
!
interface FastEthernet0/33
 shutdown
!
interface FastEthernet0/34
 shutdown
!
interface FastEthernet0/35
 shutdown
!
interface FastEthernet0/36
 shutdown
!
interface FastEthernet0/37
 shutdown
!
interface FastEthernet0/38
 shutdown
!
```

```
interface FastEthernet0/39
 shutdown
!
interface FastEthernet0/40
 shutdown
!
interface FastEthernet0/41
 shutdown
!
interface FastEthernet0/42
 shutdown
!
interface FastEthernet0/43
 shutdown
!
interface FastEthernet0/44
 shutdown
!
interface FastEthernet0/45
 shutdown
!
interface FastEthernet0/46
 shutdown
!
interface FastEthernet0/47
 shutdown
!
interface FastEthernet0/48
 shutdown
!
interface GigabitEthernet0/1
!
interface GigabitEthernet0/2
!
interface Vlan1
 no ip address
 no ip route-cache
 shutdown
!
interface Vlan200
 ip address 192.168.200.254 255.255.255.0
 no ip route-cache
!
ip default-gateway 192.168.200.2
ip http server
!
line con 0
line vty 0 4
 login
line vty 5 15
 login
!
end

ALS2#
```

LAB 3

Etherchannel Configuration and Implementation

Lab Objective:

The objective of this lab exercise is for you to learn and understand how implement Etherchannels in Cisco IOS Catalyst switches.

Lab Topology:

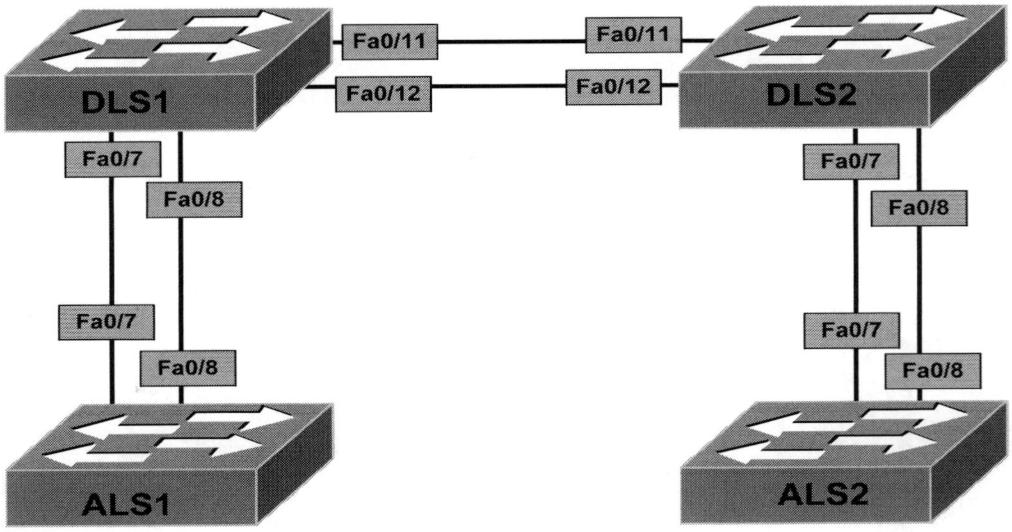

IMPORTANT NOTE

If you are using the www.howtonetwork.net racks, please begin each and every lab by shutting down all interfaces on all switches and then manually re-enabling the interfaces that are illustrated in this topology.

Task 1

Configure a VTP domain name of ETHER for all switches. Configure a VTP password of CHANNEL on all switches within the VTP domain. Enable VTP version 2 on all switches.

Task 2

Configure VLAN 4000 on all switches. This VLAN should be named PORTCHANNEL. Configure SVI 4000 on all switches using the following address assignments:

- DLS1—IP address 40.1.1.1/24
- DLS2—IP address 40.1.1.2/24
- ALS1—IP address 40.1.1.3/24
- ALS2—IP address 40.1.1.4/24

Task 3

Configure an Etherchannel between switches DLS1 and DLS2. This Etherchannel should NOT exchange PAgP or LACP packets. Configure this Etherchannel as an ISL trunk. Verify the configuration using the appropriate commands.

Task 4

Configure an Etherchannel between switches DLS1 and ALS1. This Etherchannel should be a PAgP Etherchannel that is configured as a Layer 2 802.1Q trunk. Ensure that switch ALS1 only establishes an Etherchannel if it receives PAgP packets from another PAgP-capable device. Verify the configuration using the appropriate commands.

Task 5

Configure an Etherchannel between switches DLS2 and ALS2. This Etherchannel should be an LACP Etherchannel. The ports within this Etherchannel should all be in VLAN 4000. This Etherchannel should NOT be in trunking mode. Ensure that switch ALS2 only establishes an Etherchannel if it receives LACP packets from another LACP-capable device. Verify the configuration using the appropriate commands.

Task 6

Verify your Etherchannel configuration by ensuring that all switches can ping each other.

Lab Validation

Task 1

```
DLS1(config)#vtp domain ETHER
DLS1(config)#vtp password CHANNEL
DLS1(config)#vtp version 2

DLS2(config)#vtp domain ETHER
DLS2(config)#vtp password CHANNEL
DLS2(config)#vtp version 2

ALS1(config)#vtp domain ETHER
ALS1(config)#vtp password CHANNEL
ALS1(config)#vtp version 2

ALS2(config)#vtp domain ETHER
ALS2(config)#vtp password CHANNEL
ALS2(config)#vtp version 2
```

Task 2

```
DLS1(config)#vlan 4000
DLS1(config-vlan)#name PORTCHANNEL
DLS1(config-vlan)#exit
DLS1(config)#interface vlan 4000
DLS1(config-if)#ip address 40.1.1.1 255.255.255.0
DLS1(config-if)#no shut

DLS2(config)#vlan 4000
DLS2(config-vlan)#name PORTCHANNEL
DLS2(config-vlan)#exit
DLS2(config)#interface vlan 4000
DLS2(config-if)#ip address 40.1.1.2 255.255.255.0
DLS2(config-if)#no shut

ALS1(config)#vlan 4000
ALS1(config-vlan)#name PORTCHANNEL
ALS1(config-vlan)#exit
ALS1(config)#interface vlan 4000
ALS1(config-if)#ip address 40.1.1.3 255.255.255.0
ALS1(config-if)#no shut

ALS2(config)#vlan 4000
ALS2(config-vlan)#name PORTCHANNEL
ALS2(config-vlan)#exit
ALS2(config)#interface vlan 4000
ALS2(config-if)#ip address 40.1.1.4 255.255.255.0
ALS2(config-if)#no shut
```

Task 3

```
DLS1(config)#int range f0/11 - 12
DLS1(config-if-range)#switchport
DLS1(config-if-range)#switchport trunk encapsulation isl
DLS1(config-if-range)#switchport mode trunk
DLS1(config-if-range)#channel-group 1 mode on
Creating a port-channel interface Port-channel 1

DLS1(config-if-range)#no shutdown


DLS2(config)#int range f0/11 - 12
DLS2(config-if-range)#switchport
DLS2(config-if-range)#switchport trunk encap isl
DLS2(config-if-range)#switchport mode trunk
DLS2(config-if-range)#channel-group 1 mode on
Creating a port-channel interface Port-channel 1

DLS2(config-if-range)#no shutdown
```

Verify the configuration as follows:

```
DLS1#show etherchannel 1 summary
Flags:  D - down        P - in port-channel
        I - stand-alone s - suspended
        H - Hot-standby (LACP only)
        R - Layer3      S - Layer2
        U - in use      f - failed to allocate aggregator
        u - unsuitable for bundling
        w - waiting to be aggregated
        d - default port


Number of channel-groups in use: 1
Number of aggregators:           1

Group  Port-channel  Protocol    Ports
------+-------------+-----------+----------------------------------------
1      Po1(SU)          -        Fa0/11(P)   Fa0/12(P)

DLS2#show etherchannel 1 summary
Flags:  D - down        P - bundled in port-channel
        I - stand-alone s - suspended
        H - Hot-standby (LACP only)
        R - Layer3      S - Layer2
        U - in use      f - failed to allocate aggregator

        M - not in use, minimum links not met
        u - unsuitable for bundling
        w - waiting to be aggregated
        d - default port


Number of channel-groups in use: 1
Number of aggregators:           1

Group  Port-channel  Protocol    Ports
------+-------------+-----------+----------------------------------------
1      Po1(SU)          -        Fa0/11(P)   Fa0/12(P)
```

Task 4

```
DLS1(config)#int range f0/7 - 8
DLS1(config-if-range)#switchport
DLS1(config-if-range)#switchport trunk encapsulation dot1q
DLS1(config-if-range)#switchport mode trunk
DLS1(config-if-range)#channel-group 2 mode desirable
Creating a port-channel interface Port-channel 2

DLS1(config-if-range)#no shutdown
```

```
ALS1(config)#int range f0/7 - 8
ALS1(config-if-range)#switchport mode trunk
ALS1(config-if-range)#channel-group 2 mode auto
Creating a port-channel interface Port-channel 2

ALS1(config-if-range)#no shutdown
```

Verify the configuration as follows:

```
DLS1#show etherchannel 2 summary
Flags:  D - down        P - in port-channel
        I - stand-alone s - suspended
        H - Hot-standby (LACP only)
        R - Layer3      S - Layer2
        U - in use      f - failed to allocate aggregator
        u - unsuitable for bundling
        w - waiting to be aggregated
        d - default port


Number of channel-groups in use: 2
Number of aggregators:           2

Group  Port-channel  Protocol    Ports
------+-------------+-----------+-----------------------------------------
2      Po2(SU)         PAgP      Fa0/7(P)    Fa0/8(P)

ALS1#show etherchannel 2 summary
Flags:  D - down        P - in port-channel
        I - stand-alone s - suspended
        H - Hot-standby (LACP only)
        R - Layer3      S - Layer2
        u - unsuitable for bundling
        U - in use      f - failed to allocate aggregator
        d - default port

Number of channel-groups in use: 1
Number of aggregators:           1

Group  Port-channel  Protocol    Ports
------+-------------+-----------+-----------------------------------------
2      Po2(SU)         PAgP      Fa0/7(Pd)   Fa0/8(P)
```

Task 5

```
DLS2(config)#int range f0/7 - 8
DLS2(config-if-range)#switchport
DLS2(config-if-range)#switchport access vlan 4000
DLS2(config-if-range)#switchport mode access
```

```
DLS2(config-if-range)#channel-group 2 mode active
Creating a port-channel interface Port-channel 2

DLS2(config-if-range)#no shutdown


ALS2(config)#int range f0/7 - 8
ALS2(config-if-range)#switchport access vlan 4000
ALS2(config-if-range)#switchport mode access
ALS2(config-if-range)#channel-group 2 mode passive
Creating a port-channel interface Port-channel 2

ALS2(config-if-range)#no shutdown
```

Verify the configuration as follows:

```
DLS2#show etherchannel 2 summary
Flags:  D - down        P - bundled in port-channel
        I - stand-alone s - suspended
        H - Hot-standby (LACP only)
        R - Layer3      S - Layer2
        U - in use      f - failed to allocate aggregator

        M - not in use, minimum links not met
        u - unsuitable for bundling
        w - waiting to be aggregated
        d - default port


Number of channel-groups in use: 2
Number of aggregators:           2

Group  Port-channel  Protocol    Ports
------+-------------+-----------+-----------------------------------------------
2      Po2(SU)         LACP      Fa0/7(P)    Fa0/8(P)


ALS2#show etherchannel 2 summary
Flags:  D - down        P - in port-channel
        I - stand-alone s - suspended
        H - Hot-standby (LACP only)
        R - Layer3      S - Layer2
        u - unsuitable for bundling
        U - in use      f - failed to allocate aggregator
        d - default port

Number of channel-groups in use: 1
Number of aggregators:           1

Group  Port-channel  Protocol    Ports
------+-------------+-----------+-----------------------------------------------
2      Po2(SU)         LACP      Fa0/7(P)    Fa0/8(Pd)
```

You should also use the show interfaces port-channel[number] switchport command to verify the correct Layer 2 operational mode based on the configuration.

```
DLS2#show interfaces port-channel 1 switchport
Name: Po1
Switchport: Enabled
Administrative Mode: trunk
Operational Mode: trunk
Administrative Trunking Encapsulation: isl
Operational Trunking Encapsulation: isl
Negotiation of Trunking: On
Access Mode VLAN: 1 (default)

[Truncated]

DLS2#show interfaces port-channel 2 switchport
Name: Po2
Switchport: Enabled
Administrative Mode: static access
Operational Mode: static access
Administrative Trunking Encapsulation: negotiate
Operational Trunking Encapsulation: native
Negotiation of Trunking: Off
Access Mode VLAN: 4000 (PORTCHANNEL)
Trunking Native Mode VLAN: 1 (default)
Administrative Native VLAN tagging: enabled
Voice VLAN: none

[Truncated]
```

Task 6

```
DLS1#ping 40.1.1.0

Type escape sequence to abort.
Sending 5, 100-byte ICMP Echos to 40.1.1.0, timeout is 2 seconds:
.
Reply to request 1 from 40.1.1.2, 1 ms
Reply to request 1 from 40.1.1.4, 1 ms
Reply to request 1 from 40.1.1.3, 1 ms
Reply to request 2 from 40.1.1.2, 1 ms
Reply to request 2 from 40.1.1.4, 4 ms
Reply to request 2 from 40.1.1.3, 1 ms
Reply to request 3 from 40.1.1.2, 1 ms
Reply to request 3 from 40.1.1.4, 1 ms
Reply to request 3 from 40.1.1.3, 1 ms
Reply to request 4 from 40.1.1.2, 1 ms
Reply to request 4 from 40.1.1.4, 1 ms
Reply to request 4 from 40.1.1.3, 1 ms

DLS2#ping 40.1.1.0
```

```
Type escape sequence to abort.
Sending 5, 100-byte ICMP Echos to 40.1.1.0, timeout is 2 seconds:
.
Reply to request 1 from 40.1.1.1, 1 ms
Reply to request 1 from 40.1.1.3, 4 ms
Reply to request 1 from 40.1.1.4, 4 ms
Reply to request 2 from 40.1.1.1, 1 ms
Reply to request 2 from 40.1.1.4, 8 ms
Reply to request 2 from 40.1.1.3, 1 ms
Reply to request 3 from 40.1.1.1, 1 ms
Reply to request 3 from 40.1.1.3, 1 ms
Reply to request 3 from 40.1.1.4, 1 ms
Reply to request 4 from 40.1.1.1, 1 ms
Reply to request 4 from 40.1.1.3, 1 ms
Reply to request 4 from 40.1.1.4, 1 ms

ALS1#ping 40.1.1.0

Type escape sequence to abort.
Sending 5, 100-byte ICMP Echos to 40.1.1.0, timeout is 2 seconds:
.
Reply to request 1 from 40.1.1.1, 1 ms
Reply to request 1 from 40.1.1.4, 1 ms
Reply to request 1 from 40.1.1.2, 1 ms
Reply to request 2 from 40.1.1.1, 1 ms
Reply to request 2 from 40.1.1.4, 1 ms
Reply to request 2 from 40.1.1.2, 1 ms
Reply to request 3 from 40.1.1.1, 1 ms
Reply to request 3 from 40.1.1.4, 1 ms
Reply to request 3 from 40.1.1.2, 1 ms
Reply to request 4 from 40.1.1.1, 1 ms
Reply to request 4 from 40.1.1.4, 1 ms
Reply to request 4 from 40.1.1.2, 1 ms

ALS2#ping 40.1.1.0

Type escape sequence to abort.
Sending 5, 100-byte ICMP Echos to 40.1.1.0, timeout is 2 seconds:
.
Reply to request 1 from 40.1.1.2, 1 ms
Reply to request 1 from 40.1.1.3, 4 ms
Reply to request 1 from 40.1.1.1, 1 ms
Reply to request 2 from 40.1.1.1, 1 ms
Reply to request 2 from 40.1.1.3, 1 ms
Reply to request 2 from 40.1.1.2, 1 ms
Reply to request 3 from 40.1.1.2, 1 ms
Reply to request 3 from 40.1.1.3, 1 ms
Reply to request 3 from 40.1.1.1, 1 ms
Reply to request 4 from 40.1.1.2, 1 ms
Reply to request 4 from 40.1.1.3, 1 ms
Reply to request 4 from 40.1.1.1, 1 ms
```

Final Switch Configurations

DLS1

```
DLS1#show running-config
Building configuration...

Current configuration : 4625 bytes
!
version 12.2
no service pad
service timestamps debug uptime
service timestamps log uptime
no service password-encryption
!
hostname DLS1
!
no logging console
!
no aaa new-model
ip subnet-zero
!
vtp domain ETHER
vtp mode transparent
!
no file verify auto
spanning-tree mode pvst
spanning-tree extend system-id
!
vlan internal allocation policy ascending
!
vlan 4000
 name PORTCHANNEL
!
interface Port-channel1
 switchport trunk encapsulation isl
 switchport mode trunk
!
interface Port-channel2
 switchport trunk encapsulation dot1q
 switchport mode trunk
!
interface FastEthernet0/1
 switchport mode dynamic desirable
 shutdown
!
interface FastEthernet0/2
 switchport mode dynamic desirable
 shutdown
!
interface FastEthernet0/3
```

```
 switchport mode dynamic desirable
 shutdown
!
interface FastEthernet0/4
 switchport mode dynamic desirable
 shutdown
!
interface FastEthernet0/5
 switchport mode dynamic desirable
 shutdown
!
interface FastEthernet0/6
 switchport mode dynamic desirable
 shutdown
!
interface FastEthernet0/7
 switchport trunk encapsulation dot1q
 switchport mode trunk
 channel-group 2 mode desirable
!
interface FastEthernet0/8
 switchport trunk encapsulation dot1q
 switchport mode trunk
 channel-group 2 mode desirable
!
interface FastEthernet0/9
 switchport mode dynamic desirable
 shutdown
!
interface FastEthernet0/10
 switchport mode dynamic desirable
 shutdown
!
interface FastEthernet0/11
 switchport trunk encapsulation isl
 switchport mode trunk
 channel-group 1 mode on
!
interface FastEthernet0/12
 switchport trunk encapsulation isl
 switchport mode trunk
 channel-group 1 mode on
!
interface FastEthernet0/13
 switchport mode dynamic desirable
 shutdown
!
interface FastEthernet0/14
 switchport mode dynamic desirable
 shutdown
!
interface FastEthernet0/15
```

```
 switchport mode dynamic desirable
 shutdown
!
interface FastEthernet0/16
 switchport mode dynamic desirable
 shutdown
!
interface FastEthernet0/17
 switchport mode dynamic desirable
 shutdown
!
interface FastEthernet0/18
 switchport mode dynamic desirable
 shutdown
!
interface FastEthernet0/19
 switchport mode dynamic desirable
 shutdown
!
interface FastEthernet0/20
 switchport mode dynamic desirable
 shutdown
!
interface FastEthernet0/21
 switchport mode dynamic desirable
 shutdown
!
interface FastEthernet0/22
 switchport mode dynamic desirable
 shutdown
!
interface FastEthernet0/23
 switchport mode dynamic desirable
 shutdown
!
interface FastEthernet0/24
 switchport mode dynamic desirable
 shutdown
!
interface FastEthernet0/25
 switchport mode dynamic desirable
 shutdown
!
interface FastEthernet0/26
 switchport mode dynamic desirable
 shutdown
!
interface FastEthernet0/27
 switchport mode dynamic desirable
 shutdown
!
interface FastEthernet0/28
 switchport mode dynamic desirable
 shutdown
```

```
!
interface FastEthernet0/29
 switchport mode dynamic desirable
 shutdown
!
interface FastEthernet0/30
 switchport mode dynamic desirable
 shutdown
!
interface FastEthernet0/31
 switchport mode dynamic desirable
 shutdown
!
interface FastEthernet0/32
 switchport mode dynamic desirable
 shutdown
!
interface FastEthernet0/33
 switchport mode dynamic desirable
 shutdown
!
interface FastEthernet0/34
 switchport mode dynamic desirable
 shutdown
!
interface FastEthernet0/35
 switchport mode dynamic desirable
 shutdown
!
interface FastEthernet0/36
 switchport mode dynamic desirable
 shutdown
!
interface FastEthernet0/37
 switchport mode dynamic desirable
 shutdown
!
interface FastEthernet0/38
 switchport mode dynamic desirable
 shutdown
!
interface FastEthernet0/39
 switchport mode dynamic desirable
 shutdown
!
interface FastEthernet0/40
 switchport mode dynamic desirable
 shutdown
!
interface FastEthernet0/41
 switchport mode dynamic desirable
 shutdown
!
interface FastEthernet0/42
```

```
 switchport mode dynamic desirable
 shutdown
!
interface FastEthernet0/43
 switchport mode dynamic desirable
 shutdown
!
interface FastEthernet0/44
 switchport mode dynamic desirable
 shutdown
!
interface FastEthernet0/45
 switchport mode dynamic desirable
 shutdown
!
interface FastEthernet0/46
 switchport mode dynamic desirable
 shutdown
!
interface FastEthernet0/47
 switchport mode dynamic desirable
 shutdown
!
interface FastEthernet0/48
 switchport mode dynamic desirable
 shutdown
!
interface GigabitEthernet0/1
 switchport mode dynamic desirable
!
interface GigabitEthernet0/2
 switchport mode dynamic desirable
!
interface Vlan1
 no ip address
 shutdown
!
interface Vlan4000
 ip address 40.1.1.1 255.255.255.0
!
ip classless
ip http server
ip http secure-server
!
control-plane
!
line con 0
line vty 5 15
!
end

DLS1#
```

DLS2

```
DLS2#show running-config
Building configuration...

Current configuration : 4582 bytes
!
version 12.2
no service pad
service timestamps debug uptime
service timestamps log uptime
no service password-encryption
!
hostname DLS2
!
no logging console
!
no aaa new-model
ip subnet-zero
!
vtp domain ETHER
vtp mode transparent
!
spanning-tree mode pvst
spanning-tree extend system-id
!
vlan internal allocation policy ascending
!
vlan 4000
 name PORTCHANNEL
!
interface Port-channel1
 switchport trunk encapsulation isl
 switchport mode trunk
!
interface Port-channel2
 switchport access vlan 4000
 switchport mode access
!
interface FastEthernet0/1
 switchport mode dynamic desirable
 shutdown
!
interface FastEthernet0/2
 switchport mode dynamic desirable
 shutdown
!
interface FastEthernet0/3
 switchport mode dynamic desirable
 shutdown
!
interface FastEthernet0/4
```

```
 switchport mode dynamic desirable
 shutdown
!
interface FastEthernet0/5
 switchport mode dynamic desirable
 shutdown
!
interface FastEthernet0/6
 switchport mode dynamic desirable
 shutdown
!
interface FastEthernet0/7
 switchport access vlan 4000
 switchport mode access
 channel-group 2 mode active
!
interface FastEthernet0/8
 switchport access vlan 4000
 switchport mode access
 channel-group 2 mode active
!
interface FastEthernet0/9
 switchport mode dynamic desirable
 shutdown
!
interface FastEthernet0/10
 switchport mode dynamic desirable
 shutdown
!
interface FastEthernet0/11
 switchport trunk encapsulation isl
 switchport mode trunk
 channel-group 1 mode on
!
interface FastEthernet0/12
 switchport trunk encapsulation isl
 switchport mode trunk
 channel-group 1 mode on
!
interface FastEthernet0/13
 switchport mode dynamic desirable
 shutdown
!
interface FastEthernet0/14
 switchport mode dynamic desirable
 shutdown
!
interface FastEthernet0/15
 switchport mode dynamic desirable
 shutdown
!
interface FastEthernet0/16
```

```
 switchport mode dynamic desirable
 shutdown
!
interface FastEthernet0/17
 switchport mode dynamic desirable
 shutdown
!
interface FastEthernet0/18
 switchport mode dynamic desirable
 shutdown
!
interface FastEthernet0/19
 switchport mode dynamic desirable
 shutdown
!
interface FastEthernet0/20
 switchport mode dynamic desirable
 shutdown
!
interface FastEthernet0/21
 switchport mode dynamic desirable
 shutdown
!
interface FastEthernet0/22
 switchport mode dynamic desirable
 shutdown
!
interface FastEthernet0/23
 switchport mode dynamic desirable
 shutdown
!
interface FastEthernet0/24
 switchport mode dynamic desirable
 shutdown
!
interface FastEthernet0/25
 switchport mode dynamic desirable
 shutdown
!
interface FastEthernet0/26
 switchport mode dynamic desirable
 shutdown
!
interface FastEthernet0/27
 switchport mode dynamic desirable
 shutdown
!
interface FastEthernet0/28
 switchport mode dynamic desirable
 shutdown
!
interface FastEthernet0/29
```

```
 switchport mode dynamic desirable
 shutdown
!
interface FastEthernet0/30
 switchport mode dynamic desirable
 shutdown
!
interface FastEthernet0/31
 switchport mode dynamic desirable
 shutdown
!
interface FastEthernet0/32
 switchport mode dynamic desirable
 shutdown
!
interface FastEthernet0/33
 switchport mode dynamic desirable
 shutdown
!
interface FastEthernet0/34
 switchport mode dynamic desirable
 shutdown
!
interface FastEthernet0/35
 switchport mode dynamic desirable
 shutdown
!
interface FastEthernet0/36
 switchport mode dynamic desirable
 shutdown
!
interface FastEthernet0/37
 switchport mode dynamic desirable
 shutdown
!
interface FastEthernet0/38
 switchport mode dynamic desirable
 shutdown
!
interface FastEthernet0/39
 switchport mode dynamic desirable
 shutdown
!
interface FastEthernet0/40
 switchport mode dynamic desirable
 shutdown
!
interface FastEthernet0/41
 switchport mode dynamic desirable
 shutdown
!
interface FastEthernet0/42
```

```
 switchport mode dynamic desirable
 shutdown
!
interface FastEthernet0/43
 switchport mode dynamic desirable
 shutdown
!
interface FastEthernet0/44
 switchport mode dynamic desirable
 shutdown
!
interface FastEthernet0/45
 switchport mode dynamic desirable
 shutdown
!
interface FastEthernet0/46
 switchport mode dynamic desirable
 shutdown
!
interface FastEthernet0/47
 switchport mode dynamic desirable
 shutdown
!
interface FastEthernet0/48
 switchport mode dynamic desirable
 shutdown
!
interface GigabitEthernet0/1
 switchport mode dynamic desirable
!
interface GigabitEthernet0/2
 switchport mode dynamic desirable
!
interface Vlan1
 no ip address
 shutdown
!
interface Vlan4000
 ip address 40.1.1.2 255.255.255.0
!
ip classless
ip http server
ip http secure-server
!
control-plane
!
line con 0
line vty 5 15
!
end

DLS2#
```

ALS1

```
ALS1#show running-config
Building configuration...

Current configuration : 1736 bytes
!
version 12.1
no service pad
service timestamps debug uptime
service timestamps log uptime
no service password-encryption
!
hostname ALS1
!
no logging console
!
ip subnet-zero
!
ip ssh time-out 120
ip ssh authentication-retries 3
vtp domain ETHER
vtp mode transparent
!
spanning-tree mode pvst
no spanning-tree optimize bpdu transmission
spanning-tree extend system-id
!
vlan 4000
 name PORTCHANNEL
!
interface Port-channel2
 switchport mode trunk
 flowcontrol send off
!
interface FastEthernet0/1
 shutdown
!
interface FastEthernet0/2
 shutdown
!
interface FastEthernet0/3
 shutdown
!
interface FastEthernet0/4
 shutdown
!
interface FastEthernet0/5
 shutdown
!
interface FastEthernet0/6
 shutdown
```

```
!
interface FastEthernet0/7
 switchport mode trunk
 channel-group 2 mode auto
!
interface FastEthernet0/8
 switchport mode trunk
 channel-group 2 mode auto
!
interface FastEthernet0/9
 shutdown
!
interface FastEthernet0/10
 shutdown
!
interface FastEthernet0/11
 shutdown
!
interface FastEthernet0/12
 shutdown
!
interface FastEthernet0/13
 shutdown
!
interface FastEthernet0/14
 shutdown
!
interface FastEthernet0/15
 shutdown
!
interface FastEthernet0/16
 shutdown
!
interface FastEthernet0/17
 shutdown
!
interface FastEthernet0/18
 shutdown
!
interface FastEthernet0/19
 shutdown
!
interface FastEthernet0/20
 shutdown
!
interface FastEthernet0/21
 shutdown
!
interface FastEthernet0/22
 shutdown
!
interface FastEthernet0/23
```

```
 shutdown
!
interface FastEthernet0/24
 shutdown
!
interface GigabitEthernet0/1
!
interface GigabitEthernet0/2
!
interface Vlan1
 no ip address
 no ip route-cache
 shutdown
!
interface Vlan4000
 ip address 40.1.1.3 255.255.255.0
 no ip route-cache
!
ip http server
!
line con 0
line vty 5 15
!
!
end

ALS1#
```

ALS2

```
ALS2#show running-config
Building configuration...

Current configuration : 2768 bytes
!
version 12.1
no service pad
service timestamps debug uptime
service timestamps log uptime
no service password-encryption
!
hostname ALS2
!
no logging console
!
ip subnet-zero
!
ip ssh time-out 120
ip ssh authentication-retries 3
vtp domain ETHER
vtp mode transparent
```

```
!
spanning-tree mode pvst
no spanning-tree optimize bpdu transmission
spanning-tree extend system-id
!
vlan 4000
 name PORTCHANNEL
!
interface Port-channel2
 switchport access vlan 4000
 switchport mode access
 flowcontrol send off
!
interface FastEthernet0/1
 shutdown
!
interface FastEthernet0/2
 shutdown
!
interface FastEthernet0/3
 shutdown
!
interface FastEthernet0/4
 shutdown
!
interface FastEthernet0/5
 shutdown
!
interface FastEthernet0/6
 shutdown
!
interface FastEthernet0/7
 switchport access vlan 4000
 switchport mode access
 channel-group 2 mode passive
!
interface FastEthernet0/8
 switchport access vlan 4000
 switchport mode access
 channel-group 2 mode passive
!
interface FastEthernet0/9
 shutdown
!
interface FastEthernet0/10
 shutdown
!
interface FastEthernet0/11
 shutdown
!
interface FastEthernet0/12
 shutdown
```

```
!
interface FastEthernet0/13
 shutdown
!
interface FastEthernet0/14
 shutdown
!
interface FastEthernet0/15
 shutdown
!
interface FastEthernet0/16
 shutdown
!
interface FastEthernet0/17
 shutdown
!
interface FastEthernet0/18
 shutdown
!
interface FastEthernet0/19
 shutdown
!
interface FastEthernet0/20
 shutdown
!
interface FastEthernet0/21
 shutdown
!
interface FastEthernet0/22
 shutdown
!
interface FastEthernet0/23
 shutdown
!
interface FastEthernet0/24
 shutdown
!
interface FastEthernet0/25
 shutdown
!
interface FastEthernet0/26
 shutdown
!
interface FastEthernet0/27
 shutdown
!
interface FastEthernet0/28
 shutdown
!
interface FastEthernet0/29
 shutdown
!
```

```
interface FastEthernet0/30
 shutdown
!
interface FastEthernet0/31
 shutdown
!
interface FastEthernet0/32
 shutdown
!
interface FastEthernet0/33
 shutdown
!
interface FastEthernet0/34
 shutdown
!
interface FastEthernet0/35
 shutdown
!
interface FastEthernet0/36
 shutdown
!
interface FastEthernet0/37
 shutdown
!
interface FastEthernet0/38
 shutdown
!
interface FastEthernet0/39
 shutdown
!
interface FastEthernet0/40
 shutdown
!
interface FastEthernet0/41
 shutdown
!
interface FastEthernet0/42
 shutdown
!
interface FastEthernet0/43
 shutdown
!
interface FastEthernet0/44
 shutdown
!
interface FastEthernet0/45
 shutdown
!
interface FastEthernet0/46
 shutdown
!
interface FastEthernet0/47
```

```
 shutdown
!
interface FastEthernet0/48
 shutdown
!
interface GigabitEthernet0/1
!
interface GigabitEthernet0/2
!
interface Vlan1
 no ip address
 no ip route-cache
 shutdown
!
interface Vlan4000
 ip address 40.1.1.4 255.255.255.0
 no ip route-cache
!
ip http server
!
line con 0
line vty 5 15
!
end

ALS2#
```

LAB 4

Hot Standby Redundancy Protocol (HSRP)

Lab Objective:

The objective of this lab exercise is for you to learn and understand how to implement and verify the operation of the Cisco Hot Standby Router Protocol.

Lab Topology:

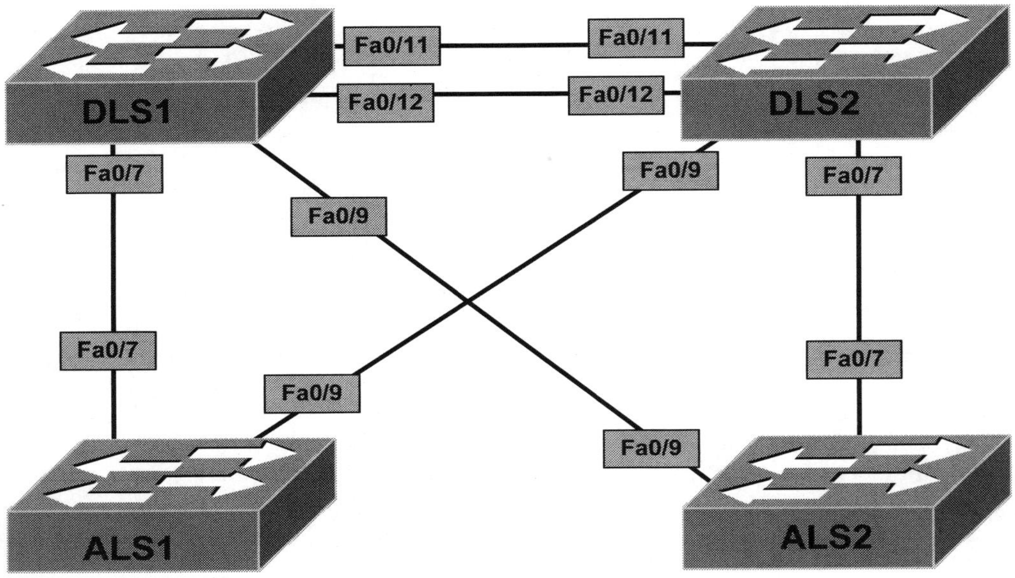

IMPORTANT NOTE

If you are using the www.howtonetwork.net racks, please begin each and every lab by shutting down all interfaces on all switches and then manually re-enabling the interfaces that are illustrated in this topology.

Task 1

Configure VTP domain name FHRP for all switches. Enable VTP v2 on all switches. Configure a VTP password of REDUNDANCY on all switches. Disable VTP on all switches.

Task 2

Configure an LACP Etherchannel between switches DLS1 and DLS2. This Etherchannel should be configured as an ISL trunk.

Task 3

Configure 802.1Q trunks on the switches within the network as follows:

- Configure an 802.1Q trunk between DLS1 and ALS1
- Configure an 802.1Q trunk between DLS1 and ALS2
- Configure an 802.1Q trunk between DLS2 and ALS1
- Configure an 802.1Q trunk between DLS2 and ALS2

Task 4

Configure Switched Virtual Interfaces on the Distribution layer switches as follows:

- Configure SVI 100 on switch DLS1. Assign this interface IP address 192.168.100.1/24
- Configure SVI 100 on switch DLS2. Assign this interface IP address 192.168.100.2/24
- Configure SVI 200 on switch DLS1. Assign this interface IP address 192.168.200.1/24
- Configure SVI 200 on switch DLS2. Assign this interface IP address 192.168.200.2/24

Verify that the Distribution layer switches can ping each other using these SVIs.

Task 5

Configure Switched Virtual Interfaces on the Access layer switches as follows:

- Configure SVI 100 on switch ALS1. Assign this interface IP address 192.168.100.5/24
- Configure SVI 200 on switch ALS2. Assign this interface IP address 192.168.200.5/24

Configure the switches with a gateway address of 192.168.100.254 (ALS1) and 192.168.200.254 (ALS2). Verify that the Access layer switches can ping both of the distribution switches.

Task 6

Configure HSRP between switches DLS1 and DLS2 as follows:

- Ensure that HSRP uses IP Multicast group address 224.0.0.102 to send packets
- Configure HSRP group 100 for SVI 100
- Authenticate HSRP using the password CISCO for plain text authentication
- Configure switch DLS1 as the primary (active) gateway using any priority value
- Configure HSRP to use a virtual address of 192.168.100.254
- Switch DLS1 should assume the role of active (primary) switch upon re-initialization

Verify your configuration using the appropriate commands.

Task 7

Configure HSRP between switches DLS1 and DLS2 as follows:

- Ensure that HSRP uses IP Multicast group address 224.0.0.102 to send packets
- Configure HSRP group 200 for SVI 200
- Authenticate HSRP using the password CISCO for MD5 authentication
- Configure switch DLS2 as the primary (active) gateway using any priority value
- Configure HSRP to use a virtual address of 192.168.100.254
- Switch DLS2 should assume the role of active (primary) switch upon re-initialization

Verify your configuration using the appropriate commands.

Task 8

Synchronize your Layer 2 and Layer 3 topologies using best practices.

Task 9

Configure the Access layer switches so that the backup port transitions to the Forwarding state in less than 5 seconds after the switch has detected that the primary link has failed. You are required to only use a single command to complete this task.

Lab Validation

Task 1

```
DLS1(config)#vtp domain FHRP
DLS1(config)#vtp password REDUNDANCY
DLS1(config)#vtp mode transparent

DLS2(config)#vtp domain FHRP
DLS2(config)#vtp password REDUNDANCY
DLS2(config)#vtp mode transparent

ALS1(config)#vtp domain FHRP
ALS1(config)#vtp password REDUNDANCY
ALS1(config)#vtp mode transparent

ALS2(config)#vtp domain FHRP
ALS2(config)#vtp password REDUNDANCY
ALS2(config)#vtp mode transparent
```

Task 2

```
DLS1(config)#interface range f0/11 - 12
DLS1(config-if-range)#switchport
DLS1(config-if-range)#switchport trunk encapsulation isl
DLS1(config-if-range)#switchport mode trunk
DLS1(config-if-range)#channel-group 1 mode on
Creating a port-channel interface Port-channel 1

DLS1(config-if-range)#no shutdown
DLS1(config-if-range)#exit

DLS2(config)#interface range f0/11 - 12
DLS2(config-if-range)#switchport
DLS2(config-if-range)#switchport trunk encap isl
DLS2(config-if-range)#switchport mode trunk
DLS2(config-if-range)#channel-group 1 mode on
Creating a port-channel interface Port-channel 1

DLS2(config-if-range)#no shutdown
DLS2(config-if-range)#exit
```

Verify your configuration as follows:

```
DLS1#show etherchannel 1 summary
Flags:  D - down        P - in port-channel
        I - stand-alone s - suspended
        H - Hot-standby (LACP only)
        R - Layer3      S - Layer2
        U - in use      f - failed to allocate aggregator
        u - unsuitable for bundling
        w - waiting to be aggregated
        d - default port


Number of channel-groups in use: 1
Number of aggregators:           1

Group  Port-channel  Protocol    Ports
------+-------------+-----------+-----------------------------------------
1      Po1(SU)          -        Fa0/11(P)   Fa0/12(P)

DLS2#show etherchannel 1 summary
Flags:  D - down        P - bundled in port-channel
        I - stand-alone s - suspended
        H - Hot-standby (LACP only)
        R - Layer3      S - Layer2
        U - in use      f - failed to allocate aggregator

        M - not in use, minimum links not met
```

```
        u - unsuitable for bundling
        w - waiting to be aggregated
        d - default port

Number of channel-groups in use: 1
Number of aggregators:           1

Group  Port-channel  Protocol    Ports
------+-------------+-----------+-----------------------------------------
1      Po1(SU)          -        Fa0/11(P)   Fa0/12(P)
```

Task 3

```
DLS1(config)#int range f0/7 , f0/9
DLS1(config-if-range)#switchport
DLS1(config-if-range)#switchport trunk encapsulation dot1q
DLS1(config-if-range)#switchport mode trunk
DLS1(config-if-range)#no shut
DLS1(config-if-range)#exit

DLS2(config)#int range f0/7 , f0/9
DLS2(config-if-range)#switchport
DLS2(config-if-range)#switchport trunk encapsulation dot1q
DLS2(config-if-range)#switchport mode trunk
DLS2(config-if-range)#no shutdown
DLS2(config-if-range)#exit

ALS1(config)#int range f0/7 , f0/9
ALS1(config-if-range)#switchport mode trunk
ALS1(config-if-range)#no shut
ALS1(config-if-range)#exit

ALS2(config)#int range f0/7 , f0/9
ALS2(config-if-range)#switchport mode trunk
ALS2(config-if-range)#no shutdown
ALS2(config-if-range)#exit
```

Task 4

```
DLS1(config)#vlan 100,200
DLS1(config-vlan)#exit
DLS1(config)#interface vlan 100
DLS1(config-if)#ip address 192.168.100.1 255.255.255.0
DLS1(config-if)#exit
DLS1(config)# exit interface vlan 200
DLS1(config-if)#ip address 192.168.200.1 255.255.255.0
DLS1(config-if)#no shut
DLS1(config-if)#

DLS2(config)#vlan 100,200
DLS2(config-vlan)#exit
```

```
DLS2(config)#interface vlan 100
DLS2(config-if)#ip address 192.168.100.2 255.255.255.0
DLS2(config-if)#no shutdown
DLS2(config-if)#exit
DLS2(config)#interface vlan 200
DLS2(config-if)#ip address 192.168.200.2 255.255.255.0
DLS2(config-if)#no shutdown
DLS2(config-if)#exit
```

Verify your configuration as follows:

```
DLS1#ping 192.168.100.2

Type escape sequence to abort.
Sending 5, 100-byte ICMP Echos to 192.168.100.2, timeout is 2 seconds:
.!!!!
Success rate is 80 percent (4/5), round-trip min/avg/max = 1/1/1 ms

DLS1#ping 192.168.200.2

Type escape sequence to abort.
Sending 5, 100-byte ICMP Echos to 192.168.200.2, timeout is 2 seconds:
.!!!!
Success rate is 80 percent (4/5), round-trip min/avg/max = 1/1/4 ms

DLS2#ping 192.168.100.1

Type escape sequence to abort.
Sending 5, 100-byte ICMP Echos to 192.168.100.1, timeout is 2 seconds:
!!!!!
Success rate is 100 percent (5/5), round-trip min/avg/max = 1/2/4 ms

DLS2#ping 192.168.200.1

Type escape sequence to abort.
Sending 5, 100-byte ICMP Echos to 192.168.200.1, timeout is 2 seconds:
!!!!!
Success rate is 100 percent (5/5), round-trip min/avg/max = 1/2/4 ms
```

Task 5

```
ALS1(config)#vlan 100
ALS1(config-vlan)#exit
ALS1(config)#interface vlan 100
ALS1(config-if)#ip address 192.168.100.5 255.255.255.0
ALS1(config-if)#no shutdown
ALS1(config-if)#exit
ALS1(config)#ip default-gateway 192.168.100.254
```

```
ALS2(config)#vlan 200
ALS2(config-vlan)#exit
ALS2(config)#interface vlan 200
ALS2(config-if)#ip address 192.168.200.5 255.255.255.0
ALS2(config-if)#no shut
ALS2(config-if)#exit
ALS2(config)#ip default-gateway 192.168.200.254
```

Verify your configuration as follows:

```
ALS1#ping 192.168.100.1

Type escape sequence to abort.
Sending 5, 100-byte ICMP Echos to 192.168.100.1, timeout is 2 seconds:
.!!!!
Success rate is 80 percent (4/5), round-trip min/avg/max = 1/2/4 ms

ALS2#ping 192.168.200.2

Type escape sequence to abort.
Sending 5, 100-byte ICMP Echos to 192.168.200.2, timeout is 2 seconds:
.!!!!
Success rate is 80 percent (4/5), round-trip min/avg/max = 1/2/4 ms
```

Task 6

```
DLS1(config)#int vlan 100
DLS1(config-if)#standby version 2
DLS1(config-if)#standby 100 authentication text CISCO
DLS1(config-if)#standby 100 priority 105
DLS1(config-if)#standby 100 ip 192.168.100.254
DLS1(config-if)#standby 100 preempt
DLS1(config-if)#exit

DLS2(config)#interface vlan 100
DLS2(config-if)#standby version 2
DLS2(config-if)#standby 100 authentication text CISCO
DLS2(config-if)#standby 100 ip 192.168.100.254
DLS2(config-if)#exit
```

Verify your configuration as follows:

```
DLS1#show standby brief
                     P indicates configured to preempt.
                     |
Interface   Grp Prio P State    Active          Standby         Virtual IP
Vl100       100 105    Active   local           192.168.100.2   192.168.100.254


DLS2#show standby
```

```
Vlan100 - Group 100 (version 2)
  State is Standby
    1 state change, last state change 00:00:21
  Virtual IP address is 192.168.100.254
  Active virtual MAC address is 0000.0c9f.f064
    Local virtual MAC address is 0000.0c9f.f064 (v2 default)
  Hello time 3 sec, hold time 10 sec
    Next hello sent in 2.620 secs
  Authentication text "CISCO"
  Preemption disabled
  Active router is 192.168.100.1, priority 105 (expires in 8.748 sec)
  Standby router is local
  Priority 100 (default 100)
  IP redundancy name is "hsrp-Vl100-100" (default)
```

Task 7

```
DLS1(config)#interface vlan 200
DLS1(config-if)#standby version 2
DLS1(config-if)#standby 200 authentication md5 key-string CISCO
DLS1(config-if)#standby 200 ip 192.168.200.254
DLS1(config-if)#exit
```

```
DLS2(config)#int vlan 200
DLS2(config-if)#standby version 2
DLS2(config-if)#standby 200 authentication md5 key-string CISCO
DLS2(config-if)#standby 200 ip 192.168.200.254
DLS2(config-if)#standby 200 preempt
DLS2(config-if)#standby 200 priority 105
DLS2(config-if)#exit
```

Verify your configuration as follows:

```
DLS1#show stand brief
                     P indicates configured to preempt.
                     |
Interface   Grp  Prio P State    Active          Standby         Virtual IP
Vl100       100  105  P Active   local           192.168.100.2   192.168.100.254
Vl200       200  100    Standby  192.168.200.2   local           192.168.200.254
```

```
DLS2#show standby brief
                     P indicates configured to preempt.
                     |
Interface   Grp  Prio P State    Active          Standby         Virtual IP
Vl100       100  100    Standby  192.168.100.1   local           192.168.100.254
Vl200       200  105  P Active   local           192.168.200.1   192.168.200.254
```

Task 8

```
DLS1(config)#spanning-tree vlan 100 priority 0

DLS2(config)#spanning-tree vlan 200 priority 0
```

Task 9

```
ALS1(config)#spanning-tree uplinkfast

ALS2(config)#spanning-tree uplinkfast
```

Verify your configuration as follows:

```
ALS1#show spanning-tree vlan 100

VLAN0100
  Spanning tree enabled protocol ieee
  Root ID    Priority    100
             Address     000d.291e.7f00
             Cost        3019
             Port        7 (FastEthernet0/7)
             Hello Time   2 sec  Max Age 20 sec  Forward Delay 15 sec

  Bridge ID  Priority    49252  (priority 49152 sys-id-ext 100)
             Address     000b.5f9e.4dc0
             Hello Time   2 sec  Max Age 20 sec  Forward Delay 15 sec
             Aging Time 300
  Uplinkfast enabled

Interface        Role Sts Cost      Prio.Nbr Type
---------------- ---- --- --------- -------- --------------------------------
Fa0/7            Root FWD 3019      128.7    P2p
Fa0/9            Altn BLK 3019      128.9    P2p

ALS1#show spanning-tree summary
Switch is in pvst mode
Root bridge for: none
EtherChannel misconfig guard is enabled
Extended system ID           is enabled
Portfast Default             is disabled
PortFast BPDU Guard Default  is disabled
Portfast BPDU Filter Default is disabled
Loopguard Default            is disabled
UplinkFast                   is enabled
BackboneFast                 is disabled
Pathcost method used         is short

Name                   Blocking Listening Learning Forwarding STP Active
---------------------- -------- --------- -------- ---------- ----------
```

```
VLAN0001                     1         0        0          1          2
VLAN0100                     1         0        0          1          2
---------------------- -------- --------- -------- ---------- ----------
2 vlans                      2         0        0          2          4

Station update rate set to 150 packets/sec.

UplinkFast statistics
-----------------------
Number of transitions via uplinkFast (all VLANs)            : 2
Number of proxy multicast addresses transmitted (all VLANs) : 8

ALS2#show spanning-tree vlan 200

VLAN0200
  Spanning tree enabled protocol ieee
  Root ID    Priority    200
             Address     000f.24ce.0d80
             Cost        3019
             Port        7 (FastEthernet0/7)
             Hello Time   2 sec  Max Age 20 sec  Forward Delay 15 sec

  Bridge ID  Priority    49352  (priority 49152 sys-id-ext 200)
             Address     0008.21a9.4f80
             Hello Time   2 sec  Max Age 20 sec  Forward Delay 15 sec
             Aging Time 300
  Uplinkfast enabled

Interface        Role Sts Cost      Prio.Nbr Type
---------------- ---- --- --------- -------- --------------------------------
Fa0/7            Root FWD 3019      128.7    P2p
Fa0/9            Altn BLK 3019      128.9    P2p

ALS2#show spanning-tree summary
Switch is in pvst mode
Root bridge for: none
EtherChannel misconfig guard is enabled
Extended system ID           is enabled
Portfast Default             is disabled
PortFast BPDU Guard Default  is disabled
Portfast BPDU Filter Default is disabled
Loopguard Default            is disabled
UplinkFast                   is enabled
BackboneFast                 is disabled
Pathcost method used         is short

Name                   Blocking Listening Learning Forwarding STP Active
---------------------- -------- --------- -------- ---------- ----------
VLAN0001                     1         0        0          1          2
VLAN0200                     1         0        0          1          2
---------------------- -------- --------- -------- ---------- ----------
2 vlans                      2         0        0          2          4
```

```
Station update rate set to 150 packets/sec.

UplinkFast statistics
-----------------------
Number of transitions via uplinkFast (all VLANs)            : 0
Number of proxy multicast addresses transmitted (all VLANs) : 0
```

Final Switch Configurations

DLS1

```
DLS1#show running-config
Building configuration...

Current configuration : 4836 bytes
!
version 12.2
no service pad
service timestamps debug uptime
service timestamps log uptime
no service password-encryption
!
hostname DLS1
!
no aaa new-model
no standby redirect
ip subnet-zero
ip routing
!
vtp domain FHRP
vtp mode transparent
!
no file verify auto
!
spanning-tree mode pvst
spanning-tree extend system-id
spanning-tree vlan 100 priority 0
!
vlan internal allocation policy ascending
!
vlan 100,200
!
interface Port-channel1
 switchport trunk encapsulation isl
 switchport mode trunk
!
interface FastEthernet0/1
 switchport mode dynamic desirable
```

```
 shutdown
!
interface FastEthernet0/2
 switchport mode dynamic desirable
 shutdown
!
interface FastEthernet0/3
 switchport mode dynamic desirable
 shutdown
!
interface FastEthernet0/4
 switchport mode dynamic desirable
 shutdown
!
interface FastEthernet0/5
 switchport mode dynamic desirable
 shutdown
!
interface FastEthernet0/6
 switchport mode dynamic desirable
 shutdown
!
interface FastEthernet0/7
 switchport trunk encapsulation dot1q
 switchport mode trunk
!
interface FastEthernet0/8
 switchport mode dynamic desirable
 shutdown
!
interface FastEthernet0/9
 switchport trunk encapsulation dot1q
 switchport mode trunk
!
interface FastEthernet0/10
 switchport mode dynamic desirable
 shutdown
!
interface FastEthernet0/11
 switchport trunk encapsulation isl
 switchport mode trunk
 channel-group 1 mode on
!
interface FastEthernet0/12
 switchport trunk encapsulation isl
 switchport mode trunk
 channel-group 1 mode on
!
interface FastEthernet0/13
 switchport mode dynamic desirable
 shutdown
!
```

```
interface FastEthernet0/14
 switchport mode dynamic desirable
 shutdown
!
interface FastEthernet0/15
 switchport mode dynamic desirable
 shutdown
!
interface FastEthernet0/16
 switchport mode dynamic desirable
 shutdown
!
interface FastEthernet0/17
 switchport mode dynamic desirable
 shutdown
!
interface FastEthernet0/18
 switchport mode dynamic desirable
 shutdown
!
interface FastEthernet0/19
 switchport mode dynamic desirable
 shutdown
!
interface FastEthernet0/20
 switchport mode dynamic desirable
 shutdown
!
interface FastEthernet0/21
 switchport mode dynamic desirable
 shutdown
!
interface FastEthernet0/22
 switchport mode dynamic desirable
 shutdown
!
interface FastEthernet0/23
 switchport mode dynamic desirable
 shutdown
!
interface FastEthernet0/24
 switchport mode dynamic desirable
 shutdown
!
interface FastEthernet0/25
 switchport mode dynamic desirable
 shutdown
!
interface FastEthernet0/26
 switchport mode dynamic desirable
 shutdown
!
```

```
interface FastEthernet0/27
 switchport mode dynamic desirable
 shutdown
!
interface FastEthernet0/28
 switchport mode dynamic desirable
 shutdown
!
interface FastEthernet0/29
 switchport mode dynamic desirable
 shutdown
!
interface FastEthernet0/30
 switchport mode dynamic desirable
 shutdown
!
interface FastEthernet0/31
 switchport mode dynamic desirable
 shutdown
!
interface FastEthernet0/32
 switchport mode dynamic desirable
 shutdown
!
interface FastEthernet0/33
 switchport mode dynamic desirable
 shutdown
!
interface FastEthernet0/34
 switchport mode dynamic desirable
 shutdown
!
interface FastEthernet0/35
 switchport mode dynamic desirable
 shutdown
!
interface FastEthernet0/36
 switchport mode dynamic desirable
 shutdown
!
interface FastEthernet0/37
 switchport mode dynamic desirable
 shutdown
!
interface FastEthernet0/38
 switchport mode dynamic desirable
 shutdown
!
interface FastEthernet0/39
 switchport mode dynamic desirable
 shutdown
!
```

```
interface FastEthernet0/40
 switchport mode dynamic desirable
 shutdown
!
interface FastEthernet0/41
 switchport mode dynamic desirable
 shutdown
!
interface FastEthernet0/42
 switchport mode dynamic desirable
 shutdown
!
interface FastEthernet0/43
 switchport mode dynamic desirable
 shutdown
!
interface FastEthernet0/44
 switchport mode dynamic desirable
 shutdown
!
interface FastEthernet0/45
 switchport mode dynamic desirable
 shutdown
!
interface FastEthernet0/46
 switchport mode dynamic desirable
 shutdown
!
interface FastEthernet0/47
 switchport mode dynamic desirable
 shutdown
!
interface FastEthernet0/48
 switchport mode dynamic desirable
 shutdown
!
interface GigabitEthernet0/1
 switchport mode dynamic desirable
!
interface GigabitEthernet0/2
 switchport mode dynamic desirable
!
interface Vlan1
 no ip address
 shutdown
!
interface Vlan100
 ip address 192.168.100.1 255.255.255.0
 standby version 2
 standby 100 ip 192.168.100.254
 standby 100 priority 105
 standby 100 preempt
```

```
 standby 100 authentication CISCO
!
interface Vlan200
 ip address 192.168.200.1 255.255.255.0
 standby version 2
 standby 200 ip 192.168.200.254
 standby 200 authentication md5 key-string CISCO
!
ip classless
ip http server
ip http secure-server
!
control-plane
!
line con 0
line vty 0 4
 no login
line vty 5 15
 no login
!
end

DLS1#
```

DLS2

```
DLS2#show running-config
Building configuration...

Current configuration : 4797 bytes
!
version 12.2
no service pad
service timestamps debug uptime
service timestamps log uptime
no service password-encryption
!
hostname DLS2
!
no aaa new-model
ip subnet-zero
ip routing
!
vtp domain FHRP
vtp mode transparent
!
spanning-tree mode pvst
spanning-tree extend system-id
spanning-tree vlan 200 priority 0
!
vlan internal allocation policy ascending
```

```
!
vlan 100,200
!
interface Port-channel1
 switchport trunk encapsulation isl
 switchport mode trunk
!
interface FastEthernet0/1
 switchport mode dynamic desirable
 shutdown
!
interface FastEthernet0/2
 switchport mode dynamic desirable
 shutdown
!
interface FastEthernet0/3
 switchport mode dynamic desirable
 shutdown
!
interface FastEthernet0/4
 switchport mode dynamic desirable
 shutdown
!
interface FastEthernet0/5
 switchport mode dynamic desirable
 shutdown
!
interface FastEthernet0/6
 switchport mode dynamic desirable
 shutdown
!
interface FastEthernet0/7
 switchport trunk encapsulation dot1q
 switchport mode trunk
!
interface FastEthernet0/8
 switchport mode dynamic desirable
 shutdown
!
interface FastEthernet0/9
 switchport trunk encapsulation dot1q
 switchport mode trunk
!
interface FastEthernet0/10
 switchport mode dynamic desirable
 shutdown
!
interface FastEthernet0/11
 switchport trunk encapsulation isl
 switchport mode trunk
 channel-group 1 mode on
!
```

```
interface FastEthernet0/12
 switchport trunk encapsulation isl
 switchport mode trunk
 channel-group 1 mode on
!
interface FastEthernet0/13
 switchport mode dynamic desirable
 shutdown
!
interface FastEthernet0/14
 switchport mode dynamic desirable
 shutdown
!
interface FastEthernet0/15
 switchport mode dynamic desirable
 shutdown
!
interface FastEthernet0/16
 switchport mode dynamic desirable
 shutdown
!
interface FastEthernet0/17
 switchport mode dynamic desirable
 shutdown
!
interface FastEthernet0/18
 switchport mode dynamic desirable
 shutdown
!
interface FastEthernet0/19
 switchport mode dynamic desirable
 shutdown
!
interface FastEthernet0/20
 switchport mode dynamic desirable
 shutdown
!
interface FastEthernet0/21
 switchport mode dynamic desirable
 shutdown
!
interface FastEthernet0/22
 switchport mode dynamic desirable
 shutdown
!
interface FastEthernet0/23
 switchport mode dynamic desirable
 shutdown
!
interface FastEthernet0/24
 switchport mode dynamic desirable
 shutdown
```

```
!
interface FastEthernet0/25
 switchport mode dynamic desirable
 shutdown
!
interface FastEthernet0/26
 switchport mode dynamic desirable
 shutdown
!
interface FastEthernet0/27
 switchport mode dynamic desirable
 shutdown
!
interface FastEthernet0/28
 switchport mode dynamic desirable
 shutdown
!
interface FastEthernet0/29
 switchport mode dynamic desirable
 shutdown
!
interface FastEthernet0/30
 switchport mode dynamic desirable
 shutdown
!
interface FastEthernet0/31
 switchport mode dynamic desirable
 shutdown
!
interface FastEthernet0/32
 switchport mode dynamic desirable
 shutdown
!
interface FastEthernet0/33
 switchport mode dynamic desirable
 shutdown
!
interface FastEthernet0/34
 switchport mode dynamic desirable
 shutdown
!
interface FastEthernet0/35
 switchport mode dynamic desirable
 shutdown
!
interface FastEthernet0/36
 switchport mode dynamic desirable
 shutdown
!
interface FastEthernet0/37
 switchport mode dynamic desirable
 shutdown
```

```
!
interface FastEthernet0/38
 switchport mode dynamic desirable
 shutdown
!
interface FastEthernet0/39
 switchport mode dynamic desirable
 shutdown
!
interface FastEthernet0/40
 switchport mode dynamic desirable
 shutdown
!
interface FastEthernet0/41
 switchport mode dynamic desirable
 shutdown
!
interface FastEthernet0/42
 switchport mode dynamic desirable
 shutdown
!
interface FastEthernet0/43
 switchport mode dynamic desirable
 shutdown
!
interface FastEthernet0/44
 switchport mode dynamic desirable
 shutdown
!
interface FastEthernet0/45
 switchport mode dynamic desirable
 shutdown
!
interface FastEthernet0/46
 switchport mode dynamic desirable
 shutdown
!
interface FastEthernet0/47
 switchport mode dynamic desirable
 shutdown
!
interface FastEthernet0/48
 switchport mode dynamic desirable
 shutdown
!
interface GigabitEthernet0/1
 switchport mode dynamic desirable
!
interface GigabitEthernet0/2
 switchport mode dynamic desirable
!
interface Vlan1
```

```
 no ip address
 shutdown
!
interface Vlan100
 ip address 192.168.100.2 255.255.255.0
 standby version 2
 standby 100 ip 192.168.100.254
 standby 100 authentication CISCO
!
interface Vlan200
 ip address 192.168.200.2 255.255.255.0
 standby version 2
 standby 200 ip 192.168.200.254
 standby 200 priority 105
 standby 200 preempt
 standby 200 authentication md5 key-string CISCO
!
ip classless
ip http server
ip http secure-server
!
control-plane
!
line con 0
line vty 0 4
 login
line vty 5 15
 login
!
end

DLS2#
```

ALS1

```
ALS1#show running-config
Building configuration...

Current configuration : 1808 bytes
!
version 12.1
no service pad
service timestamps debug uptime
service timestamps log uptime
no service password-encryption
!
hostname ALS1
!
no logging console
!
ip subnet-zero
```

```
!
no ip domain-lookup
ip ssh time-out 120
ip ssh authentication-retries 3
vtp domain FHRP
vtp mode transparent
!
!
spanning-tree mode pvst
no spanning-tree optimize bpdu transmission
spanning-tree extend system-id
spanning-tree uplinkfast
!
!
!
!
vlan 100
!
interface FastEthernet0/1
 shutdown
!
interface FastEthernet0/2
 shutdown
!
interface FastEthernet0/3
 shutdown
!
interface FastEthernet0/4
 shutdown
!
interface FastEthernet0/5
 shutdown
!
interface FastEthernet0/6
 shutdown
!
interface FastEthernet0/7
 switchport mode trunk
!
interface FastEthernet0/8
 switchport mode trunk
!
interface FastEthernet0/9
 switchport mode trunk
!
interface FastEthernet0/10
 shutdown
!
interface FastEthernet0/11
 shutdown
!
interface FastEthernet0/12
 shutdown
```

```
!
interface FastEthernet0/13
 shutdown
!
interface FastEthernet0/14
 shutdown
!
interface FastEthernet0/15
 shutdown
!
interface FastEthernet0/16
 shutdown
!
interface FastEthernet0/17
 shutdown
!
interface FastEthernet0/18
 shutdown
!
interface FastEthernet0/19
 shutdown
!
interface FastEthernet0/20
 shutdown
!
interface FastEthernet0/21
 shutdown
!
interface FastEthernet0/22
 shutdown
!
interface FastEthernet0/23
 shutdown
!
interface FastEthernet0/24
 shutdown
!
interface GigabitEthernet0/1
!
interface GigabitEthernet0/2
!
interface Vlan1
 no ip address
 no ip route-cache
 shutdown
!
interface Vlan100
 ip address 192.168.100.5 255.255.255.0
 no ip route-cache
!
interface Vlan200
 ip address 192.168.200.15 255.255.255.0
 no ip route-cache
```

```
 shutdown
!
ip default-gateway 192.168.100.254
ip http server
!
line con 0
line vty 0 4
 login
line vty 5 15
 login
!
!
end

ALS1#
```

ALS2

```
ALS2#show running-config
Building configuration...

Current configuration : 2621 bytes
!
version 12.1
no service pad
service timestamps debug uptime
service timestamps log uptime
no service password-encryption
!
hostname ALS2
!
no logging console
!
ip subnet-zero
!
ip ssh time-out 120
ip ssh authentication-retries 3
vtp domain FHRP
vtp mode transparent
!
spanning-tree mode pvst
no spanning-tree optimize bpdu transmission
spanning-tree extend system-id
spanning-tree uplinkfast
!
vlan 200
!
interface FastEthernet0/1
 shutdown
!
interface FastEthernet0/2
 shutdown
```

```
!
interface FastEthernet0/3
 shutdown
!
interface FastEthernet0/4
 shutdown
!
interface FastEthernet0/5
 shutdown
!
interface FastEthernet0/6
 shutdown
!
interface FastEthernet0/7
 switchport mode trunk
!
interface FastEthernet0/8
 shutdown
!
interface FastEthernet0/9
 switchport mode trunk
!
interface FastEthernet0/10
 shutdown
!
interface FastEthernet0/11
 shutdown
!
interface FastEthernet0/12
 shutdown
!
interface FastEthernet0/13
 shutdown
!
interface FastEthernet0/14
 shutdown
!
interface FastEthernet0/15
 shutdown
!
interface FastEthernet0/16
 shutdown
!
interface FastEthernet0/17
 shutdown
!
interface FastEthernet0/18
 shutdown
!
interface FastEthernet0/19
 shutdown
!
interface FastEthernet0/20
 shutdown
!
```

```
interface FastEthernet0/21
 shutdown
!
interface FastEthernet0/22
 shutdown
!
interface FastEthernet0/23
 shutdown
!
interface FastEthernet0/24
 shutdown
!
interface FastEthernet0/25
 shutdown
!
interface FastEthernet0/26
 shutdown
!
interface FastEthernet0/27
 shutdown
!
interface FastEthernet0/28
 shutdown
!
interface FastEthernet0/29
 shutdown
!
interface FastEthernet0/30
 shutdown
!
interface FastEthernet0/31
 shutdown
!
interface FastEthernet0/32
 shutdown
!
interface FastEthernet0/33
 shutdown
!
interface FastEthernet0/34
 shutdown
!
interface FastEthernet0/35
 shutdown
!
interface FastEthernet0/36
 shutdown
!
interface FastEthernet0/37
 shutdown
!
interface FastEthernet0/38
 shutdown
!
```

```
interface FastEthernet0/39
 shutdown
!
interface FastEthernet0/40
 shutdown
!
interface FastEthernet0/41
 shutdown
!
interface FastEthernet0/42
 shutdown
!
interface FastEthernet0/43
 shutdown
!
interface FastEthernet0/44
 shutdown
!
interface FastEthernet0/45
 shutdown
!
interface FastEthernet0/46
 shutdown
!
interface FastEthernet0/47
 shutdown
!
interface FastEthernet0/48
 shutdown
!
interface GigabitEthernet0/1
!
interface GigabitEthernet0/2
!
interface Vlan1
 no ip address
 no ip route-cache
 shutdown
!
interface Vlan200
 ip address 192.168.200.5 255.255.255.0
 no ip route-cache
!
ip default-gateway 192.168.200.254
ip http server
!
line con 0
line vty 0 4
 login
line vty 5 15
 login
!
end
ALS2#
```

LAB 5

Securing Catalyst Switch LAN Access Ports

Lab Objective:

The objective of this lab exercise is for you to learn and understand how to secure Access ports on Cisco Catalyst switches using Port Security and Identity Based Networking Services.

Lab Topology:

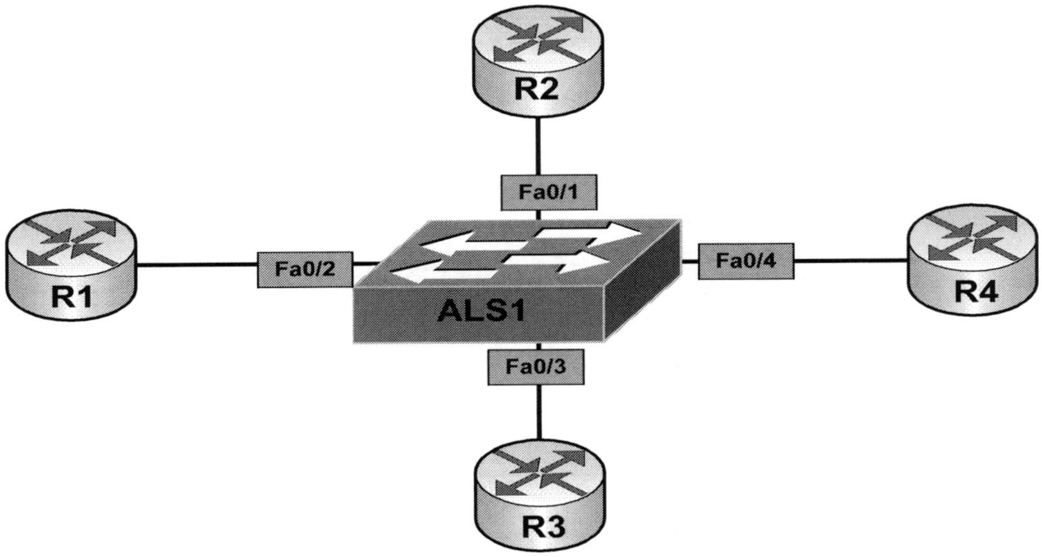

IMPORTANT NOTE

If you are using the **www.howtonetwork.net** racks, please begin each and every lab by shutting down all interfaces on all switches and then manually re-enabling the interfaces that are illustrated in this topology.

LAB SPECIFIC NOTE

If you are using the **www.howtonetwork.net** racks, the diagram is based on the physical cabling of the CCNP Rack. This is seen in the CDP output:

```
ALS1#show cdp neighbors
Capability Codes: R - Router, T - Trans Bridge, B - Source Route Bridge
                  S - Switch, H - Host, I - IGMP, r - Repeater, P - Phone

Device ID        Local Intrfce     Holdtme    Capability  Platform  Port ID
R2               Fas 0/1            169          R S I     2620XM    Fas 0/0
R3               Fas 0/3            171          R S I     2620XM    Fas 0/0
R1               Fas 0/2            172          R S I     2620XM    Fas 0/0
R4               Fas 0/4            171          R S I     2620XM    Fas 0/0
```

If using a home lab, you can substitute the routers for any other devices, such as workstations. No explicit configuration is required other than that the device port or NIC is up so as to bring up the switch port

Task 1

Enable interfaces FastEthernet0/1 to FastEthernet0/4 and verify the connected devices using or by looking at the switch CAM table entry for the specific port or ports.

Task 2

Configure port security on FastEthernet0/1 as follows:

- Only the explicit MAC address of the device connected to this port should be allowed
- This entry should be flushed exactly every 8 hours
- If another MAC is detected, a log message should be generated and the port shutdown

Task 3

Configure port security on FastEthernet0/2 as follows:

- The MAC address of the connected device should be dynamically learned by the switch
- This port should learn no more than 5 different MAC addresses
- The learned MAC addresses should be flushed following 1 hour of inactivity
- This port should discard all Unicast or Multicast frames with unknown source MACs

Task 4

Configure port security on FastEthernet0/3 as follows:

- The MAC address of the connected device should be dynamically learned by the switch
- This MAC address should be saved to NVRAM and be retained across a reboot
- The port should never age out the MAC address
- This port should drop packets with unknown MAC addresses and generate a Syslog trap

Task 5

Configure Identity Based Networking Services for FastEthernet0/4 as follows:

- The port should use 802.1x port-based authentication
- In the initial state, the port should allow only EAPOL frames to be sent and received
- The supplicant should be authenticated against RADIUS server 192.168.1.254

Lab Validation

Task 1

```
ALS1(config)#interface range fastethernet 0/1 - 4
ALS1(config-if-range)#no shutdown
ALS1(config-if-range)#exit
ALS1(config)#exit
ALS1#
ALS1#show cdp neighbors
Capability Codes: R - Router, T - Trans Bridge, B - Source Route Bridge
                  S - Switch, H - Host, I - IGMP, r - Repeater, P - Phone

Device ID        Local Intrfce     Holdtme    Capability  Platform  Port ID
R2               Fas 0/1            150         R S I     2620XM    Fas 0/0
R3               Fas 0/3            152         R S I     2620XM    Fas 0/0
R1               Fas 0/2            153         R S I     2620XM    Fas 0/0
R4               Fas 0/4            152         R S I     2620XM    Fas 0/0
```

Task 2

To determine the MAC address of the device connected to the port, perform the following:

```
ALS1#show mac-address-table int f0/1
          Mac Address Table
-------------------------------------------

Vlan    Mac Address       Type        Ports
----    -----------       --------    -----
   1    000c.85f8.1640    DYNAMIC     Fa0/1
Total Mac Addresses for this criterion: 1
```

Next, complete the task by configuring the following:

```
ALS1(config)#interface fastethernet 0/1
ALS1(config-if)#switchport mode access
ALS1(config-if)#switchport port-security
ALS1(config-if)#switchport port-security mac-address 000c.85f8.1640
ALS1(config-if)#switchport port-security aging type absolute
ALS1(config-if)#switchport port-security aging static
ALS1(config-if)#switchport port-security aging time 480
```

Verify your configuration using the appropriate show commands as follows:

```
ALS1#show port-security interface fastethernet 0/1
Port Security              : Enabled
Port Status                : Secure-up
Violation Mode             : Shutdown
```

```
Aging Time                  : 480 mins
Aging Type                  : Absolute
SecureStatic Address Aging  : Enabled
Maximum MAC Addresses       : 1
Total MAC Addresses         : 1
Configured MAC Addresses    : 1
Sticky MAC Addresses        : 0
Last Source Address         : 0000.0000.0000
Security Violation Count    : 0

ALS1#show port-security
Secure Port  MaxSecureAddr  CurrentAddr  SecurityViolation  Security Action
                (Count)       (Count)          (Count)
---------------------------------------------------------------------------
      Fa0/1              1            1                  0         Shutdown
---------------------------------------------------------------------------
Total Addresses in System (excluding one mac per port)     : 0
Max Addresses limit in System (excluding one mac per port) : 1024

ALS1#show port-security address
          Secure Mac Address Table
-------------------------------------------------------------------
Vlan    Mac Address       Type                Ports   Remaining Age
                                                         (mins)
----    -----------       ----                -----   -------------
   1    000c.85f8.1640    SecureConfigured    Fa0/1      470
-------------------------------------------------------------------
Total Addresses in System (excluding one mac per port)     : 0
Max Addresses limit in System (excluding one mac per port) : 1024
```

Task 3

```
ALS1(config)#interface fastethernet 0/2
ALS1(config-if)#switchport mode access
ALS1(config-if)#switchport port-security
ALS1(config-if)#switchport port-security maximum 5
ALS1(config-if)#switchport port-security aging type inactivity
ALS1(config-if)#switchport port-security aging time 60
ALS1(config-if)#switchport port-security violation protect
```

Verify your configuration as follows:

```
ALS1#show port-security interface fastethernet 0/2
Port Security               : Enabled
Port Status                 : Secure-up
Violation Mode              : Protect
Aging Time                  : 60 mins
Aging Type                  : Inactivity
SecureStatic Address Aging  : Disabled
Maximum MAC Addresses       : 5
```

```
Total MAC Addresses          : 1
Configured MAC Addresses     : 0
Sticky MAC Addresses         : 0
Last Source Address          : 0013.c3bc.b720
Security Violation Count     : 0

ALS1#show port-security
Secure Port  MaxSecureAddr  CurrentAddr  SecurityViolation  Security Action
                (Count)       (Count)          (Count)
---------------------------------------------------------------------------
      Fa0/1              1            1                  0         Shutdown
      Fa0/2              5            1                  0          Protect
---------------------------------------------------------------------------
Total Addresses in System (excluding one mac per port)     : 0
Max Addresses limit in System (excluding one mac per port) : 1024

ALS1#show port-security address
          Secure Mac Address Table
-------------------------------------------------------------------
Vlan    Mac Address       Type                 Ports   Remaining Age
                                                          (mins)
----    -----------       ----                 -----   -------------
   1    000c.85f8.1640    SecureConfigured     Fa0/1      454
   1    0013.c3bc.b720    SecureDynamic        Fa0/2       60 (I)
-------------------------------------------------------------------
Total Addresses in System (excluding one mac per port)     : 0
Max Addresses limit in System (excluding one mac per port) : 1024
```

Task 4

```
ALS1(config)#interface fastethernet 0/3
ALS1(config-if)#switchport mode access
ALS1(config-if)#switchport port-security
ALS1(config-if)#switchport port-security mac-address sticky
ALS1(config-if)#switchport port-security violation restrict
```

Verify your configuration as follows:

```
ALS1#show port-security interface fastethernet 0/3
Port Security                : Enabled
Port Status                  : Secure-up
Violation Mode               : Restrict
Aging Time                   : 0 mins
Aging Type                   : Absolute
SecureStatic Address Aging   : Disabled
Maximum MAC Addresses        : 1
Total MAC Addresses          : 1
Configured MAC Addresses     : 0
Sticky MAC Addresses         : 1
Last Source Address          : 0019.55b2.9520
Security Violation Count     : 0
```

```
ALS1#show port-security
Secure Port  MaxSecureAddr  CurrentAddr  SecurityViolation  Security Action
                (Count)       (Count)          (Count)
---------------------------------------------------------------------------
      Fa0/1              1            1                  0         Shutdown
      Fa0/2              5            1                  0          Protect
      Fa0/3              1            1                  0         Restrict
---------------------------------------------------------------------------
Total Addresses in System (excluding one mac per port)     : 0
Max Addresses limit in System (excluding one mac per port) : 1024

ALS1#show port-security address
          Secure Mac Address Table
-------------------------------------------------------------------
Vlan    Mac Address       Type                Ports   Remaining Age
                                                         (mins)
----    -----------       ----                -----   -------------
   1    000c.85f8.1640    SecureConfigured    Fa0/1      257
   1    0013.c3bc.b720    SecureDynamic       Fa0/2       60 (I)
   1    0019.55b2.9520    SecureSticky        Fa0/3        -
-------------------------------------------------------------------
Total Addresses in System (excluding one mac per port)     : 0
Max Addresses limit in System (excluding one mac per port) : 1024
```

Task 5

```
ALS1(config)#aaa new-model
ALS1(config)#aaa authentication dot1x default group radius
ALS1(config)#radius-server host 192.168.1.254
ALS1(config)#dot1x system-auth-control
ALS1(config)#interface fastethernet 0/4
ALS1(config-if)#switchport mode access
ALS1(config-if)#dot1x port-control auto
ALS1(config-if)#exit
```

Verify your configuration as follows:

NOTE: Unless you have an 802.1x client or supplicant, and a configured RADIUS server, the connected host won't actually be authenticated. However, you can still verify your configuration by looking at the interface state and 802.1x interface statistics for FastEthernet0/1.

```
ALS1#show dot1x interface fastethernet 0/4
Supplicant MAC <Not Applicable>
   AuthSM State       = CONNECTING
   BendSM State       = IDLE
   Posture            = N/A
PortStatus         = UNAUTHORIZED
```

```
MaxReq              = 2
MaxAuthReq          = 2
HostMode            = Single
Port Control        = Auto
ControlDirection    = Both
QuietPeriod         = 60 Seconds
Re-authentication   = Disabled
ReAuthPeriod        = 3600 Seconds
ServerTimeout       = 30 Seconds
SuppTimeout         = 30 Seconds
TxPeriod            = 30 Seconds
Guest-Vlan          = 0

ALS1#show dot1x statistics  interface fastethernet 0/4
PortStatistics Parameters for Dot1x
--------------------------------------------
TxReqId = 6     TxReq = 6       TxTotal = 8
RxStart = 0     RxLogoff = 0    RxRespId = 0    RxResp = 0
RxInvalid = 0   RxLenErr = 0    RxTotal= 0
RxVersion = 0   LastRxSrcMac 0000.0000.0000
```

Final Switch Configurations

ALS1

```
ALS1#show running-config
Building configuration...

Current configuration : 2291 bytes
!
version 12.1
no service pad
service timestamps debug uptime
service timestamps log uptime
no service password-encryption
!
hostname ALS1
!
no logging console
aaa new-model
aaa authentication dot1x default group radius
!
ip subnet-zero
!
ip ssh time-out 120
ip ssh authentication-retries 3
vtp domain ETHER
vtp mode transparent
!
spanning-tree mode pvst
```

```
no spanning-tree optimize bpdu transmission
spanning-tree extend system-id
dot1x system-auth-control
!
interface FastEthernet0/1
 switchport mode access
 switchport port-security
 switchport port-security aging time 480
 switchport port-security aging static
 switchport port-security mac-address 000c.85f8.1640
!
interface FastEthernet0/2
 switchport mode access
 switchport port-security
 switchport port-security maximum 5
 switchport port-security aging time 60
 switchport port-security violation protect
 switchport port-security aging type inactivity
!
interface FastEthernet0/3
 switchport mode access
 switchport port-security
 switchport port-security violation restrict
 switchport port-security mac-address sticky
 switchport port-security mac-address sticky 0019.55b2.9520
!
interface FastEthernet0/4
 switchport mode access
 dot1x port-control auto
 spanning-tree portfast
!
interface FastEthernet0/5
 shutdown
!
interface FastEthernet0/6
 shutdown
!
interface FastEthernet0/7
 shutdown
!
interface FastEthernet0/8
 shutdown
!
interface FastEthernet0/9
 shutdown
!
interface FastEthernet0/10
 shutdown
!
interface FastEthernet0/11
 shutdown
!
interface FastEthernet0/12
 shutdown
!
```

```
interface FastEthernet0/13
 shutdown
!
interface FastEthernet0/14
 shutdown
!
interface FastEthernet0/15
 shutdown
!
interface FastEthernet0/16
 shutdown
!
interface FastEthernet0/17
 shutdown
!
interface FastEthernet0/18
 shutdown
!
interface FastEthernet0/19
 shutdown
!
interface FastEthernet0/20
 shutdown
!
interface FastEthernet0/21
 shutdown
!
interface FastEthernet0/22
 shutdown
!
interface FastEthernet0/23
 shutdown
!
interface FastEthernet0/24
 shutdown
!
interface GigabitEthernet0/1
!
interface GigabitEthernet0/2
!
interface Vlan1
 no ip address
 no ip route-cache
 shutdown
!
ip http server
radius-server host 192.168.1.254 auth-port 1812 acct-port 1813
radius-server retransmit 3
!
line con 0
line vty 5 15
!
end

ALS1#
```

LAB 6

Spanning Tree Protocol Path Cost and Port Priority

Lab Objective:

The objective of this lab exercise is for you to learn and understand how manipulate the Spanning Tree topology using the Spanning Tree Path Cost and Port Priority values.

Lab Topology:

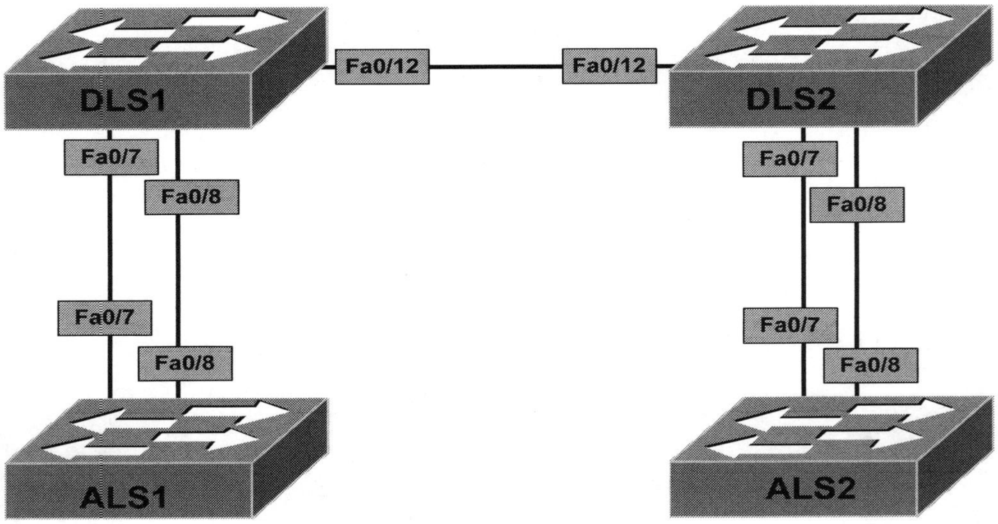

IMPORTANT NOTE

If you are using the www.howtonetwork.net racks, please begin each and every lab by shutting down all interfaces on all switches and then manually re-enabling the interfaces that are illustrated in this topology.

Task 1

Configure a VTP domain name of 802.1D for all switches. Enable VTP v2 on all switches. Configure a VTP password of STP on all switches.

Task 2

- Disable VTP on all switches

Task 3

Configure IEEE 802.1Q trunks between all switches. Disable DTP on all switch trunk ports.

Task 4

Configure VLANs 2000 and 3000 on all switches. Configure Root and Backup Root Bridge parameters for these two VLANs as follows:

- VLAN 2000—DLS1 is the Root Bridge and DLS2 is the secondary Root Bridge
- VLAN 3000—DLS2 is the Root Bridge and DLS1 is the secondary Root Bridge

DO NOT manually configure STP priorities for these VLANs. Instead, allow Cisco IOS to do so.

Task 5

Configure ALS1 and ALS2 to use only their FastEthernet0/8 interfaces to forward traffic for the configured VLANs. Only when Fa0/8 fails should the Fa0/7 interfaces on either switch be used to forward traffic for all VLANs. You should adhere to the following restrictions:

- To influence port selection on ALS1, only the Spanning Tree Port Cost can be manipulated
- To influence port selection on ALS2, only the STP Port Priority can be manipulated

Task 6

Verify your configuration using the appropriate commands.

Lab Validation

Task 1

```
DLS1(config)#vtp domain 802.1D
Changing VTP domain name from SWITCH to 802.1D
DLS1(config)#vtp version 2
DLS1(config)#vtp password STP
Setting device VLAN database password to STP

DLS2(config)#vtp domain 802.1D
Changing VTP domain name from SWITCH to 802.1D
DLS2(config)#vtp version 2
DLS2(config)#vtp pass STP
Setting device VLAN database password to STP

ALS1(config)#vtp domain 802.1D
Changing VTP domain name from SWITCH to 802.1D
ALS1(config)#vtp version 2
ALS1(config)#vtp password STP
Setting device VLAN database password to STP

ALS2(config)#vtp domain 802.1D
Changing VTP domain name from SWITCH to 802.1D
ALS2(config)#vtp version 2
ALS2(config)#vtp password STP
Setting device VLAN database password to STP
```

Task 2

```
DLS1(config)#vtp mode transparent
Setting device to VTP TRANSPARENT mode.

DLS2(config)#vtp mode transparent
Setting device to VTP TRANSPARENT mode.

ALS1(config)#vtp mode transparent
Setting device to VTP TRANSPARENT mode.

ALS2(config)#vtp mode transparent
Setting device to VTP TRANSPARENT mode.
```

Task 3

```
DLS1(config)#interface range f0/7 - 8 , fa0/12
DLS1(config-if-range)#switchport
DLS1(config-if-range)#switchport trunk encapsulation dot1q
DLS1(config-if-range)#switchport mode trunk
DLS1(config-if-range)#switchport nonegotiate
DLS1(config-if-range)#no shutdown
DLS1(config-if-range)#exit

DLS2(config)#interface range f0/7 - 8 , fa0/12
DLS2(config-if-range)#switchport
DLS2(config-if-range)#switchport trun encap dot1q
DLS2(config-if-range)#switchport mode trunk
DLS2(config-if-range)#switchport nonegotiate
DLS2(config-if-range)#no shut
DLS2(config-if-range)#exit

ALS1(config)#interface range f0/7 - 8
ALS1(config-if-range)#switchport mode trunk
ALS1(config-if-range)#switchport nonegotiate
ALS1(config-if-range)#no shut
ALS1(config-if-range)#exit

ALS2(config)#interface range f0/7 - 8
ALS2(config-if-range)#switchport mode trunk
ALS2(config-if-range)#switchport nonegotiate
ALS2(config-if-range)#no shutdown
ALS2(config-if-range)#exit
```

Task 4

```
DLS1(config)#vlan 2000
DLS1(config-vlan)#exit
DLS1(config)#vlan 3000
DLS1(config-vlan)#exit
DLS1(config)#spanning-tree vlan 2000 root primary
DLS1(config)#spanning-tree vlan 3000 root secondary
```

```
DLS2(config)#vlan 2000
DLS2(config-vlan)#exit
DLS2(config)#vlan 3000
DLS2(config-vlan)#exit
DLS2(config)#spanning-tree vlan 2000 root secondary
DLS2(config)#spanning-tree vlan 3000 root primary

ALS1(config)#vlan 2000
ALS1(config-vlan)#exit
ALS1(config)#vlan 3000
ALS1(config-vlan)#exit

ALS2(config)#vlan 2000
ALS2(config-vlan)#exit
ALS2(config)#vlan 3000
ALS2(config-vlan)#exit
```

Verify the Spanning Tree Protocol Root and Backup Root placement based on the configuration.

```
DLS1#show spanning-tree vlan 2000

VLAN2000
  Spanning tree enabled protocol ieee
  Root ID     Priority    26576
              Address     000d.291e.7f00
              This bridge is the root
              Hello Time   2 sec  Max Age 20 sec  Forward Delay 15 sec

  Bridge ID   Priority    26576  (priority 24576 sys-id-ext 2000)
              Address     000d.291e.7f00
              Hello Time   2 sec  Max Age 20 sec  Forward Delay 15 sec
              Aging Time 300

Interface        Role Sts Cost      Prio.Nbr Type
---------------- ---- --- --------- -------- --------------------------------
Fa0/7            Desg FWD 19        128.7    P2p
Fa0/8            Desg FWD 19        128.8    P2p
Fa0/12           Desg FWD 19        128.12   P2p


DLS2#show spanning-tree vlan 3000

VLAN3000
  Spanning tree enabled protocol ieee
  Root ID     Priority    27576
              Address     000f.24ce.0d80
              This bridge is the root
              Hello Time   2 sec  Max Age 20 sec  Forward Delay 15 sec

  Bridge ID   Priority    27576  (priority 24576 sys-id-ext 3000)
              Address     000f.24ce.0d80
```

```
          Hello Time   2 sec  Max Age 20 sec  Forward Delay 15 sec
          Aging Time 300

Interface          Role Sts Cost      Prio.Nbr Type
------------------ ---- --- --------- -------- ----------------------------
Fa0/7              Desg FWD 19        128.7    P2p
Fa0/8              Desg FWD 19        128.8    P2p
Fa0/12             Desg FWD 19        128.12   P2p
```

Task 5

As it stands, switches ALS1 and ALS2 elect port FastEthernet0/7 as the Root Port. This is because, all other parameters being equal, this port has a lower port ID than Fa0/8.

```
ALS1#show spanning-tree root port
VLAN2000           FastEthernet0/7
VLAN3000           FastEthernet0/7

ALS2#show spanning-tree root port
VLAN2000           FastEthernet0/7
VLAN3000           FastEthernet0/7
```

To achieve the desired result on ALS1, the Spanning Tree Port Cost should be changed. This value is only changed on the Non-Root Bridge:

```
ALS1(config)#int fa0/8
ALS1(config-if)#spanning-tree vlan 2000,3000 cost 1
ALS1(config-if)#exit
```

To achieve the desired result on ALS2, the Spanning Tree Port Priority should be changed. STP Port Priority values are locally significant between two bridges and so must be configured on the FastEthernet0/8 interface of switch DSL2. This means that the BPDUs received by ALS2 from FastEthernet0/8 will have a lower sender ID than those received from port FastEthernet0/7:

```
DLS2(config)#int f0/8
DLS2(config-if)#spanning-tree vlan 2000,3000 port-priority 16
DLS2(config-if)#exit
```

Task 6

```
ALS1#show spanning-tree root port
VLAN2000           FastEthernet0/8
VLAN3000           FastEthernet0/8

ALS1#show spanning-tree vlan 2000 root
```

```
                                        Root Hello Max Fwd
Vlan                 Root ID            Cost  Time Age Dly  Root Port
---------------- -------------------- ------ ----- --- ---  ----------------
VLAN2000         26576 000d.291e.7f00      1     2  20  15  Fa0/8

ALS1#show spanning-tree vlan 3000 root

                                        Root Hello Max Fwd
Vlan                 Root ID            Cost  Time Age Dly  Root Port
---------------- -------------------- ------ ----- --- ---  ----------------
VLAN3000         27576 000f.24ce.0d80     20     2  20  15  Fa0/8

ALS2#show spanning-tree root port
VLAN2000         FastEthernet0/8
VLAN3000         FastEthernet0/8

ALS2#show spanning-tree vlan 2000 root

                                        Root Hello Max Fwd
Vlan                 Root ID            Cost  Time Age Dly  Root Port
---------------- -------------------- ------ ----- --- ---  ----------------
VLAN2000         26576 000d.291e.7f00     38     2  20  15  Fa0/8

ALS2#show spanning-tree vlan 3000 root

                                        Root Hello Max Fwd
Vlan                 Root ID            Cost  Time Age Dly  Root Port
---------------- -------------------- ------ ----- --- ---  ----------------
VLAN3000         27576 000f.24ce.0d80     19     2  20  15  Fa0/8
```

NOTE: Configuring the port priority value on ALS2 will not work as this switch does not send BPDUs. This is why this value is configured on the Root Bridge. This is illustrated below:

```
DLS2(config)#int f0/8
DLS2(config-if)#no spanning-tree vlan 2000,3000 port-priority 16
DLS2(config-if)#exit

ALS2(config)#int f0/8
ALS2(config-if)#spanning-tree vlan 2000,3000 port-priority 16
ALS2(config-if)#exit
```

Because ALS1 is not sending BPDUs and is not the Root Bridge for the VLAN, the configuration of the Port Priority on FastEthernet0/8 of ALS1 will have no effect on the STP topology:

Final Switch Configurations

DLS1

```
DLS1#show running-config
Building configuration...

Current configuration : 4412 bytes
!
version 12.2
no service pad
service timestamps debug uptime
service timestamps log uptime
no service password-encryption
!
hostname DLS1
!
no logging console
!
no aaa new-model
ip subnet-zero
!
vtp domain 802.1D
vtp mode transparent
!
no file verify auto
!
spanning-tree mode pvst
spanning-tree extend system-id
spanning-tree vlan 2000 priority 24576
spanning-tree vlan 3000 priority 28672
!
vlan internal allocation policy ascending
!
vlan 2000,3000
!
interface FastEthernet0/1
 switchport mode dynamic desirable
 shutdown
!
interface FastEthernet0/2
 switchport mode dynamic desirable
 shutdown
!
interface FastEthernet0/3
 switchport mode dynamic desirable
 shutdown
!
interface FastEthernet0/4
 switchport mode dynamic desirable
 shutdown
```

```
!
interface FastEthernet0/5
 switchport mode dynamic desirable
 shutdown
!
interface FastEthernet0/6
 switchport mode dynamic desirable
 shutdown
!
interface FastEthernet0/7
 switchport trunk encapsulation dot1q
 switchport mode trunk
 switchport nonegotiate
!
interface FastEthernet0/8
 switchport trunk encapsulation dot1q
 switchport mode trunk
 switchport nonegotiate
!
interface FastEthernet0/9
 switchport mode dynamic desirable
 shutdown
!
interface FastEthernet0/10
 switchport mode dynamic desirable
 shutdown
!
interface FastEthernet0/11
 switchport mode dynamic desirable
 shutdown
!
interface FastEthernet0/12
 switchport trunk encapsulation dot1q
 switchport mode trunk
 switchport nonegotiate
!
interface FastEthernet0/13
 switchport mode dynamic desirable
 shutdown
!
interface FastEthernet0/14
 switchport mode dynamic desirable
 shutdown
!
interface FastEthernet0/15
 switchport mode dynamic desirable
 shutdown
!
interface FastEthernet0/16
 switchport mode dynamic desirable
 shutdown
!
```

```
interface FastEthernet0/17
 switchport mode dynamic desirable
 shutdown
!
interface FastEthernet0/18
 switchport mode dynamic desirable
 shutdown
!
interface FastEthernet0/19
 switchport mode dynamic desirable
 shutdown
!
interface FastEthernet0/20
 switchport mode dynamic desirable
 shutdown
!
interface FastEthernet0/21
 switchport mode dynamic desirable
 shutdown
!
interface FastEthernet0/22
 switchport mode dynamic desirable
 shutdown
!
interface FastEthernet0/23
 switchport mode dynamic desirable
 shutdown
!
interface FastEthernet0/24
 switchport mode dynamic desirable
 shutdown
!
interface FastEthernet0/25
 switchport mode dynamic desirable
 shutdown
!
interface FastEthernet0/26
 switchport mode dynamic desirable
 shutdown
!
interface FastEthernet0/27
 switchport mode dynamic desirable
 shutdown
!
interface FastEthernet0/28
 switchport mode dynamic desirable
 shutdown
!
interface FastEthernet0/29
 switchport mode dynamic desirable
 shutdown
!
```

```
interface FastEthernet0/30
 switchport mode dynamic desirable
 shutdown
!
interface FastEthernet0/31
 switchport mode dynamic desirable
 shutdown
!
interface FastEthernet0/32
 switchport mode dynamic desirable
 shutdown
!
interface FastEthernet0/33
 switchport mode dynamic desirable
 shutdown
!
interface FastEthernet0/34
 switchport mode dynamic desirable
 shutdown
!
interface FastEthernet0/35
 switchport mode dynamic desirable
 shutdown
!
interface FastEthernet0/36
 switchport mode dynamic desirable
 shutdown
!
interface FastEthernet0/37
 switchport mode dynamic desirable
 shutdown
!
interface FastEthernet0/38
 switchport mode dynamic desirable
 shutdown
!
interface FastEthernet0/39
 switchport mode dynamic desirable
 shutdown
!
interface FastEthernet0/40
 switchport mode dynamic desirable
 shutdown
!
interface FastEthernet0/41
 switchport mode dynamic desirable
 shutdown
!
interface FastEthernet0/42
 switchport mode dynamic desirable
 shutdown
!
```

```
interface FastEthernet0/43
 switchport mode dynamic desirable
 shutdown
!
interface FastEthernet0/44
 switchport mode dynamic desirable
 shutdown
!
interface FastEthernet0/45
 switchport mode dynamic desirable
 shutdown
!
interface FastEthernet0/46
 switchport mode dynamic desirable
 shutdown
!
interface FastEthernet0/47
 switchport mode dynamic desirable
 shutdown
!
interface FastEthernet0/48
 switchport mode dynamic desirable
 shutdown
!
interface GigabitEthernet0/1
 switchport mode dynamic desirable
!
interface GigabitEthernet0/2
 switchport mode dynamic desirable
!
interface Vlan1
 no ip address
 shutdown
!
ip classless
ip http server
ip http secure-server
!
control-plane
!
line con 0
line vty 5 15
!
end

DLS1#
```

DLS2

```
DLS2#show running-config
Building configuration...

Current configuration : 4446 bytes
!
version 12.2
no service pad
service timestamps debug uptime
service timestamps log uptime
no service password-encryption
!
hostname DLS2
!
no logging console
!
no aaa new-model
ip subnet-zero
!
vtp domain 802.1D
vtp mode transparent
!
spanning-tree mode pvst
spanning-tree extend system-id
spanning-tree vlan 2000 priority 28672
spanning-tree vlan 3000 priority 24576
!
vlan internal allocation policy ascending
!
vlan 2000,3000
!
interface FastEthernet0/1
 switchport mode dynamic desirable
 shutdown
!
interface FastEthernet0/2
 switchport mode dynamic desirable
 shutdown
!
interface FastEthernet0/3
 switchport mode dynamic desirable
 shutdown
!
interface FastEthernet0/4
 switchport mode dynamic desirable
 shutdown
!
interface FastEthernet0/5
 switchport mode dynamic desirable
 shutdown
!
```

```
interface FastEthernet0/6
 switchport mode dynamic desirable
 shutdown
!
interface FastEthernet0/7
 switchport trunk encapsulation dot1q
 switchport mode trunk
 switchport nonegotiate
!
interface FastEthernet0/8
 switchport trunk encapsulation dot1q
 switchport mode trunk
 switchport nonegotiate
 spanning-tree vlan 2000,3000 port-priority 16
!
interface FastEthernet0/9
 switchport mode dynamic desirable
 shutdown
!
interface FastEthernet0/10
 switchport mode dynamic desirable
 shutdown
!
interface FastEthernet0/11
 switchport mode dynamic desirable
 shutdown
!
interface FastEthernet0/12
 switchport trunk encapsulation dot1q
 switchport mode trunk
 switchport nonegotiate
!
interface FastEthernet0/13
 switchport mode dynamic desirable
 shutdown
!
interface FastEthernet0/14
 switchport mode dynamic desirable
 shutdown
!
interface FastEthernet0/15
 switchport mode dynamic desirable
 shutdown
!
interface FastEthernet0/16
 switchport mode dynamic desirable
 shutdown
!
interface FastEthernet0/17
 switchport mode dynamic desirable
 shutdown
!
```

```
interface FastEthernet0/18
 switchport mode dynamic desirable
 shutdown
!
interface FastEthernet0/19
 switchport mode dynamic desirable
 shutdown
!
interface FastEthernet0/20
 switchport mode dynamic desirable
 shutdown
!
interface FastEthernet0/21
 switchport mode dynamic desirable
 shutdown
!
interface FastEthernet0/22
 switchport mode dynamic desirable
 shutdown
!
interface FastEthernet0/23
 switchport mode dynamic desirable
 shutdown
!
interface FastEthernet0/24
 switchport mode dynamic desirable
 shutdown
!
interface FastEthernet0/25
 switchport mode dynamic desirable
 shutdown
!
interface FastEthernet0/26
 switchport mode dynamic desirable
 shutdown
!
interface FastEthernet0/27
 switchport mode dynamic desirable
 shutdown
!
interface FastEthernet0/28
 switchport mode dynamic desirable
 shutdown
!
interface FastEthernet0/29
 switchport mode dynamic desirable
 shutdown
!
interface FastEthernet0/30
 switchport mode dynamic desirable
 shutdown
!
```

```
interface FastEthernet0/31
 switchport mode dynamic desirable
 shutdown
!
interface FastEthernet0/32
 switchport mode dynamic desirable
 shutdown
!
interface FastEthernet0/33
 switchport mode dynamic desirable
 shutdown
!
interface FastEthernet0/34
 switchport mode dynamic desirable
 shutdown
!
interface FastEthernet0/35
 switchport mode dynamic desirable
 shutdown
!
interface FastEthernet0/36
 switchport mode dynamic desirable
 shutdown
!
interface FastEthernet0/37
 switchport mode dynamic desirable
 shutdown
!
interface FastEthernet0/38
 switchport mode dynamic desirable
 shutdown
!
interface FastEthernet0/39
 switchport mode dynamic desirable
 shutdown
!
interface FastEthernet0/40
 switchport mode dynamic desirable
 shutdown
!
interface FastEthernet0/41
 switchport mode dynamic desirable
 shutdown
!
interface FastEthernet0/42
 switchport mode dynamic desirable
 shutdown
!
interface FastEthernet0/43
 switchport mode dynamic desirable
 shutdown
!
```

```
interface FastEthernet0/44
 switchport mode dynamic desirable
 shutdown
!
interface FastEthernet0/45
 switchport mode dynamic desirable
 shutdown
!
interface FastEthernet0/46
 switchport mode dynamic desirable
 shutdown
!
interface FastEthernet0/47
 switchport mode dynamic desirable
 shutdown
!
interface FastEthernet0/48
 switchport mode dynamic desirable
 shutdown
!
interface GigabitEthernet0/1
 switchport mode dynamic desirable
!
interface GigabitEthernet0/2
 switchport mode dynamic desirable
!
interface Vlan1
 no ip address
 shutdown
!
ip classless
ip http server
ip http secure-server
!
control-plane
!
line con 0
line vty 5 15
end

DLS2#
```

ALS1

```
ALS1#show running-config
Building configuration...

Current configuration : 1610 bytes
!
version 12.1
no service pad
```

```
service timestamps debug uptime
service timestamps log uptime
no service password-encryption
!
hostname ALS1
!
no logging console
!
ip subnet-zero
!
ip ssh time-out 120
ip ssh authentication-retries 3
vtp domain 802.1D
vtp mode transparent
!
spanning-tree mode pvst
no spanning-tree optimize bpdu transmission
spanning-tree extend system-id
!
vlan 2000,3000
!
interface FastEthernet0/1
 shutdown
!
interface FastEthernet0/2
 shutdown
!
interface FastEthernet0/3
 shutdown
!
interface FastEthernet0/4
 shutdown
!
interface FastEthernet0/5
 shutdown
!
interface FastEthernet0/6
 shutdown
!
interface FastEthernet0/7
 switchport mode trunk
 switchport nonegotiate
!
interface FastEthernet0/8
 switchport mode trunk
 switchport nonegotiate
 spanning-tree vlan 2000,3000 cost 1
!
interface FastEthernet0/9
 shutdown
!
interface FastEthernet0/10
```

```
 shutdown
!
interface FastEthernet0/11
 shutdown
!
interface FastEthernet0/12
 shutdown
!
interface FastEthernet0/13
 shutdown
!
interface FastEthernet0/14
 shutdown
!
interface FastEthernet0/15
 shutdown
!
interface FastEthernet0/16
 shutdown
!
interface FastEthernet0/17
 shutdown
!
interface FastEthernet0/18
 shutdown
!
interface FastEthernet0/19
 shutdown
!
interface FastEthernet0/20
 shutdown
!
interface FastEthernet0/21
 shutdown
!
interface FastEthernet0/22
 shutdown
!
interface FastEthernet0/23
 shutdown
!
interface FastEthernet0/24
 shutdown
!
interface GigabitEthernet0/1
!
interface GigabitEthernet0/2
!
interface Vlan1
 no ip address
 no ip route-cache
 shutdown
```

```
!
ip http server
!
line con 0
line vty 5 15
!
end

ALS1#
```

ALS2

```
ALS2# show running-config

Building configuration...

Current configuration : 2509 bytes
!
version 12.1
no service pad
service timestamps debug uptime
service timestamps log uptime
no service password-encryption
!
hostname ALS2
!
no logging console
!
ip subnet-zero
!
ip ssh time-out 120
ip ssh authentication-retries 3
vtp domain 802.1D
vtp mode transparent
!
spanning-tree mode pvst
no spanning-tree optimize bpdu transmission
spanning-tree extend system-id
!
vlan 2000,3000
!
interface FastEthernet0/1
 shutdown
!
interface FastEthernet0/2
 shutdown
!
interface FastEthernet0/3
 shutdown
!
interface FastEthernet0/4
```

```
 shutdown
!
interface FastEthernet0/5
 shutdown
!
interface FastEthernet0/6
 shutdown
!
interface FastEthernet0/7
 switchport mode trunk
 switchport nonegotiate
!
interface FastEthernet0/8
 switchport mode trunk
 switchport nonegotiate
!
interface FastEthernet0/9
 shutdown
!
interface FastEthernet0/10
 shutdown
!
interface FastEthernet0/11
 shutdown
!
interface FastEthernet0/12
 shutdown
!
interface FastEthernet0/13
 shutdown
!
interface FastEthernet0/14
 shutdown
!
interface FastEthernet0/15
 shutdown
!
interface FastEthernet0/16
 shutdown
!
interface FastEthernet0/17
 shutdown
!
interface FastEthernet0/18
 shutdown
!
interface FastEthernet0/19
 shutdown
!
interface FastEthernet0/20
 shutdown
!
```

```
interface FastEthernet0/21
 shutdown
!
interface FastEthernet0/22
 shutdown
!
interface FastEthernet0/23
 shutdown
!
interface FastEthernet0/24
 shutdown
!
interface FastEthernet0/25
 shutdown
!
interface FastEthernet0/26
 shutdown
!
interface FastEthernet0/27
 shutdown
!
interface FastEthernet0/28
 shutdown
!
interface FastEthernet0/29
 shutdown
!
interface FastEthernet0/30
 shutdown
!
interface FastEthernet0/31
 shutdown
!
interface FastEthernet0/32
 shutdown
!
interface FastEthernet0/33
 shutdown
!
interface FastEthernet0/34
 shutdown
!
interface FastEthernet0/35
 shutdown
!
interface FastEthernet0/36
 shutdown
!
interface FastEthernet0/37
 shutdown
!
interface FastEthernet0/38
```

```
 shutdown
!
interface FastEthernet0/39
 shutdown
!
interface FastEthernet0/40
 shutdown
!
interface FastEthernet0/41
 shutdown
!
interface FastEthernet0/42
 shutdown
!
interface FastEthernet0/43
 shutdown
!
interface FastEthernet0/44
 shutdown
!
interface FastEthernet0/45
 shutdown
!
interface FastEthernet0/46
 shutdown
!
interface FastEthernet0/47
 shutdown
!
interface FastEthernet0/48
 shutdown
!
interface GigabitEthernet0/1
!
interface GigabitEthernet0/2
!
interface Vlan1
 no ip address
 no ip route-cache
 shutdown
!
ip http server
!
line con 0
line vty 5 15
!
end

ALS2#
```

LAB 7

Spanning Tree Protocol Timers and Diameter

Lab Objective:

The objective of this lab exercise is for you to learn and understand how manipulate the default Spanning Tree Protocol timer values and the overall network diameter.

Lab Topology:

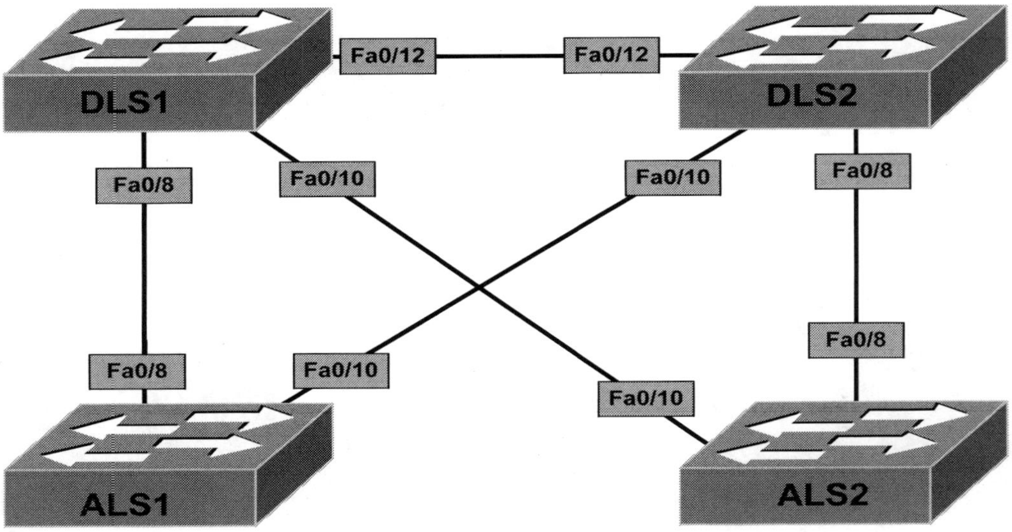

IMPORTANT NOTE

If you are using the www.howtonetwork.net racks, please begin each and every lab by shutting down all interfaces on all switches and then manually re-enabling the interfaces that are illustrated in this topology.

Task 1

Configure a VTP domain name of 802.1D for all switches. Configure a VTP password of STP on all switches within the VTP domain. All switches should be in VTP Transparent mode.

Task 2

Configure VLANs 100 and 200 in the STP domain as follows:

- Switch DLS1 should be Root for VLAN 100 and secondary Root for VLAN 200
- Switch DLS2 should be Root for VLAN 200 and secondary Root for VLAN 100
- Allow Cisco IOS software to automatically set the Root and secondary Root priority values

Task 3

Configure 802.1Q trunking between the switches. Use the default native VLAN.

Task 4

Verify that the Root Bridge and secondary Root Bridges for all switches are as required.

Task 5

Configure a Spanning Tree diameter of 4 for VLAN 100 and VLAN 200. This configuration should also be replicated on the secondary Root Bridge for both VLANs. Use the simplest method of configuring the Spanning Tree Protocol diameter that is available in IOS software.

Task 6

Verify your configuration using the appropriate commands.

Lab Validation

Task 1

```
DLS1(config)#vtp domain 802.1D
DLS1(config)#vtp password STP
DLS1(config)#vtp mode transparent

DLS2(config)#vtp domain 802.1D
DLS2(config)#vtp pass STP
DLS2(config)#vtp mode transparent

ALS1(config)#vtp domain 802.1D
ALS1(config)#vtp password STP
ALS1(config)#vtp mode transparent

ALS2(config)#vtp domain 802.1D
ALS2(config)#vtp password STP
ALS2(config)#vtp mode transparent
```

Task 2

```
DLS1(config)#vlan 100
DLS1(config-vlan)#exit
DLS1(config)#vlan 200
DLS1(config-vlan)#exit
DLS1(config)#spanning-tree vlan 100 root primary
DLS1(config)#spanning-tree vlan 200 root secondary

DLS2(config)#vlan 100
DLS2(config-vlan)#exit
DLS2(config)#vlan 200
DLS2(config-vlan)#exit
DLS2(config)#spanning-tree vlan 200 root primary
DLS2(config)#spanning-tree vlan 100 root secondary
```

```
ALS1(config)#vlan 100
ALS1(config-vlan)#exit
ALS1(config)#vlan 200
ALS1(config-vlan)#exit

ALS2(config)#vlan 100
ALS2(config-vlan)#exit
ALS2(config)#vlan 200
ALS2(config-vlan)#exit
```

Task 3

```
DLS1(config)#interface range f0/8 , f0/10 , f0/12
DLS1(config-if-range)#switchport
DLS1(config-if-range)#switchport trunk encapsulation dot1q
DLS1(config-if-range)#switchport mode trunk
DLS1(config-if-range)#no shutdown
DLS1(config-if-range)#exit

DLS2(config)#interface range f0/8 , f0/10 , f0/12
DLS2(config-if-range)#switchport
DLS2(config-if-range)#switchport trunk encapsulation dot1q
DLS2(config-if-range)#switchport mode trunk
DLS2(config-if-range)#no shut
DLS2(config-if-range)#exit

ALS1(config)#interface range f0/8 , f0/10
ALS1(config-if-range)#switchport mode trunk
ALS1(config-if-range)#no shut
ALS1(config-if-range)#exit

ALS2(config)#interface range f0/8 , f0/10
ALS2(config-if-range)#switchport mode trunk
ALS2(config-if-range)#no shutdown
ALS2(config-if-range)#exit
```

Task 4

```
DLS1#show spanning-tree vlan 100

VLAN0100
  Spanning tree enabled protocol ieee
  Root ID    Priority    24676
             Address     000d.291e.7f00
             This bridge is the root
             Hello Time   2 sec  Max Age 20 sec  Forward Delay 15 sec

  Bridge ID  Priority    24676  (priority 24576 sys-id-ext 100)
             Address     000d.291e.7f00
             Hello Time   2 sec  Max Age 20 sec  Forward Delay 15 sec
             Aging Time 300
```

```
Interface        Role Sts Cost      Prio.Nbr Type
---------------- ---- --- --------- -------- --------------------------------
Fa0/8            Desg FWD 19        128.8    P2p
Fa0/10           Desg FWD 19        128.10   P2p
Fa0/12           Desg FWD 19        128.12   P2p

DLS1#show spanning-tree vlan 200

VLAN0200
  Spanning tree enabled protocol ieee
  Root ID    Priority    24776
             Address     000f.24ce.0d80
             Cost        19
             Port        12 (FastEthernet0/12)
             Hello Time   2 sec  Max Age 20 sec  Forward Delay 15 sec

  Bridge ID  Priority    28872  (priority 28672 sys-id-ext 200)
             Address     000d.291e.7f00
             Hello Time   2 sec  Max Age 20 sec  Forward Delay 15 sec
             Aging Time 300

Interface        Role Sts Cost      Prio.Nbr Type
---------------- ---- --- --------- -------- --------------------------------
Fa0/8            Desg FWD 19        128.8    P2p
Fa0/10           Desg FWD 19        128.10   P2p
Fa0/12           Root FWD 19        128.12   P2p

DLS2#show spanning-tree vlan 100

VLAN0100
  Spanning tree enabled protocol ieee
  Root ID    Priority    24676
             Address     000d.291e.7f00
             Cost        19
             Port        12 (FastEthernet0/12)
             Hello Time   2 sec  Max Age 20 sec  Forward Delay 15 sec

  Bridge ID  Priority    28772  (priority 28672 sys-id-ext 100)
             Address     000f.24ce.0d80
             Hello Time   2 sec  Max Age 20 sec  Forward Delay 15 sec
             Aging Time 300

Interface           Role Sts Cost      Prio.Nbr Type
------------------- ---- --- --------- -------- -----------------------------
Fa0/8               Desg FWD 19        128.8    P2p
Fa0/10              Desg FWD 19        128.10   P2p
Fa0/12              Root FWD 19        128.12   P2p

DLS2#
DLS2#show spanning-tree vlan 200

VLAN0200
```

```
  Spanning tree enabled protocol ieee
  Root ID    Priority    24776
             Address     000f.24ce.0d80
             This bridge is the root
             Hello Time   2 sec  Max Age 20 sec  Forward Delay 15 sec

  Bridge ID  Priority    24776  (priority 24576 sys-id-ext 200)
             Address     000f.24ce.0d80
             Hello Time   2 sec  Max Age 20 sec  Forward Delay 15 sec
             Aging Time 300

Interface            Role Sts Cost      Prio.Nbr Type
-------------------- ---- --- --------- -------- ----------------------------
Fa0/8                Desg FWD 19        128.8    P2p
Fa0/10               Desg FWD 19        128.10   P2p
Fa0/12               Desg FWD 19        128.12   P2p

ALS1#show spanning-tree vlan 100

VLAN0100
  Spanning tree enabled protocol ieee
  Root ID    Priority    24676
             Address     000d.291e.7f00
             Cost        19
             Port        8 (FastEthernet0/8)
             Hello Time   2 sec  Max Age 20 sec  Forward Delay 15 sec

  Bridge ID  Priority    32868  (priority 32768 sys-id-ext 100)
             Address     000b.5f9e.4dc0
             Hello Time   2 sec  Max Age 20 sec  Forward Delay 15 sec
             Aging Time 300

Interface          Role Sts Cost      Prio.Nbr Type
------------------ ---- --- --------- -------- --------------------------------
Fa0/8              Root FWD 19        128.8    P2p
Fa0/10             Altn BLK 19        128.10   P2p

ALS1#show spanning-tree vlan 200

VLAN0200
  Spanning tree enabled protocol ieee
  Root ID    Priority    24776
             Address     000f.24ce.0d80
             Cost        19
             Port        10 (FastEthernet0/10)
             Hello Time   2 sec  Max Age 20 sec  Forward Delay 15 sec

  Bridge ID  Priority    32968  (priority 32768 sys-id-ext 200)
             Address     000b.5f9e.4dc0
             Hello Time   2 sec  Max Age 20 sec  Forward Delay 15 sec
             Aging Time 300
```

```
Interface        Role Sts Cost      Prio.Nbr Type
---------------- ---- --- --------- -------- --------------------------------
Fa0/8            Altn BLK 19        128.8    P2p
Fa0/10           Root FWD 19        128.10   P2p

ALS2#show spanning-tree vlan 100

VLAN0100
  Spanning tree enabled protocol ieee
  Root ID    Priority    24676
             Address     000d.291e.7f00
             Cost        19
             Port        10 (FastEthernet0/10)
             Hello Time   2 sec  Max Age 20 sec  Forward Delay 15 sec

  Bridge ID  Priority    32868  (priority 32768 sys-id-ext 100)
             Address     0008.21a9.4f80
             Hello Time   2 sec  Max Age 20 sec  Forward Delay 15 sec
             Aging Time 300

Interface        Role Sts Cost      Prio.Nbr Type
---------------- ---- --- --------- -------- --------------------------------
Fa0/8            Altn BLK 19        128.8    P2p
Fa0/10           Root FWD 19        128.10   P2p

ALS2#
ALS2#show spanning-tree vlan 200

VLAN0200
  Spanning tree enabled protocol ieee
  Root ID    Priority    24776
             Address     000f.24ce.0d80
             Cost        19
             Port        8 (FastEthernet0/8)
             Hello Time   2 sec  Max Age 20 sec  Forward Delay 15 sec

  Bridge ID  Priority    32968  (priority 32768 sys-id-ext 200)
             Address     0008.21a9.4f80
             Hello Time   2 sec  Max Age 20 sec  Forward Delay 15 sec
             Aging Time 300

Interface        Role Sts Cost      Prio.Nbr Type
---------------- ---- --- --------- -------- --------------------------------
Fa0/8            Root FWD 19        128.8    P2p
Fa0/10           Altn BLK 19        128.10   P2p
```

Task 5

```
DLS1(config)#spanning-tree vlan 100 root primary diameter 4
DLS1(config)#spanning-tree vlan 200 root secondary diameter 4

DLS2(config)#spanning-tree vlan 100 root secondary diameter 4
DLS2(config)#spanning-tree vlan 200 root primary diameter 4
```

Task 6

```
DLS1#show spanning-tree vlan 100

VLAN0100
  Spanning tree enabled protocol ieee
  Root ID    Priority    24676
             Address     000d.291e.7f00
             This bridge is the root
             Hello Time   2 sec  Max Age 14 sec  Forward Delay 10 sec

[Truncated]

DLS1#show spanning-tree vlan 200

VLAN0200
  Spanning tree enabled protocol ieee
  Root ID    Priority    24776
             Address     000f.24ce.0d80
             Cost        19
             Port        12 (FastEthernet0/12)
             Hello Time   2 sec  Max Age 14 sec  Forward Delay 10 sec

[Truncated]

DLS2#show spanning-tree vlan 100

VLAN0100
  Spanning tree enabled protocol ieee
  Root ID    Priority    24676
             Address     000d.291e.7f00
             Cost        19
             Port        12 (FastEthernet0/12)
             Hello Time   2 sec  Max Age 14 sec  Forward Delay 10 sec

[Truncated]

DLS2#show spanning-tree vlan 200

VLAN0200
  Spanning tree enabled protocol ieee
  Root ID    Priority    24776
             Address     000f.24ce.0d80
```

```
            This bridge is the root
            Hello Time   2 sec  Max Age 14 sec  Forward Delay 10 sec

[Trucated]

ALS2#show spanning-tree vlan 100

VLAN0100
  Spanning tree enabled protocol ieee
  Root ID    Priority    24676
             Address     000d.291e.7f00
             Cost        19
             Port        10 (FastEthernet0/10)
             Hello Time   2 sec  Max Age 14 sec  Forward Delay 10 sec

[Truncated]

ALS2#show spanning-tree vlan 200

VLAN0200
  Spanning tree enabled protocol ieee
  Root ID    Priority    24776
             Address     000f.24ce.0d80
             Cost        19
             Port        8 (FastEthernet0/8)
             Hello Time   2 sec  Max Age 14 sec  Forward Delay 10 sec

[Truncated]


ALS1#show spanning-tree VLAN 100

VLAN0100
  Spanning tree enabled protocol ieee
  Root ID    Priority    24676
             Address     000d.291e.7f00
             Cost        19
             Port        8 (FastEthernet0/8)
             Hello Time   2 sec  Max Age 14 sec  Forward Delay 10 sec

[Truncated]

ALS1#show spanning-tree VLAN 200

VLAN0200
  Spanning tree enabled protocol ieee
  Root ID    Priority    24776
             Address     000f.24ce.0d80
             Cost        19
             Port        10 (FastEthernet0/10)
             Hello Time   2 sec  Max Age 14 sec  Forward Delay 10 sec

[Truncated]
```

We can verify the values computed by Cisco IOS using the following equations:

- Diameter = (Max Age + 2 - (4 * Hello)) / 2
- Diameter = ((2 * Forward Delay) - (4 * Hello)) / 3

Diameter = (Max Age + 2 - (4 * Hello)) / 2 Diameter = (14 + 2 - (4 * 2)) / 2 Diameter = (16 - 8) / 2 Diameter = 8 / 2 Diameter = 4	Diameter = ((2 * Forward Delay) - (4 * Hello)) / 3 Diameter = ((2 * 10) - (4 * 2)) / 3 Diameter = (20 - 8) / 3 Diameter = 12 / 3 Diameter = 4

Final Switch Configurations

DLS1

```
DLS1#show running-config
Building configuration...

Current configuration : 4450 bytes
!
version 12.2
no service pad
service timestamps debug uptime
service timestamps log uptime
no service password-encryption
!
hostname DLS1
!
no logging console
!
no aaa new-model
ip subnet-zero
!
vtp domain 802.1D
vtp mode transparent
!
no file verify auto
!
spanning-tree mode pvst
spanning-tree extend system-id
spanning-tree vlan 100 priority 24576
spanning-tree vlan 200 priority 28672
spanning-tree vlan 100,200 forward-time 10
spanning-tree vlan 100,200 max-age 14
!
vlan internal allocation policy ascending
!
```

```
vlan 100,200
!
!
interface FastEthernet0/1
 switchport mode dynamic desirable
 shutdown
!
interface FastEthernet0/2
 switchport mode dynamic desirable
 shutdown
!
interface FastEthernet0/3
 switchport mode dynamic desirable
 shutdown
!
interface FastEthernet0/4
 switchport mode dynamic desirable
 shutdown
!
interface FastEthernet0/5
 switchport mode dynamic desirable
 shutdown
!
interface FastEthernet0/6
 switchport mode dynamic desirable
 shutdown
!
interface FastEthernet0/7
 switchport mode dynamic desirable
 shutdown
!
interface FastEthernet0/8
 switchport trunk encapsulation dot1q
 switchport mode trunk
!
interface FastEthernet0/9
 switchport mode dynamic desirable
 shutdown
!
interface FastEthernet0/10
 switchport trunk encapsulation dot1q
 switchport mode trunk
!
interface FastEthernet0/11
 switchport mode dynamic desirable
 shutdown
!
interface FastEthernet0/12
 switchport trunk encapsulation dot1q
 switchport mode trunk
!
interface FastEthernet0/13
```

```
 switchport mode dynamic desirable
 shutdown
!
interface FastEthernet0/14
 switchport mode dynamic desirable
 shutdown
!
interface FastEthernet0/15
 switchport mode dynamic desirable
 shutdown
!
interface FastEthernet0/16
 switchport mode dynamic desirable
 shutdown
!
interface FastEthernet0/17
 switchport mode dynamic desirable
 shutdown
!
interface FastEthernet0/18
 switchport mode dynamic desirable
 shutdown
!
interface FastEthernet0/19
 switchport mode dynamic desirable
 shutdown
!
interface FastEthernet0/20
 switchport mode dynamic desirable
 shutdown
!
interface FastEthernet0/21
 switchport mode dynamic desirable
 shutdown
!
interface FastEthernet0/22
 switchport mode dynamic desirable
 shutdown
!
interface FastEthernet0/23
 switchport mode dynamic desirable
 shutdown
!
interface FastEthernet0/24
 switchport mode dynamic desirable
 shutdown
!
interface FastEthernet0/25
 switchport mode dynamic desirable
 shutdown
!
interface FastEthernet0/26
```

```
 switchport mode dynamic desirable
 shutdown
!
interface FastEthernet0/27
 switchport mode dynamic desirable
 shutdown
!
interface FastEthernet0/28
 switchport mode dynamic desirable
 shutdown
!
interface FastEthernet0/29
 switchport mode dynamic desirable
 shutdown
!
interface FastEthernet0/30
 switchport mode dynamic desirable
 shutdown
!
interface FastEthernet0/31
 switchport mode dynamic desirable
 shutdown
!
interface FastEthernet0/32
 switchport mode dynamic desirable
 shutdown
!
interface FastEthernet0/33
 switchport mode dynamic desirable
 shutdown
!
interface FastEthernet0/34
 switchport mode dynamic desirable
 shutdown
!
interface FastEthernet0/35
 switchport mode dynamic desirable
 shutdown
!
interface FastEthernet0/36
 switchport mode dynamic desirable
 shutdown
!
interface FastEthernet0/37
 switchport mode dynamic desirable
 shutdown
!
interface FastEthernet0/38
 switchport mode dynamic desirable
 shutdown
!
interface FastEthernet0/39
```

```
 switchport mode dynamic desirable
 shutdown
!
interface FastEthernet0/40
 switchport mode dynamic desirable
 shutdown
!
interface FastEthernet0/41
 switchport mode dynamic desirable
 shutdown
!
interface FastEthernet0/42
 switchport mode dynamic desirable
 shutdown
!
interface FastEthernet0/43
 switchport mode dynamic desirable
 shutdown
!
interface FastEthernet0/44
 switchport mode dynamic desirable
 shutdown
!
interface FastEthernet0/45
 switchport mode dynamic desirable
 shutdown
!
interface FastEthernet0/46
 switchport mode dynamic desirable
 shutdown
!
interface FastEthernet0/47
 switchport mode dynamic desirable
 shutdown
!
interface FastEthernet0/48
 switchport mode dynamic desirable
 shutdown
!
interface GigabitEthernet0/1
 switchport mode dynamic desirable
!
interface GigabitEthernet0/2
 switchport mode dynamic desirable
!
interface Vlan1
 no ip address
 shutdown
!
ip classless
ip http server
ip http secure-server
```

```
!
control-plane
!
line con 0
line vty 0 4
 no login
line vty 5 15
 no login
!
end

DLS1#
```

DLS2

```
DLS2#show running-config
Building configuration...

Current configuration : 4431 bytes
!
version 12.2
no service pad
service timestamps debug uptime
service timestamps log uptime
no service password-encryption
!
hostname DLS2
!
no logging console
!
no aaa new-model
ip subnet-zero
!
vtp domain 802.1D
vtp mode transparent
!
spanning-tree mode pvst
spanning-tree extend system-id
spanning-tree vlan 100 priority 28672
spanning-tree vlan 200 priority 24576
spanning-tree vlan 100,200 forward-time 10
spanning-tree vlan 100,200 max-age 14
!
vlan internal allocation policy ascending
!
vlan 100,200
!
interface FastEthernet0/1
 switchport mode dynamic desirable
 shutdown
!
```

```
interface FastEthernet0/2
 switchport mode dynamic desirable
 shutdown
!
interface FastEthernet0/3
 switchport mode dynamic desirable
 shutdown
!
interface FastEthernet0/4
 switchport mode dynamic desirable
 shutdown
!
interface FastEthernet0/5
 switchport mode dynamic desirable
 shutdown
!
interface FastEthernet0/6
 switchport mode dynamic desirable
 shutdown
!
interface FastEthernet0/7
 switchport mode dynamic desirable
 shutdown
!
interface FastEthernet0/8
 switchport trunk encapsulation dot1q
 switchport mode trunk
!
interface FastEthernet0/9
 switchport mode dynamic desirable
 shutdown
!
interface FastEthernet0/10
 switchport trunk encapsulation dot1q
 switchport mode trunk
!
interface FastEthernet0/11
 switchport mode dynamic desirable
 shutdown
!
interface FastEthernet0/12
 switchport trunk encapsulation dot1q
 switchport mode trunk
!
interface FastEthernet0/13
 switchport mode dynamic desirable
 shutdown
!
interface FastEthernet0/14
 switchport mode dynamic desirable
 shutdown
!
interface FastEthernet0/15
 switchport mode dynamic desirable
```

```
 shutdown
!
interface FastEthernet0/16
 switchport mode dynamic desirable
 shutdown
!
interface FastEthernet0/17
 switchport mode dynamic desirable
 shutdown
!
interface FastEthernet0/18
 switchport mode dynamic desirable
 shutdown
!
interface FastEthernet0/19
 switchport mode dynamic desirable
 shutdown
!
interface FastEthernet0/20
 switchport mode dynamic desirable
 shutdown
!
interface FastEthernet0/21
 switchport mode dynamic desirable
 shutdown
!
interface FastEthernet0/22
 switchport mode dynamic desirable
 shutdown
!
interface FastEthernet0/23
 switchport mode dynamic desirable
 shutdown
!
interface FastEthernet0/24
 switchport mode dynamic desirable
 shutdown
!
interface FastEthernet0/25
 switchport mode dynamic desirable
 shutdown
!
interface FastEthernet0/26
 switchport mode dynamic desirable
 shutdown
!
interface FastEthernet0/27
 switchport mode dynamic desirable
 shutdown
!
interface FastEthernet0/28
 switchport mode dynamic desirable
 shutdown
!
```

```
interface FastEthernet0/29
 switchport mode dynamic desirable
 shutdown
!
interface FastEthernet0/30
 switchport mode dynamic desirable
 shutdown
!
interface FastEthernet0/31
 switchport mode dynamic desirable
 shutdown
!
interface FastEthernet0/32
 switchport mode dynamic desirable
 shutdown
!
interface FastEthernet0/33
 switchport mode dynamic desirable
 shutdown
!
interface FastEthernet0/34
 switchport mode dynamic desirable
 shutdown
!
interface FastEthernet0/35
 switchport mode dynamic desirable
 shutdown
!
interface FastEthernet0/36
 switchport mode dynamic desirable
 shutdown
!
interface FastEthernet0/37
 switchport mode dynamic desirable
 shutdown
!
interface FastEthernet0/38
 switchport mode dynamic desirable
 shutdown
!
interface FastEthernet0/39
 switchport mode dynamic desirable
 shutdown
!
interface FastEthernet0/40
 switchport mode dynamic desirable
 shutdown
!
interface FastEthernet0/41
 switchport mode dynamic desirable
 shutdown
!
interface FastEthernet0/42
 switchport mode dynamic desirable
```

```
 shutdown
!
interface FastEthernet0/43
 switchport mode dynamic desirable
 shutdown
!
interface FastEthernet0/44
 switchport mode dynamic desirable
 shutdown
!
interface FastEthernet0/45
 switchport mode dynamic desirable
 shutdown
!
interface FastEthernet0/46
 switchport mode dynamic desirable
 shutdown
!
interface FastEthernet0/47
 switchport mode dynamic desirable
 shutdown
!
interface FastEthernet0/48
 switchport mode dynamic desirable
 shutdown
!
interface GigabitEthernet0/1
 switchport mode dynamic desirable
!
interface GigabitEthernet0/2
 switchport mode dynamic desirable
!
interface Vlan1
 no ip address
 shutdown
!
ip classless
ip http server
ip http secure-server
!
control-plane
!
line con 0
line vty 0 4
 login
line vty 5 15
 login
!
end

DLS2#
```

ALS1

```
ALS1#show running-config
Building configuration...

Current configuration : 1550 bytes
!
version 12.1
no service pad
service timestamps debug uptime
service timestamps log uptime
no service password-encryption
!
hostname ALS1
!
no logging console
!
ip subnet-zero
!
ip ssh time-out 120
ip ssh authentication-retries 3
vtp domain 802.1D
vtp mode transparent
!
spanning-tree mode pvst
no spanning-tree optimize bpdu transmission
spanning-tree extend system-id
!
vlan 100,200
!
interface FastEthernet0/1
 shutdown
!
interface FastEthernet0/2
 shutdown
!
interface FastEthernet0/3
 shutdown
!
interface FastEthernet0/4
 shutdown
!
interface FastEthernet0/5
 shutdown
!
interface FastEthernet0/6
 shutdown
!
interface FastEthernet0/7
 shutdown
!
```

```
interface FastEthernet0/8
 switchport mode trunk
!
interface FastEthernet0/9
 shutdown
!
interface FastEthernet0/10
 switchport mode trunk
!
interface FastEthernet0/11
 shutdown
!
interface FastEthernet0/12
 shutdown
!
interface FastEthernet0/13
 shutdown
!
interface FastEthernet0/14
 shutdown
!
interface FastEthernet0/15
 shutdown
!
interface FastEthernet0/16
 shutdown
!
interface FastEthernet0/17
 shutdown
!
interface FastEthernet0/18
 shutdown
!
interface FastEthernet0/19
 shutdown
!
interface FastEthernet0/20
 shutdown
!
interface FastEthernet0/21
 shutdown
!
interface FastEthernet0/22
 shutdown
!
interface FastEthernet0/23
 shutdown
!
interface FastEthernet0/24
 shutdown
!
interface GigabitEthernet0/1
```

```
!
interface GigabitEthernet0/2
!
interface Vlan1
 no ip address
 no ip route-cache
 shutdown
!
ip http server
!
line con 0
line vty 0 4
 login
line vty 5 15
 login
!
end

ALS1#
```

ALS2

```
ALS2#show running-config
Building configuration...

Current configuration : 2486 bytes
!
version 12.1
no service pad
service timestamps debug uptime
service timestamps log uptime
no service password-encryption
!
hostname ALS2
!
no logging console
!
ip subnet-zero
!
ip ssh time-out 120
ip ssh authentication-retries 3
vtp domain 802.1D
vtp mode transparent
!
spanning-tree mode pvst
no spanning-tree optimize bpdu transmission
spanning-tree extend system-id
!
vlan 100,200
!
```

```
interface FastEthernet0/1
 shutdown
!
interface FastEthernet0/2
 shutdown
!
interface FastEthernet0/3
 shutdown
!
interface FastEthernet0/4
 shutdown
!
interface FastEthernet0/5
 shutdown
!
interface FastEthernet0/6
 shutdown
!
interface FastEthernet0/7
 shutdown
!
interface FastEthernet0/8
 switchport mode trunk
!
interface FastEthernet0/9
 shutdown
!
interface FastEthernet0/10
 switchport mode trunk
!
interface FastEthernet0/11
 shutdown
!
interface FastEthernet0/12
 shutdown
!
interface FastEthernet0/13
 shutdown
!
interface FastEthernet0/14
 shutdown
!
interface FastEthernet0/15
 shutdown
!
interface FastEthernet0/16
 shutdown
!
interface FastEthernet0/17
 shutdown
!
interface FastEthernet0/18
```

```
 shutdown
!
interface FastEthernet0/19
 shutdown
!
interface FastEthernet0/20
 shutdown
!
interface FastEthernet0/21
 shutdown
!
interface FastEthernet0/22
 shutdown
!
interface FastEthernet0/23
 shutdown
!
interface FastEthernet0/24
 shutdown
!
interface FastEthernet0/25
 shutdown
!
interface FastEthernet0/26
 shutdown
!
interface FastEthernet0/27
 shutdown
!
interface FastEthernet0/28
 shutdown
!
interface FastEthernet0/29
 shutdown
!
interface FastEthernet0/30
 shutdown
!
interface FastEthernet0/31
 shutdown
!
interface FastEthernet0/32
 shutdown
!
interface FastEthernet0/33
 shutdown
!
interface FastEthernet0/34
 shutdown
!
interface FastEthernet0/35
 shutdown
```

```
!
interface FastEthernet0/36
 shutdown
!
interface FastEthernet0/37
 shutdown
!
interface FastEthernet0/38
 shutdown
!
interface FastEthernet0/39
 shutdown
!
interface FastEthernet0/40
 shutdown
!
interface FastEthernet0/41
 shutdown
!
interface FastEthernet0/42
 shutdown
!
interface FastEthernet0/43
 shutdown
!
interface FastEthernet0/44
 shutdown
!
interface FastEthernet0/45
 shutdown
!
interface FastEthernet0/46
 shutdown
!
interface FastEthernet0/47
 shutdown
!
interface FastEthernet0/48
 shutdown
!
interface GigabitEthernet0/1
!
interface GigabitEthernet0/2
!
interface Vlan1
 no ip address
 no ip route-cache
 shutdown
!
ip http server
!
line con 0
```

```
line vty 0 4
 login
line vty 5 15
 login
!
end

ALS2#
```

LAB 8

Supporting Wireless and Voice Integrations

Lab Objective:

The objective of this lab exercise is for you to learn and understand how to implement Cisco Catalyst switch configuration to support wireless and voice solutions.

Lab Topology:

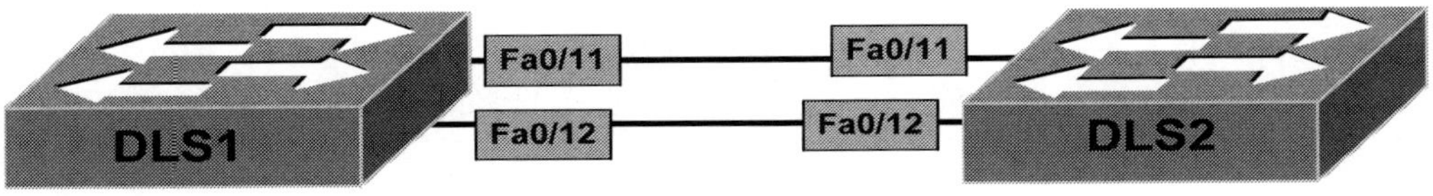

IMPORTANT NOTE

If you are using the www.howtonetwork.net racks, please begin each and every lab by shutting down all interfaces on all switches and then manually re-enabling the interfaces that are illustrated in this topology.

LAB SPECIFIC NOTE

While this lab focuses on Catalyst switch port configuration to support Wireless Access Points and Cisco IP phones, you do not actually physically need these devices. Instead, emphasis should be placed on the configuration commands required to configure the switch to support these imaginary devices as stated in the lab exercise.

Task 1

Configure VTP domain SERVICES with a password of ADVANCED on switches DLS1 and DLS2. Both switches should be configured as VTP Servers. Use VTP version 2.

Task 2

Configure a PAgP Etherchannel between switches DLS1 and DLS2. You may choose the PAgP mode that you desire; however, verify that the Etherchannel is established.

Task 3

A Cisco Wireless LAN Controller will be connected to Fa0/48 on both switches. These WLCs will be configured with the following SSID information:

- SSID Red—VLAN 100
- SSID Yellow—VLAN 103
- SSID Blue—VLAN 101
- SSID Green—VLAN 102

Configure both switches to support the WLCs.

Task 4

Cisco LAPs will be connected to both switches on interfaces FastEthernet0/1 to FastEthernet0/9. These LAPs will reside in management VLAN 104. This is the VLAN they will use to communicate with the WLC. The same VLAN is also configured on the WLC. Configure both switches to support the future LAPs and WLC.

Task 5

Some Cisco IP phones for regular employees will be connected to FastEthernet0/10 through FastEthernet0/20 of switch DLS1. These phones will reside in VLAN 105. The devices connected to the Cisco IP phones will reside in VLAN 106. It is important that the QoS settings on the phones be trusted only if connected to Cisco IP phones; however, the QoS settings from the connected devices should not be trusted. Configure switch DLS1 to support these requirements.

Task 6

Some Cisco IP phones for Management and Executives will be connected to FastEthernet0/10 through FastEthernet0/20 of switch DLS2. These phones will reside in VLAN 107. The devices connected to the Cisco IP phones will reside in VLAN 108. It is important that the QoS settings on the phones AND on the connected devices be trusted. Configure switch DLS2 to support these requirements.

Task 7

The IP phone of the CEO is connected to port FastEthernet0/30 on switch DLS1. All of the QoS settings received from this phone should be trusted. In addition to this, all data traffic received from the device connected to the CEOs IP phone should be assigned the highest Class of Service value. The IP phone will reside in VLAN 200 and the data traffic in VLAN 201. Configure switch DLS1 to support this requirement.

Task 8

Ensure that end-to-end QoS settings are honored throughout the switched domain.

Lab Validation

Task 1

```
DLS1(config)#vtp domain SERVICES
DLS1(config)#vtp password ADVANCED
DLS1(config)#vtp version 2

DLS2(config)#vtp domain SERVICES
DLS2(config)#vtp password ADVANCED
DLS2(config)#vtp version 2
```

Task 2

```
DLS1(config)#interface range fastethernet 0/11 - 12
DLS1(config-if-range)#switchport
DLS1(config-if-range)#switchport trunk encapsulation dot1q
DLS1(config-if-range)#switchport mode trunk
DLS1(config-if-range)#channel-group 1 mode desirable
Creating a port-channel interface Port-channel 1

DLS1(config-if-range)#no shutdown
DLS1(config-if-range)#exit

DLS2(config)#interface range fastethernet 0/11 - 12
DLS2(config-if-range)#switchport
DLS2(config-if-range)#switchport trunk encapsulation dot1q
DLS2(config-if-range)#switchport mode trunk
DLS2(config-if-range)#channel-group 1 mode desirable
Creating a port-channel interface Port-channel 1

DLS2(config-if-range)#no shutdown
DLS2(config-if-range)#exit
```

Verify your configuration as follows:

```
DLS1#show etherchannel summary
Flags:  D - down        P - in port-channel
        I - stand-alone s - suspended
        H - Hot-standby (LACP only)
        R - Layer3      S - Layer2
        U - in use      f - failed to allocate aggregator
        u - unsuitable for bundling
        w - waiting to be aggregated
        d - default port


Number of channel-groups in use: 1
Number of aggregators:           1
```

```
Group  Port-channel  Protocol    Ports
------+-------------+-----------+-----------------------------------------------
---
1      Po1(SU)         PAgP      Fa0/11(P)   Fa0/12(P)

DLS2#show pagp neighbor
Flags:  S - Device is sending Slow hello.  C - Device is in Consistent state.
        A - Device is in Auto mode.        P - Device learns on physical
port.

Channel group 1 neighbors
          Partner              Partner          Partner         Partner Group
Port      Name                 Device ID        Port       Age  Flags   Cap.
Fa0/11    DLS1                 000d.291e.7f00   Fa0/11      4s  SC      10001
Fa0/12    DLS1                 000d.291e.7f00   Fa0/12      3s  SC      10001
```

Task 3

```
DLS1(config)#vlan 100
DLS1(config-vlan)#name Red
DLS1(config-vlan)#exit
DLS1(config)#vlan 103
DLS1(config-vlan)#name Yellow
DLS1(config-vlan)#exit
DLS1(config)#vlan 101
DLS1(config-vlan)#name Blue
DLS1(config-vlan)#exit
DLS1(config)#vlan 102
DLS1(config-vlan)#name Green
DLS1(config-vlan)#exit
DLS1(config)#interface fastethernet 0/48
DLS1(config-if)#description 'To Be Connected To WLC'
DLS1(config-if)#switchport
DLS1(config-if)#switchport trunk encapsulation dot1q
DLS1(config-if)#switchport mode trunk
DLS1(config-if)#switchport trunk allowed vlan 100-103
DLS2(config-if)#spanning-tree portfast trunk
%Warning: portfast should only be enabled on ports connected to a single
 host. Connecting hubs, concentrators, switches, bridges, etc... to this
 interface  when portfast is enabled, can cause temporary bridging loops.
 Use with CAUTION
DLS1(config-if)#no shutdown
DLS1(config-if)#exit

DLS2(config)#vlan 100
DLS2(config-vlan)#name Red
DLS2(config-vlan)#exit
DLS2(config)#vlan 103
DLS2(config-vlan)#name Yellow
DLS2(config-vlan)#exit
DLS2(config)#vlan 101
```

```
DLS2(config-vlan)#name Blue
DLS2(config-vlan)#exit
DLS2(config)#vlan 102
DLS2(config-vlan)#name Green
DLS2(config-vlan)#exit
DLS2(config)#interface fastethernet 0/48
DLS2(config-if)#description 'To Be Connected To WLC'
DLS2(config-if)#switchport
DLS2(config-if)#switchport trunk encapsulation dot1q
DLS2(config-if)#switchport mode trunk
DLS2(config-if)#switchport trunk allowed vlan 100-103
DLS2(config-if)#spanning-tree portfast trunk
%Warning: portfast should only be enabled on ports connected to a single
 host. Connecting hubs, concentrators, switches, bridges, etc... to this
 interface  when portfast is enabled, can cause temporary bridging loops.
 Use with CAUTION
DLS2(config-if)#no shutdown
DLS2(config-if)#exit
```

Task 4

```
DLS1(config)#vlan 104
DLS1(config-vlan)#name Management
DLS1(config-vlan)#exit
DLS1(config)#interface range fastethernet 0/1 - 9
DLS1(config-if-range)#description 'Connected To Future LAPs'
DLS1(config-if-range)#switchport
DLS1(config-if-range)#switchport access vlan 104
DLS1(config-if-range)#switchport mode access
DLS1(config-if-range)#no shut
DLS1(config-if-range)#exit
DLS1(config)#interface fastethernet 0/48
DLS1(config-if)#switchport trunk allowed vlan add 104
DLS1(config-if)#exit
```

```
DLS2(config)#vlan 104
DLS2(config-vlan)#name Management
DLS2(config-vlan)#exit
DLS2(config)#interface range fastethernet 0/1 - 9
DLS2(config-if-range)#description 'Connected to Future LAPs'
DLS2(config-if-range)#switchport
DLS2(config-if-range)#switchport access vlan 104
DLS2(config-if-range)#switchport mode access
DLS2(config-if-range)#no shutdown
DLS2(config-if-range)#exit
DLS2(config)#interface fastethernet 0/48
DLS2(config-if)#switchport trunk allowed vlan add 104
DLS2(config-if)#exit
```

Task 5

```
DLS1(config)#mls qos
QoS: ensure flow-control on all interfaces are OFF for proper operation.
DLS1(config)#interface range fastethernet 0/10 - 20
DLS1(config-if-range)#description 'Connected To Future Employee IP Phones'
DLS1(config-if-range)#switchport
DLS1(config-if-range)#switchport access vlan 106
DLS1(config-if-range)#switchport voice vlan 105
DLS1(config-if-range)#switchport mode access
DLS1(config-if-range)#spanning-tree portfast
DLS1(config-if-range)#mls qos trust device cisco-phone
DLS1(config-if-range)#mls qos trust cos
DLS1(config-if-range)#no shutdown
DLS1(config-if-range)#exit
```

Task 6

```
DLS2(config)#vlan 107,108
DLS2(config-vlan)#exit
DLS2(config)#mls qos
QoS: ensure flow-control on all interfaces are OFF for proper operation.
DLS2(config)#interface range fastethernet 0/10 - 20
DLS2(config-if-range)#$ 'Connected To Future Mgmt and Exec IP Phones'
DLS2(config-if-range)#switchport
DLS2(config-if-range)#switchport access vlan 107
DLS2(config-if-range)#switchport voice vlan 108
DLS2(config-if-range)#switchport mode access
DLS2(config-if-range)#mls qos trust cos
DLS2(config-if-range)#switchport priority extend trust
DLS2(config-if-range)#spanning-tree portfast
DLS2(config-if-range)#no shutdown
DLS2(config-if-range)#exit
```

Task 7

```
DLS1(config)#vlan 200,201
DLS1(config-vlan)#exit
DLS1(config)#interface fastethernet 0/30
DLS1(config-if)#description 'Connected To CEO IP Phone'
DLS1(config-if)#switchport
DLS1(config-if)#switchport mode access
DLS1(config-if)#switchport access vlan 201
DLS1(config-if)#switchport voice vlan 200
DLS1(config-if)#spanning-tree portfast
DLS1(config-if)#mls qos trust cos
DLS1(config-if)#switchport priority extend cos 5
DLS1(config-if)#no shutdown
DLS1(config-if)#exit
```

Task 8

```
DLS1(config)#interface range fastethernet 0/11 - 12
DLS1(config-if-range)#mls qos trust cos
DLS1(config-if-range)#exit

DLS2(config)#interface range fastethernet 0/11 - 12
DLS2(config-if-range)#mls qos trust cos
DLS2(config-if-range)#exit
```

Final Switch Configurations

DLS1

```
DLS1#show running-config
Building configuration...

Current configuration : 7106 bytes
!
version 12.2
no service pad
service timestamps debug uptime
service timestamps log uptime
no service password-encryption
!
hostname DLS1
!
no logging console
!
no aaa new-model
mls qos
ip subnet-zero
no ip domain-lookup
!
vtp domain SERVICES
vtp mode transparent
!
no file verify auto
spanning-tree mode pvst
spanning-tree extend system-id
!
vlan internal allocation policy ascending
!
vlan 100
 name Red
!
vlan 101
 name Blue
!
vlan 102
```

```
 name Green
!
vlan 103
 name Yellow
!
vlan 104
 name Management
!
vlan 105-106,200-201
!
interface Port-channel1
 switchport trunk encapsulation dot1q
 switchport mode trunk
!
interface FastEthernet0/1
 description 'Connected To Future LAPs'
 switchport access vlan 104
 switchport mode access
!
interface FastEthernet0/2
 description 'Connected To Future LAPs'
 switchport access vlan 104
 switchport mode access
!
interface FastEthernet0/3
 description 'Connected To Future LAPs'
 switchport access vlan 104
 switchport mode access
!
interface FastEthernet0/4
 description 'Connected To Future LAPs'
 switchport access vlan 104
 switchport mode access
!
interface FastEthernet0/5
 description 'Connected To Future LAPs'
 switchport access vlan 104
 switchport mode access
!
interface FastEthernet0/6
 description 'Connected To Future LAPs'
 switchport access vlan 104
 switchport mode access
!
interface FastEthernet0/7
 description 'Connected To Future LAPs'
 switchport access vlan 104
 switchport mode access
!
interface FastEthernet0/8
 description 'Connected To Future LAPs'
 switchport access vlan 104
 switchport mode access
!
```

```
interface FastEthernet0/9
 description 'Connected To Future LAPs'
 switchport access vlan 104
 switchport mode access
!
interface FastEthernet0/10
 description 'Connected To Future Employee IP Phones'
 switchport access vlan 106
 switchport mode access
 switchport voice vlan 105
 mls qos trust device cisco-phone
 mls qos trust cos
 spanning-tree portfast
!
interface FastEthernet0/11
 description 'Connected To Future Employee IP Phones'
 switchport access vlan 106
 switchport trunk encapsulation dot1q
 switchport mode access
 switchport voice vlan 105
 mls qos trust device cisco-phone
 mls qos trust cos
 channel-group 1 mode desirable
 spanning-tree portfast
!
interface FastEthernet0/12
 description 'Connected To Future Employee IP Phones'
 switchport access vlan 106
 switchport trunk encapsulation dot1q
 switchport mode access
 switchport voice vlan 105
 mls qos trust device cisco-phone
 mls qos trust cos
 channel-group 1 mode desirable
 spanning-tree portfast
!
interface FastEthernet0/13
 description 'Connected To Future Employee IP Phones'
 switchport access vlan 106
 switchport mode access
 switchport voice vlan 105
 mls qos trust device cisco-phone
 mls qos trust cos
 spanning-tree portfast
!
interface FastEthernet0/14
 description 'Connected To Future Employee IP Phones'
 switchport access vlan 106
 switchport mode access
 switchport voice vlan 105
 mls qos trust device cisco-phone
 mls qos trust cos
 spanning-tree portfast
!
```

```
interface FastEthernet0/15
 description 'Connected To Future Employee IP Phones'
 switchport access vlan 106
 switchport mode access
 switchport voice vlan 105
 mls qos trust device cisco-phone
 mls qos trust cos
 spanning-tree portfast
!
interface FastEthernet0/16
 description 'Connected To Future Employee IP Phones'
 switchport access vlan 106
 switchport mode access
 switchport voice vlan 105
 mls qos trust device cisco-phone
 mls qos trust cos
 spanning-tree portfast
!
interface FastEthernet0/17
 description 'Connected To Future Employee IP Phones'
 switchport access vlan 106
 switchport mode access
 switchport voice vlan 105
 mls qos trust device cisco-phone
 mls qos trust cos
 spanning-tree portfast
!
interface FastEthernet0/18
 description 'Connected To Future Employee IP Phones'
 switchport access vlan 106
 switchport mode access
 switchport voice vlan 105
 mls qos trust device cisco-phone
 mls qos trust cos
 spanning-tree portfast
!
interface FastEthernet0/19
 description 'Connected To Future Employee IP Phones'
 switchport access vlan 106
 switchport mode access
 switchport voice vlan 105
 mls qos trust device cisco-phone
 mls qos trust cos
 spanning-tree portfast
!
interface FastEthernet0/20
 description 'Connected To Future Employee IP Phones'
 switchport access vlan 106
 switchport mode access
 switchport voice vlan 105
 mls qos trust device cisco-phone
 mls qos trust cos
 spanning-tree portfast
!
```

```
interface FastEthernet0/21
 switchport mode dynamic desirable
 shutdown
!
interface FastEthernet0/22
 switchport mode dynamic desirable
 shutdown
!
interface FastEthernet0/23
 switchport mode dynamic desirable
 shutdown
!
interface FastEthernet0/24
 switchport mode dynamic desirable
 shutdown
!
interface FastEthernet0/25
 switchport mode dynamic desirable
 shutdown
!
interface FastEthernet0/26
 switchport mode dynamic desirable
 shutdown
!
interface FastEthernet0/27
 switchport mode dynamic desirable
 shutdown
!
interface FastEthernet0/28
 switchport mode dynamic desirable
 shutdown
!
interface FastEthernet0/29
 switchport mode dynamic desirable
 shutdown
!
interface FastEthernet0/30
 description 'Connected To CEO IP Phone'
 switchport access vlan 201
 switchport mode access
 switchport voice vlan 200
 switchport priority extend cos 5
 mls qos trust cos
 spanning-tree portfast
!
interface FastEthernet0/31
 switchport mode dynamic desirable
 shutdown
!
interface FastEthernet0/32
 switchport mode dynamic desirable
 shutdown
!
```

```
interface FastEthernet0/33
 switchport mode dynamic desirable
 shutdown
!
interface FastEthernet0/34
 switchport mode dynamic desirable
 shutdown
!
interface FastEthernet0/35
 switchport mode dynamic desirable
 shutdown
!
interface FastEthernet0/36
 switchport mode dynamic desirable
 shutdown
!
interface FastEthernet0/37
 switchport mode dynamic desirable
 shutdown
!
interface FastEthernet0/38
 switchport mode dynamic desirable
 shutdown
!
interface FastEthernet0/39
 switchport mode dynamic desirable
 shutdown
!
interface FastEthernet0/40
 switchport mode dynamic desirable
 shutdown
!
interface FastEthernet0/41
 switchport mode dynamic desirable
 shutdown
!
interface FastEthernet0/42
 switchport mode dynamic desirable
 shutdown
!
interface FastEthernet0/43
 switchport mode dynamic desirable
 shutdown
!
interface FastEthernet0/44
 switchport mode dynamic desirable
 shutdown
!
interface FastEthernet0/45
 switchport mode dynamic desirable
 shutdown
!
interface FastEthernet0/46
```

```
 switchport mode dynamic desirable
 shutdown
!
interface FastEthernet0/47
 switchport mode dynamic desirable
 shutdown
!
interface FastEthernet0/48
 description 'To Be Connected To WLC'
 switchport trunk encapsulation dot1q
 switchport trunk allowed vlan 100-104
 switchport mode trunk
 spanning-tree portfast trunk
!
interface GigabitEthernet0/1
 switchport mode dynamic desirable
!
interface GigabitEthernet0/2
 switchport mode dynamic desirable
!
interface Vlan1
 no ip address
 shutdown
!
ip classless
ip http server
ip http secure-server
!
control-plane
!
line con 0
line vty 5 15
!
end

DLS1#
```

DLS2

```
DLS2#show running-config
Building configuration...

Current configuration : 6938 bytes
!
version 12.2
no service pad
service timestamps debug uptime
service timestamps log uptime
no service password-encryption
!
hostname DLS2
!
```

```
no logging console
!
no aaa new-model
mls qos
ip subnet-zero
no ip domain-lookup
!
vtp domain SERVICES
vtp mode transparent
!
spanning-tree mode pvst
spanning-tree extend system-id
!
vlan internal allocation policy ascending
!
vlan 100
 name Red
!
vlan 101
 name Blue
!
vlan 102
 name Green
!
vlan 103
 name Yellow
!
vlan 104
 name Management
!
vlan 107-108,200
!
interface Port-channel1
 switchport trunk encapsulation dot1q
 switchport mode trunk
!
interface FastEthernet0/1
 description 'Connected to Future LAPs'
 switchport access vlan 104
 switchport mode access
!
interface FastEthernet0/2
 description 'Connected to Future LAPs'
 switchport access vlan 104
 switchport mode access
!
interface FastEthernet0/3
 description 'Connected to Future LAPs'
 switchport access vlan 104
 switchport mode access
!
interface FastEthernet0/4
 description 'Connected to Future LAPs'
```

```
 switchport access vlan 104
 switchport mode access
!
interface FastEthernet0/5
 description 'Connected to Future LAPs'
 switchport access vlan 104
 switchport mode access
!
interface FastEthernet0/6
 description 'Connected to Future LAPs'
 switchport access vlan 104
 switchport mode access
!
interface FastEthernet0/7
 description 'Connected to Future LAPs'
 switchport access vlan 104
 switchport mode access
!
interface FastEthernet0/8
 description 'Connected to Future LAPs'
 switchport access vlan 104
 switchport mode access
!
interface FastEthernet0/9
 description 'Connected to Future LAPs'
 switchport access vlan 104
 switchport mode access
!
interface FastEthernet0/10
 description 'Connected To Future Mgmt and Exec IP Phones'
 switchport access vlan 107
 switchport mode access
 switchport voice vlan 108
 switchport priority extend trust
 mls qos trust cos
 spanning-tree portfast
!
interface FastEthernet0/11
 description 'Connected To Future Mgmt and Exec IP Phones'
 switchport access vlan 107
 switchport trunk encapsulation dot1q
 switchport mode access
 switchport priority extend trust
 mls qos trust cos
 channel-group 1 mode desirable
 spanning-tree portfast
!
interface FastEthernet0/12
 description 'Connected To Future Mgmt and Exec IP Phones'
 switchport access vlan 107
 switchport trunk encapsulation dot1q
 switchport mode access
 switchport priority extend trust
```

```
 mls qos trust cos
 channel-group 1 mode desirable
 spanning-tree portfast
!
interface FastEthernet0/13
 description 'Connected To Future Mgmt and Exec IP Phones'
 switchport access vlan 107
 switchport mode access
 switchport voice vlan 108
 switchport priority extend trust
 mls qos trust cos
 spanning-tree portfast
!
interface FastEthernet0/14
 description 'Connected To Future Mgmt and Exec IP Phones'
 switchport access vlan 107
 switchport mode access
 switchport voice vlan 108
 switchport priority extend trust
 mls qos trust cos
 spanning-tree portfast
!
interface FastEthernet0/15
 description 'Connected To Future Mgmt and Exec IP Phones'
 switchport access vlan 107
 switchport mode access
 switchport voice vlan 108
 switchport priority extend trust
 mls qos trust cos
 spanning-tree portfast
!
interface FastEthernet0/16
 description 'Connected To Future Mgmt and Exec IP Phones'
 switchport access vlan 107
 switchport mode access
 switchport voice vlan 108
 switchport priority extend trust
 mls qos trust cos
 spanning-tree portfast
!
interface FastEthernet0/17
 description 'Connected To Future Mgmt and Exec IP Phones'
 switchport access vlan 107
 switchport mode access
 switchport voice vlan 108
 switchport priority extend trust
 mls qos trust cos
 spanning-tree portfast
!
interface FastEthernet0/18
 description 'Connected To Future Mgmt and Exec IP Phones'
 switchport access vlan 107
 switchport mode access
```

```
 switchport voice vlan 108
 switchport priority extend trust
 mls qos trust cos
 spanning-tree portfast
!
interface FastEthernet0/19
 description 'Connected To Future Mgmt and Exec IP Phones'
 switchport access vlan 107
 switchport mode access
 switchport voice vlan 108
 switchport priority extend trust
 mls qos trust cos
 spanning-tree portfast
!
interface FastEthernet0/20
 description 'Connected To Future Mgmt and Exec IP Phones'
 switchport access vlan 107
 switchport mode access
 switchport voice vlan 108
 switchport priority extend trust
 mls qos trust cos
 spanning-tree portfast
!
interface FastEthernet0/21
 switchport mode dynamic desirable
 shutdown
!
interface FastEthernet0/22
 switchport mode dynamic desirable
 shutdown
!
interface FastEthernet0/23
 switchport mode dynamic desirable
 shutdown
!
interface FastEthernet0/24
 switchport mode dynamic desirable
 shutdown
!
interface FastEthernet0/25
 switchport mode dynamic desirable
 shutdown
!
interface FastEthernet0/26
 switchport mode dynamic desirable
 shutdown
!
interface FastEthernet0/27
 switchport mode dynamic desirable
 shutdown
!
interface FastEthernet0/28
 switchport mode dynamic desirable
```

```
 shutdown
!
interface FastEthernet0/29
 switchport mode dynamic desirable
 shutdown
!
interface FastEthernet0/30
 switchport mode dynamic desirable
 shutdown
!
interface FastEthernet0/31
 switchport mode dynamic desirable
 shutdown
!
interface FastEthernet0/32
 switchport mode dynamic desirable
 shutdown
!
interface FastEthernet0/33
 switchport mode dynamic desirable
 shutdown
!
interface FastEthernet0/34
 switchport mode dynamic desirable
 shutdown
!
interface FastEthernet0/35
 switchport mode dynamic desirable
 shutdown
!
interface FastEthernet0/36
 switchport mode dynamic desirable
 shutdown
!
interface FastEthernet0/37
 switchport mode dynamic desirable
 shutdown
!
interface FastEthernet0/38
 switchport mode dynamic desirable
 shutdown
!
interface FastEthernet0/39
 switchport mode dynamic desirable
 shutdown
!
interface FastEthernet0/40
 switchport mode dynamic desirable
 shutdown
!
interface FastEthernet0/41
 switchport mode dynamic desirable
 shutdown
```

```
!
interface FastEthernet0/42
 switchport mode dynamic desirable
 shutdown
!
interface FastEthernet0/43
 switchport mode dynamic desirable
 shutdown
!
interface FastEthernet0/44
 switchport mode dynamic desirable
 shutdown
!
interface FastEthernet0/45
 switchport mode dynamic desirable
 shutdown
!
interface FastEthernet0/46
 switchport mode dynamic desirable
 shutdown
!
interface FastEthernet0/47
 switchport mode dynamic desirable
 shutdown
!
interface FastEthernet0/48
 description 'To Be Connected To WLC'
 switchport trunk encapsulation dot1q
 switchport trunk allowed vlan 100-104
 switchport mode trunk
 spanning-tree portfast trunk
!
interface GigabitEthernet0/1
 switchport mode dynamic desirable
!
interface GigabitEthernet0/2
 switchport mode dynamic desirable
!
interface Vlan1
 no ip address
 shutdown
!
ip classless
ip http server
ip http secure-server
!
control-plane
!
line con 0
line vty 5 15
!
end
DLS2#
```

LAB 9

Topology Based (CEF) Switching

Lab Objective:

The objective of this lab exercise is for you to learn and understand how to implement Topology Based (CEF) switching in Cisco IOS Multilayer switches.

Lab Topology:

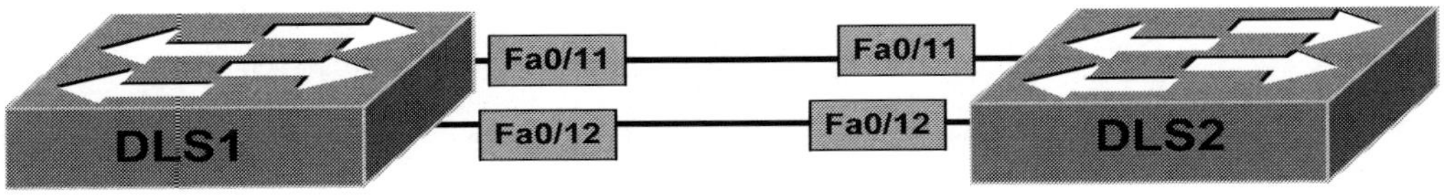

IMPORTANT NOTE

If you are using the www.howtonetwork.net racks, please begin each and every lab by shutting down all interfaces on all switches and then manually re-enabling the interfaces that are illustrated in this topology.

Task 1

Disable VTP on switches DLS1 and DSL2. Configure the VTP domain MLS with a password of CEF on both switches.

Task 2

Configure VLAN 100 on both switches. This VLAN should be named MLS-VLAN. Configure FastEthernet0/11 on both switches as an access port in this VLAN. Configure interface VLAN 100 on both switches as follows:

- DLS1—IP address 192.168.100.1/24
- DLS2—IP address 192.168.100.2/24

Verify your configuring by pinging between the switches.

Task 3

Configure FastEthernet0/12 on both switches as a ROUTED interface. Assign these interfaces IP addressing information as follows:

- DLS1—IP address 192.168.200.1/24
- DLS2—IP address 192.168.200.2/24

Verify your configuring by pinging between the switches.

Task 4

Configure the following Loopback interfaces on switch DLS1:

- Loopback 10—IP address 10.1.1.1/32
- Loopback 20—IP address 20.1.1.1/32

Configure the following Loopback interfaces on switch DLS2:

- Loopback 30—IP address 30.1.1.1/32
- Loopback 40—IP address 40.1.1.1/32

Task 5

Enable EIGRP routing on both switches using Autonomous System Number 123. Advertise all Loopback interfaces via EIGRP on both switches. Verify your configuration.

Task 6

Enable Cisco Express Forwarding (CEF) on both switches

Task 7

Verify CEF switching by viewing both the Adjacency Table and the Forwarding Information Base (FIB) on both switches. Ping between the switches and verify CEF traffic statistics.

Lab Validation

Task 1

```
DLS1(config)#vtp mode transparent
DLS1(config)#vtp domain MLS
DLS1(config)#vtp password CEF

DLS2(config)#vtp mode transparent
DLS2(config)#vtp domain MLS
DLS2(config)#vtp password CEF
```

Task 2

```
DLS1(config)#vlan 100
DLS1(config-vlan)#name MLS-VLAN
DLS1(config-vlan)#exit
DLS1(config)#interface fastethernet0/11
```

```
DLS1(config-if)#switchport
DLS1(config-if)#switchport access vlan 100
DLS1(config-if)#switchport mode access
DLS1(config-if)#no shutdown
DLS1(config-if)#exit
DLS1(config)#interface vlan 100
DLS1(config-if)#ip address 192.168.100.1 255.255.255.0
DLS1(config-if)#no shutdown
DLS1(config-if)#exit

DLS2(config)#vlan 100
DLS2(config-vlan)#name MLS-VLAN
DLS2(config-vlan)#exit
DLS2(config)#interface fastethernet 0/11
DLS2(config-if)#switchport
DLS2(config-if)#switchport access vlan 100
DLS2(config-if)#switchport mode access
DLS2(config-if)#no shut
DLS2(config-if)#exit
DLS2(config)#interface vlan 100
DLS2(config-if)#ip address 192.168.100.2 255.255.255.0
DLS2(config-if)#no shut
DLS2(config-if)#exit
```

Verify your configuration as follows:

```
DLS1#show spanning-tree vlan 100

VLAN0100
  Spanning tree enabled protocol ieee
  Root ID    Priority    32868
             Address     000d.291e.7f00
             This bridge is the root
             Hello Time   2 sec  Max Age 20 sec  Forward Delay 15 sec

  Bridge ID  Priority    32868  (priority 32768 sys-id-ext 100)
             Address     000d.291e.7f00
             Hello Time   2 sec  Max Age 20 sec  Forward Delay 15 sec
             Aging Time 300

Interface        Role Sts Cost      Prio.Nbr Type
---------------- ---- --- --------- -------- --------------------------------
Fa0/11           Desg FWD 19        128.11   P2p


DLS1#ping 192.168.100.2

Type escape sequence to abort.
Sending 5, 100-byte ICMP Echos to 192.168.100.2, timeout is 2 seconds:
.!!!!
Success rate is 80 percent (4/5), round-trip min/avg/max = 1/1/4 ms
```

```
DLS2#show spanning-tree vlan 100

VLAN0100
  Spanning tree enabled protocol ieee
  Root ID    Priority    32868
             Address     000d.291e.7f00
             Cost        19
             Port        11 (FastEthernet0/11)
             Hello Time   2 sec  Max Age 20 sec  Forward Delay 15 sec

  Bridge ID  Priority    32868  (priority 32768 sys-id-ext 100)
             Address     000f.24ce.0d80
             Hello Time   2 sec  Max Age 20 sec  Forward Delay 15 sec
             Aging Time 15

Interface           Role Sts Cost      Prio.Nbr Type
------------------- ---- --- --------- -------- ----------------------------
Fa0/11              Root FWD 19        128.11   P2p

DLS2#
DLS2#ping 192.168.100.1

Type escape sequence to abort.
Sending 5, 100-byte ICMP Echos to 192.168.100.1, timeout is 2 seconds:
!!!!!
Success rate is 100 percent (5/5), round-trip min/avg/max = 1/2/4 ms
```

Task 3

```
DLS1(config)#interface fastethernet 0/12
DLS1(config-if)#no switchport
DLS1(config-if)#ip address 192.168.200.1 255.255.255.0
DLS1(config-if)#no shutdown
DLS1(config-if)#exit

DLS2(config)#interface fastethernet 0/12
DLS2(config-if)#no switchport
DLS2(config-if)#ip address 192.168.200.2 255.255.255.0
DLS2(config-if)#no shutdown
DLS2(config-if)#exit
```

Verify your configuration as follows:

```
DLS1#ping 192.168.200.2

Type escape sequence to abort.
Sending 5, 100-byte ICMP Echos to 192.168.200.2, timeout is 2 seconds:
.!!!!
Success rate is 80 percent (4/5), round-trip min/avg/max = 1/1/4 ms
```

```
DLS2#ping 192.168.200.1

Type escape sequence to abort.
Sending 5, 100-byte ICMP Echos to 192.168.200.1, timeout is 2 seconds:
!!!!!
Success rate is 100 percent (5/5), round-trip min/avg/max = 1/2/4 ms
```

Task 4

```
DLS1(config)#interface loopback 10
DLS1(config-if)#ip address 10.1.1.1 255.255.255.255
DLS1(config)#interface loopback 20
DLS1(config-if)#ip address 20.1.1.1 255.255.255.255
DLS1(config-if)#exit

DLS2(config)#interface loopback 30
DLS2(config-if)#ip address 30.1.1.1 255.255.255.255
DLS2(config-if)#exit
DLS2(config)#interface loopback 40
DLS2(config-if)#ip address 40.1.1.1 255.255.255.255
DLS2(config-if)#exit
```

Task 5

```
DLS1(config)#ip routing
DLS1(config)#router eigrp 123
DLS1(config-router)#no auto-summary
DLS1(config-router)#network 0.0.0.0 255.255.255.255
DLS1(config-router)#exit

DLS2(config)#ip routing
DLS2(config)#router eigrp 123
DLS2(config-router)#no auto-summary
DLS2(config-router)#network 0.0.0.0 255.255.255.255
DLS2(config-router)#exit
```

Verify your configuration as follows:

```
DLS1#show ip eigrp neighbors
IP-EIGRP neighbors for process 123
H   Address                 Interface        Hold Uptime    SRTT    RTO  Q   Seq
Type
                                             (sec)          (ms)         Cnt Num
1   192.168.200.2           Fa0/12             12 00:00:35     4    200  0   10
0   192.168.100.2           Vl100              11 00:00:35     4    200  0   8

DLS1#show ip route eigrp
     40.0.0.0/32 is subnetted, 1 subnets
D       40.1.1.1 [90/130816] via 192.168.100.2, 00:00:41, Vlan100
     30.0.0.0/32 is subnetted, 1 subnets
D       30.1.1.1 [90/130816] via 192.168.100.2, 00:00:41, Vlan100
```

NOTE: An SVI is assigned a higher bandwidth value than a physical interface.

```
DLS2#show ip eigrp neighbors
EIGRP-IPv4 neighbors for process 123
H   Address                 Interface       Hold Uptime   SRTT   RTO  Q  Seq
                                            (sec)         (ms)       Cnt Num
1   192.168.200.1           Fa0/12            12 00:03:30  820  4920  0  4
0   192.168.100.1           Vl100             14 00:03:30  882  5000  0  3

DLS2#show ip route eigrp
     20.0.0.0/32 is subnetted, 1 subnets
D       20.1.1.1 [90/130816] via 192.168.100.1, 00:03:33, Vlan100
     10.0.0.0/32 is subnetted, 1 subnets
D       10.1.1.1 [90/130816] via 192.168.100.1, 00:03:33, Vlan100
```

Task 6

```
DLS1(config)#ip cef

DLS2(config)#ip cef
```

Task 7

To view basic Adjacency Table information, perform the following:

```
DLS1#show adjacency
Protocol Interface                 Address
IP       Vlan100                   192.168.100.2(10)
IP       FastEthernet0/12          192.168.200.2(6)
```

To view detailed Adjacency Table information, perform the following:

```
DLS2#show adjacency detail
Protocol Interface                 Address
IP       Vlan100                   192.168.100.1(10)
                                   0 packets, 0 bytes
                                   epoch 0
                                   sourced in sev-epoch 0
                                   Encap length 14
                                   000D291E7F00000F24CE0D800800
                                   ARP
IP       FastEthernet0/12          192.168.200.1(6)
                                   0 packets, 0 bytes
                                   epoch 0
                                   sourced in sev-epoch 0
                                   Encap length 14
                                   000D291E7F00000F24CE0D800800
                                   ARP
```

To view the contents of the FIB, perform the following:

```
DLS1#show ip cef detail
IPv4 CEF is enabled and running
VRF Default:
 18 prefixes (18/0 fwd/non-fwd)
 Table id 0, 0 resets
 Database epoch: 0 (18 entries at this epoch)

0.0.0.0/32, epoch 0, flags receive
  Special source: receive
  receive
10.1.1.1/32, epoch 0, flags attached, connected, receive
  receive
20.1.1.1/32, epoch 0, flags attached, connected, receive
  receive
30.1.1.1/32, epoch 0
  nexthop 192.168.100.2 Vlan100
40.1.1.1/32, epoch 0
  nexthop 192.168.100.2 Vlan100
192.168.100.0/24, epoch 0, flags attached, connected
  attached to Vlan100
192.168.100.0/32, epoch 0, flags receive
  receive
192.168.100.1/32, epoch 0, flags receive
  receive
192.168.100.2/32, epoch 0
  Adj source: IP adj out of Vlan100, addr 192.168.100.2
  attached to Vlan100
192.168.100.255/32, epoch 0, flags receive
  receive
192.168.200.0/24, epoch 0, flags attached, connected
  attached to FastEthernet0/12
192.168.200.0/32, epoch 0, flags receive
  receive
192.168.200.1/32, epoch 0, flags receive
  receive
192.168.200.2/32, epoch 0
  Adj source: IP adj out of FastEthernet0/12, addr 192.168.200.2
  attached to FastEthernet0/12
192.168.200.255/32, epoch 0, flags receive
  receive
224.0.0.0/4, epoch 0
  Special source: drop
  drop
224.0.0.0/24, epoch 0, flags receive
  Special source: receive
  receive
255.255.255.255/32, epoch 0, flags receive
  Special source: receive
  receive
```

To view detailed FIB information for a single interface, perform the following:

```
DLS2#show ip cef vlan 100 detail
IPv4 CEF is enabled and running
VRF Default:
 20 prefixes (20/0 fwd/non-fwd)
 Table id 0
 Database epoch:        0 (20 entries at this epoch)

10.1.1.1/32, epoch 0
  nexthop 192.168.100.1 Vlan100
20.1.1.1/32, epoch 0
  nexthop 192.168.100.1 Vlan100
192.168.100.0/24, epoch 0, flags attached, connected, cover dependents, need
deagg
  Covered dependent prefixes: 4
    need deagg: 3
    notify cover updated: 1
  attached to Vlan100
192.168.100.1/32, epoch 0, flags attached
  Adj source: IP adj out of Vlan100, addr 192.168.100.1 02B68CA0
   Dependent covered prefix type adjfib cover 192.168.100.0/24
  attached to Vlan100
```

And finally, to view CEF switching statistics, perform the following:

```
DLS1#show ip cef switching statistics

       Reason                          Drop        Punt  Punt2Host
RP RIB Packet destined for us             0         697          0
RP RIB Total                              0         697          0

RP LES Packet destined for us             0         352          0
RP LES Total                              0         352          0

All    Total                              0        1049          0
```

Final Switch Configurations

DLS1

```
DLS1#show running-config
Building configuration...

Current configuration : 4531 bytes
!
version 12.2
no service pad
```

```
service timestamps debug uptime
service timestamps log uptime
no service password-encryption
!
hostname DLS1
!
no logging console
!
no aaa new-model
ip subnet-zero
ip routing
no ip domain-lookup
!
vtp domain MLS
vtp mode transparent
!
no file verify auto
spanning-tree mode pvst
spanning-tree extend system-id
!
vlan internal allocation policy ascending
!
vlan 100
 name MLS-VLAN
!
!
interface Loopback10
 ip address 10.1.1.1 255.255.255.255
!
interface Loopback20
 ip address 20.1.1.1 255.255.255.255
!
interface FastEthernet0/1
 switchport mode dynamic desirable
 shutdown
!
interface FastEthernet0/2
 switchport mode dynamic desirable
 shutdown
!
interface FastEthernet0/3
 switchport mode dynamic desirable
 shutdown
!
interface FastEthernet0/4
 switchport mode dynamic desirable
 shutdown
!
interface FastEthernet0/5
 switchport mode dynamic desirable
 shutdown
!
```

```
interface FastEthernet0/6
 switchport mode dynamic desirable
 shutdown
!
interface FastEthernet0/7
 switchport mode dynamic desirable
 shutdown
!
interface FastEthernet0/8
 switchport mode dynamic desirable
 shutdown
!
interface FastEthernet0/9
 switchport mode dynamic desirable
 shutdown
!
interface FastEthernet0/10
 switchport mode dynamic desirable
 shutdown
!
interface FastEthernet0/11
 switchport access vlan 100
 switchport mode access
!
interface FastEthernet0/12
 no switchport
 ip address 192.168.200.1 255.255.255.0
!
interface FastEthernet0/13
 switchport mode dynamic desirable
 shutdown
!
interface FastEthernet0/14
 switchport mode dynamic desirable
 shutdown
!
interface FastEthernet0/15
 switchport mode dynamic desirable
 shutdown
!
interface FastEthernet0/16
 switchport mode dynamic desirable
 shutdown
!
interface FastEthernet0/17
 switchport mode dynamic desirable
 shutdown
!
interface FastEthernet0/18
 switchport mode dynamic desirable
 shutdown
!
```

```
interface FastEthernet0/19
 switchport mode dynamic desirable
 shutdown
!
interface FastEthernet0/20
 switchport mode dynamic desirable
 shutdown
!
interface FastEthernet0/21
 switchport mode dynamic desirable
 shutdown
!
interface FastEthernet0/22
 switchport mode dynamic desirable
 shutdown
!
interface FastEthernet0/23
 switchport mode dynamic desirable
 shutdown
!
interface FastEthernet0/24
 switchport mode dynamic desirable
 shutdown
!
interface FastEthernet0/25
 switchport mode dynamic desirable
 shutdown
!
interface FastEthernet0/26
 switchport mode dynamic desirable
 shutdown
!
interface FastEthernet0/27
 switchport mode dynamic desirable
 shutdown
!
interface FastEthernet0/28
 switchport mode dynamic desirable
 shutdown
!
interface FastEthernet0/29
 switchport mode dynamic desirable
 shutdown
!
interface FastEthernet0/30
 switchport mode dynamic desirable
 shutdown
!
interface FastEthernet0/31
 switchport mode dynamic desirable
 shutdown
!
```

```
interface FastEthernet0/32
 switchport mode dynamic desirable
 shutdown
!
interface FastEthernet0/33
 switchport mode dynamic desirable
 shutdown
!
interface FastEthernet0/34
 switchport mode dynamic desirable
 shutdown
!
interface FastEthernet0/35
 switchport mode dynamic desirable
 shutdown
!
interface FastEthernet0/36
 switchport mode dynamic desirable
 shutdown
!
interface FastEthernet0/37
 switchport mode dynamic desirable
 shutdown
!
interface FastEthernet0/38
 switchport mode dynamic desirable
 shutdown
!
interface FastEthernet0/39
 switchport mode dynamic desirable
 shutdown
!
interface FastEthernet0/40
 switchport mode dynamic desirable
 shutdown
!
interface FastEthernet0/41
 switchport mode dynamic desirable
 shutdown
!
interface FastEthernet0/42
 switchport mode dynamic desirable
 shutdown
!
interface FastEthernet0/43
 switchport mode dynamic desirable
 shutdown
!
interface FastEthernet0/44
 switchport mode dynamic desirable
 shutdown
!
```

```
interface FastEthernet0/45
 switchport mode dynamic desirable
 shutdown
!
interface FastEthernet0/46
 switchport mode dynamic desirable
 shutdown
!
interface FastEthernet0/47
 switchport mode dynamic desirable
 shutdown
!
interface FastEthernet0/48
 switchport mode dynamic desirable
 shutdown
!
interface GigabitEthernet0/1
 switchport mode dynamic desirable
!
interface GigabitEthernet0/2
 switchport mode dynamic desirable
!
interface Vlan1
 no ip address
 shutdown
!
interface Vlan100
 ip address 192.168.100.1 255.255.255.0
!
router eigrp 123
 network 0.0.0.0
 no auto-summary
!
ip classless
ip http server
ip http secure-server
!
control-plane
!
line con 0
line vty 0 4
 no login
line vty 5 15
 no login
!
end

DLS1#
```

DLS2

```
DLS2#show running-config
Building configuration...

Current configuration : 4492 bytes
!
version 12.2
no service pad
service timestamps debug uptime
service timestamps log uptime
no service password-encryption
!
hostname DLS2
!
no logging console
!
no aaa new-model
ip subnet-zero
ip routing
!
vtp domain MLS
vtp mode transparent
!
spanning-tree mode pvst
spanning-tree extend system-id
!
vlan internal allocation policy ascending
!
vlan 100
 name MLS-VLAN
!
interface Loopback30
 ip address 30.1.1.1 255.255.255.255
!
interface Loopback40
 ip address 40.1.1.1 255.255.255.255
!
interface FastEthernet0/1
 switchport mode dynamic desirable
 shutdown
!
interface FastEthernet0/2
 switchport mode dynamic desirable
 shutdown
!
interface FastEthernet0/3
 switchport mode dynamic desirable
 shutdown
!
interface FastEthernet0/4
 switchport mode dynamic desirable
```

```
 shutdown
!
interface FastEthernet0/5
 switchport mode dynamic desirable
 shutdown
!
interface FastEthernet0/6
 switchport mode dynamic desirable
 shutdown
!
interface FastEthernet0/7
 switchport mode dynamic desirable
 shutdown
!
interface FastEthernet0/8
 switchport mode dynamic desirable
 shutdown
!
interface FastEthernet0/9
 switchport mode dynamic desirable
 shutdown
!
interface FastEthernet0/10
 switchport mode dynamic desirable
 shutdown
!
interface FastEthernet0/11
 switchport access vlan 100
 switchport mode access
!
interface FastEthernet0/12
 no switchport
 ip address 192.168.200.2 255.255.255.0
!
interface FastEthernet0/13
 switchport mode dynamic desirable
 shutdown
!
interface FastEthernet0/14
 switchport mode dynamic desirable
 shutdown
!
interface FastEthernet0/15
 switchport mode dynamic desirable
 shutdown
!
interface FastEthernet0/16
 switchport mode dynamic desirable
 shutdown
!
interface FastEthernet0/17
 switchport mode dynamic desirable
```

```
 shutdown
!
interface FastEthernet0/18
 switchport mode dynamic desirable
 shutdown
!
interface FastEthernet0/19
 switchport mode dynamic desirable
 shutdown
!
interface FastEthernet0/20
 switchport mode dynamic desirable
 shutdown
!
interface FastEthernet0/21
 switchport mode dynamic desirable
 shutdown
!
interface FastEthernet0/22
 switchport mode dynamic desirable
 shutdown
!
interface FastEthernet0/23
 switchport mode dynamic desirable
 shutdown
!
interface FastEthernet0/24
 switchport mode dynamic desirable
 shutdown
!
interface FastEthernet0/25
 switchport mode dynamic desirable
 shutdown
!
interface FastEthernet0/26
 switchport mode dynamic desirable
 shutdown
!
interface FastEthernet0/27
 switchport mode dynamic desirable
 shutdown
!
interface FastEthernet0/28
 switchport mode dynamic desirable
 shutdown
!
interface FastEthernet0/29
 switchport mode dynamic desirable
 shutdown
!
interface FastEthernet0/30
 switchport mode dynamic desirable
```

```
 shutdown
!
interface FastEthernet0/31
 switchport mode dynamic desirable
 shutdown
!
interface FastEthernet0/32
 switchport mode dynamic desirable
 shutdown
!
interface FastEthernet0/33
 switchport mode dynamic desirable
 shutdown
!
interface FastEthernet0/34
 switchport mode dynamic desirable
 shutdown
!
interface FastEthernet0/35
 switchport mode dynamic desirable
 shutdown
!
interface FastEthernet0/36
 switchport mode dynamic desirable
 shutdown
!
interface FastEthernet0/37
 switchport mode dynamic desirable
 shutdown
!
interface FastEthernet0/38
 switchport mode dynamic desirable
 shutdown
!
interface FastEthernet0/39
 switchport mode dynamic desirable
 shutdown
!
interface FastEthernet0/40
 switchport mode dynamic desirable
 shutdown
!
interface FastEthernet0/41
 switchport mode dynamic desirable
 shutdown
!
interface FastEthernet0/42
 switchport mode dynamic desirable
 shutdown
!
interface FastEthernet0/43
 switchport mode dynamic desirable
 shutdown
```

```
!
interface FastEthernet0/44
 switchport mode dynamic desirable
 shutdown
!
interface FastEthernet0/45
 switchport mode dynamic desirable
 shutdown
!
interface FastEthernet0/46
 switchport mode dynamic desirable
 shutdown
!
interface FastEthernet0/47
 switchport mode dynamic desirable
 shutdown
!
interface FastEthernet0/48
 switchport mode dynamic desirable
 shutdown
!
interface GigabitEthernet0/1
 switchport mode dynamic desirable
!
interface GigabitEthernet0/2
 switchport mode dynamic desirable
!
interface Vlan1
 no ip address
 shutdown
!
interface Vlan100
 ip address 192.168.100.2 255.255.255.0
!
router eigrp 123
 network 0.0.0.0
 no auto-summary
!
ip classless
ip http server
ip http secure-server
!
control-plane
!
line con 0
line vty 0 4
 login
line vty 5 15
 login
!
end

DLS2#
```

LAB 10

VLANs and VLAN Trunking Protocol version 1

Lab Objective:

The objective of this lab exercise is for you to learn and understand how to implement a switched LAN using VLAN Trunking Protocol (VTP) version 1. With VTP version 1, Transparent mode switches do not relay received VTP information to other switches unless the VTP domain names and VTP version numbers match those of the other switches.

Lab Topology:

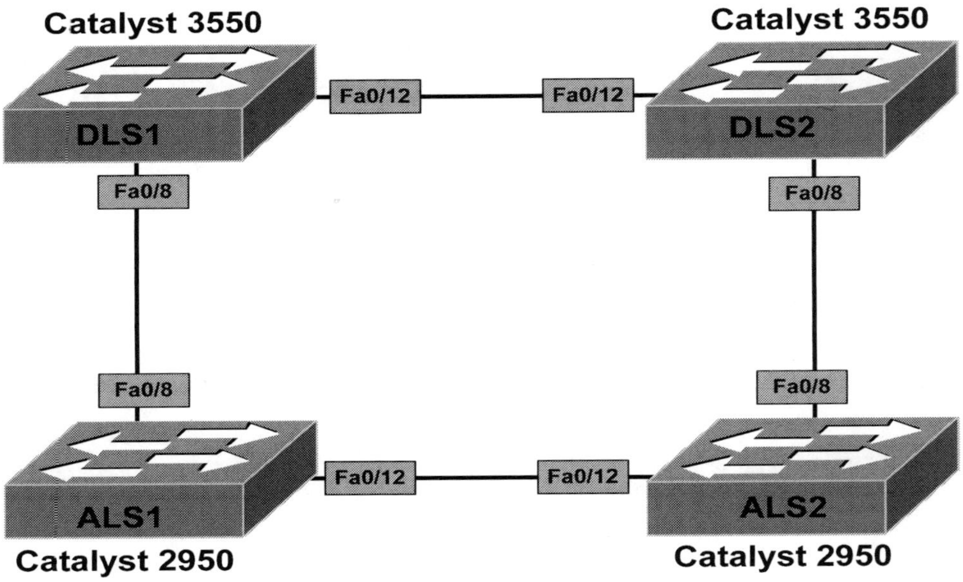

IMPORTANT NOTE

If you are using the www.howtonetwork.net racks, please begin each and every lab by shutting down all interfaces on all switches and then manually re-enabling the interfaces that are illustrated in this topology.

Task 1

Configure a VTP domain name of SWITCH for all switches illustrated in the topology. In addition to this, configure a VTP password of CISCO on all switches.

Task 2

Configure the switch VTP roles as follows:

- DLS1—Configure this switch as a VTP Server
- DLS2—Disable VTP on this switch
- ALS1—Disable VTP on this switch
- ALS2—Configure this switch as a VTP Client

Task 3

Configure IEEE 802.1Q trunks between all switches. Use the default Native VLAN.

Task 4

Configure VLAN 192 on switches DLS1, DLS2, and ALS1. Configure switch DLS1 as the Root Bridge for this VLAN and set the priority to the lowest possible allowed value.

Task 5

Configure interface VLAN 192 on all switches using the 192.168.1.0/24 subnet. Allocate the switch IP addresses as follows:

- DLS1—192.168.1.1/24
- DLS2—192.168.1.2/24
- ALS1—192.168.1.3/24
- ALS2—192.168.1.4/24

Task 6

Verify that the VTP Client (ALS2) successfully received the VTP advertisement with the VLAN 192 information from the VTP Server (DLS1).

Lab Validation

Task 1

```
DLS1#conf t
Enter configuration commands, one per line.  End with CNTL/Z.
DLS1(config)#vtp domain SWITCH
Changing VTP domain name from NULL to SWITCH
DLS1(config)#vtp password CISCO
Setting device VLAN database password to CISCO
DLS1(config)#exit

DLS2#conf t
Enter configuration commands, one per line.  End with CNTL/Z.
DLS2(config)#vtp domain SWITCH
Changing VTP domain name from NULL to SWITCH
DLS2(config)#vtp password CISCO
Setting device VLAN database password to CISCO
DLS2(config)#exit

ALS1#conf t
```

```
Enter configuration commands, one per line.  End with CNTL/Z.
ALS1(config)#vtp domain SWITCH
Changing VTP domain name from Cisco to SWITCH
ALS1(config)#vtp password CISCO
Setting device VLAN database password to CISCO
ALS1(config)#exit


ALS2#conf t
Enter configuration commands, one per line.  End with CNTL/Z.
ALS2(config)#vtp domain SWITCH
Changing VTP domain name from Cisco to SWITCH
ALS2(config)#vtp password CISCO
Setting device VLAN database password to CISCO
ALS2(config)#exit
```

Task 2

NOTE: By default, all switches are VTP servers so no configuration on DLS1 is required.

```
DLS2#conf t
Enter configuration commands, one per line.  End with CNTL/Z.
DLS2(config)#vtp mode transparent
Setting device to VTP TRANSPARENT mode.
DLS2(config)#exit

ALS1#conf t
Enter configuration commands, one per line.  End with CNTL/Z.
ALS1(config)#vtp mode transparent
Setting device to VTP TRANSPARENT mode.
ALS1(config)#exit

ALS2#conf t
Enter configuration commands, one per line.  End with CNTL/Z.
ALS2(config)#vtp mode client
Setting device to VTP CLIENT mode.
ALS2(config)#exit
```

Task 3

```
DLS1(config)#interface range fa0/8, fa0/12
DLS1(config-if-range)#switchport
DLS1(config-if-range)#switchport trunk encapsulation dot1q
DLS1(config-if-range)#switchport mode trunk
DLS1(config-if-range)#no shutdown
DLS1(config-if-range)#exit
```

```
DLS2(config)#interface range f0/8, f0/12
DLS2(config-if-range)#switchport
DLS2(config-if-range)#switchport trunk encap dot1q
DLS2(config-if-range)#switchport mode trunk
DLS2(config-if-range)#no shut

ALS1(config)#int range f0/8 , f0/12
ALS1(config-if-range)#switchport mode trunk
ALS1(config-if-range)#no shut
ALS1(config-if-range)#exit

ALS2(config)#int range f0/8 , f0/12
ALS2(config-if-range)#switchport mode trunk
ALS2(config-if-range)#no shut
ALS2(config-if-range)#exit
```

Task 4

```
DLS1(config)#vlan 192
DLS1(config-vlan)#exit
DLS1(config)#spanning-tree vlan 192 priority 0
DLS1(config)#exit

DLS2(config)#vlan 192
DLS2(config-vlan)#exit

ALS1(config)#vlan 192
ALS1(config-vlan)#exit
```

Task 5

```
DLS1(config)#int vlan 192
DLS1(config-if)#ip add 192.168.1.1 255.255.255.0
DLS1(config-if)#no shut
DLS1(config-if)#exit

DLS2(config)#int vlan 192
DLS2(config-if)#ip add 192.168.1.2 255.255.255.0
DLS2(config-if)#no shut
DLS2(config-if)#exit

ALS1(config)#int vlan 192
ALS1(config-if)#ip add 192.168.1.3 255.255.255.0
ALS1(config-if)#no shut
ALS1(config-if)#exit

ALS2(config)#int vlan 192
ALS2(config-if)#ip add 192.168.1.4 255.255.255.0
ALS2(config-if)#exit
```

Task 6

In VTP version 1, Transparent mode switches do not relay received VTP information to other switches unless the VTP domain names and VTP version numbers match those of the other switches. Because all switches are in the same VTP domain and are running VTP version 1, switch ALS2 is able to receive information on VLAN 192 from VTP Server DLS1, through the Transparent mode switches DLS2 and ALS1.

```
ALS2#show vlan brief | include 192
192  VLAN0192                         active

ALS2#show spanning-tree vlan 192

VLAN0192
  Spanning tree enabled protocol ieee
  Root ID    Priority    192
             Address     000d.291e.7f00
             Cost        38
             Port        12 (FastEthernet0/12)
             Hello Time   2 sec  Max Age 20 sec  Forward Delay 15 sec

  Bridge ID  Priority    32918  (priority 32768 sys-id-ext 150)
             Address     0008.21a9.4f80
             Hello Time   2 sec  Max Age 20 sec  Forward Delay 15 sec
             Aging Time 300

Interface        Role Sts Cost      Prio.Nbr Type
---------------- ---- --- --------- -------- --------------------------------
Fa0/8            Altn BLK 19        128.8    P2p
Fa0/12           Root FWD 19        128.12   P2p
```

IP connectivity between the switches can be validated by performing a simple ping to the IP subnet/network address 192.168.1.0 from any switch within the network as shown in ALS2.

```
ALS2#ping 192.168.1.0

Type escape sequence to abort.
Sending 5, 100-byte ICMP Echos to 192.168.1.0, timeout is 2 seconds:
.
Reply to request 1 from 192.168.1.1, 1 ms
Reply to request 1 from 192.168.1.3, 1 ms
Reply to request 1 from 192.168.1.2, 1 ms
Reply to request 2 from 192.168.1.1, 1 ms
Reply to request 2 from 192.168.1.3, 1 ms
Reply to request 2 from 192.168.1.2, 1 ms
Reply to request 3 from 192.168.1.1, 1 ms
Reply to request 3 from 192.168.1.3, 1 ms
Reply to request 3 from 192.168.1.2, 1 ms
Reply to request 4 from 192.168.1.1, 1 ms
Reply to request 4 from 192.168.1.3, 1 ms
Reply to request 4 from 192.168.1.2, 1 ms
```

Final Switch Configurations

DLS1

```
DLS1#show running-config
Building configuration...

Current configuration : 4330 bytes
!
version 12.2
no service pad
service timestamps debug uptime
service timestamps log uptime
no service password-encryption
!
hostname DLS1
!
no logging console
!
no aaa new-model
ip subnet-zero
!
no file verify auto
!
spanning-tree mode pvst
spanning-tree extend system-id
spanning-tree vlan 192 priority 0
!
vlan internal allocation policy ascending
!
interface FastEthernet0/1
 switchport mode dynamic desirable
 shutdown
!
interface FastEthernet0/2
 switchport mode dynamic desirable
 shutdown
!
interface FastEthernet0/3
 switchport mode dynamic desirable
 shutdown
!
interface FastEthernet0/4
 switchport mode dynamic desirable
 shutdown
!
interface FastEthernet0/5
 switchport mode dynamic desirable
 shutdown
!
interface FastEthernet0/6
```

```
 switchport mode dynamic desirable
 shutdown
!
interface FastEthernet0/7
 switchport mode dynamic desirable
 shutdown
!
interface FastEthernet0/8
 switchport trunk encapsulation dot1q
 switchport mode trunk
!
interface FastEthernet0/9
 switchport mode dynamic desirable
 shutdown
!
interface FastEthernet0/10
 switchport mode dynamic desirable
 shutdown
!
interface FastEthernet0/11
 switchport mode dynamic desirable
 shutdown
!
interface FastEthernet0/12
 switchport trunk encapsulation dot1q
 switchport mode trunk
!
interface FastEthernet0/13
 switchport mode dynamic desirable
 shutdown
!
interface FastEthernet0/14
 switchport mode dynamic desirable
 shutdown
!
interface FastEthernet0/15
 switchport mode dynamic desirable
 shutdown
!
interface FastEthernet0/16
 switchport mode dynamic desirable
 shutdown
!
interface FastEthernet0/17
 switchport mode dynamic desirable
 shutdown
!
interface FastEthernet0/18
 switchport mode dynamic desirable
 shutdown
!
interface FastEthernet0/19
```

```
 switchport mode dynamic desirable
 shutdown
!
interface FastEthernet0/20
 switchport mode dynamic desirable
 shutdown
!
interface FastEthernet0/21
 switchport mode dynamic desirable
 shutdown
!
interface FastEthernet0/22
 switchport mode dynamic desirable
 shutdown
!
interface FastEthernet0/23
 switchport mode dynamic desirable
 shutdown
!
interface FastEthernet0/24
 switchport mode dynamic desirable
 shutdown
!
interface FastEthernet0/25
 switchport mode dynamic desirable
 shutdown
!
interface FastEthernet0/26
 switchport mode dynamic desirable
 shutdown
!
interface FastEthernet0/27
 switchport mode dynamic desirable
 shutdown
!
interface FastEthernet0/28
 switchport mode dynamic desirable
 shutdown
!
interface FastEthernet0/29
 switchport mode dynamic desirable
 shutdown
!
interface FastEthernet0/30
 switchport mode dynamic desirable
 shutdown
!
interface FastEthernet0/31
 switchport mode dynamic desirable
 shutdown
!
interface FastEthernet0/32
```

```
 switchport mode dynamic desirable
 shutdown
!
interface FastEthernet0/33
 switchport mode dynamic desirable
 shutdown
!
interface FastEthernet0/34
 switchport mode dynamic desirable
 shutdown
!
interface FastEthernet0/35
 switchport mode dynamic desirable
 shutdown
!
interface FastEthernet0/36
 switchport mode dynamic desirable
 shutdown
!
interface FastEthernet0/37
 switchport mode dynamic desirable
 shutdown
!
interface FastEthernet0/38
 switchport mode dynamic desirable
 shutdown
!
interface FastEthernet0/39
 switchport mode dynamic desirable
 shutdown
!
interface FastEthernet0/40
 switchport mode dynamic desirable
 shutdown
!
interface FastEthernet0/41
 switchport mode dynamic desirable
 shutdown
!
interface FastEthernet0/42
 switchport mode dynamic desirable
 shutdown
!
interface FastEthernet0/43
 switchport mode dynamic desirable
 shutdown
!
interface FastEthernet0/44
 switchport mode dynamic desirable
 shutdown
!
interface FastEthernet0/45
```

```
 switchport mode dynamic desirable
 shutdown
!
interface FastEthernet0/46
 switchport mode dynamic desirable
 shutdown
!
interface FastEthernet0/47
 switchport mode dynamic desirable
 shutdown
!
interface FastEthernet0/48
 switchport mode dynamic desirable
 shutdown
!
interface GigabitEthernet0/1
 switchport mode dynamic desirable
!
interface GigabitEthernet0/2
 switchport mode dynamic desirable
!
interface Vlan1
 no ip address
 shutdown
!
interface Vlan192
 ip address 192.168.1.1 255.255.255.0
!
ip classless
ip http server
ip http secure-server
!
control-plane
!
line con 0
line vty 0 4
 no login
line vty 5 15
 no login
!
end
```

DLS2

```
DLS2#show running-config
Building configuration...

Current configuration : 4347 bytes
!
version 12.2
no service pad
```

```
service timestamps debug uptime
service timestamps log uptime
no service password-encryption
!
hostname DLS2
!
no logging console
!
no aaa new-model
ip subnet-zero
!
vtp domain SWITCH
vtp mode transparent
!
spanning-tree mode pvst
spanning-tree extend system-id
!
vlan internal allocation policy ascending
!
vlan 192
!
interface FastEthernet0/1
 switchport mode dynamic desirable
 shutdown
!
interface FastEthernet0/2
 switchport mode dynamic desirable
 shutdown
!
interface FastEthernet0/3
 switchport mode dynamic desirable
 shutdown
!
interface FastEthernet0/4
 switchport mode dynamic desirable
 shutdown
!
interface FastEthernet0/5
 switchport mode dynamic desirable
 shutdown
!
interface FastEthernet0/6
 switchport mode dynamic desirable
 shutdown
!
interface FastEthernet0/7
 switchport mode dynamic desirable
 shutdown
!
interface FastEthernet0/8
 switchport trunk encapsulation dot1q
 switchport mode trunk
```

```
!
interface FastEthernet0/9
 switchport mode dynamic desirable
 shutdown
!
interface FastEthernet0/10
 switchport mode dynamic desirable
 shutdown
!
interface FastEthernet0/11
 switchport mode dynamic desirable
 shutdown
!
interface FastEthernet0/12
 switchport trunk encapsulation dot1q
 switchport mode trunk
!
interface FastEthernet0/13
 switchport mode dynamic desirable
 shutdown
!
interface FastEthernet0/14
 switchport mode dynamic desirable
 shutdown
!
interface FastEthernet0/15
 switchport mode dynamic desirable
 shutdown
!
interface FastEthernet0/16
 switchport mode dynamic desirable
 shutdown
!
interface FastEthernet0/17
 switchport mode dynamic desirable
 shutdown
!
interface FastEthernet0/18
 switchport mode dynamic desirable
 shutdown
!
interface FastEthernet0/19
 switchport mode dynamic desirable
 shutdown
!
interface FastEthernet0/20
 switchport mode dynamic desirable
 shutdown
!
interface FastEthernet0/21
 switchport mode dynamic desirable
 shutdown
```

```
!
interface FastEthernet0/22
 switchport mode dynamic desirable
 shutdown
!
interface FastEthernet0/23
 switchport mode dynamic desirable
 shutdown
!
interface FastEthernet0/24
 switchport mode dynamic desirable
 shutdown
!
interface FastEthernet0/25
 switchport mode dynamic desirable
 shutdown
!
interface FastEthernet0/26
 switchport mode dynamic desirable
 shutdown
!
interface FastEthernet0/27
 switchport mode dynamic desirable
 shutdown
!
interface FastEthernet0/28
 switchport mode dynamic desirable
 shutdown
!
interface FastEthernet0/29
 switchport mode dynamic desirable
 shutdown
!
interface FastEthernet0/30
 switchport mode dynamic desirable
 shutdown
!
interface FastEthernet0/31
 switchport mode dynamic desirable
 shutdown
!
interface FastEthernet0/32
 switchport mode dynamic desirable
 shutdown
!
interface FastEthernet0/33
 switchport mode dynamic desirable
 shutdown
!
interface FastEthernet0/34
 switchport mode dynamic desirable
 shutdown
```

```
!
interface FastEthernet0/35
 switchport mode dynamic desirable
 shutdown
!
interface FastEthernet0/36
 switchport mode dynamic desirable
 shutdown
!
interface FastEthernet0/37
 switchport mode dynamic desirable
 shutdown
!
interface FastEthernet0/38
 switchport mode dynamic desirable
 shutdown
!
interface FastEthernet0/39
 switchport mode dynamic desirable
 shutdown
!
interface FastEthernet0/40
 switchport mode dynamic desirable
 shutdown
!
interface FastEthernet0/41
 switchport mode dynamic desirable
 shutdown
!
interface FastEthernet0/42
 switchport mode dynamic desirable
 shutdown
!
interface FastEthernet0/43
 switchport mode dynamic desirable
 shutdown
!
interface FastEthernet0/44
 switchport mode dynamic desirable
 shutdown
!
interface FastEthernet0/45
 switchport mode dynamic desirable
 shutdown
!
interface FastEthernet0/46
 switchport mode dynamic desirable
 shutdown
!
interface FastEthernet0/47
 switchport mode dynamic desirable
 shutdown
```

```
!
interface FastEthernet0/48
 switchport mode dynamic desirable
 shutdown
!
interface GigabitEthernet0/1
 switchport mode dynamic desirable
!
interface GigabitEthernet0/2
 switchport mode dynamic desirable
!
interface Vlan1
 no ip address
 shutdown
!
interface Vlan192
 ip address 192.168.1.2 255.255.255.0
!
ip classless
ip http server
ip http secure-server
!
control-plane
!
line con 0
line vty 0 4
 login
line vty 5 15
 login
!
end
```

ALS1

```
ALS1#show running-config
Building configuration...

Current configuration : 1626 bytes
!
version 12.1
no service pad
service timestamps debug uptime
service timestamps log uptime
no service password-encryption
!
hostname ALS1
!
no logging console
!
ip subnet-zero
!
```

```
ip ssh time-out 120
ip ssh authentication-retries 3
vtp domain SWITCH
vtp mode transparent
!
spanning-tree mode pvst
no spanning-tree optimize bpdu transmission
spanning-tree extend system-id
!
vlan 192
!
interface FastEthernet0/1
 shutdown
!
interface FastEthernet0/2
 shutdown
!
interface FastEthernet0/3
 shutdown
!
interface FastEthernet0/4
 shutdown
!
interface FastEthernet0/5
 shutdown
!
interface FastEthernet0/6
 shutdown
!
interface FastEthernet0/7
 shutdown
!
interface FastEthernet0/8
 switchport mode trunk
!
interface FastEthernet0/9
 shutdown
!
interface FastEthernet0/10
 shutdown
!
interface FastEthernet0/11
!
interface FastEthernet0/12
 switchport mode trunk
!
interface FastEthernet0/13
 shutdown
!
interface FastEthernet0/14
 shutdown
!
```

```
interface FastEthernet0/15
 shutdown
!
interface FastEthernet0/16
 shutdown
!
interface FastEthernet0/17
 shutdown
!
interface FastEthernet0/18
 shutdown
!
interface FastEthernet0/19
 shutdown
!
interface FastEthernet0/20
 shutdown
!
interface FastEthernet0/21
 shutdown
!
interface FastEthernet0/22
 shutdown
!
interface FastEthernet0/23
 shutdown
!
interface FastEthernet0/24
 shutdown
!
interface GigabitEthernet0/1
!
interface GigabitEthernet0/2
!
interface Vlan1
 no ip address
 no ip route-cache
 shutdown
!
interface Vlan192
 ip address 192.168.1.3 255.255.255.0
 no ip route-cache
!
ip http server
!
line con 0
line vty 0 4
 login
line vty 5 15
 login
!
end
```

ALS2

```
ALS2#show running-config
Building configuration...

Current configuration : 2281 bytes
!
version 12.1
no service pad
service timestamps debug uptime
service timestamps log uptime
no service password-encryption
!
hostname ALS2
!
no logging console
!
ip subnet-zero
!
ip ssh time-out 120
ip ssh authentication-retries 3
!
spanning-tree mode pvst
no spanning-tree optimize bpdu transmission
spanning-tree extend system-id
!
interface FastEthernet0/1
 shutdown
!
interface FastEthernet0/2
 shutdown
!
interface FastEthernet0/3
 shutdown
!
interface FastEthernet0/4
 shutdown
!
interface FastEthernet0/5
 shutdown
!
interface FastEthernet0/6
 shutdown
!
interface FastEthernet0/7
 shutdown
!
interface FastEthernet0/8
 switchport mode trunk
!
interface FastEthernet0/9
 shutdown
```

```
!
interface FastEthernet0/10
 shutdown
!
interface FastEthernet0/11
 shutdown
!
interface FastEthernet0/12
 switchport mode trunk
!
interface FastEthernet0/13
 shutdown
!
interface FastEthernet0/14
 shutdown
!
interface FastEthernet0/15
 shutdown
!
interface FastEthernet0/16
 shutdown
!
interface FastEthernet0/17
 shutdown
!
interface FastEthernet0/18
 shutdown
!
interface FastEthernet0/19
 shutdown
!
interface FastEthernet0/20
 shutdown
!
interface FastEthernet0/21
 shutdown
!
interface FastEthernet0/22
 shutdown
!
interface FastEthernet0/23
 shutdown
!
interface FastEthernet0/24
 shutdown
!
interface FastEthernet0/25
!
interface FastEthernet0/26
!
interface FastEthernet0/27
!
```

```
interface FastEthernet0/28
!
interface FastEthernet0/29
!
interface FastEthernet0/30
!
interface FastEthernet0/31
!
interface FastEthernet0/32
!
interface FastEthernet0/33
!
interface FastEthernet0/34
!
interface FastEthernet0/35
!
interface FastEthernet0/36
!
interface FastEthernet0/37
!
interface FastEthernet0/38
!
interface FastEthernet0/39
!
interface FastEthernet0/40
!
interface FastEthernet0/41
!
interface FastEthernet0/42
!
interface FastEthernet0/43
!
interface FastEthernet0/44
!
interface FastEthernet0/45
!
interface FastEthernet0/46
!
interface FastEthernet0/47
!
interface FastEthernet0/48
!
interface GigabitEthernet0/1
!
interface GigabitEthernet0/2
!
interface Vlan1
 no ip address
 no ip route-cache
 shutdown
!
interface Vlan192
```

```
 ip address 192.168.1.4 255.255.255.0
 no ip route-cache
!
ip http server
!
line con 0
line vty 0 4
 login
line vty 5 15
 login
!
end
```

LAB 11

VLANs and VLAN Trunking Protocol version 2

Lab Objective:

The objective of this lab exercise is for you to learn and understand how to implement a switched LAN using VLAN Trunking Protocol (VTP) version 1. With VTP version 2, Transparent mode switches will forward received VTP advertisements out of their trunk ports and act as VTP relays. This happens even if the VTP version is not the same.

Lab Topology:

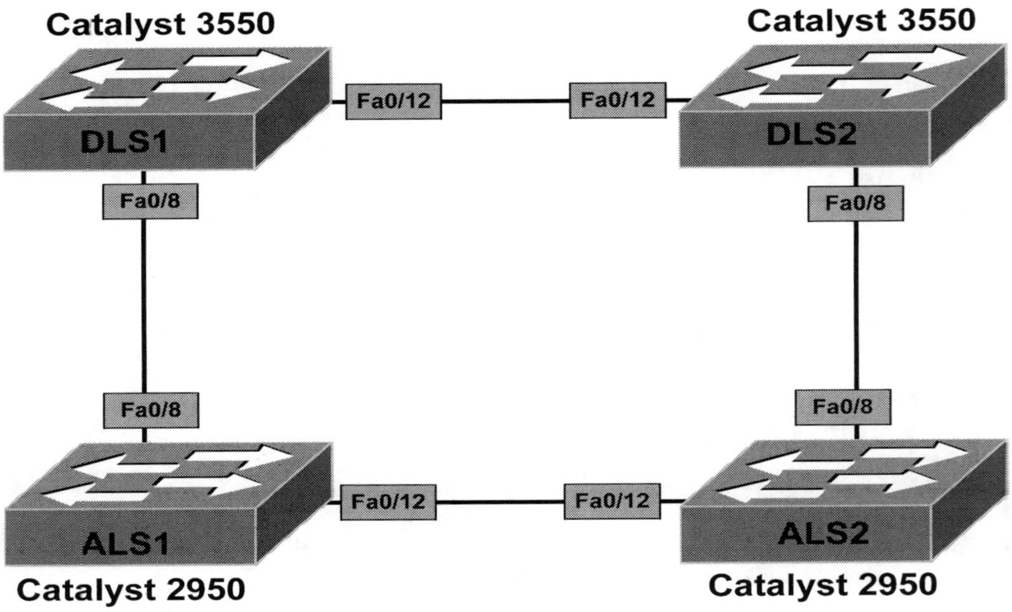

IMPORTANT NOTE

If you are using the www.howtonetwork.net racks, please begin each and every lab by shutting down all interfaces on all switches and then manually re-enabling the interfaces that are illustrated in this topology.

Task 1

Configure a VTP domain name of SWITCH for all switches. Enable VTP v2 on DLS2 and ALS1. Configure a VTP password of CISCO on all switches.

Task 2

Configure the switch VTP roles as follows:

- DLS1—Configure this switch as a VTP Server
- DLS2—Disable VTP on this switch

- ALS1—Disable VTP on this switch
- ALS2—Configure this switch as a VTP Client

Task 3

Configure IEEE 802.1Q trunks between all switches. Use the default Native VLAN.

Task 4

Configure VLAN 192 on switches DLS1, DLS2, and ALS1. Configure switch DLS1 as the Root Bridge for this VLAN and set the priority to the lowest possible allowed value.

Task 5

Configure interface VLAN 192 on all switches using the 192.168.1.0/24 subnet. Allocate the switch IP addresses as follows:

- DLS1—192.168.1.1/24
- DLS2—192.168.1.2/24
- ALS1—192.168.1.3/24
- ALS2—192.168.1.4/24

Task 6

Verify that the VTP Client (ALS2) successfully received the VTP advertisement with the VLAN 192 information from the VTP Server (DLS1).

Lab Validation

Task 1

```
DLS1#conf t
Enter configuration commands, one per line.  End with CNTL/Z.
DLS1(config)#vtp domain SWITCH
Changing VTP domain name from NULL to SWITCH
DLS1(config)#vtp password CISCO
Setting device VLAN database password to CISCO
DLS1(config)#exit

DLS2#conf t
Enter configuration commands, one per line.  End with CNTL/Z.
DLS2(config)#vtp domain SWITCH
Changing VTP domain name from NULL to SWITCH
DLS2(config)#vtp password CISCO
Setting device VLAN database password to CISCO
DLS2(config)#exit
```

```
ALS1#conf t
Enter configuration commands, one per line.  End with CNTL/Z.
ALS1(config)#vtp domain SWITCH
Changing VTP domain name from Cisco to SWITCH
ALS1(config)#vtp password CISCO
Setting device VLAN database password to CISCO
ALS1(config)#exit

ALS2#conf t
Enter configuration commands, one per line.  End with CNTL/Z.
ALS2(config)#vtp domain SWITCH
Changing VTP domain name from Cisco to SWITCH
ALS2(config)#vtp password CISCO
Setting device VLAN database password to CISCO
ALS2(config)#exit
```

Task 2

NOTE: By default, all switches are VTP servers so no configuration on DLS1 is required.

```
DLS2#conf t
Enter configuration commands, one per line.  End with CNTL/Z.
DLS2(config)#vtp mode transparent
Setting device to VTP TRANSPARENT mode.
DLS2(config)#exit

ALS1#conf t
Enter configuration commands, one per line.  End with CNTL/Z.
ALS1(config)#vtp mode transparent
Setting device to VTP TRANSPARENT mode.
ALS1(config)#exit

ALS2#conf t
Enter configuration commands, one per line.  End with CNTL/Z.
ALS2(config)#vtp mode client
Setting device to VTP CLIENT mode.
ALS2(config)#exit
```

Task 3

```
DLS1(config)#interface range fa0/8, fa0/12
DLS1(config-if-range)#switchport
DLS1(config-if-range)#switchport trunk encapsulation dot1q
DLS1(config-if-range)#switchport mode trunk
DLS1(config-if-range)#no shutdown
DLS1(config-if-range)#exit

DLS2(config)#interface range f0/8, f0/12
DLS2(config-if-range)#switchport
DLS2(config-if-range)#switchport trunk encap dot1q
```

```
DLS2(config-if-range)#switchport mode trunk
DLS2(config-if-range)#no shut

ALS1(config)#int range f0/8 , f0/12
ALS1(config-if-range)#switchport mode trunk
ALS1(config-if-range)#no shut
ALS1(config-if-range)#exit

ALS2(config)#int range f0/8 , f0/12
ALS2(config-if-range)#switchport mode trunk
ALS2(config-if-range)#no shut
ALS2(config-if-range)#exit
```

Task 4

```
DLS1(config)#vlan 192
DLS1(config-vlan)#exit
DLS1(config)#spanning-tree vlan 192 priority 0
DLS1(config)#exit

DLS2(config)#vlan 192
DLS2(config-vlan)#exit

ALS1(config)#vlan 192
ALS1(config-vlan)#exit
```

Task 5

```
DLS1(config)#int vlan 192
DLS1(config-if)#ip add 192.168.1.1 255.255.255.0
DLS1(config-if)#no shut
DLS1(config-if)#exit

DLS2(config)#int vlan 192
DLS2(config-if)#ip add 192.168.1.2 255.255.255.0
DLS2(config-if)#no shut
DLS2(config-if)#exit

ALS1(config)#int vlan 192
ALS1(config-if)#ip add 192.168.1.3 255.255.255.0
ALS1(config-if)#no shut
ALS1(config-if)#exit

ALS2(config)#int vlan 192
ALS2(config-if)#ip add 192.168.1.4 255.255.255.0
ALS2(config-if)#exit
```

Task 6

With VTP version 2, Transparent mode switches will forward received VTP advertisements out of their trunk ports and act as VTP relays. This happens even if the VTP version is not the same. Because all switches are in the same VTP domain, VTP version 1 switch ALS2 is able to receive information on VLAN 192 from VTP version 1 Server DLS1, through the VTP version 2 Transparent mode switches DLS2 and ALS1.

```
ALS2#show vlan brief | include 192
192  VLAN0192                         active


ALS2#show spanning-tree vlan 192

VLAN0192
  Spanning tree enabled protocol ieee
  Root ID    Priority    192
             Address     000d.291e.7f00
             Cost        38
             Port        12 (FastEthernet0/12)
             Hello Time   2 sec  Max Age 20 sec  Forward Delay 15 sec

  Bridge ID  Priority    32960  (priority 32768 sys-id-ext 192)
             Address     0008.21a9.4f80
             Hello Time   2 sec  Max Age 20 sec  Forward Delay 15 sec
             Aging Time 300

Interface        Role Sts Cost      Prio.Nbr Type
---------------- ---- --- --------- -------- --------------------------------
Fa0/8            Altn BLK 19        128.8    P2p
Fa0/12           Root FWD 19        128.12   P2p
```

Issue the `debug sw-vlan vtp` packets and `debug sw-vlan vtp events` commands on all switches to see the sending and relaying of VTP packets in the domain.

```
DLS1#debug sw-vlan vtp pac
vtp packets debugging is on
DLS1#debug sw-vlan vtp eve
vtp events debugging is on
DLS1#
00:13:06: VTP LOG RUNTIME: Transmit vtp summary, domain SWITCH, rev 3,
followers 0
   MD5 digest calculated = 5D 43 E1 42 94 73 A5 57 08 83 6B 5E 71 16 CE C4

00:13:48: VTP LOG RUNTIME: Transmit vtp summary, domain SWITCH, rev 3,
followers 0
   MD5 digest calculated = 5D 43 E1 42 94 73 A5 57 08 83 6B 5E 71 16 CE C4
```

```
DLS2#debug sw-vlan vtp pac
vtp packets debugging is on
DLS2#debug sw-vlan vtp eve
vtp events debugging is on
DLS2#
10:24:10: VTP LOG RUNTIME: Relaying packet received on trunk Fa0/8 - in
TRANSPARENT MODE (nc = false)

10:29:15: VTP LOG RUNTIME: Relaying packet received on trunk Fa0/12 - in
TRANSPARENT MODE (nc = false)


ALS1#debug sw-vlan vtp pa
vtp packets debugging is on
ALS1#debug sw-vlan vtp eve
vtp events debugging is on
ALS1#
10:25:36: VTP LOG RUNTIME: Relaying packet received on trunk Fa0/8 - in
TRANSPARENT MODE (nc = false)

10:30:41: VTP LOG RUNTIME: Relaying packet received on trunk Fa0/12 - in
TRANSPARENT MODE (nc = false)

ALS2#debug sw-vlan vtp pack
vtp packets debugging is on
ALS2#debug sw-vlan vtp eve
vtp events debugging is on
ALS2#
10:24:44: VTP LOG RUNTIME: Summary packet received, domain = SWITCH, rev = 3,
followers = 0

10:24:44:
10:24:44: summary: 01 01 00 06 53 57 49 54 43 48 00 00 00 00 00 00    ....
SWITCH......
10:24:44: summary: 00 00 00 00 00 00 00 00 00 00 00 00 00 00 00 00
................
10:24:44: summary: 00 00 00 00 00 00 00 03 00 00 00 00 39 33 30 33
............9303
10:24:44: summary: 30 31 30 30 30 31 31 31 5D 43 E1 42 94 73 A5 57
01000111]CaB.s%W
10:24:44: summary: 08 83 6B 5E 71 16 CE C4 01 01 00 02 00             ..k^q.
ND.....
10:24:44:
10:24:44: VTP LOG RUNTIME: Summary packet rev 3 equal to domain SWITCH rev 3

10:25:26: VTP LOG RUNTIME: Summary packet received, domain = SWITCH, rev = 3,
followers = 0

10:25:26:
10:25:26: summary: 01 01 00 06 53 57 49 54 43 48 00 00 00 00 00 00    ....
SWITCH......
10:25:26: summary: 00 00 00 00 00 00 00 00 00 00 00 00 00 00 00 00
```

```
................
10:25:26: summary: 00 00 00 00 00 00 00 03 00 00 00 00 39 33 30 33
............9303
10:25:26: summary: 30 31 30 30 30 31 31 31 5D 43 E1 42 94 73 A5 57
01000111]CaB.s%W
10:25:26: summary: 08 83 6B 5E 71 16 CE C4 01 01 00 02 00          ..k^q.
ND.....
10:25:26:
10:25:26: VTP LOG RUNTIME: Summary packet rev 3 equal to domain SWITCH rev 3
```

IP connectivity between the switches can be validated by performing a simple ping to the IP subnet/network address 192.168.1.0 from any switch within the network as shown in ALS2.

```
DLS1#ping 192.168.1.0

Type escape sequence to abort.
Sending 5, 100-byte ICMP Echos to 192.168.1.0, timeout is 2 seconds:
.
Reply to request 1 from 192.168.1.2, 1 ms
Reply to request 1 from 192.168.1.4, 4 ms
Reply to request 1 from 192.168.1.3, 1 ms
Reply to request 2 from 192.168.1.2, 1 ms
Reply to request 2 from 192.168.1.4, 1 ms
Reply to request 2 from 192.168.1.3, 1 ms
Reply to request 3 from 192.168.1.2, 1 ms
Reply to request 3 from 192.168.1.4, 1 ms
Reply to request 3 from 192.168.1.3, 1 ms
Reply to request 4 from 192.168.1.2, 1 ms
Reply to request 4 from 192.168.1.4, 1 ms
Reply to request 4 from 192.168.1.3, 1 ms
```

Final Switch Configurations

DLS1

```
DLS1#show running-config
Building configuration...

Current configuration : 4295 bytes
!
version 12.2
no service pad
service timestamps debug uptime
service timestamps log uptime
no service password-encryption
!
hostname DLS1
!
no aaa new-model
```

```
ip subnet-zero
!
no file verify auto
!
spanning-tree mode pvst
spanning-tree extend system-id
spanning-tree vlan 192 priority 0
!
vlan internal allocation policy ascending
!
interface FastEthernet0/1
 switchport mode dynamic desirable
 shutdown
!
interface FastEthernet0/2
 switchport mode dynamic desirable
 shutdown
!
interface FastEthernet0/3
 switchport mode dynamic desirable
 shutdown
!
interface FastEthernet0/4
 switchport mode dynamic desirable
 shutdown
!
interface FastEthernet0/5
 switchport mode dynamic desirable
 shutdown
!
interface FastEthernet0/6
 switchport mode dynamic desirable
 shutdown
!
interface FastEthernet0/7
 switchport mode dynamic desirable
 shutdown
!
interface FastEthernet0/8
 switchport trunk encapsulation dot1q
 switchport mode trunk
!
interface FastEthernet0/9
 switchport mode dynamic desirable
 shutdown
!
interface FastEthernet0/10
 switchport mode dynamic desirable
 shutdown
!
interface FastEthernet0/11
 switchport mode dynamic desirable
 shutdown
!
```

```
interface FastEthernet0/12
 switchport trunk encapsulation dot1q
 switchport mode trunk
!
interface FastEthernet0/13
 switchport mode dynamic desirable
 shutdown
!
interface FastEthernet0/14
 switchport mode dynamic desirable
 shutdown
!
interface FastEthernet0/15
 switchport mode dynamic desirable
 shutdown
!
interface FastEthernet0/16
 switchport mode dynamic desirable
 shutdown
!
interface FastEthernet0/17
 switchport mode dynamic desirable
 shutdown
!
interface FastEthernet0/18
 switchport mode dynamic desirable
 shutdown
!
interface FastEthernet0/19
 switchport mode dynamic desirable
 shutdown
!
interface FastEthernet0/20
 switchport mode dynamic desirable
 shutdown
!
interface FastEthernet0/21
 switchport mode dynamic desirable
 shutdown
!
interface FastEthernet0/22
 switchport mode dynamic desirable
 shutdown
!
interface FastEthernet0/23
 switchport mode dynamic desirable
 shutdown
!
interface FastEthernet0/24
 switchport mode dynamic desirable
 shutdown
!
interface FastEthernet0/25
 switchport mode dynamic desirable
```

```
 shutdown
!
interface FastEthernet0/26
 switchport mode dynamic desirable
 shutdown
!
interface FastEthernet0/27
 switchport mode dynamic desirable
 shutdown
!
interface FastEthernet0/28
 switchport mode dynamic desirable
 shutdown
!
interface FastEthernet0/29
 switchport mode dynamic desirable
 shutdown
!
interface FastEthernet0/30
 switchport mode dynamic desirable
 shutdown
!
interface FastEthernet0/31
 switchport mode dynamic desirable
 shutdown
!
interface FastEthernet0/32
 switchport mode dynamic desirable
 shutdown
!
interface FastEthernet0/33
 switchport mode dynamic desirable
 shutdown
!
interface FastEthernet0/34
 switchport mode dynamic desirable
 shutdown
!
interface FastEthernet0/35
 switchport mode dynamic desirable
 shutdown
!
interface FastEthernet0/36
 switchport mode dynamic desirable
 shutdown
!
interface FastEthernet0/37
 switchport mode dynamic desirable
 shutdown
!
interface FastEthernet0/38
 switchport mode dynamic desirable
 shutdown
!
```

```
interface FastEthernet0/39
 switchport mode dynamic desirable
 shutdown
!
interface FastEthernet0/40
 switchport mode dynamic desirable
 shutdown
!
interface FastEthernet0/41
 switchport mode dynamic desirable
 shutdown
!
interface FastEthernet0/42
 switchport mode dynamic desirable
 shutdown
!
interface FastEthernet0/43
 switchport mode dynamic desirable
 shutdown
!
interface FastEthernet0/44
 switchport mode dynamic desirable
 shutdown
!
interface FastEthernet0/45
 switchport mode dynamic desirable
 shutdown
!
interface FastEthernet0/46
 switchport mode dynamic desirable
 shutdown
!
interface FastEthernet0/47
 switchport mode dynamic desirable
 shutdown
!
interface FastEthernet0/48
 switchport mode dynamic desirable
 shutdown
!
interface GigabitEthernet0/1
 switchport mode dynamic desirable
!
interface GigabitEthernet0/2
 switchport mode dynamic desirable
!
interface Vlan1
 no ip address
 shutdown
!
interface Vlan192
 ip address 192.168.1.1 255.255.255.0
!
ip classless
ip http server
```

```
ip http secure-server
!
control-plane
!
line con 0
line vty 0 4
 no login
line vty 5 15
 no login
!
end

DLS1#
```

DLS2

```
DLS2#show running-config
Building configuration...

Current configuration : 3804 bytes
!
version 12.2
no service pad
service timestamps debug uptime
service timestamps log uptime
no service password-encryption
!
hostname DLS2
!
no aaa new-model
ip subnet-zero
!
vtp domain SWITCH
vtp mode transparent
!
spanning-tree mode pvst
spanning-tree extend system-id
!
vlan internal allocation policy ascending
!
vlan 192
!
interface FastEthernet0/1
 switchport mode dynamic desirable
!
interface FastEthernet0/2
 switchport mode dynamic desirable
!
interface FastEthernet0/3
 switchport mode dynamic desirable
!
interface FastEthernet0/4
 switchport mode dynamic desirable
!
```

```
interface FastEthernet0/5
 switchport mode dynamic desirable
!
interface FastEthernet0/6
 switchport mode dynamic desirable
!
interface FastEthernet0/7
 switchport mode dynamic desirable
!
interface FastEthernet0/8
 switchport trunk encapsulation dot1q
 switchport mode trunk
!
interface FastEthernet0/9
 switchport mode dynamic desirable
!
interface FastEthernet0/10
 switchport mode dynamic desirable
!
interface FastEthernet0/11
 switchport mode dynamic desirable
!
interface FastEthernet0/12
 switchport trunk encapsulation dot1q
 switchport mode trunk
!
interface FastEthernet0/13
 switchport mode dynamic desirable
!
interface FastEthernet0/14
 switchport mode dynamic desirable
!
interface FastEthernet0/15
 switchport mode dynamic desirable
!
interface FastEthernet0/16
 switchport mode dynamic desirable
!
interface FastEthernet0/17
 switchport mode dynamic desirable
!
interface FastEthernet0/18
 switchport mode dynamic desirable
!
interface FastEthernet0/19
 switchport mode dynamic desirable
!
interface FastEthernet0/20
 switchport mode dynamic desirable
!
interface FastEthernet0/21
 switchport mode dynamic desirable
!
interface FastEthernet0/22
```

```
 switchport mode dynamic desirable
!
interface FastEthernet0/23
 switchport mode dynamic desirable
!
interface FastEthernet0/24
 switchport mode dynamic desirable
!
interface FastEthernet0/25
 switchport mode dynamic desirable
!
interface FastEthernet0/26
 switchport mode dynamic desirable
!
interface FastEthernet0/27
 switchport mode dynamic desirable
!
interface FastEthernet0/28
 switchport mode dynamic desirable
!
interface FastEthernet0/29
 switchport mode dynamic desirable
!
interface FastEthernet0/30
 switchport mode dynamic desirable
!
interface FastEthernet0/31
 switchport mode dynamic desirable
!
interface FastEthernet0/32
 switchport mode dynamic desirable
!
interface FastEthernet0/33
 switchport mode dynamic desirable
!
interface FastEthernet0/34
 switchport mode dynamic desirable
!
interface FastEthernet0/35
 switchport mode dynamic desirable
!
interface FastEthernet0/36
 switchport mode dynamic desirable
!
interface FastEthernet0/37
 switchport mode dynamic desirable
!
interface FastEthernet0/38
 switchport mode dynamic desirable
!
interface FastEthernet0/39
 switchport mode dynamic desirable
!
interface FastEthernet0/40
```

```
 switchport mode dynamic desirable
!
interface FastEthernet0/41
 switchport mode dynamic desirable
!
interface FastEthernet0/42
 switchport mode dynamic desirable
!
interface FastEthernet0/43
 switchport mode dynamic desirable
!
interface FastEthernet0/44
 switchport mode dynamic desirable
!
interface FastEthernet0/45
 switchport mode dynamic desirable
!
interface FastEthernet0/46
 switchport mode dynamic desirable
!
interface FastEthernet0/47
 switchport mode dynamic desirable
!
interface FastEthernet0/48
 switchport mode dynamic desirable
!
interface GigabitEthernet0/1
 switchport mode dynamic desirable
!
interface GigabitEthernet0/2
 switchport mode dynamic desirable
!
interface Vlan1
 no ip address
 shutdown
!
interface Vlan192
 ip address 192.168.1.2 255.255.255.0
!
ip classless
ip http server
ip http secure-server
!
control-plane
!
line con 0
line vty 5 15
!
end

DLS2#
```

ALS1

```
ALS1#more system:running-config
!
version 12.1
no service pad
service timestamps debug uptime
service timestamps log uptime
no service password-encryption
!
hostname ALS1
!
!
ip subnet-zero
!
ip ssh time-out 120
ip ssh authentication-retries 3
vtp domain SWITCH
vtp mode transparent
!
spanning-tree mode pvst
no spanning-tree optimize bpdu transmission
spanning-tree extend system-id
!
!
!
!
vlan 192
!
interface FastEthernet0/1
 shutdown
!
interface FastEthernet0/2
 shutdown
!
interface FastEthernet0/3
 shutdown
!
interface FastEthernet0/4
 shutdown
!
interface FastEthernet0/5
 shutdown
!
interface FastEthernet0/6
 shutdown
!
interface FastEthernet0/7
 shutdown
!
interface FastEthernet0/8
 switchport mode trunk
!
interface FastEthernet0/9
```

```
 shutdown
!
interface FastEthernet0/10
 shutdown
!
interface FastEthernet0/11
 shutdown
!
interface FastEthernet0/12
 switchport mode trunk
!
interface FastEthernet0/13
 shutdown
!
interface FastEthernet0/14
 shutdown
!
interface FastEthernet0/15
 shutdown
!
interface FastEthernet0/16
 shutdown
!
interface FastEthernet0/17
 shutdown
!
interface FastEthernet0/18
 shutdown
!
interface FastEthernet0/19
 shutdown
!
interface FastEthernet0/20
 shutdown
!
interface FastEthernet0/21
 shutdown
!
interface FastEthernet0/22
 shutdown
!
interface FastEthernet0/23
 shutdown
!
interface FastEthernet0/24
 shutdown
!
interface GigabitEthernet0/1
!
interface GigabitEthernet0/2
!
interface Vlan1
 no ip address
```

```
 no ip route-cache
 shutdown
!
interface Vlan192
 ip address 192.168.1.3 255.255.255.0
 no ip route-cache
!
ip http server
!
line con 0
line vty 5 15
!
!
end

ALS1#
```

ALS2

```
ALS2#show running-config
Building configuration...

Current configuration : 2462 bytes
!
version 12.1
no service pad
service timestamps debug uptime
service timestamps log uptime
no service password-encryption
!
hostname ALS2
!
ip subnet-zero
!
ip ssh time-out 120
ip ssh authentication-retries 3
!
spanning-tree mode pvst
no spanning-tree optimize bpdu transmission
spanning-tree extend system-id
!
interface FastEthernet0/1
 shutdown
!
interface FastEthernet0/2
 shutdown
!
interface FastEthernet0/3
 shutdown
!
interface FastEthernet0/4
```

```
 shutdown
!
interface FastEthernet0/5
 shutdown
!
interface FastEthernet0/6
 shutdown
!
interface FastEthernet0/7
 shutdown
!
interface FastEthernet0/8
 switchport mode trunk
!
interface FastEthernet0/9
 shutdown
!
interface FastEthernet0/10
 shutdown
!
interface FastEthernet0/11
 shutdown
!
interface FastEthernet0/12
 switchport mode trunk
!
interface FastEthernet0/13
 shutdown
!
interface FastEthernet0/14
 shutdown
!
interface FastEthernet0/15
 shutdown
!
interface FastEthernet0/16
 shutdown
!
interface FastEthernet0/17
 shutdown
!
interface FastEthernet0/18
 shutdown
!
interface FastEthernet0/19
 shutdown
!
interface FastEthernet0/20
 shutdown
!
interface FastEthernet0/21
 shutdown
```

```
!
interface FastEthernet0/22
 shutdown
!
interface FastEthernet0/23
 shutdown
!
interface FastEthernet0/24
 shutdown
!
interface FastEthernet0/25
 shutdown
!
interface FastEthernet0/26
 shutdown
!
interface FastEthernet0/27
 shutdown
!
interface FastEthernet0/28
 shutdown
!
interface FastEthernet0/29
 shutdown
!
interface FastEthernet0/30
 shutdown
!
interface FastEthernet0/31
 shutdown
!
interface FastEthernet0/32
 shutdown
!
interface FastEthernet0/33
 shutdown
!
interface FastEthernet0/34
 shutdown
!
interface FastEthernet0/35
 shutdown
!
interface FastEthernet0/36
 shutdown
!
interface FastEthernet0/37
 shutdown
!
interface FastEthernet0/38
 shutdown
!
```

```
interface FastEthernet0/39
 shutdown
!
interface FastEthernet0/40
 shutdown
!
interface FastEthernet0/41
 shutdown
!
interface FastEthernet0/42
 shutdown
!
interface FastEthernet0/43
 shutdown
!
interface FastEthernet0/44
 shutdown
!
interface FastEthernet0/45
 shutdown
!
interface FastEthernet0/46
 shutdown
!
interface FastEthernet0/47
 shutdown
!
interface FastEthernet0/48
 shutdown
!
interface GigabitEthernet0/1
!
interface GigabitEthernet0/2
!
interface Vlan1
 no ip address
 no ip route-cache
 shutdown
!
interface Vlan192
 ip address 192.168.1.4 255.255.255.0
 no ip route-cache
!
ip http server
!
line con 0
line vty 5 15
!
!
end

ALS2#
```

Printed in Dunstable, United Kingdom

91336860R00433